The Key to Your Success in Three Easy Steps!

1 Take a Sample Test to assess your knowledge.

2 Review your personalized Study Plan to see where you need more work.

3 Use the Study Plan exercises and step-by-step tutorials to get practice—and individualized feedback—where you need it.

If your Instructor assigns homework and tests using MyFinanceLab...

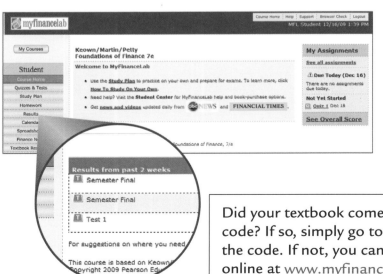

The MyFinanceLab Course Home page makes it easy for you to stay on track by displaying class announcements and automatic reminders of upcoming assignments.

Did your textbook come bundled with a MyFinanceLab access code? If so, simply go to www.myfinancelab.com to register using the code. If not, you can purchase access to MyFinanceLab online at www.myfinancelab.com.

Frequently Used Notations
Foundations of Finance, Seventh Edition

β	=	beta
EAR	=	effective annual rate
EBIT	=	earnings before interest and taxes
EBITDA	=	earnings before interest, taxes, depreciation, and amortization
EVA®	=	Economic Value Added
FCFt	=	the annual free cash flow in time period t
FVi	=	the future value of \$1 at the end of year i
IO	=	the initial outlay
IRR	=	internal rate of return
K_{wacc}	=	weighted average cost of capital
K_e	=	cost of common equity
k_{ne}	=	cost of new common equity
K_d	=	cost of debt financing
MIRR	=	the modified internal rate of return
n	=	the number of years until payment will be received or during which compounding occurs
NPV	=	net present value
OROA	=	operating return on assets
P	=	current selling price of a security
PI	=	profitability index
PMT	=	the annuity payment deposited or received each period over the life of the annuity.
PV	=	the present value of a future sum of money
r	=	required rate of return of an investor.
rf	=	risk free rate of interest.
rm	=	expected rate of return on the market portfolio of all risky investments.
ROA	=	return on assets
σ	=	standard deviation

Foundations of Finance

The Logic and Practice of Financial Management

Seventh Edition

The Prentice Hall Series in Finance

Alexander/Sharpe/Bailey
Fundamentals of Investments

Bear/Moldonado-Bear
Free Markets, Finance, Ethics, and Law

Berk/DeMarzo
Corporate Finance*

Berk/DeMarzo
Corporate Finance: The Core*

Berk/DeMarzo/Harford
Fundamentals of Corporate Finance*

Bierman/Smidt
The Capital Budgeting Decision: Economic Analysis of Investment Projects

Bodie/Merton/Cleeton
Financial Economics

Brooks
Financial Management: Core Concepts*

Click/Coval
The Theory and Practice of International Financial Management

Copeland/Weston/Shastri
Financial Theory and Corporate Policy

Cox/Rubinstein
Options Markets

Dietrich
Financial Services and Financial Institutions: Value Creation in Theory and Practice

Dorfman
Introduction to Risk Management and Insurance

Dufey/Giddy
Cases in International Finance

Eakins
Finance in .learn

Eiteman/Stonehill/Moffett
Multinational Business Finance

Emery/Finnerty/Stowe
Corporate Financial Management

Fabozzi
Bond Markets: Analysis and Strategies

Fabozzi/Modigliani
Capital Markets: Institutions and Instruments

Fabozzi/Modigliani/Jones/Ferri
Foundations of Financial Markets and Institutions

Finkler
Financial Management for Public, Health, and Not-for-Profit Organizations

Francis/Ibbotson
Investments: A Global Perspective

Fraser/Ormiston
Understanding Financial Statements

Geisst
Investment Banking in the Financial System

Gitman
Principles of Managerial Finance*

Gitman
Principles of Managerial Finance—Brief Edition*

Gitman/Joehnk
Fundamentals of Investing*

Gitman/Madura
Introduction to Finance

Guthrie/Lemon
Mathematics of Interest Rates and Finance

Haugen
The Inefficient Stock Market: What Pays Off and Why

Haugen
Modern Investment Theory

Haugen
The New Finance: Overreaction, Complexity, and Uniqueness

Holden
Excel Modeling and Estimation in Corporate Finance

Holden
Excel Modeling and Estimation in the Fundamentals of Corporate Finance

Holden
Excel Modeling and Estimation in the Fundamentals of Investments

Holden
Excel Modeling and Estimation in Investments

Hughes/MacDonald
International Banking: Text and Cases

Hull
Fundamentals of Futures and Options Markets

Hull
Options, Futures, and Other Derivatives

Hull
Risk Management and Financial Institutions

Keown
Personal Finance: Turning Money into Wealth*

Keown/Martin/Petty/Scott
Financial Management: Principles and Applications

Keown/Martin/Petty
Foundations of Finance: The Logic and Practice of Financial Management*

Kim/Nofsinger
Corporate Governance

Levy/Post
Investments

Madura
Personal Finance*

Marthinsen
Risk Takers: Uses and Abuses of Financial Derivatives

May/May/Andrew
Effective Writing: A Handbook for Finance People

McDonald
Derivatives Markets

McDonald
Fundamentals of Derivatives Markets

Megginson
Corporate Finance Theory

Melvin
International Money and Finance

Mishkin/Eakins
Financial Markets and Institutions

Moffett
Cases in International Finance

Moffett/Stonehill/Eiteman
Fundamentals of Multinational Finance

Nofsinger
Psychology of Investing

Ogden/Jen/O'Connor
Advanced Corporate Finance

Pennacchi
Theory of Asset Pricing

Rejda
Principles of Risk Management and Insurance

Schoenebeck
Interpreting and Analyzing Financial Statements

Scott/Martin/Petty/Keown/Thatcher
Cases in Finance

Seiler
Performing Financial Studies: A Methodological Cookbook

Shapiro
Capital Budgeting and Investment Analysis

Sharpe/Alexander/Bailey
Investments

Solnik/McLeavey
Global Investments

Stretcher/Michael
Cases in Financial Management

Titman/Martin
Valuation: The Art and Science of Corporate Investment Decisions

Trivoli
Personal Portfolio Management: Fundamentals and Strategies

Van Horne
Financial Management and Policy

Van Horne
Financial Market Rates and Flows

Van Horne/Wachowicz
Fundamentals of Financial Management

Vaughn
Financial Planning for the Entrepreneur

Welch
Corporate Finance: An Introduction*

Weston/Mitchel/Mulherin
Takeovers, Restructuring, and Corporate Governance

Winger/Frasca
Personal Finance

Foundations of Finance

The Logic and Practice of Financial Management

Seventh Edition

Arthur J. Keown

Virginia Polytechnic Institute and State University
R. B. Pamplin Professor of Finance

John D. Martin

Baylor University
Professor of Finance
Carr P. Collins Chair in Finance

J. William Petty

Baylor University
Professor of Finance
W. W. Caruth Chair in Entrepreneurship

Prentice Hall

Boston Columbus Indianapolis New York San Francisco Upper Saddle River
Amsterdam Cape Town Dubai London Madrid Milan Munich Paris Montreal Toronto
Delhi Mexico City Sao Paulo Sydney Hong Kong Seoul Singapore Taipei Tokyo

Editor in Chief: Donna Battista
Acquisitions Editor: Tessa O'Brien
Assistant Development Editor: Sara Holliday
Project Manager: Kerri McQueen
Editorial Assistant: Anne Cardi
Senior Managing Editor: Nancy Fenton
Senior Production Project Managers: Meredith Gertz and Heather McNally
Production Coordinator: Alison Eusden
Senior Marketing Manager: Elizabeth A. Averbeck
Marketing Assistant: Ian Gold
Director of Media: Susan Schoenberg
Media Producer: Nicole Sackin

MyFinanceLab Content Lead: Miguel Leonarte
Permissions Project Manager: Shannon Barbe
Senior Manufacturing Buyer: Carol Melville
Art Director: Linda Knowles
Cover Designer: Jodi Notowitz
Manager, Rights and Permission: Zina Arabia
Manager, Research Development: Elaine Soares
Manager, Visual Research: Beth Brenzel
Image Permission Coordinator: Nancy Seise
Photo Researcher: Sheila Norman
Project Coordination, Composition, Text Design, Illustrations, and Alterations: Nesbitt Graphics, Inc.

Credits and acknowledgments borrowed from other sources and reproduced, with permission, in this textbook appear on appropriate page within text.

Photo Credits p. 3, © Dorling Kindersley; p. 19, AP Wide World Photos; p. 47, © Paul Sakuma/AP Wide World Photos; p. 85, Ace Stock Limited; p. 119, Mira.com/ Terry Smith; p. 157 © Nell Redmond/AP Wide World Photos; p. 189, Scott Olson/Getty Images; p. 213, © Christinne Muschi/ Reuters Limited; p. 235, SuperStock Inc.; p. 265, Sunnymok/ChinaFotoPress/Newscom; p. 303, Toyota Motor Sales, USA, Inc.; p. 337, KAREN BLEIER/AFP/Getty Images; p. 373, AP Wide World Photos; p. 393, © Chuck Pefley/Alamy Images; p. 413, © Joe Raedle / Getty Images, Inc.; p. 437, Alamy Images Royalty Free; p. 467, © Les Stone/Corbis Sygma

1 2 3 4 5 6 7 8 9 10—CRK—14 13 12 11 10

Prentice Hall
is an imprint of

ISBN-13: 978-0-13-512236-5
ISBN-10: 0-13-512236-8

To my parents, from whom I learned the most.
Arthur J. Keown

*To the Martin women—wife Sally and daughter-in-law Mel,
the Martin men—sons Dave and Jess, and
Martin boys—grandsons Luke and Burke.*
John D. Martin

*To my grandchildren, Mackenzie Kate, Ashley Kate,
Cameron Petty, John Carter, and Erin Marie, who bless
me every day and make my life so much fun.*
J. William Petty

About the Authors

Arthur J. Keown is the R. B. Pamplin Professor of Finance at Virginia Polytechnic Institute and State University. He received his bachelor's degree from Ohio Wesleyan University, his M.B.A. from the University of Michigan, and his doctorate from Indiana University. An award-winning teacher, he is a member of the Academy of Teaching Excellence; has received five Certificates of Teaching Excellence at Virginia Tech, the W. E. Wine Award for Teaching Excellence, and the Alumni Teaching Excellence Award; and in 1999 received the Outstanding Faculty Award from the State of Virginia. Professor Keown is widely published in academic journals. His work has appeared in *The Journal of Finance*, the *Journal of Financial Economics*, the *Journal of Financial and Quantitative Analysis*, *The Journal of Financial Research*, the *Journal of Banking and Finance*, *Financial Management*, the *Journal of Portfolio Management*, and many others. In addition to *Foundations of Finance*, two other of his books are widely used in college finance classes all over the country—*Basic Financial Management* and *Personal Finance: Turning Money into Wealth*. Professor Keown is a Fellow of the Decision Sciences Institute, a member of the Board of Directors of the Financial Management Association, and former head of the finance department at Virginia Tech. In addition, he recently served as the co-editor of *The Journal of Financial Research* for six and a half years and as the co-editor of the Financial Management Association's *Survey and Synthesis* series for six years. He lives with his wife and two children in Blacksburg, Virginia, where he collects original art from *Mad Magazine*.

John D. Martin is Professor of Finance and the holder of the Carr P. Collins Chair of Finance at Baylor University. Dr. Martin came to Baylor University in 1998 from the University of Texas at Austin where he taught for nineteen years and was the Margaret and Eugene McDermott Centennial Professor of Finance. He teaches corporate finance and his research interests are in corporate governance, the evaluation of firm performance, and the design of incentive compensation plans. Dr. Martin has published widely in academic journals including the *Journal of Financial Economics*, *The Journal of Finance*, *Journal of Monetary Economics*, *Journal of Financial and Quantitative Analysis*, *Journal of Corporate Finance*, *Financial Management*, and *Management Science*. His work has also appeared in a number of professional publications including *Directors and Boards*, the *Financial Analysts' Journal*, the *Journal of Portfolio Management*, and the *Journal of Applied Corporate Finance*. In addition to this book Dr. Martin is co-author of nine books including *Financial Management* (9th ed., Prentice Hall), *The Theory of Finance* (Dryden Press), *Financial Analysis* (2nd ed., McGraw Hill), and *Value Based Management* (Harvard Business School Press), and he is currently writing a book on interest rate modeling. He serves on the editorial boards of eight journals and has delivered executive education programs for a number of firms including Shell Chemical, Shell E&P, Texas Instruments, and The Associates.

J. William Petty, PhD, University of Texas at Austin, is Professor of Finance and W. W. Caruth Chair of Entrepreneurship. Dr. Petty teaches entrepreneurial finance, both at the undergraduate and graduate levels. He is a University Master Teacher. In 2008, the Acton Foundation for Entrepreneurship Excellence selected him as the National Entrepreneurship Teacher of the Year. His research interests include the financing of entrepreneurial firms and shareholder value-based management. He has served as the co-editor for the *Journal of Financial Research* and the editor of the *Journal of Entrepreneurial Finance*. He has published articles in various academic and professional journals including *Journal of Financial and Quantitative Analysis, Financial Management, Journal of Portfolio Management, Journal of Applied Corporate Finance,* and *Accounting Review.* Dr. Petty is co-author of a leading textbook in small business and entrepreneurship, *Small Business Management: Launching and Growing Entrepreneurial Ventures.* He also co-authored *Value-Based Management: Corporate America's Response to the Shareholder Revolution,* 2010. Finally, he serves on the Board of Directors of a publicly-traded oil and gas firm.

Brief Contents

Contents

Preface

The study of finance focuses on making decisions that enhance the value of the firm. This is done by providing customers with the best products and services in a cost-effective way. In a sense we, the authors of *Foundations of Finance*, are trying to do the same thing. That is, we have tried to present the study of financial management in a way that makes your study as easy and productive as possible by using a step-by-step approach to walking you through each new concept or problem.

We are very proud of the history of this volume as it was the first "shortened book" of financial management when it was published in its first edition. The book broke new ground by reducing the number of chapters down to the foundational materials and by trying to present the subject in understandable terms. We continue our quest for readability with the Seventh Edition.

Pedagogy That Works

This book provides students with a conceptual understanding of the financial decision-making process, rather than just an introduction to the tools and techniques of finance. For the student, it is all too easy to lose sight of the logic that drives finance and focus instead on memorizing formulas and procedures. As a result, students have a difficult time understanding the interrelationships among the topics covered. Moreover, later in life when the problems encountered do not match the textbook presentation, students may find themselves unprepared to abstract from what they learned. To overcome this problem, the opening chapter presents 5 underlying principles of finance, which serve as a springboard for the chapters and topics that follow. In essence, the student is presented with a cohesive, inter-related perspective from which future problems can be approached.

With a focus on the big picture, we provide an introduction to financial decision making rooted in current financial theory and in the current state of world economic conditions. This focus is perhaps most apparent in the attention given to the capital markets and their influence on corporate financial decisions. What results is an introductory treatment of a discipline rather than the treatment of a series of isolated problems that face the financial manager. The goal of this text is not merely to teach the tools of a discipline or trade but also to enable students to abstract what is learned to new and yet unforeseen problems—in short, to educate the student in finance.

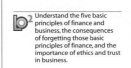

Understand the five basic principles of finance and business, the consequences of forgetting those basic principles of finance, and the importance of ethics and trust in business.

Five Principles that Form the Foundations of Finance

To the first-time student of finance, the subject matter may seem like a collection of unrelated decision rules. This could not be further from the truth. In fact, our decision rules, and the logic that underlies them, spring from five simple principles that do not require knowledge of finance to understand. These five principles guide the financial manager in the creation of value for the firm's owners (the stockholders).

As you will see, while it is not necessary to understand finance to understand these principles, it is necessary to understand these principles in order to understand finance. Although these principles may at first appear simple or even trivial, they provide the driving force behind all that follows, weaving together the concepts and techniques presented in this text, and thereby allowing us to focus on the logic underlying the practice of financial management. Now let's introduce the five principles.

Principle 1: Cash Flow Is What Matters

You probably recall from your accounting classes that a company's profits can differ dramatically from its cash flows which we will review in Chapter 3. But for now understand that cash flows, not profits, represent money that can be spent. Consequently, it is cash flow, not profits that determines the value of a business. For this reason when we analyze the consequences of a managerial decision we focus on the resulting cash flows, not profits.

In the movie industry, there is a big difference between accounting profits and cash flow.

Innovations and Distinctive Features in the Seventh Edition

"Cautionary Tale" Boxes

These give students insights into how the core concepts of finance apply in the real world. Each "Cautionary Tale" box goes behind the headlines of finance pitfalls in the news to show how one of the Five Principles was forgotten or violated.

Real-World Opening Vignettes

Each chapter begins with a story about a current, real-world company faced with a financial decision related to the chapter material that follows. These vignettes have been carefully prepared to stimulate student interest in the topic to come and can be used as a lecture tool to provoke class discussion.

New and Improved Problem Sets

The end-of-chapter study problem sets have been improved and expanded to allow for a wider range of student problems.

Use of an Integrated Learning System

The text is organized around the learning objectives that appear at the beginning of each chapter to provide the instructor and student with an easy-to-use integrated learning system. Numbered icons identifying each objective appear next to the related material throughout the text and in the summary, allowing easy location of material related to each objective.

"Can You Do It?" and "Did You Get It?"

The text provides examples for the students to work at the conclusion of each major section of a chapter, which we call, "Can You Do It?" followed by "Did You Get It?" several pages later in the text. This tool provides an essential ingredient to the building-block approach to the material that we use.

CAN YOU DO IT?
SOLVING FOR THE REAL RATE OF INTEREST

Your banker just called and offered you the chance to invest your savings for 1 year at a quoted rate of 10 percent. You also saw on the news that the inflation rate is 6 percent. What is the real rate of interest you would be earning if you made the investment? (The solution can be found on page 38.)

DID YOU GET IT?
SOLVING FOR THE REAL RATE OF INTEREST

Nominal or quoted = rate of interest	=	real rate of interest	+	inflation rate	+	product of the real rate of interest and the inflation rate
0.10	=	(real rate of interest)	+	0.06	+	0.06 × real rate of interest
0.04	=	1.06 × (real rate of interest)				

Solving for the real rate of interest :
(real rate of interest) =   0.0377   =   3.77%

Concept Check

At the end of most major sections, this tool highlights the key ideas just presented and allows students to test their understanding of the material.

Concept Check _____

1. According to Principle 3, how do investors decide where to invest their money?
2. What is an efficient market?
3. What is the a
4. Why are ethi

Integrated Examples

These provide students with real-world examples to help them apply the concepts presented in each chapter.

EXAMPLE 4.1

Firms A and B are identical in size. Both have $1,000 in total assets, and both have an operating return on assets of 14 percent. However, they are different in one respect: Firm A uses all equity and no debt financing; Firm B finances 60 percent of its investments with debt and 40 percent with equity. (For the sake of simplicity, we will assume that both firms pay interest at an interest cost of 6 percent, and there are no income taxes.) The financial statements for the two companies would be as follows:

	FIRM A	FIRM B
BALANCE SHEET		
Total assets	$1,000	$1,000
Debt (6% interest rate)	$ 0	$ 600
Equity	1,000	400
Total debt and equity	$1,000	$1,000
INCOME STATEMENT		
Operating income (OROA = 14%)	$ 140	$ 140
Interest expense (6%)	(0)	(36)
Net income	$ 140	$ 104

Extensive Coverage of Ethics

Ethics is covered as a core principle and "Ethics in Financial Management" boxes appear throughout. These show students that ethical behavior is doing the right thing and that ethical dilemmas are everywhere in finance.

ETHICS IN FINANCIAL MANAGEMENT

THE WALL STREET JOURNAL WORKPLACE-ETHICS QUIZ

Without question, when you enter the workforce you will be faced with a number of ethical dilemmas that you have never considered. The spread of technology into the workplace has raised a variety of new ethical questions, and many old ones still linger. The following is a quiz dealing with ethical questions that will both give you some questions to think about, and also allow you to compare your answers with those of other Americans surveyed.

Office Technology

1. Is it wrong to use company email for personal reasons?

   Yes   No

2. Is it wrong to play computer games on office equipment during the workday?

   Yes   No

3. Is it unethical to blame an error you made on a technological glitch?

   Yes   No

Gifts and Entertainment

4. Is a $50 gift to a boss unacceptable?

   Yes   No

8. Can you accept a $75 prize won at a raffle at a supplier's conference?

   Yes   No

Truth and Lies

9. Due to on-the-job pressure, have you ever abused or lied about sick days?

   Yes   No

10. Due to on-the-job pressure, have you ever taken credit for someone else's work or idea?

    Yes   No

Sources: Ethics Officer Association, Belmont, Mass.; Ethical Leadership Group, Wilmette, Ill.; surveys sampled a cross-section of workers at large companies and nationwide

Ethics Quiz Answers

1. 34% said personal email on company computers is wrong
2. 49% said playing computer games at work is wrong
3. 61% said it's unethical to blame your error on technology
4. 35% said a $50 gift to the boss is unacceptable
5. 12% said a $50 gift from the boss is unacceptable
6. 70% said it's unacceptable to take the $200 football tickets
7. 35% said it's unacceptable to take the $100 food basket
8. 40% said it's unacceptable to take the $75 raffle prize
9. 11% reported they lie about sick days
10. 4% reported they take credit for the work or ideas of others

Source: *The Wall Street Journal*, October 21, 1999, page B1 (Copyright © 1999, Dow Jones & Company, Inc.) All Rights Reserved.

Remember Your Principles

These in-text inserts appear throughout to allow the student to take time out and reflect on the meaning of the material just presented. The use of these inserts, coupled with the use of the 5 principles, keeps the student focused on the interrelationships and motivating factors behind the concepts.

REMEMBER YOUR PRINCIPLES

Principle In this chapter, we cover material that introduces the financial manager to the process involved in raising funds in the nation's capital markets and how interest rates in those markets are determined.

Without question the United States has a highly developed, complex, and competitive system of financial markets that allows for the quick transfer of savings from people and organizations with a surplus of savings to those with a savings deficit. Such a system of highly developed financial markets allows great ideas (such as the personal computer) to be financed and increases the overall wealth of the economy. Consider your wealth, for example, compared to that of the average family in Russia. Russia lacks the complex system of financial markets to facilitate securities transactions. As a result, real capital formation there has suffered.

Thus, we return now to **Principle 4: Market Prices Are Generally Right**. Financial managers like the U.S. system of capital markets because they trust it. This trust stems from the fact that the markets are efficient, and so prices quickly and accurately reflect all available information about the value of the underlying securities. This means that the expected risks and expected cash flows matter more to market participants than do simpler things such as accounting changes and the sequence of past price changes in a specific security. With security prices and returns (such as interest rates) competitively determined, more financial managers (rather than fewer) participate in the markets and help ensure the basic concept of efficiency.

Mini Case

The final stage in the interview process for an assistant financial analyst at Caledonia Products involves a test of your understanding of basic financial concepts. You are given the following memorandum and asked to respond to the questions. Whether you are offered a position at Caledonia will depend on the accuracy of your response.

To: Applicants for the position of Financial Analyst
From: Mr. V. Morrison, CEO, Caledonia Products
Re: A test of your understanding of basic financial concepts and of the corporate tax code

Please respond to the following questions:

a. What is the appropriate goal for the firm and why?
b. What does the risk–return trade-off mean?
c. Why are we interested in cash flows rather than accounting profits in determining the value of an asset?
d. What is an efficient market and what are the implications of efficient markets for us?
e. What is the cause of the agency problem and how do we try to solve it?
f. What do ethics and ethical behavior have to do with fin
g. Define (1) sole proprietorship, (2) partnership, and (3)

Comprehensive End-of-Chapter Problems

A comprehensive Mini Case appears at the end of almost every chapter, covering all the major topics included in that chapter. This Mini Case can be used as a lecture or review tool by the professor. For the students, it provides an opportunity to apply all the concepts presented within the chapter in a realistic setting, thereby strengthening their understanding of the material.

CALCULATOR SOLUTION

Data Input	Function Key
10	N
6	I/Y
−500	FV
0	PMT

Function Key	Answer
CPT	
PV	279.20

Financial Calculators

The use of financial calculators has been integrated throughout this text, especially with respect to the presentation of the time value of money. Where appropriate, calculator solutions appear in the margin.

Content Updates

In response to both the continued development of financial thought and reviewer comments, changes have been made in the text. Some of these changes include:

Chapter 1
An Introduction to the Foundations of Financial Management

- Updated and revised to make it as intuitive as possible.
- The principles that form the Foundations of Finance were simplified and consolidated from 10 principles down to 5 principles. In addition, a section titled Avoiding Financial Crisis—Back to the Principles was introduced. This section examines each of the principles individually and how ignoring them helped bring on the recent financial crisis.
- A new section on the importance of ethics and trust in financial management was introduced.
- In addition, new examples were added.

Chapter 2
The Financial Markets and Interest Rates

- This chapter was significantly revised to reflect the recent changes in the financial markets.
- The chapter was simplified to make it livelier and more relevant to students.
- A new section titled The Financing of Business: The Movement of Funds Through the Economy was added. This section illustrates the role of finance in our economy.
- The discussion of investment banking was revised to reflect the dramatic impact of the recent financial crisis on investment banking firms.
- A Cautionary Tale—Forgetting Principle 5: Conflicts of Interest Cause Agency Problems was introduced illustrating the impact of ignoring the principles of finance on the recent financial crisis.
- The discussion of interest rates determinants was also simplified and made more intuitive.
- This chapter was rewritten with an eye toward providing the student with need-to-know information that is used as building blocks to understand and introduce material in subsequent chapters.

Chapter 3
Understanding Financial Statements and Cash Flows

- A cautionary tale illustrating the peril of forgetting the principle that cash flows determine value.
- A new **Finance at Work** drawing from a recent *Fortune* magazine article that highlights how the world of finance may change as a result of the recent financial crisis.
- A presentation of Hewlett-Packard's financial statements to let a student see a real-world example.
- An improved figure that visually presents the make-up of a balance sheet was added.
- A totally new presentation of cash flows was added.
- The addition of a new section explaining the relevance and computation of income taxes was added.

Chapter 4
Evaluating A Firm's Financial Performance

- A cautionary tale that shows the danger of forgetting the principle that risk requires reward was added.
- A new **Ethics in Financial Management** that describes frequent rationalizations for acting unethically was added.

Chapter 5
The Time Value of Money

- A new section on the use of timelines to visualize cash flows was added.
- This chapter was revised with an eye toward making it more accessible to math-phobic students.
- Coverage of the time value of money tables was dropped.
- Alternative approaches to solving time value of money problems were provided.
- A Cautionary Tale—Forgetting Principle 3: Risk Requires a Reward and Principle 4: Market Prices Are Generally Right was introduced.
- An increased emphasis on the intuition behind the time value of money was provided stressing visualizing and setting up the problem.

Chapter 6
The Meaning and Measurement of Risk and Return

- The chapter provides an expanded presentation of holding-period returns to insure that students understand the foundation concept of returns.
- When explaining how to compute a standard deviation of returns, we developed a step-by-step approach instead of simply presenting an equation.
- There is a new **Ethics in Financial Management** box that tells the story of Aaron Beam, former CFO of HealthSouth Corporation, who explains how he gradually slipped in committing fraud, and what life is like for him today.
- The chapter offers a new presentation of risk and diversification, using Google as an example.
- There is a new presentation in the chapter showing the relationship between risk and return and the length of the holding period.

Chapter 7
The Valuation and Characteristics of Bonds

- This chapter has been revised to provide an updated explanation with examples of the nature and characteristics of bonds.
- There are all new real-world examples of how to compute the value and expected rates of returns of a bond.

Chapter 8
The Characteristics and Value of Stocks

- The chapter presents a cautionary tale that lets a student see some of the foolish ways investors try to outperform the market, usually with disastrous results, suggesting that Principle 4, Market Prices Are Generally Right, is active and working.
- We have simplified the presentation of stock valuation that better fits the needs of a student in a beginning finance class.

Chapter 9
The Cost of Capital

- This chapter was moved to appear before the discussion of capital budgeting.
- The new placement provides a logical transition from the discussion of the determinants of capital market rates of return in Chapter 8 to the application of this material to the estimation of the firm's cost of capital.
- The plight of Goldman Sachs when the credit markets seized up in 2008 is used to illustrate the volatile nature of a firm's cost of capital.

Chapter 10
Capital Budgeting Techniques and Practice
- Added coverage of the discounted payback period was included.
- The number of worked out examples were increased in this chapter since this is one of the key chapters in the book and one that traditionally provides students with a great deal of difficulty.
- Additional problems were added.

Chapter 11
Cash Flows and Other Topics in Capital Budgeting
- The discussion of the calculation of a project's free cash flows was simplified and made more intuitive in nature, while additional worked out problems were added to the chapter.

Chapter 12
Determining the Financing Mix
- Increased the discussion linking operating, financial, and combined leverage.

Chapter 13
Dividend Policy and Internal Financing
- Additional coverage of the practical considerations underlying the determination of a firm's dividend policy.

Chapter 14
Short-Term Financing
- Increased emphasis on percent of sales forecasting as well as its inherent limitations.

Chapter 15
Working Capital Management
- Revised discussion of the cash conversion cycle and its role in reducing a firm's investment in working capital.

Chapter 16
Current Asset Management
- Streamlined coverage of the methods used to speed up collections of accounts receivable.

Chapter 17
International Business Finance
- This chapter was revised and updated to reflect changes in exchange rates and in the global financial markets in general.
- The section on interest rate parity was streamlined and simplified.

A Complete Support Package for the Student and Instructor

MyFinanceLab

This fully integrated online homework system gives students the hands-on practice and tutorial help they need to learn finance efficiently. Ample opportunities for online practice and assessment in MyFinanceLab are seamlessly integrated into each chapter. For more details, see the inside front cover.

Instructor's Resource Center

This password-protected site is accessible at www.pearsonhighered.com/keown and hosts all of the instructor resources that follow. Instructors should click on the "Help Downloading Instructor Resources" link for easy-to-follow instructions on getting access or may contact their sales representative for further information.

Test Item File

This Online Test Item File, prepared by Alan D. Eastman of Indiana University of Pennsylvania, provides more than 1,600 multiple-choice, true/false, and short-answer questions with complete and detailed answers. The online Test Item File is designed for use with the TestGen-EQ test generating software. This computerized package allows instructors to custom design, save, and generate classroom tests. The test program permits instructors to edit, add, or delete questions from the test bank; edit existing graphics and create new graphics; analyze test results; and organize a database of tests and student results. This new software allows for greater flexibility and ease of use. It provides many options for organizing and displaying tests, along with a search and sort feature.

Instructor's Manual with Solutions

Written by the authors, the Online Instructor's Manual follows the textbook's organization and represents a continued effort to serve the teacher in his or her goal of being effective in the classroom. Each chapter contains a chapter orientation, an outline of each chapter (also suitable for lecture notes), answers to end-of-chapter questions, and an extensive problem set for each chapter, including a large number of alternative problems along with answers.

　The Instructor's Manual is available electronically and instructors can download this file from the Instructor's Resource Center by visiting www.pearsonhighered.com/keown.

The PowerPoint Lecture Presentation

This lecture presentation tool, prepared by Philip Samuel Russel of Philadelphia University, provides the instructor with individual lecture outlines to accompany the text. The slides include many of the figures and tables from the text. These lecture notes can be used as is or instructors can easily modify them to reflect specific presentation needs.

Study Guide

The Study Guide to accompany *Foundations of Finance: The Logic and Practice of Financial Management*, 7th Edition, was written by the authors with the objective of providing a student-oriented supplement to the text. Each chapter of the Study Guide contains an orientation of each chapter along with a chapter outline of key topics; problems (with detailed solutions) and self-tests, which can be used to aid in the preparation of outside assignments and in studying for exams; a tutorial on capital budgeting; and a set of tables that not only gives compound sum and present value interest factors but also shows how to compute the interest using a financial calculator.

Companion Website

(www.pearsonhighered.com/keown) The Website contains various activities related specifically to the Seventh Edition of *Foundations of Finance: The Logic and Practice of Financial Management*.

Excel Spreadsheets

Created by the authors, these spreadsheets correspond with the end-of-chapter problems from the text. This student resource is available on both the companion Website and MyFinanceLab.

CourseSmart for Instructors

CourseSmart goes beyond traditional teaching resources to provide instant, online access to the textbooks and course materials you need at a lower cost to students. And while students save money, you can save time and hassle with a digital textbook that allows you to search the most relevant content at the very moment you need it. Whether it's for evaluating textbooks or creating lecture notes to help students with difficult concepts, CourseSmart can make life a little easier. See how by visiting the CourseSmart Web site at www.coursesmart.com/instructors.

CourseSmart for Students

CourseSmart goes beyond traditional expectations providing instant, online access to the textbooks and course materials students need at lower cost. Students can also search, highlight, and take notes anywhere at any time. See all the benefits to students at www.coursesmart.com/students.

Subscriptions

Analyzing current events is an important skill for economic students to develop. To sharpen this skill and further support the book's theme of exploration and application, Prentice Hall offers you and your student's three news subscription offers:

The *Wall Street Journal* Print and Interactive Editions Subscription

Prentice Hall has formed a strategic alliance with the *Wall Street Journal*, the most respected and trusted daily source for information on business and economics. For a small additional charge, Prentice Hall offers students a 15-week subscription to the *Wall Street Journal* Interactive Edition (wsj.com) and a 15-week complimentary print edition subscription. Upon receipt of 10 student registrations from an adopting institution, a professor can receive a one-year subscription of the print and interactive versions as well as weekly subject-specific *Wall Street Journal* educators' lesson plans.

The *Financial Times*

We are pleased to announce a special partnership with the *Financial Times*. For a small additional charge, Prentice Hall offers your students a 15-week subscription to the *Financial Times*. Upon adoption of a special package containing the book and the subscription booklet, professors will receive a free one-year subscription. Please contact your Prentice Hall representative for details and ordering information.

Economist.com

Through a special arrangement with Economist.com, Prentice Hall offers your students a 12-week subscription to Economist.com for a small additional charge. Upon adoption of a special package containing the book and the subscription booklet, professors will receive a free six-month subscription. Please contact your Prentice Hall representative for further details and ordering information.

Acknowledgments

We gratefully acknowledge the assistance, support, and encouragement of those individuals who have contributed to the Seventh Edition of *Foundations of Finance*. Specifically, we wish to recognize the very helpful insights provided by many of our colleagues. For their careful comments and helpful reviews of the text, we are indebted to:

Haseeb Ahmed, Johnson C. Smith University
Joan Anderssen, Arapahoe Community College
Chris Armstrong, Draughons Junior College
Curtis Bacon, Southern Oregon University
Deb Bauer, University of Oregon
Pat Bernson, County College of Morris
Ed Boyer, Temple University
Joe Brocato, Tarleton State University
Joseph Brum, Fayetteville Technical Community College
Lawrence Byerly, Thomas More College
Janice Caudill, Auburn University
David Daglio, Newbury College
Julie Dahlquist, University of Texas at San Antonio
David Darst, Central Ohio Technical College
Maria de Boyrie, New Mexico State University
Kate Demarest, Carroll Community College
Khaled Elkhal, University of Southern Indiana
Cheri Etling, University of Tampa
Cheryl Fetterman, Cape Fear Community College
David R. Fewings, Western Washington University
Dr. Charles Gahala, Benedictine University
Harry Gallatin, Indiana State University
Deborah Giarusso, University of Northern Iowa
Gregory Goussak, University of Nevada, Las Vegas
Lori Grady, Bucks County Community College
Ed Graham, University of North Carolina Wilmington
Barry Greenberg, Webster University
Gary Greer, University of Houston Downtown
Bruce Hadburg, University of Tampa
Thomas Hiebert, University of North Carolina, Charlotte
Marlin Jensen, Auburn University

John Kachurick, Misericordia University
Okan Kavuncu, University of California at Santa Cruz
Gary Kayakachoian, Rhode Island College
Lynn Phillips Kugele, University of Mississippi
Mary LaPann, Adirondack Community College
Carlos Liard-Muriente, Central Connecticut State University
Christopher Liberty, College of St Rose, Empire State College
Edmund Mantell, Pace University
Peter Marks, Rhode Island College
Mario Mastrandrea, Cleveland State University
Anna McAleer, Arcadia University
Robert Meyer, Parkland College
Ronald Moy, St. John's University
Elisa Muresan, Long Island University
Anthony Pondillo, Siena College
Walter Purvis, Coastal Carolina Community College
Emil Radosevich, Central New Mexico Community College
Deana Ray, Forsyth Technical Community College
Clarence Rose, Radford University
Ahmad Salam, Widener University
Jeffrey Schultz, Christian Brothers University
Ken Shakoori, California State University, Bakersfield
Michael Slates, Bowling Green State University
Suresh Srivastava, University of Alaska Anchorage
Maurry Tamarkin, Clark University
Fang Wang, West Virginia University
Paul Warrick, Westwood College
Jill Wetmore, Saginaw Valley State University
Kevin Yost, Auburn University
Jingxue Yuan, Texas Tech University
Mengxin Zhao, Bentley College

We also thank our friends at Prentice Hall. We offer our personal expression of appreciation to our editor-in-chief Donna Battista who provided the leadership and direction to this project. We would also like to thank Tessa O'Brien, our finance editor. Tessa has been a pleasure to work with, always full of ideas and driven to help us produce the best book possible. We would also like to thank Sara Holliday, our project manager, for her administrative deftness. With Sara watching over us, there was no way the ball could be dropped. Our hats are off to you, Sara. We would also like to extend our thanks to Heather McNally, who served as our production supervisor; we express a very special thank you for seeing the book through a very complex production process and keeping it all on schedule while maintaining extremely high quality. Our thanks also go to Liz Averbeck for her marketing prowess. Liz has an amazing understanding of the market, coupled with an intuitive understanding of what the market is looking for. In addition to being a joy to work with, she is also the hardest working person in America. We also thank Nicole Sackin, our media producer, who did a great job of making sure we are on the cutting edge in terms of web applications and offerings.

As a final word, we express our sincere thanks to those using *Foundations of Finance* in the classroom. We thank you for making us a part of your team. Always feel free to give any of us a call or contact us through the Internet when you have questions or needs.

—A.J.K. / J.D.M. / J.W.P.

Chapter 1

An Introduction to the Foundations of Financial Management

Learning Objectives

After reading this chapter, you should be able to:

 Identify the goal of the firm.

 Understand the five basic principles of finance and business, the consequences of forgetting those basic principles of finance, and the importance of ethics and trust in business.

 Describe the role of finance in business.

 Distinguish between the different legal forms of business.

 Explain what has led to the era of the multinational corporation.

Apple Computer (AAPL) ignited the personal computer revolution in the 1970s with the Apple II and reinvented the personal computer in the 1980s with the Macintosh. But by 1997, it looked like it might be nearing the end for Apple. Mac users were on the decline, and the company didn't seem to be headed in any real direction. It was at that point that Steve Jobs reappeared, taking back his old job as CEO of Apple, the company he cofounded in 1976. To say the least, things began to change. In fact, between then and September 2009, the price of Apple's common stock has climbed by over forty-one-fold!

How did Apple accomplish this? The company did it by going back to what it does best, which is to produce products that make the optimal trade-off between ease of use, complexity, and features. Apple took its special skills and applied them to more than just computers, introducing new products such as the iPod, iTunes, the sleek iMac, the MacBook Air, iPod Touch, and the iPhone along with its unlimited "apps." Although all these products have done well, the success of the iPod has been truly amazing. Between the introduction of the iPod in October 2001 and the beginning of 2005, Apple sold more than 6 million of the devices. Then, in 2004, it came out with the iPod Mini, about the length and width of a business card, which has also been a huge success, particularly among women. How successful has this new product been? By 2004, Apple was selling more iPods than its signature Macintosh desktop and notebook computers.

How do you follow up on the success of the iPod? You keep improving your products and you keep developing and introducing new products that consumers want. With this in mind, in March 2009, Apple unveiled its latest version of the iPod Shuffle. At half the size of the previous generation iPod Shuffle, it has 4GB of storage, is able to hold up to 1,000 songs, and is less than the size of a house key. It even has a new feature called VoiceOver that, with the press of a button, tells you the song title or artist.

How did Apple make a decision to introduce the original iPod and now the tiny iPod Shuffle? The answer is by identifying a customer need, combined with sound financial management. Financial management deals with the maintenance and creation of economic value or wealth by focusing on decision making with an eye toward creating wealth. As such, this text deals with financial decisions such as when to introduce a new product, when to invest in new assets, when to replace existing assets, when to borrow from banks, when to sell stocks or bonds, when to extend credit to a customer, and how much cash and inventory to maintain. All of these aspects of financial management were factors in Apple's decision to introduce and continuously improve the iPod, iPod Shuffle, and iPhone, and the end result is having a major financial impact on Apple.

In this chapter, we lay the foundation for the entire book by explaining the key goal that guides financial decision making: maximizing shareholder wealth. From there we introduce the thread that ties everything together: the five basic principles of finance. Finally, we discuss the legal forms of business. We close the chapter with a brief look at what has led to the rise in multinational corporations.

The Goal of the Firm

 Identify the goal of the firm.

The fundamental goal of a business is to create value for the company's owners (that is, its shareholders). This goal is frequently stated as "maximization of shareholder wealth." Thus, the goal of the financial manager is to create wealth for the shareholders, by making decisions that will maximize the price of the existing common stock. Not only does this goal directly benefit the shareholders of the company, but it also provides benefits to society as scarce resources are directed to their most productive use by businesses competing to create wealth.

We have chosen maximization of shareholder wealth—that is, maximizing the market value of the existing shareholders' common stock—because the effects of all financial decisions ultimately affect the firm's stock price. Investors react to poor investment or dividend decisions by causing the total value of the firm's stock to fall, and they react to good decisions by pushing up the price of the stock. In effect, under this goal, good decisions are those that create wealth for the shareholder.

Obviously, there are some serious practical problems in using changes in the firm's stock to evaluate financial decisions. Many things affect stock prices; to attempt to identify a reaction to a particular financial decision would simply be impossible, but fortunately that is unnecessary. To employ this goal, we need not consider every stock price change to be a market interpretation of the worth of our decisions. Other factors, such as changes in the economy, also affect stock prices. What we do focus on is the effect that our decision *should have* on the stock price if everything else were held constant. The market price of the firm's stock reflects the value of the firm as seen by its owners and takes into account the complexities and complications of the real-world risk. As we follow this goal throughout our discussions, we must keep in mind one more question: Who exactly are the shareholders? The answer: Shareholders are the legal owners of the firm.

Concept Check

1. What is the goal of the firm?
2. How would you apply this goal in practice?

 Understand the five basic principles of finance and business, the consequences of forgetting those basic principles of finance, and the importance of ethics and trust in business.

Five Principles that Form the Foundations of Finance

To the first-time student of finance, the subject matter may seem like a collection of unrelated decision rules. This could not be further from the truth. In fact, our decision rules, and the logic that underlies them, spring from five simple principles that do not require knowledge of finance to understand. These five principles guide the financial manager in the creation of value for the firm's owners (the stockholders).

As you will see, while it is not necessary to understand finance to understand these principles, it is necessary to understand these principles in order to understand finance. Although these principles may at first appear simple or even trivial, they provide the driving force behind all that follows, weaving together the concepts and techniques presented in this text, and thereby allowing us to focus on the logic underlying the practice of financial management. Now let's introduce the five principles.

Principle 1: Cash Flow Is What Matters

You probably recall from your accounting classes that a company's profits can differ dramatically from its cash flows which we will review in Chapter 3. But for now understand that cash flows, not profits, represent money that can be spent. Consequently, it is cash flow, not profits that determines the value of a business. For this reason when we analyze the consequences of a managerial decision we focus on the resulting cash flows, not profits.

In the movie industry, there is a big difference between accounting profits and cash flow. Many a movie is crowned a success and brings in plenty of cash flow for the studio, but doesn't produce a profit. Even some of the most successful box office hits—*Forrest Gump*, *Coming to America*, and *Batman*—realized no accounting profits at all after accounting for various movie studio costs. That's because "Hollywood Accounting" allows for overhead costs not associated with the movie to be added on to the true cost of the movie. In fact, the movie *My Big Fat Greek Wedding*, which was the fifth highest grossing movie of 2002, actually lost $20 million according to the accountants. Was *My Big Fat Greek Wedding* a successful movie? It sure was—in fact it grossed over $370 million on a budget of only $5 million. Without question it produced cash, but it didn't make any profits. Unfortunately for most of the cast, their contracts entitled them to a cut of the profits, not the cash flows. They learned a bitter lesson about the difference in cash flows and profits.

incremental cash flow the difference between the cash flows a company will produce both with and without the investment it is thinking about making.

There is another important point we need to make about cash flows. Recall from your economics classes that we should always look at marginal, or **incremental cash flows** when making a financial decision. The incremental cash flow to the company as a whole is *the difference between the cash flows the company will produce both with and without the investment it's thinking about making.* To understand this concept let's think about the incremental cash flows of a movie like *Pirates of the Caribbean.* Not only did Disney make money on the movie, the movie also increased the number of people attracted to Disney theme parks to go on the "Pirates of the Caribbean" ride. So, if you were to evaluate that movie, you'd want to include its impact on sales throughout the entire company.

Principle 2: Money Has a Time Value

Perhaps the most fundamental principle of finance is that money has a "time" value. Very simply, a dollar received today is more valuable than a dollar received one year from now because we can invest the dollar we have today to earn interest so that at the end of one year we will have more than one dollar.

For example, suppose you have a choice of receiving $1,000 either today or one year from now. If you decide to receive it a year from now, you will have passed up the opportunity to earn a year's interest on the money. Economists would say you suffered an "opportunity loss" or an "opportunity cost." The cost is the interest you could have earned on the $1,000 if you invested it for one year. The concept of opportunity costs is fundamental to the study of finance and economics. Very simply, the **opportunity cost** of any choice you make *is the highest-valued alternative that you had to give up when you made the choice.* So if you loan money to your brother at no interest, money that otherwise would have been loaned to a friend for 8 percent interest (who is equally likely to repay you), then the opportunity cost of making the loan to your brother is 8 percent.

In the study of finance, we focus on the creation and measurement of value. To measure value, we use the concept of the time value of money to bring the future benefits and costs of a project, measured by its cash flows, back to the present. Then, if the benefits or cash inflows outweigh the costs, the project creates wealth and should be accepted; if the costs or cash outflows outweigh the benefits or cash inflows, the project destroys wealth and should be rejected. Without recognizing the existence of the time value of money, it is impossible to evaluate projects with future benefits and costs in a meaningful way.

opportunity cost the next best alternative available to the decision maker for a given level of risk.

Principle 3: Risk Requires a Reward

Even the novice investor knows there are an unlimited number of investment alternatives to consider. But without exception, investors will not invest if they do not expect to receive a return on their investment. They will want a return that satisfies two requirements:

◆ *A return for delaying consumption.* Why would anyone make an investment that would not at least pay them something for delaying consumption? They won't—even if there is no risk. In fact, investors will want to receive at least the same return that is available for risk-free investments, such as the rate of return being earned on U.S. government securities.

◆ *An additional return for taking on risk.* Investors generally don't like risk. Thus, risky investments are less attractive—*unless* they offer the prospect of higher returns. That said, the more unsure people are about how an investment will perform, the higher the return they will demand for making that investment. So, if you are trying to persuade investors to put money into a risky venture you are pursuing, you will have to offer them a higher expected rate of return.

Figure 1-1 depicts the basic notion that an investor's rate of return should equal a rate of return for delaying consumption plus an additional return for assuming risk. For example, if you have $5,000 to invest and are considering either buying stock in International

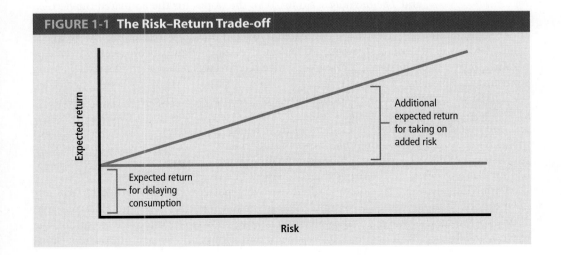

FIGURE 1-1 The Risk–Return Trade-off

Business Machines (IBM) or investing in a new bio-tech startup firm that has no past record of success, you would want the startup investment to offer the prospect of a higher expected rate of return than the investment in an established company like IBM.

Notice that we keep referring to the *expected* return rather than the *actual* return. As investors, we have expectations about what returns our investments will earn. However, we can't know for certain what they *will* be. For example, if investors could have seen into the future, no one would have bought stock in the women's retailer Ann Taylor Stores (XETRA: AAK.DE) on March 6, 2009. Why, because on that day, Ann Taylor announced a larger than expected fourth quarter loss. The result was that in minutes of the announcement, the company's stock price dropped a whopping 38 percent.

The risk–return relationship will be a key concept as we value stocks, bonds, and proposed new investment projects throughout this text. We will also spend some time determining how to measure risk. Interestingly, much of the work for which the 1990 Nobel Prize for economics was awarded centered on the graph in Figure 1-1 and how to measure risk. Both the graph and the risk-return relationship it depicts will reappear often in our study of finance.

Principle 4: Market Prices Are Generally Right

efficient market a market in which the prices of securities at any instant in time fully reflect all publicly available information about the securities and their actual public values.

To understand how securities such as bonds and stocks are valued or priced in the financial markets, it is necessary to have an understanding of the concept of an efficient market. An **efficient market** is *one where the prices of the assets traded in that market fully reflect all available information at any instant in time.*

Security markets such as the stock and bond markets are particularly important to our study of finance since these markets are the place where firms can go to raise money to finance their investments. Whether a security market such as the New York Stock Exchange (NYSE) is efficient depends on the speed with which newly released information is impounded into prices. Specifically, an efficient stock market is characterized by a large number of profit-driven individuals who act very quickly by buying (or selling) shares of stock in response to the release of new information.

If you are wondering just how vigilant investors in the stock market are in watching for good and bad news, consider the following set of events. While Nike (NKE) CEO William Perez flew aboard the company's Gulfstream jet one day in November 2005, traders on the ground sold off a significant amount of Nike's stock. Why? Because the plane's landing gear was malfunctioning, and they were watching TV coverage of the event! Before Perez landed safely, Nike's stock dropped 1.4 percent. Once Perez's plane landed, Nike's stock price immediately bounced back. This example illustrates that in the financial market there are ever-vigilant investors who are looking to act even *in the anticipation* of the release of new information.

Another example of the speed with which stock prices react to new information deals with Disney. Beginning with *Toy Story* in 1995, Disney (DIS) and Pixar (PIXR) were on a roll, making animated hits one after another including *A Bug's Life, Toy Story 2, Monsters, Inc., Finding Nemo,* and *The Incredibles.* So in 2006, the hopes for the animated movie *Cars* were very high. However, in the movie's opening weekend, it grossed only $60 million or about $10 million less than investors expected. How did the stock market respond? On the Monday following the opening weekend, Disney stock opened over two percent lower. Apparently, the news of the disappointing box office receipts was reflected in Disney's opening stock price, even before it traded!

The key learning point here is the following: Stock market prices are a useful barometer of the value of a firm. Specifically, managers can expect their company's share prices to respond quickly to investors' assessment of their decisions. If investors on the whole agree that the decision is a good one that creates value, then they will push up the price of the firm's stock to reflect that added value. On the other hand, if investors feel that a decision is bad for share prices, then the firm's share value will be driven down.

Unfortunately, this principle doesn't always work perfectly in the real world. You just need to look at the housing price bubble that helped bring on the economic downturn in 2008–2009 to realize that prices and value don't always move in lockstep. Like it or not, the psychological biases of individuals impact decision making, and as a result, our decision-making process is not always rational. Behavioral finance considers this type of behavior, and takes what we already know about financial decision making and adds in human behavior with all its apparent irrationality.

We'll try and point out the impact of human behavior on decisions throughout our study. But understand that the field of behavioral finance is a work in progress—we understand only a small portion of what may be going on. We can say, however, that behavioral biases have an impact on our financial decisions. As an example, people tend to be overconfident, and many times mistake skill for luck. As Robert Shiller, a well-known economics professor at Yale put it, "people think they know more than they do."[1] This overconfidence applies to their abilities, their knowledge and understanding, and in forecasting the future. Since they have confidence in their valuation estimates, they may take on more risk than they should. These behavioral biases impact everything in finance, from investment analysis, to analyzing new projects, to forecasting the future.

Principle 5: Conflicts of Interest Cause Agency Problems

P5
Principle

Throughout this book we will describe how to make financial decisions that increase the value of a firm's shares. However, managers do not always follow through with these decisions. Often they make decisions that actually lead to a decrease in the value of the firm's shares. When this happens, it is frequently because the manager's own interest is best served by ignoring shareholder interests. In other words, there is a conflict of interest between what is best for the managers and the stockholders. For example, it may be the case that shutting down an unprofitable plant is in the best interests of the firm's stockholders but in so doing the managers will find themselves out of a job or having to transfer to a different job. This very clear conflict of interest might lead the management of the plant to continue running the plant at a loss.

Conflicts of interest lead to what are referred to by economists as an agency cost or **agency problem**. That is, managers are the agents of the firm's stockholders (the owners) and if the agents do not act in the best interests of their principal this leads to an agency cost. Although the goal of the firm is to maximize shareholder value, in reality the agency problem may interfere with the implementation of this goal. *The agency problem results from the separation of management and the ownership of the firm.* For example, a large firm may be run by professional managers or agents who have little or no ownership in the firm. Because of this separation of the decision makers and owners, managers may make decisions that are not in line with the goal of maximizing shareholder wealth. They may approach work less energetically and attempt to benefit themselves in terms of salary and perquisites at the expense of shareholders.

agency problem problems and conflicts resulting from the separation of the management and ownership of the firm.

Managers might also avoid any projects that have risk associated with them—even if they are great projects with huge potential returns and a small chance of failure. Why is this so? Because if the project doesn't turn out, these agents of the shareholders may lose their jobs.

The costs associated with the agency problem are difficult to measure, but occasionally we see the problem's effect in the marketplace. If the market feels management is damaging shareholder wealth, there may be a positive reaction in stock price to the removal of that management. For example, on the announcement of the death of Roy Farmer, the CEO of Farmer Brothers (FARM), a seller of coffee-related products, Farmer Brothers' stock price rose about 28 percent. Generally, the tragic loss of a company's top executive raises concerns over a leadership void, causing the share price to drop, but in the case of Farmer Brothers, investors thought a change in management would have a positive impact on the company.

If the firm's management works for the owners, who are the shareholders, why doesn't the management get fired if it doesn't act in the shareholders' best interest? In theory, the shareholders pick the corporate board of directors and the board of directors in turn picks the management. Unfortunately, in reality the system frequently works the other way around. Management selects the board of director nominees and then distributes the ballots. In effect, shareholders are offered a slate of nominees selected by the management.

---

[1]See Robert J. Shiller, *Irrational Exuberance*, Broadway Books, 2000, page 142.

The end result is that management effectively selects the directors, who then may have more allegiance to managers than to shareholders. This, in turn, sets up the potential for agency problems, with the board of directors not monitoring managers on behalf of the shareholders as they should.

The root cause of agency problems is conflicts of interest. Whenever they exist in business, there is a chance that individuals will do what is in their best interests rather than the best interests of the organization. For example, in 2000 Edgerrin James was a running back for the Indianapolis Colts and was told by his coach to get a first down and then fall down. That way the Colts wouldn't be accused of running up the score against a team they were already beating badly. However, since James' contract included incentive payments associated with rushing yards and touchdowns, he acted in his own self-interest and ran for a touchdown on the very next play.

We will spend considerable time discussing monitoring managers and trying to align their interests with shareholders. As an example, managers can be monitored by rating agencies and by auditing financial statements, and compensation packages may be used to align the interests of managers and shareholders. For example, the interests of managers and shareholders can be aligned by establishing management stock options, bonuses, and perquisites that are directly tied to how closely their decisions coincide with the interest of shareholders. In other words, what is good for shareholders must also be good for managers. If that is not the case, managers will make decisions in their best interest rather than maximizing shareholder wealth.

Avoiding Financial Crisis—Back to the Principles

Four significant economic events that have occurred during the last decade all point to the importance of keeping our eye closely affixed to the five principles of finance: the dot.com bubble; the accounting scandals headlined by Enron and WorldCom; the housing bubble; and, finally, the recent meltdown of the credit markets. Specifically, the problems that firms encounter in times of crisis are often brought on by, and made worse as a result of not paying close attention to the foundational principles of finance. To illustrate, consider the following:

◆ **Forgetting Principle 1: Cash Flow Is What Matters** (*Focusing on earnings instead of cash flow*).   The financial fraud committed by WorldCom and others at the turn of the 21st century was a direct result of managerial efforts to manage the firm's reported earnings to the detriment of the firm's cash flows. The belief in the importance of current period earnings as the most important determinant of the market valuation of the firm's shares led some firms to sacrifice future cash flows in order to maintain the illusion of high and growing earnings.

◆ **Forgetting Principle 2: Money Has a Time Value** (*Focusing on the short run*). When trying to put in place a system that would align the interests of managers and shareholders, many firms tied managerial compensation to short-run performance. Consequently, the focus shifted in many firms from what was best in the long run to what was best in the short run.

◆ **Forgetting Principle 3: Risk Requires a Reward** (*Excessive risk taking due to underestimation of risk*).   Relying on historical evidence, managers often underestimated the real risks that their decisions entailed. This underestimation of the underlying riskiness of their decisions led managers to borrow excessively. This excessive use of borrowed money (or financial leverage) led to financial disaster and bankruptcy for many firms as the economy slipped into recession. Moreover, the financial crisis was exacerbated by the fact that many times companies simply didn't understand how much risk they were taking on. For example, AIG (AIG), the giant insurance company that the government bailed out, was involved in investments whose value is based on the price of oil in 50 years. Let's face it, no one knows what the price of oil will be in a half a century—being involved in this type of investment is blind risk.

◆ **Forgetting Principle 4: Market Prices Are Generally Right** (*Ignoring the efficiency of financial markets*).   Huge numbers of so-called hedge funds sprang up over the last decade and entered into investment strategies that pre-supposed that security prices could be predicted. Many of these same firms borrowed heavily in an effort to boost their returns and later discovered that security markets were a lot smarter than they thought and consequently realized huge losses on their highly-leveraged portfolios.

◆ **Forgetting Principle 5: Conflicts of Interest Cause Agency Problems** (*Executive compensation is out of control*).   Executive compensation in the U.S. is dominated by performance-based compensation in the form of stock options and grants. The use of these forms of compensation over the last decade in the face of one of the longest bull markets in history has resulted in tremendous growth in executive compensation. The motivations behind these methods of compensation are primarily tied to a desire to make managers behave like stockholders (owners). Unfortunately, this practice has resulted in pay for non-performance in many cases and a feeling among the general public that executive compensation is excessive. We are reminded again that solving the principal-agent problem is not easy to do, but it has to be done!

In this edition of *Foundations of Finance* we believe that now, perhaps more than at any time in our memory, adhering to the fundamental principles of finance is critical. In addition, to further emphasize the "back to principles theme" we have created a new feature called "Cautionary Tales" that highlights specific examples where a failure to adhere to one or more of the five principles led to problems.

The Essential Elements of Ethics and Trust

While not one of the five principles of finance, ethics and trust are essential elements of the business world. In fact, without ethics and trust nothing works. This statement could be applied to almost everything in life. Virtually everything we do involves some dependence on others. Although businesses frequently try to describe the rights and obligations of their dealings with others using contracts, it is impossible to write a perfect contract. Consequently, business dealings between people and firms ultimately depend on the willingness of the parties to trust one another.

Ethics or rather a lack of ethics in finance is a recurring theme in the news. Financial scandals at Enron, WorldCom, and Arthur Andersen demonstrate the fact that ethical lapses are not forgiven in the business world. Not only is acting in an ethical manner morally correct, it is a necessary ingredient to long-term business and personal success.

Ethical behavior is easily defined. It's simply "doing the right thing." But what is the right thing? For example, Bristol-Myers Squibb (BMY) gives away heart medication to people who can't afford it. Clearly, the firm's management feels this is socially responsible and the right thing to do. But is it? Should companies give away money and products or should they leave such acts of benevolence to the firm's shareholders? Perhaps the shareholders should decide if they personally want to donate some of their wealth to worthy causes.

Like most ethical questions, there is no clear-cut answer to the dilemma posited above. We acknowledge that people have a right to disagree about what "doing the right thing" means, and that each of us has his or her personal set of values. These values form the basis for what we think is right and wrong. Moreover, every society adopts a set of rules or laws that prescribe what it believes constitutes "doing the right thing." In a sense, we can think of laws as a set of rules that reflect the values of a society as a whole.

You might ask yourself, "As long as I'm not breaking society's laws, why should I care about ethics?" The answer to this question lies in consequences. Everyone makes errors of judgment in business which is to be expected in an uncertain world. But ethical errors are different. Even if they don't result in anyone going to jail, they tend to end careers and thereby terminate future opportunities. Why? Because unethical behavior destroys trust, and businesses cannot function without a certain degree of trust.

Throughout this book, we will point out some of the ethical pitfalls that have tripped up managers. We encourage you to do the same so these mistakes don't happen to you. Taking "The Wall Street Journal Workplace-Ethics Quiz" in the Ethics in Financial Management box is a good place for you to begin.

ETHICS IN FINANCIAL MANAGEMENT

THE WALL STREET JOURNAL WORKPLACE-ETHICS QUIZ

Without question, when you enter the workforce you will be faced with a number of ethical dilemmas that you have never considered. The spread of technology into the workplace has raised a variety of new ethical questions, and many old ones still linger. The following is a quiz dealing with ethical questions that will both give you some questions to think about, and also allow you to compare your answers with those of other Americans surveyed.

Office Technology

1. Is it wrong to use company email for personal reasons?

   Yes   No

2. Is it wrong to play computer games on office equipment during the workday?

   Yes   No

3. Is it unethical to blame an error you made on a technological glitch?

   Yes   No

Gifts and Entertainment

4. Is a $50 gift to a boss unacceptable?

   Yes   No

5. Is a $50 gift FROM the boss unacceptable?

   Yes   No

6. Of gifts from suppliers: Is it OK to take a $200 pair of football tickets?

   Yes   No

7. Is it OK to take a $100 holiday food basket?

   Yes   No

8. Can you accept a $75 prize won at a raffle at a supplier's conference?

   Yes   No

Truth and Lies

9. Due to on-the-job pressure, have you ever abused or lied about sick days?

   Yes   No

10. Due to on-the-job pressure, have you ever taken credit for someone else's work or idea?

    Yes   No

Sources: Ethics Officer Association, Belmont, Mass.; Ethical Leadership Group, Wilmette, Ill.; surveys sampled a cross-section of workers at large companies and nationwide

Ethics Quiz Answers

1. 34% said personal email on company computers is wrong
2. 49% said playing computer games at work is wrong
3. 61% said it's unethical to blame your error on technology
4. 35% said a $50 gift to the boss is unacceptable
5. 12% said a $50 gift from the boss is unacceptable
6. 70% said it's unacceptable to take the $200 football tickets
7. 35% said it's unacceptable to take the $100 food basket
8. 40% said it's unacceptable to take the $75 raffle prize
9. 11% reported they lie about sick days
10. 4% reported they take credit for the work or ideas of others

Concept Check

1. According to Principle 3, how do investors decide where to invest their money?
2. What is an efficient market?
3. What is the agency problem and why does it occur?
4. Why are ethics and trust important in business?

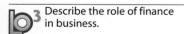 **3** Describe the role of finance in business.

The Role of Finance in Business

Finance is the study of how people and businesses evaluate investments and raise capital to fund them. Our interpretation of an investment is quite broad. When Google designed its G1 Cell Phone, it was clearly making a long-term investment. The firm had to devote considerable expenses to designing, producing, and marketing the cell phone with the hope that the cell phone would eventually capture a sufficient amount of market share from the iPhone to make the investment worthwhile. Similarly, Google is making an investment decision whenever it hires a fresh new graduate, knowing that it will be paying a salary for at least 6 months before the employee will have much to contribute.

Thus, there are three basic types of issues that are addressed by the study of finance:

1. What long-term investments should the firm undertake? This area of finance is generally referred to as **capital budgeting**.
2. How should the firm raise money to fund these investments? The firm's funding choices are generally referred to as **capital structure decisions**.
3. How can the firm best manage its cash flows as they arise in its day-to-day operations? This area of finance is generally referred to as **working capital management**.

We'll be looking at each of these three areas of business finance—capital budgeting, capital structure, and working capital management—in the chapters ahead.

capital budgeting the decision-making process with respect to investment in fixed assets.

capital structure decision the decision-making process with funding choices and the mix of long-term sources of funds.

working capital management the management of the firm's current assets and short-term financing.

Why Study Finance?

Even if you're not planning a career in finance, a working knowledge of finance will take you far in both your personal and professional life.

Those interested in management will need to study topics like strategic planning, personnel, organizational behavior, and human relations, all of which involve spending money today in the hopes of generating more money in the future. For example, GM made a strategic decision to introduce an electric car and invested $740 million to produce the Chevy Volt, a decision GM expects to pay off in the future and save the company. Similarly, marketing majors need to understand and decide how aggressively to price products and the amount to spend on advertising. Since aggressive marketing today costs money, but allows firms to reap rewards in the future, it should be viewed as an investment that the firm needs to finance. Production and operations management majors need to understand how best to manage a firm's production and control its inventory and supply chain. These are all topics that involve risky choices that relate to the management of money over time, which is the central focus of finance. *While finance is primarily about the management of money, a key component of finance is the management and interpretation of information.* Indeed, if you pursue a career in management information systems or accounting, the finance managers are likely to be your most important clients. For the student with entrepreneurial aspirations, an understanding of finance is essential—after all, if you can't manage your finances, you won't be in business very long.

Finally, an understanding of finance is important to you as an individual. The fact that you are reading this book indicates that you understand the importance of investing in yourself. By obtaining a higher education degree, you are clearly making sacrifices in the hopes of making yourself more employable and improving your chances of having a rewarding and challenging career. Some of you are relying on your own earnings and the earnings of your parents to finance your education, whereas others are raising money or borrowing it from the **financial markets**, or *institutions and procedures that facilitate financial transactions*.

Although the primary focus of this book is on developing corporate finance tools that are used in business, much of the logic and tools we develop apply to the decisions you will have to make regarding your own personal finances. Financial decisions are everywhere, both for you and the firm you work for. In the future, both your business and personal life will be spent in the world of finance. Since you're going to be living in that world, it's time to learn the basics about it.

financial markets those institutions and procedures that facilitate transactions in all types of financial claims.

The Role of the Financial Manager

A firm can assume many different organizational structures. Figure 1-2 shows a typical presentation of how the finance area fits into a firm. The vice president for finance, also called the chief financial officer (CFO), serves under the firm's chief executive officer (CEO) and is responsible for overseeing financial planning, strategic planning, and controlling the firm's cash flow. Typically, a treasurer and controller serve under the CFO. In a smaller firm, the same person may fill both roles, with just one office handling all the duties. The treasurer generally handles the firm's financial activities, including cash and credit management, making capital expenditure decisions, raising funds, financial planning, and managing any foreign currency received by the firm. The controller is responsible for managing the firm's

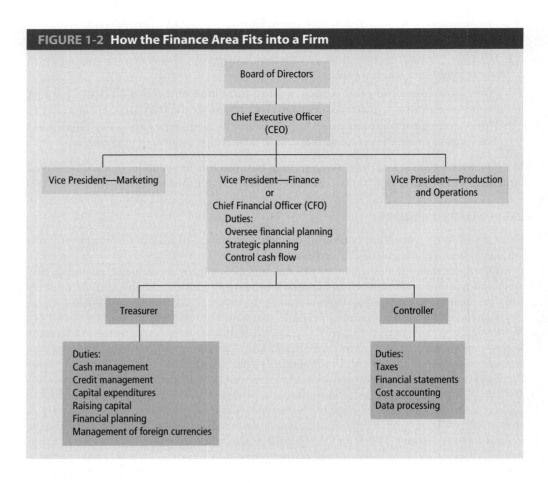

FIGURE 1-2 How the Finance Area Fits into a Firm

accounting duties, including producing financial statements, cost accounting, paying taxes, and gathering and monitoring the data necessary to oversee the firm's financial well-being. In this textbook, we focus on the duties generally associated with the treasurer and on how investment decisions are made.

Concept Check

1. What are the basic types of issues that are addressed by the study of finance?
2. What are the duties of a treasurer? Of a controller?

4 Distinguish between the different legal forms of business.

The Legal Forms of Business Organization

In the chapters ahead we focus on financial decisions for corporations because, although the corporation is not the only legal form of business available, it is the most logical choice for a firm that is large or growing. It is also the dominant business form in terms of sales in this country. In this section we explain why this is so.

Although numerous and diverse, the legal forms of business organization fall into three categories: the sole proprietorship, the partnership, and the corporation. To understand the basic differences between each form, we need to define each one and understand its advantages and disadvantages. As the firm grows, the advantages of the corporation begin to dominate. As a result, most large firms take on the corporate form.

Sole Proprietorships

sole proprietorship a business owned by a single individual.

A **sole proprietorship** is *a business owned by an individual*. The owner retains the title to the business's assets and is responsible, generally without limitation, for the liabilities incurred.

The proprietor is entitled to the profits from the business but must also absorb any losses. This form of business is initiated by the mere act of beginning the business operations. Typically, no legal requirement must be met in starting the operation, particularly if the proprietor is conducting the business in his or her own name. If a special name is used, an assumed-name certificate should be filed, requiring a small registration fee. Termination of the sole proprietorship occurs on the owner's death or by the owner's choice. Briefly stated, the sole proprietorship is for all practical purposes the absence of any formal *legal* business structure.

Partnerships

The primary difference between a partnership and a sole proprietorship is that the partnership has more than one owner. A **partnership** is *an association of two or more persons coming together as co-owners for the purpose of operating a business for profit.* Partnerships fall into two types: (1) general partnerships and (2) limited partnerships.

partnership an association of two or more individuals joining together as co-owners to operate a business for profit.

General Partnerships   In a **general partnership** *each partner is fully responsible for the liabilities incurred by the partnership.* Thus, any partner's faulty conduct, even having the appearance of relating to the firm's business, renders the remaining partners liable as well. The relationship among partners is dictated entirely by the partnership agreement, which may be an oral commitment or a formal document.

general partnership a partnership in which all partners are fully liable for the indebtedness incurred by the partnership.

Limited Partnerships   In addition to the general partnership, in which all partners are jointly liable without limitation, many states provide for **limited partnerships**. The state statutes permit *one or more of the partners to have limited liability, restricted to the amount of capital invested in the partnership.* Several conditions must be met to qualify as a limited partner. First, at least one general partner must have unlimited liability. Second, the names of the limited partners may not appear in the name of the firm. Third, the limited partners may not participate in the management of the business. Thus, a limited partnership provides limited liability for a partner who is purely an investor.

limited partnership a partnership in which one or more of the partners has limited liability, restricted to the amount of capital he or she invests in the partnership.

Corporations

The **corporation** has been a significant factor in the economic development of the United States. As early as 1819, U.S. Supreme Court Chief Justice John Marshall set forth the legal definition of a corporation as "an artificial being, invisible, intangible, and existing only in the contemplation of law."[2] This entity *legally functions separate and apart from its owners.* As such, the corporation can individually sue and be sued and purchase, sell, or own property, and its personnel are subject to criminal punishment for crimes. However, despite this legal separation, the corporation is composed of owners who dictate its direction and policies. The owners elect a board of directors, whose members in turn select individuals to serve as corporate officers, including the company's president, vice president, secretary, and treasurer. Ownership is reflected in common stock certificates, each designating the number of shares owned by its holder. The number of shares owned relative to the total number of shares outstanding determines the stockholder's proportionate ownership in the business. Because the shares are transferable, ownership in a corporation may be changed by a shareholder simply remitting the shares to a new shareholder. The shareholder's liability is confined to the amount of the investment in the company, thereby preventing creditors from confiscating stockholders' personal assets in settlement of unresolved claims. This is an extremely important advantage of a corporation. After all, would you be willing to invest in USAirways if you would be held liable if one of its planes crashed? Finally, the life of a corporation is not dependent on the status of the investors. The death or withdrawal of an investor does not affect the continuity of the corporation. Its managers continue to run the corporation when stock is sold or when it is passed on through inheritance.

corporation an entity that legally functions separate and apart from its owners.

---

[2]*The Trustees of Dartmouth College v. Woodard*, 4 Wheaton 636 (1819).

Organizational Form and Taxes: The Double Taxation on Dividends

Historically, one of the drawbacks of the corporate form was the double taxation of dividends. This occurs when a corporation earns a profit, pays taxes on those profits (the first taxation of earnings), and pays some of those profits back to the shareholders in the form of dividends, and then the shareholders pay personal income taxes on those dividends (the second taxation of those earnings). This double taxation of earnings does not take place with proprietorships and partnerships. Needless to say, that had been a major disadvantage of corporations. However, in an attempt to stimulate the economy, the tax rate on dividends was cut with the passage of the Tax Act of 2003.

Before the 2003 tax changes, you paid your regular, personal income tax rate on your dividend income, which could be as high as 35 percent. However, with the new law, qualified dividends from domestic corporations and qualified foreign corporations are now taxed at a maximum rate of 15 percent. Moreover, if your personal income puts you in the 10 percent or 15 percent income rate bracket, your dividends will be taxed at only 5 percent, and in 2008, this rate dropped to 0 percent. Unless Congress takes further action, this tax break on dividends will end after 2011 and individuals will once again be taxed at their regular personal tax rate.

S-Corporations and Limited Liability Companies (LLC)

One of the problems that entrepreneurs and small business owners face is that they need the benefits of the corporate form to expand, but the double taxation of earnings that comes with the corporate form makes it difficult to accumulate the necessary wealth for expansion. Fortunately, the government recognizes this problem and has provided two business forms that are, in effect, crosses between a partnership and a corporation with the tax benefits of partnerships (no double taxation of earnings) and the limited liability benefit of corporations (your liability is limited to what you invest).

S-corporation a corporation that, because of specific qualifications, is taxed as though it were a partnership.

The first is the **S-corporation**, which *provides limited liability while allowing the business's owners to be taxed as if they were a partnership*—that is, distributions back to the owners are not taxed twice as is the case with dividends distributed by regular corporations. Unfortunately, a number of restrictions accompany the S-corporation that detract from the desirability of this business form. Thus, an S-corporation cannot be used for a joint venture between two corporations. As a result, this business form has been losing ground in recent years in favor of the limited liability company.

limited liability company (LLC) a cross between a partnership and a corporation under which the owners retain limited liability but the company is run and is taxed like a partnership.

The **limited liability company (LLC)** is also *a cross between a partnership and a corporation*. Just as with the S-corporation, the LLC retains limited liability for its owners but runs and is taxed like a partnership. In general, it provides more flexibility than the S-corporation. For example, corporations can be owners in an LLC. However, because LLCs operate under state laws, both states and the IRS have rules for what qualifies as an LLC, and different states have different rules. But the bottom line in all this is that the LLC must not look too much like a corporation or it will be taxed as one.

Which Organizational Form Should Be Chosen?

Owners of new businesses have some important decisions to make in choosing an organizational form. Whereas each business form seems to have some advantages over the others, the advantages of the corporation begin to dominate as the firm grows and needs access to the capital markets to raise funds.

Because of the limited liability, the ease of transferring ownership through the sale of common shares, and the flexibility in dividing the shares, the corporation is the ideal business entity in terms of attracting new capital. In contrast, the unlimited liabilities of the sole proprietorship and the general partnership are deterrents to raising equity capital. Between the extremes, the limited partnership does provide limited liability for limited partners, which has a tendency to attract wealthy investors. However, the impracticality of having a large number of partners and the restricted marketability of an interest in a partnership prevent this form of organization from competing effectively with the corporation. Therefore, when developing our decision models we assume we are dealing with the corporate form and corporate tax codes.

Concept Check

1. What are the primary differences between a sole proprietorship, a partnership, and a corporation?
2. Explain why large and growing firms tend to choose the corporate form.
3. What is an LLC?

Finance and the Multinational Firm: The New Role

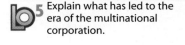
5 Explain what has led to the era of the multinational corporation.

In the search for profits, U.S. corporations have been forced to look beyond our country's borders. This movement has been spurred on by the collapse of communism and the acceptance of the free market system in third world countries. All this has taken place at a time when information technology has experienced a revolution brought on by the personal computer and the Internet. Concurrently, the United States went through an unprecedented period of deregulation of industries. These changes resulted in the opening of new international markets, and U.S. firms experienced a period of price competition here at home that made it imperative that businesses look across borders for investment opportunities. The end result is that many U.S. companies, including General Electric, IBM, Walt Disney, and American Express have restructured their operations to expand internationally.

The bottom line is what you think of as a U.S. firm may be much more of a multinational firm than you would expect. For example, Coca-Cola earns over 80 percent of its profits from overseas sales and more money from its sales in Japan than it does from all its domestic sales. This is not uncommon. In fact, in 2008, 45 percent of the sales of S&P 500 listed companies came from outside the United States.

In addition to U.S. firms venturing abroad, foreign firms have also made their mark in the United States. You need only look to the auto industry to see what changes the entrance of Toyota, Honda, Nissan, BMW, and other foreign car manufacturers have had on the auto industry. In addition, foreigners have bought and now own such companies as Brooks Brothers, RCA, Pillsbury, A&P, 20th Century Fox, Columbia Pictures, and Firestone Tire & Rubber. Consequently, even if we wanted to, we couldn't keep all our attention focused on the United States, and even more important, we wouldn't want to ignore the opportunities that are available across international borders.

Concept Check

1. What has brought on the era of the multinational corporation?
2. Has looking beyond U.S. borders been a profitable experience for U.S. corporations?

Summary

This chapter outlines the framework for the maintenance and creation of shareholder wealth, which should be the goal of the firm and its managers. The goal of maximization of shareholder wealth is chosen because it deals well with uncertainty and time in a real-world environment. As a result, the maximization of shareholder wealth is found to be the proper goal for the firm.

1 Identify the goal of the firm.

The five basic principles of finance are:

2 Understand the five basic principles of finance and business, the consequences of forgetting those basic principles of finance, and the importance of ethics and trust in business.

1. **Cash Flow Is What Matters**—incremental cash received and not accounting profits drives value.
2. **Money Has a Time Value**—a dollar received today is more valuable to the recipient than a dollar received in the future.

3. **Risk Requires a Reward**—the greater the risk of an investment, the higher will be the investor's required rate of return, and, other things remaining the same, the lower will be its value.

4. **Market Prices Are Generally Right**—For example, product market prices are often *slower* to react to important news than are prices in financial markets which tend to be very efficient and quick to respond to news.

5. **Conflicts of Interest Cause Agency Problems**—Large firms are typically run by professional managers who own a small fraction of the firms' equity. The individual actions of these managers are often motivated by self-interest, which may result in managers not acting in the best interests of the firm's owners. When this happens, the firm's owners will lose value.

While not one of the five principles of finance, ethics and trust are also essential elements of the business world, and without them, nothing works.

Finance is the study of how people and businesses evaluate investments and raise capital to fund them. There are three basic types of issues that are addressed by the study of finance: (1) What long-term investments should the firm undertake? This area of finance is generally referred to as capital budgeting. (2) How should the firm raise money to fund these investments? The firm's funding choices are generally referred to as capital structure decisions. (3) How can the firm best manage its cash flows as they arise in its day-to-day operations? This area of finance is generally referred to as working capital management.

The legal forms of business are examined. The sole proprietorship is a business operation owned and managed by an individual. Initiating this form of business is simple and generally does not involve any substantial organizational costs. The proprietor has complete control of the firm but must be willing to assume full responsibility for its outcomes.

The general partnership, which is simply a coming together of two or more individuals, is similar to the sole proprietorship. The limited partnership is another form of partnership sanctioned by states to permit all but one of the partners to have limited liability if this is agreeable to all partners.

The corporation increases the flow of capital from public investors to the business community. Although larger organizational costs and regulations are imposed on this legal entity, the corporation is more conducive to raising large amounts of capital. Limited liability, continuity of life, and ease of transfer in ownership, which increase the marketability of the investment, have contributed greatly in attracting large numbers of investors to the corporate environment. The formal control of the corporation is vested in the parties who own the greatest number of shares. However, day-to-day operations are managed by the corporate officers, who theoretically serve on behalf of the firm's stockholders.

With the collapse of communism and the acceptance of the free market system in third world countries, U.S. firms have been spurred on to look beyond their own boundaries for new business. The end result has been that it is not uncommon for major U.S. companies to earn over half their income from sales abroad. Foreign firms are also increasingly investing in the United States.

 3 Describe the role of finance in business.

 4 Distinguish between the different legal forms of business.

5 Explain what has led to the era of the multinational corporation.

Key Terms

Agency problem   7

Capital budgeting   11

Capital structure decision   11

Corporation   13

Efficient market   6

Financial markets   11

General partnership   13

Incremental cash flow   4

Limited liability company (LLC)   14

Limited partnership   13

Opportunity cost   5

Partnership   13

Sole proprietorship   12

S-corporation   14

Working capital management   11

Review Questions

myfinancelab   *All Review Questions and Study Problems are available in MyFinanceLab.*

1-1. What are some of the problems involved in implementing the goal of maximization of shareholder wealth?

1-2. Firms often involve themselves in projects that do not result directly in profits. For example, IBM and ExxonMobil frequently support public television broadcasts. Do these projects contradict the goal of maximization of shareholder wealth? Why or why not?

1-3. What is the relationship between financial decision making and risk and return? Would all financial managers view risk–return trade-offs similarly?

1-4. What is the agency problem and how might it impact the goal of maximization of shareholder wealth?

1-5. Define (a) sole proprietorship, (b) partnership, and (c) corporation.

1-6. Identify the primary characteristics of each form of legal organization.

1-7. Using the following criteria, specify the legal form of business that is favored: (a) organizational requirements and costs, (b) liability of the owners, (c) the continuity of the business, (d) the transferability of ownership, (e) management control and regulations, (f) the ability to raise capital, and (g) income taxes.

1-8. There are a lot of great business majors. Check out the Careers in Business Web site at www .careers-in-business.com. It covers not only finance but also marketing, accounting, and management. Find out about and provide a short write-up describing the opportunities investment banking and financial planning offer.

1-9. Like it or not, ethical problems seem to crop up all the time in finance. Some of the worst financial scandals are examined on the Financial Scandals Web site www.ex.ac.uk/~RDavies/arian/scandals/classic.html. Take a look at the write-ups dealing with "The Credit Crunch," "The Dot-Com Bubble and Investment Banks" and "Bernard L. Madoff Investment Securities." Provide a short write-up on these events.

1-10. We know that if a corporation is to maximize shareholder wealth, the interests of the managers and the shareholders must be aligned. The simplest way to align these interests is to structure executive compensation packages appropriately to encourage managers to act in the best interests of shareholders. However, has executive compensation gotten out of control? Take a look at the Executive Pay Watch Web site at www.aflcio.org/corporatewatch/paywatch to see to whom top salaries have gone. What are the most recent total compensation packages for the head of Oracle (ORCL), Home Depot (HD), Disney (DIS), and ExxonMobil (XOM)?

Mini Case

The final stage in the interview process for an assistant financial analyst at Caledonia Products involves a test of your understanding of basic financial concepts. You are given the following memorandum and asked to respond to the questions. Whether you are offered a position at Caledonia will depend on the accuracy of your response.

To: Applicants for the position of Financial Analyst
From: Mr. V. Morrison, CEO, Caledonia Products
Re: A test of your understanding of basic financial concepts and of the corporate tax code

Please respond to the following questions:

a. What is the appropriate goal for the firm and why?
b. What does the risk–return trade-off mean?
c. Why are we interested in cash flows rather than accounting profits in determining the value of an asset?
d. What is an efficient market and what are the implications of efficient markets for us?
e. What is the cause of the agency problem and how do we try to solve it?
f. What do ethics and ethical behavior have to do with finance?
g. Define (1) sole proprietorship, (2) partnership, and (3) corporation.

Chapter 2

The Financial Markets and Interest Rates

Learning Objectives

After reading this chapter, you should be able to:

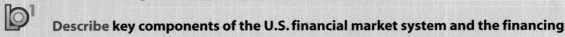

1 Describe **key components of the U.S. financial market system and the financing of business.**

2 Understand **the role of the investment-banking business in the context of raising corporate capital.**

3 Understand **private debt placements and flotation costs.**

4 Be acquainted **with recent interest rate levels.**

5 Explain **the fundamentals of interest rate determination and the popular theories of the term structure of interest rates.**

6 Understand **the relationships among the multinational firm, efficient financial markets, and intercountry risk.**

Back in 1995, when they first met, Larry Page and Sergey Brin were not particularly fond of one another. Larry was on a weekend visit to Stanford University, and Sergey was in a group of students assigned to show him around. Nonetheless, in short time the two began to collaborate and even built their own computer housings in Larry's dorm room. That computer housing later became Google's first data center. From there things didn't move as smoothly as one might expect, there just wasn't the interest from the search-engine players of the day, so Larry and Sergey decided to go it alone. Stuck in a dorm room with maxed-out credit cards, the problem they faced was money—they didn't have any. So they put together a business plan and went looking for money. Fortunately for all of us that use Google today, they met up with one of the founders of Sun Microsystems, and after a short demo he had to run off somewhere and upon leaving said, "Instead of us discussing all the details, why don't I just write you a check?" It was made out to Google Inc. and was for $100,000.

With that, Google Inc. (GOOG) was founded, and over the next 10 years it became anything but a conventional company, with an official motto of "don't be evil"; a goal to make the world a better place; on-site meals prepared by a former caterer for the Grateful Dead; lava lamps; and a fleet of Segways to move employees about

the Google campus to roller-hockey games in the parking lot and to other on-site diversions. It was not unexpected that when Google needed more money in 2004 it would raise that money in an unusual way—through a "Dutch auction." With a Dutch auction investors submit bids, saying how many shares they'd like and at what price. Next, Google used these bids to calculate an issue price that was just low enough to ensure that all the shares were sold, and everyone who bid at least that price got to buy shares at the issue price.

Eventually, Google settled on an issue price of $85 per share, and on August 19, 2004, it raised $1.76 billion dollars. How did those initial investors do? On the first day of trading Google's shares rose by 18 percent, and by mid-March 2005 the price of Google stock had risen to about $340 per share! In September 2005, Google went back to the financial markets and sold another 14.18 million shares at $295 per share, and by September 2009 it was selling at around $474 per share.

As you read this chapter you will learn about how funds are raised in the financial markets. This will help you, as an emerging business executive specializing in accounting, finance, marketing, or strategy, understand the basics of acquiring financial capital in the funds marketplace.

Long-term sources of financing, such as bonds and common stock, are raised in the capital markets. By the term **capital markets**, we mean *all the financial institutions that help a business raise long-term capital*, where "long term" is defined as a security with a maturity date of more than one year. After all, most companies are in the business of selling products and services to their customers and do not have the expertise on their own to raise money to finance the business. Examples of these financial institutions that you may have heard of would include Bank of America (BAC), Goldman Sachs (GS), Citigroup (C), Morgan Stanley (MS), UBS AG (UBS), and Deutsche Bank (DB).

This chapter focuses on the procedures by which businesses raise money in the capital markets. It helps us understand how the capital markets work. We will introduce the logic of how investors determine their required rate of return for making an investment. In addition, we will study the historical rates of returns in the capital markets so that we have a perspective on what to expect. This knowledge of financial market history will permit you as both a financial manager and an investor to realize that earning, say, a 40 percent annual return on a common stock investment does not occur very often.

As you work through this chapter, be on the lookout for direct applications of several of our principles from Chapter 1 that form the basics of business financial management. Specifically, your attention will be directed to: Principle 3: Risk Requires a Reward and Principle 4: Market Prices Are Generally Right.

capital markets all institutions and procedures that facilitate transactions in long-term financial instruments.

Financing of Business: The Movement of Funds through the Economy

 Describe key components of the U.S. financial market system and the financing of business.

Financial markets play a critical role in a capitalist economy. In fact, when money quit flowing through the financial markets in 2008, our economy ground to a halt. When our economy is healthy, funds move from saving surplus units—that is, those who spend less money than they take in—to saving deficit units—that is, those who have a need for additional funding. What are some examples of savings deficit units? Our federal government, which is running a huge deficit, taking much less in from taxes than it is spending. Hulu, the on-line video service, which would like to build new facilities, but does not have the $50 million it needs to fund the expansion. Rebecca Swank, the sole proprietor of the Sip and Stitch, a yarn and coffee shop, who would like to open a second store, but needs $100,000 to finance a second shop. Emily and Michael Dimmick, who would like to buy a house for $240,000, but only have $50,000 saved up. In each case, our government, a large company, a small business owner, and a family are all in the same boat—they would like to spend more than they take in.

Where will this money come from? It will come from savings surplus units in the economy—that is, from those who spend less than they take in. Examples of savings surplus units might include individuals, companies, and governments. For example, John and Sandy Randolph have been saving for retirement and earn $10,000 more each year than they spend. In addition, the firm John works for contributes $5,000 every year to his retirement plan. Likewise, ExxonMobil (XOM) generates about $50 billion in cash annually from its operations and invests about half of that on new exploration—the rest is available to invest. Also, there are a number of governments around the world that bring in more money than they spend—countries like China, the United Arab Emirates, and Saudi Arabia.

Now let's take a look at how savings are transferred to those who need the money. Actually, there are three ways that savings can be transferred through the financial markets to those in need of funds. These are displayed in Figure 2-1.

Let's take a closer look at these three methods:

1. **Direct transfer of funds** Here the firm seeking cash sells its securities directly to savers (investors) who are willing to purchase them in hopes of earning a large return. A startup company is a good example of this process at work. The new business may go directly to *a wealthy private investor* called an **angel investor** or business angel for funds or it may go to a **venture capitalist** for early funding. That's how Koofers.com got up and running. The founders of Koofers were students at Virginia Tech who put

angel investor a wealthy private investor who provides capital for a business start-up.

venture capitalist an investment firm (or individual investor) that provides money to business start-ups.

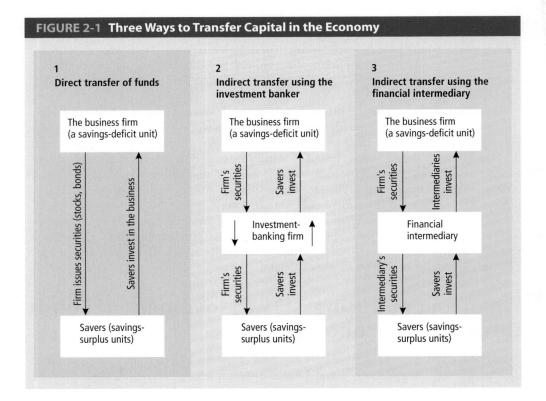

FIGURE 2-1 Three Ways to Transfer Capital in the Economy

together an interactive Web site that provides a place for students to share class notes, course and instructor ratings/grade distributions, along with study guides and past exams. The Web site proved to be wildly popular, and in 2009 received $2 million of funding to expand from two venture capitalists, who, in return, received part ownership of Koofers.

2. **Indirect transfer using an investment-banking firm** An investment-banking firm is a financial institution that helps companies raise capital, trades in securities, and provides advice on transactions such as mergers and acquisitions. When they help firms raise capital, an investment banker frequently works together with other investment bankers in what is called a syndicate. The syndicate will buy the entire issue of securities from the firm that is in need of financial capital. The syndicate will then sell the securities at a higher price to the investing public (the savers) than it paid for them. Morgan Stanley and Goldman Sachs are examples of banks that perform investment-banking duties. Notice that under this second method of transferring savings, the securities being issued just pass through the investment-banking firm. They are not transformed into a different type of security.

3. **Indirect transfer using the financial intermediary** This is the type of system life insurance companies, mutual funds, and pension funds operate within. The financial intermediary collects the savings of individuals and issues its own (indirect) securities in exchange for these savings. The intermediary then uses the funds collected from the individual savers to acquire the business firm's (direct) securities, such as stocks and bonds.

A good financial system is one that efficiently takes money from savers and gets it to the individuals who can best put that money to use, and that's exactly what our system does. This may seem like common sense, but it is not necessarily common across the world. In spite of the fact that in 2008–2009 the U.S. financial system experienced some problems, it provides more choices for both borrowers and savers than most other financial systems, and as a result, it does a better job of allocating capital to those who can more productively use it. As a result, we all benefit from the three transfer mechanisms displayed in Figure 2-1, and capital formation and economic wealth are greater than they would be in the absence of this financial market system.

There are numerous ways to classify the financial markets. These markets can take the form of anything from an actual building on Wall Street in New York City to an electronic hookup among security dealers all over the world. Let's take a look at six sets of dichotomous terms that are used to describe the financial markets.

Public Offerings Versus Private Placements

When a corporation decides to raise external capital, those funds can be obtained by making a public offering or a private placement. In a **public offering**, both *individual and institutional investors have the opportunity to purchase the securities*. The securities are usually made available to the public at large by an investment-banking firm, which is a firm that specializes in helping other firms raise money. This process of acting as an intermediary between an issuer of a security and the investing public is called underwriting, and the investment firm that does this is referred to as an underwriter. This is a very impersonal market, and the issuing firm never actually meets the ultimate purchasers of the securities.

public offering a security offering where all investors have the opportunity to acquire a portion of the financial claims being sold.

In a **private placement**, also called a direct placement, the *securities are offered and sold directly to a limited number of investors*. The firm will usually hammer out, on a face-to-face basis with the prospective buyers, the details of the offering. In this setting, the investment-banking firm may act as a finder by bringing together potential lenders and borrowers. The private placement market is a more personal market than its public counterpart.

private placement a security offering limited to a small number of potential investors.

A venture capital firm is an example of investors who are active in the private placement market. A **venture capital firm** first *raises money from institutional investors and high net worth individuals, to then pool the funds and invest in startups and early-stage companies* that have high-return potential, but also are very risky investments. These companies are not appealing to the broader public markets owing to their (1) small absolute size, (2) very limited or no historical track record of operating results, (3) obscure growth prospects, and

venture capital firm an investment firm that provides money to business start-ups.

(4) the inability to sell the stock easily or quickly. Most venture capitalists invest for five to seven years, in the hopes of selling the firms or taking them public through an IPO.

Due to the high risk, the venture capitalist will occupy a seat or seats on the young firm's board of directors and will take an active part in monitoring the company's management activities. *This situation should remind you of* **Principle 3: Risk Requires a Reward**.

Primary Markets Versus Secondary Markets

primary market a market in which securities are offered for the first time for sale to potential investors.

A **primary market** is a *market in which new, as opposed to previously issued, securities are traded.* For example, if Google issues a new batch of stock, this issue would be considered a primary market transaction. In this case, Google would issue new shares of stock and receive money from investors. The primary market is akin to the new car market. For example, the only time that Ford ever gets money for selling a car is the first time the car is sold to the public. The same is true with securities in the primary market. That's the only time the issuing firm ever gets any money for the securities, and it is the type of transaction that introduces new financial assets—for example, stocks and bonds—into the economy. The *first time a company issues stock to the public* is referred to as an **initial public offering** or **IPO**. This is what happened with Google on August 19, 2004, when it first sold its common stock to the public at $85 per share and raised $1.76 billion dollars. When Google went back to the primary market in September 2005 and sold more Google stock worth an addition $4.18 billion, it was considered a **seasoned equity offering**, or **SEO**. A seasoned equity offering is *the sale of additional shares by a company whose shares are already publicly traded* and is also called a secondary share offering.

initial public offering, IPO the first time a company issues its stock to the public.

seasoned equity offering, SEO the sale of additional stock by a company whose shares are already publicly traded.

secondary market a market in which currently outstanding securities are traded.

The **secondary market** is *where currently outstanding securities are traded.* You can think of it as akin to the used car market. If a person who bought some shares of the Google stock subsequently sells them, he or she does so in the secondary market. Those shares can go from investor to investor, and Google never receives any money when they are traded. In effect, all transactions after the initial purchase in the primary market take place in the secondary market. These sales do not affect the total amount of financial assets that exists in the economy.

money market all institutions and procedures that facilitate transactions for short-term instruments issued by borrowers with very high credit ratings.

The job of regulation of the primary and secondary markets falls on the Security and Exchange Commission, or SEC. For example, before a firm can offer its securities for sale in the primary markets, it must register them with the SEC, and it is the job of the SEC to make sure that the information provided to investors is adequate and accurate. The SEC also regulates the secondary markets, making sure that investors are provided with enough accurate information to make intelligent decisions when buying and selling in the secondary markets.

REMEMBER YOUR PRINCIPLES

Principle In this chapter, we cover material that introduces the financial manager to the process involved in raising funds in the nation's capital markets and how interest rates in those markets are determined.

Without question the United States has a highly developed, complex, and competitive system of financial markets that allows for the quick transfer of savings from people and organizations with a surplus of savings to those with a savings deficit. Such a system of highly developed financial markets allows great ideas (such as the personal computer) to be financed and increases the overall wealth of the economy. Consider your wealth, for example, compared to that of the average family in Russia. Russia lacks the complex system of financial markets to facilitate securities transactions. As a result, real capital formation there has suffered.

Thus, we return now to **Principle 4: Market Prices Are Generally Right**. Financial managers like the U.S. system of capital markets because they trust it. This trust stems from the fact that the markets are efficient, and so prices quickly and accurately reflect all available information about the value of the underlying securities. This means that the expected risks and expected cash flows matter more to market participants than do simpler things such as accounting changes and the sequence of past price changes in a specific security. With security prices and returns (such as interest rates) competitively determined, more financial managers (rather than fewer) participate in the markets and help ensure the basic concept of efficiency.

The Money Market Versus the Capital Market

The key distinguishing feature between the money and capital markets is the maturity period of the securities traded in them. The **money market** refers to *transactions in short-term debt instruments*, with short-term meaning maturity periods of 1 year or less. Short-term securities are generally issued by borrowers with very high credit ratings. The major instruments issued and traded in the money market are U.S. Treasury bills, various federal agency securities, bankers' acceptances, negotiable certificates of deposit, and commercial paper. Stocks, either common or preferred, are not traded in the money market. Keep in mind that the money market isn't a physical place. You do not walk into a building on Wall Street that has the words "Money Market" etched in stone over its arches. Rather, the money market is primarily a telephone and computer market.

As we explained, the capital market refers to the market for long-term financial instruments. Long-term here means having maturity periods that extend beyond 1 year. In the broad sense, this encompasses term loans, financial leases, and corporate stocks and bonds.

Spot Markets Versus Futures Markets

Cash markets are where something sells today, right now, on the spot—in fact, *cash markets* are often called **spot markets**. **Futures markets** are where you can *buy or sell something at some future date*—in effect, you sign a contract that states what you're buying, how much of it you're buying, at what price you're buying it, and when you will actually make the purchase. The difference between purchasing something in the spot market and purchasing it in the futures market is when it is delivered and when you pay for it. For example, say it is May right now and you need 250,000 euros in December. You could purchase 125,000 euros today in the spot market and another 125,000 euros in the futures market for delivery in December. You get the euros you purchased in the spot market today, and you get the euros you purchased in the futures market seven months later.

spot market cash market.

futures markets markets where you can buy or sell something at a future date.

Organized Security Exchanges Versus Over-the-Counter Markets

Important elements of the capital market are the organized security exchanges and the over-the-counter markets. **Organized security exchanges** are tangible entities; that is, they physically occupy space (such as a building or part of a building), and *financial instruments are traded on their premises*. The **over-the-counter markets** include *all security markets except the organized exchanges*. The money market, then, is an over-the-counter market because it doesn't occupy a physical location. Because both markets are important to financial officers concerned with raising long-term capital, some additional discussion is warranted.

organized security exchange formal organizations that facilitate the trading of securities.

over-the-counter market all security markets except organized exchanges. The money market is an over-the-counter market. Most corporate bonds also are traded in this market.

Organized Security Exchanges   There are seven organized exchanges in the United States, starting with the New York Stock Exchange (NYSE) and the American Stock Exchange (AMEX), and smaller exchanges in Philadelphia, Boston, Chicago (both the Chicago and National Stock Exchange), and the Pacific Stock Exchange, which is headquartered in San Francisco, but doesn't actually have a trading floor—it's a totally electronic exchange. The New York Stock Exchange and the American Stock Exchange are considered national stock exchanges, and the others are generally termed *regional stock exchanges*. If a firm's stock trades on a particular exchange, it is said to be *listed* on that exchange. Securities can be listed on more than one exchange. All of these seven active exchanges are registered with the Securities and Exchange Commission (SEC). Firms whose securities are traded on the registered exchanges must comply with reporting requirements of both the specific exchange and the SEC.

The NYSE, also called the "Big Board," is the oldest of all the organized exchanges. Without question, the NYSE is the big player, with over half of the typical trading volume taking place there. An example of the prominent stature of the NYSE is provided by the sheer number of companies that have stocks listed on this exchange. In 2009, the NYSE listed over 4,000 U.S. and non-U.S. issuers, which included operating companies, along with some mutual funds and exchange-traded funds. The total value of the shares of stock listed on the NYSE opened 2009 at just over $10 trillion, down from over $18 trillion in 2007. Today the NYSE is a hybrid market, allowing for face-to-face trading between individuals on the floor of the stock exchange in addition to automated, electronic trading. As a result, during times of extreme flux in the market, at the opening or close of the market, or on large trades, human judgment can be called on to make sure that the trade is executed appropriately.

Stock Exchange Benefits   Both corporations and investors enjoy several benefits provided by the existence of organized security exchanges. These include

1. **Providing a continuous market** This may be the most important function of an organized security exchange. A continuous market provides a series of continuous security prices. Price changes from trade to trade tend to be smaller than they would be

in the absence of organized markets. The reasons are that there is a relatively large sales volume of each security traded, trading orders are executed quickly, and the range between the price asked for a security and the offered price tends to be narrow. The result is that price volatility is reduced.

2. **Establishing and publicizing fair security prices** An organized exchange permits security prices to be set by competitive forces. They are not set by negotiations off the floor of the exchange, where one party might have a bargaining advantage. The bidding process flows from the supply and demand underlying each security. This means the specific price of a security is determined in the manner of an auction. In addition, the security prices determined at each exchange are widely publicized.

3. **Helping business raise new capital** Because a continuous secondary market exists, it is easier for firms to float, or issue, new security offerings at competitively determined prices. This means that the comparative values of securities offered in these markets are easily observed.

Listing Requirements To receive the benefits provided by an organized exchange, the firm must seek to have its securities listed on the exchange. An application for listing must be filed and a fee paid. The requirements for listing vary from exchange to exchange; those of the NYSE are the most stringent. The general criteria for listing fall into these categories: (1) profitability, (2) size, (3) market value, and (4) public ownership.

Over-the-Counter Markets Many publicly held firms do not meet the listing requirements of major stock exchanges. Others may want to avoid the reporting requirements and fees required to maintain a listing. As an alternative, their securities may trade in the over-the-counter markets. On the basis of sheer numbers (not dollar volume), more stocks are traded over the counter than on organized exchanges. As far as secondary trading in corporate bonds is concerned, the over-the-counter markets are where the action is. In a typical year, more than 90 percent of corporate bond business takes place over the counter.

Most over-the-counter transactions are done through a loose network of security traders who are known as broker-dealers and brokers. Brokers do not purchase securities for their own account, whereas dealers do. Broker-dealers stand ready to buy and sell specific securities at selected prices. They are said to "make a market" in those securities. Their profit is the "spread," or difference, between the price they will pay for a security (bid price) and the price at which they will sell the security (asked price).

Price Quotes and the NASDAQ The availability of prices is not as continuous in the over-the-counter market as it is on an organized exchange. Since February 8, 1971, however, when a computerized network called NASDAQ came into existence, the availability of prices in this market has improved substantially. NASDAQ stands for National Association of Security Dealers Automated Quotation System. It is a telecommunications system that provides a national information link among the brokers and dealers operating in the over-the-counter markets. Subscribing traders have a terminal that allows them to obtain representative bids and ask prices for thousands of securities traded over the counter. NASDAQ is a quotation system, not a transactions system. The final trade is still consummated by direct negotiation between traders.

The NASDAQ system has become an increasingly important element of the U.S. financial market system in recent years. It provides a nationwide communications element that was lacking in the over-the-counter side of the securities markets. The Nasdaq Stock Market Inc. describes itself as a "screen-based, floorless market." In 2009 some 3,900 companies were listed on the NASDAQ, after reaching a peak of 5,556 in 1996. It has become highly popular as the trading mechanism of choice for several fast-growth sectors in the United States, including the high-technology sector. The common stock of computer chip maker Intel Corporation (INTC), for example, is traded via the NASDAQ, as is that of Dell (DELL), Starbucks (SBUX), Whole Foods Market (WFMI), and Google (GOOG).

NASDAQ price quotes are published daily in the online version of the *Wall Street Journal* (www.wsj.com).

Concept Check

1. Explain the difference between (a) public offerings and private placements, (b) primary markets and secondary markets, (c) the money market and the capital market, and (d) organized security exchanges and over-the-counter markets.
2. Name the benefits derived from the existence of stock exchanges.
3. Briefly describe what is meant by the "NASDAQ system."

The Investment-Banking Function

Most corporations do not frequently raise long-term capital. The activities of working-capital management go on daily, but attracting long-term capital is, by comparison, episodic. The sums involved can be huge, so these situations are considered of great importance to financial managers. Because most managers are unfamiliar with the subtleties of raising long-term funds, they enlist the help of an expert, an investment banker. It is with the help of an **investment banker** serving as the underwriter that stocks and bonds are generally sold in the primary markets. An **underwriter** is a middleperson who buys the entire stock or bond issue from the issuing company and resells it to the general public in individual shares. The *difference between the price the corporation gets and the public offering price* is called the **underwriter's spread**.

Table 2-1 gives us some idea who the major players are within the investment-banking industry. It lists the top 10 houses in 2008 based on the dollar volume of security issues that were managed. Notice that there have been some name changes, with Merrill Lynch now part of Bank of America (BAC) and Wachovia now part of Wells Fargo (WFC). In addition, Lehman Brothers and Bear Stearns, two financial firms that also did investment banking, didn't make it through 2008. Today, there are no very large, stand-alone investment-banking firms; they are all banks that are also investment bankers. You'll notice that the top five bankers with regard to underwriting volume during 2008 accounted for over half of the total market share—this became even more concentrated as some of the investment-banking firms combined.

Actually, we use the term "investment banker" to describe both the firm itself and the individuals who work for it in that capacity. Just what does this intermediary role involve? The easiest way to understand it is to look at the basic investment-banking functions.

Functions

The investment banker performs three basic functions: (1) underwriting, (2) distributing, and (3) advising.

 2 Understand the role of the investment-banking business in the context of raising corporate capital.

investment banker a financial specialist who underwrites and distributes new securities and advises corporate clients about raising new funds.

underwriting the purchase and subsequent resale of a new security issue. The risk of selling the new issue at a satisfactory (profitable) price is assumed (underwritten) by the investment banker.

underwriter's spread the difference between the price the corporation raising money gets and the public offering price of a security.

TABLE 2-1 Initial Public Offerings of Stock, Global Offerings by U.S. Issuers, Ranked by 2008 Proceeds			
Manager	Amount (Billions)	Market Share	No. of Issues
Merrill Lynch (now Bank of America Merrill Lynch)	$3.8	14.3%	8
Citi	3.5	13.3	9
Goldman Sachs	3.5	13.2	6
UBS	3.0	11.5	6
Banc of America Securities	2.8	10.6	4
Wachovia Corp (now part of Wells Fargo)	2.6	9.9	3
JP Morgan	2.6	9.8	3
HSBC Holdings	2.5	9.3	1
Credit Suisse	0.8	2.9	8
Morgan Stanley	0.5	2.1	4
Top 10 Totals	$25.5	96.9%	52
Industry Totals	26.4	100.0	29

Source: Wall Street Journal, 2008 Underwriting Rankings, December 31, 2008, R10. Copyright 2008 by Dow Jones & Company, Inc. Reproduced with permission of Dow Jones & Company, Inc.

Underwriting   The term underwriting is borrowed from the field of insurance. It means *assuming a risk*. The investment banker assumes the risk of selling a security issued at a satisfactory price. A satisfactory price is one that generates a profit for the investment-banking house.

The procedure goes like this. The managing investment banker and its syndicate will buy the security issue from the corporation in need of funds. The **syndicate** is *a group of other investment bankers that is invited to help buy and resell the issue*. The managing house is the investment-banking firm that originated the business because its corporate client decided to raise external funds. On a specific day, the client that is raising capital is presented with a check from the managing house in exchange for the securities being issued. At this point the investment-banking syndicate owns the securities. The client has its cash, so it is immune from the possibility that the security markets might turn sour. That is, if the price of the newly issued security falls below that paid to the firm by the syndicate, the syndicate will suffer a loss. The syndicate, of course, hopes that the opposite situation will result. Its objective is to sell the new issue to the investing public at a price per security greater than its cost.

> **syndicate** a group of investment bankers who contractually assist in the buying and selling of a new security issue.

Distributing   Once the syndicate owns the new securities, it must get them into the hands of the ultimate investors. This is the distribution or selling function of investment banking. The investment banker may have branch offices across the United States, or it may have an informal arrangement with several security dealers who regularly buy a portion of each new offering for final sale. It is not unusual to have 300 to 400 dealers involved in the selling effort. The syndicate can properly be viewed as the security wholesaler, and the dealer organization can be viewed as the security retailer.

Advising   The investment banker is an expert in the issuance and marketing of securities. A sound investment-banking house will be aware of prevailing market conditions and can relate those conditions to the particular type of security and the price at which it should be sold at a given time. For example, business conditions may be pointing to a future increase in interest rates, so the investment banker might advise the firm to issue its bonds in a timely fashion to avoid the higher interest rates that are forthcoming. The banker can analyze the firm's capital structure and make recommendations about what general source of capital should be issued. In many instances the firm will invite its investment banker to sit on the board of directors. This permits the banker to observe corporate activity and make recommendations on a regular basis.

The Demise of the Stand-Alone Investment-Banking Industry

From the time of George Washington until the Great Depression that occurred in the 1930s, the U.S. economy experienced a recurring financial panic and banking crisis about every 15 years. During the Great Depression and the banking failures of 1933, some 4,004 banks closed their doors and Congress enacted a series of reforms that were designed to put an end to these recurring financial crises. The lynchpin of this reform was the Glass-Steagall Act or the Banking Act of 1933. An important component of the Glass-Steagall Act was the creation of the Federal Deposit Insurance Corporation (FDIC) which provides deposit insurance for bank deposits in member banks of up to $250,000[1] per depositor per bank. The creation of the FDIC was an effort to provide assurance to depositors that their deposits were secure, thereby preventing runs on banks. Another key element of Glass-Steagall was the separation of the commercial-banking and investment-banking industries. The purpose of this was to keep banks safe by prohibiting them from entering the securities industry where it is possible to incur large losses, and as a result, a strong "stand-alone" investment-banking industry emerged with names like Lehman Brothers, Bear Stearns, and J.P. Morgan.

With the repeal of Glass-Steagall in 1999, many commercial banks merged with large investment-banking firms, for example, Chase Manhattan Bank merged with J.P. Morgan, forming JPMorgan-Chase & Co. (JPM). The advantage of this to the investment banks was the access to stable funding through bank deposits along with the ability to borrow from the

---

[1]On December 31, 2013, the standard coverage limit will return to $100,000 for all deposit categories except IRAs and Certain Retirement Accounts, which will continue to be insured up to $250,000 per owner.

Fed in the case of an emergency, while the commercial bank gained access to the more lucrative, albeit more risky, securities industry. Then in 2008 as a result of the financial crisis and banking meltdown, the remaining stand-alone investment-banking firms that did not fail in the crisis, including Morgan Stanley and Goldman Sachs, quickly found commercial bank partners. At the end of the day, there were no stand-alone investment-banking firms left. Today, the investment-banking function is provided by "universal banks," that is, commercial banks that also provide investment banking services.

Distribution Methods

Several methods are available to the corporation for placing new security offerings in the hands of investment bankers followed by final investors. The investment banker's role is different in each of these. Sometimes, in fact, it is possible to bypass the investment banker. These methods are described in this section. Private placements, because of their importance, are treated later in the chapter.

A Negotiated Purchase   In a negotiated underwriting, the firm that needs funds makes contact with an investment banker, and deliberations concerning the new issue begin. If all goes well, a *method* is negotiated for determining the price the investment banker and the syndicate will pay for the securities. For example, the agreement might state that the syndicate will pay $2 less than the closing price of the firm's common stock on the day before the offering date of a new stock issue. The negotiated purchase is the most prevalent method of securities distribution in the private sector. It is generally thought to be the most profitable technique as far as investment bankers are concerned.

A Competitive Bid Purchase   The method by which the underwriting group is determined distinguishes the competitive bid purchase from the negotiated purchase. In a competitive underwriting, several underwriting groups bid for the right to purchase the new issue from the corporation that is raising funds. The firm does not directly select the investment banker. Instead, the investment banker that underwrites and distributes the issue is chosen by an auction process. The one willing to pay the greatest dollar amount per new security will win the competitive bid.

Most competitive bid purchases are confined to three situations, compelled by legal regulations: (1) railroad issues, (2) public utility issues, and (3) state and municipal bond issues. The argument in favor of competitive bids is that any undue influence of an investment banker over the firm is mitigated and the price received by the firm for each security should be higher. Thus, we would intuitively suspect that the cost of capital in a competitive bidding situation would be less than in a negotiated purchase situation. Evidence on this question, however, is mixed. One problem with the competitive bidding purchase as far as the fund-raising firm is concerned is that the benefits gained from the advisory function of the investment banker are lost. It may be necessary to use an investment banker for advisory purposes and then by law exclude the banker from the competitive bid process.

A Commission or Best-Efforts Basis   Here, the investment banker acts as an agent rather than as a principal in the distribution process. The securities are *not* underwritten. The investment banker attempts to sell the issue in return for a fixed commission on each security actually sold. Unsold securities are then returned to the corporation. This arrangement is typically used for more speculative issues. The issuing firm may be smaller or less established than the banker would like. Because the underwriting risk is not passed on to the investment banker, this distribution method is less costly to the issuer than a negotiated or competitive bid purchase. On the other hand, the investment banker only has to give it his or her "best effort." A successful sale is not guaranteed.

A Privileged Subscription   Occasionally, the firm may feel that a distinct market already exists for its new securities. When a *new issue is marketed to a definite and select group of investors*, it is called a **privileged subscription**. Three target markets are typically involved: (1) current stockholders, (2) employees, or (3) customers of the firm. Of these, distributions directed at current stockholders are the most prevalent. Such offerings are called *rights*

privileged subscription the process of marketing a new security issue to a select group of investors.

offerings. In a privileged subscription the investment banker may act only as a selling agent. It is also possible that the issuing firm and the investment banker might sign a *standby agreement*, which obligates the investment banker to underwrite the securities that are not purchased by the privileged investors.

Dutch Auction   As we explained at the beginning of the chapter, with a **Dutch auction**, investors first bid on the number of shares they would like to buy and the price they are willing to pay for them. Once all the bids are in, the prices that were bid along with the number of shares are ranked from the highest price to the lowest price. The selling price for the stock is then calculated, and it is calculated as the highest price that allows for all the stock to be sold. Although Google really brought this method to the public's eye, it has been used by a number of other companies including Overstock.com (OSTK) and Salon (SLNM). Figure 2-2 explains in more detail how a Dutch auction works.

A Direct Sale   In a **direct sale** *the issuing firm sells the securities directly to the investing public without involving an investment banker*. Even among established corporate giants, this procedure is relatively rare. A variation of the direct sale involves the private placement of a new issue by the fund-raising corporation *without* the use of an investment banker as an intermediary. Texaco (now Chevron (CVX)), Mobil Oil (now ExxonMobil (XOM)), and International Harvester (now Navistar (NAV)) are examples of large firms that have followed this procedure.

Dutch auction a method of issuing securities (common stock) where investors place bids indicating how many shares they are willing to buy and at what price. The price the stock is then sold for becomes the lowest price at which the issuing company can sell all the available shares.

direct sale the sale of securities by a corporation to the investing public without the services of an investment-banking firm.

Concept Check

1. What is the main difference between an investment banker and a commercial banker?
2. What are the three major functions that an investment banker performs?
3. What are the five key methods by which securities are distributed to final investors?

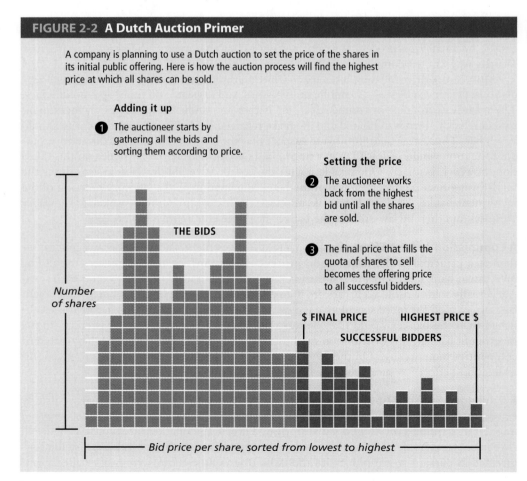

FIGURE 2-2   A Dutch Auction Primer

A company is planning to use a Dutch auction to set the price of the shares in its initial public offering. Here is how the auction process will find the highest price at which all shares can be sold.

Adding it up

❶ The auctioneer starts by gathering all the bids and sorting them according to price.

Setting the price

❷ The auctioneer works back from the highest bid until all the shares are sold.

❸ The final price that fills the quota of shares to sell becomes the offering price to all successful bidders.

THE BIDS

Number of shares

$ FINAL PRICE   HIGHEST PRICE $

SUCCESSFUL BIDDERS

Bid price per share, sorted from lowest to highest

Private Debt Placements

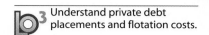
Understand private debt placements and flotation costs.

Earlier in this chapter we discussed the private placement market. Here we take a closer look at the debt side of the private placement market and how it is used by seasoned corporations as distinct from startups. Thus, when we talk of private placements in this section, we are focusing on debt contracts rather than stock offerings. This debt side of the private placement market makes up a significant portion of the total private market.

Private placements are an alternative to the sale of securities to the public or to a restricted group of investors through a privileged subscription. Any type of security can be privately placed (directly placed). The major investors in private placements are large financial institutions. Based on the volume of securities purchased, the three most important investor groups are (1) life insurance companies, (2) state and local retirement funds, and (3) private pension funds.

In arranging a private placement, the firm may (1) avoid the use of an investment banker and work directly with the investing institutions or (2) engage the services of an investment banker. If the firm does not use an investment banker, of course, it does not have to pay a fee. However, investment bankers can provide valuable advice in the private placement process. They are usually in contact with several major institutional investors; thus, they will know who the major buyers able to invest in the proposed offering are, and they can help the firm evaluate the terms of the new issue.

Private placements have advantages and disadvantages compared with public offerings. The financial manager must carefully evaluate both sides of the question. The advantages associated with private placements are:

1. **Speed** The firm usually obtains funds more quickly through a private placement than a public offering. The major reason is that registration of the issue with the SEC is not required.

2. **Reduced costs** These savings result because the lengthy registration statement for the SEC does not have to be prepared, and the investment-banking underwriting and distribution costs do not have to be absorbed.

3. **Financing flexibility** In a private placement the firm deals on a face-to-face basis with a small number of investors. This means that the terms of the issue can be tailored to meet the specific needs of the company. For example, if the investors agree to loan $50 million to a firm, the management does not have to take the full $50 million at one time. They may instead borrow as they need it, and thereby pay interest only on the amount actually borrowed. However, the company may have to pay a commitment fee of say one percent on the unused portion of the loan. That is, if the company only borrows $35 million, it will have to pay interest on that amount, and pay a commitment fee of one percent or so on the remaining $15 million. This provides some insurance against capital market uncertainties, and the firm does not have to borrow the funds if the need does not arise. There is also the possibility of renegotiation. The terms of the debt issue can be altered. The term to maturity, the interest rate, or any restrictive covenants can be discussed among the affected parties.

The following disadvantages of private placements must be evaluated.

1. **Interest costs** It is generally conceded that interest costs on private placements exceed those of public issues. Whether this disadvantage is enough to offset the reduced costs associated with a private placement is a determination the financial manager must make. There is some evidence that on smaller issues, say $500,000 as opposed to $30 million, the private placement alternative would be preferable.

2. **Restrictive covenants** A firm's dividend policy, working-capital levels, and the raising of additional debt capital may all be affected by provisions in the private-placement debt contract. This is not to say that such restrictions are always absent in public debt contracts. Rather, the firm's financial officer must be alert to the tendency for these covenants to be especially burdensome in private contracts.

3. **The possibility of future SEC registration** If the lender (investor) should decide to sell the issue to a public buyer before maturity, the issue must be registered with the SEC. Some lenders, then, require that the issuing firm agree to a future registration at their option.

Flotation Costs

flotation costs the transaction cost incurred when a firm raises funds by issuing a particular type of security.

The firm raising long-term capital incurs two types of **flotation costs**: (1) the underwriter's spread and (2) issuing costs. Of these two costs, the underwriter's spread is the larger. The *underwriter's spread* is simply the difference between the gross and net proceeds from a given security issue expressed as a percent of the gross proceeds. The *issue costs* include (1) the printing and engraving of the security certificates, (2) legal fees, (3) accounting fees, (4) trustee fees, and (5) several other miscellaneous components. The two most significant issue costs are printing and engraving and legal fees.

Data published by the SEC have consistently revealed two relationships about flotation costs. First, the costs associated with issuing common stock are notably greater than the costs associated with preferred stock offerings. In turn, preferred stock costs exceed those of bonds. Second, flotation costs (expressed as a percentage of gross proceeds) decrease as the size of the security issue increases.

In the first instance, the stated relationship reflects the fact that issue costs are sensitive to the risks involved in successfully distributing a security issue. Common stock is riskier to own than corporate bonds. Underwriting risk is, therefore, greater with common stock than with bonds. Thus, flotation costs just mirror these risk relationships as identified in **Principle 3: Risk Requires a Reward**. In the second case, a portion of the issue costs is fixed. Legal fees and accounting costs are good examples. So, as the size of the security issue rises, the fixed component is spread over a larger gross proceeds base. As a consequence, average flotation costs vary inversely with the size of the issue.

CAUTIONARY TALE

FORGETTING PRINCIPLE 5: CONFLICTS OF INTEREST CAUSE AGENCY PROBLEMS

In 2004, America found itself in the midst of a housing boom. Fueled by low interest rates and government legislation aimed at allowing more people to qualify for housing loans, including those who wouldn't ordinarily qualify, new home construction rates were at a 20-year high. Homeownership was on the rise. And before long, even more first-time homebuyers would realize the American dream.

That was good news for investment bankers like Michael Francis, whose business entailed working with lenders on the West Coast who supplied him with mortgages he could package up as securities and sell to investors who, in turn, collected the interest monthly. For Francis, it didn't matter if the mortgages defaulted; after all, he collected his fees as soon as the mortgages were packaged up and sold as securities. If the mortgages went bad, it wasn't the bank that experienced a loss, it was the last one holding them.

But Francis could only sell the mortgages to big investors once they had been approved by a credit rating agency. The agency's appraisal signaled to investors that the securities were "safe" investments. However, the rating agencies were paid by the people selling the securities, and the more securities that were issued, the more they got paid, and that created a huge temptation to go easy.

Michael Francis admits he had doubts about the risk level of these securities, but the economy was booming and housing prices continued to climb. At the time, the mortgages seemed like safe enough investments to earn the "safe" rating from credit rating agencies. Besides, the investment bank Francis worked for (which he declined to name) was making oodles of money.

If this is starting to sound like one too many conflicts of interest, it should. The acts (or failures to act) of these investment banks and rating agencies are prime examples of how conflicts of interest can lead to agency problems and unethical behavior. Looking back, Francis says the judgment of many in the financial institutions was cloudy. He summed up the way lenders failed to adequately qualify borrowers as, "we removed the litmus test. No income, no asset. Not verifying income ... breathe on a mirror and if there's fog you sort of get a loan."

Many players had a hand in the eventual housing bust that followed, but the credit rating agencies that gave risky securities a "safe" rating, investment banks that failed to question those ratings, and lenders who offered bad loans to homebuyers in the first place are all key players. The appeal of short-term profits and a massive failure to self-regulate caused these institutions to lose sight of the long-term interests of their clients. Many think these conflicts of interest and failure of self-governance all led to the financial crisis of 2009.

Source: MSNBC documentary, "House of Cards."

Regulation Aimed at Making the Goal of the Firm Work: The Sarbanes-Oxley Act

Because of growing concerns about both agency and ethical issues, in 2002 Congress passed the Sarbanes-Oxley Act, or SOX as it is commonly called. One of the primary inspirations for this new law was Enron, which failed financially in December 2001. Prior to bankruptcy, Enron's board of directors actually voted on two occasions to temporarily suspend its own "code of ethics" to permit its CFO to engage in risky financial ventures that benefited the CFO personally while exposing the corporation to substantial risk.

SOX holds corporate advisors who have access to or influence on company decisions (such as a firm's accountants, lawyers, company officers, and boards of directors), legally accountable for any instances of misconduct. The act very simply and directly identifies its purpose as being "to protect investors by improving the accuracy and reliability of corporate disclosures made pursuant to the securities laws, and for other purposes," and mandates that senior executives take individual responsibility for the accuracy and completeness of the firm's financial reports.

SOX safeguards the interests of the shareholders by providing greater protection against accounting fraud and financial misconduct. Unfortunately, all this has not come without a price. While SOX has received praise from the likes of the former Federal Reserve Chairman Alan Greenspan and has increased investor confidence in financial reporting, it has also been criticized. The demanding reporting requirements are quite costly, and as a result, may inhibit firms listing on U.S. stock markets.

Concept Check

1. Within the financial markets, explain what we mean by "private placements."
2. What are the possible advantages and disadvantages of private placements?
3. What are the two major categories of flotation costs?
4. Are flotation costs greater for a new bond issue or a new common stock issue?

Rates of Return in the Financial Markets

 4 Be acquainted with recent interest rate levels.

In this chapter we've discussed the process of raising funds to finance new projects. As you might expect, to raise those funds a firm must offer a rate of return *competitive* with the next-best investment alternative available to that saver (investor).

This *rate of return on the next-best investment alternative to the saver* is known as the investor's **opportunity cost of funds**. The opportunity cost concept is crucial in financial management and is referred to often.

opportunity cost of funds the next-best rate of return available to the investor for a given level of risk.

Next we review the levels and variability in rates of return that have occurred over the lengthy period of 1926 through 2008. This review focuses on returns from a wide array of financial instruments. In Chapter 6, we will explain the relationship of rates of return and risk more completely. Then in Chapter 9 we discuss at length the concept of an *overall* cost of capital. Part of that overall cost of capital is attributed to interest rate levels at given points in time. So we follow this initial broad look at interest rate levels with a discussion of the more recent period of 1981 through 2008.

Rates of Return over Long Periods

History can tell us a great deal about the returns that investors earn in the financial markets. Let's look at what has taken place since 1926. First, what should we expect in terms of return and risk? From **Principle 3: Risk Requires a Reward** we know that with higher returns we should expect to see higher risk, and that's exactly the case. Common stocks of small firms have more risk and produce higher average annual returns than large stock, with the annual return on small-company stocks averaging 16.40 percent and the annual return on large-company stocks averaging 11.70 percent.

 3
Principle

The data is summarized visually in Figure 2-3, which presents the relationship between the average annual observed rates of return for different types of securities along with the

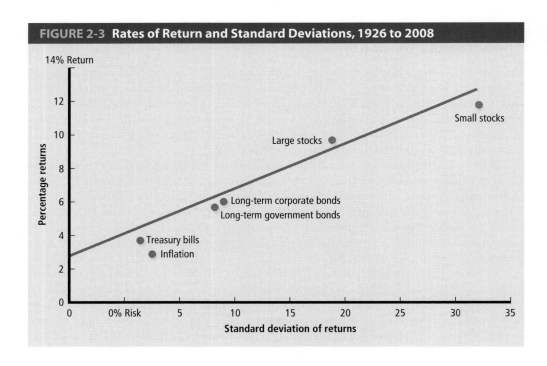

FIGURE 2-3 Rates of Return and Standard Deviations, 1926 to 2008

average annual rate of inflation. Over this period, the average inflation rate was 3.0 percent. We refer to this rate as the "inflation-risk premium." The investor who earns only the rate of inflation has earned no "real return." That is, the *real* return is the return earned above the rate of increase in the general price level for goods and services in the economy, which is the inflation rate. In addition to the danger of not earning above the inflation rate, investors are concerned about the risk of the borrower defaulting, or failing to repay the loan when due. Thus, we would expect investors to earn a default-risk premium for investing in long-term corporate bonds versus long-term government bonds because corporate bonds are considered more risky. The premium for 1926 to 2008, as shown in Figure 2-3, was 0.2 percent, or what is called 20 basis points (5.9 percent on long-term corporate bonds minus 5.7 percent on long-term government bonds). We would also expect an even greater risk premium for common stocks vis-à-vis long-term corporate bonds, because the variability in average returns is greater for common stocks. The results show such a risk premium: Common stocks earned 3.7 percent more than long-term corporate bonds (9.6 percent for common stocks minus 5.9 percent for long-term corporate bonds).

Remember that these returns are "averages" across many securities and over an extended period of time. However, these averages reflect the conventional wisdom regarding risk premiums: The greater the risk, the greater will be the expected returns. Such a relationship is shown in Figure 2-3, where the average returns are plotted against their standard deviations; note that higher average returns have historically been associated with higher dispersion in these returns.

Interest Rate Levels in Recent Periods

The *nominal* interest rates on some key fixed-income securities are displayed within both Table 2-2 and Figure 2-4 for the 1984–2008 time frame. The rate of inflation at the consumer level is also presented in those two exhibits. This allows us to observe quite easily several concepts that were mentioned in the previous section. Specifically, we can observe (1) the inflation-risk premium, (2) the default-risk premium across the several instruments, and (3) the approximate real return for each instrument. Looking at the mean (average) values for each security and the inflation rate at the bottom of Table 2-2 will facilitate the discussion.

Year	3-month Treasury Bills %	30-yr Treasury Bonds %	30-yr Aaa-Rated Corporate Bonds %	Inflation Rate %
1984	9.54	12.41	12.71	3.9
1985	7.47	10.79	11.37	3.8
1986	5.97	7.78	9.02	1.1
1987	5.78	8.59	9.38	4.4
1988	6.67	8.96	9.71	4.4
1989	8.11	8.45	9.26	4.6
1990	7.5	8.61	9.32	6.1
1991	5.38	8.14	8.77	3.1
1992	3.43	7.67	8.14	2.9
1993	3	6.59	7.22	2.7
1994	4.25	7.37	7.97	2.7
1995	5.49	6.88	7.59	2.5
1996	5.01	6.71	7.37	3.3
1997	5.06	6.61	7.27	1.7
1998	4.78	5.58	6.53	1.6
1999	4.64	5.87	7.05	2.7
2000	5.82	5.94	7.62	3.4
2001	3.4	5.49	7.08	1.6
2002	1.61	5.43	6.49	2.4
2003	1.01	4.93	5.66	1.9
2004	1.37	4.86	5.63	3.3
2005	3.15	4.51	5.23	3.4
2006	4.73	4.91	5.59	2.5
2007	4.36	4.84	5.56	4.1
2008	1.37	4.28	5.63	0.1
Mean	4.76	6.89	7.73	2.97

TABLE 2-2 Interest Rate Levels and Inflation Rates, 1984 through 2008

Source: Federal Reserve System, Release H-15, Selected Interest Rates.

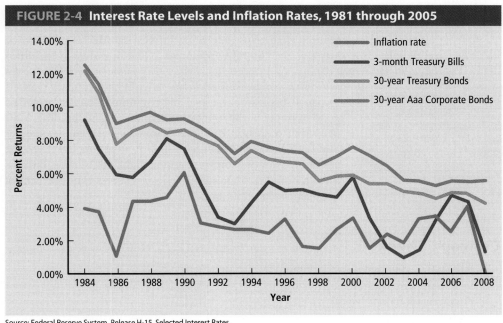

FIGURE 2-4 Interest Rate Levels and Inflation Rates, 1981 through 2005

Source: Federal Reserve System, Release H-15, Selected Interest Rates.

Notice that the average inflation between 1984 and 2008 was slightly higher than it was over the 1926 through 2008 period. This was largely because of the high inflation rates in the 1980s. In recent years, this has changed and inflation rates have dropped dramatically from their levels in the 1980s, and as inflation has dropped, interest rates have come down. This only makes sense according to the logic of the financial markets. Investors *require* a **nominal (or quoted) rate of interest** that exceeds the inflation rate or else their realized *real* return will be negative.

Table 2-2 indicates that investor rationality prevailed. For example, the average return premium demanded on U.S. Treasury bills with a 3-month maturity was 1.79 percent (or 179 basis points, where a basis point is one one-hundredth of 1 percent) in excess of the inferred **inflation-risk premium** of 2.97 percent. That is, an average 4.76 percent yield on Treasury bills over the period *minus* the average inflation rate of 2.97 percent over the same period produces a premium of 1.79 percent. This 1.79 percent can be thought of as the real risk-free short-term interest rate that prevailed over the 1984–2008 period.

The **default-risk premium** is also evident in Table 2-2 and Figure 2-4:

SECURITY	AVERAGE YIELD
30-year Treasury bonds	6.89
30-year Aaa corporate bonds	7.73

Again, the basic rationale of the financial markets prevailed. The default-risk premium on 30-year high-rated (Aaa) corporate bonds relative to long-term Treasury bonds of 30-year maturity was 0.84 percent (7.73 percent minus 6.89 percent), or 84 basis points.

The preceding array of numbers can also be used to identify another factor that affects interest rate levels. It is referred to as the *maturity premium*. The **maturity premium** can be defined as *the additional return required by investors in longer-term securities (bonds in this case) to compensate them for the greater risk of price fluctuations on those securities caused by interest rate changes.* This maturity premium arises even if securities possess equal (or approximately equal) odds of default. Notice that Treasury bonds with a 30-year maturity commanded a 2.13 percent yield differential over the shorter, 3-month-to-maturity Treasury bonds. (Both types of bonds are considered risk-free because they are issued and backed by the U.S. government.) This provides an estimate of the maturity premium demanded by all investors over this specific 1984–2008 period.

When you study the basic mathematics of financial decisions and the characteristics of fixed-income securities in later chapters, you will learn how to quantify this maturity premium that is imbedded in nominal interest rates.

One other type of risk premium that helps determine interest rate levels needs to be identified and defined. It is known as the "liquidity premium." The **liquidity premium** is defined as *the additional return required by investors in securities that cannot be quickly converted into cash at a reasonably predictable price.* The secondary markets for small-bank stocks, especially community banks, provide a good example of the liquidity premium. A bank holding company that trades on the New York Stock Exchange, such as SunTrust Bank, will be more liquid to investors than, say, the common stock of Century National Bank of Orlando, Florida. Such a liquidity premium is reflected across the spectrum of financial assets, from bonds to stocks.

nominal (or quoted) rate of interest the interest rate paid on debt securities without an adjustment for any loss in purchasing power.

inflation-risk premium a premium to compensate for anticipated inflation that is equal to the price change expected to occur over the life of the bond or investment instrument.

default-risk premium the additional return required by investors to compensate them for the risk of default. It is calculated as the difference in rates between a U.S. Treasury bond and a corporate bond of the same maturity and marketability.

maturity premium the additional return required by investors in longer-term securities to compensate them for the greater risk of price fluctuations on those securities caused by interest rate changes.

liquidity premium the additional return required by investors for securities that cannot be quickly converted into cash at a reasonably predictable price.

> **P**rinciple **REMEMBER YOUR PRINCIPLES**
> Our third principle, **Principle 3: Risk Requires a Reward**, established the fundamental risk–return relationship that governs the financial markets. We are now trying to provide you with an understanding of the kinds of risks that are rewarded in the risk–return relationship presented in **Principle 3**.

Concept Check

1. What is the "opportunity cost of funds"?
2. Over long periods of time is the "real rate of return" higher on 30-year Treasury bonds or 30-year Aaa corporate bonds?
3. Distinguish between the concepts of the "inflation-risk premium" and the "default-risk premium."
4. Distinguish between the concepts of the "maturity premium" and the "liquidity premium."

Interest Rate Determinants in a Nutshell

Using the logic from **Principle 3: Risk Requires a Reward**, we can decompose the interest rate paid on a security into a simple equation with the nominal interest rate equal to the sum of the real risk-free interest rate plus compensation for taking on several different types of risk and several risk premiums, where the **real risk-free interest rate** is *a required rate of return on a fixed-income security that has no risk in an economic environment of zero inflation*. The real risk-free interest rate can be thought of as the return demanded by investors in U.S. Treasury securities during periods of no inflation. The equation for the nominal interest rate is

$$
\begin{aligned}
\text{nominal interest rate} = \ & \text{real risk-free interest rate} \\
& + \text{inflation-risk premium} \\
& + \text{default-risk premium} \\
& + \text{maturity premium} \\
& + \text{liquidity premium}
\end{aligned} \tag{2-1}
$$

5 Explain the fundamentals of interest rate determination and the popular theories of the term structure of interest rates.

3 Principle

real risk-free interest rate the required rate of return on a fixed-income security that has no risk in an economic environment of zero inflation.

Estimating Specific Interest Rates Using Risk Premiums: An Example

By using our knowledge of various risk premia as contained in equation (2-1), the financial manager can generate useful information for the firm's financial planning process. For instance, if the firm is about to offer a new issue of corporate bonds to the investing marketplace, it is possible for the financial manager or analyst to estimate what interest rate (yield) would satisfy the market to help ensure that the bonds are actually bought by investors. It would be unwise for the firm to offer too high of a yield because it will incur unnecessary interest expenses that will negatively impact earnings. On the other hand, offering too low of a yield will hinder the bonds from being attractive to investors (savers) in a competitive marketplace. The following example should help clarify and illustrate this situation.

Real and Nominal Rates of Interest

As we just learned, when a rate of interest is quoted, it is generally the nominal, or observed, rate. The nominal rate of interest tells you how much more money you will have. The **real rate of interest**, in contrast, represents *the rate of increase in your actual purchasing power, after adjusting for inflation*. In effect, the real rate of interest tells you how much more purchasing power you will have. The real rate of interest is not necessarily a risk-free rate of interest,

real rate of interest the nominal (quoted) rate of interest less any loss in purchasing power of the dollar during the time of the investment.

CAN YOU DO IT?

You have been asked to provide a reasonable estimate of the nominal interest rate for a new issue of 30-year Aaa-rated bonds (that is, very high quality corporate bonds) to be offered by Big Truck Producers Inc. The final format that the CFO of Big Truck has requested is that of equation (2-1) in the text.

After some thought, you decided to estimate the different premiums in equation (2-1) as follows:

1. The real risk-free rate of interest is the difference between the calculated average yield on 3-month Treasury bills and the inflation rate.

2. The inflation-risk premium is the rate of inflation expected to occur over the life of the bond under consideration.

3. The default-risk premium is estimated by the difference between the average yield on 30-year Aaa-rated corporate bonds and 30-year Treasury bonds.

4. The maturity premium is estimated by the difference between the calculated average yield on 30-year Treasury bonds and 3-month Treasury bills.

You next conducted research and found the following: The current 3-month Treasury bill rate is 4.89 percent, the 30-year Treasury bond rate is 5.38 percent, the 30-year Aaa-rated corporate bond rate is 6.24 percent, and the inflation rate is 3.60 percent. Finally, you have estimated that Big Truck's bonds will have a slight liquidity premium of 0.03 percent. While the bonds will be traded on the New York Exchange for Bonds, the secondary market for the firm's bonds is more uncertain than that of some other truck producers.

Now place your output into the format of equation (2-1) so that the nominal interest rate can be estimated and the size of each variable can also be inspected for reasonableness and discussion with the chief financial officer. (Solution can be found on page 36.)

DID YOU GET IT?

Let's now look at the building blocks that will comprise our forecast of the nominal interest rate on Big Truck's new issue of bonds. The nominal rate that is forecast to satisfy the market turns out be 6.27 percent. The following tables illustrate how we obtained this estimate.

(1) 3-month Treasury Bills %	(2) 30-year Treasury Bonds %	(3) 30-year Aaa-Rated Corporate Bonds %	(4) Inflation Rate %
4.89	5.38	6.24	3.60

Table Columns Shown Above	Equation (2-1)	
(1)–(4)	real risk-free interest rate	1.29
	+	+
(4)	inflation-risk premium	3.60
	+	+
(3)–(2)	default-risk premium	0.86
	+	+
(2)–(1)	maturity premium	0.49
	+	+
Given	liquidity premium	0.03
	=	=
	nominal interest rate	6.27

Thus, we see that:

1. The real risk-free rate of interest is 1.29 percent, which is the difference between the average yield on a 3-month Treasury bill and the inflation rate (column 1 less column 4).

2. The inflation-risk premium of 3.60 percent is the inflation rate (column 4).

3. The default-risk premium of 0.86 is the difference in the average rate available to investors in the least risky (30-year Aaa-rated) corporate bonds that mature in 30 years and the average return for a Treasury bond that matures in 30 years (column 3 minus column 2).

4. The maturity premium of 0.49 percent is the rate earned by investors on 30-year Treasury bonds less the rate on 3-month Treasury bills (column 2 minus column 1).

5. The liquidity premium is 0.03 percent, based on your earlier assumption.

When we put this all together as an estimate of the nominal interest rate needed to satisfy the financial markets on Big Truck's new bond issue, we have

nominal rate on Big Truck's bonds $= 1.29 + 3.60 + 0.86 + 0.49 + 0.03 = 6.27\%$

Understanding this analysis will help you deal with the Mini Case at the end of this chapter. We move now to an examination of the relationship between real and nominal interest rates.

---

although it can be. In effect, there are real rates of interest for all different levels of risk. Because the real rate of interest is not necessarily a risk-free rate, it can include both the real risk-free rate of interest and any appropriate risk premiums (default-risk premium, maturity premium, and liquidity premium). The nominal risk-free rate can be calculated to be approximately

$$\text{nominal interest rate} \approx \text{(approximately equals) real rate of interest} + \text{inflation-risk premium} \qquad (2\text{-}2)$$

This equation just says that the nominal rate of interest is approximately equal to the real interest rate plus the inflation premium and provides a quick and *approximate* way of estimating the real rate of interest by solving directly for this rate. You'll notice it is very similar to equation (2-1), except it lumps all the different risk premiums in with the real risk-free rate of interest to come up with the real rate of interest. This basic relationship in equation (2-2) contains important information for the financial decision maker. It has also been for years the subject of fascinating and lengthy discussions among financial economists. We will look more at the substance of the real rate of interest in the second section that follows here. In that discussion, we will improve on equation (2-2) by making it more precise.

As we saw in equation (2-2), a quick approximation for the nominal rate of interest is the real interest rate plus the inflation premium. Let's take a closer look at this relationship. Let's begin by assuming that you have $100 today and lend it to someone for one year at a nominal rate of interest of 11.3 percent. This means you will get back $111.30 in 1 year. But if during the year, the prices of goods and services rise by 5 percent, it will take $105 at year-end to purchase the same goods and services that $100 purchased at the beginning of the year. What was your increase in purchasing power over the year? The quick and dirty answer is found by subtracting the inflation rate from the nominal rate, $11.3\% - 5\% = 6.3\%$, but this is not exactly correct. We can also express the relationship among the nominal interest rate, the rate of inflation, and the real rate of interest as follows:

$$1 + \text{nominal interest rate} = (1 + \text{real rate of interest})(1 + \text{rate of inflation}) \qquad (2\text{-}3)$$

Solving for the nominal rate of interest, nominal interest rate = real rate of interest + rate of inflation + (real rate of interest)(rate of inflation)

Consequently, the nominal rate of interest is equal to the sum of the real rate of interest, the inflation rate, and the product of the real rate and the inflation rate. This relationship among nominal rates, real rates, and the rate of inflation has come to be called the *Fisher effect*.[2] What does the product of the real rate of interest and the inflation rate represent? It represents the fact that the money you earn on your investment is worth less because of inflation. All this demonstrates that the observed nominal rate of interest includes both the real rate and an *inflation premium*.

Substituting into equation (2-3) using a nominal rate of 11.3 percent and an inflation rate of 5 percent, we can calculate the real rate of interest as follows:

Nominal or quoted rate of interest	=	real rate of interest	+	inflation rate	+	product of the real rate of interest and the inflation rate
0.113	=	(real rate of interest)	+	0.05	+	0.05 × real rate of interest
0.063	=	1.05 × (real rate of interest)				

Solving for the real rate of interest:

(real rate of interest) =	0.06	=	6%

Thus, at the new higher prices, your purchasing power will have increased by only 6 percent, although you have $11.30 more than you had at the start of the year. To see why, let's assume that at the outset of the year, one unit of the market basket of goods and services costs $1, so you could purchase 100 units with your $100. At the end of the year, you have $11.30 more, but each unit now costs $1.05 (remember the 5 percent rate of inflation). How many units can you buy at the end of the year? The answer is $111.30 ÷ $1.05 = 106, which represents a 6 percent increase in real purchasing power.[3]

Inflation and Real Rates of Return: The Financial Analyst's Approach

Although the algebraic methodology presented in the previous section is strictly correct, few practicing analysts or executives use it. Rather, they employ some version of the following

CAN YOU DO IT?

SOLVING FOR THE REAL RATE OF INTEREST

Your banker just called and offered you the chance to invest your savings for 1 year at a quoted rate of 10 percent. You also saw on the news that the inflation rate is 6 percent. What is the real rate of interest you would be earning if you made the investment? (The solution can be found on page 38.)

---

[2]This relationship was analyzed many years ago by Irving Fisher. For those who want to explore Fisher's theory of interest in more detail, a fine overview is contained in Peter N. Ireland, "Long-Term Interest Rate and Inflation: A Fisherian Approach," Federal Reserve Bank of Richmond, *Economic Quarterly*, 82 (Winter 1996), pp. 22–26.

[3]In Chapter 5, we will study more about the time value of money.

DID YOU GET IT?
SOLVING FOR THE REAL RATE OF INTEREST

Nominal or quoted rate of interest	=	real rate of interest	+	inflation rate	+	product of the real rate of interest and the inflation rate
0.10	=	(real rate of interest)	+	0.06	+	0.06 × real rate of interest
0.04	=	1.06 × (real rate of interest)				

Solving for the real rate of interest :

(real rate of interest) =   0.0377   =   3.77%

relationship, an approximation method, to estimate the real rate of interest over a selected past time frame.

(nominal interest rate) − (inflation rate) = real interest rate

The concept is straightforward, but its implementation requires that several judgments be made. For example, which interest rate series and maturity period should be used? Suppose we settle for using some U.S. Treasury security as a surrogate for a nominal risk-free interest rate. Then, should we use the yield on 3-month U.S. Treasury bills or, perhaps, the yield on 30-year Treasury bonds? There is no absolute answer to the question.

So, we can have a real risk-free short-term interest rate, as well as a real risk-free long-term interest rate, and several variations in between. In essence, it just depends on what the analyst wants to accomplish. We could also calculate the real rate of interest on some rating class of 30-year corporate bonds (such as Aaa-rated bonds) and have a risky real rate of interest as opposed to a real risk-free interest rate.

Furthermore, the choice of a proper inflation index is equally challenging. Again, we have several choices. We could use the consumer price index, the producer price index for finished goods, or some price index out of the national income accounts, such as the gross domestic product chain price index. Again, there is no precise scientific answer as to which specific price index to use. Logic and consistency do narrow the boundaries of the ultimate choice.

Let's tackle a very basic (simple) example. Suppose that an analyst wants to estimate the approximate real interest rate on (1) 3-month Treasury bills, (2) 30-year Treasury bonds, and (3) 30-year Aaa-rated corporate bonds over the 1984–2008 time frame. Furthermore, the annual rate of change in the consumer price index (measured from December to December) is considered a logical measure of past inflation experience. Most of our work is already done for us in Table 2-2. Some of the data from Table 2-2 are displayed here.

SECURITY	MEAN NOMINAL YIELD (%)	MEAN INFLATION RATE (%)	INFERRED REAL RATE (%)
3-month Treasury bills	4.76	2.97	1.79
30-year Treasury bonds	6.89	2.97	3.92
30-year Aaa-rated corporate bonds	7.73	2.97	4.76

Notice that the mean yield over the 25 years from 1984 to 2008 on all three classes of securities has been used. Likewise, the mean inflation rate over the same time period has been used as an estimate of the inflation-risk premium. The last column provides the approximation for the real interest rate on each class of securities.

Thus, over the 25-year examination period the real rate of interest on 3-month Treasury bills was 1.79 percent versus 3.92 percent on 30-year Treasury bonds, versus 4.76 percent on 30-year Aaa-rated corporate bonds. These three estimates (approximations) of the real interest rate provide a rough guide to the increase in real purchasing power associated with an investment position in each security. Remember that the real rate on the corporate bonds is expected to be greater than that on long-term government bonds because of the default-risk premium placed on the corporate securities. We move in the next section to a more detailed discussion of the maturity-risk premium.

Concept Check

1. What is the "nominal rate of interest"? Explain how it differs from the "real rate of interest."
2. Write an equation that includes the building blocks of the nominal rate of interest.

The Term Structure of Interest Rates

The relationship between a debt security's rate of return and the length of time until the debt matures is known as the **term structure of interest rates** or the **yield to maturity**. For the relationship to be meaningful to us, all the factors other than maturity, meaning factors such as the chance of the bond defaulting, must be held constant. Thus, *the term structure reflects observed rates or yields on similar securities, except for the length of time until maturity, at a particular moment in time.*

Figure 2-5 shows an example of the term structure of interest rates. The curve is upward sloping, indicating that longer terms to maturity command higher returns, or yields. In this hypothetical term structure, the rate of interest on a 5-year note or bond is 7.5 percent, whereas the comparable rate on a 20-year bond is 9 percent.

term structure of interest rates the relationship between interest rates and the term to maturity, where the risk of default is held constant.

yield to maturity the rate of return a bondholder will receive if the bond is held to maturity.

Observing the Historical Term Structures of Interest Rates

As we might expect, the term structure of interest rates changes over time, depending on the environment. The particular term structure observed today may be quite different from the term structure 1 month ago and different still from the term structure 1 month from

---

CAN YOU DO IT?

SOLVING FOR THE NOMINAL RATE OF INTEREST

If you would like to earn a real rate of interest of 6 percent while the inflation rate is 4 percent, what nominal rate of interest would you have? (The solution can be found on page 40.)

FIGURE 2-5 The Term Structure of Interest Rates

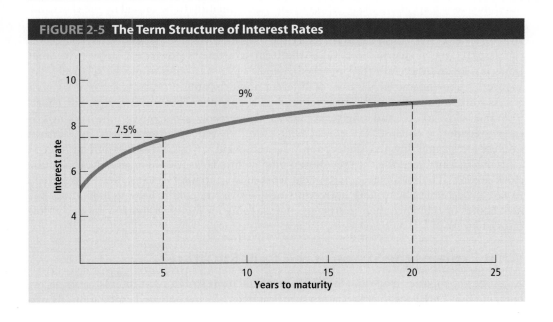

DID YOU GET IT?

SOLVING FOR THE NOMINAL RATE OF INTEREST

Nominal or quoted rate of interest	=	real rate of interest	+	inflation rate	+	product of the real rate of interest and the inflation rate
	=	0.06	+	0.04	+	(0.06 × 0.04)
	=	0.1024	=	10.24%		

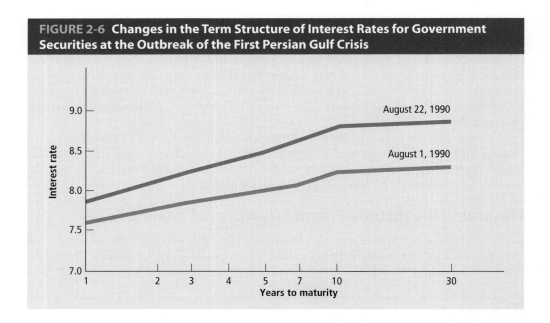

FIGURE 2-6 Changes in the Term Structure of Interest Rates for Government Securities at the Outbreak of the First Persian Gulf Crisis

now. A perfect example of the changing term structure, or yield curve, was witnessed during the early days of the first Persian Gulf Crisis, which occurred in August 1990. Figure 2-6 shows the yield curves 1 day before the Iraqi invasion of Kuwait and then again just 3 weeks later. The change is noticeable, particularly for long-term interest rates. Investors quickly developed new fears about the prospect of increased inflation to be caused by the crisis and, consequently, increased their required rates of return. Although the upward-sloping term-structure curves in Figures 2-5 and 2-6 are the ones most commonly observed, yield curves can assume several shapes. Sometimes the term structure is downward sloping; at other times it rises and then falls (humpbacked); and at still other times it may be relatively flat. Figure 2-7 shows some yield curves at different points in time.

As you can see in Figure 2-7, the yield curve in September 2009 was very low, with short-term rates close to zero and long-term rates at 4.24 percent. In response to the banking crisis and economic collapse, the government moved to reduce interest rates. In addition, interest rates came down as the economy slowed, while investors further pushed interest rates on Treasury securities as they moved money into Treasuries to escape the risk of the stock market. The reason the government worked to keep interest rates down was to help restart the economy by making borrowing inexpensive—hopefully helping individuals buy new homes or refinance their mortgages and allowing businesses to borrow money at low rates to invest.

What Explains the Shape of the Term Structure?

A number of theories may explain the shape of the term structure of interest rates at any point in time. Three possible explanations are prominent: (1) the unbiased expectations theory,

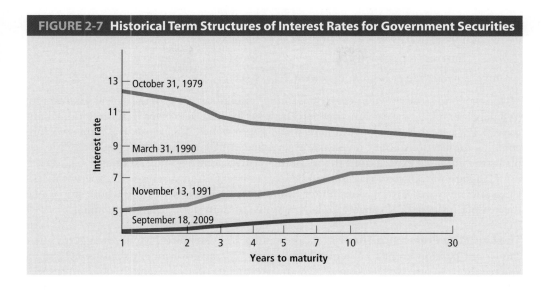

FIGURE 2-7 Historical Term Structures of Interest Rates for Government Securities

(2) the liquidity preference theory, and (3) the market segmentation theory.[4] Let's look at each in turn.

The Unbiased Expectations Theory   The **unbiased expectations theory** says that *the term structure is determined by an investor's expectations about future interest rates.*[5] To see how this works, consider the following investment problem faced by Mary Maxell. Mary has $10,000 that she wants to invest for 2 years, at which time she plans to use her savings to make a down payment on a new home. Wanting not to take any risk of losing her savings, she decides to invest in U.S. government securities. She has two choices. First, she can purchase a government security that matures in 2 years, which offers her an interest rate of 9 percent per year. If she does this, she will have $11,881 in 2 years, calculated as follows:[6]

Principal amount	$10,000
Plus year 1 interest (.09 × $10,000)	900
Principal plus interest at the end of year 1	$10,900
Plus year 2 interest (.09 × $10,900)	981
Principal plus interest at the end of year 2	$11,881

Alternatively, Mary could buy a government security maturing in 1 year that pays an 8 percent rate of interest. She would then need to purchase another 1-year security at the end of the first year. Which alternative Mary chooses obviously depends in part on the rate of interest she expects to receive on the government security she will purchase a year from now. We cannot tell Mary what the interest rate will be in a year; however, we can at least calculate the rate that will give her the same 2-year total savings she would get from her first choice, or $11,881. The interest rate can be calculated as follows:

Savings needed in 2 years	$11,881
Savings at the end of year 1 [$10,000(1 + .08)]	$10,800
Interest needed in year 2	$ 1,081

unbiased expectations theory the theory that the shape of the term structure of interest rates is determined by an investor's expectations about future interest rates.

[4]See Richard Roll, *The Behavior of Interest Rates: An Application of the Efficient Market Model to U.S. Treasury Bills* (New York: Basic Books, 1970).
[5]Irving Fisher thought of this idea in 1896. The theory was later refined by J. R. Hicks in *Value and Capital* (London: Oxford University Press, 1946) and F. A. Lutz and V. C. Lutz in *The Theory of Investment in the Firm* (Princeton, NJ: Princeton University Press, 1951).
[6]We could also calculate the principal plus interest for Mary's investment using the following compound interest equation: $10,000(1 + 0.09)^2 = $11,881. We study the mathematics of compound interest in Chapter 5.

For Mary to receive $1,081 in the second year, she would have to earn about 10 percent on her second-year investment, computed as follows:

$$\frac{\text{interest received in year 2}}{\text{investment made at beginning of year 2}} = \frac{\$1,081}{\$10,800} = 10\%$$

So the term structure of interest rates for our example consists of the 1-year interest rate of 8 percent and the 2-year rate of 9 percent. This exercise also gives us information about the *expected* 1-year rate for investments made 1 year hence. In a sense, the term structure contains implications about investors' expectations of future interest rates; thus, this explains the unbiased expectations theory of the term structure of interest rates.

Although we can see a relationship between current interest rates with different maturities and investors' expectations about future interest rates, is this the whole story? Are there other influences? Probably, so let's continue to think about Mary's dilemma.

The Liquidity Preference Theory   In presenting Mary's choices, we have suggested that she would be indifferent to a choice between the 2-year government security offering a 9 percent return and two consecutive 1-year investments offering 8 and 10 percent, respectively. However, that would be so only if she is unconcerned about the risk associated with not knowing the rate of interest on the second 1-year security as of today. If Mary is risk averse (that is, she dislikes risk), she might not be satisfied with expectations of a 10 percent return on the second 1-year government security. She might require some additional expected return to be truly indifferent. Mary might in fact decide that she will expose herself to the uncertainty of future interest rates only if she can reasonably *expect* to earn an additional 0.5 percent in interest, or 10.5 percent, on the second 1-year investment. This *risk premium* (additional required interest rate) to compensate for the risk of changing future interest rates is nothing more than the maturity premium introduced earlier, and this concept underlies the liquidity preference theory of the term structure.[7] According to the **liquidity preference theory**, *investors require maturity premiums to compensate them for buying securities that expose them to the risks of fluctuating interest rates.*

The Market Segmentation Theory   The **market segmentation theory** of the term structure of interest rates is built on the notion that legal restrictions and personal preferences limit choices for investors to certain ranges of maturities. For example, commercial banks prefer short- to medium-term maturities as a result of the short-term nature of their deposit liabilities. They prefer not to invest in long-term securities. Life insurance companies, on the other hand, have long-term liabilities, so they prefer longer maturities in investments. At the extreme, the market segmentation theory implies that *the rate of interest for a particular maturity is determined solely by demand and supply for a given maturity and that it is independent of the demand and supply for securities having different maturities.* A more moderate version of the theory allows investors to have strong maturity preferences, but it also allows them to modify their feelings and preferences if significant yield changes occur.

liquidity preference theory the theory that the shape of the term structure of interest rates is determined by an investor's additional required interest rate in compensation of additional risks.

market segmentation theory the theory that the shape of the term structure of interest rates implies that the rate of interest for a particular maturity is determined solely by demand and supply for a given maturity. This rate is independent of the demand and supply for securities having different maturities.

Concept Check

1. Identify three prominent theories that attempt to explain the term structure of interest rates.
2. Which shape of the yield curve is considered to be the most typical?

LO6 Understand the relationships among the multinational firm, efficient financial markets, and intercountry risk.

Finance and the Multinational Firm: Efficient Financial Markets and Intercountry Risk

In this chapter we have discussed and demonstrated that the United States has a highly developed, complex, and competitive system of financial markets that allows for the quick transfer of savings from people and organizations with a surplus of savings to people and

---

[7]This theory was first presented by John R. Hicks in *Value and Capital* (London: Oxford University Press, 1946), pp. 141–145, with the risk premium referred to as the liquidity premium. For our purposes we use the term *maturity premium* to describe this risk premium, thereby keeping our terminology consistent within this chapter.

organizations with a savings deficit. Such a system of robust and credible financial markets allows great ideas (such as the personal computer) to be financed and increases the overall wealth of the given economy.

One major reason underdeveloped countries are indeed underdeveloped is that they lack a financial market system that has the confidence of those who must use it—such as the multinational firm. The multinational firm with cash to invest in foreign markets will weigh heavily the integrity of both the financial system and the political system of the prospective foreign country.

A lack of integrity on either the financial side or the political stability side retards direct investment in the lesser-developed nation. Consider the Walt Disney Company, headquartered in Burbank, California. Disney common stock trades on the NYSE (DIS), although the firm has significant overseas real investments such as Disneyland Paris Resort, Tokyo Disneyland, Hong Kong Disneyland, and Shanghai Disneyland. Disney has confidence in China's financial markets and those of western Europe and Japan. Disney would be less inclined to invest in a country like North Korea because it is less politically and financially stable.

Concept Check

1. Identify one major reason why underdeveloped countries remain underdeveloped.

Summary

This chapter centers on the market environment in which corporations raise long-term funds, including the structure of the U.S. financial markets, the institution of investment banking, and the various methods for distributing securities. It also discusses the role interest rates play in allocating savings to ultimate investment.

Describe key components of the U.S. financial market system and the financing of business.

Corporations can raise funds through public offerings or private placements. The public market is impersonal in that the security issuer does not meet the ultimate investors in the financial instruments. In a private placement, the securities are sold directly to a limited number of institutional investors.

The primary market is the market for new issues. The secondary market represents transactions in currently outstanding securities. Both the money and capital markets have primary and secondary sides. The money market refers to transactions in short-term debt instruments. The capital market, on the other hand, refers to transactions in long-term financial instruments. Trading in the capital markets can occur in either the organized security exchanges or the over-the-counter market. The money market is exclusively an over-the-counter market.

Understand the role of the investment-banking business in the context of raising corporate capital.

The investment banker is a financial specialist involved as an intermediary in the merchandising of securities. He or she performs the functions of (1) underwriting, (2) distributing, and (3) advising. Major methods for the public distribution of securities include (1) the negotiated purchase, (2) the competitive bid purchase, (3) the commission or best-efforts basis, (4) privileged subscriptions, and (5) direct sales. The direct sale bypasses the use of an investment banker. The negotiated purchase is the most profitable distribution method to the investment banker. It also provides the greatest amount of investment-banking services to the corporate client. Today, there are no major stand-alone investment bankers.

Understand private debt placements and flotation costs.

Privately placed debt provides an important market outlet for corporate bonds. Major investors in this market are (1) life insurance firms, (2) state and local retirement funds, and (3) private pension funds. Several advantages and disadvantages are associated with private placements. The financial officer must weigh these attributes and decide if a private placement is preferable to a public offering.

Be acquainted with recent interest rate levels.

Flotation costs consist of the underwriter's spread and issuing costs. The flotation costs of common stock exceed those of preferred stock, which, in turn, exceed those of debt. Moreover, flotation costs as a percent of gross proceeds are inversely related to the size of the security issue.

On July 30, 2002, President Bush signed into law the Sarbanes-Oxley Act of 2002. Its intended purpose as stated in the act is "to protect investors by improving the accuracy and reliability of corporate disclosures made pursuant to the securities laws, and for other purposes."

Explain the fundamentals of interest rate determination and the popular theories of the term structure of interest rates.

The financial markets give managers an informed indication of investors' opportunity costs. The more efficient the market, the more informed the indication. This information is a useful input about the rates of return that investors require on financial claims. In turn, this becomes useful to financial managers as they estimate the overall cost of capital the firm will have to pay for its financing needs.

From **Principle 3: Risk Requires a Reward**, you know that the rates of return on various securities are based on the risks that investors face when they invest in those securities. In addition to a

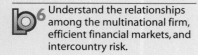

LO6 Understand the relationships among the multinational firm, efficient financial markets, and intercountry risk.

risk-free return, investors will want to be compensated for the potential loss of purchasing power resulting from inflation. Moreover, investors require a greater return the greater the default risk, maturity premium, and liquidity premium are on the securities being analyzed.

A system of robust and credible financial markets allows great ideas to be financed and increases the overall wealth of a given economy. The multinational firm with cash to invest in foreign markets will weigh heavily the integrity of both the financial system and the political system of the prospective foreign country where the proposed investment project will be domiciled. A lack of integrity on either the financial side or the political stability side retards direct investment in a less-developed nation.

Key Terms

Angel investor   20

Capital market   19

Default-risk premium   34

Direct sale   28

Dutch auction   28

Flotation costs   30

Futures market   23

Inflation-risk premium   34

Initial public offering, IPO   22

Investment banker   25

Liquidity preference theory   42

Liquidity premium   34

Market segmentation theory   42

Maturity premium   34

Money market   22

Nominal (or quoted) rate of interest   34

Opportunity cost of funds   31

Organized security exchange   23

Over-the-counter market   23

Primary market   22

Private placement   21

Privileged subscription   27

Public offering   21

Real rate of interest   35

Real risk-free interest rate   35

Seasoned equity offering, SEO   22

Secondary market   22

Spot market   23

Syndicate   26

Term structure of interest rates   39

Unbiased expectations theory   41

Underwriter's spread   25

Underwriting   25

Venture capital firm   21

Venture capitalist   20

Yield to maturity   39

Review Questions

All Review Questions and Study Problems are available in MyFinanceLab.

2-1. Distinguish between the money and capital markets.

2-2. What major benefits do corporations and investors enjoy because of the existence of organized security exchanges?

2-3. What general criteria does an organized exchange examine to determine whether a firm's securities can be listed on the exchange? (Specific numbers are not needed here but rather areas of investigation.)

2-4. Why do you think most secondary-market trading in bonds takes place over the counter?

2-5. What is an investment banker, and what major functions does he or she perform?

2-6. What is the major difference between a negotiated purchase and a competitive bid purchase?

2-7. Why is an investment-banking syndicate formed?

2-8. Why might a large corporation want to raise long-term capital through a private placement rather than a public offering?

2-9. As a recent business school graduate, you work directly for the corporate treasurer. Your corporation is going to issue a new security and is concerned with the probable flotation costs. What tendencies about flotation costs can you relate to the treasurer?

2-10. Identify three distinct ways that savings are ultimately transferred to business firms in need of cash.

2-11. Explain the term *opportunity cost* with respect to the cost of funds to the firm.

2-12. Compare and explain the historical rates of return for different types of securities.

2-13. Explain the impact of inflation on rates of return.

2-14. Define the *term structure of interest rates.*

2-15. Explain the popular theories for the rationale of the term structure of interest rates.

Study Problems

2-1. (*Calculating the default-risk premium*) At present, 10-year Treasury bonds are yielding 4% while a 10-year corporate bond was yielding 6.8%. If the liquidity premium on the corporate bond was 0.4%, what is the corporate bond's default-risk premium?

2-2. (*Real interest rates: financial analyst's method*) The CFO of your firm has asked you for an approximate answer to this question: What was the increase in real purchasing power associated with both 3-month Treasury bills and 30-year Treasury bonds? Assume that the current 3-month Treasury bill rate is 4.34 percent, the 30-year Treasury bond rate is 7.33 percent, and the inflation rate is 2.78 percent. Also, the chief financial officer wants a short explanation should the 3-month real rate turn out to be *less* than the 30-year real rate.

2-3. (*Inflation and interest rates*) What would you expect the nominal rate of interest to be if the real rate is 4 percent and the expected inflation rate is 7 percent?

2-4. (*Inflation and interest rates*) Assume the expected inflation rate to be 4 percent. If the current real rate of interest is 6 percent, what ought the nominal rate of interest be?

2-5. (*Calculating the maturity premium*) At present, the real risk-free rate of interest is 2%, while inflation is expected to be 2% for the next two years. If a 2-year Treasury note yields 4.5%, what is the maturity premium for this 2-year Treasury note?

2-6. (*Term structure of interest rates*) You want to invest your savings of $20,000 in government securities for the next 2 years. Currently, you can invest either in a security that pays interest of 8 percent per year for the next 2 years or in a security that matures in 1 year but pays only 6 percent interest. If you make the latter choice, you would then reinvest your savings at the end of the first year for another year.

    a. Why might you choose to make the investment in the 1-year security that pays an interest rate of only 6 percent, as opposed to investing in the 2-year security paying 8 percent? Provide numerical support for your answer. Which theory of term structure have you supported in your answer?

    b. Assume your required rate of return on the second-year investment is 11 percent; otherwise, you will choose to go with the 2-year security. What rationale could you offer for your preference?

Mini Case

On the first day of your summer internship, you've been assigned to work with the Chief Financial Officer (CFO) of SanBlas Jewels Inc. Not knowing how well trained you are, the CFO has decided to test your understanding of interest rates. Specifically, she asked you to provide a reasonable estimate of the nominal interest rate for a new issue of Aaa-rated bonds to be offered by SanBlas Jewels Inc. The final format that the chief financial officer of SanBlas Jewels has requested is that of equation (2-1) in the text. Your assignment also requires that you consult the data in Table 2-2.

    Some agreed-upon procedures related to generating estimates for key variables in equation (2-1) follow.

    a. The current 3-month Treasury bill rate is 2.96 percent, the 30-year Treasury bond rate is 5.43 percent, the 30-year Aaa-rated corporate bond rate is 6.71 percent, and the inflation rate is 2.33 percent.

    b. The real risk-free rate of interest is the difference between the calculated average yield on 3-month Treasury bills and the inflation rate.

    c. The default-risk premium is estimated by the difference between the average yield on Aaa-rated bonds and 30-year Treasury bonds.

    d. The maturity premium is estimated by the difference between the average yield on 30-year Treasury bonds and 3-month Treasury bills.

    e. SanBlas Jewels' bonds will be traded on the New York Bond Exchange, so the liquidity premium will be slight. It will be greater than zero, however, because the secondary market for the firm's bonds is more uncertain than that of some other jewel sellers. It is estimated at 4 basis points. A basis point is one one-hundredth of 1 percent.

Now place your output into the format of equation (2-1) so that the nominal interest rate can be estimated and the size of each variable can also be inspected for reasonableness and discussion with the CFO.

Chapter 3

Understanding Financial Statements and Cash Flows

Learning Objectives

After reading this chapter, you should be able to:

 Compute a company's profits, as reflected by its income statement.

 Determine a firm's financial position at a point in time based on its balance sheet.

Measure a company's cash flows.

Compute taxable income and income taxes owed.

In Hewlett-Packard's (HP) 2008 annual report, Mark Hurd (CEO) describes the firm as follows:

> We are a leading global provider of products, technologies, software, solutions and services to individual consumers, small- and medium-sized businesses ("SMBs"), and large enterprises, including customers in the public and education sectors.

In his letter to the shareholders in the annual report, Hurd discusses the economic difficulties he believes the company will face in 2009, given the severe economic downturn.

> In the near term, we expect that economic conditions in 2009 will be extremely challenging. It will take continued discipline and tough decision making to stay the course and continue executing our strategy in the coming months.

In response to the anticipated challenges, he describes the firm's competitive advantages that he says will carry the firm through the difficult times:

> [O]ur company has significant competitive advantages:
>
> ◆ A strong balance sheet
> ◆ Diversified revenues with one-third of our revenue and well over half of our profits from recurring sources such as services and supplies
> ◆ A lean, variable cost structure and commitment to continue to eliminate all costs that are not core to the company's success
> ◆ Proven financial and operational discipline

> These advantages will be put to good use by our outstanding executive leadership team . . . Our plan is to get through this period without losing any muscle in the organization or changing our swing in the marketplace . . . We expect that HP's ability to execute in a challenging marketplace will differentiate us from our competitors and enable HP to emerge from the current environment as a stronger force in the industry.

In essence, Hurd is saying that when it comes to tough times, having strong financial statements is critical, and will provide a competitive advantage during these times. This chapter lays a foundation for your understanding financial statements, which in some ways is the "language" of business.

In Chapter 2, we explained the workings of the financial markets. We found that these markets provide the means for bringing together investors (savers) with the users of capital (businesses that provide products and services to the consumer). There we looked at the world as the economist sees it, with an eye for understanding the marketplace where managers go to acquire capital. It is the investors in these financial markets who determine the value of a firm, and given our goal of maximizing shareholder value, no issue is more fundamental to our study. However, we want to alter our perspective for the time being.

In this chapter, we view the world of finance more as an accountant sees it. To begin, we examine the three basic financial statements that are used to understand how a firm is doing financially: the income statement, or what is sometimes called the profit and loss statement, the balance sheet, and the statement of cash flows. Our goal is not to make you an accountant, but instead to provide you with the tools to understand a firm's financial situation. With this knowledge, you will be able to understand the financial consequences of a company's decisions and actions—as well as your own.

The financial performance of a firm matters to a lot of groups—the company's management, its employees, and its investors, just to name a few. If you are an employee, the firm's performance is important to you because it may determine your annual bonus, your job security, and your opportunity to advance your professional career. This is true whether you are in the firm's marketing, finance, or human resources department. Moreover, an employee who can see how decisions affect a firm's finances has a competitive advantage. So regardless of your position in the firm, it is in your own best interest to know the basics of financial statements—even if accounting is not your greatest love.

Let's begin our review of financial statements by looking at the format and content of the income statement.

The Income Statement

An **income statement**, or **profit and loss statement**, indicates the amount of profits generated by a firm over a given time period, often 1 year. In its most basic form, the income statement may be represented as follows:

$$\textbf{Sales} - \textbf{expenses} = \textbf{profits} \qquad (3\text{-}1)$$

Compute a company's profits, as reflected by its income statement.

income statement (profit and loss statement) a basic accounting statement that measures the results of a firm's operations over a specified period, commonly 1 year. Also known as the profit and loss statement. The bottom line of the income statement shows the firm's profit or loss for the period.

cost of goods sold the cost of producing or acquiring a product or service to be sold in the ordinary course of business.

gross profit sales or revenue minus the cost of goods sold.

operating expenses marketing and selling expenses, general and administrative expenses, and depreciation expense.

operating income (earnings before interest and taxes) sales less the cost of goods sold less operating expenses.

The format for an income statement is shown in Figure 3-1. The income statement begins with sales or revenue, from which we subtract the **cost of goods sold** (the cost of producing or acquiring the product or service to be sold) to yield **gross profits**. Next, **operating expenses** are deducted to determine **operating income** (also called **operating profits** or **earnings before interest and taxes** or **EBIT**). Notice that the operating expenses in the income statement consist of:

1. Marketing and selling expenses—the cost of promoting the firm's products or services to customers.
2. General and administrative expenses—the firm's overhead expenses, such as executive salaries and rent expense.
3. Depreciation expense—a noncash expense to allocate the cost of depreciable assets, such as plant and equipment, over the life of the asset.

In Figure 3-1, we see that operating income is the result of management's decisions relating only to the *operations* of the business, not its financing. In other words, the firm's

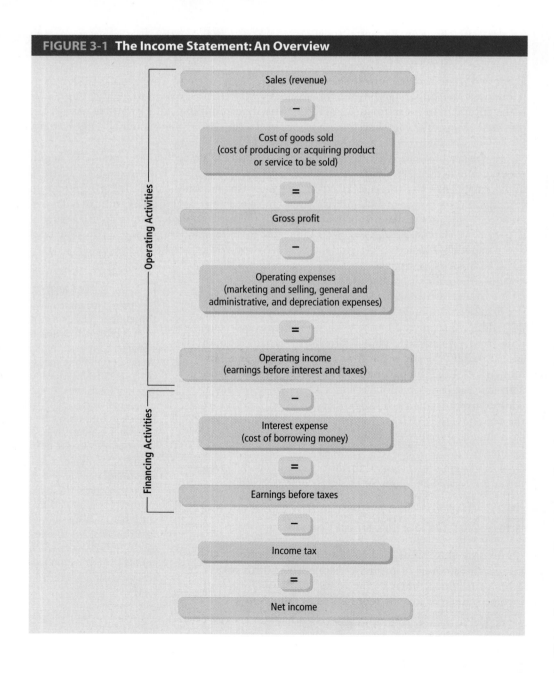

FIGURE 3-1 The Income Statement: An Overview

FINANCE AT WORK

THE LESSONS OF ADVERSITY

What has been learned from the most recent economic crisis? In the May 4, 2009 issue of *Fortune Magazine*, Rick Tetzeli concludes that "the survivors have been taught a few things about thinking long term and sticking to principles." He then suggests some lessons learned.

Gorging on easy profits can be fatal. Wall Street and Detroit tumbled for a lot of reasons, but high on the list is the fact that they thought the free buffet would be open indefinitely.

On Wall Street myriad bets were made on the belief that somehow accepting increasing risk would always pay off. Any reader of the account of the failure of Bear Stearns, *House of Cards*, by William Cohan will come away astonished at how little thought was given to the question, What if it doesn't last? The cabal of mega-losers on this list, led by AIG, answers that question pretty clearly.

As for Detroit, the more the bailout process exposes its decision-making process, the more we realize that, at least at GM, the assumption was that consumer preferences would be slow to change. Well, guess what?

Highly disciplined companies can thrive in all seasons. That doesn't mean they didn't suffer. From Apple to Berkshire, they did. But they didn't suffer nearly as much as others. . . . IBM has become the model for pushing itself up the technology learning curve, while Johnson & Johnson has relentlessly taken the long view. The average annual return on its stock since it went public in 1944 is 17.1%.

The next five years may redefine everything. Banking and automaking aren't the only industries that will be changed for good. Entertainment, publishing, and airlines face threats to their survival. And consider homebuilding—five companies fell right off the list this year: Hovnanian, KB Home, Lennar, NVR, and Toll Brothers.

In retailing, department stores like Macy's got clobbered, while discounters from Wal-Mart to Dollar Tree made new inroads. You won't find any $4.99 items for sale in Dollar Tree's stores—it only sells items for a buck, like tape, party supplies, and writing utensils. Says CEO Bob Sasser, "We are positioned well for any economy. We sell things people need every day." The American consumer's focus on value versus prestige may be changing in a lasting way.

American business—we hope—has been tempered by fire. If the next five years will be defining ones, they will also be years where we should see U.S. companies apply what they've learned from 2008. Robert Coury, CEO of Mylan a pharma maker new to the [Fortune 500] list, guided his company through two acquisitions in three years and increased his headcount from 3,500 to 15,000. "We've already gone through the most tumultuous change in the history of our company," he says. "We're tested warriors and tested leaders." Right now, the stock market agrees—Mylan's stock is up 143% since October.

Businesses will be more accountable. Anytime a business magazine writes something like this, it's worth noting the date, since these predictions are so often wishful thinking. But right now it's not such a reach. For starters, one result of the broad populist anger [against corporations] is that government is getting involved, with an eye toward restraining the worst corporate behavior. But even without federal involvement, businesses will have to answer to a higher authority.

According to Ram Charan, a consultant to CEOs of many Fortune 500 companies, the executives he works with "are very sensitive to the societal pressure, and you will see change." For starters, Charan foresees a shift in the composition of executive pay. Corporate boards will try to ease the grip of Wall Street by adopting pay structures that consider all stakeholders, including employees and customers. That would be a change we could all live with. And a sign that we actually learned something from the disaster.

Source: Rick Tetzeli, "The Lessons of Adversity," *Fortune Magazine*, May 4, 2009, pp. 62–63.

financing expenses (its interest expense resulting from the use of debt financing) have not been subtracted to this point. Thus, the operating income of a firm reports the results of the following activities:

1. The selling price of the products or services to be sold and the number of units sold (selling price × units sold = total sales)

2. The cost of producing or acquiring the goods or services that were sold (cost of goods sold)

3. Selling and marketing expenses (the expenses related to marketing, selling, and distributing the products or services)

4. The firm's overhead expenses (general and administrative expenses, and depreciation expenses)

We then determine the **earnings before taxes**, or **taxable income**, by deducting the **financing cost** (the interest expense on the firm's debt financing) from the operating income.[1]

earnings before taxes (taxable income) operating income minus interest expense.

financing cost cost incurred by a company that often includes interest expenses and preferred dividends.

---

[1]If a firm has issued preferred stock, it would pay preferred stock dividends, which would be shown in the income statement as an expense along with any interest paid on debt. For our purposes, we will assume that there is no preferred stock being used to finance the firm's assets.

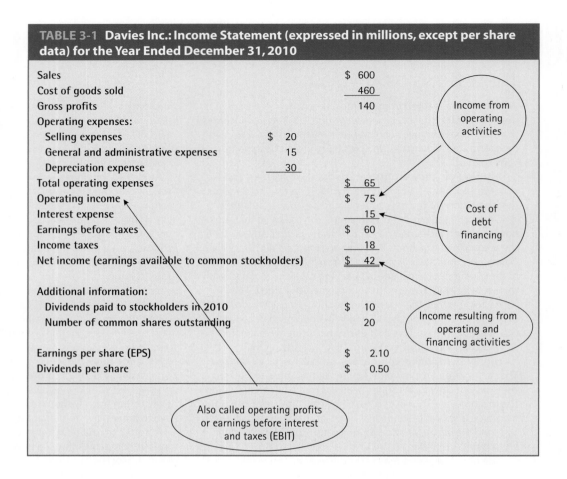

TABLE 3-1 Davies Inc.: Income Statement (expressed in millions, except per share data) for the Year Ended December 31, 2010

Sales		$ 600
Cost of goods sold		460
Gross profits		140
Operating expenses:		
Selling expenses	$ 20	
General and administrative expenses	15	
Depreciation expense	30	
Total operating expenses		$ 65
Operating income		$ 75
Interest expense		15
Earnings before taxes		$ 60
Income taxes		18
Net income (earnings available to common stockholders)		$ 42
Additional information:		
Dividends paid to stockholders in 2010		$ 10
Number of common shares outstanding		20
Earnings per share (EPS)		$ 2.10
Dividends per share		$ 0.50

Income from operating activities

Cost of debt financing

Income resulting from operating and financing activities

Also called operating profits or earnings before interest and taxes (EBIT)

Next, the firm's income taxes are calculated, based on its earnings before taxes and the applicable tax rate for the amount of income reported. For instance, if a firm had earnings before taxes of $100,000, and its tax rate is 28 percent, then it would owe $28,000 in taxes (0.28 × $100,000 = $28,000).

net income (earnings available to common stockholders) a figure representing a firm's profit or loss for the period. It also represents the earnings available to the firm's common and preferred stockholders.

The resulting number is the **net income**, or **earnings available to common stockholders**, which represents income that may be reinvested in the firm or distributed to its owners—provided, of course, the cash is available to do so. As you will come to understand, a positive net income on an income statement does not necessarily mean that a firm has generated positive cash flows.

Table 3-1 contains the 2010 income statement for Davies Inc., a manufacturer of accessories for small technology products. We see that the firm had *sales* of $600 million for the 12-month period ended December 31, 2010. The *cost of goods sold* was $460 million, resulting in *gross profits* of $140 million. The firm then had $65 million of operating expenses. After deducting the operating expenses, the firm's *operating income* (*earnings before interest and taxes*) was $75 million. To this point, we have calculated the profits resulting only from operating the business, without regard for any financing costs, such as the interest paid on money borrowed.

We next deduct the $15 million in interest expense (the amount paid for borrowing money) to arrive at the company's *earnings before taxes* (*taxable income*) of $60 million. We then subtract the income taxes of $18 million to determine the company's *net income*, or *earnings available to common stockholders*, of $42 million.

earnings per share net income on a per share basis.

At this point, we have completed the income statement. However, the firm's owners (common stockholders) like to know how much income the firm made on a *per share* basis, or what is called **earnings per share**. We calculate earnings per share as net income divided

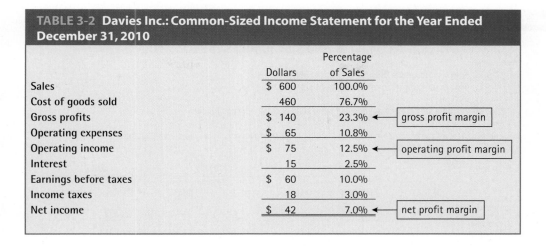

TABLE 3-2 Davies Inc.: Common-Sized Income Statement for the Year Ended December 31, 2010

	Dollars	Percentage of Sales	
Sales	$ 600	100.0%	
Cost of goods sold	460	76.7%	
Gross profits	$ 140	23.3% ←	gross profit margin
Operating expenses	$ 65	10.8%	
Operating income	$ 75	12.5% ←	operating profit margin
Interest	15	2.5%	
Earnings before taxes	$ 60	10.0%	
Income taxes	18	3.0%	
Net income	$ 42	7.0% ←	net profit margin

by the number of common stock shares outstanding. Because Davies Inc. had 20 million shares outstanding in 2010 (see Table 3-1), its earnings per share was $2.10 ($2.10 = $42 million net income ÷ 20 million shares).

Investors also want to know the amount of dividends a firm pays for each share outstanding, or the **dividends per share**. In Table 3-1 we see that Davies Inc. paid $10 million in dividends during 2010. We can then determine that the firm paid $0.50 in dividends per share ($0.50 = $10 million total dividends ÷ 20 million shares outstanding).

What conclusions can we draw from Davies Inc.'s income statement? To answer this question, it is helpful to restate the numbers in the income statement as a percentage of sales. Such a revision is called a **common-sized income statement** and is presented in Table 3-2 for Davies Inc. The common-sized income statement allows us to express expenses and profits on a relative basis, so that we can more easily compare a firm's income performance across time and with competitors. The profits-to-sales relationships are defined as **profit margins**. For Davies Inc. we see that the firm earned

1. A 23.3 percent **gross profit margin** (23.3% = $140 million of gross profits ÷ $600 million of sales)
2. A 12.5 percent **operating profit margin** (12.5% = $75 million of operating income ÷ $600 million of sales)
3. A 7 percent **net profit margin** (7% = $42 million of net income ÷ $600 million of sales)

dividends per share the amount of dividends a firm pays for each share outstanding.

common-sized income statement an income statement in which a firm's expenses and profits are expressed as a percentage of its sales.

profit margins financial ratios (sometimes simply referred to as margins) that reflect the level of the firm's profits relative to its sales. Examples include the gross profit margin (gross profit divided by sales), operating profit margin (operating income divided by sales), and the net profit margin (net income).

gross profit margin gross profit divided by net sales. It is a ratio denoting the gross profit earned by the firm as a percentage of its net sales.

operating profit margin operating income divided by sales. This ratio serves as an overall measure of the company's operating effectiveness.

net profit margin net income divided by sales. A ratio that measures the net income of the firm as a percent of sales.

CAN YOU DO IT?

PREPARING AN INCOME STATEMENT

Given the information below for Menielle Inc., construct an income statement. What are the firm's gross profits, operating income, and net income? What is the firm's noncash expense? Calculate earnings per share and dividends per share assuming that there are 20,000 shares outstanding.

Interest expense	$35,000	Sales	$400,000
Cost of goods sold	$150,000	Common stock dividends	$15,000
Selling and marketing expenses	$40,000	Income taxes	$40,000
Administrative expenses	$30,000	Depreciation expense	$20,000

(The solution can be found on page 53.)

FIGURE 3-2 Hewlett-Packard's Income Statement

HEWLETT-PACKARD COMPANY AND SUBSIDIARIES

**Management's Discussion and Analysis of
Financial Condition and Results of Operations**

Hewlett-Packard's income statement was reported in its 2008 annual report as follows

Results of operations in dollars and as a percentage of net revenue were as follows for the following fiscal years ended October 31:

	2008		2007[2]		2006[2]	
			In millions			
Net revenue	$118,364	100.0%	$104,286	100.0%	$ 91,658	100.0%
Cost of sales[1]	89,921	76.0%	76,887	75.6%	69,427	75.7%
Gross profit	$ 28,443	24.0%	$ 25,399	24.4%	$ 22,231	24.3%
Research and development	3,543	3.0%	3,611	3.5%	3,591	3.9%
Selling, general and administrative	13,104	11.1%	12,226	11.7%	11,266	12.3%
Amortization of purchased intangible assets	967	0.9%	783	0.7%	604	0.7%
In-process research and development charges	45	—	190	0.2%	52	—
Restructuring charges	270	0.2%	387	0.4%	158	0.2%
Acquisition-related charges	41	—	—	—	—	—
Pension curtailments and pension settlements, net	—	—	(517)	(0.5)%	—	—
Earnings from operations	$ 10,473	8.8%	$ 8,719	8.4%	$ 6,560	7.2%
Interest and other, net	—	—	458	0.4%	631	0.6%
Earnings before taxes	$ 10,473	8.8%	$ 9,177	8.8%	$ 7,191	7.8%
Provision for taxes	2,144	1.8%	1,913	1.8%	993	1.0%
Net earnings	$ 8,329	7.0%	$ 7,264	7.0%	$ 6,198	6.8%

(1) Cost of products, cost of services and financing interest.
(2) Certain reclassifications have been made to prior year amounts in order to conform to the current year presentation.

Net Revenue

The components of weighted-average net revenue growth as compared to prior-year periods were as follows for the following fiscal years ended October 31:

	2008	2007
	Percentage points	
Personal Systems Group	5.6	7.9
HP Services	5.6	1.1
Imaging and Printing Group	0.9	1.8
Enterprise Storage and Servers	0.7	1.5
HP Software	0.5	1.2
HP Financial Services	0.4	0.3
Corporate Investments/Other	(0.2)	—
Total HP	13.5	13.8

In practice, managers pay close attention to the firm's profit margins. Profit margins are considered to be an important measurement of how well the firm is doing financially. Managers carefully watch for any changes in margins, up or down. They also compare the firm's margins with those of competitors—something we will discuss in Chapter 4. For the time being, simply remember that profit-to-sales relationships, or *profit margins*, are important in assessing a firm's performance. To observe the income statement from an actual company, Hewlett-Packard, see Figure 3-2

DID YOU GET IT?

PREPARING AN INCOME STATEMENT

On page 51, we provided data for Menielle Inc. and asked you to prepare an income statement based on the information. Your results should be as follows:

Sales		$400,000
Cost of goods sold		150,000
Gross profit		$250,000
Operating expenses:		
Selling and marketing expenses	$40,000	
Administrative expenses	30,000	
Depreciation expense	20,000	
Total operating expenses		$ 90,000
Operating income		$160,000
Interest expense		35,000
Earnings before tax		$125,000
Income taxes		40,000
Net income		$ 85,000
Earnings per share ($85,000 net income ÷ 20,000 shares)		$ 4.25
Dividends per share ($15,000 dividends ÷ 20,000 shares)		$ 0.75

Concept Check

1. What can we learn by reviewing a firm's income statement?
2. What basic relationship can we see in an income statement?
3. How are gross profits, operating income, and net income different as they relate to the areas of business activity reported in the income statement?
4. What are earnings per share and dividends per share?
5. What is a profit margin? What are the different types of profit margins?

The Balance Sheet

A firm's income statement reports the results from operating the business *for a period of time*, such as 1 year. The firm's **balance sheet**, on the other hand, provides a snapshot of the firm's financial position *at a specific point in time*, presenting its asset holdings, liabilities, and owner-supplied capital (stockholders' equity). Figure 3-3 shows the difference in time perspectives

 Determine a firm's financial position at a point in time based on its balance sheet.

balance sheet a statement that shows a firm's assets, liabilities, and shareholder equity at a given point in time. It is a snapshot of the firm's financial position on a particular date.

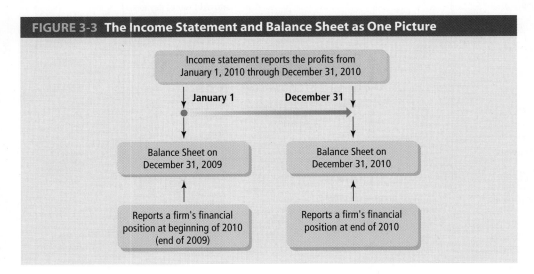

FIGURE 3-3 The Income Statement and Balance Sheet as One Picture

between an income statement and a balance sheet. By examining two balance sheets, one at the beginning of a year and one at the end of the year, along with the income statement for the year, we have a more complete picture of a firm's operations. For instance, we could see what a company looked like at the beginning of 2010 (by looking at its balance sheet on December 31, 2009), what happened during the year (by looking at its income statement for 2010), and the final outcome at the end of 2010 (by looking at its balance sheet on December 31, 2010).

In its simplest form, a balance sheet is represented by the following balance sheet "equation":

$$\textbf{Total assets = total liabilities (debt) + total shareholders' equity} \qquad (3\text{-}2)$$

where *total assets* represent the resources owned by the firm, and *total liabilities* and *total shareholders' equity* indicate how those resources were financed.

The conventional practice is to report the value of the firm's various assets in the balance sheet by using the actual cost of acquiring them. Thus, the balance sheet does not represent the current market value of the company's assets, and consequently does not reflect the value of the company itself. Rather, *it reports historical transactions at their cost.* Therefore, the balance sheet reports a company's **accounting book value**, which is simply equal to a firm's total assets as listed in its balance sheet. It's important for you to understand that a company's accounting book value is not the same as the market value of the assets. Determining a fair or market value of a business or its assets is a different matter—an issue that we will give great attention to throughout future chapters.

Figure 3-4 shows us the basic components of a balance sheet. On the left side of Figure 3-4, the firm's assets are listed according to their type; on the right side, we see a listing of the different sources of financing a company could use to finance its assets.

accounting book value the value of an asset as shown on a firm's balance sheet. It represents the historical cost of the asset rather than its current market value or replacement cost.

Types of Assets

As shown in Figure 3-4, a company's assets fall into two categories: (1) current assets and (2) long-term (fixed) assets.

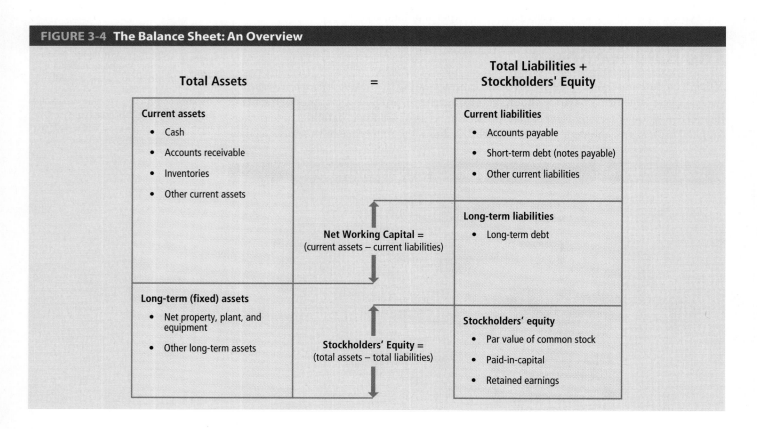

FIGURE 3-4 The Balance Sheet: An Overview

Total Assets = **Total Liabilities + Stockholders' Equity**

Current assets
- Cash
- Accounts receivable
- Inventories
- Other current assets

Long-term (fixed) assets
- Net property, plant, and equipment
- Other long-term assets

Current liabilities
- Accounts payable
- Short-term debt (notes payable)
- Other current liabilities

Long-term liabilities
- Long-term debt

Stockholders' equity
- Par value of common stock
- Paid-in-capital
- Retained earnings

Net Working Capital =
(current assets − current liabilities)

Stockholders' Equity =
(total assets − total liabilities)

Current Assets   **Current assets**, or **gross working capital**, as it is sometimes called, are those assets that are relatively *liquid*, that is, those that are expected to be converted into cash within 12 months. Current assets include a firm's cash, accounts receivable, inventories, and other current assets.

◆ **Cash.**   Every firm must have **cash** to conduct its business operations. A reservoir of cash is needed because of the unequal flow of funds into (cash receipts) and out of (cash expenditures) the business.

◆ **Accounts receivable.**   A firm's **accounts receivable** are the amounts owed to the firm by its customers who buy on credit.

◆ **Inventories.**   A company's **inventories** consist of raw materials, works in process, and finished goods held by the firm for eventual sale.

◆ **Other current assets.**   Other current assets include such items as prepaid expenses. For example, a company's insurance premium might be due before the actual insurance coverage begins; or the firm's rent might have to be paid in advance. These expenditures are considered assets because they represent an investment that's been made by the company. Only when, for example, the insurance premium is used up following the coverage period is the premium considered an expense.

Fixed Assets   **Fixed assets** are long term in nature, such as machinery and equipment, buildings, and land. These assets will be used over a number of years.

When a firm purchases a fixed asset, it does not immediately report the cost of the asset as an expense in its income statement. Instead, it is considered to be an asset and included in the balance sheet. Some of these assets, such as machinery and equipment, will depreciate in value over time due to obsolescence or daily wear and tear; others may not, such as land.

With depreciable assets, the original cost of an asset is allocated in the income statement over the asset's expected useful life. The amount allocated as the cost each year is shown as a **depreciation expense** in the income statement. The sum of all depreciation taken over the entire life of the asset is shown as **accumulated depreciation** in the balance sheet.

To illustrate, assume that a truck purchased for $20,000 is to be evenly depreciated over a 4-year life.[2] The depreciation expense to be reported in the income statement for each year would be $5,000 ($20,000 asset cost ÷ 4 years = $5,000). When a firm buys the truck, the $20,000 original cost of the asset is added to the balance sheet as a **gross fixed asset**. The cumulative depreciation taken over the asset's life is reported as *accumulated depreciation*. We subtract the accumulated depreciation each year from the gross fixed assets to determine **net fixed assets**. In this example, the income statements for each year and balance sheets over time would appear as follows:

current assets (gross working capital) current assets consist primarily of cash, marketable securities, accounts receivable, inventories, and prepaid expenses.

cash cash on hand, demand deposits, and short-term marketable securities that can quickly be converted into cash.

accounts receivable money owed by customers who purchased goods or services from the firm on credit.

inventories raw materials, work in progress, and finished goods held by the firm for eventual sale.

fixed assets assets such as equipment, buildings, and land.

depreciation expense a noncash expense to allocate the cost of depreciable assets, such as plant and equipment, over the life of the asset.

accumulated depreciation the sum of all depreciation taken over the entire life of a depreciable asset.

gross fixed assets the original cost of a firm's fixed assets.

net fixed assets gross fixed assets minus the accumulated depreciation taken over the life of the assets.

Income Statement

	FOR THE YEAR ENDING			
	1	2	3	4
Depreciation expense	$5,000	$5,000	$5,000	$5,000

Balance Sheet

	END OF YEAR			
	1	2	3	4
Gross fixed assets	$20,000	$20,000	$20,000	$20,000
Accumulated depreciation	5,000	10,000	15,000	20,000
Net fixed assets	$15,000	$10,000	$ 5,000	$0

[2]In this instance, we are using a straight-line depreciation method. Other methods allow a firm to accelerate the depreciation expenses in the early years of the asset's life and report less in the later years.

FINANCE AT WORK

GOLDMAN SACHS ANNOUNCES FIRST QUARTER 2009 EARNINGS

Goldman Sachs Group, Inc. is a global investment-banking firm. Below are excerpts from the press release Goldman Sachs issued to report its first-quarter earnings for 2009. The excerpts are followed by parts of a *Wall Street Journal* article reporting on the release.

PRESS RELEASE
　Relations: Lucas van Praag
　Investor Relations: Dane E. Holmes

Goldman Sachs Reports First Quarter Earnings per Common Share of $3.39

NEW YORK, April 13, 2009—The Goldman Sachs Group, Inc. (NYSE: GS) today reported net revenues of $9.43 billion and net earnings of $1.81 billion for its first quarter ended March 27, 2009. Diluted earnings per common share were $3.39 compared with $3.23 for the first quarter ended February 29, 2008 and a diluted loss per common share of $4.97 for the fourth quarter ended November 28, 2008. Annualized return on average common shareholders' equity was 14.3% for the first quarter of 2009.

"Given the difficult market conditions, we are pleased with this quarter's performance," said Lloyd C. Blankfein, Chairman and Chief Executive Officer. "Our results reflect the strength and diversity of our client franchise, the resilience of our business model and the dedication and focus of our people. We believe these attributes position the firm to continue to create value for our clients and actively fulfill our role in the capital markets."

A conference call to discuss the firm's results, outlook and related matters will be held Tuesday, April 14, 2009 at 7:00 A.M. (ET). The call will be open to the public. Members of the public who would like to listen to the conference call should dial 1-888-281-7154 (U.S. Domestic) or 1-706-679-5627 (international). The number should be dialed at least 10 minutes prior to the start of the conference call. The conference call will also be accessible as an audio webcast through the Investor Relations section of the firm's Web site, www.gs.com/shareholders. There is no charge to access the call.

And What Did the *Wall Street Journal* Have to Say?

Goldman Sachs Group Inc. announced robust earnings, along with its plan that would make it the first big financial firm to pay back the money it received from the government last fall. The Wall Street firm announced better-than-expected profit ahead of schedule after the close of trading Monday. The firm reported net income of $1.81 billion, or $3.39 a share, for the period ended March 27, compared with $1.51 billion, or $3.23, during the first quarter of last year. The firm had been scheduled to announce results Tuesday morning.

Driving the earnings was record performance in the fixed-income, currency, and commodities division, where the trading of products tied to interest rates and strength in commodities helped generate $6.56 billion in net revenue, a 34% rise from the comparable period last year. Those results offset a downturn in investment banking and money management.

Sources: http://www2.goldmansachs.com/our-firm/press/press-releases/current/2009-q1-results.html, accessed May 31, 2009; and Kate Kelly and Susanne Craig. "Goldman Flexes Its Profit Muscle—Share Sale Is Set as Better-Than-Expected Results Get Released Early," *Wall Street Journal*. (Eastern Edition). New York, N.Y.: April 14, 2009, p. C.1.

It is important to understand the distinction between *gross* fixed assets and *net* fixed assets and how depreciation expense in the income statement relates to accumulated depreciation in the balance sheet.

Other Assets　Other assets are all of the firm's assets that are not current assets or fixed assets. They include, for example, long-term investments and intangible assets such as the company's patents, copyrights, and goodwill.

Types of Financing

We now turn to the right side of the balance sheet in Figure 3-4 labeled "Total Liabilities + Stockholders' Equity," which indicates how the firm finances its assets. **Debt** is money that has been borrowed and must be repaid at some predetermined date. **Equity**, on the other hand, represents the shareholders' (owners') investment in the company.

debt liabilities consisting of such sources as credit extended by suppliers or a loan from a bank.

equity stockholders' investment in the firm and the cumulative profits retained in the business up to the date of the balance sheet.

current debt (short-term liabilities) due to be paid within 12 months.

accounts payable money owed to suppliers for goods or services purchased in the ordinary course of business.

Debt (Liabilities)　Debt capital is financing provided by a creditor. As shown in Figure 3-4, it is divided into (1) current or short-term debt and (2) long-term debt.

Current Debt　The firm's **current debt**, or **short-term liabilities**, includes borrowed money that must be repaid within the next 12 months. The sources of a firm's current debt include the following:

◆ **Accounts payable.**　The firm's **accounts payable** represents the credit suppliers have extended the firm when it purchased inventories. The purchasing firm may have 30, 60, or even 90 days to pay for the inventory. This form of credit extension is also called **trade credit**.

◆ **Accrued expenses.** **Accrued expenses** are short-term liabilities that have been incurred in the firm's operations but not yet paid. For example, the company's employees might have done work for which they will not be paid until the following week or month, and these are recorded as accrued wages.

◆ **Short-term notes.** **Short-term notes** represent amounts borrowed from a bank or other lending source that are due and payable within 12 months.

Long-Term Debt   The firm's **long-term debt** includes loans from banks or other sources that lend money for longer than 12 months. A firm might borrow money for 5 years to buy equipment, or it might borrow money for as long as 25 or 30 years to purchase real estate, such as land and buildings. Usually a loan to finance real estate is called a **mortgage**, where the lender has first claim on the property in the event the borrower is unable to repay the loan.

Equity   Equity includes the shareholders' investment—both preferred stockholders and common stockholders—in the firm.

◆ **Preferred stockholders** generally receive a dividend that is fixed in amount. In the event of the firm being liquidated, these stockholders are paid after the firm's creditors but before the common stockholders.

◆ **Common stockholders** are the *residual owners* of a business. They receive whatever income is left over after paying all expenses. In the event the firm is liquidated, the common stockholders receive only what is left over—good or bad—after the creditors and preferred stockholders are paid. The amount of a firm's common equity as reported in the balance sheet is equal to the sum of two items:

1. **The amount a company receives from selling stock to investors.** This amount may simply be shown as **common stock** in the balance sheet or it may be divided into **par value** (the arbitrary value a firm puts on each share of stock prior to its being offered for sale) and **additional paid-in capital** above par (or just **paid-in capital** for short). Paid-in capital is the additional amount of capital the firm raises when buyers pay more than par value for the firm's stock. The amount of common stock issued will be offset by any stock that has been repurchased by the company, which is shown as **treasury stock**.

2. **The amount of the firm's retained earnings. Retained earnings** are the earnings (net income, to be exact) that have been retained in the business rather than being distributed to the shareholders. In other words, we take the *cumulative total of all the net income over the firm's life less the common stock dividends that have been paid over the years*. More simply, we can compute retained earnings at the end of a given year by taking the retained earnings at the end of the previous year, adding net income and subtracting dividends paid for the current year.[3] But remember, profits and cash are not the same; *so do not think of retained earnings as a big bucket of cash*. It is not!

Balance sheets for Davies Inc. are presented in Table 3-3 as of December 31, 2009, and December 31, 2010, along with the changes in each account between the two years. The balance sheet data shows that the firm ended 2010 with $438 million in assets, compared to $392 million at the end of 2009, for an increase of $46 million. As shown in the far right-hand column in Table 3-3, the increase resulted from (1) the additional investment in current assets (gross working capital) of $37 million (mostly from the increase in inventories), and (2) $39 million of new investments in fixed assets (based on the change in *gross* fixed assets, not *net* fixed assets). However, $30 million of the firm's fixed assets were depreciated during the year, as reflected by the increase in accumulated depreciation. Thus, the $46 million

---

trade credit credit made available by a firm's suppliers in conjunction with the acquisition of materials. Trade credit appears in the accounts payable section of the balance sheet.

accrued expenses expenses that have been incurred but not yet paid in cash.

short-term notes (debt) amounts borrowed from lenders, mostly financial institutions such as banks, where the loan is to be repaid within 12 months.

long-term debt loans from banks or other sources that lend money for longer than 12 months.

mortgage a loan to finance real estate where the lender has first claim on the property in the event the borrower is unable to repay the loan.

preferred stockholders stockholders who have claims on the firm's income and assets after creditors, but before common stockholders.

common stockholders investors who own the firm's common stock. Common stockholders are the residual owners of the firm.

common stock shares that represent ownership in a corporation.

par value the arbitrary value a firm puts on each share of stock prior to its being offered for sale.

additional paid-in capital the amount a company receives from selling stock to investors above par value.

treasury stock the firm's stock that has been issued and then repurchased by the firm.

retained earnings cumulative profits retained in a business up to the date of the balance sheet.

---

[3]Sometimes retained earnings will be affected by some unusual or extraordinary accounting transactions in addition to the reported net income and the dividends paid to stockholders. However, we are ignoring this possibility when explaining retained earnings.

TABLE 3-3 Davies Inc. Balance Sheets ($ millions) December 31, 2009 and 2010						
		2009		2010		Change
ASSETS						
Cash		$ 21		$ 20		$ (1)
Accounts receivable		31		36		5
Inventory		51		84		33
Other current assets		3		3		0
Total current assets		$106		$143		$37
Gross plant and equipment	$ 371		$ 410		$ 39	
Less accumulated depreciation	(85)		(115)		(30)	
Net plant and equipment		$286		$295		$ 9
Total assets		$392		$438		$46
DEBT AND EQUITY						
Accounts payable		$ 41		$ 42		$ 1
Accrued expenses		10		10		0
Short-term notes		14		12		(2)
Total current liabilities		$ 65		$ 64		$ (1)
Long-term debt		160		171		11
Total debt		$225		$235		$10
Common stockholders' equity						
Common stock—par value		$ 10		$ 11		$ 1
Paid-in capital		72		75		3
Retained earnings		85		117		32
Total common stockholders' equity		$167		$203		$36
Total liabilities and equity		$392		$438		$46

increase in total assets can be reconciled as follows: A $37 million increase in current assets, *plus* $39 million invested in new fixed assets, *less* $30 million in the depreciation of the firm's fixed assets.

In the debt and equity section of Table 3-3, notice that the $46 million increase in total debt and equity is exactly the same amount as the increase in total assets—as it must be. (Remember total assets = total debt + total equity.) The additional financing came primarily from a $36 million increase in common equity and secondarily from borrowing $11 million in long-term debt. The increase in common equity can be explained as follows (in $ millions):

December 31, 2009, common equity		$167
Sale of common stock		
Increase in par value	$ 1	
Increase in additional paid-in capital	3	
Total amount received from selling stock		$ 4
Increase in retained earnings		
Net income for 2010	$42	
Less 2010 common stock dividends	(10)	
Total increase in retained earnings		$ 32
Increase in common equity		$ 36
December 31, 2010, common equity		$203

There are two other issues revealed in the balance sheet that deserve special note: (1) the amount of a firm's working capital and (2) the mix of debt to equity used in financing the company. Let's consider each for Davies Inc.

Working Capital

Earlier we noted that the term *current assets* is also referred to as *gross working capital*. These two terms are used interchangeably. As we explained, gross working capital is equal to a company's current assets. By contrast, **net working capital** is equal to a company's current assets *less* its current liabilities. That is,

$$\textbf{Net working capital} = \textbf{current assets} - \textbf{current liabilities} \qquad (3\text{-}4)$$

Thus, net working capital compares the amount of current assets (assets that should convert into cash within the next 12 months) to the current liabilities (debt that must be paid within 12 months). The larger the net working capital a firm has, the more able the firm will be to pay its debt as it comes due. Thus, the amount of net working capital is important to a company's lenders who are always concerned about a company's ability to repay its loans. For Davies Inc. net working capital is computed as follows:

	2009	2010
Gross working capital (current assets)	$106,000,000	$143,000,000
Current liabilities	65,000,000	64,000,000
Net working capital	$41,000,000	$79,000,000

We see that the firm's net working capital increased $38 million, from $41 million to $79 million, mostly the result of increased amounts of inventories. The increase would prompt a lender or investor to know exactly why there was such a large increase in inventories, which could be good or bad. On one hand, it might mean that the firm is anticipating higher future sales and is stocking up on inventory. On the other hand, it might mean that firm's sales have declined and unsold inventory is piling up.

Most firms have a positive amount of net working capital because their current assets are greater than their current debts. There are a few exceptions. Take Disney and Starbucks, for example. These two firms actually have more current liabilities than current assets, which results in a negative net working capital position for each. How do you think this could happen? Very simply, these businesses involve mostly cash sales: The firms collect cash immediately from their customers and then quickly use it up again to keep their businesses operating. However, Disney's and Starbucks' suppliers have probably granted them 30 days or more to pay their bills. In other words, the two firms collect early and pay late.

Debt Ratio

A firm's **debt ratio** is *the percentage of a company's assets financed by debt*. Looking at Davies Inc., the debt ratios for 2009 and 2010 were 57.4 percent and 53.7 percent, respectively.

		2009	2010
Debt ratio $=$	$\dfrac{\text{total debt}}{\text{total assets}}$	$\dfrac{\$225M}{\$392M} = 57.4\%$	$\dfrac{\$235M}{\$438M} = 53.7\%$

CAN YOU DO IT?

PREPARING A BALANCE SHEET

Given the information below for Menielle Inc., construct a balance sheet. What are the firm's current assets, net fixed assets, total assets, current or short-term debt, long-term debt, total equity, and total debt and equity?

Gross fixed assets	$75,000	Accounts receivable	$50,000
Cash	10,000	Long-term bank note	5,000
Other assets	15,000	Mortgage	20,000
Accounts payable	40,000	Common stock	100,000
Retained earnings	15,000	Inventories	70,000
Accumulated depreciation	20,000	Short-term notes	20,000

(The solution can be found on page 60.)

TABLE 3-4 Davies Inc. Common-Sized Balance Sheet ($ millions) December 31, 2009 and 2010					
		2009	**2010**		**Change**
ASSETS					
Cash		5.4%	4.6%		−0.8%
Accounts receivable		7.9%	8.2%		0.3%
Inventory		13.0%	19.2%		6.2%
Other current assets		0.8%	0.7%		−0.1%
Total current assets		27.0%	32.6%		5.6%
Gross plant and equipment	94.6%		93.6%	−1.0%	
Less accumulated depreciation	−21.7%		−26.3%	−4.6%	
Net plant and equipment		73.0%	67.4%		−5.6%
Total assets		100.0%	100.0%		0.0%
DEBT AND EQUITY					
Accounts payable and accrued expenses		13.0%	11.9%		−1.1%
Short-term notes		3.6%	2.7%		−0.8%
Total current liabilities		16.6%	14.6%		−2.0%
Long-term debt		40.8%	39.0%		−1.8%
Total debt		57.4%	53.7%		−3.7%
Common stockholders' equity					
Common stock—par value		2.6%	2.5%		0.0%
Paid-in capital		18.4%	17.1%		−1.2%
Retained earnings		21.7%	26.7%		5.0%
Total common stockholders' equity		42.6%	46.3%		3.7%
Total liabilities and equity		100.0%	100.0%		0.0%

The debt ratio is an important measure to lenders and investors because it indicates the amount of financial risk the company is bearing—the more debt a company uses to finance its assets, the greater is its financial risk. We will discuss this topic in detail in Chapter 12.

Finally, we can gain additional perspective of a company's financial position by converting the balance sheet into a **common-sized balance sheet**. On a common-sized balance sheet, each item is shown as a percentage of total assets (and total debt and equity). Table 3-4 shows common-sized balance sheets for Davies Inc.

common-sized balance sheet a balance sheet in which a firm's assets and sources of debt and equity are expressed as a percentage of its total assets.

DID YOU GET IT?
PREPARING A BALANCE SHEET

On page 59, we provided balance sheet data for Menielle Inc. and asked you to develop the balance sheet based on the information. Your results should be as follows:

Cash		$ 10,000	Accounts payable		$ 40,000
Accounts receivable		50,000	Short-term notes		20,000
Inventories		70,000	Total short-term debt		$ 60,000
Total current assets		$130,000	Long-term bank note	$5,000	
Gross fixed assets	$ 75,000		Mortgage	20,000	
Accumulated depreciation	(20,000)		Total long-term debt		$ 25,000
Net fixed assets		$ 55,000	Total debt		$ 85,000
Other assets		15,000	Common stock	100,000	
Total assets		$200,000	Retained earnings	15,000	
			Total equity		$115,000
			Total debt and equity		$200,000

Now we can observe that inventories increased from 13 percent of total assets to over 19 percent. Gross fixed assets declined 1 percent, whereas net fixed assets decreased 5.6 percent as a result of the additional depreciation taken on the assets. As already noted, the firm is using a bit less debt financing on a percentage basis due to the increase in equity, specifically, its retained earnings.

Earlier we showed the income statement for Hewlett-Packard. Now see Figure 3-5 for Hewlett-Packard's balance sheets.

Concept Check

1. Regarding the time frame reported, how is the balance sheet different from the income statement?
2. What does the basic balance sheet equation state, and what does it mean?
3. What is a firm's "accounting book value"?
4. What are a firm's two principal sources of financing? Of what do these sources consist?
5. What is gross working capital? Net working capital?
6. What is a debt ratio?

Measuring Cash Flows

 3 Measure a company's cash flows.

Although an income statement measures a company's profits, profits are not the same as cash flows; profits are calculated on an accrual basis rather than a cash basis. **Accrual basis accounting** records revenue when it is earned, whether or not the revenue has been received in cash, and records expenses when they are incurred, even if the money has not actually been paid out. For example, sales reported in the income statement include both cash sales and credit sales. Therefore, sales for a given year do not correspond exactly to the actual cash collected from sales. Similarly, a firm must purchase inventory, but some of the purchases are financed by trade credit rather than by an immediate cash payment, so the firm's expenses are not equal to its actual "out of pocket" cash flows. Also, under the accrual system, the purchase of equipment that will last for more than 1 year is not shown as an expense in the income statement. Instead, the amount is recorded as an asset and then expensed as depreciation over the useful life of the equipment. An annual depreciation expense (this is not a cash flow) is recorded as a way to match the use of the asset with sales generated from its service.

accrual basis accounting a method of accounting whereby revenue is recorded when it is earned, whether or not the revenue has been received in cash. Likewise, expenses are recorded when they are incurred, even if the money has not actually been paid out.

We could give you more examples to show why a firm's profits differ from its cash flows, but the point should be clear: *Profits and cash flows are not the same thing*. In fact, a business could be profitable but have negative cash flows, even to the point of going bankrupt. So, understanding a firm's cash flows is very important to its managers.

There are two common approaches used to measure a firm's cash flows. First, we can calculate a company's **free cash flows**. Once a firm has paid all of its operating expenses and taxes and made all of its investments, the remaining cash flows are *free* to be distributed to the creditors and shareholders—thus, the term *free cash flows*. Alternatively, we can use the conventional accountant's presentation called a *statement of cash flows*, which is always included in the financial section of a firm's annual report. This method for presenting cash flows focuses on identifying the sources and uses of cash that explain the change in a firm's cash balance reported in the balance sheet.

free cash flows the amount of cash available from operations after the firm pays for the investments it has made in operating working capital and fixed assets. This cash is available to distribute to the firm's creditors and owners.

During recent years, free cash flow has come to be viewed by many executives as an important measure of a firm's performance. Jack Welch, the former CEO of General Electric, explains the importance of free cash flows to management in these words:

> [T]here's cash flow, which is valuable because it just does not lie. All your other profit-and-loss numbers, like net income, have some art to them. They've been massaged through the accounting process, which is filled with assumptions. But free cash flow tells you the true condition of the business. It gives you a sense of your maneuverability—whether you can return cash to shareholders, pay down debt, borrow more to grow faster, or any combination of these options. Cash flow helps you understand and control your destiny.

We will use free cash flows in later chapters to evaluate capital investment opportunities. As we will see numerous times, the value of an investment is the present value of

FIGURE 3-5 Hewlett-Packard's Balance Sheet

HEWLETT-PACKARD COMPANY AND SUBSIDIARIES

Consolidated Balance Sheets

Hewlett-Packard reported the following balance sheet in its 2008 annual report.

	October 31	
	2008	**2007**
	In millions, except par value	
ASSETS		
Current assets:		
....	$ 10,153	$11,293
Short-term investments	93	152
Accounts receivable	16,928	13,420
Financing receivables	2,314	2,507
Inventory	7,879	8,033
Other current assets	14,361	11,997
Total current assets	$ 51,728	$47,402
Property, plant and equipment	10,838	7,798
Long-term financing receivables and other assets	10,468	7,647
Goodwill	32,335	21,773
Purchased intangible assets	7,962	4,079
Total assets	$113,331	$88,699
LIABILITIES AND STOCKHOLDERS EQUITY		
Current liabilities:		
Notes payable and short-term borrowings	$ 10,176	$ 3,186
Accounts payable	14,138	11,787
Employee compensation and benefits	4,159	3,465
Taxes on earnings	869	1,891
Deferred revenue	6,287	5,025
Accrued restructuring	1,099	123
Other accrued liabilities	16,211	13,783
Total current liabilities	$ 52,939	$39,260
Long-term debt	7,676	4,997
Other liabilities	13,774	5,916
Stockholders equity:		
Common stock, $0.01 par value (9,600 shares authorized; 2,415 and 2,580 shares issued and outstanding, respectively)	$ 24	$ 26
Additional paid-in capital	14,012	16,381
Retained earnings	24,971	21,560
Accumulated other comprehensive (loss) income ..	(65)	559
Total stockholders' equity	$ 38,942	$38,526
Total liabilities and stockholders' equity	$113,331	$88,699

FIGURE 3-6 Statement of Cash Flows: An Overview

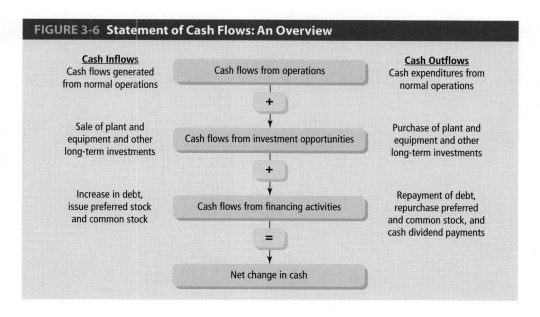

its free cash flows. But for now we will learn about the *statement of cash flows*. After all, it is a key financial statement, and we need to know what it is telling us, whether we are part of the management team, creditors, or shareholders.

As shown in Figure 3-6 above, there are three key activities that explain the cash inflows and outflows of a business, these being:

1. **Generating cash flows from day-to-day business operations.** It is informative to know how much cash is being generated in the normal course of operating a business on a daily basis, beginning with purchasing inventories on credit, selling on credit, paying for the inventories, and finally collecting on the sales made on credit.

2. **Investing in fixed assets and other long-term investments.** When a company purchases or sells fixed assets, like equipment and buildings, there can be significant cash inflows and outflows.

3. **Financing the business.** Cash inflows and outflows occur from borrowing or repaying debt, paying dividends, and from issuing stock (equity) or repurchasing stock from the shareholders.

If we know the cash flows from the activities above, we can easily explain a firm's cash flows in total. To understand how this is done, let's return to Davies' income statement (Table 3-1 on page 50) and balance sheets (Table 3-3 on page 58) to explain this process.

Cash Flows from Operations   Here we want to convert the company's income statement from an *accrual* basis to a *cash* basis. This conversion can be accomplished in two steps: (1) add back depreciation to net income since depreciation is not a cash expense, and (2) subtract any uncollected sales (increase in accounts receivables) and cash payments for inventories (increases in inventories less increases in accounts payables).

Why we add back depreciation should be clear. The changes in accounts receivables, inventories, and accounts payables may be less intuitive. Two comments might be helpful:

1. A firm's sales either are cash sales or credit sales. If accounts receivables increase, that means customers did not pay for everything they purchased. Thus, any increase in accounts receivables, as in the case for Davies Inc., needs to be subtracted from total sales to determine the cash that has been collected from customers.

2. The other activity occurring in the daily course of business is purchasing inventories. An increase in inventories shows that we bought inventories, but if accounts payables (credit extended by a supplier) increase, then we know that the firm did not pay for all

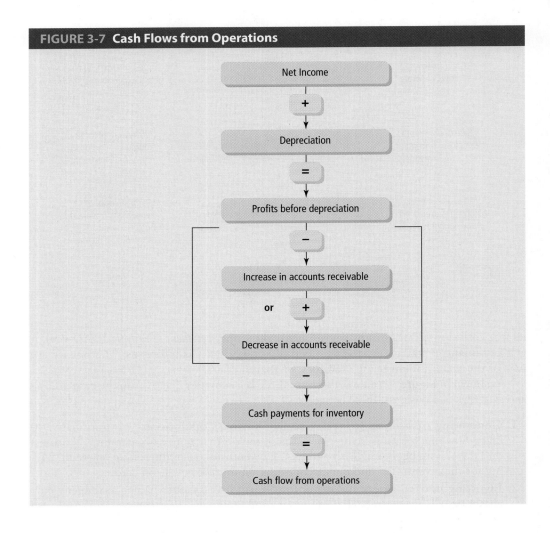

FIGURE 3-7 Cash Flows from Operations

the inventories purchased. Thus, the net payment for inventories is equal to the increase in inventories less what we have not paid for yet (increase in accounts payables).

Figure 3-7 shows a graphical presentation of the procedure for computing a firm's cash flows from operations.

Referring back to Davies Inc. income statement and balance sheets, we can compute the cash flows from operations (expressed in $ millions) as follows:

Net income	$42	
Plus depreciation	30	
Profits before depreciation		$72
Less the increase in accounts receivable (uncollected sales)		($ 5)
Less payments for inventories consisting of:		
Increase in inventories	(33)	
Less increase in accounts payable (inventories purchased on credit)	1	
Payments for inventories		($32)
Cash flows from operations		$35

Investing in Fixed Assets   When a company purchases fixed assets, such as equipment or buildings, these expenditures are shown as an increase in *gross* fixed assets (not the increase in *net* fixed assets) in the balance sheet. For instance, Davies Inc. spent $39 million on new plant and equipment in 2010, based on the change in *gross* fixed assets from $371 million to $410 million, as shown in their balance sheets (Table 3-3).

Financing a Business   Financing a business involves (1) paying dividends to the owners; (2) increasing or decreasing short-term and long-term debt, which means borrowing more money (an increase in debt) or paying off debt (a decrease in debt); and (3) selling shares of stock (source of cash) or repurchasing stock (use of cash).

Continuing with Davies Inc., we know from the income statement (Table 3-1) that they paid $10 million in dividends to the shareholders. Then from their balance sheets (Table 3-3), we see that short-term notes decreased $2 million (a use of cash) and long-term debt increased $11 million (a source of cash). Finally, Davies Inc. issued $4 million in common stock. This increase is reflected in the balance sheets in the combined increase in common stock par value of $1 million and additional paid in capital of $3 million. Thus, in net, Davies Inc. raised $3 million in financing cash flows:

Cash inflows from borrowing money	
Decrease in short-term notes	($ 2)
Increase in long-term debt	11
Issued new common stock (increase in par value and additional paid in capital)	4
Less dividends paid to owners	(10)
Financing cash flows	$ 3

To summarize, Davies Inc. generated $35 million in cash flows from operations; invested $39 million in plant and equipment; and received $3 million from financing activities, for a net decrease in cash of $1 million. This can be verified from the balance sheets (see Table 3-3), which show that Davies Inc.'s cash decreased $1 million during 2010 (from $21 million to $20 million). The complete statement of cash flows is provided in Table 3-5 below.

TABLE 3-5 Davies Inc. Statement of Cash Flows ($ millions) Year Ending December 31, 2010

Operating activities:		
Net income	$42	
Plus depreciation	30	
Profits before depreciation		$72
Less increase in accounts receivable (uncollected sales)		($ 5)
Less payments for inventories consisting of:		
Increase in inventories	(33)	
Less increase in accounts payables (inventories purchased on credit)	1	
Payments for inventories		($32)
Cash flows from operations		$35
Investment activities:		
Less increase in gross fixed assets		($39)
Financing activities:		
Cash inflows from borrowing money		
Decrease in short-term notes	($ 2)	
Increase in long-term debt	11	
Issued new common stock (increase in par value and additional paid in capital)	4	
Less dividends paid to owners	(10)	
Financing cash flows		$ 3
Decrease in cash		($ 1)
Beginning cash		21
Ending cash		$20

CAN YOU DO IT?

HOW MUCH CAN YOU TRUST A BROTHER-IN-LAW?

Your brother-in-law has asked you to help him finance what he considers to be a "great investment opportunity." He plans to sell a new brand of European clothing that is becoming popular in the United States. He thinks that the university located nearby, from which you both graduated, would be an ideal location. He estimates that the financing can come mostly from a bank loan and credit from suppliers. However, the two of you will need to chip in a total of $5,000 to get the business going. He will invest $3,000, he says, and he wants you to invest the remaining $2,000.

It's not that you don't trust your brother-in-law, but you have decided to undertake your own investigation of the opportunity. After a few hours of work, you develop what you think are realistic estimates of the profits that can be earned from the venture. You also estimate how much money it will take to start the business.

There is a slight problem, however: Your new puppy chewed up your papers. After putting the dog in the backyard without any supper, you pick up the pieces and begin reconstructing your work. The remnants of your hard work—at least most of it—look as follows (numbers are in thousands):

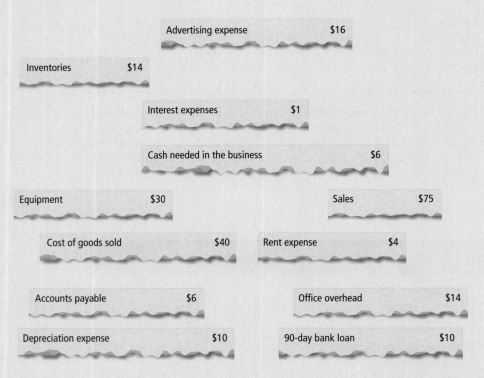

Advertising expense	$16		
Inventories	$14		
Interest expenses	$1		
Cash needed in the business	$6		
Equipment	$30	Sales	$75
Cost of goods sold	$40	Rent expense	$4
Accounts payable	$6	Office overhead	$14
Depreciation expense	$10	90-day bank loan	$10

Can you reconstruct the income statement and balance sheet using the bits of information provided above? What do you conclude about your brother-in-law's great opportunity?

See page 68 for the solution to your brother-in-law problem—hopefully after you have made a good-faith effort to solve it yourself.

In addition to the statement of cash flows for Davies Inc., see Figure 3-8 on the next page to see the statement of cash flows for Hewlett-Packard.

Based on our review of Davies Inc.'s financial statements, we can now draw some conclusions. To this point, we have learned that:

◆ For every dollar of sales, Davies earned 12.5 cents in operating income and 7 cents in net income.

◆ The firm finances its assets more with debt than with equity.

◆ The company's primary investments in 2010 were in additional inventories and fixed assets.

◆ Davies made significant investments ($39 million) in long-term assets that were financial from cash flows from operations and additional financing.

FIGURE 3-8 Hewlett-Packard's Consolidated Statements of Cash Flows

HEWLETT-PACKARD COMPANY AND SUBSIDIARIES
Consolidated Statements of Cash Flows

Hewlett-Packard reported the following statement of cash flows in its 2008 annual report.

	For the fiscal years ended October 31		
	2008	2007	2006
	In millions		
Cash flows from operating activities:			
Net earnings	$ 8,329	$ 7,264	$ 6,198
Adjustments to reconcile net earnings to net cash provided by operating activities:			
Depreciation and amortization	3,356	2,705	2,353
Stock-based compensation expense	606	629	536
Provision for doubtful accounts—accounts and financing receivables	275	47	4
Provision for inventory	214	362	267
Restructuring charges	270	387	158
Pension curtailments and pension settlements, net	—	(517)	—
In-process research and development charges	45	190	52
Acquisition-related charges	41	—	—
Deferred taxes on earnings	1,035	415	693
Excess tax benefit from stock-based compensation	(293)	(481)	(251)
Losses (gains) on investments	11	(14)	(25)
Other, net	(83)	(86)	18
Changes in assets and liabilities:			
Accounts and financing receivables	(261)	(2,808)	(882)
Inventory	89	(633)	(1,109)
Accounts payable	1,630	(346)	1,879
Taxes on earnings	(43)	502	(513)
Restructuring	(165)	(606)	(810)
Other assets and liabilities	(465)	2,605	2,785
Net cash provided by operating activities	$ 14,591	$ 9,615	$ 11,353
Cash flows from investing activities:			
Investment in property, plant and equipment	(2,990)	(3,040)	(2,536)
Proceeds from sale of property, plant and equipment	425	568	556
Purchases of available-for-sale securities and other investments	(178)	(283)	(46)
Maturities and sales of available-for-sale securities and other investments	280	425	94
Payments made in connection with business acquisitions, net	(11,248)	(6,793)	(855)
Net cash used in investing activities	$(13,711)	$ (9,123)	$ (2,787)
Cash flows from financing activities:			
Issuance (repayment) of commercial paper and notes payable, net	5,015	1,863	(55)
Issuance of debt	3,121	4,106	1,121
Payment of debt	(1,843)	(3,419)	(1,259)
Issuance of common stock under employee stock plans	1,810	3,103	2,538
Repurchase of common stock	(9,620)	(10,887)	(6,057)
Prepayment of common stock repurchase	—	—	(1,722)
Excess tax benefit from stock-based compensation	293	481	251
Dividends	(796)	(846)	(894)
Net cash used in financing activities	$ (2,020)	$ (5,599)	$ (6,077)
(Decrease) increase in cash and cash equivalents	(1,140)	(5,107)	2,489
Cash and cash equivalents at beginning of period	11,293	16,400	13,911
Cash and cash equivalents at end of period	$ 10,153	$ 11,293	$ 16,400

DID YOU GET IT?
HOW MUCH CAN YOU TRUST A BROTHER-IN-LAW?

Now that you understand how a firm's income statement and balance sheet are used, let's return to your brother-in-law's clothing-business proposition described on page 66. You have constructed the business's projected income statement and balance sheet from the fragments of paper your dog chewed up and found the following results (in $ thousands):

PROJECTED INCOME STATEMENT			PROJECTED BALANCE SHEET	
Sales		$ 75	Cash needed in the business	$ 6
Cost of goods sold		40	Inventories	14
Gross profit		$ 35	Equipment	30
			Total assets	$50
Operating expenses:				
Office overhead	$14		Accounts payable	$ 6
Advertising expense	16		90-day bank loan	10
Rent expense	4		Total debt	$16
Depreciation expense	10		Equity:	
Total operating expenses		$ 44	Brother-in-law	$ 3
Operating income		$ (9)	Your investment	2
Interest expense		1	Total equity	$ 5
Loss before taxes		$(10)	Total projected debt and equity	$21
Taxes		0	Additional financing needed	29
Net income		$(10)	Total debt and equity needed	$50

So, based on your estimates, the venture would expect to incur a loss of $10,000. Furthermore, the balance sheet suggests you will need $50,000 to purchase the business's assets. This would have to come from $16,000 in debt financing that you hope you can obtain, $3,000 from your brother-in-law, and $2,000 from you, which totals $21,000. However, this is still less than the $50,000 you actually need. Thus, the business will need an additional $29,000. Maybe, just maybe, this is not quite the opportunity your brother-in-law perceives it to be.

CAN YOU DO IT?
MEASURING CASH FLOWS

Given the following information for Menielle Inc., prepare a statement of cash flows.

Increase in accounts receivable	13		Dividends	5
Increase in inventories	25		Change in common stock	0
Net income	33		Increase in gross fixed assets	55
Beginning cash	15		Depreciation expense	7
Increase in accounts payable	20			
Increase in accrued expenses	5			
Increase in long-term notes payable	28			

(The solution can be found on page 69.)

We will use the information included in this chapter in Chapter 4 to dig deeper and conduct a financial analysis of Davies Inc. Read on.

Concept Check

1. Why doesn't an income statement provide a measure of a firm's cash flows?
2. What are the three main parts of a statement of cash flows?
3. What does each part tell us about a company?

DID YOU GET IT?

MEASURING CASH FLOWS

On page 67 we asked you to calculate Menielle Inc.'s cash flows. Your results should be as follows:

Net income		$ 33
Depreciation expense		7
Income before depreciation		$ 40
Less increase in accounts receivable		(13)
Less payments for inventories consisting of:		
Increase in inventories	$(25)	
Less increase in accounts payable	20	
Payments for inventories		$(5)
Less increase in accrued expenses		5
Cash flow from operations		$ 27
Investment activity		
Increase in fixed assets		$(55)
Financing activity		
Increase in long-term notes payable		$ 28
Change in common stock		0
Common stock dividends		(5)
Total financing activities		$ 23
Change in cash		$ (5)
Beginning cash		15
Ending Cash		$ 10

Income Taxes and Finance

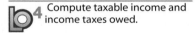

4 Compute taxable income and income taxes owed.

Income tax is one of the largest expenses that a business encounters, and as a result, it must be considered in making investment and financing decisions. But understanding income taxes is a profession unto itself. Tax accountants spend a lifetime attempting to remain current with the tax laws. So we will limit our discussion to the basic issue of computing a corporation's income taxes and let the tax accountants provide us counsel on the rest.

For our purposes, we simply need to know that **taxable income** for a corporation consists of two basic components: operating income and capital gains. Operating income, as we have already defined, is essentially gross profits less any operating expenses, such as marketing expenses, administrative expenses and so forth. **Capital gains** occur when a firm sells a capital asset, which is any asset that is not part of its ordinary operations. For example, when a company sells a piece of equipment or land, any gain (sales price less the cost of the asset) is thought to be a capital gain. Also, the *interest expense* paid on the firm's outstanding debt is a tax-deductible expense. However, dividends paid to the firm's stockholders are *not* deductible expenses, but rather distributions of income. Other taxable income includes the interest income and dividend income that the corporation receives.

taxable income gross income from all sources, except for allowable exclusions, less any tax-deductible expenses.

capital gains gains from selling any asset that is not part of the ordinary operations.

Computing Taxable Income

To demonstrate how to compute a corporation's taxable income, consider the J and S Corporation, a manufacturer of home accessories. The firm, originally established by Kelly Stites, had sales of $50 million for the year. The cost of producing the accessories totaled $23 million. Operating expenses were $10 million. The corporation has $12.5 million in debt outstanding, with an 8 percent interest rate, which resulted in $1 million interest expense ($12,500,000 × 0.08 = $1,000,000). Management paid $1 million in dividends to the firm's common stockholders. No other income, such as interest or dividend income, was received. The taxable income for the J and S Corporation would be $16 million, as shown in Table 3-6.

Once we know J and S Corporation's taxable income, we can determine the amount of taxes the firm owes.

TABLE 3-6 J and S Corporation Taxable Income

Sales		$50,000,000
Cost of goods sold		23,000,000
Gross profit		$27,000,000
Operating expenses		
Administrative expenses	$4,000,000	
Depreciation expenses	1,500,000	
Marketing expenses	4,500,000	
Total operating expenses		$10,000,000
Operating income		
(earnings before interest and taxes)		$17,000,000
Other income		0
Interest expense		1,000,000
Taxable income		$16,000,000

Dividends paid to common stockholders ($1,000,000) are not tax-deductible expenses.

Computing the Taxes Owed

The taxes to be paid by the corporation on its taxable income are based on the corporate tax rate structure. The specific rates for corporations, as of early 2007, are given in Table 3-7.

marginal tax rate the tax rate that would be applied to the next dollar of income.

The tax rates shown in Table 3-7 are defined as the **marginal tax rates**, or *rates applicable to the next dollar of income*. For instance, if a firm has earnings of $60,000 and is contemplating an investment that would yield $10,000 in additional profits, the tax rate to be used in calculating the taxes on this added income is 25 percent; that is, the marginal tax rate is 25 percent.

TABLE 3-7 Corporate Tax Rates

15%	$0–$50,000
25%	$50,001–$75,000
34%	$75,001–$10,000,000
35%	over $10,000,000
Additional surtax:	

- 5% on income between $100,000 and $335,000
- 3% on income between $15,000,000 and $18,333,333

The rates in Table 3-7 go up to a top marginal corporate tax rate of 35 percent for taxable income in excess of $10 million, and a surtax of 3 percent on taxable income between $15 million and $18,333,333. This means the corporation's marginal tax rate on income between $15 million and $18,333,333 is 38 percent (the 35 percent rate plus the 3 percent surtax). There is also a 5 percent surtax on taxable income between $100,000 and $335,000, which means the marginal rate on income between $100,000 and $335,000 is 39 percent (the 34 percent rate plus the 5 percent surtax). For example, the tax liability for J and S Corporation, which had $16 million in taxable earnings, would be $5,530,000, calculated as follows:

EARNINGS	×	MARGINAL TAX RATE	=	TAXES
$ 50,000	×	15%	=	$ 7,500
25,000	×	25%	=	6,250
9,925,000	×	34%	=	3,374,500
6,000,000	×	35%	=	2,100,000
				$5,488,250

Additional surtaxes:

• Add 5% surtax on income between $100,000 and $335,000 (5% × [$335,000 − $100,000])	11,750
• Add 3% surtax on income between $15,000,000 and $18,333,333 (3% × [$16,000,000 − $15,000,000])	30,000
Total tax liability	$5,530,000

CAN YOU DO IT?

COMPUTING A CORPORATION'S INCOME TAXES

Assume that the Griggs Corporation had sales during the past year of $5 million; its cost of goods sold was $3 million; and it incurred operating expenses of $950,000. In addition, it received $185,000 in interest income. In turn, it paid $40,000 in interest and $75,000 in common stock dividends.

J and S Corporation's marginal tax rate is 38 percent (this is because $16 million falls into the 35% tax bracket *with* a 3% surtax); that is, any additional income will be taxed at a rate of 38 percent. However, after taxable income exceeds $18,333,333, the marginal tax rate declines to 35 percent, and the 3 percent surtax no longer applies.

For financial decision making, it's the *marginal tax rate* rather than the average tax rate that we are concerned with. Why? Because, generally speaking, the marginal rate is the rate that corporation pays on the next dollar that is earned. We always want to consider the tax consequences of any financial decision. The marginal tax rate is the rate that will be applicable for any changes in earnings that occur as a result of the decision being made. Thus, when making financial decisions involving taxes, always use the marginal tax rate in your calculations.[4]

DID YOU GET IT?

COMPUTING A CORPORATION'S INCOME TAXES

Sales		$5,000,000
Cost of goods sold		($ 3,000,000)
Gross profit		$2,000,000
Operating expenses		($ 950,000)
Operating income		$1,050,000
Other taxable income and expenses:		
Interest income	$185,000	
Interest expense	($ 40,000)	$ 145,000
Taxable income		$1,195,000
Tax computation		
15% × $ 50,000 =	$ 7,500	
25% × $ 25,000 =	$ 6,250	
34% × $1,120,000 =	380,800	
$1,195,000	$394,550	
Add 5% surtax for income		
Between $100,000 and		
$335,000	$ 11,750	
Tax liability	$406,300	

Analysis:
Note that the $75,000 Griggs paid in common stock dividends is not tax deductible. The marginal tax rate and the average tax rate both equal 34 percent; thus, we could have computed Griggs's tax liability as 34 percent of $1, 195,000 or $406,300.

---

[4]On taxable income between $335,000 and $10 million, both the marginal and average tax rates equal 34 percent because of the imposition of the 5 percent surtax that applies to taxable income between $100,000 and $335,000. After the company's taxable income exceeds $18,333,333, both the marginal and average tax rates equal 35 percent because the 3 percent surtax on income between $15 million and $18,333,333 eliminates the benefits of having the first $10 million of income taxed at 34 percent rather than 35 percent.

1 Compute a company's profits, as reflected by its income statement.

Summary

A firm's profits may be viewed as follows:

Gross profit = sales − cost of goods sold

Earnings before interest and tax (operating profit) = sales − cost of goods sold − operating expenses

Net profit (net income) = sales − cost of goods sold − operating expenses − interest expense − taxes

The following five activities determine a company's net income:

1. The revenue derived from selling the company's product or service
2. The cost of producing or acquiring the goods or services to be sold
3. The operating expenses related to (1) marketing and distributing the product or service to the customer and (2) administering the business
4. The financing costs of doing business—namely, the interest paid to the firm's creditors
5. The payment of taxes

2 Determine a firm's financial position at a point in time based on its balance sheet.

The balance sheet presents a company's assets, liabilities, and equity on a specific date. Its total assets represent all the investments that the firm has made in the business. The total assets must equal the firm's total debt and equity because every dollar of assets has been financed by the firm's lenders or stockholders. The firm's assets include its current assets, fixed assets, and other assets. Its debt includes both its short-term and long-term debt. The firm's equity includes (1) common stock, which may be shown as par value plus additional paid-in capital, and (2) retained earnings. All the numbers in a balance sheet are based on historical costs, rather than current market values.

3 Measure a company's cash flows.

A firm's profits are not an adequate measure of its cash flows. To measure a company's cash flows requires that we look both at the income statement and the changes in the balance sheet. There are three main parts of a statement of cash flows: cash flows from operations, investment cash flows, and financing cash flows. Examining these three parts of the statement of cash flows helps us understand where cash came from and how it was used.

4 Compute taxable income and income taxes owed.

For the most part, taxable income for the corporation is equal to the firm's operating income plus capital gains less any interest expense. Tax consequences, particularly marginal tax rates, have a direct bearing on the decisions of the financial manager.

Key Terms

Accounting book value   54

Accounts payable   56

Accounts receivable   55

Accrual basis accounting   61

Accrued expenses   57

Accumulated depreciation   55

Additional paid-in capital   57

Balance sheet   53

Capital gains   69

Cash   55

Common-sized balance sheet   60

Common-sized income statement   51

Common stock   57

Common stockholders   57

Cost of goods sold   48

Current assets (gross working capital)   55

Current debt   56

Debt   56

Debt ratio   59

Depreciation expense   55

Dividends per share   51

Earnings before interest and taxes or EBIT   48

Earnings before taxes (taxable income)   49

Earnings per share   50

Equity   56

Financing cost   49

Fixed assets   55

Free cash flows   61

Gross fixed assets   55

Gross profit   48

Gross profit margin   51

Review Questions

All Review Questions and Study Problems are available in MyFinanceLab.

3-1. A company's financial statements consist of the balance sheet, income statement, and statement of cash flows. Describe what each statement tells us.

3-2. How do gross profits, operating profits, and net income differ?

3-3. How do dividends and interest expense differ?

3-4. Why is it that the preferred stockholders' equity section of the balance sheet changes only when new shares are sold or repurchased, whereas the common stockholders' equity section changes from year to year regardless of whether new shares are bought or sold?

3-5. What is net working capital?

3-6. Why might one firm have positive cash flows and be headed for financial trouble, whereas another firm with negative cash flows could actually be in a good financial position?

3-7. Why is the examination of only the balance sheet and income statement not adequate in evaluating a firm?

3-8. Why are dividends paid to a firm's owners not a tax-deductible expense?

3-9. See the annual report for the Dell Corporation by going to www.dell.com. Scroll to the bottom of the page, then click "About Dell," then "Investors," and finally the link "Annual Reports." Scan the list to determine which year you would like to review. Alternatively, select one of the other links (such as "Financial History") to learn additional financial information about Dell Inc.

3-10. Go to www.homedepot.com for the home page of the Home Depot Corporation. Scroll to the bottom of the page and select the "Corporate Info" option, then "Investor Relations," and finally "Financial Reports." Look for key words in the income statement that appear in this chapter, such as sales, gross profits, and net income. What do you learn about the firm from its financial statements that you find interesting?

3-11. Go to the *Wall Street Journal* home page at www.wsj.com. Search for Barnes & Noble (ticker symbol BKS). Find the firm's earnings announcements. What did you learn about the company from the announcements? Also, search www.barnesandnoble.com to find the same information.

Self-Test Problems

The solution to this problem is provided at the end of the chapter.

ST-1. (*Interpreting financial statements and measuring cash flows*) Given the following information for the M & G Corporation:

   a. How much is the firm's net working capital and what is the debt ratio for 2010?

   b. Complete (1) a common-sized income statement and (2) a common-sized balance sheet. Interpret your results for 2010.

   c. Prepare a statement of cash flows for 2010. Interpret your results.

M & G Corporation Balance Sheet for December 31, 2009 and 2010

	2009	2010
Cash	$ 9,000	$ 500
Accounts receivable	12,500	16,000
Inventories	29,000	45,500
Total current assets	$ 50,500	$ 62,000
Land	·20,000	26,000
Buildings and equipment	70,000	100,000
Less accumulated depreciation	(28,000)	(38,000)
Total fixed assets	$ 62,000	$ 88,000
Total assets	$112,500	$150,000
Accounts payable	$ 6,500	$ 17,000
Accrued expenses	4,000	5,000
Short-term bank notes	17,000	47,000
Total current liabilities	$ 27,500	$ 69,000
Long-term debt	28,750	22,950
Common stock	31,500	31,500
Retained earnings	24,750	26,550
Total debt and equity	$112,500	$150,000

M & G Corporation Income Statement for the Year Ending December 31, 2010

	2010
Sales (all credit)	$160,000
Cost of goods sold	96,000
Gross profit	$ 64,000
Operating expenses	
Fixed cash operating expenses	$ 21,000
Variable operating expenses	16,000
Depreciation	10,000
Total operating expenses	$ 47,000
Earnings before interest and taxes	$ 17,000
Interest expense	6,100
Earnings before taxes	$ 10,900
Income taxes	3,900
Net income	$ 7,000

ST-2. (*Corporate income tax*) The Dana Flatt Corporation had sales of $2 million this past year. Its cost of goods sold was $1.2 million and its operating expenses were $400,000. Interest expenses on outstanding debts were $164,000, and the company paid $40,000 in preferred stock dividends. The corporation received interest income of $12,000. Determine the corporation's taxable income and its tax liability.

Study Problems

3-1. (*Review of financial statements*) Prepare a balance sheet and income statement for Belmond Inc. from the following information.

Inventory	$ 6,500
Common stock	45,000
Cash	16,550
Operating expenses	1,350
Short-term notes payable	600
Interest expense	900
Depreciation expense	500
Net sales	12,800
Accounts receivable	9,600
Accounts payable	4,800
Long-term debt	55,000
Cost of goods sold	5,750
Buildings and equipment	$122,000
Accumulated depreciation	34,000
Taxes	1,440
General and administrative expense	850
Retained earnings	?

3-2. (*Computing cash flows*) Given the following information, prepare a statement of cash flows.

Increase in accounts receivable	$25
Increase in inventories	30
Operating income	75
Interest expense	25
Increase in accounts payable	25
Dividends	15
Increase in common stock	20
Increase in net fixed assets	23
Depreciation expense	12
Income taxes	17
Beginning cash	20

3-3. (*Review of financial statements*) Prepare a balance sheet and income statement for the Warner Company from the following scrambled list of items.

a. What is the firm's net working capital and debt ratio?
b. Complete a common-sized income statement and a common-sized balance sheet. Interpret your findings.

Depreciation expense	$ 66,000
Cash	225,000
Long-term debt	334,000
Sales	573,000
Accounts payable	102,000
General and administrative expense	79,000
Buildings and equipment	895,000
Notes payable	75,000
Accounts receivable	153,000
Interest expense	4,750
Accrued expenses	7,900
Common stock	289,000
Cost of goods sold	297,000
Inventory	99,300
Taxes	50,500
Accumulated depreciation	263,000
Prepaid expenses	14,500
Taxes payable	53,000
Retained earnings	262,900

3-4. (*Statement of cash flows*) Interpret the following information regarding Westlake Corporation's cash flows.

Net income	$ 680
Depreciation expense	125
Profits before depreciation	805
Increase in accounts receivables	(200)
Increase in inventories	(240)
Increase in accounts payables	120
Increase in accrued expenses	81
Cash flow from operations	$ 566
Investment activity	
Change in fixed assets	$(1,064)
Financing activity	
Increase in long-term debt	$ 640
Common stock dividends	(120)
Total financing activities	$ 520
Change in cash	$ 22
Beginning cash	500
Ending cash	$ 522

3-5. (*Computing cash flows*) Given the following information, prepare a statement of cash flows.

Dividends	$ 25
Increase in common stock	27
Increase in accounts receivable	65
Increase in inventories	5
Operating income	215
Increase in accounts payables	40
Interest expense	50
Depreciation expense	20
Increase in bank debt	48
Increase in accrued expenses	15
Increase in gross fixed assets	55
Income taxes	45

3-6. (*Cash flow analysis*) Interpret the following information regarding Maness Corporation's statement of cash flows.

Net income	$ 370
Depreciation expense	60
Profits before depreciation	430
Increase in accounts receivables	(300)
Increase in inventories	(400)
Increase in accounts payables	200
Increase in accrued expenses	40
Cash flow from operations	$ (30)
Investment activity	
Change in fixed assets	$(1,500)
Financing activity	
Increase in short-term notes	$ 100
Repayment of long-term debt	(250)
Repurchase common stock	(125)
Common stock dividends	(75)
Total financing activities	$ (350)
Change in cash	$(1,880)
Beginning cash	3,750
Ending cash	$ 1,870

3-7. (*Interpreting financial statements and measuring cash flows*) Given the information below for Pamplin Inc.:

   a. How much is the firm's net working capital and what is the debt ratio?
   b. Complete a common-sized income statement, a common-sized balance sheet, and a statement of cash flows for 2010. Interpret your results.

Pamplin Inc. Balance Sheet at 12/31/2009 and 12/31/2010

ASSETS

	2009	2010
Cash	$ 200	$ 150
Accounts receivable	450	425
Inventory	550	625
Current assets	$ 1,200	$ 1,200
Plant and equipment	$ 2,200	$ 2,600
Less accumulated depreciation	(1,000)	(1,200)
Net plant and equipment	$ 1,200	$ 1,400
Total assets	$ 2,400	$ 2,600

LIABILITIES AND OWNERS' EQUITY

	2009	2010
Accounts payable	$ 200	$ 150
Notes payable—current (9%)	0	150
Current liabilities	$ 200	$ 300
Bonds	$ 600	$ 600
Owners' equity		
Common stock	$ 900	$ 900
Retained earnings	700	800
Total owners' equity	$1,600	$1,700
Total liabilities and owners' equity	$2,400	$2,600

Pamplin Inc. Income Statement for Years Ending 12/31/2009 and 12/31/2010

	2009		2010	
Sales		$ 1,200		$ 1,450
Cost of goods sold		700		850
Gross profit		$ 500		$ 600
Selling, general, and administrative expenses	$ 30		$ 40	
Depreciation	220	250	200	240
Operating income		$ 250		$ 360
Interest expense		$ 50		64
Net income before taxes		$ 200		$ 296
Taxes (40%)		80		118
Net income		$ 120		$ 178

3-8. (*Interpreting financials statements and measuring cash flows*) Based on the information for T. P. Jarmon Company for the year ended December 31, 2010:

   a. How much is the firm's net working capital and what is the debt ratio?
   b. Complete a statement of cash flows for the period. Interpret your results.
   c. Compute the changes in the balance sheets from 2009 to 2010. What do you learn about T. P. Jarmon from these computations? How do these numbers relate to the statement of cash flows?

T. P. Jarmon Company Balance Sheet for 12/31/2009 and 12/31/2010

ASSETS

	2009	2010
Cash	$ 15,000	$ 14,000
Marketable securities	6,000	6,200
Accounts receivable	42,000	33,000
Inventory	51,000	84,000
Prepaid rent	$ 1,200	$ 1,100
Total current assets	$ 115,200	$ 138,300
Net plant and equipment	286,000	270,000
Total assets	$ 401,200	$ 408,300

LIABILITIES AND EQUITY

	2009	2010
Accounts payable	$ 48,000	$ 57,000
Accruals	6,000	5,000
Notes payable	15,000	13,000
Total current liabilities	$ 69,000	$ 75,000
Long-term debt	$ 160,000	$ 150,000
Common stockholders' equity	$ 172,200	$ 183,300
Total liabilities and equity	$ 401,200	$ 408,300

T. P. Jarmon Company Income Statement for the Year Ended 12/31/2010

Sales		$ 600,000
Less cost of goods sold		460,000
Gross profit		$ 140,000
Operating and interest expenses		
General and administrative	$ 30,000	
Interest	10,000	
Depreciation	30,000	
Total operating and interest expenses		70,000
Earnings before taxes		$ 70,000
Taxes		27,100
Net income available to common stockholders		$ 42,900
Cash dividends		31,800
Change in retained earnings		$ 11,100

3-9. (*Measuring cash flows*) Prepare a statement of cash flows for Abrahams Manufacturing Company for the year ended December 31, 2010. Interpret your results.

Abrahams Manufacturing Company Balance Sheet for 12/31/2009 and 12/31/2010

	2009	2010
Cash	$ 89,000	$ 100,000
Accounts receivable	64,000	70,000
Inventory	112,000	100,000
Prepaid expenses	10,000	10,000
Total current assets	275,000	280,000
Gross plant and equipment	238,000	311,000
Accumulated depreciation	(40,000)	(66,000)
Total assets	$ 473,000	$ 525,000
Accounts payable	$ 85,000	$ 90,000
Accrued liabilities	68,000	63,000
Total current debt	153,000	153,000
Mortgage payable	70,000	0
Preferred stock	0	120,000
Common stock	205,000	205,000
Retained earnings	45,000	47,000
Total debt and equity	$ 473,000	$ 525,000

Abrahams Manufacturing Company Income Statement for the Year Ended 12/31/2010

	2010
Sales	$ 184,000
Cost of goods sold	60,000
Gross profit	$ 124,000
Selling, general, and administrative expenses	44,000
Depreciation expense	26,000
Operating income	$ 54,000
Interest expense	4,000
Earnings before taxes	$ 50,000
Taxes	16,000
Preferred stock dividends	10,000
Earnings available to common shareholders	$ 24,000

Additional Information

1. The only entry in the accumulated depreciation account is for 2010 depreciation.

2. The firm paid $22,000 in common stock dividends during 2010.

3-10. (*Corporate income tax*) The William B. Waugh Corporation is a regional Toyota dealer. The firm sells new and used trucks and is actively involved in the parts business. During the most recent year, the company generated sales of $3 million. The combined cost of goods sold and the operating expenses were $2.1 million. Also, $400,000 in interest expense was paid during the year. Calculate the corporation's tax liability.

3-11. (*Corporate income tax*) Sales for L. B. Menielle Inc. during the past year amounted to $5 million. The firm provides parts and supplies for oil field service companies. Gross profits for the year were $3 million. Operating expenses totaled $1 million. The interest income from the securities it owned was $20,000. The firm's interest expense was $100,000. Compute the corporation's tax liability.

3-12. (*Corporate income tax*) Sandersen Inc. sells minicomputers. During the past year, the company's sales were $3 million. The cost of its merchandise sold came to $2 million, and cash operating expenses were $400,000; depreciation expense was $100,000, and the firm paid $150,000 in interest on its bank loans. Also, the corporation paid $25,000 in the form of dividends to its own common stockholders. Calculate the corporation's tax liability.

Mini Case

In 2009, the auto industry was being devastated by the economic downturn. General Motors filed for bankruptcy and was renamed Motors Liquidation, an event that could not have been imagined in prior times. Toyota, historically a tough competitor for Detroit, was beginning to be affected as well, but not nearly to the same extent as GM. Below are the financial statements for the two firms. GM's fiscal year ends on December 31; thus, the statements are for the end-of-year for 2007 and 2008. Toyota, on the other hand, has a March 31 fiscal year; therefore the statements are for fiscal years 2008 and 2009. As a result, Toyota's financials are three months later than the financials for General Motors.

a. Prepare a common-sized income statement and common-sized balance sheet for each firm for both years.

b. How much profit (loss) was each company making per dollar of sales? To what would you attribute any differences?

c. What differences do you notice in the common-sized balance sheets that could account for the problems of GM relative to Toyota?

d. Conduct an Internet search on the two firms to gain additional insights as to causes of the financial differences between the firms in 2008 and continuing into 2009.

e. How are the two companies doing financially today?

Toyota Corp. Annual Income Statement
for Years Ending March 31, 2008 and 2009 (in $ millions except earnings per share)

	2008	2009
Sales	$262,394	$208,995
Cost of goods sold	199,912	172,663
Gross profits	$ 62,482	$ 36,332
Selling, general, and administrative expenses	24,938	25,804
Depreciation and amortization	14,883	15,221
Operating income	$ 22,661	$ (4,693)
Interest expense	460	477
Nonoperating income (expenses)	4,043	147
Earnings before tax	$ 26,244	$ (5,023)
Income taxes	9,098	(575)
Net income (loss)	$ 17,146	$ (4,448)
Common shares outstanding	1,589	1,570
Earnings per share	$ 10.79	$ (2.83)

Toyota Corp. Balance Sheet
for Years Ending March 31, 2008 and 2009 ($ millions)

ASSETS	MARCH 31, 2008	MARCH 31, 2009
Cash and short-term investments	$ 23,012	30,386
Receivables	68,519	57,181
Inventories	18,222	14,857
Other current assets	10,880	12,601
Total current assets	$120,633	$115,025
Gross fixed assets	$173,633	175,027
Accumulated depreciation and amortization	(95,661)	(99,677)
Net fixed assets	$ 77,972	$ 75,350
Other assets	125,363	105,482
TOTAL ASSETS	$323,968	$295,857

LIABILITIES		
Notes payable	$ 46,124	48,627
Accounts payable	22,086	13,229
Income taxes payable	3,050	522
Accrued expenses	16,039	15,684
Other current liabilities	31,882	29,739
Total current liabilities	$ 119,181	$ 107,801
Long-term debt	59,706	64,150
Deferred taxes	10,969	6,539
Other liabilities	15,642	14,942
TOTAL LIABILITIES	$205,498	$193,432

EQUITY		
Common stock	$ 3,963	4,042
Capital surplus	4,966	5,102
Retained earnings	121,443	106,117
Less: Treasury stock—total dollar amount	(11,902)	(12,836)
Total common equity	$ 118,470	$ 102,425
TOTAL LIABILITIES AND STOCKHOLDERS' EQUITY	$ 323,968	$ 295,857

General Motors Corp. Annual Income Statement
for Years Ending December 31, 2007 and December 31, 2008 (in $ millions except per share data)

	2007	2008
Sales	$179,984	$148,979
Cost of goods sold	160,856	149,311
Gross profits	$ 19,128	$ (332)
Selling, general, and administrative expenses	14,412	14,801
Depreciation and amortization	9,513	9,931
Operating income	$ (4,797)	$ (25,064)
Interest expense	3,307	3,055
Nonoperating income (expenses)	1,969	(975)
Taxable income	$ (6,135)	$ (29,094)
Income taxes	37,162	1,766
Income before extraordinary items	(43,297)	(30,860)
Extraordinary items	4,565	
Net income (loss)	$ (38,732)	$ (30,860)
Common shares outstandings	566	579
Earnings per share	$ (68.43)	$ (53.30)

General Motors Corp. Balance Sheets
for Years Ending December 31, 2007 and 2009 ($ millions)

ASSETS

Cash and short-term investments	$ 26,956	$ 14,066
Receivables	9,659	7,711
Inventories—total	14,939	13,042
Other current assets	8,849	6,505
Total current assets	$ 60,403	$ 41,324
Gross fixed assets	97,319	86,919
Accumulated depreciation	(47,590)	(45,042)
Net fixed assets	$ 49,729	$ 41,877
Other assets—sundry	38,751	7,846
TOTAL ASSETS	$ 148,883	$ 91,047

LIABILITIES

Notes payable	$ 6,047	$ 15,754
Accounts payable	29,439	22,236
Accrued expenses	34,024	35,921
Other current liabilities	5,813	1,822
Total current liabilities	$ 75,323	$ 75,733
Long-term debt	33,384	29,594
Post-retirement benefits	47,375	28,919
Pension	11,381	25,178
Other liabilities	18,514	17,777
Total liabilities	$ 185,977	$177,201

COMMON EQUITY

Common stock	$ 943	$ 1,017
Capital surplus	15,319	15,755
Retained earnings	(53,356)	(102,926)
Total common equity	$ (37,094)	$ (86,154)
TOTAL DEBT AND EQUITY	$ 148,883	$ 91,047

Self-Test Solution

SS-1.

 a. 2010 net working capital = current assets − current liabilities

$$= \$62{,}000 - \$69{,}000$$
$$= \$(7{,}000)$$

   2010 debt ratio = total liabilities ÷ total assets

$$= \$91{,}950 \div 150{,}000$$
$$= 0.613 \text{ or } 61.3\%$$

(1)b. Common-sized income statement

	2010	% OF SALES
Sales (all credit)	$160,000	100.0%
Cost of goods sold	96,000	60.0%
Gross profit	$ 64,000	40.0%
Operating expenses		
Fixed cash operating expenses	$ 21,000	13.1%
Variable operating expenses	16,000	10.0%
Depreciation	10,000	6.3%
Total operating expenses	$ 47,000	29.4%
Earnings before interest and taxes	$ 17,000	10.6%
Interest expense	6,100	3.8%
Earnings before taxes	$ 10,900	6.8%
Income taxes	3,900	2.4%
Net income	$ 7,000	4.4%

From the common-sized income statement, we see that M & G Corporation's gross profit margin was 40 percent of sales. Furthermore, the firm earned an operating profit margin of 10.6 percent and a net profit margin of 4.4 percent.

(2) Common-sized balance sheet

Cash	$ 500	0.3%
Accounts receivable	16,000	10.7%
Inventories	45,500	30.3%
Total current assets	$ 62,000	41.3%
Land	$ 26,000	17.3%
Plant and equipment	100,000	66.7%
Accumulated depreciation	(38,000)	− 25.3%
Total fixed assets	$ 88,000	58.7%
Total assets	$150,000	100.0%
Accounts payable	$ 17,000	11.3%
Accrued expenses	$ 5,000	3.3%
Short-term bank notes	47,000	31.3%
Total current liabilities	$ 69,000	46.0%
Long-term debt	22,950	15.3%
Total debt	$ 91,950	61.3%
Common stock	$ 31,500	21.0%
Retained earnings	26,550	17.7%
Total common equity	$ 58,050	38.7%
Total liabilities and equity	$150,000	100.0%

M & G Corporation has about 41 percent in current assets and 59 percent in long-term assets. A large part of its debt is short term, mostly in the form of short-term bank notes.

c. Complete a statement of cash flows for the period. Interpret your results.

Net income	$ 7,000
Depreciation expense	10,000
Profits before depreciation	17,000
Increase in accounts receivables	(3,500)
Increase in inventories	(16,500)
Increase in accounts payables	10,500
Increase in accrued expenses	1,000
Cash flow from operations	$ 8,500
Investment activity	
Change in fixed assets	$(36,000)
Financing activity	
Increase in short-term bank notes	30,000
Decrease in long-term debt	$ (5,800)
Common stock dividends	(5,200)
Total financing activities	$ 19,000
Change in cash	$ (8,500)
Beginning cash	9,000
Ending cash	$ 500

Thus, M & G Corporation's managers invested more in fixed assets and land than was generated in cash flows from operations. The company then borrowed enough in short-term financing to cover its shortfall to make up the difference and to pay down its long-term debt, pay interest expense, and pay dividends.

SS-2.

Sales		$2,000,000
Cost of goods sold		(1,200,000)
Gross profits		$ 800,000
Operating expenses		(400,000)
Operating income		$ 400,000
Interest expense		(164,000)
Interest income		12,000
Taxable income		$ 248,000
Tax computation		
15% ×	$ 50,000	$ 7,500
25% ×	$ 25,000	$ 6,250
34% ×	$173,000	$ 58,820
	$248,000	$ 72,570
Add 5% surcharge for income		
between $100,000 and $248,000		$ 7,400
Tax liability		$ 79,970

Chapter 4

Evaluating a Firm's Financial Performance

Learning Objectives

After reading this chapter, you should be able to:

Explain the purpose and importance of financial analysis.

Calculate and use a comprehensive set of measurements to evaluate a company's performance.

Describe the limitations of financial ratio analysis.

The previous chapter was most likely a review for many students using this text, having taken a basic financial accounting course earlier in their studies. But hopefully the chapter served as a good refresher if some time has elapsed since studying accounting. After all, it is easy to forget.

In this chapter, we want to answer the question, "So what?" What significance do the financial statements tell the firm's managers, as well as its other stakeholders, such as suppliers, creditors, and stockholders, about the firm's financial performance? We now want to use the data in the financial statements to gain greater insights into a company's operations, just as Paul Polman did when he became the new chief executive of Unilever in January 2009.

Unilever—whose products include Ben & Jerry's ice cream, Dove soap, Lipton teas, and Hellmann's mayonnaise—increased prices in 2008, just as the recession was taking root. As a result, some consumers stopped buying its products, driving down sales volume in the first quarter of 2009.

As Unilever's new CEO, Polman vowed to drive volume with lower prices and aggressive marketing spending. The impact was immediate. Second-quarter sales rose 4.1 percent, a strong result given the global recession. (By comparison, at rival Procter & Gamble Co., sales over the same period fell 1 percent.) But at the same time, Unilever's profit margins fell to 12.6 percent in the second quarter from 13.2 percent in the year-earlier period, due to the lower prices and increases in the firm's advertising budget. Thus, dollar profits essentially remained unchanged.

In response, Polman intends to reverse the declining profit margins by reducing costs. "We're looking at opportunities to drive costs out of the system to reinvest the savings back in growth," Polman said at a media briefing in London. For example, since taking over, Polman has tried to increase the speed of decision making in the company, known for its sprawling bureaucracy and cautious culture. After his arrival, the company introduced "Thirty-Day Action Plans," for instance. The plans are designed to make executives take quick action to fix problems with individual products.

Polman is Unilever's first CEO who wasn't brought up from the company's internal ranks. The executive spent most of his career at Procter & Gamble Co. Analysts said it could take years to change the Unilever culture. "I believe [Mr. Polman] is the right man to do so but I am not so optimistic it will go through quickly," said Claudia Lenz, an analyst at Bank Vontobel in Switzerland.

It will be interesting to follow Unilever's performance in future years under Polman's leadership. His dilemma between increasing sales and lowering profit margins is one that all managers face.

In this chapter, we will see that either increasing sales alone or increasing profit margins alone will *not* give a manager the complete picture. Management should consider them together as they impact a firm's return on investment. Thus, understanding the relationships between decisions and the financial consequences are critical for managers, and is the topic of this chapter.

Source: Adapted from Aaron O. Patrick, "Unilever CEO's Push to Cut Prices Drives Increase in Sales," *Wall Street Journal*, August 5, 2009, p. B1.

This chapter is a natural extension of Chapter 3. In this chapter, we restate financial statements in relative terms to understand how a firm is performing. Specifically, we look at key financial relationships in the form of ratios to understand three basic attributes of the firm's performance:

◆ The ability of the firm to meet its current liabilities as they come due, or what financial analysts refer to as *liquidity*

◆ Whether the firm's managers deliver acceptable, and hopefully, even superior profits on the capital entrusted to the firm

◆ Whether the firm's managers create or destroy shareholder value

In this chapter, we look at financial measurements, or metrics, used to manage a business. Is using metrics to help us manage a business important? John Thompson, CEO, Symantec Corporation, a high-growth Internet security firm, thinks so:

I don't believe you can manage what you don't measure. A firm needs metrics that serve as an indication for the team about what you're paying attention to. If employees know you're measuring market growth and customer satisfaction, they'll pay attention to those considerations and will behave based on indicators that you, as the leader, provide to the organization. Metrics help the team focus on what's important for an organization.

The best metrics are simple to understand, are simple to communicate, and make it relatively easy for everyone to get access to the data that represents the results. That makes your metrics an effective management tool. If you make your metrics difficult to gather, manage, or communicate, they won't be effective. Simplicity is key.

My experience has proven to me the importance of picking a few metrics that are the most critical for running the business. Stick with them—and communicate them to both internal and external audiences.[1]

With this advice from an experienced CEO, we begin our study of the key financial metrics that can and must be used by companies, both large and small.

[1]David Liss, "Ask the CEO: Management by the Numbers," *Business Week Online*, New York: McGraw-Hill, at www .businessweek.com/technology/content/jul2003/tc20030721_6130.htm, accessed May 15, 2009.

LO1   Explain the purpose and importance of financial analysis.

The Purpose of Financial Analysis

As explained in Chapter 1, the fundamental and core objective of financial management is to create shareholder value, as opposed to focusing on accounting numbers, such as earnings. In a perfect world, we would rely on market values relating to a firm's assets rather than its accounting data. However, we rarely have market values to guide decision making. Thus, accounting information can be very useful for this purpose.

However, financial analysts use accounting information differently than accountants do. Accountants focus on using the information to prepare financial statements according to generally accepted accounting principles (GAAP). By contrast, financial analysts use the information to measure a company's performance and make projections about and improve its future financial performance. The analysis is primarily based on the use of ratios that help us see critical relationships that might not otherwise be readily identifiable. Ratios are used to standardize financial information so that we can make comparisons. Otherwise, it is really difficult to compare the financial statements of two firms of different sizes or even the same firm at different times.

financial ratios accounting data restated in relative terms in order to help people identify some of the financial strengths and weaknesses of a company.

Financial ratios give us two ways of making meaningful comparisons of a firm's financial data: (1) We can examine the ratios across time (say, for the past 5 years) to compare a firm's current and past performance; and (2) we can compare the firm's ratios with those of other firms. In comparing a firm with other companies, we could select a peer group of companies, or we could use industry norms published by firms such as Dun & Bradstreet, Risk Management Association, Standard & Poor's, Value Line, and Prentice Hall. Dun & Bradstreet, for instance, annually publishes a set of 14 key ratios for each of 125 lines of business. The Risk Management Association (the association of bank loan and credit officers) publishes a set of 16 key ratios for more than 350 lines of business. The firms are grouped according to the North American Industrial Classification System (NAICS) codes. They are also segmented by firm size to provide the basis for more meaningful comparisons.

Figure 4-1 shows the financial statement information as reported by Risk Management Association (RMA) for new car dealers. The report shows the information by two asset-size and sales-size categories. In the complete report (not provided here), other size categories are presented. The balance sheet data in the report are provided as a percentage of total assets, or what we called in Chapter 3 a *common-sized balance sheet.* Likewise, the income statement data are reported as a percentage of sales, referred to as a *common-sized income statement.*[2] In presenting the financial ratios in the bottom portion of the report, RMA gives three results for each ratio—the firms at the 75th, 50th, and 25th percentiles, respectively.

Financial analysis is not just a tool for financial managers but also can be used effectively by investors, lenders, suppliers, employees, and customers. Within the firm, managers use financial ratios to:

REMEMBER YOUR PRINCIPLES

Principle As in Chapter 3 when we talked about financial statements, a primary rationale for evaluating a company's financial performance relates to **Principle 5: Conflicts of Interest Cause Agency Problems.** Thus, the firm's common stockholders need information that can be used to monitor managers' actions. Interpreting the firm's financial statements through the use of financial ratios is a key tool used in this monitoring. Of course, the firm's managers also need metrics to monitor the company's performance so corrective actions can be taken when necessary.

Principle 4: Market Prices Are Generally Right is also relevant when it comes to evaluating a firm's financial performance. By exceptionally profitable markets, we mean markets in which investments earn rates of return that exceed the opportunity cost of the money invested. Thus, rates of return are critical measures of whether or not managers are creating shareholder value. In addition, certain financial ratios can help us better know if managers are pursuing exceptionally good investments or bad ones.

Finally, **Principle 3: Risk Requires a Reward** is also at work in this chapter. As we will see, how managers choose to finance the business affects the company's risk and, as a result, the rate of return stockholders receive on their investments.

◆ Identify deficiencies in the firm's performance and take corrective action.

◆ Evaluate employee performance and determine incentive compensation.

◆ Compare the financial performance of the firm's different divisions.

[2]In Chapter 3, we presented a common-sized income statement and common-sized balance sheet for Davies Inc. (See pages 51 and 60.)

FIGURE 4-1   Financial Statement Data by Industry: Norms for New Car Dealers

RETAIL—NEW CAR DEALERS NAICS 4411 (SIC 5511)

CURRENT DATA SORTED BY ASSETS			CURRENT DATA SORTED BY SALES	
50-100MM	100-250MM		10-25MM	25MM and OVER
%	%	ASSETS	%	%
7.3	8.7	Cash and Equivalents	8.1	10.3
10.0	10.9	Trade Receivables (net)	7.3	8.7
48.3	45.5	Inventory	67.9	60.0
4.4	2.5	All Other Current	2.7	2.9
70.0	67.6	Total Current	85.9	81.9
16.3	20.9	Fixed Assets (net)	8.3	10.9
2.6	1.5	Intangibles (net)	1.4	1.6
11.1	10.0	All Other Non-current	4.3	5.6
100.0	100.0	Total	100.0	100.0
		LIABILITIES		
42.2	42.5	Notes Payable Short Term	56.5	51.8
3.5	2.4	Cur. Mat.-L/T/D	2.0	2.4
3.5	4.2	Trade Payables	4.3	4.4
.1	.2	Income Taxes Payable	.1	.2
9.7	12.8	All Other Current	9.5	11.2
59.0	62.2	Total Current	72.3	70.0
14.6	16.0	Long Term Debt	6.5	7.5
.6	.3	Deferred Taxes	.1	.2
3.4	2.3	All Other Non-current	2.7	2.2
22.5	19.2	Net Worth	18.5	20.1
100.0	100.0	Total Liabilities and Net Worth	100.0	100.0
		INCOME DATA		
100.0	100.0	Net Sales	100.0	100.0
15.6	15.6	Gross Profit	12.3	12.1
13.2	14.0	Operating Expenses	11.9	11.2
2.4	1.6	Operating Profit	.3	.9
-.3	.3	All Other Expenses (net)	-.6	-.5
2.6	1.3	Profit Before Taxes	.9	1.4
		RATIOS		
1.3	1.2		1.3	1.3
1.2	1.1	Current	1.2	1.1
1.1	.9		1.1	1.0
.4	.4		.3	.4
.3	.3	Quick	(768) .2 (1302) .2	
.2	.2		.1	.2
5 67.2	6 61.0		3 127.5	4 102.8
10 36.1	11 33.1	Sales/Receivables	5 70.6	6 60.7
17 21.6	17 21.9		9 38.6	10 37.5

CURRENT DATA SORTED BY ASSETS			CURRENT DATA SORTED BY SALES	
50-100MM	100-250MM		10-25MM	25MM and OVER
%	%	RATIOS	%	%
52 7.1	53 6.9		60 6.1	46 8.0
67 5.4	62 5.9	Cost of Sales/Inventory	76 4.8	59 6.2
80 4.5	74 5.0		93 3.9	73 5.0
3 142.6	3 111.0		1 257.4	2 209.2
4 84.3	4 81.3	Cost of Sales/Payables	3 140.6	3 123.4
8 43.8	8 43.5		5 71.2	5 77.8
16.7	30.5		17.5	21.9
29.7	95.3	Sales/Working Capital	30.6	39.4
53.0	-98.0		88.5	134.2
8.4	12.7		6.8	11.3
(32) 4.0	(20) 4.1	EBIT/Interest	(597) 2.4	(938) 4.5
1.5	2.5		1.0	1.9
8.4			4.6	6.7
(10) 1.5		Net Profit+Depr., Dep., Amort./Cur. Mat. L/T/D	(64) 1.8	(174) 2.2
1.0			.6	.9
.2	.4		.2	.2
.8	1.3	Fixed Assets/Net Worth	.4	.5
1.3	4.9		1.2	1.2
2.4	3.2		3.0	2.6
3.7	5.3	Debt/Net Worth	5.8	4.8
6.6	17.0		14.0	9.8
39.3	77.4		36.4	50.4
(36) 23.2	(25) 22.2	% Profit Before Taxes/Tangible Net Worth	(692) 17.4	(1223) 28.0
10.5	13.3		3.0	12.2
8.6	7.7		6.1	9.2
4.4	5.0	% Profit Before Taxes/Total Assets	2.3	4.8
1.5	2.9		.1	1.6
84.2	74.0		163.6	126.3
22.9	17.7	Sales/Net Fixed Assets	77.4	67.2
9.6	8.2		37.0	27.0
4.0	3.9		4.5	5.2
3.3	3.1	Sales/Total Assets	3.8	4.2
1.9	2.5		3.0	3.4
.3	.2		.1	.1
(37) .4	(21) .5	% Depr., Dep., Amort./Sales	(679) .3	(1214) .3
1.0	.8		.4	.4
.1			.4	.2
(17) .3		% Officers', Directors', Owners' Comp/Sales	(501) .6	(760) .4
1.1			1.1	1.0
7968935M	13431196M	Net Sales ($)	13318098M	95427461M
2604956M	3948948M	Total Assets ($)	3876849M	24306019M

M = $ thousand   MM = $ million

◆ Prepare, at both the firm and division levels, financial projections, such as those associated with the launch of a new product.

◆ Understand the financial performance of the firm's competitors.

◆ Evaluate the financial condition of a major supplier.

Outside the company, financial ratios can be used by:

◆ Lenders to decide whether or not to make a loan to the company
◆ Credit-rating agencies to determine the firm's creditworthiness
◆ Investors to decide whether or not to invest in a company
◆ Major suppliers to decide whether or not to grant credit terms to a company

The conclusion: Financial analysis tools can help a wide group of individuals for a variety of purposes. However, in this chapter we will focus on how the firm itself uses financial ratios to evaluate its performance. But remember that personnel in marketing, human resources, information systems, and other groups within a firm can use financial ratios for a variety of other reasons.

Concept Check

1. What is the basic purpose of doing a financial analysis?
2. How does a firm use financial ratios? Who else might use financial ratios and why?
3. Where can we find financial ratios for different companies or for peer groups?

LO2 Calculate and use a comprehensive set of measurements to evaluate a company's performance.

Measuring Key Financial Relationships

Instructors usually take one of two approaches to teach students about financial ratios. The first approach reviews the different types or categories of ratios, whereas the second approach uses ratios to answer important questions about a firm's operations. We prefer the latter approach and have chosen the following five questions to help you map out the process of using financial ratios:

1. How liquid is the firm?
2. Are the firm's managers generating adequate operating profits on the company's assets?
3. How is the firm financing its assets?
4. Are the firm's managers providing a good return on the capital provided by the shareholders?
5. Are the firm's managers creating shareholder value?

Let's look at each of these five questions in turn. In doing so, we will use Davies Inc. to illustrate the use of financial ratios. The company's financial statements, which were originally presented in Chapter 3, are shown again in Table 4-1 and Table 4-2.

TABLE 4-1 Davies Inc. Income Statement for Year Ending December 31, 2010 ($ millions)		
Sales		$ 600
Cost of goods sold		460
Gross profits		$ 140
Operating expenses:		
Selling expenses	$ 20	
General and administrative expenses	15	
Depreciation expense	30	
Total operating expenses		$ 65
Operating income (EBIT)		$ 75
Interest		15
Earnings before taxes		$ 60
Income taxes		18
Net income		$ 42
Number of common shares outstanding (millions)		20
Earnings per share (EPS)		$ 2.10
Dividends per share (DPS)		$ 0.50

TABLE 4-2 Davies Inc. Balance Sheets ($ millions) December 31, 2010

Assets		
Cash		$ 20
Accounts receivable		36
Inventories		84
Other current assets		3
Total current assets		$ 143
Gross fixed assets	$ 410	
Accumulated depreciation	(115)	
Net fixed assets		$ 295
Total assets		$ 438
Debt and Equity		
Accounts payable		$ 42
Accrued expenses		10
Short-term notes		12
Total current liabilities		$ 64
Long-term debt		$ 171
Total liabilities		$ 235
Equity		
Common stockholders' equity		
Common stock—par value		$ 11
Paid-in capital		75
Retained earnings		117
Total common equity		$ 203
Total liabilities and equity		$ 438

To give us a basis for comparison, we also provide the average financial ratios for a peer group of businesses similar to Davies Inc. In the ratio computations, we have color coded the numbers so that you can readily determine whether a particular number is coming from the income statement (red numbers) or the balance sheet (blue numbers).

Question 1: How Liquid Is the Firm—Can It Pay Its Bills?

A liquid asset is one that can be converted quickly and routinely into cash at the current market price. So the **liquidity** of a business is a function of its ability to have cash available when needed to meet its financial obligations. Very simply, can we expect the company to be able to pay creditors on a timely basis?

This question can be answered by taking a look at two complementary perspectives: (1) by comparing the firm's assets that are relatively liquid (those that can be converted quickly and easily into cash) with the firm's debt owed in the near term, and (2) by examining the timeliness with which the firm's primary liquid assets—accounts receivable and inventories—are being converted into cash. Let's consider these two approaches.

liquidity a firm's ability to pay its bills on time. Liquidity is related to the ease and quickness with which a firm can convert its noncash assets into cash, as well as the size of the firm's investment in noncash assets relative to its short-term liabilities.

Measuring Liquidity: Perspective 1   The first angle for measuring liquidity is to look at the company's balance sheet and compare the firm's "liquid" assets (current assets) to its current (short-term) liabilities. Thus, the most commonly used measure of a firm's short-term solvency is the **current ratio**:

$$\text{Current ratio} = \frac{\text{current assets}}{\text{current liabilities}} \qquad (4\text{-}1)$$

current ratio a firm's current assets divided by its current liabilities. This ratio indicates the firm's degree of liquidity by comparing its current assets to its current liabilities.

For Davies Inc.:

$$\text{Current ratio} = \frac{\$143M}{\$64M} = 2.23$$

Peer group current ratio   1.80

CAUTIONARY TALE

FORGETTING PRINCIPLE 3: RISK REQUIRES A REWARD

Clearly, borrowing money carries risk—after all, you eventually have to pay off any debt you take on. Yet every day, forgetting this simple principle gets Americans in trouble. Between the mid-1980s and the early 2000s, the American household debt-to-income ratio doubled. In fact, this debt ratio spiked from between 45 and 60 percent to 135 percent! Interest on this household debt also increased substantially. At the same time, because interest on home mortgages is tax deductible, households had an incentive to borrow excessive amounts for home loans. This heavy debt burden—the risk of borrowing—meant that any unexpected expense, loss of a job, or increase in mortgage payments resulted in defaults.

Based on the current ratio, Davies Inc. is more liquid than the average firm in the peer group. The company has $2.23 in current assets for every $1 in short-term debt, compared to a peer-group average current ratio of $1.80.

When we use the current ratio, we assume that the firm's accounts receivable will be collected and turned into cash on a timely basis and that its inventories can be sold without any extended delay. However, a company's inventory is generally less liquid than its accounts receivable because inventory must first be sold before any cash can be collected. So, if we want to have a more stringent test of a firm's liquidity, we include only the firm's cash and accounts receivable in the numerator of our liquidity measure (and not its inventory). This revised ratio is called the **acid-test** (or **quick**) **ratio**. It is calculated as follows:

acid-test (quick) ratio a firm's cash and accounts receivable divided by its current liabilities. This ratio is a more stringent measure of liquidity than the current ratio in that it excludes inventories and other current assets (those that are least liquid) from current assets.

$$\text{Acid-test ratio} = \frac{\text{cash} + \text{accounts receivable}}{\text{current liabilities}} \tag{4-2}$$

For Davies Inc.:

$$\text{Acid-test ratio} = \frac{\$20M + \$36M}{\$64M} = 0.88$$

Peer group acid-test ratio	0.94

Based on the acid-test ratio, Davies Inc. appears to be slightly *less* liquid. It has $0.88 in cash and accounts receivable per $1 in current debt, compared to $0.94 for the average company in the peer group.

Measuring Liquidity: Perspective 2   The second angle for measuring liquidity examines the quality of a firm's accounts receivable and inventories in terms of the firm's ability to convert these assets into cash on a timely basis. A firm might have a higher current ratio or acid-test ratio than its competitors. However, it might also have more uncollectible receivables and/or be carrying a lot of obsolete inventory. So knowing the quality of these assets is necessary if we are to have a more complete understanding of a firm's liquidity.

Converting Accounts Receivable to Cash   The conversion of accounts receivable into cash can be measured by computing how long it takes to collect the firm's receivables. We can answer this question by computing a firm's days of sales outstanding, or its **average collection period**, as follows:[3]

average collection period a firm's accounts receivable divided by the company's average daily credit sales (annual credit sales ÷ 365). This ratio expresses how rapidly the firm is collecting its credit accounts.

$$\text{Average collection period} = \frac{\text{accounts receivable}}{\text{annual credit sales}/365} = \frac{\text{accounts receivable}}{\text{daily credit sales}} \tag{4-3}$$

---

[3]When computing a given ratio that uses information from both the income statement and the balance sheet, we should remember that the income statement is for a given time period (e.g., 2010), whereas balance sheet data are at a point in time (e.g., December 31, 2010). If there has been a significant change in an asset from the beginning of the period to the end of the period, it would be better to use the average balance for the year. For example, if the accounts receivable for a company have increased from $1,000 at the beginning of the year to $2,000 at the end of the year, it would be more appropriate to use the average accounts receivable of $1,500 in our computations. Nevertheless, in an effort to simplify, we will use year-end amounts from the balance sheet in our computations.

Assuming that Davies Inc. sells entirely on credit, the firm's average collection period would be found as follows:

$$\text{Average collection period} = \frac{\text{accounts receivable}}{\text{daily credit sales}}$$

For Davies Inc.:

$$\text{Average collection period} = \frac{\$36M}{\$600M/365} = \frac{\$36M}{\$1.64M/day} = 21.95 \text{ days}$$

Peer group average collection period	25.00 days

On average Davies Inc. collects its accounts receivable in 22 days compared to 25 days for the peer group, which suggests that the firm's receivables are more liquid than those of competing firms.

We could have reached the same conclusion by measuring how many times accounts receivable are "rolled over" during a year, using the **accounts receivable turnover ratio**. If Davies Inc. collects its accounts receivable every 21.90 days, then it is collecting 16.67 times per year (16.67 times = 365 days ÷ 21.90 days). The accounts receivable turnover can also be calculated as follows:

accounts receivable turnover ratio a firm's credit sales divided by its accounts receivable. This ratio expresses how often accounts receivable are "rolled over" during a year.

$$\text{Accounts receivable turnover} = \frac{\text{annual credit sales}}{\text{accounts receivable}} \qquad (4\text{-}4)$$

For Davies Inc.:

$$\text{Accounts receivable turnover} = \frac{\$600M}{\$36M} = 16.67X$$

Peer group accounts receivable turnover	14.60X

Whether we use the average collection period or the accounts receivable turnover ratio, the conclusion is the same. Davies Inc. collects its accounts receivable more quickly than competing firms. In other words, Davies Inc.'s accounts receivable are of better quality than the peer group average.

Converting Inventories to Cash   We now want to know the quality of Davies Inc.'s inventory, as indicated by how long the inventory is held before being sold; stated differently, we want to know how many times the company is turning over its inventory during the year. **Inventory turnover** is calculated as follows:[4]

inventory turnover a firm's cost of goods sold divided by its inventory. This ratio measures the number of times a firm's inventories are sold and replaced during the year, that is, the relative liquidity of the inventories.

$$\text{Inventory turnover} = \frac{\text{cost of goods sold}}{\text{inventory}} \qquad (4\text{-}5)$$

For Davies Inc.:

$$\text{Inventory turnover} = \frac{\$460M}{\$84M} = 5.48X$$

Peer group inventory turnover	7.00X

We see that Davies Inc. is moving (turning over) its inventory more slowly than the average peer group firm—5.48 times per year at Davies Inc., compared with 7.0 times for the peer group, which suggests that the firm's inventory is less liquid than that of the peer group on average.

---

[4]Note that sales has been replaced by cost of goods sold in the numerator. Because inventory (the denominator) is measured at cost, we want to use the cost-based measure of sales in the numerator. Otherwise our answer will vary from one firm to the next solely because of differences in how each firm marks up its sales over cost. However, some of the industry norms provided by financial services are computed using sales in the numerator. In those cases, we will want to use sales in our computation of inventory turnover.

CAN YOU DO IT?

EVALUATING DISNEY'S LIQUIDITY

The following information (expressed in $ millions) is taken from the Walt Disney Company's 2008 financial statements:

Current assets	$ 11,666
Accounts receivable	5,373
Cash	3,001
Inventories	1,124
Sales	37,843
Cost of goods sold	30,439
Total current liabilities	11,591

Evaluate Disney's liquidity based on the following norms in the broadcasting and entertainment industry:

Current ratio	1.17
Acid-test ratio	0.92
Accounts receivable turnover	10.08
Inventory turnover	18.32

(The solution can be found on page 93.)

We could also express the inventory turnover in terms of the number of days of sales in inventory. Davies Inc. turns its inventory over 5.48 times per year, so on average, it is carrying its inventory for 67 days (365 days ÷ 5.48 times per year), whereas the average peer firm carries its inventory only 52 days (365 days ÷ 7.0 times per year) on average.

To conclude, the current ratio indicates that Davies Inc. is more liquid than the competing firms on average, but this result assumes that the firm's inventory are of similar quality as the competitors, which is not the case given Davies' slower inventory turnover. The acid-test ratio, on the other hand, suggests that the firm is less liquid than its competitors, but we know that Davies' accounts receivable are more liquid than the average peer group firm. So we have a mixed outcome and cannot say definitely whether Davies Inc. is more or less liquid. Judgment suggests that Davies Inc. is probably similar in its liquidity to other firms on average.

Concept Check

1. What information about the firm is provided by liquidity measures?
2. Describe the two perspectives available for measuring liquidity.
3. Why might a very high current ratio actually indicate there's a problem with a firm's inventory or accounts receivable management? What might be another reason for a high current ratio?
4. Why might a successful (liquid) firm have an acid-test ratio that is less than 1?

Question 2: Are the Firm's Managers Generating Adequate Operating Profits on the Company's Assets?

We now switch to a different dimension of performance—the firm's profitability. The question is, "Do the firm's managers produce adequate profits from the company's assets?" From the perspective of the firm's shareholders, there is no more important question to be asked. One of the most important ways managers create shareholder value is to earn strong profits on the assets in which they have invested.

To answer this all-important question, think about the process of financing a company. In its simplest form, a firm's shareholders invest in a business. The company might also borrow additional money from other sources (banks and so forth). The cumulative effects of this process are reflected in a firm's balance sheet. For example, Figure 4-2 indicates that Davies Inc.'s shareholders have invested $203 million in the company, and the company has borrowed another $235 million to finance $438 million of assets. These assets were then used to produce $75 million in operating profits.

DID YOU GET IT?
EVALUATING DISNEY'S LIQUIDITY

	DISNEY	INDUSTRY
Current ratio	1.01	1.17
Acid-test ratio	0.72	0.92
Accounts receivable turnover	7.04X	10.1X
Inventory turnover	27.08X	18.3X

Based on these results, Disney is not as liquid as the average firm in the industry! The company has less liquid assets relative to its current liabilities than do its competitors on average. Nor does the firm convert its receivables to cash as quickly as its competitors. However, Disney's inventories turn over more quickly than those of its competitors.

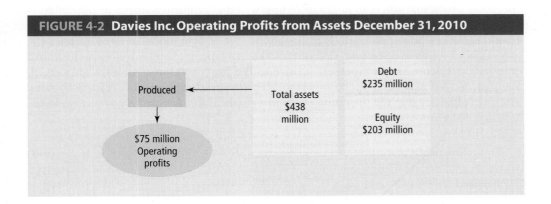

FIGURE 4-2 Davies Inc. Operating Profits from Assets December 31, 2010

Notice that we are using *operating profits* (the same as *operating income* or *earnings before interest and taxes*) rather than *net income*. Operating profits is the income generated from the firm's assets without regard to how the assets are financed. The effect of financing will be explicitly considered in the two questions that follow, but for now we want to isolate only the operating aspects of the company's profits.

To examine the level of operating profits relative to the firm's total assets, we use the **operating return on assets (OROA)**:

$$\text{Operating return on assets} = \frac{\text{operating profits}}{\text{total assets}} \qquad (4\text{-}6)$$

operating return on assets (OROA) the ratio of a firm's operating income divided by its total assets. This ratio indicates the rate of return being earned on the firm's assets.

For Davies Inc.:

$$\text{Operating return on assets} = \frac{\$75M}{\$438M} = 0.171 = 17.1\%$$

Peer group operating return on assets	17.8%

Davies Inc. is earning a slightly lower return on its assets relative to the average firm in the peer group. Managers are generating 17.1 cents of operating profits for every $1 of assets, compared to 17.8 cents on average for the peer group.

Because Davies Inc. is generating a return on the firm's assets that is less than the competition, the company's managers will want to know why the firm is not earning a competitive return on the assets. The answer lies in two areas: (1) *operations management*, which includes the day-to-day buying and selling of a firm's goods or services as reflected in the income statement, and (2) *asset management*, which relates to the balance sheet. We can relate operations management and asset management through a firm's *operating return on assets* using the product of two ratios; that is,

		OPERATIONS		ASSET MANAGEMENT	

$$\underset{\text{on assets}}{\text{Operating return}} = \underset{\text{margin}}{\text{operating profit}} \times \underset{\text{turnover}}{\text{total asset}} \qquad (4\text{-}7a)$$

which is calculated as follows:

$$\underset{\text{on assets}}{\text{Operating return}} = \frac{\text{operating profits}}{\text{sales}} \times \frac{\text{sales}}{\text{total assets}} \qquad (4\text{-}7b)$$

Managing Operations   The first component of the operating return on assets (OROA), the **operating profit margin**, is an indicator of how well the company manages its operations— that is, how well revenues are being generated and costs controlled. The operating profit margin measures how well a firm is managing its cost of operations, in terms of both the cost of goods sold and operating expenses (marketing expenses, general and administrative expenses, and depreciation expenses) relative to the firm's revenues. All else being equal, the objective for managing operations is to keep costs and expenses low relative to sales. Thus, we often say that the operating profit margin measures *how well the firm is managing its income statement.*

operating profit margin a firm's operating income (earnings before interest and taxes) divided by sales. This ratio serves as an overall measure of operating effectiveness.

$$\text{Operating profit margin} = \frac{\text{operating profits}}{\text{sales}} \qquad (4\text{-}8)$$

For Davies Inc.:

$$\text{Operating profit margin} = \frac{\$75M}{\$600M} = 0.125 = 12.5\%$$

Peer group operating profit margin	15.5%

The foregoing result clearly suggests that Davies Inc.'s managers are not as good at managing its cost of goods sold and operating expenses as comparable firms. The company has higher costs per sales dollar, which result in a lower operating profit margin. Put another way, Davies Inc. is not as good as competitors at managing its income statement.

Managing Assets   The second component in equation (4-7) is the **total asset turnover**. This ratio indicates how well the firm is managing its assets, or **asset efficiency**. It measures how efficiently a firm is using its assets to generate sales. To clarify, assume that Company A generates $3 in sales for every $1 invested in assets, whereas Company B generates the same $3 in sales but has invested $2 in assets. We can therefore conclude that Company A is using its assets more efficiently to generate sales, which leads to a higher return on the firm's investment in assets.

total asset turnover a firm's sales divided by its total assets. This ratio is an overall measure of asset efficiency based on the relation between a firm's sales and the total assets.

asset efficiency how well a firm is managing its assets.

$$\text{Total asset turnover} = \frac{\text{sales}}{\text{total assets}} \qquad (4\text{-}9)$$

For Davies Inc.:

$$\text{Total asset turnover} = \frac{\$600M}{\$438M} = 1.37X$$

Peer group total asset turnover	1.15X

Davies Inc. is using its assets more efficiently than its competitors because it generates about $1.37 in sales per dollar of assets, whereas the competition produces only $1.15 in sales per every dollar of assets.

However, we should not stop here with our analysis of Davies Inc.'s asset utilization. We have learned that, in general, Davies Inc.'s managers are making effective use of the firm's assets, but this may not be the case for each and every type of asset. So we also want to know how well the firm is managing its accounts receivable, inventories, and fixed assets, respectively.

To answer the preceding question, we examine the turnover ratios for each asset category. Of course, we already calculated the turnover ratios for the company's accounts receivable and inventories, and concluded that Davies Inc.'s managers are managing the firm's accounts receivable more efficiently than its competitors, but not its inventories. But, we still need to compute the **fixed asset turnover** as follows:

$$\text{Fixed asset turnover} = \frac{\text{sales}}{\text{net fixed assets}} \qquad (4\text{-}10)$$

fixed asset turnover a firm's sales divided by its net fixed assets. This ratio indicates how efficiently the firm is using its fixed assets.

For Davies Inc.:

$$\text{Fixed asset turnover} = \frac{\$600M}{\$295M} = 2.03X$$

Peer group fixed asset turnover	1.75X

Thus, Davies Inc. has a smaller investment in fixed assets relative to the firm's sales than the average peer group firm.

We can now look at all the asset efficiency ratios together to summarize Davies Inc.'s asset management:

	DAVIES INC.	PEER GROUP
Total asset turnover	1.37X	1.15X
Accounts receivable turnover	16.67X	14.60X
Inventory turnover	5.48X	7.00X
Fixed asset turnover	2.03X	1.75X

Davies Inc.'s situation with respect to asset management is now clear. Overall, Davies Inc.'s managers are utilizing the firm's assets efficiently, as based on the firm's total asset turnover. This overall asset efficiency results from better management of the firm's accounts

FINANCE AT WORK

MANAGING BY THE NUMBERS

Dorian S. Boyland is taking care of business as he bustles about his 29,000-square-foot Honda dealership, located in Greenfield, Wisconsin. He is preparing for a grand opening, even though the store has been open since 2001.

Boyland, 48, is excited about the festivities, but he intends to get a return on this investment. Make no mistake about it; he is meticulous about how he spends money, keeping the company's advertising and sales salaries less than 10 percent of gross profits, respectively. No more than 10 percent of gross profits are paid in commissions to managers, and no more than 15 percent of gross profits are paid in commissions to sales managers.

The auto dealer operates with one goal in mind: net a 3 percent to 3.5 percent profit on sales from all seven of his auto dealerships. "I never ask how many cars we sold," says Boyland. "I ask my sales managers how much profit did we make. I operate on the premise that if I sell a car for $20,000, I know that 3 percent (or $600) of that amount is going to go to my bottom line. Now, how

I get that 3 percent is how we operate the store—from the bottom up."

Boyland's cost controls are a never-ending process. A financial analysis is generated monthly and reviewed by all store managers. This information sharing allows every general manager and sales manager to critique one another, exchange ideas, and establish goals and guidelines.

Volume is very important to dealers because manufacturers expect them to achieve a certain level of market penetration. But as Boyland sees it, "You can be No. 1 in terms of volume, but if you are constantly losing money, you'll be taken out of business."

Boyland grows excited when discussing business strategies. "You have to have a passion for this business," he says. "There's a lot of money to be made and a lot of money to be lost. But whether you are selling cars or shoes, you go into business to make money. That's the bottom line."

Source: Carolyn M. Brown, "Maximum Overdrive," *Black Enterprise*, Vol. 33, No. 11 (June 2003), pp. 156–162. Copyright 2003 by Graves Ventures LLC.

CAN YOU DO IT?

EVALUATING DISNEY'S OPERATING RETURN ON ASSETS

Given the following financial information for the Walt Disney Company (expressed in $ millions), evaluate the firm's operating return on its assets (OROA).

Accounts receivable	$ 5,373
Inventories	1,124
Sales	37,843
Operating profits	4,427
Cost of goods sold	30,439
Net fixed assets	21,723
Total assets	62,497

The industry norms are as follows:

Operating return on assets	5.09%
Operating profit margin	11.30%
Total asset turnover	0.45X
Accounts receivable turnover	10.08X
Inventory turnover	18.32X
Fixed assets turnover	1.05X

(The solution can be found on page 98.)

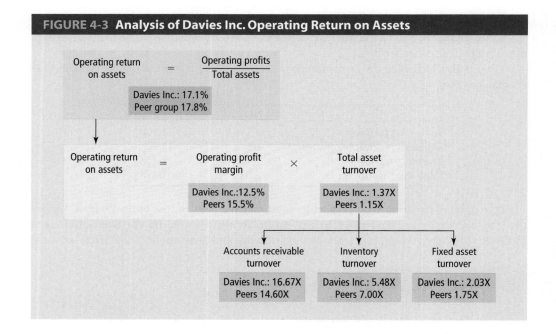

FIGURE 4-3 Analysis of Davies Inc. Operating Return on Assets

receivable and fixed assets (which have higher turnovers than the peer group), but the firm is not managing its inventories as well (which has a lower turnover than the peer group).

Figure 4-3 provides a summary of our evaluation of Davies Inc.'s operating and asset management performance. We began by computing the operating return on assets to determine if managers are producing good returns on the assets. We then broke the operating return on assets into its two pieces, operations management (operating profit margin) and asset management (asset turnover ratios), to explain why Davies Inc.'s operating return on assets is lower than the peer group.

Concept Check

1. Which number in a company's income statement should be used to measure its profitability relative to its total assets? Why?

2. What two broad areas of the firm's management does the operating return on assets assess?

3. What factors influence the operating profit margin?

4. A low total asset turnover indicates that a firm's total assets are not being managed efficiently. What additional information would you want to know when this is the case?

ETHICS IN FINANCIAL MANAGEMENT

FRAUD'S RED FLAGS

Directors and CEOs are more concerned than ever about understanding the corporate culture of their companies, and, if necessary, doing something to improve it. The consequences of lapses earlier in the decade that led to the great accounting scandals are still being felt today, both for those who are serving time in "Club Fed" and those serving on public boards.

Following are some examples of indicators that something might be amiss.

- **The old rules don't apply.** Most companies encourage creativity and value innovation. Yet when it comes to compliance with laws and regulations, and conducting business ethically, the old rules may be the best rules.
- **It seems too good to be true.** How many times do we say this or think it to ourselves? How often does it turn out that it was too good to be true?

One example is MassMutual's CEO's deferred-compensation account. According to press reports, its phenomenal success was not the result of investment acumen, but rather 20-20 hindsight in allocating portions of the account to hypothetical investments in companies whose shares had already appreciated in value.

- **We will do it just this once.** Robbing Peter to pay Paul is still robbery, and it's a slippery slope. The reports from the trials of WorldCom and HealthSouth executives contain numerous examples of this red flag.
- **Everybody else does it.** This is one of the most dangerous red flags because it is so common and it reflects an utter lack of thought about right and wrong. This is a rationale that is often used to justify accounting practices that may be technically defensible but do not result in "fair presentation" of financial results or conditions.
- **The lawyers, or accountants, said it is okay.** Here is another red flag that was apparently flown at Enron and WorldCom. You can just imagine how many times at each of these companies some senior or middle manager was told that something was okay because the attorneys, auditors, or boss said so. Yet, in many cases, the person asked to falsify the financial records or pass judgment on the special-purpose corporations knew better.
- **Conflicts of interest.** Dozens of companies have suffered serious scandals and shareholder revolt because management has had financial interests in enterprises that do business with, or compete against, their company. Just consider the "special-purpose entities" at Enron that created conflicts of interest for the company's CFO Andrew Fastow.
- **Too many euphemisms.** Labels are important. Would we eat as much sushi if it were called "raw fish," carpaccio if it were called "raw beef," or sweetbreads if they were called "organ meat"? The same idea is at work in the business world.

One of the recent reminders of the dangers of euphemisms is the Hewlett-Packard scandal over the investigation by the chairman of the board of outside directors' alleged leaks of confidential information. It seems unlikely that the company officers who were involved would have proceeded with "pretexting" if it were called "obtaining private, personal information under false pretenses."

Source: Excerpts from Michael Ross, "Fraud's Red Flags," *Directorship*, July 25, 2008, http://www.businessweek.com/managing/content/jul2008/ca20080725_953586.htm, accessed June 4, 2009.

Question 3: How Is the Firm Financing Its Assets?

We now turn to the matter of how a firm is financed. (We will return to the issue of profitability shortly.) Is it financed through debt or equity? To answer this question, we use two ratios. First, we ask *what percentage of the firm's assets is financed by debt*, including both short-term and long-term debt, realizing that the remaining percentage must be financed by equity. We compute the **debt ratio** as follows:[5]

$$\text{Debt ratio} = \frac{\text{total debt}}{\text{total assets}} \qquad (4\text{-}11)$$

For Davies Inc.:

$$\text{Debt ratio} = \frac{\$235\text{M}}{\$438\text{M}} = 0.54 = 54\%$$

Peer group debt ratio	35%

debt ratio a firm's total liabilities divided by its total assets. This ratio measures the extent to which a firm has been financed with debt.

---

[5]Instead of using the debt ratio, we could use the debt–equity ratio. The debt–equity ratio is simply a transformation of the debt ratio:

$$\text{Debt–equity ratio} = \frac{\text{total debt}}{\text{total equity}} = \frac{\text{debt ratio}}{1 - \text{debt ratio}} \text{ and the debt ratio} = \frac{\text{debt/equity}}{1 + \text{debt/equity}}$$

DID YOU GET IT?

EVALUATING DISNEY'S OPERATING RETURN ON ASSETS

Disney generates a higher return on its assets than the average firm in the industry, 7.08 percent compared to 5.09 percent on average for the industry. Disney provided a higher operating return on its assets, both by managing its operations better (achieving a slightly higher operating profit margin) and by making better use of its assets. The company's higher total asset turnover is due to a higher fixed asset and inventory turnover, which makes up for the less efficient management of the firm's accounts receivable, which have a lower turnover.

	DISNEY	INDUSTRY
Operating return on assets	7.08%	5.09%
Operating profit margin	11.69%	11.30%
Total asset turnover	0.61	0.45X
Accounts receivable turnover	7.04X	10.08X
Inventory turnover	27.08X	18.32X
Fixed assets turnover	1.74X	1.05X

Davies Inc. finances 54 percent of its assets with debt (taken from Davies Inc.'s balance sheet in Table 4-2), compared with the peer group average of 35 percent. Stated differently, Davies Inc. finances with 46 percent equity, whereas the average for the peer group is 65 percent equity. Thus, Davies Inc. uses significantly more debt than the peer group average. As we will see at several points in our study, more debt financing results in more financial risk.

Our second perspective regarding the firm's financing decisions comes by looking at the income statement. When the firm borrows money, it must at least pay the interest on what it has borrowed. Thus, it is informative to compare (1) the amount of operating income that is available to pay the interest with (2) the amount of interest that has to be paid. Stated as a ratio, we compute the number of times we are earning our interest. The **times interest earned** ratio is commonly used when examining a firm's debt position and is computed in the following manner:

> **times interest earned** a firm's earnings before interest and taxes (EBIT) divided by interest expense. This ratio measures a firm's ability to meet its interest payments from its annual operating earnings.

$$\text{Times interest earned} = \frac{\text{operating profits}}{\text{interest expense}} \tag{4-12}$$

For Davies Inc.:

$$\text{Times interest earned} = \frac{\$75M}{\$15M} = 5.0X$$

Peer group times interest earned   7.0X

Davies Inc.'s interest expense is $15 million, which when compared to its operating income of $75 million, indicates that its interest expense is consuming 1/5 (20.0%) of its operating profits compared to 1/7 (14.29%) for the average peer group firm.

Why would Davies Inc. have a lower times interest earned ratio than the peer group? For one thing, Davies Inc. uses significantly more debt than the average company in the peer group, which leads to more interest expense. Second, its operating return on assets is slightly less than competitors, which means the firm has less operating income to cover the interest.

Before concluding our discussion regarding times interest earned, we should understand that interest is not paid with income but with cash. Moreover, in addition to the interest that must be paid, the firm might be required to repay some of the debt principal. Thus, the times interest earned ratio is only a crude measure of the firm's capacity to service its debt. Nevertheless, it does give us a general indication of a company's financial risk and its capacity to borrow.

CAN YOU DO IT?

EVALUATING DISNEY'S FINANCING DECISIONS

Given the information to the right (expressed in $ millions) for the Disney Corporation, calculate the firm's debt ratio and the times interest earned. How do Disney's ratios compare to those of the industry in which it operates? What are the implications of your findings?

Total debt	$30,174
Total common equity	
Common stock	3,991
Retained earnings	28,332
Total liabilities and equity	62,497
Operating profits	4,427
Interest expense	524
Industry norms:	
Debt ratio	34.21%
Times interest earned	4.50X

(The solution can be found on page 100.)

Concept Check

1. What information is provided by the debt ratio?

2. Why is it important to calculate the times interest earned ratio, even for firms that have low debt ratios?

3. Why does operating income not give a complete picture of a firm's ability to service its debt?

Question 4: Are the Firm's Managers Providing a Good Return on the Capital Provided by the Company's Shareholders?

We now want to look at the *accounting return on the common stockholders' investment*, or the **return on equity** (frequently shortened to ROE). We want to know if the earnings available to the firm's owners (shareholders) are attractive when compared with the returns earned for the owners of companies in the peer group. We measure the return on equity (ROE) as follows:

return on equity a firm's net income divided by its common book equity. This ratio is the accounting rate of return earned on the common stockholders' investment.

$$\text{Return on equity} = \frac{\text{net income}}{\text{common equity}} \qquad (4\text{-}13)$$

For Davies Inc.:

$$\text{Return on equity} = \frac{\$42M}{\$203M} = 0.207 = 20.7\%$$

Peer group return on equity	18.0%

In the preceding computation, the common equity includes all common equity in the balance sheet, including both common stock and retained earnings. (Understand that profits retained within the business are as much of an investment for the common stockholders as when the shareholders bought the company's stock.)

The return on equity for Davies Inc. and the peer group are 20.7 percent and 18.0 percent, respectively. Hence, the owners of Davies Inc. are receiving a higher return on their equity investment than the shareholders in the peer group firms on average. How are they doing it? To answer, we need to draw on what we have already learned, namely, that:

1. Davies Inc. is receiving a lower operating return on its assets. We learned earlier that the operating return on assets was 17.1 percent for Davies Inc., compared to 17.8 percent for the competition. A lower (higher) return on the firm's assets will always result in a lower (higher) return on equity.

DID YOU GET IT?
EVALUATING DISNEY'S FINANCING DECISIONS

A comparison of Disney's debt ratio and times interest earned with the industry is as follows:

	DISNEY	INDUSTRY
Debt ratio	48.28%	34.21%
Times interest earned	8.45X	4.50X

Disney uses significantly more debt financing than the average firm in the industry. The higher debt ratio implies that the firm has greater financial risk. Even so, Disney appears to have no difficulty servicing its debt, covering its interest 8.45 times compared only to 4.50 times for the average firm in the industry. Disney's higher times interest earned is attributable to a significantly higher operating return on assets, which more than offsets the higher debt ratio.

2. Davies Inc. uses significantly more debt (less equity) financing than the average firm in the industry—54 percent debt for Davies Inc. and 35 percent debt for the peer group. As we will see shortly, the more debt a firm uses, the higher its return on equity will be, provided that the firm is earning a return on assets greater than the interest rate on its debt. Conversely, the less debt a firm uses, the lower its return on equity will be (again, provided that the firm is earning a return on assets greater than the interest rate on its debt). Thus, Davies Inc. has increased its return for its shareholders by using more debt. That's the good news. The bad news for Davies Inc.'s shareholders is that the more debt a firm uses, the greater is the company's financial risk, which translates into more risk for the shareholders.

To help us understand the foregoing reason for Davies Inc.'s higher return on equity and its implications, consider the following example.

EXAMPLE 4.1

Firms A and B are identical in size. Both have $1,000 in total assets, and both have an operating return on assets of 14 percent. However, they are different in one respect: Firm A uses all equity and no debt financing; Firm B finances 60 percent of its investments with debt and 40 percent with equity. (For the sake of simplicity, we will assume that both firms pay interest at an interest cost of 6 percent, and there are no income taxes.) The financial statements for the two companies would be as follows:

	FIRM A	FIRM B
BALANCE SHEET		
Total assets	$1,000	$1,000
Debt (6% interest rate)	$ 0	$ 600
Equity	1,000	400
Total debt and equity	$1,000	$1,000
INCOME STATEMENT		
Operating income (OROA = 14%)	$ 140	$ 140
Interest expense (6%)	(0)	(36)
Net income	$ 140	$ 104

Computing the return on equity for both companies, we see that Firm B has a more attractive return of 26 percent compared with Firm A's 14 percent. The calculations are as follows:

			FIRM A	FIRM B
Return on common equity	$=$	net income / common equity	$= \dfrac{\$140}{\$1,000} = 14\%$	$\dfrac{\$104}{\$400} = 26\%$

Why the difference? The answer is straightforward. Firm B is earning 14 percent on all of its $1,000 in assets, but only having to pay 6 percent to the lenders on the $600 debt principal. The difference between the 14 percent return on the firm's assets (operating return on assets) and the 6 percent interest rate goes to the owners, thus boosting Firm B's return on equity above that of Firm A.

This is an illustration of favorable financial leverage. What's favorable, you might ask? Well, you earn 14 percent on your investments while paying only 6 percent to the bankers, thus capturing an 8 percent spread on each dollar of debt financing. The result is an increase in the return on equity to Firm B when compared to Firm A. What a great deal for Firm B's shareholders! So if debt enhances owners' returns, why doesn't Firm A borrow money or Firm B borrow even more money?

The good outcome for Firm B shareholders is based on the assumption that the firm does in fact earn 14 percent operating return on the assets. But what if the economy falls into a deep recession, business declines sharply, and Firms A and B only earn a 2 percent operating return on their assets? Let's recompute the return on equity given the new conditions:

	FIRM A	FIRM B
Operating income (OROA = 2%)	$ 20	$ 20
Less interest expense	(0)	(36)
Net income	$ 20	($ 16)
Return on equity:		
net income / common equity	$ 20 / $1,000	($ 16) / $ 400
Equals:	2%	−4%

Now the use of financial leverage has a negative influence on the return on equity, with Firm B earning less than Firm A for its owners. This results from Firm B earning less than the interest rate of 6 percent; consequently, the equity investors have to make up the difference. Thus, financial leverage is a two-edged sword; when times are good, financial leverage can make them very, very good, but when times are bad, financial leverage makes them very, very bad. Financial leverage can enhance the returns of the equity investors, but it also increases the possibility of losses, thereby increasing the uncertainty, or risk, for the owners. Chapter 12 will address financial leverage in greater detail.

Figure 4-4 on the next page provides a summary of our discussion of the return on equity relative to Davies Inc. and helps us visualize the two fundamental factors affecting a firm's return on equity:

1. There is a direct relationship between a firm's operating return on assets (OROA) and the resulting return on equity (ROE). As we have explained, the higher the

operating return on assets (OROA), the higher will be the return on equity (ROE). Even more precisely, the greater the difference between the firm's operating return on assets (OROA) and the interest rate (i) being paid on the firm's debt, the higher the return on equity will be. So increasing the operating return on assets relative to the interest rate (OROA-i) increases the return on equity (ROE). But if OROA-i decreases, then ROE will decrease as well.

2. Increasing the amount of debt financing relative to the amount of equity (increasing the debt ratio) increases the return on equity if the operating return on assets is higher than the interest rate being paid. If the operating return on assets falls below the interest rate, more debt financing will decrease the return on equity.

In short, the return on equity is driven by (1) the spread between the operating return on assets and the interest rate (OROA-i) and (2) changes in the debt ratio.

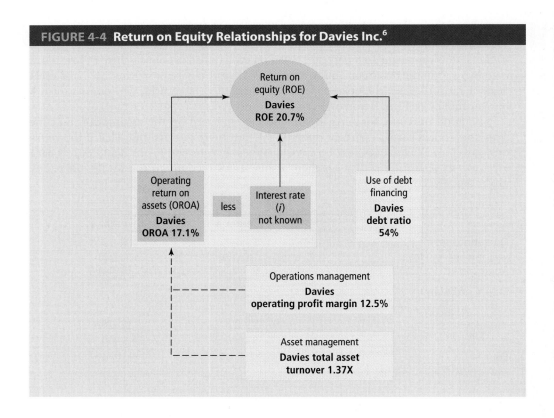

FIGURE 4-4 Return on Equity Relationships for Davies Inc.[6]

CAN YOU DO IT?

EVALUATING DISNEY'S RETURN ON EQUITY

The net income and also the common equity invested by Disney's shareholders (expressed in $ millions) are provided here, along with the average return on equity for the industry. Evaluate the rate of return being earned on the common stockholders' equity investment. In addition to comparing the Disney Corporation's return on equity to the industry, consider the implications Disney's operating return on assets and its debt financing practices have on the firm's return on equity.

Net income	$4,427
Common equity	
Common stock	3,991
Retained earnings	28,332
Industry average return on equity	4.31%

(The solution can be found on page 103.)

(The solution can be found on page 103.)

[6]This figure is a modified format of the "DuPont Analysis."

Concept Check

1. How is a company's return on equity related to the firm's operating return on assets?
2. How is a company's return on equity related to the firm's debt ratio?
3. What is the upside of debt financing? What is the downside?

DID YOU GET IT?
EVALUATING DISNEY'S RETURN ON EQUITY

Disney's return on equity is 13.7 percent (13.7% = $4,427 million net income/$32,323 million common equity), compared to 4.31 percent for the industry average. Disney's return on equity is due to the firm having a higher operating return on assets and using a lot more debt financing than the average firm in the industry.

Question 5: Are the Firm's Managers Creating Shareholder Value?

To this point, we have relied exclusively on accounting data to assess the performance of a firm's managers. We now want to look at management's performance in terms of creating or destroying shareholder value. To answer this question, we use two approaches: (1) We examine market-value ratios, and (2) we estimate the value being created for shareholders, as measured by a popular technique called Economic Value Added (EVA™).

Market-Value Ratios   There are two commonly used ratios that compare the firm's stock price to the firm's earnings and the accounting book value of the equity. These two ratios indicate what investors think of management's past performance and future prospects.

Price/Earnings Ratio   The **price/earnings** (P/E) **ratio** indicates how much investors are willing to pay for $1 of reported earnings. Returning to Davies Inc., the firm had net income in 2010 of $42 million and 20 million shares of common stock outstanding. (See Table 4-1.) Accordingly, its earnings per share were $2.10 ($2.10 = $42 million net income ÷ 20 million shares). At the time, the firm's stock was selling for $32 per share. Thus, the price/earnings ratio was 15.24 times, calculated as follows:

price/earnings ratio the price the market places on $1 of a firm's earnings. For example, if a firm has an earnings per share of $2, and a stock price of $30 per share, its price/earnings ratio is 15 ($30 ÷ $2).

$$\text{Price/earnings ratio} = \frac{\text{price per share}}{\text{earnings per share}} \qquad (4\text{-}14)$$

For Davies Inc.:

$$\text{Price/earning ratio} = \frac{\$32.00}{\$2.10} = 15.24\text{X}$$

Peer group average price/earnings ratio 19.0X

Davies Inc.'s price/earnings ratio tells us that the investors were willing to pay $15.24 for every dollar of earnings per share that Davies Inc. produced, compared to an average price/earnings ratio of 19 times for the firms making up the peer group. Thus, investors were not willing to pay as much for Davies Inc.'s earnings as were shareholders of the average peer group firm. Why might that be? The price/earnings ratio will be higher for companies that investors think have strong earnings growth prospects with less risk. Thus, investors must perceive Davies Inc. to have less growth potential and/or greater risk compared to the average company in the peer group.

Price/Book Ratio   A second frequently used indicator of investors' assessment of the firm is its **price/book ratio**. This ratio compares the market value of a share of stock to the book

price/book ratio the market value of a share of the firm's stock divided by the book value per share of the firm's reported equity in the balance sheet.

CAN YOU DO IT?
COMPUTING DISNEY'S PRICE/EARNINGS RATIO AND PRICE/BOOK RATIO

Disney's stock was selling for $23, while its net income was $4.427 billion ($4,427 million) and its common equity in the balance sheet (book equity) was $32.323 billion ($32,323 million). There were 1.823 billion shares outstanding. What was the firm's earnings per share and its book value per share? Calculate the price/earnings ratio and the price/book ratio. The average firm in the industry sold for 11 times earnings and 1.6 times book value. What do the shareholders think about the firm's performance and future growth prospects?
    (The solution can be found on page 105.)

value per share of the firm's reported equity in its balance sheet. We already know that the market price of Davies Inc.'s common stock was $32. To determine the equity book value per share, we divide the firm's equity book value by the number of shares of stock outstanding. From Davies Inc.'s balance sheet (Table 4-2), we see that the equity book value was $203 million (including both common stock and retained earnings). Given that Davies Inc. had 20 million shares outstanding, the equity book value per share is $10.15 ($10.15 = $203 million book equity value ÷ 20 million shares). With this information, we determine the price/book ratio to be:

$$\text{Price/book ratio} = \frac{\text{market price per share}}{\text{equity book value per share}} \qquad (4\text{-}15)$$

For Davies Inc.:

$$\text{Price/book ratio} = \frac{\$32.00}{\$10.15} = 3.15X$$

Peer group 500 price/book ratio 3.7X

Given that the book value per share is an accounting number that reflects historical costs, we can roughly think of it as the amount shareholders have invested in the business over its lifetime. So, a ratio greater than 1 indicates that investors believe the firm is more valuable than the amount shareholders have invested in it. Conversely, a ratio less than 1 suggests that investors do not believe the stock is worth the amount shareholders have invested in it. Clearly, investors believe the stock of Davies Inc. is now worth more than shareholders paid, because they are now paying $3.15 for each dollar of book value. In comparison, the average firm in the peer group was selling for $3.70 for every $1 in book equity. Again, the investors are signaling that they believe that Davies Inc. has less growth prospects relative to its riskiness.

Economic Value Added (EVA™)   The price/book ratio, as just described, indicates whether the shareholders value the firm's equity above or below the amount of capital they originally invested. If the firm's market value is above the accounting book value (price/book > 1), then management has created value for shareholders, but if the firm's market value is below book value (price/book < 1), then management has destroyed shareholder value.

How is shareholder value created or destroyed? Quite simply, shareholder value is created when a firm earns a rate of return on the capital invested that is greater than the investors' required rate of return. If we invest in a firm and have a 12 percent required rate of return, and the firm earns 15 percent on our capital, then the firm's managers have created value for investors. If instead, the firm earns only 10 percent, then value has been destroyed. This concept is regularly applied by firms when they decide whether or not to make large capital investments in plant and equipment; however, it has not been generally applied to the analysis of a firm's day-to-day operating results. Instead, managers have traditionally focused on accounting results, such as earnings growth, profit margins, and the return on equity.

DID YOU GET IT?

COMPUTING DISNEY'S PRICE/EARNINGS RATIO AND PRICE/BOOK RATIO

We compute Disney's price/earnings ratio and price/book ratio as follows:

$$\text{Earnings per share} = \frac{\text{net income}}{\text{number of shares}}$$

$$= \frac{4.427 \text{ billion}}{1.823 \text{ billion shares}} = \$2.43$$

$$\text{Equity book value per share} = \frac{\text{common equity}}{\text{number of shares}}$$

$$= \frac{\$32.323 \text{ billion}}{1.823 \text{ billion shares}} = \$17.73$$

$$\text{Price/earnings ratio} = \frac{\text{market price per share}}{\text{earning per share}} = \frac{\$23}{\$2.43} = 9.47$$

$$\text{Price/book ratio} = \frac{\text{market price per share}}{\text{equity book value per share}}$$

$$= \frac{\$23}{\$17.73} = 1.30$$

Disney's stock is selling for 9.47 times its earnings and 1.30 times its book value. At the same time, the average firm in the industry was selling for 11 times its earnings and 1.6 times its book value. Thus, investors see Disney as having lower growth prospects and/or greater risk.

More recently, however, people have begun assessing whether or not a firm's managers are creating shareholder value and then linking this assessment to managers' compensation, mostly through bonuses. Although several techniques have been developed for making this assessment, the one that has received the most attention is Economic Value Added (EVA™).

Economic Value Added is a financial performance measure developed by the investment consulting firm, Stern Stewart & Co. EVA attempts to measure a firm's economic profit, rather than accounting profit, in a given year. Economic profits assign a cost to the equity capital (the opportunity cost of the funds provided by the shareholders) in addition to the interest cost on the firm's debt—even though accountants recognize only the interest expense as a financing cost when calculating a firm's net income.

For example, assume a firm has total assets of $1,000; 40 percent ($400) is financed with debt, and 60 percent ($600) is financed with equity. If the interest rate on the debt is 5 percent, the firm's interest expense is $20 ($20 = $400 × 0.05) and would be reported in the firm's income statement. However, there would be no cost shown for the equity financing. To compute economic profits, we compute not only the $20 in interest expense but also the opportunity cost of the $600 equity capital invested in the firm. That is, if the shareholders could earn 15 percent on another investment of similar risk (their opportunity cost is, therefore, 15 percent), then we should count this cost just as surely as we do the interest expense. This would involve subtracting not only the $20 in interest but also $90 ($90 = $600 equity × 0.15) as the cost of equity. Thus, the firm has earned an economic profit only if its operating profit exceeds $110 ($20 + $90). Stated as a percentage, the firm must earn at least an 11 percent operating return on its assets (11% = $110 ÷ $1,000) in order to meet the investors' required rate of return.

We can calculate Economic Value Added (EVA)—the value created for the shareholders for a given year—as follows:

$$\text{EVA} = \left(\begin{matrix} \text{operating return} \\ \text{on assets} \end{matrix} - \begin{matrix} \text{cost of} \\ \text{all capital} \end{matrix} \right) \times \text{total assets} \qquad (4\text{-}16)$$

where the cost of capital is the cost of all the firm's capital, both debt and equity. That is, the value created by management is determined by the amount the firm earns on its invested capital relative to the cost of these funds—both debt and equity—and the amount of capital invested in the firm, which are the total assets.[7]

---

[7]In Chapter 9, we will explain how the firm's cost of capital is calculated.

TABLE 4-3 Davies Inc. Financial Ratio Analysis

FINANCIAL RATIOS		DAVIES INC.	PEER GROUP
1. FIRM LIQUIDITY			
Current ratio	$\dfrac{\text{Current assets}}{\text{Current liabilities}}$	$\dfrac{\$143M}{\$64M}=2.23$	1.80
Acid-test ratio	$\dfrac{\text{Cash + Accounts Receivable}}{\text{Current liabilities}}$	$\dfrac{\$20M+\$36M}{\$64M}=.88$	.94
Average collection period	$\dfrac{\text{Accounts receivable}}{\text{Daily credit sales}}$	$\dfrac{\$36M}{\$600M \div 365}=21.90$	25
Accounts receivable turnover	$\dfrac{\text{Credit sales}}{\text{Accounts receivable}}$	$\dfrac{\$600M}{\$36M}=16.67$	14.6
Inventory turnover	$\dfrac{\text{Cost of goods sold}}{\text{Inventory}}$	$\dfrac{\$460M}{\$84M}=5.48$	7.00
2. OPERATING PROFITABILITY			
Operating return on assets	$\dfrac{\text{Operating profit}}{\text{Total assets}}$	$\dfrac{\$75M}{\$438M}=17.1\%$	17.8
Operating profit margin	$\dfrac{\text{Operating profit}}{\text{Sales}}$	$\dfrac{\$75M}{\$600M}=12.5\%$	15.5
Total asset turnover	$\dfrac{\text{Sales}}{\text{Total assets}}$	$\dfrac{\$600M}{\$438M}=1.37$	1.15
Accounts receivable turnover	$\dfrac{\text{Credit sales}}{\text{Accounts receivable}}$	$\dfrac{\$600M}{\$36M}=16.67$	14.6
Inventory turnover	$\dfrac{\text{Cost of goods sold}}{\text{Inventory}}$	$\dfrac{\$460M}{\$84M}=5.48$	7.00
Fixed assets turnover	$\dfrac{\text{Sales}}{\text{Fixed assets}}$	$\dfrac{\$600M}{\$295M}=2.03$	1.75
3. FINANCING DECISIONS			
Debt ratio	$\dfrac{\text{Total debt}}{\text{Total assets}}$	$\dfrac{\$235M}{\$438M}=53.7\%$	35%
Times interest earned	$\dfrac{\text{Operating income}}{\text{Interest expense}}$	$\dfrac{\$75M}{\$15M}=5.0X$	7.0X
4. RETURN ON EQUITY			
Return on equity	$\dfrac{\text{Net income}}{\text{Common equity}}$	$\dfrac{\$42M}{\$203M}=20.7\%$	18%
5. MARKET-VALUE RATIOS			
Price/earnings ratio	$\dfrac{\text{Market price per share}}{\text{Earnings per share}}$	$\dfrac{\$32.00}{\$2.10}=15.24X$	19.0X
Price/book ratio	$\dfrac{\text{Market price per share}}{\text{Equity book value per share}}$	$\dfrac{\$32.00}{\$10.15}=3.15X$	3.7X

CAN YOU DO IT?

CALCULATING DISNEY'S ECONOMIC VALUE ADDED

Earlier in the chapter, we determined that Disney's operating return on assets (OROA) was 7.08 percent. If Disney's cost of capital (the cost of both its debt and equity capital) was 10 percent at that time, what was the Economic Value Added for the firm when its total assets were approximately $62.497 billion?

(The solution can be found on page 108.)

Continuing with our previous example, assume that our company is earning a 16 percent operating return on its assets (total invested capital). Then the firm's economic value added is $50, calculated as follows:

$$\text{EVA} = \left(\begin{array}{cc} \text{operating return} & \text{cost of} \\ \text{on assets} & \text{all capital} \end{array} \right) \times \text{total assets}$$

$$\text{EVA} = (0.16 - 0.11) \times \$1000 = \$50$$

The foregoing explains the EVA concept in its simplest form. However, computing EVA requires converting a firm's financial statements from an accountant's perspective (GAAP) to an economic book value. This process is much more involved than we will go into here, but the basic premise involved in its computation is the same.

To conclude, with the exception of Economic Value Added, a summary of all the ratios we used to analyze the financial performance of Davies Inc. is provided in Table 4-3.

Concept Check

1. What determines if a firm is creating or destroying shareholder value?
2. What measures can we use to determine whether a firm is creating shareholder value?
3. What is indicated by a price/book ratio that is greater than 1? Less than 1?
4. How does the information provided by a firm's price/book ratio differ from that provided by its price/earnings ratio?
5. How do the profits shown in an income statement differ from economic profits?
6. What is Economic Value Added? What does it tell you?

The Limitations of Financial Ratio Analysis

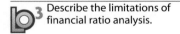 Describe the limitations of financial ratio analysis.

We conclude this chapter by offering several caveats about using financial ratios. We have described how financial ratios can be used to understand a company's financial position. That said, anyone who works with these ratios needs to be aware of the limitations related to their use. The following list includes some of the more important pitfalls you will encounter as you compute and interpret financial ratios:

1. It is sometimes difficult to determine the industry to which a firm belongs when the firm engages in multiple lines of business. In this case, you must select your own set of peer firms and construct your own norms.
2. Published peer group or industry averages are only approximations. They provide the user with general guidelines, rather than scientifically determined averages of the ratios for all, or even a representative sample, of the firms within an industry.
3. An industry average is not necessarily a desirable target ratio or norm. There is nothing magical about an industry norm. At best, an industry average provides an indication as to the financial position of the average firm within the industry. It does not mean it is the ideal or best value for the ratio. For various reasons, a well-managed company might be above the average, whereas another equally good firm might choose to be below the average.

DID YOU GET IT?
CALCULATING DISNEY'S ECONOMIC VALUE ADDED

Disney's Economic Value Added (EVA) is calculated as follows:

$$EVA = \left(\begin{array}{c} \text{operating return} \\ \text{on assets} \end{array} - \begin{array}{c} \text{cost of} \\ \text{all capital} \end{array} \right) \times \text{total assets}$$

$$= (7.08\% - 10\%) \times \$62.497 \text{ billion} = (\$1.824 \text{ billion})$$

Wow! In the year we are calculating Disney's EVA, 2008, the firm destroyed $1.824 billion in shareholder value by earning a rate of return on the firm's assets that was less than the investors' required rate of return.

4. Accounting practices differ widely among firms. For example, different firms choose different methods to depreciate their fixed assets. Differences such as these can make the computed ratios of different firms difficult to compare.

5. Financial ratios can be too high or too low. For example, a current ratio that exceeds the industry norm might signal the presence of excess liquidity, resulting in lower profits relative to the firm's investment in assets. On the other hand, a current ratio that falls below the norm might indicate (1) the possibility that the firm has inadequate liquidity and may at some future date be unable to pay its bills on time, or (2) the firm is managing its accounts receivable and inventories more efficiently than other similar firms.

6. Many firms experience seasonal changes in their operations. As a result, their balance sheet entries and their corresponding ratios will vary with the time of year the statements are prepared. To avoid this problem, an average account balance should be used (one calculated on the basis of several months or quarters during the year) rather than the year-end account balance. For example, an average of the firm's month-end inventory balance might be used to compute its inventory turnover ratio versus a year-end inventory balance.

In spite of their limitations, financial ratios provide us with a very useful tool for assessing a firm's financial condition. We should, however, be aware of their potential weaknesses. In many cases, the "real" value derived from the ratios is that they tell us what additional questions we need to ask about the firm.

Concept Check

1. When comparing a firm to its peers, why is it difficult to determine the industry to which the firm belongs?

2. Why do differences in the accounting practices of firms limit the usefulness of financial ratios?

3. Why should you be careful when comparing a firm with industry norms?

 Explain the purpose and importance of financial analysis.

 Calculate and use a comprehensive set of measurements to evaluate a company's performance.

Summary

A variety of groups find financial ratios useful. For instance, both managers and shareholders use them to measure and track a company's performance over time. Financial analysts outside of the firm who have an interest in its economic well-being also use financial ratios. An example of this group would be a loan officer of a commercial bank who wishes to determine the creditworthiness of a loan applicant and its ability to pay the interest and principal associated with the loan request.

Financial ratios are the principal tool of financial analysis. Sometimes referred to simply as benchmarks, ratios standardize the financial information of firms so comparisons can be made between firms of varying sizes.

Financial ratios can be used to answer at least five questions: (1) How liquid is the company? (2) Are the company's managers effectively generating profits on the firm's assets? (3) How is the firm financed? (4) Are the firm's managers providing a good return on the capital provided by the shareholders? (5) Are the firm's managers creating or destroying shareholder value?

Two methods can be used to analyze a firm's financial ratios. (1) We can examine the firm's ratios across time (say, for the past 5 years) to compare its current and past performance; and (2) we can compare the firm's ratios with those of other firms. In our example, a peer group was chosen for analyzing the financial position of Davies Inc.

Financial ratios provide a popular way to evaluate a firm's financial performance. However, when evaluating a company's use of its assets (capital) to create firm value, a financial ratio analysis based entirely on the firm's financial statements may not be enough. If we want to understand how the shareholders assess the performance of a company's managers, we can use the market price of the firm's stock relative to its accounting earnings and equity book value.

Economic Value Added (EVA™) provides another approach to evaluate a firm's performance in terms of shareholder value creation. EVA is equal to the return on a company's invested capital less the investors' opportunity cost of the funds times the total amount of the capital invested.

 3 Describe the limitations of financial ratio analysis.

The following are some of the limitations that you will encounter as you compute and interpret financial ratios:

1. It is sometimes difficult to determine an appropriate industry within which to place the firm.
2. Published industry averages are only approximations rather than scientifically determined averages.
3. Accounting practices differ widely among firms and can lead to differences in computed ratios.
4. Some financial ratios can be too high or too low, which makes the results more difficult to interpret.
5. An industry average may not be a desirable target ratio or norm.
6. Many firms experience seasonal business conditions. As a result, the ratios calculated for them will vary with the time of year the statements are prepared.

In spite of their limitations, financial ratios provide us with a very useful tool for assessing a firm's financial condition.

Key Terms

Accounts receivable turnover ratio   91

Acid-test (quick) ratio   90

Asset efficiency   94

Average collection period   90

Current ratio   89

Debt ratio   97

Financial ratios   86

Fixed asset turnover   95

Inventory turnover   91

Liquidity   89

Operating profit margin   94

Operating return on assets (OROA)   93

Price/book ratio   103

Price/earnings ratio   103

Return on equity   99

Times interest earned   98

Total asset turnover   94

Review Questions

All Review Questions and Study Problems are available in MyFinanceLab.

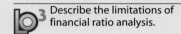

4-1. Describe the "five-question approach" to using financial ratios.

4-2. Discuss briefly the two perspectives that can be taken when performing a ratio analysis.

4-3. Where can we obtain industry norms?

4-4. What are the limitations of industry average ratios? Discuss briefly.

4-5. What is liquidity, and what is the rationale for its measurement?

4-6. Distinguish between a firm's operating return on assets and operating profit margin.

4-7. Why is a firm's operating return on assets a function of its operating profit margin and total asset turnover?

4-8. What is the difference between a firm's gross profit margin, operating profit margin, and net profit margin?

4-9. What information do the price/earnings ratio and the price/book ratio give us about the firm and its investors?

4-10. Explain what determines a company's return on equity.

4-11. What is Economic Value Added? Why is it used?

4-12. Go to the Web site for IBM at www.ibm.com/investor. Click "Investor tools" and then "Investment guides" for a guide to reading financial statements. How does the guide differ from the presentation in Chapter 3 and this chapter?

Self-Test Problems

ST-1. (*Ratio analysis and short-term liquidity*) Ray's Tool and Supply Company in Austin, Texas, has been expanding its level of operation for the past 2 years. The firm's sales have grown rapidly as a result of the expansion of the Austin economy. However, Ray's is a privately held company, and the only source of available funds is a line of credit with the firm's bank. The company needs to expand its inventories to meet the needs of its growing customer base but also wishes to maintain a current ratio of at least 3. If Ray's current assets are $6 million, and its current ratio is now 4, how much can it expand its inventories (finance the expansion with its line of credit) before its target current ratio is violated?

ST-2. (*Ratio analysis*) The statements for M & G Industries are presented below:

M & G Industries Balance Sheet for December 31, 2009 and 2010

		2009		2010
Cash		$ 9,000		$ 500
Accounts receivable		12,500		16,000
Inventories		29,000		45,500
Total current assets		$ 50,500		$ 62,000
Land	20,000		26,000	
Buildings and equipment	70,000		100,000	
Less accumulated depreciation	(28,000)		(38,000)	
Total fixed assets		$ 62,000		$ 88,000
Total assets		$ 112,500		$150,000
Accounts payable		$ 10,500		$ 22,000
Short-term bank notes		17,000		47,000
Total current liabilities		$ 27,500		$ 69,000
Long-term debt		28,750		22,950
Common stock		31,500		31,500
Retained earnings		24,750		26,550
Total debt and equity		$ 112,500		$150,000

M & G Industries Income Statement for the Years Ended December 31, 2009 and 2010

		2009		2010
Sales (all credit)		$125,000		$160,000
Cost of goods sold		75,000		96,000
Gross profit		$ 50,000		$ 64,000
Operating expenses				
Fixed cash operating expenses	$ 21,000		$ 21,000	
Variable operating expenses	$ 12,500		16,000	
Depreciation	4,500		10,000	
Total operating expenses		$ 38,000		$ 47,000
Earnings before interest and taxes		$ 12,000		$ 17,000
Interest expense		$ 3,000		$ 6,100
Earnings before taxes		$ 9,000		10,900
Taxes		$ 4,500		$ 5,450
Net income		$ 4,500		$ 5,450

a. Based on the preceding statements, complete the following table:

M & G Industries Ratio Analysis

	INDUSTRY AVERAGES	ACTUAL 2009	ACTUAL 2010
Current ratio	1.80		
Acid-test ratio	0.70		
Average collection period	37.00		
Inventory turnover	2.50		
Debt ratio	58.0%		
Times interest earned	3.80		
Operating profit margin	10.0%		
Total asset turnover	1.14		
Fixed asset turnover	1.40		
Operating return on assets	11.4%		
Return on common equity	9.5%		

b. Evaluate the firm's financial position at the end of 2010 in terms of liquidity, operating return on assets, financing, and return on equity.
c. If in 2010 the firm has 5,000 shares of common stock outstanding selling for $15, what is the (1) firm's earnings per share, (2) price/earnings ratio, and (3) price/book ratio?

Study Problems

4-1. (*Ratio analysis*) Brashear Inc. currently has $2,145,000 in current assets and $858,000 in current liabilities. The company's managers want to increase the firm's inventory, which will be financed by a short-term note with the bank. What level of inventories can the firm carry without its current ratio falling below 2.0?

4-2. (*Ratio analysis*) The Allen Corporation had sales in 2008 of $65 million, total assets of $42 million, and total liabilities of $20 million. The interest rate on the company's debt is 6 percent and its tax rate is 30 percent. The operating profit margin was 12 percent. What was the 2008 operating income and net income? What was operating return on assets and return on equity? Assume that interest must be paid on all of the debt.

4-3. (*Ratio analysis*) Last year, Davies Inc. had sales of $400,000, with a cost of goods sold of $112,000. The firm's operating expenses were $130,000, and its increase in retained earnings was $58,000. There are currently 22,000 common stock shares outstanding and the firm pays a $1.60 dividend per share.

a. Assuming the firm's earnings are taxed at 34 percent, construct the firm's income statement.
b. Compute the firm's operating profit margin.
c. What was the times interest earned?

4-4. (*Ratio analysis*) Greene Inc.'s balance sheet shows a stockholders' equity value of $750,500. The firm's earnings per share was $3, resulting in a price/earnings ratio of 12.25. There are 50,000 shares of common stock outstanding. What is the price/book ratio? What does this indicate about how shareholders view Greene Inc.?

4-5. (*Ratio analysis*) The Mitchem Marble Company has a target current ratio of 2.0 but has experienced some difficulties financing its expanding sales in the past few months. At present the firm has a current ratio of 2.5 and current assets of $2.5 million. If Mitchem expands its receivables and inventories using its short-term line of credit, how much additional short-term funding can it borrow before its current ratio standard is reached?

4-6. (*Ratio analysis*) The balance sheet and income statement for the J. P. Robard Mfg. Company are as follows:

Balance Sheet ($000)

Cash	$ 500
Accounts receivable	2,000
Inventories	1,000
Current assets	3,500
Net fixed assets	4,500
Total assets	$ 8,000
Accounts payable	$ 1,100
Accrued expenses	600
Short-term notes payable	300
Current liabilities	$ 2,000
Long-term debt	2,000
Owners' equity	4,000
Total liabilities and owners' equity	$ 8,000

Income Statement ($000)

Net sales (all credit)	$ 8,000
Cost of goods sold	(3,300)
Gross profit	4,700
Operating expenses	
(includes $500 depreciation)	(3,000)
Operating income	$ 1,700
Interest expense	(367)
Earnings before taxes	$ 1,333
Income taxes (40%)	(533)
Net income	$ 800

Calculate the following ratios:

Current ratio	Operating return on assets
Times interest earned	Debt ratio
Inventory turnover	Average collection period
Total asset turnover	Fixed asset turnover
Operating profit margin	Return on equity

4-7. (*Analyzing operating return on assets*) The R. M. Smithers Corporation earned an operating profit margin of 10 percent based on sales of $10 million and total assets of $5 million last year.

a. What was Smithers' total asset turnover ratio?

b. During the coming year the company president has set a goal of attaining a total asset turnover of 3.5. How much must firm sales rise, other things being the same, for the goal to be achieved? (State your answer in both dollars and percentage increase in sales.)

c. What was Smithers' operating return on assets last year? Assuming the firm's operating profit margin remains the same, what will the operating return on assets be next year if the total asset turnover goal is achieved?

4-8. (*Using financial ratios*) The Brenmar Sales Company had a gross profit margin (gross profits ÷ sales) of 30 percent and sales of $9 million last year. Seventy-five percent of the firm's sales are on credit and the remainder are cash sales. Brenmar's current assets equal $1.5 million, its current liabilities equal $300,000, and it has $100,000 in cash plus marketable securities.

a. If Brenmar's accounts receivable are $562,500, what is its average collection period?

b. If Brenmar reduces its average collection period to 20 days, what will be its new level of accounts receivable?

c. Brenmar's inventory turnover ratio is 9 times. What is the level of Brenmar's inventories?

4-9. (*Ratio analysis*) Using Pamplin Inc.'s financial statements shown here:

a. Compute the following ratios for both 2009 and 2010.

	INDUSTRY NORM	2009	2010
Current ratio	5.00		
Acid-test (quick) ratio	3.00		
Inventory turnover	2.20		
Average collection period	90.00		
Debt ratio	0.33		
Times interest earned	7.00		
Total asset turnover	0.75		
Fixed asset turnover	1.00		
Operating profit margin	20%		
Return on common equity	9%		

b. How liquid is the firm?
c. Are its managers generating an adequate operating profit on the firm's assets?
d. How is the firm financing its assets?
e. Are its managers generating a good return on equity?

Pamplin Inc. Balance Sheet at 12/31/2009 and 12/31/2010

ASSETS

	2009		2010	
Cash		$ 200		$ 150
Accounts receivable		450		425
Inventory		550		625
Current assets		$ 1,200		$ 1,200
Plant and equipment	$ 2,200		$ 2,600	
Less accumulated depreciation	(1,000)		(1,200)	
Net plant and equipment		$ 1,200		$ 1,400
Total assets		$ 2,400		$ 2,600

Liabilities and Owners' Equity

	2009		2010	
Accounts payable		$ 200		$ 150
Notes payable—current (9%)		0		150
Current liabilities		$ 200		$ 300
Bonds (8.33% interest)		600		600
Total debt		$ 800		$ 900
Owners' equity				
Common stock	$ 300		$ 300	
Paid-in capital	600		600	
Retained earnings	700		800	
Total owners' equity		$ 1,600		$ 1,700
Total liabilities and owners' equity		$ 2,400		$ 2,600

Pamplin Inc. Income Statement for Years Ending 12/31/2009 and 12/31/2010

	2009		2010	
Sales (all credit)		$1,200		$1,450
Cost of goods sold		700		850
Gross profit		$ 500		$ 600
Operating expenses	30		40	
Depreciation	220	250	200	240
Operating income		$ 250		$ 360
Interest expense		50		64
Net income before taxes		$ 200		$ 296
Taxes (40%)		80		118
Net income		$ 120		$ 178

4-10. (*Financial ratios—investment analysis*) The annual sales for Salco Inc. were $4.5 million last year. The firm's end-of-year balance sheet was as follows:

Current assets	$ 500,000	Liabilities	$1,000,000
Net fixed assets	1,500,000	Owners' equity	1,000,000
	$2,000,000		$2,000,000

The firm's income statement for the year was as follows:

Sales	$ 4,500,000
Less cost of goods sold	(3,500,000)
Gross profit	$ 1,000,000
Less operating expenses	(500,000)
Operating income	$ 500,000
Less interest expense	(100,000)
Earnings before taxes	$ 400,000
Less taxes (50%)	(200,000)
Net income	$ 200,000

a. Calculate Salco's total asset turnover, operating profit margin, and operating return on assets.
b. Salco plans to renovate one of its plants, which will require an added investment in plant and equipment of $1 million. The firm will maintain its present debt ratio of .5 when financing the new investment and expects sales to remain constant. The operating profit margin will rise to 13 percent. What will be the new operating return on assets for Salco after the plant's renovation?
c. Given that the plant renovation in part b occurs and Salco's interest expense rises by $50,000 per year, what will be the return earned on the common stockholders' investment? Compare this rate of return with that earned before the renovation.

4-11. (*Financial analysis*) The T. P. Jarmon Company manufactures and sells a line of exclusive sportswear. The firm's sales were $600,000 for the year just ended, and its total assets exceeded $400,000. The company was started by Mr. Jarmon just 10 years ago and has been profitable every year since its inception. The chief financial officer for the firm, Brent Vehlim, has decided to seek a line of credit from the firm's bank totaling $80,000. In the past, the company has relied on its suppliers to finance a large part of its needs for inventory. However, in recent months tight money conditions have led the firm's suppliers to offer sizable cash discounts to speed up payments for purchases. Mr. Vehlim wants to use the line of credit to replace a large portion of the firm's payables during the summer, which is the firm's peak seasonal sales period.

The firm's two most recent balance sheets were presented to the bank in support of its loan request. In addition, the firm's income statement for the year just ended was provided. These statements are found in the following tables:

T. P. Jarmon Company, Balance Sheet for 12/31/2009 and 12/31/2010

	2009	2010
Cash	$ 15,000	$ 14,000
Marketable securities	6,000	6,200
Accounts receivable	42,000	33,000
Inventory	51,000	84,000
Prepaid rent	1,200	1,100
Total current assets	$ 115,200	$ 138,300
Net plant and equipment	286,000	270,000
Total assets	$ 401,200	$ 408,300
Accounts payable	$ 48,000	$ 57,000
Notes payable	15,000	13,000
Accruals	6,000	5,000
Total current liabilities	$ 69,000	$ 75,000
Long-term debt	160,000	150,000
Common stockholders' equity	172,200	183,300
Total liabilities and equity	$ 401,200	$ 408,300

T. P. Jarmon Company, Income Statement for the Year Ended 12/31/2010

Sales (all credit)		$ 600,000
Less cost of goods sold		460,000
Gross profit		$ 140,000
Less operating and interest expenses		
General and administrative	$ 30,000	
Interest	10,000	
Depreciation	30,000	
Total		70,000
Earnings before taxes		$ 70,000
Less taxes		27,100
Net income available to common stockholders		$ 42,900
Less cash dividends		31,800
Change in retained earnings		$ 11,100

Jan Fama, associate credit analyst for the Merchants National Bank of Midland, Michigan, was assigned the task of analyzing Jarmon's loan request.

a. Calculate the financial ratios for 2010 corresponding to the industry norms provided as follows:

RATIO	NORM
Current ratio	1.8
Acid-test ratio	0.9
Debt ratio	0.5
Times interest earned	10.0
Average collection period	20.0
Inventory turnover (based on cost of goods sold)	7.0
Return on common equity	12.0%
Operating return on assets	16.8%
Operating profit margin	14.0%
Total asset turnover	1.20
Fixed asset turnover	1.80

b. Which of the ratios reported in the industry norms do you feel should be most crucial in determining whether the bank should extend the line of credit?

c. Prepare Jarmon's statement of cash flows for the year ended December 31, 2010. Interpret your findings.

d. Use the information provided by the financial ratios and the cash flow statement to decide if you would support making the loan.

4-12. (*Economic Value Added*) Stegemoller Inc.'s managers want to evaluate the firm's prior-year performance in terms of its contribution to shareholder value. This past year, the firm earned an operating income return on investment of 12 percent, compared to an industry norm of 11 percent. It has been estimated that the firm's investors have an opportunity cost on their funds of 14 percent. The firm's total assets for the year were $100 million. Compute the amount of economic value created or destroyed by the firm. How does your finding support or fail to support what you would conclude using ratio analysis to evaluate the firm's performance?

4-13. (*Ratio analysis*)

a. Go to www.investor.reuters.com. (You will need to sign up for a free membership before being able to access all the information on the site.) Type in the symbol for Starbucks (SBUX) in the "Quote" box and then click "Go." Click the "Financial Statements" link on the left side of the Web page and examine Starbucks' financial statements.

b. After becoming familiar with the financial statements for Starbucks, click on the "Ratios" link in the left margin to see a large number of ratios that have been calculated for the company. There are many more ratios than what we presented, and some have been calculated differently than we did—a problem that occurs frequently when using different sources of ratios. Which ratios are familiar to you? How have the ratios changed for Starbucks Corporation over the past 5 years (look at the 5-year averages)?

4-14. Being able to identify an industry to use for benchmarking your firm's results with similar companies is frequently not easy. Choose a type of business and go to www.naics.com. This Web site allows you to do a free search for the NAICS (North American Industry Classification System, pronounced Nakes) number for different types of businesses. Choose keywords such as "athletic shoes" or "auto dealers" and others to see to which industry they have been assigned.

4-15. (*Market-value ratios*) Bremmer Industries has a price per earnings ratio of 16.29X.

   a. If Bremmer's earnings per share is $1.35, what is the price per share of Bremmer's stock?

   b. Using the price per share you found in part (a), determine the price per book ratio if Bremmer's equity book value per share is $9.58.

4-16. (*Financing decisions*) Ellie's Electronics Incorporated has total assets of $63 million and total debt of $42 million. The company also has operating income of $21 million with interest expenses of $6 million.

   a. What is Ellie's debt ratio?

   b. What is Ellie's times interest earned?

   c. Based on the information above, would you recommend to Ellie's management that the firm is in a strong enough position to assume more debt and increase interest expense to $9 million?

4-17. (*Economic value added*) Callaway Concrete uses Economic Value Added as a financial performance measure. Callaway has $240 million in assets, and the firm has financed its assets with 37% equity and 63% debt with an interest rate of 6%. The firm's opportunity cost on its funds is 12%, while the operating return on the firm's assets is 14%.

   a. What is the Economic Value Added created or destroyed by Callaway Concrete?

   b. What does Economic Value Added measure?

Mini Case

Go to http://finance.yahoo.com/and locate current financial information for GM and Toyota, both in terms of the company's current financial statements and stock market prices. With this information:

   a. Compute the financial ratios for both firms for the most recent year, and evaluate the relative performance of the two firms in the following areas:

     1. Liquidity

     2. Operating profitability

     3. Financing practices

     4. Return on the shareholders' investment

   b. What is each firm's price/earnings ratio and market/book ratio? What do these ratios tell you?

   c. Assume that the cost of capital (investors' required rate of return) is 8 percent for both companies. Calculate the EVA for each company. Interpret your findings.

Self-Test Solutions

SS-1. Note that the current ratio for Ray's Tool and Supply Company before its inventory expansion is as follows:

   current ratio = $6,000,000/current liabilities = 4

Thus, the firm's level of current liabilities is $1.5 million. If the expansion in inventories is financed entirely with borrowed funds, then the change in inventories is equal to the change in the firm's current liabilities. Thus, the firm's current ratio after the expansion can be defined as follows:

$$\text{current ratio} = \frac{\$6,000,000 + \text{change in inventory}}{\$1,500,000 + \text{change in inventory}} = 3$$

Note that we set the new current ratio equal to the firm's target of 3. Solving for the change in inventory in the equation, we determine that the firm can expand its inventories by $750,000, finance the expansion with current liabilities, and still maintain its target current ratio.

SS-2.

a. M & G Industries Ratio Analysis

	INDUSTRY AVERAGES	ACTUAL 2009	ACTUAL 2010
Current ratio	1.80	1.84	0.90
Acid-test ratio	0.70	0.78	0.24
Average collection period (based on a 365-day year and end-of-year figures)	37.00	36.50	36.50
Inventory turnover	2.50	2.59	2.11
Debt ratio	58%	50%	61.3%
Times interest earned	3.80	4.00	2.79
Operating profit margin	10%	9.6%	10.6%
Total asset turnover	1.14	1.11	1.07
Fixed asset turnover	1.40	2.02	1.82
Operating return on assets	11.4%	10.67%	11.3%
Return on common equity	9.5%	8.0%	9.4%

b. M & G's liquidity is poor, as suggested by its low current ratio and acid-test ratio in 2010; also, the firm's inventories are turning over slowly compared to the industry norm. In 2010, M & G's managers are doing a satisfactory job of generating profits on the firm's operating assets, as indicated by the operating return on assets. Note that the operating return on assets in 2010 is about the same as the industry average, owing to a slightly above-average operating profit margin combined with a slightly below-average total asset turnover ratio. The problem with the total asset turnover ratio comes from slow inventory turnover. M & G has increased its use of debt to the point of using slightly more debt than the average company in the industry. As a result, the firm's coverage of interest has decreased to a point well below the industry norm.

c.

1. $\text{Earnings per share} = \dfrac{\text{net income}}{\text{number of shares outstanding}} = \dfrac{\$5,450}{5,000} = \$1.09$

2. $\text{Price/earnings ratio} = \dfrac{\text{market price share}}{\text{earnings per share}} = \dfrac{\$15.00}{\$1.09} = 13.76$

3. $\text{Price/book ratio} = \dfrac{\text{market price share}}{\text{book value per share}} = \dfrac{\$15.00}{\$11.61} = 1.29$

where

$$\text{book value per share} = \dfrac{\text{total book equity value}}{\text{number of shares outstanding}}$$

$$= \dfrac{\$31,500 + \$26,550}{5,000 \text{ shares}}$$

$$= \dfrac{\$58,050}{5,000 \text{ shares}} = \$11.61$$

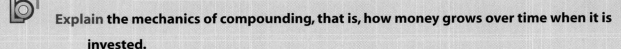

Chapter 5

The Time Value of Money

Learning Objectives

After reading this chapter, you should be able to:

1. Explain the mechanics of compounding, that is, how money grows over time when it is invested.

2. Discuss the relationship between compounding and bringing the value of money back to the present.

3. Understand annuities.

4. Determine the future or present value of a sum when there are nonannual compounding periods.

5. Determine the present value of an uneven stream of payments and understand perpetuities.

6. Explain how the international setting complicates the time value of money.

In business, there is probably no other single concept with more power or applications than that of the time value of money. In his landmark book, *A History of Interest Rates*, Sidney Homer noted that if $1,000 was invested for 400 years at 8 percent interest, it would grow to $23 quadrillion—that would work out to approximately $5 million per person on earth. He was not giving a plan to make the world rich but effectively pointing out the power of the time value of money.

The time value of money is certainly not a new concept. Benjamin Franklin had a good understanding of how it worked when he left £1,000 each to Boston and Philadelphia. With the gift, he left instructions that the cities were to lend the money, charging the going interest rate, to worthy apprentices. Then, after the money had been invested in this way for 100 years, they were to use a portion of the investment to build something of benefit to the city and hold some back for the future. Two hundred years later, Franklin's Boston gift resulted in the construction of the Franklin Union, has helped countless medical students with loans, and still has over $3 million left in the account. Philadelphia, likewise, has reaped a significant reward from his gift with its portion of the gift growing to over $2 million. Bear in mind that all this has come from a gift of £2,000 with some serious help from the time value of money.

The power of the time value of money can also be illustrated through a story Andrew Tobias tells in his book *Money Angles*. There he tells of a peasant who wins a chess tournament put on by the king. The king asks the peasant what he would like as the prize. The peasant answers that he would like for his village one piece of grain to be placed on the first square of his chessboard, two pieces of grain on the second square, four pieces on the third, eight on the fourth, and so forth. The king, thinking he was getting off easy, pledged on his word of honor that it would be done. Unfortunately for the king, by the time all 64 squares on the chessboard were filled, there were 18.5 million trillion grains of wheat on the board—the kernels were compounding at a rate of 100 percent over the 64 squares of the chessboard. Needless to say, no one in the village ever went hungry; in fact, that is so much wheat that if each kernel were one-quarter inch long (quite frankly, I have no idea how long a kernel of wheat is, but Andrew Tobias's guess is one-quarter inch), if laid end to end, they could stretch to the sun and back 391,320 times.

Understanding the techniques of compounding and moving money through time is critical to almost every business decision. It will help you to understand such varied things as how stocks and bonds are valued, how to determine the value of a new project, how much you should save for your children's education, and how much your mortgage payments will be.

In the next six chapters, we focus on determining the value of the firm and the desirability of the investments it considers making. A key concept that underlies this material is the time value of money; that is, a dollar today is worth more than a dollar received a year from now. Intuitively this idea is easy to understand. We are all familiar with the concept of interest. This concept illustrates what economists call an opportunity cost of passing up the earning potential of a dollar today. This opportunity cost is the time value of money.

To evaluate and compare investment proposals, we need to examine how dollar values might accrue from accepting these proposals. To do this, all the dollar values must first be comparable. In other words, we must move all dollar flows back to the present or out to a common future date. An understanding of the time value of money is essential, therefore, to an understanding of financial management, whether basic or advanced.

Compound Interest and Future Value

 Explain the mechanics of compounding, that is, how money grows over time when it is invested.

We begin our study of the time value of money with some basic tools for visualizing the time pattern of cash flows. While timelines seem simple at first glance, they can be a tremendous help for more complicated problems.

Using Timelines to Visualize Cash Flows

As a first step in visualizing cash flows, we can construct a timeline, a linear representation of the timing of cash flows. A timeline identifies the timing and amount of a stream of cash flows—both cash received and cash spent—along with the interest rate it earns. Timelines are a critical first step used by financial analysts to solve financial problems. We will refer to them often throughout this text.

To illustrate how to construct a timeline, consider the following example, where we receive annual cash flows over the course of four years. The following timeline shows our cash inflows and outflows from time period 0 (the present) until the end of year 4:

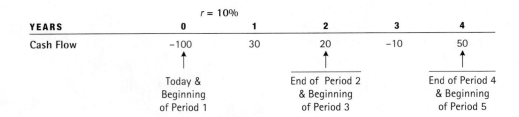

For our purposes, time periods are identified on the top of the timeline, and in this example, the time periods are measured in years, which are indicated on the far left of the timeline. Thus, time period 0 is both today and the beginning of the first year. The dollar amount of the cash flow received or spent at each time period is shown below the timeline. Positive values represent *cash inflows*. Negative values represent *cash outflows*. For example, in the timeline shown, a $100 cash outflow occurs today, or at time 0, followed by cash inflows of $30 and $20 at the end of years 1 and 2, a negative cash flow (a cash outflow) of $10 at the end of year 3, and finally a cash inflow of $50 at the end of year 4.

The units of measurement on the timeline are time periods and are typically expressed in years, but could be expressed as months, days, or any unit of time. However, for now, let's assume we're looking at cash flows that occur annually. Thus, the distance between 0 and 1 represents the period between today and the end of the first year. Consequently, time period 0 indicates today, while time period 1 represents the end of the first year, which is also the beginning of the second year. (You can think of it as being both the last second of the first year and the first second of the second year.) The interest rate, which is 10% in this example, is listed above the timeline.

In this chapter and throughout the text, we will often refer to the idea of moving money through time. Because this concept is probably not familiar to everyone, we should take a moment to explain it. Most business investments involve investing money today. Then, in subsequent years, the investment produces cash that comes back to the business. To evaluate an investment, you need to compare the amount of money the investment requires today with the amount of money the investment will return to you in the future, and adjust these numbers for the fact that a dollar today is worth more than a dollar in the future. Timelines simplify solving time value of money problems, and they are not just for beginners; experienced financial analysts use them as well. In fact, the more complex the problem you're trying to solve, the more valuable a timeline will be in terms of helping you visualize exactly what needs to be done.

Most of us encounter the concept of compound interest at an early age. Anyone who has ever had a savings account or purchased a government savings bond has received compound interest. **Compound interest** occurs when *interest paid on the investment during the first period is added to the principal; then, during the second period, interest is earned on this new sum.*

For example, suppose we place $100 in a savings account that pays 6 percent interest, compounded annually. How will our savings grow? At the end of the first year we have earned 6 percent, or $6 on our initial deposit of $100, giving us a total of $106 in our savings account, thus,

$$\text{value at the end of year 1} = \text{present value} \times (1 + \text{interest rate})$$
$$= \$100(1 + 0.06)$$
$$= \$100(1.06)$$
$$= \$106$$

Carrying these calculations one period further, we find that we now earn the 6 percent interest on a principal of $106, which means we earn $6.36 in interest during the second

compound interest the situation in which interest paid on an investment during the first period is added to the principal. During the second period, interest is earned on the original principal plus the interest earned during the first period.

year. Why do we earn more interest during the second year than we did during the first? Simply because we now earn interest on the sum of the original principal and the interest we earned in the first year. In effect we are now earning interest on interest; this is the concept of compound interest. Examining the mathematical formula illustrating the earning of interest in the second year, we find

> **REMEMBER YOUR PRINCIPLES**
> **Principle** In this chapter we develop the tools to incorporate **Principle 2: Money Has a Time Value** into our calculations. In coming chapters we use this concept to measure value by bringing the benefits and costs from a project back to the present.

value at the end of year 2 = value at the end of year 1 × (1 + r)

where r = the annual interest (or discount) rate

which, for our example, gives

value at the end of year 2 = $106 × (1.06)
= $112.36

Looking back, we can see that the **future value** at the end of year 1, or $106, is actually equal to the present value times (1 + r), or $100(1 + 0.06). Moving forward to year 2 we find,

future value the amount to which your investment will grow.

value at the end of year 2 = present value × (1 + r) × (1 + r)
= present value × (1 + r)²

Carrying this forward into the third year, we find that we enter the year with $112.36 and we earn 6 percent, or $6.74 in interest, giving us a total of $119.10 in our savings account. This can be expressed as

value at the end of year 3 = present value × (1 + r) × (1 + r) × (1 + r)
= present value × (1 + r)³

By now a pattern is becoming apparent. We can generalize this formula to illustrate the future value of our investment if it is compounded annually at a rate of r for n years to be

future value = present value × (1 + r)ⁿ

Letting FV_n stand for the future value at the end of n periods and PV stand for the present value, we can rewrite this equation as,

$$FV_n = PV(1 + r)^n \qquad (5\text{-}1)$$

We also refer to $(1 + r)^n$ as the **future value factor**. Thus, to find the future value of a dollar amount, all you need to do is multiply that dollar amount times the appropriate future value factor,

future value factor the value of $(1 + r)^n$ used as a multiple to calculate an amount's future value.

future value = present value × (future value factor)

where future value factor = $(1 + r)^n$.

Figure 5-1 illustrates how this investment of $100 would continue to grow for the first 20 years at a compound interest rate of 6 percent. Notice how the amount of interest earned annually increases each year. Again, the reason is that each year interest is received on the sum of the original investment plus any interest earned in the past. The situation in which interest is earned on interest that was earned in the past is referred to as compound interest. *If you only earned interest on your initial investment*, it would be referred to as **simple interest**.

simple interest if you only earned interest on your initial investment it would be referred to as simple interest.

When we examine the relationship between the number of years an initial investment is compounded for and its future value, as shown graphically in Figure 5-2, we see that we can increase the future value of an investment by either increasing the number of years for which we let it compound or by compounding it at a higher interest rate. We can also see this from equation (5-1) because an increase in either r or n while the present value is held constant results in an increase in the future value.

FIGURE 5-1 $100 Compounded at 6 Percent Over 20 Years

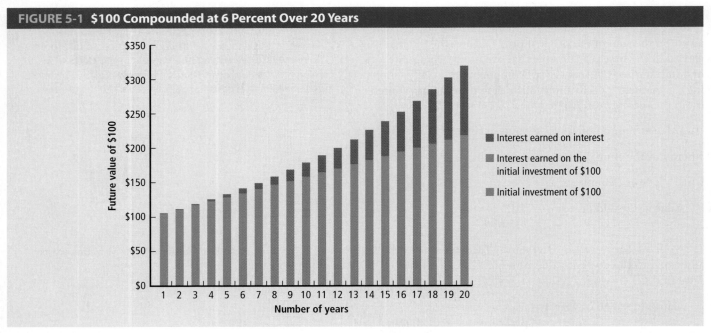

FIGURE 5-2 The Future Value of $100 Initially Deposited and Compounded at 0, 5, 10, and 15 Percent

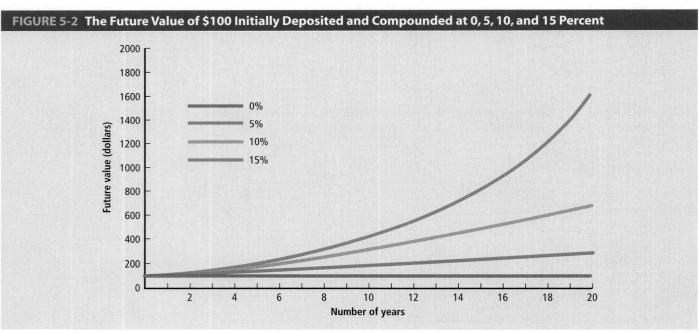

EXAMPLE 5.1

If we place $1,000 in a savings account paying 5 percent interest compounded annually, how much will our account accrue to in 10 years? Substituting present value = $1,000, r = 5 percent, and n = 10 years into equation (5-1), we get

$$\text{future value} = \text{present value} \times (1 + r)^n \tag{5-1}$$
$$FV_n = PV(1 + r)^n$$
$$= \$1,000(1 + 0.05)^{10}$$
$$= \$1,000(1.62889)$$
$$= \$1,628.89$$

Thus, at the end of 10 years we will have $1,628.89 in our savings account.

Techniques for Moving Money Through Time

There are three different approaches that you can use to solve a time value of money problem. The first is to simply do the math. Financial calculators are a second alternative, and there are a number of them that do a good job of solving time value of money problems. Based on many years of experience, the Texas Instruments BA II Plus or the Hewlett-Packard 10BII calculators would be excellent choices. Finally, spreadsheets can move money through time, and in the real world, they are without question the tool of choice. Now let's take a look at all three alternatives.

Mathematical Calculations   If we want to calculate the future value of an amount of money, the mathematical calculations are relatively straightforward. However, as we will see, time value of money calculations are easier using a financial calculator or spreadsheet. Those are the chosen methods in the real world.

EXAMPLE 5.2

If we invest $500 in a bank where it will earn 8 percent interest compounded annually, how much will it be worth at the end of 7 years? Plugging in $n = 7$, $r = 8$ percent, and present value = $500 into equation (5-1), we find

$$\text{future value} = \text{present value} \times (1 + r)^n \tag{5-1}$$
$$= \$500(1 + 0.08)^7$$
$$= \$500(1.71382)$$
$$= \$856.91$$

Thus, we will have $856.91 at the end of 7 years.

In the future we will find several uses for equation (5-1); not only can we find the future value of an investment, but we can also solve for the present value, r, or n.

Using a Financial Calculator   Before we review the use of the financial calculator, let's review the five "time value of money" keys on a financial calculator. Although the specific keystrokes used to perform time value of money calculations differ slightly when using financial calculators made by different companies, the symbols used are basically the same. Below are the keystrokes as they appear on a Texas Instruments BA II Plus calculator.

MENU KEY	DESCRIPTION
Menu Keys we will use in this chapter include:	
N	Stores (or calculates) the total number of payments or compounding periods.
I/Y	Stores (or calculates) the interest (or discount or growth) rate per period.
PV	Stores (or calculates) the present value of a cash flow (or series of cash flows).
FV	Stores (or calculates) the future value, that is, the dollar amount of a final cash flow (or the compound value of a single flow or series of cash flows).
PMT	Stores (or calculates) the dollar amount of each annuity (or equal) payment deposited or received.

The keys shown here correspond to the TI BA II Plus calculator. Other financial calculators have essentially the same keys. They are simply labeled a little differently. We should stop and point out that the labels on the keys of financial calculators are slightly different than what we have been using in our mathematical formulas. For example, we have used a lower case n to refer to the number of compounding periods, whereas an uppercase N appears on the Texas Instruments BA II Plus calculator. Likewise, the I/Y key refers to the rate of interest per period, whereas we have used r. Some financial calculators also have a CPT key, which stands for "compute." It is simply the key you press when you want the calculator to begin solving your problem. Finally, the PMT key refers to a fixed payment received or paid each period.

At this point you might be wondering exactly why we are using different symbols in this book than are used on calculators. The answer is that, unfortunately, the symbols used by the different companies that design and make financial calculators are not consistent. The symbols in Microsoft Excel are somewhat different as well.

An important thing to remember when using a financial calculator is that cash outflows (investments you make rather than receive) generally have to be entered as negative numbers. In effect, a financial calculator sees money as "leaving your hands" and therefore taking on a *negative* sign when you invest it. The calculator then sees the money "returning to your hands" and therefore taking on a *positive* sign after you've earned interest on it. Also, every calculator operates a bit differently with respect to entering variables. Needless to say, it is a good idea to familiarize yourself with exactly how your calculator functions.[1]

Once you've entered all the variables you know, including entering a zero for any variable with a value of zero, you can let the calculator do the math for you. If you own a Texas Instruments BA II Plus calculator, press the compute key (CPT), followed by the key corresponding to the unknown variable you're trying to determine. With a Hewlett-Packard calculator, once the known variables are entered, you need only press the key corresponding to the final variable to calculate its value.

A good starting place when working a problem is to write down all the variables you know. Then assign a value of zero to any variables that are not included in the problem. Once again, make sure that the sign you give to the different variables reflects the direction of the cash flow.

Calculator Tips—Getting It Right   Calculators are pretty easy to use. But there are some common mistakes that are often made. So, before you take a crack at solving a problem using a financial calculator ensure that you take the following steps:

1. **Set your calculator to one payment per year.** Some financial calculators use monthly payments as the default. Change it to annual payments. Then consider n to be the number of periods and r the interest rate per period.
2. **Set your calculator to display at least four decimal places or to floating decimal place (nine decimal places).** Most calculators are preset to display only two decimal places. Because interest rates are so small, change your decimal setting to at least four.
3. **Set your calculator to the "end" mode.** Your calculator will assume cash flows occur at the end of each time period.

When you're ready to work a problem, remember:

1. **Every problem must have at least one positive and one negative number.** The pre-programming within the calculator assumes that you are analyzing problems in which money goes out (outflows) and comes in (inflows) so you have to be sure to enter the sign appropriately. If you are using a BA II Plus calculator and get an "Error 5" message, that means you are solving for either r or n and you input both the present and future values as positive numbers—correct that and re-solve the problem.
2. **You must enter a zero for any variable that isn't used in a problem, or you have to clear the calculator before beginning a new problem.** If you don't clear your calculator or enter a value for one of the variables, your calculator won't assume that that variable is zero. Instead, your calculator will assume it carries the same number as it did during the previous problem. So be sure to clear out the memory (CLR, TVM) or enter zeros for variables not included in the problem.
3. **Enter the interest rate as a percent, not a decimal.** That means 10% must be entered as 10 rather than 0.10.

Two popular financial calculators are the Texas Instruments BA II Plus (TI BA II Plus) and the Hewlett-Packard 10BII (HP 10BII). If you're using one of these calculators and encounter

---

[1]Appendix A in the back of the book provides a tutorial that covers both the Texas Instruments BA II Plus and the Hewlett-Packard 10BII calculators.

any problems, take a look at Appendix A at the end of the book. It provides a tutorial for both of these calculators.

Spreadsheets   Practically speaking, most time value of money calculations are now done on computers with the help of spreadsheet software. Although there are competing spreadsheet programs, the most popular is Microsoft Corporation's Excel®. Just like financial calculators, Excel has "built-in" functions that make it really easy to do future value calculations.

Excel Tips—Getting It Right

1. **Take advantage of the formula help that Excel offers.** All Excel functions are set up the same way: First, with the "=" sign; second, with the function's name (for example, FV or PV); and third, with the inputs into that function enclosed in parentheses. The following, for example, is how the future value function looks:

   =FV(rate,nper,pmt,pv)

   When you begin typing in your Excel function in a spreadsheet cell (that is, a box where you enter a single piece of data), all the input variables will appear at the top of the spreadsheet in their proper order so you will know what variable must be entered next. For example, =FV(**rate**,nper,pmt,pv,type) will come into view, with **rate** appearing in bold because rate is the next variable to enter. This means you don't really need to memorize the functions because they will appear when you begin entering them.

2. **If you're lost, click on "Help."** On the top row of your Excel spreadsheet you'll notice the word *Help* listed—another way to get to the help link is to hit the F1 button. When you're lost, the help link is your friend. Click on it and enter "PV" or "FV" in the search bar, and the program will explain how to calculate each. All of the other financial calculations you might want to find can be found the same way.

3. **Be careful about rounding the *r* variable.** For example, suppose you're dealing with the interest rate 6.99% compounded monthly. This means you will need to enter the interest rate per month, which is =6.99%/12, and since you are performing division in the cell, you need to put an "=" sign before the division is performed. Don't round the result of 0.0699/12 to 0.58 and enter 0.58 as *r*. Instead, enter =6.99%/12 or as a decimal =0.0699/12 for *r*.

   Also, you'll notice that while the inputs using an Excel spreadsheet are almost identical to those on a financial calculator, the interest rate in Excel is entered *either* as a decimal (0.06) *or* a whole number followed by a % sign (6%) rather than a 6 (as you would enter if you were using a financial calculator).

4. **Don't let the Excel notation fool you.** Excel doesn't use *r* or I/Y to note the interest rate. Instead, it uses the term *rate*. Don't let this bother you. All of these notations refer to the same thing—the interest rate. Similarly, Excel doesn't use *n* to denote the number of periods. Instead, it uses *nper*. Once again, don't let this bother you. Both *n* and *nper* refer to the number of periods.

5. **Don't be thrown off by the "type" input variable.** You'll notice that Excel asks for a new variable that we haven't talked about yet, "type." Again, if you type "=FV(" in a cell, "=FV(**rate**,nper,pmt,pv,type)" will immediately appear just below that cell. Don't let this new variable, "type," throw you off. The variable "type" refers to whether the payments, pmt, occur at the end of each period (which is considered type=0) or the beginning of each period (which is considered type=1). But you don't have to worry about it at all because the default on "type" is 0. *Thus, if you don't enter a value for "type," it will assume that the payments occur at the end of each period.* We're going to assume they occur at the end of each period, and if they don't, we'll deal with them another way which will be introduced later in this chapter. You'll also notice that since we assume that all payments occur at the end of each period unless otherwise stated, we ignore the "type" variable.

Some of the more important Excel functions that we will be using throughout the book include the following (again, we are ignoring the "type" variable because we are assuming cash flows occur at the end of the period):

CALCULATION (WHAT IS BEING SOLVED FOR)	FORMULA
Present value	=PV(rate, nper, pmt, fv)
Future value	=FV(rate, nper, pmt, pv)
Payment	=PMT(rate, nper, pv, fv)
Number of periods	=NPER(rate, pmt, pv, fv)
Interest rate	=RATE(nper, pmt, pv, fv)

Reminders: First, just like using a financial calculator, the outflows have to be entered as negative numbers. In general, each problem will have two cash flows—one positive and one negative. Second, a small, but important, difference between a spreadsheet and a financial calculator. When using a financial calculator, you enter the interest rate as a percent. For example, 6.5% is entered as 6.5. However, with the spreadsheet, the interest rate is entered as a decimal, thus 6.5 percent would be entered as 0.065 or, alternatively, as 6.5 followed by a % sign.

EXAMPLE 5.3

If you put $1,000 in an investment paying 20 percent interest compounded annually, how much will your account grow to in 10 years?

Let's start with a timeline to help you visualize the problem:

	$r = 20\%$										
YEARS	0	1	2	3	4	5	6	7	8	9	10
Cash Flows	−1,000										Future Value = ?

USING THE MATHEMATICAL FORMULAS

Substituting present value = $1,000, r = 20 percent, and n = 10 years into equation (5-1), we get

$$\text{future value} = \text{present value} \times (1 + r)^n \qquad (5\text{-}1)$$
$$= \$1,000(1 + 0.20)^{10}$$
$$= \$1,000(6.19174)$$
$$= \$6,191.74$$

Thus, at the end of ten years, you will have $6,191.74 in your investment. In this problem we've invested $1,000 at 20 percent and found that it will grow to $6,191.74 after ten years. These are actually equivalent values expressed in terms of dollars from different time periods where we've assumed a 20 percent compound rate.

USING A FINANCIAL CALCULATOR

A financial calculator makes this even simpler. If you are not familiar with the use of a financial calculator, or if you have any problems with these calculations, you should immediately go to Appendix A at the back of the book. There you'll find an introduction to financial calculators and the time value of money along with calculator tips to make sure that you come up with the right answers.

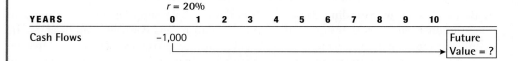

Enter	10.	20.0	−1,000.	0	
	N	I/Y	PV	PMT	FV
Solve for					6,191.74

Notice that you input the present value with a negative sign. In effect, a financial calculator sees money as "leaving your hands" and therefore taking on a negative sign when you invest it. In this case you are investing $1,000 right now, so it takes on a negative sign—as a result, the answer takes on a positive sign.

USING AN EXCEL SPREADSHEET

You'll notice the inputs using an Excel spreadsheet are almost identical to those on a financial calculator. The only difference is that the interest rate in Excel is entered *either* as a decimal (0.20) *or* a whole number followed by a % sign (20%) rather than a 20 (as you would enter if you were using a financial calculator). Again, the present value should be entered with a negative value so that the answer takes on a positive sign.

	A	B
1	interest rate (rate) =	20.00%
2	number of periods (nper) =	10
3	payment (pmt) =	$0
4	present value (pv) =	($1,000)
5		
6	future value (fv) =	$6,191.74
7		
8	Excel formula =FV(rate,nper,pmt,pv)	
9	Entered in cell b6: =FV(b1,b2,b3,b4)	

Two Additional Types of Time Value of Money Problems

Sometimes the time value of money does not involve determining either the present value or future value of a sum, but instead deals with either the number of periods in the future, n, or the rate of interest, r. For example, to answer the following question you will need to calculate the value for n.

◆ How many years will it be before the money I have saved will be enough to buy a second home?

Similarly, questions such as the following must be answered by solving for the interest rate, r.

◆ What rate do I need to earn on my investment to have enough money for my newborn child's college education ($n = 18$ years)?
◆ What interest rate has my investment earned?

Fortunately, with the help of a financial calculator or an Excel spreadsheet, you can easily solve for r or n in any of the above situations. It can also be done using the mathematical formulas, but it's much easier with a calculator or spreadsheet, so we'll stick to them.

Solving for the Number of Periods   Suppose you want to know how many years it will take for an investment of $9,330 to grow to $20,000 if it's invested at 10 percent annually. Let's take a look at solving this using a financial calculator and an Excel spreadsheet.

Using a Financial Calculator   With a financial calculator, all you do is substitute in the values for I/Y, PV, and FV, and solve for N:

Enter		10.0	–9,330.	0	20,000.
	N	I/Y	PV	PMT	FV
Solve for	8.0				

You'll notice that *PV* is input with a negative sign. In effect the financial calculator is programmed to assume that the $9,330 is a cash outflow, whereas the $20,000 is money that you receive. If you don't give one of these values a negative sign, you can't solve the problem.

Using an Excel Spreadsheet   With Excel, solving for *n* is straightforward. You simply use the =NPER function and input values for rate, pmt, pv, and fv.

	A	B
1	interest rate (rate) =	0.10
2	payment (pmt) =	0
3	present value (pv) =	($9,330)
4	future value (fv) =	$20,000
5		
6	number of periods (nper) =	8
7		
8	Excel formula =nper(rate,pmt,pv,fv)	
9	Entered in cell b6: =nper(b1,b2,b3,b4)	

Solving for the Rate of Interest   You have just inherited $34,946 and want to use it to fund your retirement in 30 years. If you have estimated that you will need $800,000 to fund your retirement, what rate of interest would you have to earn on your $34,946 investment? Let's take a look at solving this using a financial calculator and an Excel spreadsheet to calculate the interest rate.

Using a Financial Calculator   With a financial calculator, all you do is substitute in the values for N, PV, and FV, and solve for I/Y:

Enter	30.		−34,946.	0.	800,000.
	N	I/Y	PV	PMT	FV
Solve for		11.0			

Using an Excel Spreadsheet   With Excel, the problem is also very easy. You simply use the =RATE function and input values for nper, pmt, pv, and fv.

	A	B
1	number of periods (nper) =	30
2	payment (pmt) =	0
3	present value (pv) =	($34,946)
4	future value (fv) =	$800,000
5		
6	interest rate (rate) =	11.00%
7		
8	Excel formula =rate(nper,pmt,pv,fv)	
9	Entered in cell b6: =rate(b1,b2,b3,b4)	

Applying Compounding to Things Other Than Money

While this chapter focuses on moving money through time at a given interest rate, the concept of compounding applies to almost anything that grows. For example, let's assume you're interested in knowing how big the market for wireless printers will be in five years and assume the demand for them is expected to grow at a rate of 25 percent per year over the next five years. We can calculate the future value of the market for printers using the same formula we used to calculate future value for a sum of money. If the market is currently 25,000 printers per year, then 25,000 would be the present value, *n* would be 5, *r* would be 25%, and substituting into equation (5-1) you would be solving *FV*,

$$\text{future value} = \text{present value} \times (1 + r)^n \tag{5-1}$$
$$= 25,000(1 + 0.25)^5 = 76,293$$

In effect, you can view the interest rate, r, as a compound growth rate, and solve for the number of periods it would take for something to grow to a certain level—what something will grow to in the future. Or you could solve for r, that is, solve for the rate that something would have to grow at in order to reach a target level.

Concept Check

1. Principle 2 states that "money has a time value." Explain this statement.
2. How does compound interest differ from simple interest?
3. Explain the formula $FV_n = PV(1 + r)^n$.

Present Value

Up to this point we have been moving money forward in time; that is, we know how much we have to begin with and are trying to determine how much that sum will grow in a certain number of years when compounded at a specific rate. We are now going to look at the reverse question: What is the value in today's dollars of a sum of money to be received in the future? The answer to this question will help us determine the desirability of investment projects in Chapters 10 and 11. In this case we are moving future money back to the present. We will determine the **present value** of a lump sum, which in simple terms is the *current value of a future payment*. In fact, we will be doing nothing other than inverse compounding. The differences in these techniques come about merely from the investor's point of view. In compounding, we talked about the compound interest rate and the initial investment; in determining the present value, we will talk about the discount rate and present value of future cash flows. Determining the discount rate is the subject of Chapter 9 and can be defined as the rate of return available on an investment of equal risk to what is being discounted. Other than that, the technique and the terminology remain the same, and the mathematics are simply reversed. In equation (5-1) we were attempting to determine the future value of an initial investment. We now want to determine the initial investment or present value. By dividing both sides of equation (5-1) by $(1 + r)^n$, we get

$$\text{present value} = \text{future value at the end of year } n \times \left[\frac{1}{(1 + r)^n} \right]$$

or

$$PV = FV_n \left[\frac{1}{(1 + r)^n} \right] \tag{5-2}$$

The term in the brackets in equation (5-2) is referred to as the **present value factor**. Thus, to find the present value of a future dollar amount, all you need to do is multiply that future dollar amount times the appropriate present value factor,

$$\text{present value} = \text{future value (present value factor)}$$

$$\text{where present value factor} = \left[\frac{1}{(1 + r)^n} \right]$$

Because the mathematical procedure for determining the present value is exactly the inverse of determining the future value, we also find that the relationships among n, r, and present value are just the opposite of those we observed in future value. The present value of a future sum of money is inversely related to both the number of years until the payment will be received and the discount rate. This relationship is shown in Figure 5-3. Although the present value equation [equation (5-2)] is used extensively to evaluate new investment proposals, it should be stressed that the equation is actually the same as the future value, or compounding equation [equation (5-1)], only solves for present value instead of future value.

 2 Discuss the relationship between compounding and bringing the value of money back to the present.

present value the value in today's dollars of a future payment discounted back to present at the required rate of return.

present value factor the value of $\frac{1}{(1 + r)^n}$ used as a multiplier to calculate an amount's present value.

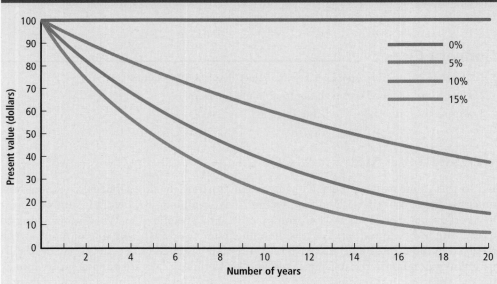

FIGURE 5-3 The Present Value of $100 to Be Received at a Future Date and Discounted Back to the Present at 0, 5, 10, and 15 Percent

EXAMPLE 5.4

What is the present value of $500 to be received 10 years from today if our discount rate is 6 percent? Substituting $FV_{10} = \$500$, $n = 10$, and $r = 6$ percent into equation (5-2), we find

$$\text{present value} = \$500\left[\frac{1}{(1 + 0.06)^{10}}\right]$$

$$= \$500\left(\frac{1}{1.791}\right)$$

$$= \$500(0.5584)$$

$$= \$279.20$$

Thus, the present value of the $500 to be received in 10 years is $279.20.

CALCULATOR SOLUTION

Data Input	Function Key
10	N
6	I/Y
−500	FV
0	PMT

Function Key	Answer
CPT	
PV	279.20

EXAMPLE 5.5

You're on vacation in a rather remote part of Florida and see an advertisement stating that if you take a sales tour of some condominiums "you will be given $100 just for taking the tour." However, the $100 that you get is in the form of a savings bond that will not pay you the $100 for 10 years. What is the present value of $100 to be received 10 years from today if your discount rate is 6 percent? Substituting $FV_{10} = \$100$, $n = 10$, and $r = 6\%$ into equation (5-2) you find,

$$\text{present value} = \$100\left[\frac{1}{(1 + 0.06)^{10}}\right]$$

$$= \$100(0.5584)$$

$$= \$55.84$$

Thus, the value in today's dollars of that $100 savings bond is only $55.84.

CALCULATOR SOLUTION

Data Input	Function Key
10	N
6	I/Y
−100	FV
0	PMT

Function Key	Answer
CPT	
PV	55.84

CAUTIONARY TALE

FORGETTING PRINCIPLE 4: MARKET PRICES ARE GENERALLY RIGHT

In the Cautionary Tale for Chapter 2, we looked at the role the mortgage crisis played in the financial collapse of 2009 from the viewpoint of conflicts of interest and failed corporate governance. But there are many lenses through which we can look to analyze the crisis. One such lens is the principle of efficient markets.

In 2007, several U.S. real estate markets entered a housing bubble. To look more closely at the underlying factors that led to the recent housing bubble (and burst), let's take a step back for a moment.

Beginning in the mid-1990s, the federal government made moves to relax conventional lending standards. In one such move, the government required the Federal National Mortgage Association, commonly known as Fannie Mae, and the Federal Home Loan Mortgage Corporation, known as Freddie Mac, to increase their holdings of loans to low- and moderate-income borrowers. Then in 1999, the U.S. Department of Housing and Urban Development (HUD) regulations required Fannie Mae and Freddie Mac to accept more loans with little or no down payment. As a result, the government had opened the door to very risky loans that would not have been made without this government action.

After the 2001 terrorist attack on the World Trade Center, the government made another move which acted against what we know about competitive markets. The Fed lowered short-term interest rates to insure that the economy did not seize up. These low, short-term interest rates made adjustable rate loans with low down payments highly attractive to homebuyers. As a result of the low interest rate, when individuals took out variable rate mortgages, they often qualified for bigger mortgages than they could have afforded during a normal interest rate period. But in 2005 and 2006, to control inflation, the Fed returned these short-term interest rates to higher levels and the adjustable rates reset, causing the monthly payments on these loans to increase. Housing prices began to fall and defaults soared.

These actions prevented supply and demand from acting naturally. As a result, housing prices were unnaturally inflated and the listed value of the mortgages, when packaged as securities, was a poor indicator of their actual worth. When homeowners defaulted on their loans in spades, investors were left holding the bad mortgages. These defaulted mortgages also led to a lot more houses on the market that the banks couldn't sell, which led to the market drying up, as it then became very difficult for anyone to get a *new* loan.

We now know that these events put into motion the housing bubble that contributed to the 2009 financial crisis. Competitive markets operate with natural forces of supply and demand, and while they tend to eliminate huge returns, competitive markets can also help to prevent the occurrence of short-lived false values—such as the temporarily low monthly interest payments for new homebuyers—that lead to an eventual crash. If we take one lesson away from this, it should be this: Don't mess with efficient markets. If the markets move interest rates to higher levels, it's for a reason.

Again, we have only one present-value–future-value equation; that is, equations (5-1) and (5-2) are different formats of the same equation. We have introduced them as separate equations to simplify our calculations; in one case we are determining the value in future dollars, and in the other case the value in today's dollars. In either case the reason is the same: to compare values on alternative investments and to recognize that the value of a dollar received today is not the same as that of a dollar received at some future date. In other words, we must measure the dollar values in dollars of the same time period. For example, if we looked at these projects—one that promised $1,000 in 1 year, one that promised $1,500 in 5 years, and one that promised $2,500 in 10 years—the concept of present value allows us to bring their flows back to the present and make those projects comparable. Moreover, because all present values are comparable (they are all measured in dollars of the same time period), we can add and subtract the present value of inflows and outflows to determine the present value of an investment. Let's now look at an example of an investment that has two cash flows in different time periods and determine the present value of this investment.

CAN YOU DO IT?

SOLVING FOR THE PRESENT VALUE WITH TWO FLOWS IN DIFFERENT YEARS

What is the present value of an investment that yields $500 to be received in 5 years and $1,000 to be received in 10 years if the discount rate is 4 percent?

(The solution can be found on page 133.)

STEP 1
CALCULATOR SOLUTION

Data Input	Function Key
7	N
6	I/Y
−1,000	FV
0	PMT

Function Key	Answer
CPT	
PV	665.06

STEP 2
CALCULATOR SOLUTION

Data Input	Function Key
10	N
6	I/Y
−1,000	FV
0	PMT

Function Key	Answer
CPT	
PV	558.39

STEP 3
Add the two present values that you just calculated together:

$ 665.06
  558.39
$1,223.45

EXAMPLE 5.6

What is the present value of an investment that yields $1,000 to be received in 7 years and $1,000 to be received in 10 years if the discount rate is 6 percent? Substituting the values of $n = 7$, $r = 6$ percent, and $FV_7 = \$1,000$; and $n = 10$, $r = 6$ percent, and $FV_{10} = \$1,000$ into equation (5-2) and adding these values together, we find

$$\text{present value} = \$1,000\left[\frac{1}{(1 + 0.06)^7}\right] + \$1,000\left[\frac{1}{(1 + 0.06)^{10}}\right]$$

$$= \$1,000(0.66506) + \$1,000(0.55839)$$

$$= \$665.06 + \$558.39 = \$1,223.45$$

Again, present values are comparable because they are measured in the same time period's dollars.

With a financial calculator, this becomes a three-step solution, as shown in the margin. First, you'll solve for the present value of the $1,000 received at the end of 7 years, then you'll solve for the present value of the $1,000 received at the end of 10 years, and finally, you'll add the two present values together. Remember, once you've found the present value of those future cash flows you can add them together because they're measured in the same period's dollars.

Concept Check

1. What is the relationship between the present-value equation (5-2) and the future-value, or compounding, equation (5-1)?
2. Why is the present value of a future sum always less than that sum's future value?

Annuities

 3 Understand annuities.

annuity a series of equal dollar payments made for a specified number of years.

ordinary annuity an annuity where the cash flows occur at the end of each period.

An **annuity** is a *series of equal dollar payments for a specified number of years*. When we talk about annuities, we are referring to **ordinary annuities** unless otherwise noted. With an ordinary annuity *the payments occur at the end of each period*. Because annuities occur frequently in finance—for example, as bond interest payments—we treat them specially. Although compounding and determining the present value of an annuity can be dealt with using the methods we have just described, these processes can be time consuming, especially for larger annuities. Thus, we have modified the single cash flow formulas to deal directly with annuities.

Compound Annuities

compound annuity depositing an equal sum of money at the end of each year for a certain number of years and allowing it to grow.

A **compound annuity** involves *depositing or investing an equal sum of money at the end of each year for a certain number of years and allowing it to grow*. Perhaps we are saving money for education, a new car, or a vacation home. In any case, we want to know how much our savings will have grown at some point in the future.

Actually, we can find the answer by using equation (5-1), our compounding equation, and compounding each of the individual deposits to its future value. For example, if to provide for a college education we are going to deposit $500 at the end of each year for the next 5 years in a bank where it will earn 6 percent interest, how much will we have at the end of 5 years? Compounding each of these values using equation (5-1), we find that we will have $2,818.50 at the end of 5 years.

$$FV_5 = \$500(1 + 0.6)^4 + \$500(1 + 0.6)^3 + \$500(1 + 0.6)^2 + \$500(1 + 0.6) + \$500$$
$$= \$500(1.262) + \$500(1.191) + \$500(1.124) + \$500(1.060) + \$500$$
$$= \$631.00 + \$595.50 + \$562.00 + \$530.00 + \$500.00$$
$$= \$2,818.50$$

DID YOU GET IT?
SOLVING FOR THE PRESENT VALUE WITH TWO FLOWS IN DIFFERENT YEARS

There are several different ways you can solve this problem—using the mathematical formulas, a financial calculator, or a spreadsheet—each one giving you the same answer.

1. **Using the Mathematical Formula.** Substituting the values of $n = 5, r = 4$ percent, and $FV_5 = \$500$; and $n = 10, r = 4$ percent, and $FV_{10} = \$1,000$ into equation (5-2) and adding these values together, we find

$$\text{present value} = \$500\left[\frac{1}{(1 + 0.04)^5}\right] + \$1,000\left[\frac{1}{(1 + 0.04)^{10}}\right]$$
$$= \$500(0.822) + \$1,000(0.676)$$
$$= \$411 + \$676 = \$1,087$$

2. **Using a Financial Calculator.** Again, it is a three-step process. First calculate the present value of each cash flow individually, and then add the present values together.

STEP 1
CALCULATOR SOLUTION

Data Input	Function Key
5	N
4	I/Y
−500	FV
0	PMT

Function Key	Answer
CPT	
PV	410.96

STEP 2
CALCULATOR SOLUTION

Data Input	Function Key
10	N
4	I/Y
−1,000	FV
0	PMT

Function Key	Answer
CPT	
PV	675.56

STEP 3
Add the two present values that you just calculated together:

$ 410.96
675.56
$1,086.52

3. **Using an Excel Spreadsheet.** Using Excel, the cash flows are brought back to the present using the =PV function. If the future values were entered as positive values, our answer will come out as a negative number.

By examining the mathematics involved and the graph of the movement of money through time in Table 5-1, we can see that all we are really doing is adding up the future values of different cash flows that initially occurred in different time periods. Fortunately, there is also an equation that helps us calculate the future value of an annuity:

$$\text{future value of an annuity} = PMT\left[\frac{\text{future value factor} - 1}{r}\right]$$
$$= PMT\left[\frac{(1 + r)^n - 1}{r}\right] \tag{5-3}$$

To simplify our discussion, we will refer to the value in brackets in equation (5-3) as the **annuity future value factor**. It is defined as $\left[\frac{(1 + r)^n - 1}{r}\right]$.

Using this new notation, we can rewrite equation (5-3) as follows:

$$FV_n = PMT\left[\frac{(1 + r)^n - 1}{r}\right] = PMT(\text{annuity future value factor})$$

annuity future value factor the value of $\left[\frac{(1 + r)^n - 1}{r}\right]$ used as a multiplier to calculate the future value of an annuity.

Rather than asking how much we will accumulate if we deposit an equal sum in a savings account each year, a more common question to ask is how much we must deposit each

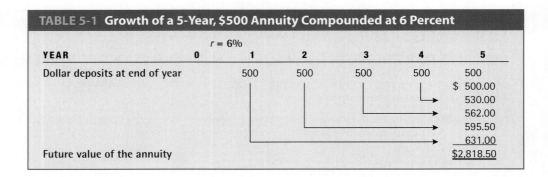

TABLE 5-1 Growth of a 5-Year, $500 Annuity Compounded at 6 Percent

YEAR		0	1	2	3	4	5
Dollar deposits at end of year			500	500	500	500	500
							$ 500.00
							530.00
							562.00
							595.50
							631.00
Future value of the annuity							$2,818.50

year to accumulate a certain amount of savings. This problem frequently occurs with respect to saving for large expenditures.

For example, if we know that we need $10,000 for college in 8 years, how much must we deposit in the bank at the end of each year at 6 percent interest to have the college money ready? In this case we know the values of n, r, and FV_n in equation (5-3); what we do not know is the value of PMT. Substituting these example values in equation (5-3), we find

$$\$10,000 = PMT\left[\frac{(1 + 0.06)^8 - 1}{0.06}\right]$$

$$\$10,000 = PMT(9.8975)$$

$$\frac{\$10,000}{9.8975} = PMT$$

$$\$1,010.36 = PMT$$

Thus, we must deposit $1,010.36 in the bank at the end of each year for 8 years at 6 percent interest to accumulate $10,000 at the end of 8 years.

EXAMPLE 5.7

How much must we deposit in an 8 percent savings account at the end of each year to accumulate $5,000 at the end of 10 years? Substituting the values $FV_{10} = \$5,000$, $n = 10$, and $r = 8$ percent into equation (5-3), we find

$$\$5,000 = PMT\left[\frac{(1 + 0.08)^{10} - 1}{0.08}\right]$$

$$\$5,000 = PMT(14.4866)$$

$$\frac{5,000}{14.4866} = PMT$$

$$\$345.15 = PMT$$

Thus, we must deposit $345.15 per year for 10 years at 8 percent to accumulate $5,000.

The Present Value of an Annuity

Pension payments, insurance obligations, and the interest owed on bonds all involve annuities. To compare these three types of investments we need to know the present value of each. For example, if we wish to know what $500 received at the end of each of the next 5 years is worth today given a discount rate of 6 percent, we can simply substitute the

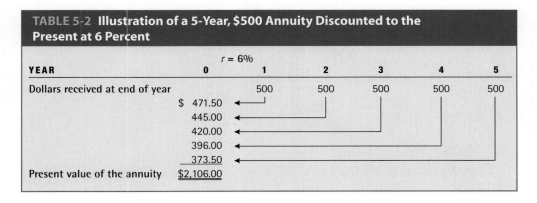

TABLE 5-2 **Illustration of a 5-Year, $500 Annuity Discounted to the Present at 6 Percent**

appropriate values into equation (5-2), such that

$$PV = \$500\left[\frac{1}{(1 + 0.06)^1}\right] + \$500\left[\frac{1}{(1 + 0.06)^2}\right] + \$500\left[\frac{1}{(1 + 0.06)^3}\right]$$

$$+ \$500\left[\frac{1}{(1 + 0.06)^4}\right] + \$500\left[\frac{1}{(1 + 0.06)^5}\right]$$

$$= \$500(0.943) + \$500(0.890) + \$500(0.840) + \$500(0.792) + \$500(0.747)$$

$$= \$2,106$$

Thus, the present value of this annuity is $2,106.00. By examining the mathematics involved and the graph of the movement of money through time in Table 5-2, we can see that all we are really doing is adding up the present values of different cash flows that initially occurred in different time periods. Fortunately, there is also an equation that helps us calculate the present value of an annuity:

$$\text{present value of an annuity} = PMT\left[\frac{1 - \text{present value factor}}{r}\right]$$

$$= PMT\left[\frac{1 - (1 + r)^{-n}}{r}\right] \qquad (5\text{-}4)$$

To simplify our discussion, we will refer to the value in the brackets in equation (5-4) as the **annuity present value factor**. It is defined as $\left[\dfrac{1 - (1 + r)^{-n}}{r}\right]$.

annuity present value factor the value of $\left[\dfrac{1 - (1 + r)^{-n}}{r}\right]$ used as a multiplier to calculate the present value of an annuity

EXAMPLE 5.8

What is the present value of a 10-year $1,000 annuity discounted back to the present at 5 percent? Substituting $n = 10$ years, $r = 5$ percent, and $PMT = \$1,000$ into equation (5-4), we find

$$PV = \$1,000\left[\frac{1 - (1 + 0.05)^{-10}}{0.05}\right]$$

$$PV = \$1,000(7.722)$$

$$= \$7,722$$

Thus, the present value of this annuity is $7,722.

CALCULATOR SOLUTION

Data Input	Function Key
10	N
5	I/Y
−1,000	PMT
0	PV

Function Key	Answer
CPT	
PV	7,722

When we solve for *PMT*, the financial interpretation of this action would be: How much can be withdrawn, perhaps as a pension or to make loan payments, from an account that earns

r percent compounded annually for each of the next n years if we wish to have nothing left at the end of n years? For example, if we have $5,000 in an account earning 8 percent interest, how large of an annuity can we draw out each year if we want nothing left at the end of 5 years? In this case the present value, PV, of the annuity is $5,000, $n = 5$ years, $r = 8$ percent, and PMT is unknown. Substituting this into equation (5-4), we find

$$\$5,000 = PMT\left[\frac{1 - (1 + 0.08)^{-5}}{0.08}\right] = PMT(3.993)$$

$$\$1,252 = PMT$$

Thus, this account will fall to zero at the end of 5 years if we withdraw $1,252 at the end of each year.

Annuities Due

annuity due an annuity in which the payments occur at the beginning of each period.

Annuities due are really just *ordinary annuities in which all the annuity payments have been shifted forward by 1 year*. Compounding them and determining their future and present value is actually quite simple. With an annuity due, each annuity payment occurs at the beginning of each period rather than at the end of the period. Let's first look at how this affects our compounding calculations.

Because an annuity due merely shifts the payments from the end of the year to the beginning of the year, we now compound the cash flows for one additional year. Therefore, the compound sum of an annuity due is simply

future value of an annuity due = future value of an annuity $\times$ (1 + r)

$$FV_n(\text{annuity due}) = PMT\left[\frac{(1 + r)^n - 1}{r}\right](1 + r) \tag{5-5}$$

In an earlier example on saving for college, we calculated the value of a 5-year ordinary annuity of $500 invested in the bank at 6 percent to be $2,818.50. If we now assume this to be a 5-year annuity due, its future value increases from $2,818.50 to $2,987.66.

$$FV_5 = \$500\left[\frac{(1 + 0.06)^5 - 1}{0.06}\right](1 + 0.06)$$

$$= \$500(5.637093)(1.06)$$

$$= \$2,987.66$$

Likewise, with the present value of an annuity due, we simply receive each cash flow 1 year earlier—that is, we receive it at the beginning of each year rather than at the end of each year. Thus, because each cash flow is received 1 year earlier, it is discounted back for one less period. To determine the present value of an annuity due, we merely need to find the present value of an ordinary annuity and multiply that by (1 + r), which in effect cancels out 1 year's discounting.

present value of an annuity due = present value of an annuity $\times$ (1 + r)

$$PV(\text{annuity due}) = PMT\left[\frac{1 - (1 + r)^{-n}}{r}\right](1 + r) \tag{5-6}$$

Reexamining the earlier college saving example in which we calculated the present value of a 5-year ordinary annuity of $500 given a discount rate of 6 percent, we now find that if it is an annuity due rather than an ordinary annuity, the present value increases from $2,106 to $2,232.55.

$$PV = \$500\left[\frac{1 - (1 + 0.06)^{-5}}{0.06}\right](1 + 0.06)$$

$$= \$500(4.21236)(1.06)$$

$$= \$2,232.55$$

With a financial calculator, first treat it as if it were an ordinary annuity and find the future or present value. Then multiply the present value times $(1 + r)$, in this case times 1.06; this is shown in the margin.

The result of all this is that both the future and present values of an annuity due are larger than those of an ordinary annuity because in each case all payments are received earlier. Thus, when *compounding*, an annuity due compounds for one additional year, whereas when *discounting*, an annuity due discounts for one less year. Although annuities due are used with some frequency in accounting, their usage is quite limited in finance. Therefore, in the remainder of this text, whenever the term *annuity* is used, you should assume that we are referring to an ordinary annuity.

EXAMPLE 5.9

The Virginia State Lottery runs like most other state lotteries: You must select 6 out of 44 numbers correctly in order to win the jackpot. If you come close, there are some significantly lesser prizes, which we ignore for now. For each million dollars in the lottery jackpot, you receive $50,000 per year for 20 years, and your chance of winning is 1 in 7.1 million. A recent advertisement for the Virginia State Lottery went as follows: "Okay, you got two kinds of people. You've got the kind who play Lotto all the time, and the kind who play Lotto some of the time. You know, like only on a Saturday when they stop in at the store on the corner for some peanut butter cups and diet soda and the jackpot happens to be really big. I mean, my friend Ned? He's like 'Hey, it's only $2 million this week.' Well, hellloooo, anybody home? I mean, I don't know about you, but I wouldn't mind having a measly 2 mill coming *my* way. . . ."

What is the present value of these payments? The answer to this question depends on what assumption you make about the time value of money. In this case, let's assume that your required rate of return on an investment with this level of risk is 10 percent. Keeping in mind that the Lotto is an annuity due—that is, on a $2 million lottery you would get $100,000 immediately and $100,000 at the end of each of the next 19 years. Thus, the present value of this 20-year annuity due discounted back to present at 10 percent becomes:

$$PV\text{(annuity due)} = PMT\left[\frac{1 - (1 + r)^{-n}}{r}\right](1 + r) \tag{5-6}$$

$$= \$100,000\left[\frac{1 - (1 + 0.10)^{-20}}{0.10}\right](1 + 0.10)$$

$$= \$100,000(8.51356)(1.10)$$

$$= \$851,356(1.10)$$

$$= \$936,492$$

Present value of an annuity due:

STEP 1
CALCULATOR SOLUTION

Data Input	Function Key
20	N
10	I/Y
−100,000	PMT
0	FV

Function Key	Answer
CPT	
PV	851,356

STEP 2

$851,356
×1.10
$936,492

Solving this is a two-step process. In step 1, you treat the jackpot as if it were an ordinary annuity and find the present value. Then multiply the present value times $(1 + r)$, in this case times 1.10; this is shown in the margin.

Thus, the present value of the $2 million Lotto jackpot is less than $1 million if 10 percent is the discount rate. Moreover, because the chance of winning is only 1 in 7.1 million, the expected value of each dollar "invested" in the lottery is only (1/7.1 million) × ($936,492) = 13.19¢. That is, for every dollar you spend on the lottery you should expect to get, on average, about 13 cents back—not a particularly good deal. Although this ignores the minor payments for coming close, it also ignores taxes. In this case, it looks like "my friend Ned" is doing the right thing by staying clear of the lottery. Obviously, the main value of the lottery is entertainment. Unfortunately, without an understanding of the time value of money, it can sound like a good investment.

Amortized Loans

amortized loan a loan that is paid off in equal periodic payments.

The procedure of solving for *PMT*, the annuity payment value when *r*, *n*, and *PV* are known, is also used to determine what payments are associated with paying off a loan in equal installments over time. *Loans that are paid off this way, in equal periodic payments,* are called **amortized loans**. Actually, the word *amortization* comes from the Latin word meaning "about to die." When you pay off a loan using regular, fixed payments, that loan is amortized. Although the payments are fixed, different amounts of each payment are applied toward the principal and the interest. With each payment you owe a bit less toward the principal. As a result, the amount that has to go toward the interest payment declines with each payment, whereas the portion of each payment that goes toward the principal increases. Figure 5-4 illustrates the process of amortization.

For example, suppose a firm wants to purchase a piece of machinery. To do this, it borrows $6,000 to be repaid in four equal payments at the end of each of the next 4 years, and the interest rate that is paid to the lender is 15 percent on the outstanding portion of the loan. To determine what the annual payments associated with the repayment of this debt will be, we simply use equation (5-4) and solve for the value of *PMT*, the annual annuity. In this case, we know *PV*, *r*, and *n*. *PV*, the present value of the annuity, is $6,000; *r*, the annual interest rate, is 15 percent; and *n*, the number of years for which the annuity will last, is 4 years. *PMT*, the annuity payment received (by the lender and paid by the firm) at the end of each year, is unknown. Substituting these values into equation (5-4), we find

$$\$6,000 = PMT\left[\frac{1 - (1 + 0.15)^{-4}}{0.15}\right]$$

$$\$6,000 = PMT(2.85498)$$

$$\$2,101.59 = PMT$$

CALCULATOR SOLUTION

Data Input	Function Key
4	N
15	I/Y
−6,000	PV
0	FV

Function Key	Answer
CPT	
PMT	2,101.59

Concept Check

1. How does an annuity due differ from an ordinary annuity?
2. Why are both the future and present values greater for an annuity?

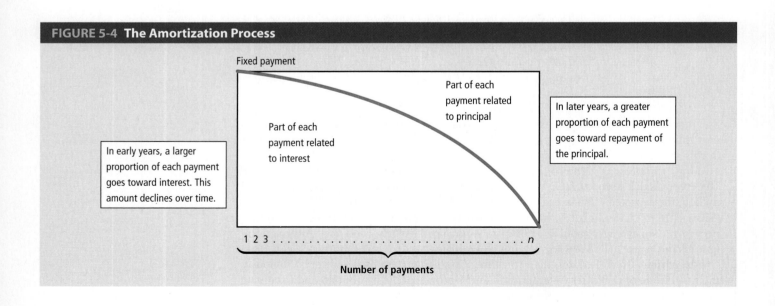

FIGURE 5-4 The Amortization Process

Fixed payment

In early years, a larger proportion of each payment goes toward interest. This amount declines over time.

Part of each payment related to interest

Part of each payment related to principal

In later years, a greater proportion of each payment goes toward repayment of the principal.

1 2 3 . . . . *n*

Number of payments

TABLE 5-3 Loan Amortization Schedule Involving a $6,000 Loan at 15 Percent to Be Repaid in 4 Years

Year	Annuity	Interest Portion of the Annuity[a]	Repayment of the principal Portion of the Annuity[b]	Outstanding Loan Balance After the Annuity Payment
0	0	0	0	$6,000.00
1	$2,101.59	$900.00	$1,201.59	4,798.41
2	2,101.59	719.76	1,381.83	3,416.58
3	2,101.59	512.49	1,589.10	1,827.48
4	2,101.59	274.12	1,827.48	

[a]The interest portion of the annuity is calculated by multiplying the outstanding loan balance at the beginning of the year by the interest rate of 15 percent. Thus, for year 1 it was $6,000 × 0.15 = $900.00, for year 2 it was $4,798.41 × 0.15 = $719.76, and so on.

[b]Repayment of the principal portion of the annuity was calculated by subtracting the interest portion of the annuity (column 2) from the annuity (column 1).

To repay the principal and interest on the outstanding loan in 4 years, the annual payments would be $2,101.59. The breakdown of interest and principal payments is given in the *loan amortization schedule* in Table 5-3, with very minor rounding error. As you can see, the interest portion of the payment declines each year as the loan outstanding balance declines.

Now let's use a spreadsheet to look at a loan amortization problem and calculate the monthly mortgage payment, and then determine how much of a specific payment goes toward interest and principal.

To buy a new house you take out a 25-year mortgage for $100,000. What will your monthly payments be if the interest rate on your mortgage is 8 percent? To solve this problem, you must first convert the annual rate of 8 percent into a monthly rate by dividing it by 12. Second, you have to convert the number of periods into months by multiplying 25 years times 12 months per year for a total of 300 months.

	A	B
1	interest rate (rate) =	0.6667%
2	number of periods (nper) =	300
3	present value (pv) =	$100,000
4	future value (fv) =	$0
5		
6	payment (pmt) =	($771.82)
7		
8	Excel formula =pmt(rate,nper,pv,fv)	
9	Entered in cell b6: =pmt((8/12)%,b2,b3,b4	

You can also use Excel to calculate the interest and principal portion of any loan amortization payment. You can do this using the following Excel functions:

CALCULATION	FUNCTION
Interest portion of payment	=IPMT(rate, per, nper, pv, fv)
Principal portion of payment	=PPMT(rate, per, nper, pv, fv)
where per refers to the number of an individual periodic payment	

For this example, you can determine how much of the 48th monthly payment goes toward interest and principal as follows,

	A	B
1	interest rate (rate) =	0.6667%
2	payment number (per) =	48
3	number of periods (nper) =	300
4	present value (pv) =	$100,000
5	future value (fv) =	$0
6		
7	Interest portion of the 48th payment =	($628.12)
8	Principal portion of the 48th loan payment =	($143.69)
9		
10	Entered values in cell b7: =IPMT((8/12)%,b2,b3,b4,b5)	
11	Entered values in cell b8: =PPMT((8/12)%,b2,b3,b4,b5)	

Concept Check

1. What is an amortized loan?
2. What functions in Excel help determine the amount of interest and principal in a mortgage payment?

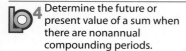

4 Determine the future or present value of a sum when there are nonannual compounding periods.

Making Interest Rates Comparable

In order to make intelligent decisions about where to invest or borrow money, it is important that we make the stated interest rates comparable. Unfortunately, some rates are quoted as compounded annually, whereas others are quoted as compounded quarterly or compounded daily. But it is not fair to compare interest rates with different compounding periods to each other. Thus, the only way interest rates can logically be compared is to convert them to a common compounding period.

In order to understand the process of making different interest rates comparable, it is first necessary to define the nominal, or quoted, interest rate. The nominal, or quoted, rate is the rate of interest stated on the contract. For example, if you shop around for loans and are quoted 8 percent compounded annually and 7.85 percent compounded quarterly, then 8 percent and 7.85 percent would both be nominal rates. Unfortunately, because on one rate the interest is compounded annually, but on the other interest is compounded quarterly, the two rates are not comparable. In fact, it is never appropriate to compare nominal rates *unless* they include the same number of compounding periods per year. To make them comparable, we must calculate their equivalent rate at some common compounding period. We do this by calculating the **effective annual rate (EAR)**. This is *the annual compound rate that produces the same return as the nominal or quoted rate.*

Let's assume that you are considering borrowing money from a bank at 12 percent compounded monthly. If you borrow $1 at 1 percent per month for 12 months you'd owe,

$$\$1.00(1.01)^{12} = \$1.126825$$

In effect, you are borrowing at 12.6825 percent rather than just by 12 percent. Thus, the EAR for 12 percent compounded monthly is 12.6825. It tells us the annual rate that would produce the same loan payments as the nominal rate. In other words, you'll end up with the same monthly payments if you borrow at 12.6825 percent compounded annually, or 12 percent compounded monthly. Thus, 12.6825 is the effective annual rate (EAR) for 12 percent compounded monthly.

Generalizing on this process, we can calculate the EAR using the following equation:

$$EAR = \left(1 + \frac{quoted\ rate}{m}\right)^{m} - 1 \tag{5-7}$$

where *EAR* is the effective annual rate and *m* is the number of compounding periods within a year. Given the wide variety of compounding periods used by businesses and banks,

effective annual rate (EAR) the annual compound rate that produces the same return as the nominal, or quoted, rate when something is compounded on a nonannual basis. In effect, the EAR provides the true rate of return.

it is important to know how to make these rates comparable so that logical decisions can be made.

> **EXAMPLE 5.10**
>
> You've just received your first credit card and the problem is the rate. It looks pretty high to you. The quoted rate is 21.7 percent, and when you look closer, you notice that the interest is compounded daily. What's the EAR, or effective annual rate, on your credit card?
>
> To calculate the EAR we can use equation (5-7)
>
> $$EAR = \left[1 + \frac{\text{quoted rate}}{m}\right]^m - 1 \tag{5-7}$$
>
> where the quoted rate is 21.7 percent, or 0.217, and m is 365. Substituting, we get
>
> $$EAR = \left[1 + \frac{0.217}{365}\right]^{365} - 1$$
>
> $$EAR = 1.242264 - 1 = 0.242264 \text{ or } 24.2264 \text{ percent}$$
>
> Thus, in reality, the effective annual rate is actually 24.2264 percent.

Finding Present and Future Values with Nonannual Periods

The same logic that applies to calculating the EAR also applies to calculating present and future values when the periods are semiannual, quarterly, or any other nonannual period. Previously when we moved money through time we assumed that the cash flows occurred annually and the compounding or discounting period was always annual. However, it need not be, as evidenced by the fact that bonds generally pay interest semiannually and most mortgages require monthly payments.

For example, if we invest our money for 5 years at 8 percent interest compounded semiannually, we are really investing our money for 10 6-month periods during which we receive 4 percent interest each period. If it is 8 percent compounded quarterly for 5 years, we receive 2 percent interest per period for 20 3-month periods. This process can easily be generalized, giving us the following formula for finding the future value of an investment for which interest is compounded in nonannual periods:

$$FV_n = PV\left[1 + \frac{r}{m}\right]^{m \cdot n} \tag{5-8}$$

where FV_n = the future value of the investment at the end of n years
n = the number of years during which the compounding occurs
r = annual interest (or discount) rate
PV = the present value or original amount invested at the beginning of the first year
m = the number of times compounding occurs during the year

In fact, all the formulas for moving money through time can be easily modified to accommodate nonannual periods. In each case, we begin with the formulas we introduced in this chapter, and make two adjustments—the first where n, the number of years appears, and the second where r, the annual interest rate appears. Thus, the adjustment involves two steps:

◆ n becomes the number of periods or n (the number of years) times m (the number of times compounding occurs per year). Thus, if it is monthly compounding for 10 years, n becomes $10 \times 12 = 120$ months in 10 years, and if it is daily compounding over 10 years, it becomes $10 \times 365 = 3,650$ days in 10 years.

◆ r becomes the interest rate per period or r (the annual interest rate) divided by m (the number of times compounding occurs per year). Thus, if it is a 6 percent annual rate with monthly compounding, r becomes $6\% \div 12 = 0.5$ percent per month, and if it is a 6 percent annual rate compounded daily, then r becomes $(6\% \div 365)$ per day.

CAN YOU DO IT?

HOW MUCH CAN YOU AFFORD TO SPEND ON A HOUSE?
AN AMORTIZED LOAN WITH MONTHLY PAYMENTS

You've been house shopping and aren't sure how big a house you can afford. You figure you can handle monthly mortgage payments of $1,250, and you can get a 30-year loan at 6.5 percent. How big of a mortgage can you afford? In this problem, you are solving for *PV*, which is the amount of money you can borrow today.

(The solution can be found on page 143.)

TABLE 5-4 The Value of $100 Compounded at Various Intervals

	FOR 1 YEAR AT *r* PERCENT			
r =	2%	5%	10%	15%
Compounded annually	$102.00	$105.00	$110.00	$115.00
Compounded semiannually	102.01	105.06	110.25	115.56
Compounded quarterly	102.02	105.09	110.38	115.87
Compounded monthly	102.02	105.12	110.47	116.08
Compounded weekly (52)	102.02	105.12	110.51	116.16
Compounded daily (365)	102.02	105.13	110.52	116.18
	FOR 10 YEARS AT *r* PERCENT			
r =	2%	5%	10%	15%
Compounded annually	$121.90	$162.89	$259.37	$404.56
Compounded semiannually	122.02	163.86	265.33	424.79
Compounded quarterly	122.08	164.36	268.51	436.04
Compounded monthly	122.10	164.70	270.70	444.02
Compounded weekly (52)	122.14	164.83	271.57	447.20
Compounded daily (365)	122.14	164.87	271.79	448.03

We can see the value of intrayear compounding by examining Table 5-4. Because "interest is earned on interest" more frequently as the length of the compounding period declines, there is an inverse relationship between the length of the compounding period and the effective annual interest rate: The shorter the compounding period is, the higher the effective interest rate will be. Conversely, the longer the compounding period is, the lower the effective interest rate will be.

CALCULATOR SOLUTION

Data Input	Function Key
20	N
12/4	I/Y
100	PV
0	PMT

Function Key	Answer
CPT	
FV	−180.61

EXAMPLE 5.11

If we place $100 in a savings account that yields 12 percent compounded quarterly, what will our investment grow to at the end of 5 years? Substituting $n = 5$, $m = 4$, $r = 12$ percent, and $PV = \$100$ into equation (5-8), we find

$$FV_5 = \$100\left(1 + \frac{0.12}{4}\right)^{4 \cdot 5}$$

$$= \$100(1 + 0.03)^{20}$$

$$= \$100(1.8061)$$

$$= \$180.61$$

Thus, we will have $180.61 at the end of 5 years. In this problem, N becomes the number of quarters in 5 years while I/Y becomes the interest rate per period. In effect 3 percent per quarter for 20 quarters.

DID YOU GET IT?

HOW MUCH CAN YOU AFFORD TO SPEND ON A HOUSE? AN AMORTIZED LOAN WITH MONTHLY PAYMENTS

There are several different ways you can solve this problem—using the mathematical formulas, a financial calculator, or a spreadsheet—each one giving you the same answer.

1. **Using the Mathematical Formulas.** Again, you need to multiply n times m, and divide r by m, where m is the number of compounding periods per year. Thus,

$$PV = \$1{,}250 \left[\frac{1 - \dfrac{1}{\left(1 + \dfrac{.065}{12}\right)^{30 \cdot 12}}}{\dfrac{.065}{12}} \right]$$

$$PV = \$1{,}250 \left[\frac{1 - \dfrac{1}{(1 + .00541667)^{360}}}{.00541667} \right]$$

$$PV = \$1{,}250 \left[\frac{1 - \dfrac{1}{6.99179797}}{.00541667} \right]$$

$$PV = \$1{,}250(158.210816)$$

$$PV = \$197{,}763.52$$

2. **Using a Financial Calculator.** First, you must convert everything to months. To do this you would first convert n into months by multiplying n times m (30 times 12) and enter this into $\boxed{N}$. Next you would enter the interest rate as a monthly rate by dividing r by m and entering this number into $\boxed{I/Y}$. Finally, make sure that the value entered as $\boxed{PMT}$ is a monthly figure, that is, it is the monthly payment value.

CALCULATOR SOLUTION

Data Input	Function Key
360	$\boxed{N}$
6.5/12	$\boxed{I/Y}$
−1,250	$\boxed{PMT}$
0	$\boxed{FV}$

Function Key	Answer
$\boxed{CPT}$	
$\boxed{PV}$	197,763.52

3. **Using an Excel Spreadsheet.**

	A	B
1	interest rate (rate) =	0.5417%
2	number of periods (nper) =	360
3	payment (pmt) =	1250
4	future value (fv) =	0
5		
6	present value (pv) =	($197,763.52)
7	Entered values in cell b6: =PV((6.5/12)%,b2,b3,b4)	
8		

EXAMPLE 5.12

In 2009 the average U.S. household owed about $10,000 in credit card debt, and the average interest rate on credit card debt was 13.0 percent. On many credit cards the minimum monthly payment is 4 percent of the debt balance. If the average household paid off 4 percent of the initial amount it owed each month, that is, made payments of $400 each month, how many months would it take to repay this credit card debt? Use a financial calculator to solve this problem.

You'll notice in the solution that appears in the margin that the value for *PMT* goes in as a negative. The answer is over 29 months.

CALCULATOR SOLUTION

Data Input	Function Key
13.0/12	$\boxed{I/Y}$
10,000	$\boxed{PV}$
−400	$\boxed{PMT}$
0	$\boxed{FV}$

Function Key	Answer
$\boxed{CPT}$	
$\boxed{N}$	29.3

Concept Check

1. Why does the future value of a given amount increase when interest is compounded nonannually as opposed to annually?

2. How do you adjust the present- and future-value formulas when interest is compounded monthly?

5 Determine the present value of an uneven stream of payments and understand perpetuities.

STEP 1

Bring the $200 at the end of year 2 back to present:

CALCULATOR SOLUTION

Data Input	Function Key
2	N
6	I/Y
200	FV
0	PMT

Function Key	Answer
CPT	
PV	−178.00

STEP 2

Bring the negative $400 at the end of year 3 back to present:

CALCULATOR SOLUTION

Data Input	Function Key
3	N
6	I/Y
0	PMT
−400	FV

Function Key	Answer
CPT	
PV	335.85

STEP 3

Bring the 7-year, $500 annuity beginning at the end of year 4 back to the beginning of year 4, which is the same as the end of year 3:

CALCULATOR SOLUTION

Data Input	Function Key
7	N
6	I/Y
500	PMT
0	FV

Function Key	Answer
CPT	
PV	−2,791.19

The Present Value of an Uneven Stream

Although some projects will involve a single cash flow, and some will involve annuities, many projects will involve uneven cash flows over several years. Chapter 10, which examines investments in fixed assets, presents this situation repeatedly. There we will be comparing not only the present value of cash flows generated by different projects but also the cash inflows and outflows generated by a particular project to determine that project's present value. However, this will not be difficult because the present value of any cash flow is measured in today's dollars and thus can be compared, through addition for inflows and subtraction for outflows, to the present value of any other cash flow also measured in today's dollars. For example, if we wished to find the present value of the following cash flows

YEAR	CASH FLOW	YEAR	CASH FLOW
1	$ 0	6	500
2	200	7	500
3	−400	8	500
4	500	9	500
5	500	10	500

given a 6 percent discount rate, we would merely discount the flows back to the present and total them by adding in the positive flows and subtracting the negative ones. However, this problem is complicated by the annuity of $500 that runs from years 4 through 10. To accommodate this, we can first discount the annuity back to the beginning of period 4 (or end of period 3) and get its present value at that point in time. We then bring this single cash flow (which is the present value of the 7-year annuity) back to the present. In effect we discount twice, first back to the end of period 3, then back to the present. This is shown graphically in Table 5-5 and numerically in Table 5-6. Thus, the present value of this uneven stream of cash flows is $2,185.69.

Remember, once the cash flows from an investment have been brought back to the present, they can be combined by adding and subtracting to determine the project's total present value.

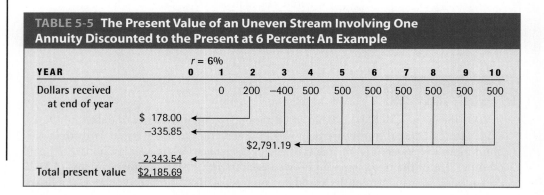

TABLE 5-5 The Present Value of an Uneven Stream Involving One Annuity Discounted to the Present at 6 Percent: An Example

YEAR	0	1	2	3	4	5	6	7	8	9	10
Dollars received at end of year	0	200	−400	500	500	500	500	500	500	500	

$r = 6\%$

$ 178.00
−335.85
$2,791.19
2,343.54
Total present value $2,185.69

TABLE 5-6 Determining the Present Value of an Uneven Stream Involving One Annuity Discounted to the Present at 6 Percent: An Example

1. Present value of $200 received at the end of 2 years at 6% =	$178.00
2. Present value of a $400 outflow at the end of 3 years at 6% =	−335.85
3. (a) Value at end of year 3 of a $500 annuity, years 4–10 at 6% = $2,791.19	
(b) Present value of $2,791.19 received at the end of year 3 at 6% =	2,343.54
4. Total present value =	$2,185.69

Concept Check

1. How would you calculate the present value of an investment that produced cash flows of $100 received at the end of year 1 and $700 at the end of year 2?

Perpetuities

A **perpetuity** is *an annuity that continues forever*; that is, every year following its establishment this investment pays the same dollar amount. An example of a perpetuity is preferred stock that pays a constant dollar dividend infinitely. Determining the present value of a perpetuity is delightfully simple; we merely need to divide the constant flow by the discount rate. For example, the present value of a $100 perpetuity discounted back to the present at 5 percent is $100/0.05 = $2,000. Thus, the equation representing the present value of a perpetuity is

$$PV = \frac{PP}{r} \tag{5-9}$$

where: PV = the present value of the perpetuity
PP = the constant dollar amount provided by the perpetuity
r = the annual interest (or discount) rate

EXAMPLE 5.13

What is the present value of a $500 perpetuity discounted back to the present at 8 percent? Substituting PP = $500 and r = 0.08 into equation (5-9), we find

$$PV = \frac{\$500}{0.08} = \$6,250$$

Thus, the present value of this perpetuity is $6,250.

Concept Check

1. What is a perpetuity?
2. When r, the annual interest (or discount) rate, increases, what happens to the present value of a perpetuity? Why?

The Multinational Firm: The Time Value of Money

6 Explain how the international setting complicates the time value of money.

P3
Principle

From **Principle 3: Risk Requires a Reward**, we found that investors demand a return for delaying consumption, as well as an additional return for taking on added risk. The discount rate that we use to move money through time should reflect this return for delaying consumption; and as the Fisher Effect showed in Chapter 2, this discount rate should reflect anticipated inflation. In the United States, anticipated inflation has historically been quite low, although it does tend to fluctuate over time. Elsewhere in the world, however, the inflation rate is difficult to predict because it can be dramatically high and fluctuate tremendously.

Let's look at Argentina, keeping in mind that similar examples abound in Central and South America and Eastern Europe. At the beginning of 1992, Argentina introduced its fifth currency in 22 years, the new peso. The austral, the currency that was replaced, was introduced in June 1985 and was initially equal in value to $1.25 U.S. currency. Five and a half

---

Sidebar (right column)

STEP 4
Bring the value we just calculated, which is the value of the 7-year annuity of $500 at the end of year 3, back to present.

CALCULATOR SOLUTION

Data Input	Function Key
3	N
6	I/Y
2,791.19	FV
0	PMT

Function Key	Answer
CPT	
PV	−2,343.54

STEP 5
Add the present value of the cash inflows and subtract the present value of the cash outflow (the $400 from the end of year 3) calculated in steps 1, 2, and 4.

$ 178.00
−335.85
+2,343.54
$ 2,185.69

perpetuity an annuity with an infinite life.

years later, it took 100,000 australs to equal $1. Inflation had reached the point at which the stack of money needed to buy a candy bar was bigger and weighed more than the candy bar itself, and many workers received their week's wages in grocery bags. Needless to say, if we were to move australs through time, we would have to use an extremely high interest or discount rate.

Unfortunately, in countries suffering from hyperinflation, inflation rates tend to fluctuate dramatically, and this makes estimating the expected inflation rate even more difficult. For example, in 1989 the inflation rate in Argentina was 4,924 percent; in 1990 it dropped to 1,344 percent; in 1991 it was only 84 percent; in 1992, only 18 percent; in 2000 it was close to zero, and by 2009 it was back up again, with some forecasts for 2010 putting it in the 20 percent range. Finally, here are two cases at the extreme: In July 1946 in Hungary, the rate of inflation was so high that prices doubled every 15 hours; while in November 2008, the *daily* inflation rate hit 98% in Zimbabwe with prices doubling virtually every day.

The bottom line on all this is that for companies doing business internationally, dramatic fluctuations in inflation rates can make choosing the appropriate discount rate to move money through time an extremely difficult process.

Concept Check

1. How does the international setting complicate the choice of the appropriate interest rate to use when discounting cash flows back to the present?

TABLE 5-7 Summary of Time Value of Money Equations

Calculation	Equation
Future value of a single payment	$FV_n = PV(1 + r)^n$
Present value of a single payment	$PV = FV_n \left[\dfrac{1}{(1 + r)^n} \right]$
Future value of an annuity	$FV \text{ of an annuity} = PMT \left[\dfrac{(1 + r)^n - 1}{r} \right]$
Present value of an annuity	$PV \text{ of an annuity} = PMT \left[\dfrac{1 - (1 + r)^{-n}}{r} \right]$
Future value of an annuity due	$FV_n(\text{annuity due}) = \text{future value of an annuity} \times (1 + r)$
Present value of an annuity due	$PV(\text{annuity due}) = \text{present value of an annuity} \times (1 + r)$
Effective annual return (EAR) =	$\left[1 + \dfrac{\text{quoted rate}}{m} \right]^m - 1$
Future value of a single payment with nonannual compounding	$FV_n = PV \left(1 + \dfrac{r}{m} \right)^{mn}$
Present value of a perpetuity	$PV = \dfrac{PP}{r}$

Notations: FV_n = the future value of the investment at the end of n years
  n = the number of years until payment will be received or during which compounding occurs
  r = the annual interest or discount rate
  PV = the present value of the future sum of money
  m = the number of times compounding occurs during the year
  PMT = the annuity payment deposited or received at the end of each year
  PP = the constant dollar amount provided by the perpetuity

Summary

Compound interest occurs when interest paid on an investment during the first period is added to the principal; then, during the second period, interest is earned on this new sum. The formula for this appears in Table 5-7.

Although there are several ways to move money through time, they all give you the same result. In the business world, the primary method is through the use of a financial spreadsheet, with Excel being the most popular. If you can use a financial calculator, you can easily apply your skills to a spreadsheet.

Actually, we have only one formula with which to calculate both present value and future value—we simply solve for different variables—FV and PV. This single compounding formula is $FV_n = PV(1 + r)^n$ and is presented in Table 5-7.

An annuity is a series of equal payments made for a specified number of years. In effect, it is calculated as the sum of the present or future value of the individual cash flows over the life of the annuity. The formulas for several types of annuities are given in Table 5-7.

If the cash flows from an annuity occur at the end of each period, the annuity is referred to as an ordinary annuity. If the cash flows occur at the beginning of each period, the annuity is referred to as an annuity due. We will assume that cash flows occur at the end of each period unless otherwise stated.

The procedure for solving for PMT, the annuity payment value when r, n, and PV are known, is also used to determine what payments are associated with paying off a loan in equal installments over time. Loans that are paid off this way, in equal periodic payments, are called amortized loans. Although the payments are fixed, different amounts of each payment are applied toward the principal and the interest. With each payment you make, you owe a bit less on the principal. As a result, the amount that goes toward the interest payment declines with each payment made, whereas the portion of each payment that goes toward the principal increases.

With nonannual compounding, interest is earned on interest more frequently because the length of the compounding period is shorter. As a result, there is an inverse relationship between the length of the compounding period and the effective annual interest rate. The formula for solving for the future value of a single payment with nonannual compounding is given in Table 5-7.

Although some projects will involve a single cash flow, and some will involve annuities, many projects will involve uneven cash flows over several years. However, finding the present or future value of these flows is not difficult because the present value of any cash flow measured in today's dollars can be compared, by adding the inflows and subtracting the outflows, to the present value of any other cash flow also measured in today's dollars.

A perpetuity is an annuity that continues forever; that is, every year following its establishment the investment pays the same dollar amount. An example of a perpetuity is preferred stock, which pays a constant dollar dividend infinitely. Determining the present value of a perpetuity is delightfully simple. We merely need to divide the constant flow by the discount rate.

For companies doing business internationally, dramatic fluctuations in inflation rates from country to country can make choosing the appropriate discount rate to move money through time an extremely difficult process.

 1 Explain the mechanics of compounding, that is, how money grows over time when it is invested.

 2 Discuss the relationship between compounding and bringing the value of money back to the present.

 3 Understand annuities.

 4 Determine the future or present value of a sum when there are nonannual compounding periods.

5 Determine the present value of an uneven stream of payments and understand perpetuities.

 6 Explain how the international setting complicates the time value of money.

Key Terms

Amortized loan   138

Annuity   132

Annuity due   136

Annuity future value factor   133

Annuity present value factor   135

Compound annuity   132

Compound interest   120

Effective annual rate (EAR)   140

Future value   121

Future value factor   121

Ordinary annuity   132

Perpetuity   145

Present value   129

Present value factor   129

Simple interest   121

Review Questions

All Review Questions and Study Problems are available in MyFinanceLab.

5-1. What is the time value of money? Why is it so important?

5-2. The process of discounting and compounding are related. Explain this relationship.

5-3. How would an increase in the interest rate (r) or a decrease in the holding period (n) affect the future value (FV_n) of a sum of money? Explain why.

5-4. Suppose you were considering depositing your savings in one of three banks, all of which pay 5 percent interest; bank A compounds annually, bank B compounds semiannually, and bank C compounds daily. Which bank would you choose? Why?

5-5. What is an annuity? Give some examples of annuities. Distinguish between an annuity and a perpetuity.

5-6. Compare some of the different financial calculators that are available on the Internet. Look at *Kiplinger Online calculators* (www.kiplinger.com/tools/index.html) which include saving and investing, mutual funds, bonds, stocks, home, auto, credit cards, and budgeting online calculators. Also go to www.dinkytown.net, www.bankrate.com/calculators.aspx, and www.interest.com and click on the "Calculators" link. Which financial calculators do you find to be the most useful? Why?

Self-Test Problems

Solutions to these problems are provided at the end of the chapter.

ST-1. You place $25,000 in a savings account paying an annual compound interest of 8 percent for 3 years and then move it into a savings account that pays 10 percent interest compounded annually. By how much will your money have grown at the end of 6 years?

ST-2. You purchase a boat for $35,000 and pay $5,000 down. You also agree to pay the rest over the next 10 years in 10 equal end-of-the-year payments plus 13 percent compound interest on the unpaid balance. What will be the amount of each payment?

Study Problems

5-1. (*Compound interest*) To what amount will the following investments accumulate?
  a. $5,000 invested for 10 years at 10 percent compounded annually
  b. $8,000 invested for 7 years at 8 percent compounded annually
  c. $775 invested for 12 years at 12 percent compounded annually
  d. $21,000 invested for 5 years at 5 percent compounded annually

5-2. (*Compound value solving for n*) How many years will the following take?
  a. $500 to grow to $1,039.50 if invested at 5 percent compounded annually
  b. $35 to grow to $53.87 if invested at 9 percent compounded annually
  c. $100 to grow to $298.60 if invested at 20 percent compounded annually
  d. $53 to grow to $78.76 if invested at 2 percent compounded annually

5-3. (*Compound value solving for r*) At what annual rate would the following have to be invested?
  a. $500 to grow to $1,948.00 in 12 years
  b. $300 to grow to $422.10 in 7 years
  c. $50 to grow to $280.20 in 20 years
  d. $200 to grow to $497.60 in 5 years

5-4. (*Present value*) What is the present value of the following future amounts?
  a. $800 to be received 10 years from now discounted back to the present at 10 percent
  b. $300 to be received 5 years from now discounted back to the present at 5 percent
  c. $1,000 to be received 8 years from now discounted back to the present at 3 percent
  d. $1,000 to be received 8 years from now discounted back to the present at 20 percent

5-5. (*Compound annuity*) What is the accumulated sum of each of the following streams of payments?
  a. $500 a year for 10 years compounded annually at 5 percent
  b. $100 a year for 5 years compounded annually at 10 percent
  c. $35 a year for 7 years compounded annually at 7 percent
  d. $25 a year for 3 years compounded annually at 2 percent

5-6. (*Present value of an annuity*) What is the present value of the following annuities?

    a. $2,500 a year for 10 years discounted back to the present at 7 percent

    b. $70 a year for 3 years discounted back to the present at 3 percent

    c. $280 a year for 7 years discounted back to the present at 6 percent

    d. $500 a year for 10 years discounted back to the present at 10 percent

5-7. (*Compound value*) Stanford Simmons, who recently sold his Porsche, placed $10,000 in a savings account paying annual compound interest of 6 percent.

    a. Calculate the amount of money that will have accrued if he leaves the money in the bank for 1, 5, and 15 years.

    b. If he moves his money into an account that pays 8 percent or one that pays 10 percent, rework part (a) using these new interest rates.

    c. What conclusions can you draw about the relationship between interest rates, time, and future sums from the calculations you have completed in this problem?

5-8. (*Future value*) Sarah Wiggum would like to make a single investment and have $2 million at the time of her retirement in 35 years. She has found a mutual fund that will earn 4 percent annually. How much will Sarah have to invest today? What if Sarah were a finance major and learned how to earn a 14 percent annual return, how much would she have to invest today?

5-9. (*Compound interest with nonannual periods*)

    a. Calculate the future sum of $5,000, given that it will be held in the bank 5 years at an annual interest rate of 6 percent.

    b. Recalculate part (a) using compounding periods that are (1) semiannual and (2) bimonthly.

    c. Recalculate parts (a) and (b) for a 12 percent annual interest rate.

    d. Recalculate part (a) using a time horizon of 12 years (annual interest rate is still 6 percent).

    e. With respect to the effect of changes in the stated interest rate and holding periods on future sums in parts (c) and (d), what conclusions do you draw when you compare these figures with the answers found in parts (a) and (b)?

5-10. (*Solving for r with annuities*) Nicki Johnson, a sophomore mechanical engineering student, receives a call from an insurance agent, who believes that Nicki is an older woman ready to retire from teaching. He talks to her about several annuities that she could buy that would guarantee her an annual fixed income. The annuities are as follows:

ANNUITY	INITIAL PAYMENT INTO ANNUITY (AT t = 0)	AMOUNT OF MONEY RECEIVED PER YEAR	DURATION OF ANNUITY (YEARS)
A	$50,000	$8,500	12
B	$60,000	$7,000	25
C	$70,000	$8,000	20

If Nicki could earn 11 percent on her money by placing it in a savings account, should she place it instead in any of the annuities? Which ones, if any? Why?

5-11. (*Future value*) Sales of a new finance book were 15,000 copies this year and were expected to increase by 20 percent per year. What are expected sales during each of the next 3 years? Graph this sales trend and explain.

5-12. (*Future value*) Albert Pujols hit 47 home runs in 2009. If his home-run output grew at a rate of 12 percent per year, what would it have been over the following 5 years?

5-13. (*Loan amortization*) Mr. Bill S. Preston, Esq., purchased a new house for $80,000. He paid $20,000 down and agreed to pay the rest over the next 25 years in 25 equal end-of-year payments plus 9 percent compound interest on the unpaid balance. What will these equal payments be?

5-14. (*Solving for PMT of an annuity*) To pay for your child's education, you wish to have accumulated $15,000 at the end of 15 years. To do this you plan on depositing an equal amount into the bank at the end of each year. If the bank is willing to pay 6 percent compounded annually, how much must you deposit each year to reach your goal?

5-15. (*Solving for r in compound interest*) If you were offered $1,079.50 10 years from now in return for an investment of $500 currently, what annual rate of interest would you earn if you took the offer?

5-16. (*Future value of an annuity*) In 10 years you are planning on retiring and buying a house in Oviedo, Florida. The house you are looking at currently costs $100,000 and is expected to increase in value each year at a rate of 5 percent. Assuming you can earn 10 percent annually on your investments, how much must you invest at the end of each of the next 10 years to be able to buy your dream home when you retire?

5-17. (*Compound value*) The Aggarwal Corporation needs to save $10 million to retire a $10 million mortgage that matures in 10 years. To retire this mortgage, the company plans to put a fixed amount into an account at the end of each year for 10 years, with the first payment occurring at the end of 1 year. The Aggarwal Corporation expects to earn 9 percent annually on the money in this account. What equal annual contribution must it make to this account to accumulate the $10 million in 10 years?

5-18. (*Compound interest with nonannual periods*) After examining the various personal loan rates available to you, you find that you can borrow funds from a finance company at 12 percent compounded monthly or from a bank at 13 percent compounded annually. Which alternative is more attractive?

5-19. (*Present value of an uneven stream of payments*) You are given three investment alternatives to analyze. The cash flows from these three investments are as follows:

	INVESTMENT		
END OF YEAR	**A**	**B**	**C**
1	$10,000		$10,000
2	10,000		
3	10,000		
4	10,000		
5	10,000	$10,000	
6		10,000	50,000
7		10,000	
8		10,000	
9		10,000	
10		10,000	10,000

Assuming a 20 percent discount rate, find the present value of each investment.

5-20. (*Present value*) The Kumar Corporation is planning on issuing bonds that pay no interest but can be converted into $1,000 at maturity, 7 years from their purchase. To price these bonds competitively with other bonds of equal risk, it is determined that they should yield 10 percent, compounded annually. At what price should the Kumar Corporation sell these bonds?

5-21. (*Perpetuities*) What is the present value of the following?

    a. A $300 perpetuity discounted back to the present at 8 percent
    b. A $1,000 perpetuity discounted back to the present at 12 percent
    c. A $100 perpetuity discounted back to the present at 9 percent
    d. A $95 perpetuity discounted back to the present at 5 percent

5-22. (*Solving for n with nonannual periods*) About how many years would it take for your investment to grow fourfold if it were invested at 16 percent compounded semiannually?

5-23. (*Complex present value*) How much do you have to deposit today so that beginning 11 years from now you can withdraw $10,000 a year for the next 5 years (periods 11 through 15) plus an *additional* amount of $20,000 in that last year (period 15)? Assume an interest rate of 6 percent.

5-24. (*Loan amortization*) On December 31, Beth Klemkosky bought a yacht for $50,000, paying $10,000 down and agreeing to pay the balance in 10 equal end-of-year installments and 10 percent interest on the declining balance. How big would the annual payments be?

5-25. (*Solving for r of an annuity*) You lend a friend $30,000, which your friend will repay in five equal annual end-of-year payments of $10,000, with the first payment to be received 1 year from now. What rate of return does your loan receive?

5-26. (*Solving for r in compound interest*) You lend a friend $10,000, for which your friend will repay you $27,027 at the end of 5 years. What interest rate are you charging your "friend"?

5-27. (*Loan amortization*) A firm borrows $25,000 from the bank at 12 percent compounded annually to purchase some new machinery. This loan is to be repaid in equal installments at the end of each year over the next 5 years. How much will each annual payment be?

5-28. (*Present-value comparison*) You are offered $1,000 today, $10,000 in 12 years, or $25,000 in 25 years. Assuming that you can earn 11 percent on your money, which should you choose?

5-29. (*Compound annuity*) You plan on buying some property in Florida 5 years from today. To do this you estimate that you will need $20,000 at that time for the purchase. You would like to accumulate these funds by making equal annual deposits in your savings account, which pays 12 percent annually. If you make your first deposit at the end of this year, and you would like your account to reach $20,000 when the final deposit is made, what will be the amount of your deposits?

5-30. (*Complex present value*) You would like to have $50,000 in 15 years. To accumulate this amount you plan to deposit each year an equal sum in the bank, which will earn 7 percent interest compounded annually. Your first payment will be made at the end of the year.

    a. How much must you deposit annually to accumulate this amount?

    b. If you decide to make a large lump-sum deposit today instead of the annual deposits, how large should this lump-sum deposit be? (Assume you can earn 7 percent on this deposit.)

    c. At the end of 5 years you will receive $10,000 and deposit this in the bank toward your goal of $50,000 at the end of 15 years. In addition to this deposit, how much must you deposit in equal annual deposits to reach your goal? (Again assume you can earn 7 percent on this deposit.)

5-31. (*Comprehensive present value*) You are trying to plan for retirement in 10 years, and currently you have $100,000 in a savings account and $300,000 in stocks. In addition you plan on adding to your savings by depositing $10,000 per year in your savings account at the end of each of the next 5 years and then $20,000 per year at the end of each year for the final 5 years until retirement.

    a. Assuming your savings account returns 7 percent compounded annually, and your investment in stocks will return 12 percent compounded annually, how much will you have at the end of 10 years? (Ignore taxes.)

    b. If you expect to live for 20 years after you retire, and at retirement you deposit all of your savings in a bank account paying 10 percent, how much can you withdraw each year after retirement (20 equal withdrawals beginning 1 year after you retire) to end up with a zero balance upon your death?

5-32. (*Loan amortization*) On December 31, Son-Nan Chen borrowed $100,000, agreeing to repay this sum in 20 equal end-of-year installments and 15 percent interest on the declining balance. How large must the annual payments be?

5-33. (*Loan amortization*) To buy a new house you must borrow $150,000. To do this you take out a $150,000, 30-year, 10 percent mortgage. Your mortgage payments, which are made at the end of each year (one payment each year), include both principal and 10 percent interest on the declining balance. How large will your annual payments be?

5-34. (*Present value*) The state lottery's million-dollar payout provides for $1 million to be paid over 19 years in 20 payments of $50,000. The first $50,000 payment is made immediately, and the 19 remaining $50,000 payments occur at the end of each of the next 19 years. If 10 percent is the appropriate discount rate, what is the present value of this stream of cash flows? If 20 percent is the appropriate discount rate, what is the present value of the cash flows?

5-35. (*Solving for r in compound interest—financial calculator needed*) In September 1963, the first issue of the comic book *X-MEN* was issued. The original price for that issue was $0.12. By September 2009, 46 years later, the value of this comic book had risen to $22,000. What annual rate of interest would you have earned if you had bought the comic in 1963 and sold it in 2009?

5-36. (*Comprehensive present value*) You have just inherited a large sum of money, and you are trying to determine how much you should save for retirement and how much you can spend now. For retirement, you will deposit today (January 1, 2011) a lump sum in a bank account paying 10 percent compounded annually. You don't plan on touching this deposit until you retire in 5 years (on January 1, 2016), and you plan on living for 20 additional years and then dropping dead on December 31, 2035. During your retirement you would like to receive income of $50,000 per year to be received the first day of each year, with the first payment on January 1, 2016, and the last payment on January 1, 2035. Complicating this objective is your desire to have one final 3-year fling during which time you'd like to track down all the living original cast members of *Leave It to Beaver* and *The Brady Bunch* and get their autographs. To finance this effort you want to receive $250,000 on January 1, 2031, and *nothing* on January 1, 2032, and January 1, 2033, as you will be on the road. In addition, after you pass on (January 1, 2036), you would like to have a total of $100,000 to leave to your children.

    a. How much must you deposit in the bank at 10 percent on January 1, 2011, to achieve your goal? (Use a timeline to answer this question.)

    b. What kinds of problems are associated with this analysis and its assumptions?

5-37. (*Spreadsheet problem*) If you invest $900 in a bank in which it will earn 8 percent compounded annually, how much will it be worth at the end of 7 years? Use a spreadsheet to do your calculations.

5-38. (*Spreadsheet problem*) In 20 years you'd like to have $250,000 to buy a vacation home, but you have only $30,000. At what rate must your $30,000 be compounded annually for it to grow to $250,000 in 20 years? Use a spreadsheet to calculate your answer.

5-39. (*Spreadsheet problem*) To buy a new house you take out a 25-year mortgage for $300,000. What will your monthly payments be if the interest rate on your mortgage is 8 percent? Use a spreadsheet to calculate your answer. Now, calculate the portion of the 48th monthly payment that goes toward interest and principal.

5-40. (*Future and present value using a calculator*) Over the past few years Microsoft founder Bill Gates's net worth has fluctuated between $20 billion and $130 billion. In 2010 Gates was worth about $28 billion after he reduced his stake in Microsoft from 21 percent to around 14 percent by moving billions into his charitable foundation. Let's see what Bill Gates can do with his money in the following problems.

    a. I'll take Manhattan? Manhattan's native tribe sold Manhattan Island to Peter Minuit for $24 in 1626. Now, 384 years later in 2010, Bill Gates wants to buy the island from the "current natives." How much would Bill have to pay for Manhattan if the "current natives" want a 6 percent annual return on the original $24 purchase price? Could he afford it?

    b. (*Nonannual compounding using a calculator*) How much would Bill have to pay for Manhattan if the "current natives" want a 6% return compounded monthly on the original $24 purchase price?

    c. Microsoft Seattle? Bill Gates decides to pass on Manhattan and instead plans to buy the city of Seattle, Washington, for $60 billion in 10 years. How much would Mr. Gates have to invest today at 10 percent compounded annually in order to purchase Seattle in 10 years?

    d. Now assume Bill Gates wants to invest only about half his net worth today, $14 billion, in order to buy Seattle for $60 billion in 10 years. What annual rate of return would he have to earn in order to complete his purchase in 10 years?

    e. Margaritaville? Instead of buying and running large cities, Bill Gates is considering quitting the rigors of the business world and retiring to work on his golf game. To fund his retirement, Bill Gates would invest his $28 billion fortune in safe investments with an expected annual rate of return of 7 percent. Also, Mr. Gates wants to make 40 equal annual withdrawals from this retirement fund beginning a year from today. How much can Mr. Gates's annual withdrawal be in this case?

5-41. (*Compounding using a calculator*) Bart Simpson, age 10, wants to be able to buy a really cool new car when he turns 16. His really cool car costs $15,000 today, and its cost is expected to increase 3 percent annually. Bart wants to make one deposit today (he can sell his mint-condition original *Nuclear Boy* comic book) into an account paying 7.5 percent annually in order to buy his car in 6 years. How much will Bart's car cost, and how much does Bart have to save today in order to buy this car at age 16?

5-42. (*Compounding using a calculator*) Lisa Simpson wants to have $1 million in 45 years by making equal annual end-of-the-year deposits into a tax-deferred account paying 8.75 percent annually. What must Lisa's annual deposit be?

5-43. (*Compounding using a calculator and annuities due*) Springfield mogul Montgomery Burns, age 80, wants to retire at age 100 in order to steal candy from babies full time. Once Mr. Burns retires, he wants to withdraw $1 billion at the beginning of each year for 10 years from a special offshore account that will pay 20 percent annually. In order to fund his retirement, Mr. Burns will make 20 equal end-of-the-year deposits in this same special account that will pay 20 percent annually. How much money will Mr. Burns need at age 100, and how large of an annual deposit must he make to fund this retirement account?

5-44. (*Compounding using a calculator and annuities due*) Imagine Homer Simpson actually invested $100,000 5 years ago at a 7.5 percent annual interest rate. If he invests an additional $1,500 a year at the beginning of each year for 20 years at the same 7.5 percent annual rate, how much money will Homer have 20 years from now?

5-45. (*Nonannual compounding using a calculator*) Prof. Finance is thinking about trading cars. He estimates he will still have to borrow $25,000 to pay for his new car. How large will Prof. Finance's monthly car loan payment be if he can get a 5-year (60 equal monthly payments) car loan from the university's credit union at 6.2 percent?

5-46. (*Nonannual compounding using a calculator*) Bowflex's television ads say you can get a fitness machine that sells for $999 for $33 a month for 36 months. What rate of interest are you paying on this Bowflex loan?

5-47. (*Nonannual compounding using a calculator*) Ford's current incentives include 4.9 percent financing for 60 months or $1,000 cash back for a Mustang. Let's assume Suzie Student wants to buy the premium Mustang convertible, which costs $25,000, and she has no down payment other than the cash back from Ford. If she chooses the $1,000 cash back, Suzie can borrow from the VTech Credit Union at 6.9 percent for 60 months (Suzie's credit isn't as good as Prof. Finance's). What will Suzie Student's monthly payment be under each option? Which option should she choose?

5-48. (*Nonannual compounding using a calculator*) Ronnie Rental plans to invest $1,000 at the end of each quarter for 4 years into an account that pays 6.4 percent compounded quarterly. He will use this money as a down payment on a new home at the end of the 4 years. How large will his down payment be 4 years from today?

5-49. (*Nonannual compounding using a calculator*) Dennis Rodman has a $5,000 debt balance on his Visa card that charges 12.9 percent compounded monthly. Dennis's current minimum monthly payment is 3 percent of his debt balance, which is $150. How many months (round up) will it take Dennis to pay off his credit card if he pays the current minimum payment of $150 at the end of each month?

5-50. (*Nonannual compounding using a calculator*) Should we have bet the kids' college fund at the dog track? In the downturn of 2008–2009 investors suffered substantial declines on tax-sheltered college savings plans (called 529 plans) around the country. Let's look at one specific case of a college professor (let's call him Prof. ME) with two young children. Two years ago Prof. ME invested $160,000 hoping to have $420,000 available 12 years later when the first child started college. However, the account's balance is now only $140,000. Let's figure out what is needed to get Prof. ME's college savings plan back on track.

   a. What was the original annual rate of return needed to reach Prof. ME's goal when he started the fund 2 years ago?
   b. Now with only $140,000 in the fund and 10 years remaining until his first child starts college, what annual rate of return would the fund have to earn to reach Prof. ME's $420,000 goal if he adds nothing to the account?
   c. Shocked by his experience of the past 2 years, Prof. ME feels the college mutual fund has invested too much in stocks. He wants a low-risk fund in order to ensure he has the necessary $420,000 in 10 years, and he is willing to make end-of-the-month deposits to the fund as well. He later finds a fund that promises to pay a guaranteed return of 6 percent compounded monthly. Prof. ME decides to transfer the $140,000 to this new fund and make the necessary monthly deposits. How large of a monthly deposit must Prof. ME make into this new fund to meet his $420,000 goal?
   d. Now Prof. ME gets sticker shock from the necessary monthly deposit he has to make into the guaranteed fund in the preceding question. He decides to invest the $140,000 today and $500 at the end of each month for the next 10 years into a fund consisting of 50 percent stock and 50 percent bonds and hope for the best. What annual rate of return would the fund have to earn in order to reach Prof. ME's $420,000 goal?

5-51. (*Complex annuity*) Upon graduating from college 35 years ago, Dr. Nick Riviera was already thinking of retirement. Since then he has made deposits into his retirement fund on a quarterly basis in the amount of $300. Nick has just completed his final payment and is at last ready to retire. His retirement fund has earned 9% interest compounded quarterly.

   a. How much has Nick accumulated in his retirement account?
   b. In addition to all this, 15 years ago, Nick received an inheritance check for $20,000 from his beloved uncle. He decided to deposit the entire amount into his retirement fund. What is his current balance in the fund?

5-52. (*Solving for r in an annuity*) Your folks just called and would like some advice from you. An insurance agent just called them and offered them the opportunity to purchase an annuity for $21,074.25 that will pay them $3,000 per year for 20 years, but they don't have the slightest idea what return they would be making on their investment of $21,074.25. What rate of return will they be earning?

5-53. (*Complex annuity and future value*) Milhouse, 22, is about to begin his career as a rocket scientist for a NASA contractor. Being a rocket scientist, Milhouse knows that he should begin saving for retirement immediately. Part of his inspiration came from reading an article on Social Security in *Newsweek*, where he saw that the ratio of workers paying taxes to retirees collecting checks will drop dramatically in the future. In fact the ratio was 8.6 workers for every retiree in 1955; today the ratio is 3.3, and it will drop to 2 workers for every retiree in 2040. Milhouse's retirement plan pays 9 percent interest annually and allows him to make equal yearly contributions. Upon retirement Milhouse plans to buy a new boat, which he estimates will cost him $300,000 in 43 years (he plans to retire at age 65). He also estimates that in order to live comfortably he will require a yearly income of $80,000 for each year after he retires. Based on family history, Milhouse expects to live until age 80 (that is, he would like to receive 15 payments of $80,000 at the end of each year). When he retires, Milhouse will purchase his boat in one lump sum and place the remaining balance into an account, which pays 6% interest, from which he will withdraw his $80,000 per year. If Milhouse's first contribution is made 1 year from today, and his last is made the day he retires, how much money must he contribute each year to his retirement fund?

5-54. (*Future value*) Bob Terwilliger received $12,345 for his services as financial consultant to the mayor's office of his hometown of Springfield. Bob says that his consulting work was his civic duty and that he should not receive any compensation. So, he has invested his paycheck into an account paying 3.98 percent annual interest and left the account in his will to the city of Springfield on the condition that the city could not collect any money from the account for 200 years. How much money will the city receive from Bob's generosity in 200 years?

5-55. (*Solving for r*) Kirk Van Houten, who has been married for 23 years, would like to buy his wife an expensive diamond ring with a platinum setting on their 30-year wedding anniversary. Assume that the cost of the ring will be $12,000 in 7 years. Kirk currently has $4,510 to invest. What annual rate of return must Kirk earn on his investment to accumulate enough money to pay for the ring?

5-56. (*Solving for n*) Jack asked Jill to marry him, and she has accepted under one condition: Jack must buy her a new $330,000 Rolls-Royce Phantom. Jack currently has $45,530 that he may invest. He has found a mutual fund that pays 4.5% annual interest in which he will place the money. How long will it take Jack to win Jill's hand in marriage?

5-57. (*Present value*) Ronen Consulting has just realized an accounting error which has resulted in an unfunded liability of $398,930 due in 28 years. Toni Flanders, the company's CEO, is scrambling to discount the liability to the present to assist in valuing the firm's stock. If the appropriate discount rate is 7 percent, what is the present value of the liability?

Mini Case

For your job as the business reporter for a local newspaper, you are given the task of putting together a series of articles that explain the power of the time value of money to your readers. Your editor would like you to address several specific questions in addition to demonstrating for the readership the use of time value of money techniques by applying them to several problems. What would be your response to the following memorandum from your editor?

> To: Business Reporter
> From: Perry White, Editor, *Daily Planet*
> Re: Upcoming Series on the Importance and Power of the Time Value of Money

In your upcoming series on the time value of money, I would like to make sure you cover several specific points. In addition, before you begin this assignment, I want to make sure we are all reading from the same script, as accuracy has always been the cornerstone of the *Daily Planet*. In this regard, I'd like a response to the following questions before we proceed:

a. What is the relationship between discounting and compounding?
b. What is the relationship between the present value factor and the annuity present value factor?
c. 1. What will $5,000 invested for 10 years at 8 percent compounded annually grow to?
   2. How many years will it take $400 to grow to $1,671 if it is invested at 10 percent compounded annually?
   3. At what rate would $1,000 have to be invested to grow to $4,046 in 10 years?
d. Calculate the future sum of $1,000, given that it will be held in the bank for 5 years and earn 10 percent compounded semiannually.
e. What is an annuity due? How does this differ from an ordinary annuity?
f. What is the present value of an ordinary annuity of $1,000 per year for 7 years discounted back to the present at 10 percent? What would be the present value if it were an annuity due?
g. What is the future value of an ordinary annuity of $1,000 per year for 7 years compounded at 10 percent? What would be the future value if it were an annuity due?
h. You have just borrowed $100,000, and you agree to pay it back over the next 25 years in 25 equal end-of-year payments plus 10 percent compound interest on the unpaid balance. What will be the size of these payments?
i. What is the present value of a $1,000 perpetuity discounted back to the present at 8 percent?

j. What is the present value of a $1,000 annuity for 10 years, with the first payment occurring at the end of year 10 (that is, ten $1,000 payments occurring at the end of year 10 through year 19), given a discount rate of 10 percent?

k. Given a 10 percent discount rate, what is the present value of a perpetuity of $1,000 per year if the first payment does not begin until the end of year 10?

Self-Test Solutions

SS-1. This is a compound interest problem in which you must first find the future value of $25,000 growing at 8 percent compounded annually for 3 years and then allow that future value to grow for an additional 3 years at 10 percent. First, the value of the $25,000 after 3 years growing at 8 percent is

$$FV_3 = PV(1 + r)^n$$
$$FV_3 = \$25,000(1 + 0.8)^3$$
$$FV_3 = \$31,492.80$$

Thus, after 3 years you have $31,492.80. Now this amount is allowed to grow for 3 years at 10 percent. Plugging this into equation (5-1), with $PV = \$31,492.80$, $r = 10$ percent, and $n = 3$ years, we solve for FV_3.

$$FV_3 = \$31,492.80(1 + 0.10)^3$$
$$FV_3 = \$41,916.92$$

Thus, after 6 years the $25,000 will have grown to $41,916.92.

SS-2. This loan amortization problem is actually just a present-value-of-an-annuity problem in which we know the values of r, n, and PV and are solving for PMT. In this case the value of r is 13 percent, n is 10 years, and PV is $30,000. Substituting these values into equation (5-4) we find

$$\$30,000 = PMT\left[\frac{1 - (1 + 0.13)^{-10}}{0.13}\right]$$

$$\$5,528.69 = PMT$$

STEP 1
Determine the value of $25,000 growing at 8 percent for 3 years:

CALCULATOR SOLUTION

Data Input	Function Key
3	N
8	I/Y
25,000	PV
0	PMT

Function Key	Answer
CPT	
FV	−31,492.80

STEP 2
Determine the value of the $31,492.80, calculated in step 1, growing at 10 percent for 3 years.

CALCULATOR SOLUTION

Data Input	Function Key
3	N
10	I/Y
31,492.80	PV
0	PMT

Function Key	Answer
CPT	
FV	−41,916.92

CALCULATOR SOLUTION

Data Input	Function Key
10	N
13	I/Y
30,000	PV
0	FV

Function Key	Answer
CPT	
PMT	−5,528.69

Chapter 6

The Meaning and Measurement of Risk and Return

Learning Objectives

After reading this chapter, you should be able to:

  Define and measure **the expected rate of return of an individual investment.**

Define and measure **the riskiness of an individual investment.**

Compare **the historical relationship between risk and rates of return in the capital markets.**

Explain **how diversifying investments affects the riskiness and expected rate of return of a portfolio or combination of assets.**

 Explain **the relationship between an investor's required rate of return on an investment and the riskiness of the investment.**

One of the most important concepts in finance is *risk and return,* which is the total focus of our third principle of finance—**Risk Requires a Reward**. You only have to consider what happened in the capital markets, especially stocks, from late 2007 to early 2009 to see the overwhelming presence of risk and returns. For example, if you had been so unfortunate as to buy a portfolio of stocks consisting of the Standard & Poor's 500 in October 2007 and sold in February 2009, you would have lost 53 percent of your money. Even worse, if you had held Bank of America stock during that time period, you would have lost 94 percent of your money! However, if you had been so astute as to buy Bank of America stock in February 2009 and sold four months later in June 2009, you would have earned a whopping 333 percent return on your investment. Even investing in the S&P stocks would have earned you 29 percent on your investment—not bad for a few months.

Clearly, owning stocks in recent times has not been for the faint of heart, where in a single day you could have earned as much as five percent on your investment, or lost even more. The market crash and extreme volatility in stock prices in 2008 and 2009 are what Nassim Nicholas Taleb would call a black swan—a highly improbable event that has a massive impact.[1] As a consequence, our confidence in forecasting the future has been undermined. Furthermore, our lives have been impacted and future plans delayed. We are much more cognizant of the financial risks that we face, both individually and in business.

[1]In his book *The Black Swan: The Impact of the Highly Improbable* (New York: Random House, 2007), Nassim Nicholas Taleb uses the analogy of a black swan, which represents a highly unlikely event. Until black swans were discovered in Australia, everyone assumed that all swans were white. Thus, for Taleb, the black swan symbolizes an event that no one thinks possible.

In this chapter, we will help you understand the nature of risk and how risk *should* relate to expected returns on investments. We will look back beyond the past few years to see what we can learn about long-term historical risk-and-return relationships. These are topics that should be of key interest to us all in this day and age.

The need to recognize risk in financial decisions has already been apparent in earlier chapters. In Chapter 2, we referred to the discount rate, or the interest rate, as the opportunity cost of funds, but we did not look at the reasons why that rate might be high or low. For example, we did not explain why in June 2009 you could buy bonds issued by General Electric that promised to pay a 6.3 percent rate of return, or why you could buy Dow Chemical bonds that would give you an 8.7 percent rate of return, provided that both firms make the payments to the investors as promised.

In this chapter, we learn that risk is an integral force underlying rates of return. To begin our study, we define expected return and risk and offer suggestions about how these important concepts of return and risk can be measured quantitatively. We also compare the historical relationship between risk and rates of return. We then explain how diversifying investments can affect the expected return and riskiness of those investments. We also consider how the riskiness of an investment should affect the required rate of return on an investment.

Let's begin our study by looking at what we mean by the expected rate of return and how it can be measured.

Expected Return Defined and Measured

 Define and measure the expected rate of return of an individual investment.

The expected benefits, or returns, an investment generates come in the form of cash flows. Cash flow, not accounting profit, is the relevant variable the financial manager uses to measure returns. This principle holds true regardless of the type of security, whether it is a debt instrument, preferred stock, common stock, or any mixture of these (such as convertible bonds).

To begin our discussion about an asset's expected rate of return, let's first understand how to compute an **historical** or **realized rate of return** on an investment. It may also be called a **holding-period return**. For instance, consider the dollar return you would have earned had you purchased a share of Apple stock on April 1, 2009 for $104.50 and sold one month later on May 1 for $125.80. The dollar return from your investment would have been $21.30 ($21.30 = $125.80 − $104.50), assuming that the company paid no dividend. In addition to the dollar gain, we can calculate the rate of return as a percentage. It is useful to summarize the return on an investment in terms of a percentage because that way we can see the return per dollar invested which is independent of how much we actually invest.

The rate of return earned from the investment in Apple can be calculated as the ratio of the dollar return of $21.30 divided by your $104.50 investment in the stock at the beginning of the month, or 20.4 percent (0.204 = $21.30 ÷ $104.50).

holding-period return (historical or realized rate of return) the rate of return earned on an investment, which equals the dollar gain divided by the amount invested.

We can formalize the return calculations using equations (6-1) and (6-2):

Holding-Period Dollar Gain would be:

$$\text{Holding-period dollar gain, DG} = \text{Price}_{\text{end of period}} + \text{cash distribution (dividend)} - \text{Price}_{\text{beginning of period}} \quad (6\text{-}1)$$

and for the holding-period rate of return

$$\text{Rate of return, } r = \frac{\text{dollar gain}}{P_{\text{beginning of period}}} = \frac{P_{\text{end of period}} + \text{Dividend} - P_{\text{beginning of period}}}{P_{\text{beginning of period}}} \quad (6\text{-}2)$$

The method we have just used to compute the holding-period return on our investment in Apple tells us the return we actually earned during an historical time period. However, the risk–return trade-off that investors face on a day-to-day basis is based *not* on realized rates of return, but on what the investor *expects* to earn on an investment in the future. We can think of the rate of return that will ultimately be realized from making a risky investment in terms of a range of possible return outcomes, much like the distribution of grades for this class at the end of the term. To describe this range of possible returns, it is customary to use the average of the different possible returns. We refer to the average of the possible rates of return as the investment's **expected rate of return**.

expected rate of return The arithmetic mean or average of all possible outcomes where those outcomes are weighted by the probability that each will occur.

Accurately measuring expected future cash flows is not easy in a world of uncertainty. To illustrate, assume you are considering an investment costing $10,000, for which the future cash flows from owning the security depend on the state of the economy, as estimated in Table 6-1.

In any given year, the investment could produce any one of three possible cash flows, depending on the particular state of the economy. With this information, how should we select the cash flow estimate that means the most for measuring the investment's expected rate of return? One approach is to calculate an *expected* cash flow. The expected cash flow is simply the weighted average of the *possible* cash flow outcomes such that the weights are the probabilities of the various states of the economy occurring. Stated as an equation:

$$\text{Expected cash flow, } \overline{CF} = \begin{pmatrix} \text{cash flow} & & \text{probability} \\ \text{in state 1} & \times & \text{of state 1} \\ (CF_1) & & (Pb_1) \end{pmatrix} + \begin{pmatrix} \text{cash flow} & & \text{probability} \\ \text{in state 2} & \times & \text{of state 2} \\ (CF_2) & & (Pb_2) \end{pmatrix}$$

$$+ \begin{pmatrix} \text{cash flow} & & \text{probability} \\ \text{in state 3} & \times & \text{of state 3} \\ (CF_3) & & (Pb_3) \end{pmatrix} \quad (6\text{-}3)$$

> **REMEMBER YOUR PRINCIPLES**
>
> **Principle** Remember that future cash flows, not reported earnings, determine the investor's rate of return. That is, **Principle 1: Cash Flow Is What Matters**.

For the present illustration:

$$\begin{aligned}\text{Expected cash flow} &= (0.2)(\$1,000) + (0.3)(\$1,200) \\ &\quad + (0.5)(\$1,400) \\ &= \$1,260\end{aligned}$$

In addition to computing an expected dollar return from an investment, we can also calculate an expected rate of return

TABLE 6-1 Measuring the Expected Return of an Investment			
State of the Economy	Probability of the States[a]	Cash Flows from the Investment	Percentage Returns (Cash Flow ÷ Investment Cost)
Economic recession	20%	$1,000	10% ($1,000 ÷ $10,000)
Moderate economic growth	30%	1,200	12% ($1,200 ÷ $10,000)
Strong economic growth	50%	1,400	14% ($1,400 ÷ $10,000)

[a]The probabilities assigned to the three possible economic conditions have to be determined subjectively, which requires managers to have a thorough understanding of both the investment cash flows and the general economy.

CAN YOU DO IT?

COMPUTING EXPECTED CASH FLOW AND EXPECTED RETURN

You are contemplating making a $5,000 investment that would have the following possible outcomes in cash flow each year. What is the expected value of the future cash flows and the expected rate of return?

PROBABILITY	CASH FLOW
0.30	$350
0.50	625
0.20	900

(The solution can be found on page 160.)

earned on the $10,000 investment. Similar to the expected cash flow, the expected rate of return is *a weighted average of all the possible returns, weighted by the probability that each return will occur*. As the last column in Table 6-1 shows, the $1,400 cash inflow, assuming strong economic growth, represents a 14 percent return ($1,400 ÷ $10,000). Similarly, the $1,200 and $1,000 cash flows result in 12 percent and 10 percent returns, respectively. Using these percentage returns in place of the dollar amounts, the expected rate of return can be expressed as follows:

$$\text{Expected rate of return, } \bar{r} = \begin{pmatrix} \text{rate of return} \\ \text{for state 1} \\ (r_1) \end{pmatrix} \times \begin{pmatrix} \text{probability} \\ \text{of state 1} \\ (Pb_1) \end{pmatrix} + \begin{pmatrix} \text{rate of return} \\ \text{for state 2} \\ (r_2) \end{pmatrix} \times \begin{pmatrix} \text{probability} \\ \text{of state 2} \\ (Pb_2) \end{pmatrix}$$

$$+ \begin{pmatrix} \text{rate of return} \\ \text{for state 3} \\ (r_3) \end{pmatrix} \times \begin{pmatrix} \text{probability} \\ \text{of state 3} \\ (Pb_3) \end{pmatrix} \tag{6-4}$$

In our example:

$$\bar{r} = (0.2)(10\%) + (0.3)(12\%) + (0.5)(14\%) = 12.6\%$$

With our concept and measurement of expected returns, let's consider the other side of the investment coin: risk.

Concept Check

1. When we speak of "benefits" from investing in an asset, what do we mean?
2. Why is it difficult to measure future cash flows?
3. Define *expected rate of return*.

Risk Defined and Measured

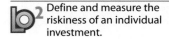 Define and measure the riskiness of an individual investment.

Because we live in a world where events are uncertain, the way we see risk is vitally important in almost all dimensions of our life. The Greek poet and statesman Solon, writing in the sixth century B.C., put it this way:

> There is risk in everything that one does, and no one knows where he will make his landfall when his enterprise is at its beginning. One man, trying to act effectively, fails to foresee something and falls into great and grim ruination, but to another man, one who is acting ineffectively, a god gives good fortune in everything and escape from his folly.[2]

Solon would have given more of the credit to Zeus than we would for the outcomes of our ventures. However, his insight reminds us that little is new in this world, including the

---

[2]Translated by Arthur W. H. Adkins from the Greek text of Solon's poem "Prosperity, Justice, and the Hazards of Life," in M. L. West, ed., *Iambi et Elegi Graeci ante Alexandrum Cantati*, vol. 2 (Oxford: Clarendon Press, 1972).

DID YOU GET IT?
COMPUTING EXPECTED CASH FLOW AND EXPECTED RETURN

PROBABILITY	POSSIBLE		EXPECTED	
	CASH FLOW	RETURN	CASH FLOW	RETURN
0.30	$350	7.0%	$105.00	2.1%
0.50	625	12.5%	312.50	6.3%
0.20	900	18.0%	180.00	3.6%
Expected cash flow and rate of return			$597.50	12.0%

The possible returns are equal to the possible cash flows divided by the $5,000 investment. The expected cash flow and return are equal to the possible cash flows and possible returns multiplied by the probabilities.

need to acknowledge and compensate as best we can for the risks we encounter. In fact, the significance of risk and the need for understanding what it means in our lives is noted by Peter Bernstein in the following excerpt:

> What is it that distinguishes the thousands of years of history from what we think of as modern times? The answer goes way beyond the progress of science, technology, capitalism, and democracy.
>
> The distant past was studded with brilliant scientists, mathematicians, inventors, technologists, and political philosophers. Hundreds of years before the birth of Christ, the skies had been mapped, the great library of Alexandria built, and Euclid's geometry taught. Demand for technological innovation in warfare was as insatiable then as it is today. Coal, oil, iron, and copper have been at the service of human beings for millennia, and travel and communication mark the very beginnings of recorded civilization.
>
> The revolutionary idea that defines the boundary between modern times and the past is the mastery of risk: the notion that the future is more than a whim of the gods and that men and women are not passive before nature. Until human beings discovered a way across that boundary, the future was a mirror of the past or the murky domain of oracles and soothsayers who held a monopoly over knowledge of anticipated events.[3]

In our study of risk, we want to consider these questions:

1. What is risk?
2. How do we know the amount of risk associated with a given investment; that is, how do we measure risk?
3. If we choose to diversify our investments by owning more than one asset, as most of us do, will such diversification reduce the riskiness of our combined portfolio of investments?

Without intending to be trite, risk means different things to different people, depending on the context and on how they feel about taking chances. For the student, risk is the possibility of failing an exam or the chance of not making his or her best grades. For the coal miner or the oil field worker, risk is the chance of an explosion in the mine or at the well site. For the retired person, risk means perhaps not being able to live comfortably on a fixed income. For the entrepreneur, risk is the chance that a new venture will fail.

While certainly acknowledging these different kinds of risk, we limit our attention to the risk inherent in an investment. In this context, **risk** is the *potential variability in future cash flows*. The wider the range of possible events that can occur, the greater the risk.[4] If we think about it, this is a relatively intuitive concept.

risk potential variability in future cash flows.

---

[3]Peter Bernstein, *Against the Gods: The Remarkable Story of Risk*. John Wiley & Sons, Inc., New York, 1996, p. 1.
[4]When we speak of possible events, we must not forget that it is the highly unlikely event that we cannot anticipate that may have the greatest impact on the outcome of an investment. So, we evaluate investment opportunities based on the best information available, but there may be a *black swan* that we cannot anticipate.

To help us grasp the fundamental meaning of risk within this context, consider two possible investments:

1. The first investment is a U.S. Treasury bill, a government security that matures in 90 days and promises to pay an annual return of 3 percent. If we purchase and hold this security for 90 days, we are virtually assured of receiving no more and no less than 3 percent on an annualized basis. For all practical purposes, the risk of loss is nonexistent.

2. The second investment involves the purchase of the stock of a local publishing company. Looking at the past returns of the firm's stock, we have made the following estimate of the annual returns from the investment:

CHANCE OF OCCURRENCE	RATE OF RETURN ON INVESTMENT
1 chance in 10 (10% chance)	0%
2 chances in 10 (20% chance)	5%
4 chances in 10 (40% chance)	15%
2 chances in 10 (20% chance)	25%
1 chance in 10 (10% chance)	30%

Investing in the publishing company could conceivably provide a return as high as 30 percent if all goes well, or no return (0 percent) if everything goes against the firm. However, in future years, both good and bad, we could expect a 15 percent return on average.[5]

$$\begin{aligned} \text{Expected return} &= (0.10)(0\%) + (0.20)(5\%) + (0.40)(15\%) + (0.20)(25\%) \\ &\quad + (0.10)(30\%) \\ &= 15\% \end{aligned}$$

Comparing the Treasury bill investment with the publishing company investment, we see that the Treasury bill offers an expected 3 percent annualized rate of return, whereas the publishing company has an expected rate of return of 15 percent. However, our investment in the publishing firm is clearly more "risky"—that is, there is greater uncertainty about the final outcome. Stated somewhat differently, there is a greater variation or dispersion of possible returns, which in turn implies greater risk.[6] Figure 6-1 shows these differences graphically in the form of discrete probability distributions.

FIGURE 6-1 The Probability Distribution of the Returns on Two Investments

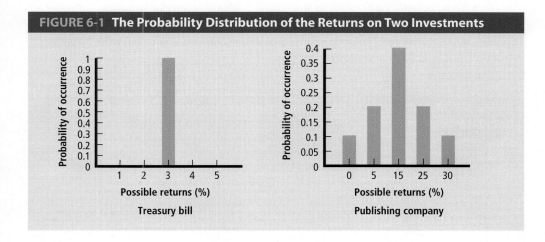

Treasury bill

Publishing company

---

[5]We assume that the particular outcome or return earned in 1 year does *not* affect the return earned in the subsequent year. Technically speaking, the distribution of returns in any year is assumed to be independent of the outcome in any prior year.

[6]How can we possibly view variations above the expected return as risk? Should we even be concerned with the positive deviations above the expected return? Some would say "no," viewing risk as only the negative variability in returns from a predetermined minimum acceptable rate of return. However, as long as the distribution of returns is symmetrical, the same conclusions will be reached.

Although the return from investing in the publishing firm is clearly less certain than for Treasury bills, quantitative measures of risk are useful when the difference between two investments is not so evident. We can quantify the risk of an investment by computing the variance in the possible investment returns and its square root, the **standard deviation** (σ). For the case where there are n possible returns (i.e., states of the economy) we calculate the variance as follows:

standard deviation a statistical measure of the spread of a probability distribution calculated by squaring the difference between each outcome and its expected value, weighting each value by its probability, summing over all possible outcomes, and taking the square root of this sum.

$$\begin{array}{l} \text{Variance in} \\ \text{rates of return} \\ (\sigma^2) \end{array} = \left[\left(\begin{array}{c} \text{rate of return} \\ \text{for state 1} \\ (r_1) \end{array} - \begin{array}{c} \text{expected rate} \\ \text{of return} \\ \bar{r} \end{array} \right)^2 \times \begin{array}{c} \text{probability} \\ \text{of state 1} \\ (Pb_1) \end{array} \right]$$

$$+ \left[\left(\begin{array}{c} \text{rate of return} \\ \text{for state 2} \\ (r_2) \end{array} - \begin{array}{c} \text{expected rate} \\ \text{of return} \\ \bar{r} \end{array} \right)^2 \times \begin{array}{c} \text{probability} \\ \text{of state 2} \\ (Pb_2) \end{array} \right]$$

$$+ \cdots + \left[\left(\begin{array}{c} \text{rate of return} \\ \text{for state } n \\ (r_n) \end{array} - \begin{array}{c} \text{expected rate} \\ \text{of return} \\ \bar{r} \end{array} \right)^2 \times \begin{array}{c} \text{probability} \\ \text{of state } n \\ (Pb_n) \end{array} \right]$$

$$(6\text{-}5)$$

For the publishing company's common stock, we calculate the standard deviation using the following five-step procedure:

STEP 1 Calculate the expected rate of return of the investment, which was calculated above to be 15%.

STEP 2 Subtract the expected rate of return of 15% from each of the possible rates of return and square the difference.

STEP 3 Multiply the squared differences calculated in step 2 by the probability that those outcomes will occur.

STEP 4 Sum all the values calculated in step 3 together. The sum is the variance of the distribution of possible rates of return. Note that the variance is actually the *average squared difference between the possible rates of return and the expected rate of return.*

STEP 5 Take the square root of the variance calculated in step 4 to calculate the standard deviation of the distribution of possible rates of return.

Table 6-2 illustrates the application of this process, which results in an estimated standard deviation for the common stock investment of 9.2%. This compared to the Treasury bill investment, which is risk free, has a standard deviation of 0%. The more risky the investment, the higher is its standard deviation.

TABLE 6-2 Measuring the Variance and Standard Deviation of the Publishing Company Investment

State of the World	Rate of Return	Chance or Probability		Step 2	Step 3
A	B	C	D = B × C	E = (B − $\bar{r}$)²	F = E × C
1	0%	0.10	0%	225%	22.5%
3	5%	0.20	1%	100%	20.0%
4	15%	0.40	6%	0%	0%
4	25%	0.20	5%	100%	20.0%
5	30%	0.10	3%	225%	22.5%

Step 1: Expected Return ($\bar{r}$) = ⟶ 15%

Step 4: Variance = ⟶ 85%

Step 5: Standard Deviation = ⟶ 9.2%

CAN YOU DO IT?

COMPUTING THE STANDARD DEVIATION

In the preceding "Can You Do It?" on page 159, we computed the expected cash flow of $597.50 and the expected return of 12 percent on a $5,000 investment. Now let's calculate the standard deviation of the returns. The probabilities of possible returns are given as follows:

PROBABILITY	RETURNS
0.30	7.0%
0.50	12.5%
0.20	18.0%

(The solution can be found on page 165.)

Alternatively, we could use equation (6-5) to calculate the standard deviation in investment returns as follows:

$$\sigma = \left[\begin{array}{l} (\ 0\% - 15\%)^2(.10) + (\ 5\% - 15\%)^2(.20) \\ + (15\% - 15\%)^2(.40) + (25\% - 15\%)^2(.20) \\ + (30\% - 15\%)^2(.10) \end{array} \right]^{\frac{1}{2}}$$

$$= \sqrt{85\%} = 9.22\%$$

Although the standard deviation of returns provides us with a quantitative measure of an asset's riskiness, how should we interpret the result? What does it mean? Is the 9.22 percent standard deviation for the publishing company investment good or bad? First, we should remember that statisticians tell us that two-thirds of the time, an event will fall within one standard deviation of the expected value (assuming the distribution is normally distributed; that is, it is shaped like a bell). Thus, given a 15 percent expected return and a standard deviation of 9.22 percent for the publishing company investment, we can reasonably anticipate that the actual returns will fall between 5.78 percent and 24.22 percent (15% ± 9.22%) two-thirds of the time. In other words, there is not much certainty with this investment.

A second way of answering the question about the meaning of the standard deviation comes by comparing the investment in the publishing firm against other investments. Obviously the attractiveness of a security with respect to its return and risk cannot be determined in isolation. Only by examining other available alternatives can we reach a conclusion about a particular investment's risk. For example, if another investment, say, an investment in a firm that owns a local radio station, has the same expected return as the publishing company, 15 percent, but with a standard deviation of 7 percent, we would consider the risk associated with the publishing firm, 9.22 percent, to be excessive. In the technical jargon of modern portfolio theory, the radio station investment is said to "dominate" the publishing firm investment. In common sense terms, this means that the radio station investment has the same expected return as the publishing company investment, but is less risky.

FINANCE AT WORK

A DIFFERENT PERSPECTIVE OF RISK

The first Chinese symbol shown here represents danger; the second stands for opportunity. The Chinese define risk as the combination of danger and opportunity. Greater risk, according to the Chinese, means we have greater opportunity to do well, but also greater danger of doing badly.

ETHICS IN FINANCIAL MANAGEMENT

"I SHOULD HAVE SAID NO"

At 66, Aaron Beam is getting on with his life. Six years ago Beam made headlines by admitting that he cooked the books at HealthSouth Corp., the Birmingham, Alabama-based provider of inpatient and outpatient rehabilitation services that he co-founded.

Released after three months in a minimum-security prison, Beam retreated to his small hometown of Loxley, Alabama. Having sold his $3 million dream home to pay restitution and legal fees, Beam now lives modestly and mows lawns for a living. But he is also developing another career: educational speaker.

In a recent interview with Beam, Edward Teach reports the following conversation:

Most CFOs can probably tell stories about the CEOs they've worked with, but in your case it sounds like an especially difficult relationship.
Unless you were there and experienced it, it's hard to understand. You couldn't tell [Scrushy] no on anything. I have seen him so mad over minor things that I actually feared for my physical safety. I often joke with students that if Richard Scrushy and Hannibal Lecter were in a fight, I would bet on Richard Scrushy.

How did the fraud begin?
By 1994 or 1995 we were a *Fortune* 500 company and the largest company in Alabama; we had 40,000 employees in all 50 states. But as we matured, it got more and more difficult to make our numbers. You can't keep growing at 20% to 30% every year on the bottom line. To keep the Street from lowering its estimates, we started lowering our reserves for bad debts; when we did acquisitions we would change the estimates of the companies we were acquiring so we could apply those estimates to our earnings as we went forward.

We committed fraud in the summer of 1996, when we could no longer change estimates to make earnings. We thought we could make a lot of entries small enough that the auditors wouldn't detect them. So one night, during the second quarter of 1996, I said, "OK, let's do it," and we credited revenue that did not exist and we debited assets that did not exist.

You kept committing fraud until you quit in 1997. How did you feel during that time?
I felt rotten. It was terrible. My hope was that after we had done it once, we wouldn't have to do it again. But after doing it for four quarters, I felt like it wasn't going to end, so that's when I left. We had dug ourselves [into] a hole.

Weston Smith finally blew the whistle. Do you regret not having done so yourself?
The correct thing I should have done was, at the critical point when we weren't going to make our numbers, I should have said no [to any illegal actions]. If I got fired, I got fired. Once you actually commit fraud and have blood on your hands, getting out of the trap is very difficult.

Today you travel to business schools and talk to students about your experience at HealthSouth. What do you hope to accomplish?
I'm trying to turn a big negative into a positive, because there is such a need for ethics in the business world today, and I'm in a unique position to talk about it. If we can teach college students that they're going to face these kinds of temptations every day in the business world, we can make a difference.

What's life like for you now?
It's actually pretty good, even though I basically have no wealth now. I'm just back to being an ordinary guy. I went back to college and took a two-year certificate program in turf management. I have a lawn-service business—it's one man and a lawn mower. I'm cutting grass and doing public speaking and working on a book about my experiences.

Are you at peace with yourself?
I am. My marriage survived through it all. People seem to respect what I'm doing in my speaking. It's sad, though, and I tell people this: I was a founder of one of the most successful health-care companies in the history of the United States. Today HealthSouth is trading on the New York Stock Exchange and doing well. But I won't be remembered for that. I will be remembered as one of the guys who committed the fraud. That hurts, and it hurt my family a lot. But, you know, you heal over time, and I'm OK today.

Source: Edward Teach, "I Should Have Said No," *CFO Magazine*, June 1, 2009, pp. 34–36.

What if we compare the investment in the publishing company with one in a quick oil-change franchise, an investment in which the expected rate of return is an attractive 24 percent but the standard deviation is estimated at 13 percent? Now what should we do? Clearly, the oil-change franchise has a higher expected rate of return, but it also has a larger standard deviation. In this example, we see that the real challenge in selecting the better investment comes when one investment has a higher expected rate of return but also exhibits greater risk. *Here the final choice is determined by our attitude toward risk, and there is no single right answer.* You might select the publishing company, whereas I might choose the oil-change investment, and neither of us would be wrong. We would simply be expressing our tastes and preferences about risk and return.

DID YOU GET IT?
COMPUTING THE STANDARD DEVIATION

DEVIATION (POSSIBLE RETURN − 12% EXPECTED RETURN)	DEVIATION SQUARED	PROBABILITY	PROBABILITY × DEVIATION SQUARED
−5.0%	0.25%	0.30	0.075%
0.5%	0.0025%	0.50	0.00125%
6.0%	0.36%	0.20	0.072%
Sum of squared deviations × probability (variance)			0.14825%
Standard deviation			3.85%

Concept Check

1. How is risk defined?

2. How does the standard deviation help us measure the riskiness of an investment?

3. Does greater risk imply a bad investment?

Rates of Return: The Investor's Experience

 Compare the historical relationship between risk and rates of return in the capital markets.

So far, we have mostly used hypothetical examples of expected rates of return and risk; however, it is also interesting to look at returns that investors have actually received on different types of securities. For example, Ibbotson Associates publishes the long-term historical annual rates of return for the following types of investments beginning in 1926 and continuing to the present:

1. Common stocks of large companies
2. Common stocks of small firms
3. Long-term corporate bonds
4. Long-term U.S. government bonds
5. Intermediate-term U.S. government bonds
6. U.S. Treasury bills (short-term government securities)

Before comparing these returns, we should think about what to expect. First, we would intuitively expect a Treasury bill (short-term government securities) to be the least risky of the six portfolios. Because a Treasury bill has a short-term maturity date, the price is less volatile (less risky) than the price of an intermediate- or long-term government security. In turn, because there is a chance of default on a corporate bond, which is essentially nonexistent for government securities, a long-term government bond is less risky than a long-term corporate bond. Finally, the common stocks of large companies are more risky than corporate bonds, with small-company stocks being more risky than large-firm stocks.

With this in mind, we could reasonably expect different rates of return to the holders of these varied securities. If the market rewards an investor for assuming risk, the average annual rates of return should increase as risk increases.

A comparison of the annual rates of return for the six respective portfolios for the years 1926 to 2008 is provided in Figure 6-2. Four aspects of these returns are included: (1) the nominal average annual rate of return; (2) the standard deviation of the returns, which measures the volatility, or riskiness, of the returns; (3) the real average annual rate of return, which is the nominal return less the inflation rate; and (4) the risk premium, which represents the additional return received beyond the risk-free rate (Treasury bill rate) for assuming risk. Looking at the first two columns of nominal average annual returns and standard deviations, we get a good overview of the risk–return relationships that have existed over the 83 years ending in 2008. In every case, there has been a positive relationship between risk and return, with Treasury bills being least risky and small-company stocks being most risky.

FINANCE AT WORK

HARD LESSONS

When Anthony Dombrowik was promoted from controller to CFO of the Red Lion Hotel Group in 2008, he knew the role would be challenging. What he didn't know was that his first year would essentially be a trial-by-fire, requiring him to navigate through some of the most daunting times ever faced by American business. During Dombrowik's first 16 months on the job, Red Lion's revenues dropped some 13% with no recovery in sight. The company cut 10% of its workforce, including finance staffers, and combed its operations for any and all cost-cutting ideas, even switching to cheaper guest-room soaps. Dombrowik is thankful that none of the commercial mortgage-backed securities (CMBS) that finance the bulk of Red Lion's business have come due recently—there's no chance of rolling them over when they do—but soon he will have to find a new source of outside funding. At the same time, he is looking for opportunity in the ashes, hoping to grow the business by acquiring or franchising distressed hotel properties that may come up for sale.

Since September 2008, when the bankruptcy of Lehman Brothers triggered the near-meltdown of the nation's financial system, the CFO's role was reshaped in new and sometimes unnerving ways. Thanks to the post-September credit crunch and steep falloff in consumer demand, thousands of finance chiefs like Dombrowik have restructured their businesses, executed layoffs, hoarded cash, and begged for financing. Many such actions are standard operating procedure in tough times, and

some will be reversed when the economy finally turns around. But [the most recent] recession—the longest and nastiest since the Great Depression—[promised] to leave a lasting impact on business in general and corporate finance in particular.

Indeed, more than 85 percent of finance executives responding to a *CFO Magazine* survey said they don't expect their companies to return to business as usual after the economy recovers. They predict that substantial adjustments will be necessary, whether that means shuttering business units, responding to new competitive challenges, or dealing with new (and generally unwelcome) regulation.

Ironically, even though the vast majority anticipate what some refer to as a "new normal," nearly half expected their current business model to serve the company well going forward; a substantial number, however, expected their firm's strategy to change once they can shift their attention away from short-term survival.

One thing is clear: No CFO is likely to forget the hard lessons he or she has learned in areas like cash management, forecasting, risk, and human capital. "Those who lived through the Depression were forever more frugal, and I think you'll see something similar this time in the business world", says Dombrowik. He for one is planning to retain as much of Red Lion's recent cost-cutting as possible when demand picks up again (although the soaps will likely be upgraded).

Source: Alix Stuart, "Hard Lessons," *CFO Magazine*, September 1, 2009, pp. 42–44.

The return information in Figure 6-2 clearly demonstrates that only common stock has in the long run served as an inflation hedge and provided any substantial risk premium. However, it is equally apparent that the common stockholder is exposed to a sizable amount of risk, as is demonstrated by the 20.6 percent standard deviation for large-company stocks

FIGURE 6-2	Historical Rates of Return			
Securities	Nominal Average Annual Returns	Standard Deviation of Returns	Real Average Annual Returns[a]	Risk Premium[b]
Large-company stocks	11.7%	20.6%	8.6%	7.9%
Small-company stocks	16.4%	33.0%	13.3%	14.6%
Corporate bonds	6.2%	8.4%	3.1%	2.4%
Government bonds	6.1%	9.4%	3.0%	2.3%
U.S. Treasury bills	3.8%	3.1%	0.7%	0.0%
Inflation	3.1%	4.2%		

[a]The real return equals the nominal returns less the inflation rate of 3.1 percent.
[b]The risk premium equals the nominal security return than the average risk-free rate (Treasury bills) of 3.8 percent.

and the 33 percent standard deviation for small-company stocks. In fact, in the 1926 to 2008 time frame, common shareholders of large firms received negative returns in 23 of the 83 years, compared with only 1 (1938) in 83 years for Treasury bills.

Concept Check

1. What is the additional compensation for assuming greater risk called?
2. In Figure 6-2, which rate of return is the risk-free rate? Why?

Risk and Diversification

 4 Explain how diversifying investments affects the riskiness and expected rate of return of a portfolio or combination of assets.

More can be said about risk, especially about its nature, when we own more than one asset in our investment portfolio. Let's consider for the moment how risk is affected if we diversify our investment by holding a variety of securities.

Let's assume that you graduated from college in December 2008. Not only did you get the good job you had hoped for, but you also finished the year with a little nest egg—not enough to take that summer fling to Europe like some of your college friends but a nice surplus. Besides, you suspected that they used credit cards to go anyway. So, you made two stock investments with your nest egg—one in Harley Davidson and one in Starbucks. (As the owner of a Harley Softail motorcycle, you've had a passion for riding since your high school days. And you give Starbucks credit for helping you get through many long study sessions.) You then focused on your career and seldom thought about your investments. Your first extended break from work came June 2009. After a lazy Saturday morning, you decided to get on the Internet to see how your investments did over the previous several months. You bought Starbucks for $9, and the stock was now trading at almost $15. "Not bad," you thought. But then the bad news—Harley-Davidson was selling for $16, compared to the $20 that you paid for the stock.

Clearly, what we have described about Harley Davidson and Starbucks were events unique to these two companies, and as we would expect, investors reacted accordingly; that is, the value of the stock changed in light of the new information. Although we might have wished we had owned only Starbucks stock at the time, most of us would prefer to avoid such uncertainties; that is, we are risk averse. Instead, we would like to reduce the risk associated with our investment portfolio, without having to accept a lower expected return. Good news: It is possible by diversifying your portfolio!

Diversifying Away the Risk

If we diversify our investments across different securities rather than invest in only one stock, the variability in the returns of our portfolio should decline. The reduction in risk will occur if the stock returns within our portfolio do not move precisely together over time—that is, if they are not perfectly correlated. Figure 6-3 shows graphically what we could

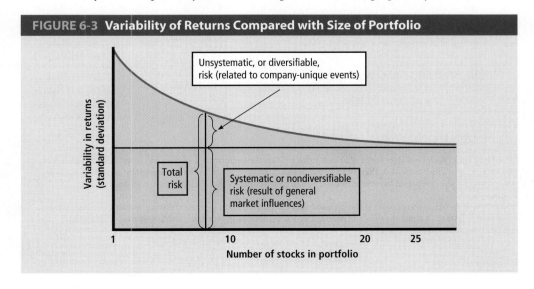

FIGURE 6-3 Variability of Returns Compared with Size of Portfolio

Unsystematic, or diversifiable, risk (related to company-unique events)

Variability in returns (standard deviation)

Total risk

Systematic or nondiversifiable risk (result of general market influences)

1   10   20   25

Number of stocks in portfolio

expect to happen to the variability of returns as we add additional stocks to the portfolio. The reduction occurs because some of the volatility in returns of a stock are unique to that security. The unique variability of a single stock tends to be countered by the uniqueness of another security. However, we should not expect to eliminate all risk from our portfolio. In practice, it would be rather difficult to cancel all the variations in returns of a portfolio, because stock prices have some tendency to move together. Thus, we can divide the total risk (total variability) of our portfolio into two types of risk: (1) **company-unique risk**, or **unsystematic risk**, and (2) **market risk**, or **systematic risk**. Company-unique risk might also be called **diversifiable risk**, in that it *can be diversified away*. Market risk is **nondiversifiable risk**; it *cannot be eliminated through random diversification*. These two types of risk are shown graphically in Figure 6-3. Total risk declines until we have approximately 20 securities, and then the decline becomes very slight.

    The remaining risk, which would typically be about 40 percent of the total risk, is the portfolio's systematic, or market, risk. At this point, our portfolio is highly correlated with all securities in the marketplace. Events that affect our portfolio now are not so much unique events as changes in the general economy, major political events, and sociological changes. Examples include changes in interest rates in the economy, changes in tax legislation that affect all companies, or increasing public concern about the effect of business practices on the environment. Our measure of risk should, therefore, measure how responsive a stock or portfolio is to changes in a market portfolio, such as the New York Stock Exchange or the S&P 500 Index.[7]

Measuring Market Risk

To help clarify the idea of systematic risk, let's examine the relationship between the common stock returns of Google and the returns of the S&P 500 Index.

    The monthly returns for Google and the S&P 500 Index for the 12 months ending May 2009 are presented in Table 6-3 and Figure 6-4. These *monthly returns*, or **holding-period returns**, as they are often called, are calculated as follows.[8]

$$\text{Monthly holding return} = \frac{\text{Price}_{\text{end of month}} - \text{Price}_{\text{beginning of month}}}{\text{Price}_{\text{beginning of month}}}$$

$$= \frac{\text{Price}_{\text{end of month}}}{\text{Price}_{\text{beginning of month}}} - 1 \qquad (6\text{-}6)$$

For instance, the holding-period return for Google and the S&P 500 Index for March 2009 is computed as follows:

$$\text{The Google return} = \frac{\text{stock price at end of March 2009}}{\text{stock price at end of February 2009}} - 1$$

$$= \frac{\$395.97}{\$348.06} - 1 = 0.138 = 13.8\%$$

$$\text{The S\&P 500 Index return} = \frac{\text{index value at end of March 2009}}{\text{index value at end of February 2009}} - 1$$

$$= \frac{\$872.81}{\$797.87} - 1 = 0.0939 = 9.4\%$$

company-unique risk see unsystematic risk.

unsystematic risk the risk related to an investment return that can be eliminated through diversification. Unsystematic risk is the result of factors that are unique to the particular firm. Also called company-unique risk or diversifiable risk.

market risk see systematic risk.

systematic risk (1) the risk related to an investment return that cannot be eliminated through diversification. Systematic risk results from factors that affect all stocks. Also called market risk or nondiversifiable risk. (2) The risk of a project from the viewpoint of a well-diversified shareholder. This measure takes into account that some of the project's risk will be diversified away as the project is combined with the firm's other projects, and, in addition, some of the remaining risk will be diversified away by shareholders as they combine this stock with other stocks in their portfolios.

diversifiable risk see Unsystematic risk.

nondiversifiable risk see Systematic risk.

holding-period return the return an investor would receive from holding a security for a designated period of time. For example, a monthly holding-period return would be the return for holding a security for a month.

---

[7]The New York Stock Exchange Index is an index that reflects the performance of all stocks listed on the New York Stock Exchange. The Standard & Poor's (S&P) 500 Index is similarly an index that measures the combined stock-price performance of the companies that constitute the 500 largest companies in the United States, as designated by Standard & Poor's.

[8]For simplicity's sake, we are ignoring the dividend that the investor receives from the stock as part of the total return. In other words, letting D_t equal the dividend received by the investor in month t, the holding-period return would more accurately be measured as

$$r_1 = \frac{P_t + D_t}{P_{t-1}} - 1 \qquad (6\text{-}7)$$

TABLE 6-3 Monthly Holding-Period Returns, Google versus the S&P 500 Index, June 2008 through May 2009

Month and Year	Google Price	Google Returns (%)	S&P 500 Index Price	S&P 500 Index Returns (%)
2008				
May	$526.42		$1,280.00	
June	473.75	−10.0%	1,267.38	−1.0%
July	463.29	−2.2%	1,282.83	1.2%
August	400.52	−13.5%	1,164.74	−9.2%
September	359.36	−10.3%	968.75	−16.8%
October	292.96	−18.5%	896.24	−7.5%
November	307.65	5.0%	903.25	0.8%
December	338.53	10.0%	825.88	−8.6%
2009				
January	337.99	−0.2%	735.09	−11.0%
February	348.06	3.0%	797.87	8.5%
March	395.97	13.8%	872.81	9.4%
April	417.23	5.4%	919.14	5.3%
May	426.56	2.2%	942.87	2.6%
Average return		−1.3%		−2.2%
Standard deviation		9.9%		8.3%

At the bottom of Table 6-3, we have also computed the averages of the returns for the 12 months, for both Google and the S&P 500 Index, and the standard deviation for these returns. Because we are using historical return data, we assume each observation has an equal probability of occurrence. Thus, the average holding-period return is found by summing the returns and dividing by the number of months; that is,

$$\text{Average holding period return} = \frac{\text{return in month 1} + \text{return in month 2} + \cdots + \text{return in last month}}{\text{number of monthly returns}} \tag{6-8}$$

FIGURE 6-4 Monthly Holding-Period Returns: Google versus the S&P 500 Index, June 2008 through May 2009

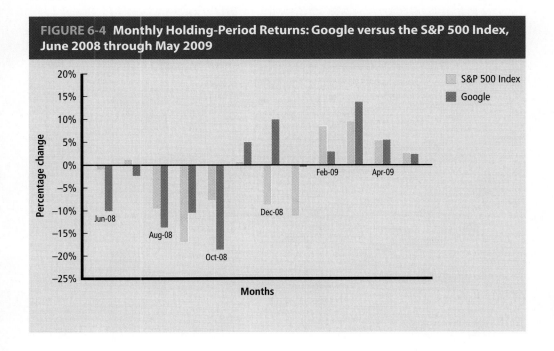

and the standard deviation is computed as follows:

Standard
deviation

$$= \sqrt{\frac{(\text{return in month 1} - \text{average return})^2 + (\text{return in month 2} - \text{average return})^2 + \cdots (\text{return in last month} - \text{average return})^2}{\text{number of monthly returns} - 1}}$$

(6-9)

In looking at Table 6-3 and Figure 6-4, we notice the following things about Google's holding-period returns over the 12 months ending in May 2009.

1. Google's owners experienced significant negative monthly holding-period returns, mostly from June through October 2008, losing 1.3 percent on average per month for the entire 12-month period. During the same time period, the general market, as represented by the Standard & Poor's 500 Index, declined 2.2 percent on average each month. Remember that the returns in Table 6-3 are historical or realized, and not expected. No investor would invest if she expected to lose money in an investment. But in a world of risk, your returns may not match your expectations. In fact, referring back to Figure 6-1, we see that over the long term (83 years to be exact) investors in large companies earned almost a 1 percent monthly return. What will happen in the future, no one can say. Hopefully, the old "normal" will return.

2. The second bad news is the high volatility of the returns, which is a measure of the risk. As shown at the bottom of Table 6-3, Google's standard deviation is 9.9 percent, compared to 8.3 percent for the S&P 500 Index. Both these numbers are high relative to the average monthly returns. These results, which are again based on the second half of 2008 and the first half of 2009, are far higher than in previous years, especially for the S&P 500 Index. For example, the 8.3 percent for the S&P 500 Index compares to about 2 percent during 2005–2006. So not only did values decline during 2008 and 2009, but the fluctuations of the returns from month to month have been high. Negative historical returns and high volatility—not exactly an investor's idea of fun.

3. We should also notice the tendency, although far from perfect, of Google's stock price to increase when the value of the S&P 500 Index increases and vice versa. This was the case in 10 of the 12 months. That is, there is a moderate positive relationship between Google's stock returns and the S&P 500 Index returns.

With respect to our third observation, that there is a relationship between the stock returns of Google and the S&P 500 Index, it is helpful to see this relationship by graphing Google's

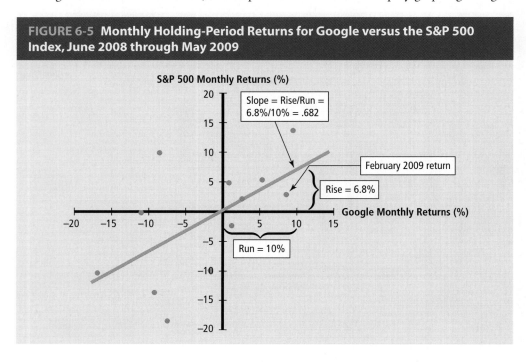

FIGURE 6-5 Monthly Holding-Period Returns for Google versus the S&P 500 Index, June 2008 through May 2009

returns against the S&P 500 Index returns. We provide such a graph in Figure 6-5. In the figure, we have plotted Google's returns on the vertical axis and the returns for the S&P 500 Index on the horizontal axis. Each of the 12 dots in the figure represents the returns of Google and the S&P 500 Index for a particular month. For instance, the returns for February 2009 for Google and the S&P 500 Index were 3.0 percent and 8.5 percent, respectively, which are noted in the figure.

In addition to the dots in the graph, we have drawn a line of "best fit," which we call the **characteristic line**. *The slope of the characteristic line measures the average relationship between a stock's returns and those of the S&P 500 Index*: or stated differently, *the slope of the line indicates the average movement in a stock's price in response to a movement in the S&P 500 Index price*. We can estimate the slope of the line visually by fitting a line that appears to cut through the middle of the dots. We then compare the rise (increase of the line on the vertical axis) to the run (increase on the horizontal axis). Alternatively, we can enter the return data into a financial calculator or Excel spreadsheet, which will calculate the slope based on statistical analysis. For Google, the slope of the line is 0.68, which means that on average that as the market returns (S&P 500 Index returns) increase or decrease 1 percent, the return for Google on average increases or decreases 0.68 percentage points.

We can also think of the 0.68 slope of the characteristic line as indicating that Google's returns are 0.68 times as volatile on average as those of the overall market (S&P 500 Index). This slope has come to be called **beta** (β) in investor jargon, and it *measures the average relationship between a stock's returns and the market's returns*. It is a term you will see almost any time you read an article written by a financial analyst about the riskiness of a stock.

Looking once again at Figure 6-5, we see that the dots (returns) are scattered all about the characteristic line—most of the returns do not fit neatly on the characteristic line. That is, the average relationship may be 0.68, but the variation in Google's returns is only partly explained by the stock's average relationship with the S&P 500 Index. There are other driving forces unique to Google that also affect the firm's stock returns. (Earlier, we called this company-unique risk.) If we were, however, to diversify our holdings and own, say, 20 stocks with betas of 0.68, we could essentially eliminate the variation about the characteristic line. That is, we would remove almost all the volatility in returns, except for that caused by the general market, which is represented by the slope of the line in Figure 6-5. If we plotted the returns of our 20-stock portfolio against the S&P 500 Index, the points in our new graph would fit nicely along a straight line with a slope of 0.68, which means that the beta (β) of the portfolio is also 0.68. The new graph would look something like the one shown in Figure 6-6. In other words, by diversifying our portfolio, we can essentially eliminate the variations

characteristic line the line of "best fit" through a series of returns for a firm's stock relative to the market's returns. The slope of the line, frequently called beta, represents the average movement of the firm's stock returns in response to a movement in the market's returns.

beta the relationship between an investment's returns and the market's returns. This is a measure of the investment's nondiversifiable risk.

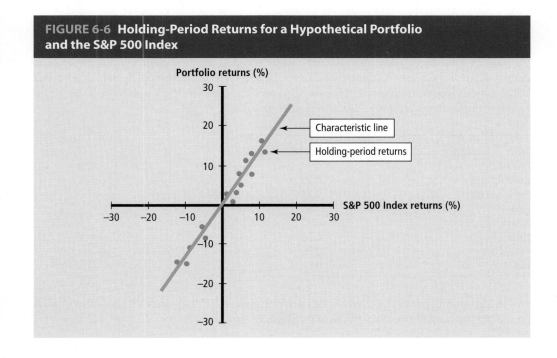

FIGURE 6-6 Holding-Period Returns for a Hypothetical Portfolio and the S&P 500 Index

CAN YOU DO IT?

ESTIMATING BETA

Below, we provide the end-of-month prices for McDonald's stock and the Standard & Poor's 500 Index for November 2008 through May 2009. Given the information, compute the following both for McDonald's and the S&P 500: (1) the monthly holding-period returns, (2) the average monthly returns, and (3) the standard deviation of the returns. Next, graph the holding-period returns of McDonald's on the vertical axis against the holding-period returns of the S&P 500 on the horizontal axis. Draw a line on your graph similar to what we did in Figure 6-5 to estimate the average relationship between the stock returns of McDonald's and the returns of the overall market as represented by the S&P 500. What is the approximate slope of your line? What does this tell you?

(In working this problem, it would be easier if you used an Excel spreadsheet including the slope function.)

	MCDONALDS CORP.	S&P 500
Nov-08	$57.73	$896.24
Dec-08	61.11	903.25
Jan-09	51.19	825.88
Feb-09	52.05	735.09
Mar-09	53.64	797.87
Apr-09	57.31	872.81
May-09	57.06	919.14

(The solution can be found on page 174.)

about the characteristic line, leaving only the variation in returns for a company that comes from variations in the general market returns.

So beta (β)—the slope of the characteristic line—is a measure of a firm's market risk or systematic risk, which is the risk that remains for a company even after we have diversified our portfolio. It is this risk—and only this risk—that matters for investors who have broadly diversified portfolios.

Although we have said that beta is a measure of a stock's systematic risk, how should we interpret a specific beta? For instance, when is a beta considered low and when is it considered high? In general, a stock with a beta of zero has no systematic risk; a stock with a beta of 1 has systematic or market risk equal to the "typical" stock in the marketplace; and a stock with a beta exceeding 1 has more market risk than the typical stock. Most stocks, however, have betas between 0.60 and 1.60.

We should also realize that calculating beta is not an exact science. The final estimate of a firm's beta is heavily dependent on one's methodology. For instance, it matters whether you use 24 months in your measurement or 60 months, as most professional investment companies do. Take our computation of Google's beta. We said Google's beta is 0.68 but Value Line, a well-known investment service, has estimated Google's beta to be 0.90. Value Line's beta estimates for a number of firms are as follows:

	BETAS
Coca-Cola	0.70
ExxonMobil	0.75
General Electric	1.15
IBM	0.90
Merck	0.70
Nike	0.90
PepsiCo	0.60
WalMart	0.60

To this point, we have talked about measuring an individual stock's beta. We will now consider how to measure the beta for a portfolio of stocks.

Measuring a Portfolio's Beta

What if we were to diversify our portfolio, as we have just suggested, but instead of acquiring stocks with the same beta as Google (0.68), we buy 8 stocks with betas of 1.0 and 12 stocks with betas of 1.5. What would the beta of our portfolio become? As it works out, the **portfolio beta** is merely the average of the individual stock betas. It is a *weighted average of the individual securities' betas, with the weights being equal to the proportion of the portfolio invested in each security.* Thus, the beta (β) of a portfolio consisting of n stocks is equal to

> **portfolio beta** the relationship between a portfolio's returns and the market returns. It is a measure of the portfolio's nondiversifiable risk.

$$
\begin{aligned}
\text{Portfolio} \atop \text{beta} &= \left(\begin{array}{c} \text{percentage of} \\ \text{portfolio invested} \\ \text{in asset 1} \end{array} \times \begin{array}{c} \text{beta for} \\ \text{asset 1}' \\ (\beta_1) \end{array} \right) \\
&+ \left(\begin{array}{c} \text{percentage of} \\ \text{portfolio invested} \\ \text{in asset 2} \end{array} \times \begin{array}{c} \text{beta for} \\ \text{asset 2}' \\ (\beta_2) \end{array} \right) + \cdots \\
&+ \left(\begin{array}{c} \text{percentage of} \\ \text{portfolio invested} \\ \text{in asset } n \end{array} \times \begin{array}{c} \text{beta for} \\ \text{asset } n \\ (\beta_n) \end{array} \right)
\end{aligned}
\tag{6-10}
$$

So, assuming we bought equal amounts of each stock in our new 20-stock portfolio, the beta would simply be 1.3, calculated as follows:

$$
\text{Portfolio beta} = \left(\frac{8}{20} \times 1.0 \right) + \left(\frac{12}{20} \times 1.50 \right) = 1.3
$$

Thus, whenever the general market increases or decreases 1 percent, our new portfolio's returns would change 1.3 percent on average, which means that our new portfolio has more systematic, or market, risk than the market has as a whole.

We can conclude that the beta of a portfolio is determined by the betas of the individual stocks. If we have a portfolio consisting of stocks with low betas, then our portfolio will have a low beta. The reverse is true as well. Figure 6-7 presents these situations graphically.

Before leaving the subject of risk and diversification, we want to share a study that demonstrates the effects of diversifying our investments, not just across different stocks but also across different types of securities.

FIGURE 6-7 Holding-Period Returns: High- and Low-Beta Portfolios and the S&P 500 Index

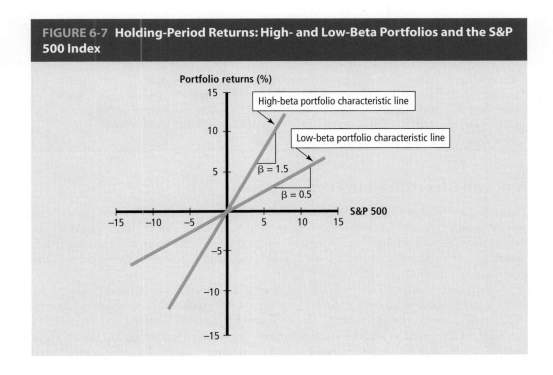

DID YOU GET IT?
ESTIMATING BETA

The holding-period returns, average monthly returns, and the standard deviations for McDonald's and the S&P 500 data are as follows:

	MCDONALDS CORP.		S&P 500	
	PRICES	RETURNS	PRICES	RETURNS
Nov-08	$57.73		$896.24	
Dec-08	61.11	5.85%	903.25	0.78%
Jan-09	51.19	−16.23%	825.88	−8.57%
Feb-09	52.05	1.68%	735.09	−10.99%
Mar-09	53.64	3.05%	797.87	8.54%
Apr-09	57.31	6.84%	872.81	9.39%
May-09	57.06	−0.44%	919.14	5.31%
Average return		0.13%		0.74%
Standard deviation		8.45%		8.73%

The graph would appear as follows:

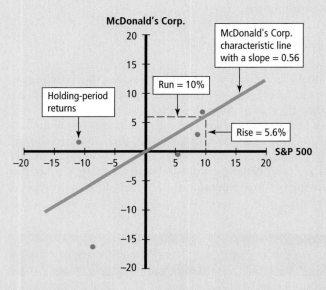

The average relationship between McDonald's stock returns and the S&P 500's returns as estimated is 0.56, where the rise of the line is 5.6 relative to a run (horizontal axis) of 10 (0.56 = 5.6/10). If our estimates fairly represent the relationships, then McDonald's stock returns are less volatile than the market's returns. When the market rises (or falls) 1 percent, McDonald's stock will rise (or fall) 0.56 percent. (We should, however, be hesitant to draw any firm conclusions here, given the limited number of return observations.)

Risk and Diversification Demonstrated

To this point, we have described the effect of diversification on risk and return in a general way. Also, when we spoke of diversification, we were diversifying by holding more stocks in our portfolio. Now let's look briefly on how risk and return change as we (1) diversify between two different types of assets—stocks and bonds, and (2) increase the length of time that we hold a portfolio of assets.

Notice that when we previously spoke about diversification, we were diversifying by holding more stock, but the portfolio still consisted of all stocks. Now we examine diversifying between a portfolio of stocks and a portfolio of bonds. Diversifying among different kinds of assets is called **asset allocation**, compared with diversification within the different asset classes, such as stocks, bonds, real estate, and commodities. We know from experience

asset allocation identifying and selecting the asset classes appropriate for a specific investment portfolio and determining the proportions of those assets within the portfolio.

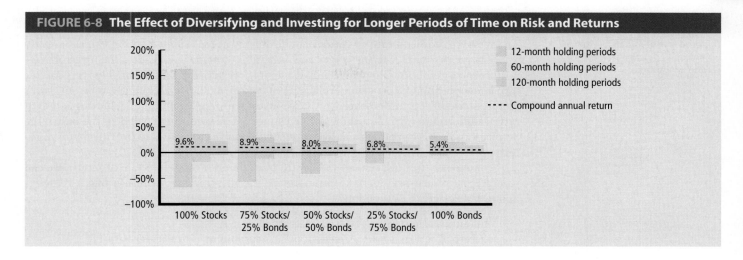

FIGURE 6-8 The Effect of Diversifying and Investing for Longer Periods of Time on Risk and Returns

that the benefit we receive from diversifying is far greater through effective asset allocation than from astutely selecting individual stocks to include with an asset category.

Figure 6-8 presents the range of rolling returns for several mixtures of stocks and bonds depending on whether we held the investments 12 months, 60 months, or 120 months between 1926 and 2008. For the 12-month holding period, we would have purchased the investment at the beginning of each year and sold at the end of each year, repeating this process every year from 1926 to 2008. Then for the 60 months, we would have invested at the beginning of the year and held the investment for 60 months. In other words, we invested at the beginning of 1926 and sold at the end 1930, then did the same for 1927–1931, repeating the process for all 60-month periods all the way through 2008. Finally, we would have invested at the beginning of each year, holding each investment for 120 months.

As we observe in Figure 6-8, moving from an all-stock portfolio to a mixture of stocks and bonds and finally to an all-bond portfolio reduces the variability of returns (our measure for risk) significantly along with declining average rates of return. Stated differently, if we want to increase our expected returns, we must assume more risk. That is, there is a clear relationship between risk and return. Reminds us of **Principle 3: Risk Requires a Reward**.

Equally important, how long we hold our investments matters greatly when it comes to reducing risk. As we move from 12 months to 60 months, and finally to 120 months, we see the range of return falling sharply, especially when we move from 12-month holding periods to 60-month holding periods. As a side note, notice that there has never been a time between 1926 and 2008 when an investor lost money if she held an all-stock portfolio—the most risky portfolio—for ten years. In other words, *the market rewards the patient investor.*

In the next section, we complete our study of risk and returns by connecting risk—market or systematic risk—to the investor's *required* rate of return. After all, although risk is an important issue, it is primarily important in its effect on the investor's required rate of return.

Concept Check

1. Give specific examples of systematic and unsystematic risk. How many different securities must be owned to essentially diversify away unsystematic risk?

2. What method is used to measure a firm's market risk?

3. After reviewing Figure 6-5, explain the difference between the plotted dots and the firm's characteristic line. What must be done to eliminate the variations?

The Investor's Required Rate of Return

In this section, we examine the concept of the investor's required rate of return, especially as it relates to the riskiness of an asset, and then we see how the required rate of return might be measured.

Explain the relationship between the investor's required rate of return on an investment and the riskiness of the investment.

The Required Rate of Return Concept

required rate of return minimum rate of return necessary to attract an investor to purchase or hold a security.

An investor's **required rate of return** can be defined as the *minimum rate of return necessary to attract an investor to purchase or hold a security*. This definition considers the investor's opportunity cost of funds of making an investment in *the next-best investment*. This forgone return is an opportunity cost of undertaking the investment and, consequently, is the investor's required rate of return. In other words, we invest with the intention of achieving a rate of return sufficient to warrant making the investment. The investment will be made only if the purchase price is low enough relative to expected future cash flows to provide a rate of return greater than or equal to our required rate of return.

To help us better understand the nature of an investor's required rate of return, we can separate the return into its basic components: the risk-free rate of return plus a risk premium. Expressed as an equation:

$$\text{Investor's required} \atop \text{rate of return} = {\text{risk-free rate of} \atop \text{return}} + {\text{risk} \atop \text{premium}} \tag{6-11}$$

risk-free rate of return the rate of return on risk-free investments. The interest rates on short-term U.S. government securities are commonly used to measure this rate.

risk premium the additional return expected for assuming risk.

The **risk-free rate of return** is the *required rate of return, or discount rate, for riskless investments*. Typically, our measure for the risk-free rate of return is the U.S. Treasury bill rate. The **risk premium** is the *additional return we must expect to receive for assuming risk*. As the level of risk increases, we will demand additional expected returns. Even though we may or may not actually receive this incremental return, we must have reason to expect it; otherwise, why expose ourselves to the chance of losing all or part of our money?

> **EXAMPLE 6.1**
>
> Assume you are considering the purchase of a stock that you believe will provide a 14 percent return over the next year. If the expected risk-free rate of return, such as the rate of return for 90-day Treasury bills, is 5 percent, then the risk premium you are demanding to assume the additional risk is 9 percent $(14\% - 5\%)$.

Measuring the Required Rate of Return

We have seen that (1) systematic risk is the only relevant risk—the rest can be diversified away, and (2) the required rate of return, k, equals the risk-free rate plus a risk premium. We will now examine how we can estimate investors' required rates of return.

The finance profession has had difficulty in developing a practical approach to measure an investor's required rate of return; however, financial managers often use a method called the **capital asset pricing model (CAPM)**. The capital asset pricing model is *an equation that equates the expected rate of return on a stock to the risk-free rate plus a risk premium for the stock's systematic risk*. Although certainly not without its critics, the CAPM provides an intuitive approach for thinking about the return that an investor should require on an investment, given the asset's systematic or market risk.

capital asset pricing model (CAPM) an equation stating that the expected rate of return on a project is a function of (1) the risk-free rate, (2) the investment's systematic risk, and (3) the expected risk premium for the market portfolio of all risky securities.

Equation (6-11) above provides the natural starting point for measuring the investor's required rate of return and sets us up for using the CAPM. Rearranging this equation to solve for the risk premium we have

$$\text{Risk} \atop \text{premium} = {\text{investor's required} \atop \text{rate of return, } r} - {\text{risk-free rate of} \atop \text{return } r_f} \tag{6-12}$$

which simply says that the risk premium for a security equals the investor's required return less the risk-free rate existing in the market. For example, if the required return is 15 percent, and the risk-free rate is 5 percent, the risk premium is 10 percent. Also, if the required return for the market portfolio is 12 percent, and the risk-free rate is 5 percent, the risk premium

FINANCE AT WORK

DOES BETA ALWAYS WORK?

At the start of 1998, Apple Computer was in deep trouble. As a result, its stock price fluctuated wildly—far more than other computer firms, such as IBM. However, based on the capital asset pricing model (CAPM) and its measure of beta, the required return of Apple's investors would have been only 8 percent, compared with 12 percent for IBM's stockholders. Equally interesting, when Apple's situation improved in the spring of that year, and its share price became less volatile, Apple's investors, at least according to the CAPM, would have required a rate of return of 11 percent—a 3 percentage point increase from the earlier required rate of return. That is not what intuition would suggest should have happened.

So what should we think? Just when Apple's future was most in doubt and its shares most volatile, its beta was only 0.47, suggesting that Apple's stock was only half as volatile as the overall stock market. In reality, beta is meaningless here. The truth is that Apple was in such a dire condition that its stock price simply "decoupled" itself from the stock market. So, as IBM and its peer stock prices moved up and down with the rest of the market, Apple shares reacted solely to news about the company, without

regard for the market's movements. The stock's beta thus created the false impression that Apple shares were more stable than the stock market.

The lesson here is that beta may at times be misleading when used with individual companies. Instead, its use is far more reliable when applied to a portfolio of companies. If a firm that was interested in acquiring Apple Computer in 1998, for instance, had used the beta in computing the required rate of return for the acquisition, it would without a doubt have overvalued Apple.

So does that mean that CAPM is worthless? No, not as long as company-unique risk is not the main driving force in a company's stock price movements or if investors are able to diversify away specific company risk. Then they would bid up the price of such shares until they reflected only market risk. For example, a mutual fund that specializes in "distressed stocks" might purchase a number of "Apple Computer-type companies," each with its own problems, but for different reasons. For such investors, betas work pretty well. Thus, the moral of the story is to exercise common sense and judgment when using a beta.

---

for the market would be 7 percent. This 7 percent risk premium would apply to any security having systematic (nondiversifiable) risk equivalent to the general market, or a beta (β) of 1.

In this same market, a security with a beta (β) of 2 should provide a risk premium of 14 percent, or twice the 7 percent risk premium existing for the market as a whole. Hence, in general, the appropriate required rate of return for a given security should be determined by

$$\begin{matrix} \text{Required return on} \\ \text{security, } r \end{matrix} = \begin{matrix} \text{risk free} \\ \text{rate of return, } r_f \end{matrix}$$
$$+ \begin{matrix} \text{beta for} \\ \text{security, } \beta \end{matrix} \times \left(\begin{matrix} \text{required return} \\ \text{on the market portfolio, } r_m \end{matrix} - \begin{matrix} \text{risk-free} \\ \text{rate of return, } r_f \end{matrix} \right)$$

$$(6\text{-}13)$$

Equation (6-13) is the CAPM. This equation designates the risk–return trade-off existing in the market, where risk is measured in terms of beta. Figure 6-9 graphs the CAPM as the **security market line**.[9] The security market line is *the graphic representation of the CAPM. It is the line that shows the appropriate required rate of return given a stock's systematic risk.*

security market line the return line that reflects the attitudes of investors regarding the minimum acceptable return for a given level of systematic risk associated with a security.

[9]Two key assumptions are made in using the security market line. First, we assume that the marketplace where securities are bought and sold is highly efficient. Market efficiency indicates that the price of an asset responds quickly to new information, thereby suggesting that the price of a security reflects all available information. As a result, the current price of a security is considered to represent the best estimate of its future price. Second, the model assumes that a perfect market exists. A perfect market is one in which information is readily available to all investors at a nominal cost. Also, securities are assumed to be infinitely divisible, with any transaction costs incurred in purchasing or selling a security being negligible. Furthermore, investors are assumed to be single-period wealth maximizers who agree on the meaning and significance of the available information. Finally, within the perfect market, all investors are *price takers*, which simply means that a single investor's actions cannot affect the price of a security. These assumptions are obviously not descriptive of reality. However, from the perspective of positive economics, the mark of a good theory is the accuracy of its predictions, not the validity of the simplifying assumptions that underlie its development.

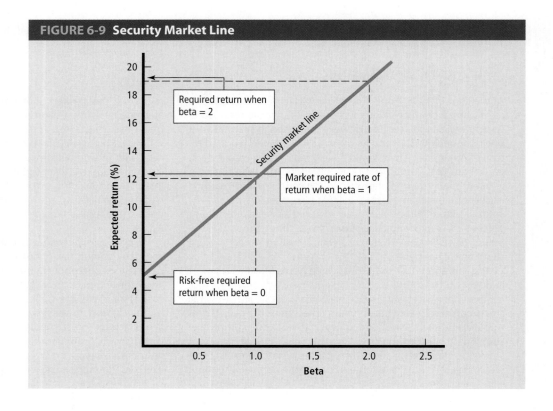

FIGURE 6-9 Security Market Line

As presented in this figure, securities with betas equal to 0, 1, and 2 should have required rates of return as follows:

If $\beta = 0$: required rate of return $= 5\% + 0(12\% - 5\%) = 5\%$

If $\beta = 1$: required rate of return $= 5\% + 1(12\% - 5\%) = 12\%$

If $\beta = 2$: required rate of return $= 5\% + 2(12\% - 5\%) = 19\%$

where the risk-free rate is 5 percent, and the required return for the market portfolio is 12 percent.

Concept Check

1. How does opportunity cost affect an investor's required rate of return?
2. What are the two components of the investor's required rate of return?
3. How does beta fit into factoring the risk premium in the CAPM equation?
4. Assuming the market is efficient, what is the relationship between a stock's price and the security market line?

CAN YOU DO IT?

COMPUTING A REQUIRED RATE OF RETURN

Determine a fair expected (or required) rate of return for a stock that has a beta of 1.25 when the risk-free rate is 5 percent, and the expected market return is 9 percent.

(The solution can be found on page 179.)

DID YOU GET IT?
COMPUTING A REQUIRED RATE OF RETURN

The appropriate rate of return would be:

Required return = risk-free rate + [beta × (market return − risk-free rate)]

= 5% + [1.25 × (9% − 5%)]

= 10%

Summary

In Chapter 2, we referred to the discount rate as the interest rate, or the opportunity cost of funds. At that point, we considered a number of important factors that influence interest rates, including the price of time, expected or anticipated inflation, the risk premium related to maturity (liquidity), and the variability of future returns. In this chapter, we have returned to our study of rates of return and looked ever so carefully at the relationship between risk and rates of return.

 Define and measure the expected rate of return of an individual investment.

In a world of uncertainty, we cannot make forecasts with certitude. Thus, we must speak in terms of *expected* events. The expected return on an investment may therefore be stated as a weighted average of all possible returns, weighted by the probability that each will occur.

 Define and measure the riskiness of an individual investment.

Risk for our purposes is the variability of returns and can be measured by the standard deviation.

Ibbotson Associates have provided us with annual rates of return earned on different types of security investments as far back as 1926. They summarize among other things, the annual returns for six portfolios of securities made up of

 Compare the historical relationship between risk and rates of return in the capital markets.

1. Common stocks of large companies
2. Common stocks of small firms
3. Long-term corporate bonds
4. Long-term U.S. government bonds
5. Intermediate-term U.S. government bonds
6. U.S. Treasury bills

 Explain how diversifying investments affects the riskiness and expected rate of return of a portfolio or combination of assets.

A comparison of the annual rates of return for these respective portfolios for the years 1926 to 2008 shows a positive relationship between risk and return, with Treasury bills being least risky and common stocks of small firms being most risky. From the data, we are able to see the benefit of diversification in terms of improving the return–risk relationship. Also, the data clearly demonstrate that only common stock has in the long run served as an inflation hedge, and that the risk associated with common stock can be reduced if investors are patient in receiving their returns.

 Explain the relationship between the investor's required rate of return on an investment and the riskiness of the investment.

We made an important distinction between nondiversifiable risk and diversifiable risk. We concluded that the only relevant risk, given the opportunity to diversify our portfolio, is a security's nondiversifiable risk, which we called by two other names: systematic risk and market-related risk.

The capital asset pricing model provides an intuitive framework for understanding the risk–return relationship. The CAPM suggests that investors determine an appropriate required rate of return, depending upon the amount of systematic risk inherent in a security. This minimum acceptable rate of return is equal to the risk-free rate plus a risk premium for assuming risk.

Key Terms

Review Questions

All Review Questions and Study Problems are available in MyFinanceLab.

6-1. a. What is meant by the investor's required rate of return?

   b. How do we measure the riskiness of an asset?

   c. How should the proposed measurement of risk be interpreted?

6-2. What is (a) unsystematic risk (company-unique or diversifiable risk) and (b) systematic risk (market or nondiversifiable risk)?

6-3. What is a beta? How is it used to calculate *r*, the investor's required rate of return?

6-4. What is the security market line? What does it represent?

6-5. How do we measure the beta of a portfolio?

6-6. If we were to graph the returns of a stock against the returns of the S&P 500 Index, and the points did not follow a very ordered pattern, what could we say about that stock? If the stock's returns tracked the S&P 500 returns very closely, then what could we say?

6-7. Over the past 8 decades, we have had the opportunity to observe the rates of return and the variability of these returns for different types of securities. Summarize these observations.

6-8. What effect will diversifying your portfolio have on your returns?

Self-Test Problems

(The solutions to the following problems are found at the end of the chapter.)

ST-1. (*Expected return and risk*) Universal Corporation is planning to invest in a security that has several possible rates of return. Given the following probability distribution of returns, what is the expected rate of return on the investment? Also compute the standard deviations of the returns. What do the resulting numbers represent?

PROBABILITY	RETURN
0.10	−10%
0.20	5%
0.30	10%
0.40	25%

ST-2. (*Capital asset pricing model*) Using the CAPM, estimate the appropriate required rate of return for the three stocks listed here, given that the risk-free rate is 5 percent, and the expected return for the market is 17 percent.

STOCK	BETA
A	0.75
B	0.90
C	1.40

ST-3. (*Average expected return and risk*) Given the holding-period returns shown here, calculate the average returns and the standard deviations for the Kaifu Corporation and for the market.

MONTH	KAIFU CORP.	MARKET
1	4%	2%
2	6	3
3	0	1
4	2	−1

ST-4. (*Holding-period returns*) From the price data that follow, compute the holding-period returns for periods 2 through 4.

PERIOD	STOCK PRICE
1	$10
2	13
3	11
4	15

ST-5. (*Security market line*)

a. Determine the expected return and beta for the following portfolio:

STOCK	PERCENTAGE OF PORTFOLIO	BETA	EXPECTED RETURN
1	40%	1.00	12%
2	25	0.75	11
3	35	1.30	15

b. Given the foregoing information, draw the security market line and show where the securities fit on the graph. Assume that the risk-free rate is 8 percent and that the expected return on the market portfolio is 12 percent. How would you interpret these findings?

Study Problems

6-1. (*Expected rate of return and risk*) Carter Inc. is evaluating a security. One-year Treasury bills are currently paying 9.1 percent. Calculate the investment's expected return and its standard deviation. Should Carter invest in this security?

PROBABILITY	RETURN
0.15	6%
0.30	9%
0.40	10%
0.15	15%

6-2. (*Expected rate of return and risk*) Summerville Inc. is considering an investment in one of two common stocks. Given the information that follows, which investment is better, based on the risk (as measured by the standard deviation) and return of each?

COMMON STOCK A		COMMON STOCK B	
PROBABILITY	RETURN	PROBABILITY	RETURN
0.30	11%	0.20	−5%
0.40	15%	0.30	6%
0.30	19%	0.30	14%
		0.20	22%

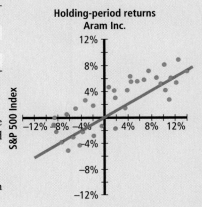

Holding-period returns
Aram Inc.

6-3. (*Required rate of return using CAPM*)

a. Compute a fair rate of return for Intel common stock, which has a 1.2 beta. The risk-free rate is 6 percent, and the market portfolio (New York Stock Exchange stocks) has an expected return of 16 percent.

b. Why is the rate you computed a fair rate?

6-4. (*Estimating beta*) From the graph in the margin relating the holding-period returns for Aram Inc. to the S&P 500 Index, estimate the firm's beta.

6-5. (*Capital asset pricing model*) Levine Manufacturing Inc. is considering several investments. The rate on Treasury bills is currently 6.75 percent, and the expected return for the market is 12 percent. What should be the required rates of return for each investment (using the CAPM)?

SECURITY	BETA
A	1.50
B	0.90
C	0.70
D	1.15

6-6. (*Capital asset pricing model*) MFI Inc. has a beta of 0.86. If the expected market return is 11.5 percent and the risk-free rate is 7.5 percent, what is the appropriate required return of MFI (using the CAPM)?

6-7. (*Capital asset pricing model*) The expected return for the general market is 12.8 percent, and the risk premium in the market is 4.3 percent. Tasaco, LBM, and Exxos have betas of 0.864, 0.693, and 0.575, respectively. What are the corresponding required rates of return for the three securities?

6-8. (*Computing holding-period returns*)

a. From the price data here, compute the holding-period returns for Jazman and Solomon for periods 2 through 4.

PERIOD	JAZMAN	SOLOMON
1	$9	$27
2	11	28
3	10	32
4	13	29

b. How would you interpret the meaning of a holding-period return?

6-9. (*Measuring risk and rates of return*)

a. Given the holding-period returns shown here, compute the average returns and the standard deviations for the Zemin Corporation and for the market.

MONTH	ZEMIN CORP.	MARKET
1	6%	4%
2	3	2
3	−1	1
4	−3	−2
5	5	2
6	0	2

b. If Zemin's beta is 1.54 and the risk-free rate is 8 percent, what would be an appropriate required return for an investor owning Zemin? (*Note:* Because the returns of Zemin Corporation are based on monthly data, you will need to annualize the returns to make them compatible with the risk-free rate. For simplicity, you can convert from monthly to yearly returns by multiplying the average monthly returns by 12.)

c. How does Zemin's historical average return compare with the return you believe to be a fair return, given the firm's systematic risk?

6-10. (*Portfolio beta and security market line*) You own a portfolio consisting of the stocks below:

STOCK	PERCENTAGE OF PORTFOLIO	BETA	EXPECTED RETURN
1	20%	1.00	16%
2	30	0.85	14
3	15	1.20	20
4	25	0.60	12
5	10	1.60	24

The risk-free rate is 7 percent. Also, the expected return on the market portfolio is 15.5 percent.

a. Calculate the expected return of your portfolio. (*Hint:* The expected return of a portfolio equals the weighted average of the individual stocks' expected returns, where the weights are the percentage invested in each stock.)

b. Calculate the portfolio beta.

c. Given the foregoing information, plot the security market line on paper. Plot the stocks from your portfolio on your graph.

d. From your plot in part c, which stocks appear to be your winners and which ones appear to be losers?

e. Why should you consider your conclusion in part d to be less than certain?

6-11. (*Expected return, standard deviation, and capital asset pricing model*) The following are the end-of-month prices for both the Standard & Poor's 500 Index and Hewlett-Packard's common stock.

a. Using the data here, calculate the holding-period returns for each of the months.

	HEWLETT-PACKARD	S&P 500 INDEX
2008		
May	$ 46.55	$ 1,400.38
June	43.81	1,280.00
July	44.39	1,267.38
August	46.49	1,282.83
September	45.90	1,164.74
October	38.00	968.75
November	35.02	896.24
December	36.10	903.25
2009		
January	34.57	825.88
February	28.88	735.09
March	31.99	797.87
April	35.90	872.81
May	34.28	919.14

b. Calculate the average monthly return and the standard deviation for both the S&P 500 and Hewlett-Packard.

c. Develop a graph that shows the relationship between the Hewlett-Packard stock returns and the S&P 500 Index. (Show the Hewlett-Packard returns on the vertical axis and the S&P 500 Index returns on the horizontal axis as done in Figure 6-5.)

d. From your graph, describe the nature of the relationship between Hewlett-Packard stock returns and the returns for the S&P 500 Index.

6-12. (*Standard deviation*) Given the following probabilities and returns for Mik's Corporation, find the standard deviation.

PROBABILITY	RETURNS
0.40	7%
0.25	4%
0.15	18%
0.20	10%

6-13. Assume you have the following portfolio.

	STOCK WEIGHT	BETA
Apple	38%	1.50
Green Mountain Coffee	15%	1.44
Disney	27%	1.15
Target	20%	1.20

What is the portfolio's beta?

6-14. (*Holding period dollar gain and return*) Suppose you purchased 16 shares of Disney stock for $24.22 per share on May 1, 2009. On September 1 of the same year, you sold 12 shares of the stock for $25.68. Calculate the holding-period dollar gain for the shares you sold, assuming no dividend was distributed, and the holding-period rate of return.

6-15. Go to www.moneychimp.com. Select the link "Volatility." Complete the retirement planning calculator, making the assumptions that you believe are appropriate for you. Then go to the Monte Carlo simulation calculator. Assume that you invest in large-company common stocks during your working years and then invest in long-term corporate bonds during retirement. Use the nominal average returns and standard deviations shown in Figure 6-2. What did you learn?

6-16. Go to www.cgi.money.cnn.com/tools. Choose "Asset Allocator." Answer the questions and click "Calculate." Try different options and see how the calculator suggests you allocate your investments.

6-17. Access http://finance.yahoo.com. On the left side of the page, scroll down to and select "Investing" and then choose "Education." Next select "Glossary" and find "Expected Return" and "Expected Value." What did you learn from the definitions of these terms?

6-18. Go to www.investopedia.com/university/beginner, where there is an article on "Investing 101: A Tutorial for Beginning Investors." Read the article and explain what it says about risk tolerance.

Mini Case

Note: Although not absolutely necessary, you are advised to use a computer spreadsheet to work the following problem.

a. Use the price data from the table that follows for the Standard & Poor's 500 Index, Walmart, and Target to calculate the holding-period returns for the 24 months from July 2007 through June 2009.

MONTH	S&P 500	WALMART	TARGET
Jun-07	1,503.35	46.32	61.86
Jul-07	1,455.27	44.24	58.91
Aug-07	1,473.99	42.22	64.28
Sep-07	1,526.75	42.24	61.98
Oct-07	1,549.38	43.75	59.83
Nov-07	1,481.14	46.35	58.62
Dec-07	1,468.36	46.20	48.88
Jan-08	1,378.55	49.32	54.17
Feb-08	1,330.63	48.21	51.56
Mar-08	1,322.70	51.45	49.67
Apr-08	1,385.59	56.63	52.07
May-08	1,400.38	56.63	52.43
Jun-08	1,280.00	55.12	45.68
Jul-08	1,267.38	57.50	44.44
Aug-08	1,282.83	58.17	52.26
Sep-08	1,164.74	58.98	48.35
Oct-08	968.75	54.96	39.54
Nov-08	896.24	55.03	33.44
Dec-08	903.25	55.45	34.21
Jan-09	825.88	46.60	30.91
Feb-09	735.09	48.70	28.20
Mar-09	797.87	51.82	34.25
Apr-09	872.81	50.13	41.10
May-09	919.14	49.74	39.30
June-09	946.21	48.68	39.00

b. Calculate the average monthly holding-period returns and the standard deviation of these returns for the S&P 500 Index, Walmart, and Target.
c. Plot (1) the holding-period returns for Walmart against the Standard & Poor's 500 Index, and (2) the Target holding-period returns against the Standard & Poor's 500 Index. (Use Figure 6-5 as the format for your graph.)
d. From your graphs in part c, describe the nature of the relationship between the stock returns for Walmart and the returns for the S&P 500 Index. Make the same comparison for Target.
e. Assume that you have decided to invest one-half of your money in Walmart and the remainder in Target. Calculate the monthly holding-period returns for your two-stock portfolio. (*Hint:* The monthly return for the portfolio is the average of the two stocks' monthly returns.)
f. Plot the returns of your two-stock portfolio against the Standard & Poor's 500 Index as you did for the individual stocks in part c. How does this graph compare to the graphs for the individual stocks? Explain the difference.
g. The following table shows the returns on an *annualized* basis that were realized from holding long-term government bonds for the same period. Calculate the average *monthly* holding-period returns and the standard deviations of these returns. (*Hint:* You will need to convert the annual returns to monthly returns by dividing each return by 12 months.)

MONTH AND YEAR	ANNUALIZED RATE OF RETURN (%)
Jul-07	5.00%
Aug-07	4.67%
Sep-07	4.52%
Oct-07	4.53%
Nov-07	4.15%
Dec-07	4.10%
Jan-08	3.74%
Feb-08	3.74%
Mar-08	3.51%
Apr-08	3.68%
May-08	3.88%
Jun-08	4.10%
Jul-08	4.01%
Aug-08	3.89%
Sep-08	3.69%
Oct-08	3.81%
Nov-08	3.53%
Dec-08	2.42%
Jan-09	2.52%
Feb-09	2.87%
Mar-09	2.82%
Apr-09	2.93%
May-09	3.29%
Jun-09	3.18%

h. Now assuming that you have decided to invest equal amounts of money in Walmart, Target, and long-term government securities, calculate the monthly returns for your three-asset portfolio. What is the average return and the standard deviation?

i. Make a comparison of the average returns and the standard deviations for all the individual assets and the two portfolios that we designed. What conclusions can be reached by your comparison?

j. According to Standard & Poor's, the betas for Walmart and Target are 0.59 and 1.02, respectively. Compare the meaning of these betas relative to the standard deviations calculated above.

k. Assume that the current treasury bill rate is 4.5 percent and that the expected market return is 10 percent. Given the betas for Walmart and Target in part j, estimate an appropriate rate of return for the two firms.

Self-Test Solutions

SS-1.

(A) PROBABILITY	(B) RETURN	EXPECTED RETURN ($\bar{r}$)	WEIGHTED DEVIATION
$P(r)$	(r)	$(A) \times (B)$	$(r - \bar{r})^2 P(r)$
0.10	−10%	−1%	52.9%
0.20	5	1	12.8
0.30	10	3	2.7
0.40	25	10	57.6
		$\bar{r} = 13\%$	$\sigma^2 = 126.0\%$
			$\sigma = 11.22\%$

From our studies in statistics, we know that if the distribution of returns were normal, then Universal could expect a return of 13 percent, with a 67 percent possibility that this return would vary up or down by 11.22 percent between 1.78 percent (13% − 11.22%) and 24.22 percent (13% + 11.22%). However, it is apparent from the probabilities that the distribution is not normal.

SS-2.

Stock A: 5% + 0.75 (17% − 5%) = 14.0%

Stock B: 5% + 0.90 (17% − 5%) = 15.8%

Stock C: 5% + 1.40 (17% − 5%) = 21.8%

SS-3.

KAIFU		MARKET	
Average return:	$\dfrac{4\% + 6\% + 0\% + 2\%}{4} = 3\%$	Average return:	$\dfrac{2\% + 3\% + 1\% - 1\%}{4} = 1.25\%$
Standard deviation:	$\sqrt{\dfrac{[(4\% - 3\%)^2 + (6\% - 3\%)^2 + (0\% - 3\%)^2 + (2\% - 3\%)^2]}{4 - 1}} = 2.58\%$	Standard deviation:	$\sqrt{\dfrac{[(2\% - 1.25\%)^2 + (3\% - 1.25\%)^2 + (1\% - 1.25\%)^2 + (-1\% - 1.25\%)^2]}{4 - 1}} = 1.71\%$

SS-4.

TIME	STOCK PRICE	HOLDING-PERIOD RETURN
1	$10	
2	13	($13 ÷ $10) − 1 = 30.0%
3	11	($11 ÷ $13) − 1 = −15.4%
4	15	($15 ÷ $11) − 1 = 36.4%

SS-5. a. Portfolio expected return:

$(0.4 \times 12\%) + (0.25 \times 11\%) + (0.35 \times 15\%) = 12.8\%$

Portfolio beta:

$(0.4 \times 1) + (0.25 \times 0.75) + (0.35 \times 1.3) = 1.04$

b.

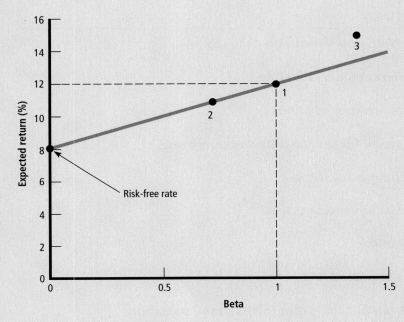

Stocks 1 and 2 seem to be right in line with the security market line, which suggest that they are earning a fair return, given their systematic risk. Stock 3, on the other hand, is earning more than a fair return (above the security market line). We might be tempted to conclude that security 3 is undervalued. However, we may be seeing an illusion; it is possible to mis-specify the security market line by using bad estimates in our data.

Chapter 7

The Valuation and Characteristics of Bonds

Learning Objectives

After reading this chapter, you should be able to:

1 Distinguish between different kinds of bonds.

2 Explain the more popular features of bonds.

3 Define the term *value* as used for several different purposes.

4 Explain the factors that determine value.

5 Describe the basic process for valuing assets.

6 Estimate the value of a bond.

7 Compute a bondholder's expected rate of return.

8 Explain three important relationships that exist in bond valuation.

If you have ever shopped at Neiman Marcus, you know it sells only very high-quality products, which for many of us means *expensive*.

For many years Neiman Marcus' stock had been traded on the New York Stock Exchange, but that ended in 2005, when a private investment group, including Texas Pacific Group and Warburg Pincus LLC, bought the firm for $5.1 billion. To buy the stock, the investors borrowed a lot of money to finance the purchase, and then they provided the equity financing to complete it. In this type of financing arrangement, known as a *leveraged buyout*, or LBO, the new owners work with the firm's managers to make it more efficient and then eventually sell it to other investors or take the firm public. By 2005, LBOs were taking on significantly more debt than in the past to make their purchases. Consequently, the owners of these firms were finding it more difficult to sell the companies or to take them public. So, they began paying themselves large dividends, which meant that there was less money available to service the companies' debt.

In announcing the sale, Richard A. Smith, Neiman Marcus' CEO and chairman of the board, remarked, "This transaction provides outstanding shareholder value and represents an endorsement of the excellent performance of our entire team." But although Smith considered the sale to be a good deal for the firm's stockholders, the firm's bondholders, who had loaned the company money, were not happy.

In the Neiman Marcus case, the bondholders made an unusual demand of the shareholders: For the interest they were to be paid as part of the buyout, they agreed to accept new bonds rather than cash—a provision known as a *payment in kind*, or PIK. But they insisted that Neiman Marcus must not pay any dividends to the new shareholders with the money that was saved by the trade, or PIK.

Although the PIK provision does provide, as CFO James Skinner notes, "a security blanket in case of financial stress," the fact is, bondholders did not want to see shareholders rewarded at their expense. "You want to make sure there's enough cash available to pay debt [rather than see it] go out to the equity holders," observed Paul Scanlon, a manager at Putnam Investments, which bought more than $13 million of the bonds.

"LBO activity has firmly established its place atop the list of bondholder concerns," wrote the authors of a Morgan Stanley report. Given the increasingly aggressive terms of the deals, they added, "All we need is Michael Douglas to squeeze back into his bespoke suit, his Gucci loafers, and release *Wall Street II*, and we'll know the end of the LBO boom can't be far behind."

Source: Adapted from Ronald Fink, "Bondholder Backlash," *CFO Magazine*, February 01, 2006, pp. 51–55, and www.neimanmarcusgroup.com

Knowing the fair value or price of an asset is no easy matter. The *Maxims* by the French writer La Rouchefoucauld, written over 3 centuries ago, still speak to us: "The greatest of all gifts is the power to estimate things at their true worth."

Understanding how to value financial securities is essential if managers are to meet the objective of maximizing the value of the firm. If they are to maximize the investors' value, they must know what drives the value of an asset. Specifically, they need to understand how bonds and stocks are valued in the marketplace; otherwise, they cannot act in the best interest of the firm's investors.

A bond is one form of a company's long-term debt. In this chapter, we begin by identifying the different kinds of bonds. We next look at the features or characteristics of most bonds. We then examine the concepts of and procedures for valuing an asset and apply these ideas to valuing bonds.

We now begin our study by considering the different kinds of bonds.

Types of Bonds

$\boxed{\textbf{lo}^1}$ Distinguish between different kinds of bonds.

A **bond** is a *type of debt or long-term promissory note, issued by the borrower, promising to pay its holder a predetermined and fixed amount of interest per year and the face value of the bond at maturity*. However, there is a wide variety of such creatures. Just to mention a few, we have

Debentures   Eurobonds
Subordinated debentures   Convertible bonds
Mortgage bonds

bond a long-term (10-year or more) promissory note issued by the borrower, promising to pay the owner of the security a predetermined, fixed amount of interest each year.

The following sections briefly explain each of these types of bonds.

Debentures

The term **debenture** applies to *any unsecured long-term debt*. Because these bonds are unsecured, the earning ability of the issuing corporation is of great concern to the bondholder.

debenture any unsecured long-term debt.

They are also viewed as being more risky than secured bonds and, as a result, must provide investors with a higher yield than secured bonds provide. Often the firm issuing debentures attempts to provide some protection to the holder of the debenture by agreeing not to issue more secured long-term debt that would further tie up the firm's assets. To the issuing firm, the major advantage of debentures is that no property has to be secured by them. This allows the firm to issue debt and still preserve some future borrowing power.

Subordinated Debentures

subordinated debenture a debenture that is subordinated to other debentures in terms of its payments in case of insolvency.

Many firms have more than one issue of debentures outstanding. In this case a hierarchy may be specified, in which some debentures are given *subordinated standing in case of insolvency*. The claims of the **subordinated debentures** are honored only after the claims of secured debt and unsubordinated debentures have been satisfied.

Mortgage Bonds

mortgage bond a bond secured by a lien on real property.

A **mortgage bond** is a *bond secured by a lien on real property*. Typically, the value of the real property is greater than that of the mortgage bonds issued. This provides the mortgage bondholders with a margin of safety in the event the market value of the secured property declines. In the case of foreclosure, *trustees*, who represent the bondholders and act on their behalf, have the power to sell the secured property and use the proceeds to pay the bondholders. The bond trustee, usually a banking institution or trust company, oversees the relationship between the bondholder and the issuing firm, protecting the bondholder and seeing that the terms of the indenture are carried out. In the event that the proceeds from this sale do not cover the bonds, the bondholders become general creditors, similar to debenture bondholders, for the unpaid portion of the debt.

Eurobonds

Eurobond a bond issued in a country different from the one in which the currency of the bond is denominated; for example, a bond issued in Europe or Asia by an American company that pays interest and principal to the lender in U.S. dollars.

Eurobonds are not so much a different type of security. They are simply securities, in this case *bonds, issued in a country different from the one in which the currency of the bond is denominated*. For example, a bond that is issued in Europe or in Asia by an American company and that pays interest and principal to the lender in U.S. dollars would be considered a Eurobond. Thus, even if the bond is not issued in Europe, it merely needs to be sold in a country different from the one in which the bond's currency is denominated to be considered a Eurobond.

The primary attractions of Eurobonds to borrowers, aside from favorable rates, are the relative lack of regulation (Eurobonds are not registered with the Securities and Exchange Commission [SEC]), less-rigorous disclosure requirements than those of the SEC, and the speed with which they can be issued. Interestingly, not only are Eurobonds not registered with the SEC, but they may not be offered to U.S. citizens and residents.

Convertible Bonds

convertible bond a debt security that can be converted into a firm's stock at a prespecified price.

Convertible bonds are debt securities that can be converted into a firm's stock at a prespecified price. For instance, you might have a convertible bond with a face, or par, value of $1,000 that pays 6 percent interest, or $60, each year. The bond matures in 5 years, at which time the company must pay the $1,000 par value to the bondholder. However, at the time the bond was issued, the firm gave the bondholder the option of either collecting the $1,000 or receiving shares of the firm's stock at a conversion price of $50. In other words, the bondholder would receive 20 shares (20 = $1,000 par value ÷ $50 conversion price). What would you do if you were the bondholder? If the stock were selling for more than $50, then you would want to give up the $1,000 par value and take the stock. Thus, it's the investor's choice either to take the $1,000 promised when the bond was issued or to convert the bond into the firm's stock.

Consider Ingersoll Rand Company, a diversified equipment manufacturer. In 2009, the firm issued $300 million of 5-percent convertible debt. The bonds can be converted at any time into Ingersoll Rand common stock at a conversion price of $17.94 per share. Because the par value for each bond is $1,000, a bondholder can convert one bond into 55.74 shares (55.74 shares = $1,000 ÷ $17.94 price per share.) This option allows the investor to be repaid the $1,000 par value or to convert into stock if the total value of the stock exceeds $1,000. Thus,

FINANCE AT WORK

ALCOA: HOW TO RAISE $1.5 BILLION AHEAD OF WEAK EARNINGS

March 16, 2009, was a day of bad news for investors. Alcoa warned of a first-quarter loss, cut its quarterly dividend to three cents a share from 17 cents and told investors it wanted to raise $1.1 billion in the capital markets to help it prepare for a long downturn in its business and pay back debt that was coming due soon. The stock fell 8.7 percent on the following day.

Still, the company wanted to raise the cash quickly, regardless of whether or not there was an overhang of bad news. "These windows are short, and when you have these few days, you have to act. I think the market has become more accustomed to the volatility. People are now so used to seeing volatility that news flow is impacting them less," said a person familiar with the deal.

Alcoa and its underwriters (Morgan Stanley, Credit Suisse Group, Citigroup, and Barclays Capital) settled on a two-pronged approach, selling stock and convertible bonds. In the end, Alcoa sold $900 million of stock and $500 million of convertible debt.

The key to getting the financing done was speed: a two-day boot camp of meetings and phone calls with investors. With the aluminum industry suffering, management emphasized that Alcoa would be a survivor and talked up the company's financial and economic position compared with peers. The executives told investors a bottom was near for the aluminum sector and particularly for plunging aluminum prices, which are near historical lows. At the same time, they maintained that demand is delayed and due to rise. In short, their "pitch" held that things were so bad that they had to get better.

With the credit markets showing signs of thawing and the stock market hitting 12-year lows in March, companies decided to sell more bonds to pay off their existing debt. But Alcoa opted for a large equity offering because it didn't want to endanger its balance sheet by piling on more debt, according to people familiar with the company's plans. "Alcoa decided to take some dilution on equity and open up the options a bit more," one person said. In addition, the company paid significantly lower fees to the underwriters to sell stock than it would for a debt offering on which it also would be shelling out interest payments.

The company pitched the offering as a chance for investors who had sold their holdings in the downturn of last year to get back in at relatively low prices.

Alcoa also had a little bit of luck on its side: As the deal was being priced, aluminum prices showed the biggest one-day uptick in more than a year, with a 7-percent boost based on optimism from research analysts.

Perhaps the biggest surprise was the success of the convertible debt. Underwriters had planned to sell only about $250 million of bonds that would convert to stock in five years. But they saw pressing investor demand for more as convertible bonds prepare to become one of the most sought-after securities by investors looking to put money to work. That demand enabled underwriters to trim the coupon payment—or interest rate—to 5.25% from 6%, reducing the cost to the company.

Source: http://blogs.wsj.com/deals/2009/03/25/alcoa-how-to-raise-15-billion-ahead-of-weak-earnings/tab/print/, accessed June 25, 2009.

with convertible bonds, the investor gets to participate in the upside if the company does well. For instance, three months after the bonds were issued, the firm's stock was selling for $27. If you had been an investor, you could have converted the bonds into 55.74 shares of stock, which would be worth about $1,500. Not bad for three months.

Now that you have an understanding of the kinds of bonds firms might issue, let's look at some of the characteristics and terminology of bonds.

Concept Check

1. How do debentures, subordinated debentures, and mortgage bonds differ with regard to their risk? How would investors respond to the varying types of risk?
2. How is a Eurobond different from a bond issued in Asia that is denominated in dollars?
3. Why would a convertible bond increase much more in value than a bond that is not convertible?

Terminology and Characteristics of Bonds

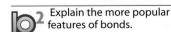

Explain the more popular features of bonds.

Before valuing bonds, we first need to understand the terminology related to bonds. Then we will be better prepared to determine the value of a bond.

When a firm or nonprofit institution needs financing, one source is bonds. As already noted, this type of financing instrument is simply a long-term promissory note, issued by the borrower, promising to pay its holder a predetermined and fixed amount of interest each year. Some of the more important terms and characteristics that you might hear about bonds are as follows:

Claims on assets and income	Call provision
Par value	Indenture
Coupon interest rate	Bond ratings
Maturity	

Let's consider each in turn.

Claims on Assets and Income

In the case of insolvency, claims of debt, including bonds, are generally honored before those of both common stock and preferred stock. In general, if the interest on bonds is not paid, the bond trustees can classify the firm as insolvent and force it into bankruptcy. Thus, the bondholders' claim on income is more likely to be honored than that of the common stockholders, whose dividends are paid at the discretion of the firm's management. However, different types of debt can have a hierarchy among themselves as to the order of their claims on assets.

Par Value

par value on the face of a bond, the stated amount that the firm is to repay upon the maturity date.

The **par value** of a bond is its *face value, which is returned to the bondholder at maturity.* In general, corporate bonds are issued in denominations of $1,000, although there are some exceptions to this rule. Also, when bond prices are quoted, either by financial managers or in the financial press, prices are generally expressed as a percentage of the bond's par value. For example, a Time-Warner Cable bond was recently quoted as selling for $116.72. That does not mean you can buy the bond for $116.72. It means that this bond is selling for 116.72 percent of its par value of $1,000. Hence, the market price of this bond is actually $1,167.20. At maturity in 2019 the bondholder will receive $1,000.

Coupon Interest Rate

coupon interest rate the interest rate contractually owed on a bond as a percent of its par value.

The **coupon interest rate** on a bond indicates the *percentage of the par value of the bond that will be paid out annually in the form of interest.* Thus, regardless of what happens to the price of a bond with an 8 percent coupon interest rate and a $1,000 par value, it will pay out $80 annually in interest until maturity (0.08 × $1,000 = $80). For the Time-Warner Cable bonds, the coupon rate is 8.25 percent; thus an investor owning the bonds would receive 8.25 percent of its par value of $1,000, or $82.50 ($82.50 = 0.0825 × $1,000) per year. The investor receives a fixed dollar income each year from the interest; thus, these bonds are called **fixed-rate bonds**.

fixed-rate bond a bond that pays a fixed amount of interest to the investor each year.

zero coupon bond a bond issued at a substantial discount from its $1,000 face value and that pays little or no interest.

Occasionally, a firm will issue bonds that have zero or very low coupon rates, thus the name **zero coupon bonds**. Instead of paying interest, the company sells the bonds at a substantial discount below the $1,000 par or face value. Thus, the investor receives a large part (or all with zero coupon bonds) of the return from the appreciation of the bond value as it moves in time to maturity. For example, Amgen, the biotech company, issued $3.95 billion face value bonds with a coupon rate of only 1/8th of 1 percent. Thus, the investors would hardly receive any interest income. But the bonds were issued to the investors at $500 for each $1,000 face value bond. Investors who purchased these bonds for $500 could hold them until they mature and would then receive the $1,000 par value.

Maturity

maturity the length of time until the bond issuer returns the par value to the bondholder and terminates the bond.

The **maturity** of a bond indicates *the length of time until the bond issuer returns the par value to the bondholder and terminates or redeems the bond.*

Call Provision

callable bond (redeemable bond) an option available to a company issuing a bond whereby the issuer can call (redeem) the bond before it matures. This is usually done if interest rates decline below what the firm is paying on the bond.

call protection period a prespecified time period during which a company cannot recall a bond.

If a company issues bonds and then later the prevailing interest rate declines, the firm may want to pay off the bonds early and then issue new bonds with a lower interest rate. To do so, the bond must be **callable**, or **redeemable**; otherwise, the firm cannot force the bondholder to accept early payment. The issuer, however, usually must pay the bondholders a premium, such as 1 year's interest. Also, there frequently is a **call protection period** where the firm cannot call the bond for a prespecified time period.

Indenture

An **indenture** is the *legal agreement between the firm issuing the bonds and the trustee who represents the bondholders*. The indenture provides the specific terms of the loan agreement, including a description of the bonds, the rights of the bondholders, the rights of the issuing firm, and the responsibilities of the trustee. This legal document may run 100 pages or more in length, with the majority of it devoted to defining protective provisions for the bondholder.

Typically, the restrictive provisions included in the indenture attempt to protect the bondholders' financial position relative to that of other outstanding securities. Common provisions involve (1) prohibiting the sale of the firm's accounts receivable, (2) limiting common stock dividends, (3) restricting the purchase or sale of the firm's fixed assets, and (4) setting limits on additional borrowing by the firm. Not allowing the sale of accounts receivable is specified because such sales would benefit the firm's short-run liquidity position at the expense of its future liquidity position. Common stock dividends may not be allowed if the firm's liquidity falls below a specified level, or the maximum dividend payout might be limited to some fraction, say, 50 or 60 percent of earnings. Fixed-asset restrictions generally require permission before they can be liquidated or used as collateral on new loans. Constraints on additional borrowing usually involve limiting the amount and type of additional long-term debt that can be issued. All these restrictions have one thing in common: They attempt to prohibit actions that would improve the status of other securities at the expense of bonds, and to protect the status of bonds from being weakened by any managerial action.

indenture the legal agreement between the firm issuing bonds and the bond trustee who represents the bondholders, providing the specific terms of the loan agreement.

Bond Ratings

John Moody first began to rate bonds in 1909. Since that time three rating agencies—Moody's, Standard & Poor's, and Fitch Investor Services—have provided ratings on corporate bonds. These ratings involve a judgment about the future risk potential of the bonds. Although they deal with expectations, several historical factors seem to play a significant role in their determination. Bond ratings are favorably affected by (1) a greater reliance on equity as opposed to debt in financing the firm, (2) profitable operations, (3) a low variability in past earnings, (4) large firm size, and (5) little use of subordinated debt. In turn, the rating a bond receives affects the interest rate demanded on the bond by the investors. The poorer the bond rating, the higher the interest rate demanded by investors. (Table 7-1 describes these ratings.) Thus, bond ratings are extremely important for the financial

> **REMEMBER YOUR PRINCIPLES**
> **Principle** When we say that a lower bond rating means a higher interest rate charged by the investors (bondholders), we are observing an application of **Principle 3: Risk Requires a Reward**.

TABLE 7-1 Standard & Poor's Corporate Bond Ratings

AAA	This is the highest rating assigned by Standard & Poor's for debt obligation and indicates an extremely strong capacity to pay principal and interest.
AA	Bonds rated AA also qualify as high-quality debt obligations. Their capacity to pay principal and interest is very strong, and in the majority of instances, they differ from AAA issues only by a small degree.
A	Bonds rated A have a strong capacity to pay principal and interest, although they are somewhat more susceptible to the adverse effects of changes in circumstances and economic conditions.
BBB	Bonds rated BBB are regarded as having an adequate capacity to pay principal and interest. Whereas they normally exhibit adequate protection parameters, adverse economic conditions or changing circumstances are more likely to lead to a weakened capacity to pay principal and interest for bonds in this category than for bonds in the A category.
BB B CCC CC	Bonds rated BB, B, CCC, and CC are regarded, on balance, as predominately speculative with respect to the issuer's capacity to pay interest and repay principal in accordance with the terms of the obligation. BB indicates the lowest degree of speculation and CC the highest. Although such bonds will likely have some quality and protective characteristics, these are outweighed by large uncertainties or major risk exposures to adverse conditions.
C	The rating C is reserved for income bonds on which no interest is being paid.
D	Bonds rated D are in default, and payment of principal and/or interest is in arrears.

Plus (+) or Minus (−): To provide more detailed indications of credit quality, the ratings from AA to BB may be modified by the addition of a plus or minus sign to show relative standing within the major rating categories.

Source: Adapted from www.standardandpoors.com, December 2005.

FINANCE AT WORK

CLEAR CHANNEL RATING IS CUT

In early 2009, faced with a decrease in advertising revenues, Clear Channel Communications eliminated about 9 percent of its workforce. On March 9, 2009, Moody's Investors Service downgraded the media conglomerate's credit rating four notches. The following is an article that appeared in the *Wall Street Journal* on March 10, 2009.

> Moody's Investors Service slashed Clear Channel Communications Inc.'s credit rating by four notches Monday, and said the downgrade reflected the "high probability" that the company will break its financial covenants this year.
>
> The covenants call for a ratio of secured debt to earnings before interest, taxes, depreciation and amortization of no more than 9.5 times. As of the end of 2008, that ratio was at 6.39 times, compared with six times at the end of September.
>
> Moody's analyst Neil Begley wrote that "compliance will be very challenging" and "a debt restructuring will be likely." Clear Channel,

the country's largest radio and outdoor advertising company, declined to comment. Clear Channel bonds due in 2018 traded at about 10 cents on the dollar Monday.

Moody's current rating for the company is Caa3, two notches away from Moody's lowest rating.

Bishop Cheen, an analyst at Wachovia Capital Markets LLC, agrees that the company will fall out of compliance, but not until 2010. While the company seems safely within its limit for now, its radio and billboard advertising is deteriorating at a rapid clip.

The company took on $15.7 billion in connection with its privatization, which closed last year. Last month, it tapped an additional $1.6 billion of a $2 billion credit facility, spooking the markets. Many investors believed that Clear Channel was drawing down the facility while it still could.

Source: Sarah McBride, "Clear Channel Rating is Cut," *Wall Street Journal*, March 10, 2009, pg. B2.

---

junk bond any bond rated BB or below.

manager. They provide an indicator of default risk that in turn affects the interest rate that must be paid on borrowed funds.

Toward the bottom end of the rating spectrum, we have **junk bonds**, which are high-risk debt with *ratings of BB or below* by Moody's and Standard & Poor's. The lower the rating, the higher the chance of default. The lowest rating is CC for Standard & Poor's and Ca for Moody's. Originally, the term "junk bonds" was used to describe firms with sound financial histories that were facing severe financial problems and suffering from poor credit ratings. Junk bonds are also called **high-yield bonds** because of the high interest rates they pay the investor. Typically, they have an interest rate of between 3 and 5 percent more than AAA-grade long-term debt.

high-yield bond see Junk bond.

We are now ready to think about bond valuation. To begin, we must first clarify precisely what we mean by value. Next, we need to understand the basic concepts of valuation and the process for valuing an asset. Then we may apply these concepts to valuing a bond, and in Chapter 8, to valuing stocks.

REMEMBER YOUR PRINCIPLES

Principle Some have thought junk bonds were fundamentally different from other securities, but they are not. They are bonds with a great amount of risk and, therefore, promise high expected returns. Thus, **Principle 3: Risk Requires a Reward**.

Concept Check

book value (1) the value of an asset as shown on the firm's balance sheet. It represents the historical cost of the asset rather than its current market value or replacement cost. (2) The depreciated value of a company's assets (original cost less accumulated depreciation) less outstanding liabilities.

1. What are some of the important features of a bond? Which features determine the cash flows associated with a bond?

2. What restrictions are typically included in an indenture in order to protect the bondholder?

3. How does the bond rating affect an investor's required rate of return? What actions could a firm take to receive a more favorable rating?

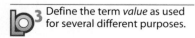 Define the term *value* as used for several different purposes.

Defining Value

The term *value* is often used in different contexts, depending on its application. **Book value** is the *value of an asset as shown on a firm's balance sheet*. It represents the historical cost of the asset rather than its current worth. For instance, the book value of a company's common stock is the amount the investors originally paid for the stock and, therefore, the amount the firm received when the stock was issued.

Liquidation value is the *dollar sum that could be realized if an asset were sold individually and not as part of a going concern*. For example, if a firm's operations were discontinued and its assets were divided up and sold, the sales price would represent the asset's liquidation value.

The **market value** of an asset is the *observed value for the asset in the marketplace*. This value is determined by supply and demand forces working together in the marketplace, whereby buyers and sellers negotiate a mutually acceptable price for the asset. For instance, the market price for Harley-Davidson's common stock on June 20, 2009, was $25 per share. This price was reached by a large number of buyers and sellers working through the New York Stock Exchange. In theory, a market price exists for all assets. However, many assets have no readily observable market price because trading seldom occurs. For instance, the market price for the common stock of Vision Research Organization, a recent start-up firm in Dallas, Texas, would be more difficult to establish than the market value of Harley-Davidson's common stock.

The **intrinsic**, or **economic**, **value** of an asset—also called the **fair value**—is the *present value of the asset's expected future cash flows*. This value is the amount an investor should be willing to pay for the asset given the amount, timing, and riskiness of its future cash flows. Once the investor has estimated the intrinsic value of a security, this value could be compared with its market value when available. If the intrinsic value is greater than the market value, then the security is undervalued in the eyes of the investor. Should the market value exceed the investor's intrinsic value, then the security is overvalued.

We hasten to add that if the securities market is working efficiently, the market value and the intrinsic value of a security will be equal. Whenever a security's intrinsic value differs from its current market price, the competition among investors seeking opportunities to make a profit will quickly drive the market price back to its intrinsic value. Thus, we may define an **efficient market** as one in which *the values of all securities at any instant fully reflect all available public information*, which results in the market value and the intrinsic value being the same. If the markets are efficient, it is extremely difficult for an investor to make extra profits from an ability to predict prices.

The idea of market efficiency has been the backdrop for an intense battle between professional investors and university professors. The academic community has contended that someone throwing darts at the list of securities in the *Wall Street Journal* could do as well as a professional money manager. Market professionals retort that academicians are grossly mistaken in this view. The war has been intense but also one that the student of finance should find intriguing.

liquidation value the dollar sum that could be realized if an asset were sold.

market value the value observed in the marketplace.

intrinsic, or economic, value the present value of an asset's expected future cash flows. This value is the amount the investor considers to be fair value, given the amount, timing, and riskiness of future cash flows.

fair value the present value of an asset's expected future cash flows.

efficient market market where the values of all securities fully recognize all available public information.

> **REMEMBER YOUR PRINCIPLES**
>
> **Principle** The fact that investors have difficulty identifying stocks that are undervalued relates to **Principle 4: Market Prices Are Generally Right**. In an efficient market, the price reflects all available public information about the security and, therefore, it is priced fairly.

Concept Check

1. Explain the different types of value.
2. Why should the market value equal the intrinsic value?

What Determines Value?

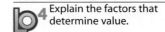 Explain the factors that determine value.

For our purposes, *the value of an asset is its intrinsic value or the present value of its expected future cash flows*, when these cash flows are discounted back to the present using the investor's required rate of return. This statement is true for valuing all assets, and it serves as the basis of almost all that we do in finance. Thus, value is affected by three elements:

1. The amount and timing of the asset's expected cash flows
2. The riskiness of these cash flows
3. The investor's required rate of return for undertaking the investment

The first two factors are characteristics of the asset. The third one, the required rate of return, is the minimum rate of return necessary to attract an investor to purchase or hold a

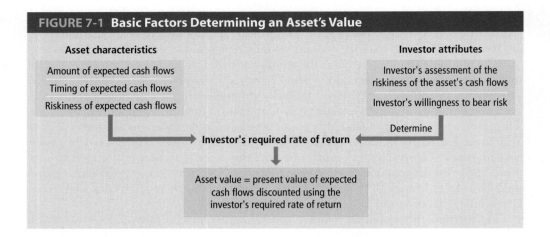

FIGURE 7-1 Basic Factors Determining an Asset's Value

Asset characteristics

Amount of expected cash flows
Timing of expected cash flows
Riskiness of expected cash flows

Investor attributes

Investor's assessment of the riskiness of the asset's cash flows
Investor's willingness to bear risk
Determine

Investor's required rate of return

Asset value = present value of expected cash flows discounted using the investor's required rate of return

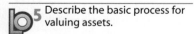 **REMEMBER YOUR PRINCIPLES**

Principle Our discussions should remind us of three of our principles that help us understand finance:

Principle 3: Risk Requires a Reward.

Principle 2: Money Has a Time Value.

Principle 1: Cash Flow Is What Matters.

Determining the economic worth or value of an asset always relies on these three principles. Without them, we would have no basis for explaining value. With them, we can know that the amount and timing of cash, not earnings, drive value. Also, we must be rewarded for taking risk; otherwise, we will not invest.

security. This rate of return is determined by *the rates of return available on similar investments*, or what we learned in Chapter 2 is called the opportunity cost of funds. This rate must be high enough to compensate the investor for risk perceived in the asset's future cash flows. (The required rate of return was explained in Chapter 6.)

Figure 7-1 depicts the basic factors involved in valuation. As the figure shows, finding the value of an asset involves the following steps:

1. Assessing the asset's characteristics, which include the amount and timing of the expected cash flows and the riskiness of these cash flows

2. Determining the investor's required rate of return, which embodies the investor's attitude about assuming risk and the investor's perception of the riskiness of the asset

3. Discounting the expected cash flows back to the present, using the investor's required rate of return as the discount rate

Thus, intrinsic value is a function of the cash flows yet to be received, the riskiness of these cash flows, and the investor's required rate of return.

Concept Check

1. What are the three important elements of asset valuation?

5 Describe the basic process for valuing assets.

Valuation: The Basic Process

The valuation process can be described as follows: It is assigning value to an asset by calculating the present value of its expected future cash flows using the investor's required rate of return as the discount rate. The investor's required rate of return, r, is determined by the level of the risk-free rate of interest and risk premium that the investor feels is necessary compensation. Therefore, a basic asset valuation model can be defined mathematically as follows:

$$\text{Asset value} = \frac{\text{Cash flow in year 1}}{\left(1 + \text{required rate of return}\right)^1} + \frac{\text{Cash flow in year 2}}{\left(1 + \text{required rate of return}\right)^2} + \cdots + \frac{\text{Cash flow in year } n}{\left(1 + \text{required rate of return}\right)^n}$$

Or stated in symbols, we have:

$$V = \frac{C_1}{(1+r)^1} + \frac{C_2}{(1+r)^2} + \cdots + \frac{C_n}{(1+r)^n} \qquad (7\text{-}1)$$

where V = the intrinsic value, or present value, of an asset producing expected future
         cash flows, C_t, in years 1 through n
     C_t = cash flow to be received at time t
       r = the investor's required rate of return

Using equation (7-1), there are three basic steps in the valuation process:

Step 1. Estimate the C_t in equation (7-1), which is the amount and timing of the future
        cash flows the security is expected to provide.
Step 2. Determine r, the investor's required rate of return.
Step 3. Calculate the intrinsic value, V, as the present value of expected future cash
        flows discounted at the investor's required rate of return.

Equation (7-1), which measures the present value of future cash flows, is the basis of the valuation process. It is the most important equation in this chapter because all the remaining equations in this chapter and in Chapter 8 are merely reformulations of this one equation. If we understand equation (7-1), all the valuation work we do, and a host of other topics as well, will be much clearer in our minds.

With the foregoing principles of valuation as our foundation, let's now look at how bonds are valued.

Valuing Bonds

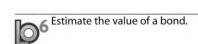
Estimate the value of a bond.

The value of a bond is the present value of both the future interest to be received and the par or maturity value of the bond. It's that simple.

The process for valuing a bond, as depicted in Figure 7-2, requires knowing three essential elements: (1) the amount and timing of the cash flows to be received by the investor, (2) the time to maturity of the bond, and (3) the investor's required rate of return. The amount of cash flows is dictated by the periodic interest to be received and by the par value to be paid at maturity. Given these elements, we can compute the value of the bond, or the present value.

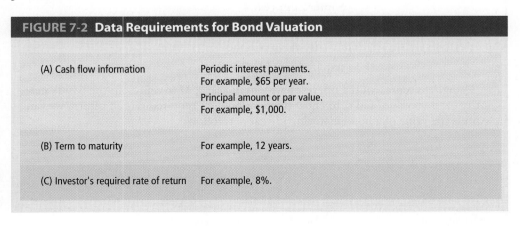

FIGURE 7-2 Data Requirements for Bond Valuation

(A) Cash flow information	Periodic interest payments. For example, $65 per year.
	Principal amount or par value. For example, $1,000.
(B) Term to maturity	For example, 12 years.
(C) Investor's required rate of return	For example, 8%.

EXAMPLE 7.1

Consider a bond issued by Walmart with a maturity date of 2013 and a stated annual coupon rate of 4.55 percent.[1] In December 2009, with 4 years left to maturity, investors owning the bonds were only requiring a 2.48 percent rate of return. We can calculate the value of the bonds to these investors using the following three-step valuation procedure:

Step 1. Estimate the amount and timing of the expected future cash flows. Two types of cash flows are received by the bondholder:
  a. Annual interest payments equal to the coupon rate of interest times the face value of the bond. In this example, the bond's coupon interest rate is 4.55 percent; thus, the annual interest payment is $45.50 = 0.0455 \times \$1,000$. Assuming that 2009 interest payments have already been made, these cash flows will be received by the bondholder in each of the 4 years before the bond matures (2010 through 2013 = 4 years).
  b. The face value of $1,000 to be received in 2013.

To summarize, the cash flows received by the bondholder are as follows:

YEARS	1	2	3	4
	$45.50	$45.50	$45.50	$ 45.50
				$1,000.00
				$1,045.50

Step 2. Determine the investor's required rate of return by evaluating the riskiness of the bond's future cash flows. A 2.48 percent required rate of return for the bondholders is given. However, we should recall from Chapter 6 that an investor's required rate of return is equal to a rate earned on a risk-free security plus a risk premium for assuming risk.

Step 3. Calculate the intrinsic value of the bond as the present value of the expected future interest and principal payments discounted at the investor's required rate of return.

In general, the present value of a bond is found as follows:

$$\text{Bond value} = V_b = \frac{\$ \text{ interest in year 1}}{(1 + \text{ required rate of return})^1} \tag{7-2a}$$

$$+ \frac{\$ \text{ interest in year 2}}{(1 + \text{ required rate of return})^2}$$

$$+ \frac{\$ \text{ interest in year 3}}{(1 + \text{ required rate of return})^3}$$

$$+ \cdots$$

$$+ \frac{\$ \text{ interest in year } n}{(1 + \text{ required rate of return})^n}$$

$$+ \frac{\$ \text{ maturity value of bond}}{(1 + \text{ required rate of return})^n}$$

Using I_t to represent the interest payment in year t, M to represent the bond's maturity (or par) value, and r_b to equal the bondholder's required rate of return, we can express the value of a bond maturing in year n as follows:

$$V_b = \frac{\$I_1}{(1 + r_b)^1} + \frac{\$I_2}{(1 + r_b)^2} + \frac{\$I_3}{(1 + r_b)^3} + \cdots + \frac{\$I_n}{(1 + r_b)^n} + \frac{\$M}{(1 + r_b)^n} \tag{7-2b}$$

(continued on next page)

---

[1]Walmart pays interest to its bondholders on a semiannual basis on June 15 and December 15. However, for the moment, assume the interest is to be received annually. The effect of semiannual payments is examined shortly.

DID YOU GET IT?

COMPUTING AN ASSET'S VALUE

The value of an asset generating $5,000 per year for 4 years, given a 12 percent required rate of return, would be $15,186.75. Using a TI BA II Plus calculator, we find the answer as follows:

CALCULATOR SOLUTION

Data Input	Function Key
12	I/Y
4	N
−5,000	+/− PMT
0	FV

Function Key	Answer
CPT	
PV	15,186.75

If an investor owns an asset that pays $5,000 in cash flows each year for 4 years, he would earn exactly his required rate of return of 12 percent if he paid $15,186.75 today.

Notice that equation (7-2b) is a restatement of equation (7-1), where now the cash flows are represented by the interest received each period and the par value of the bond when it matures. In either equation, the value of an asset is the present value of its future cash flows.

The equation for finding the value of the Walmart bonds would be as follows:

$$V_b = \frac{\$45.50}{(1 + 0.0248)^1} + \frac{\$45.50}{(1 + 0.0248)^2} + \frac{\$45.50}{(1 + 0.0248)^3} + \frac{\$45.50}{(1 + 0.0248)^4} + \frac{\$1,000}{(1 + 0.0248)^4}$$

Finding the value of the Walmart bonds can be represented graphically as follows:

YEAR	0	1	2	3	4
Dollars received at end of year		$45.50	$45.50	$45.50	$ 45.50 +$1,000.00 $1,045.50
Present value	$1,077.91				

Using a TI BA II Plus financial calculator, we find the value of the bond to be $1,077.91, as calculated in the margin.[2] Thus, if investors consider 2.48 percent to be an appropriate required rate of return in view of the risk level associated with Walmart bonds, paying a price of $1,077.91 would satisfy their return requirement.

We can also solve for the value of Walmart's bonds using a spreadsheet. The solution using Excel appears as follows:

CALCULATOR SOLUTION

Data Input	Function Key
4	N
2.48	I/Y
−45.50	+/− PMT
1000	+/− FV

Function Key	Answer
CPT	
PV	1,077.91

	A	B	C	D
1	Required rate of return	Rate	2.48%	
2	Years left to maturity	Nper	4	
3	Annual interest payment	Pmt	−45.50	
4	Future value	FV	−1,000	
5	Present value	PV	$1,077.91	
6				
7		Equation:		
8		=PV(Rate,Nper,Pmt,FV) = PV(C1,C2,C3,C4)		
9				
10				

[2]As noted in Chapter 5, we are using the TI BA II Plus. You may want to return to the Chapter 5 section "Moving Money Through Time with the Aid of a Financial Calculator" or Appendix A, to see a more complete explanation of using the TI BA II Plus. For an explanation of other calculators, see the study guide that accompanies this text.

CAN YOU DO IT?

COMPUTING A BOND'S VALUE

La Fiesta Restaurants issued bonds that have a 6 percent coupon interest rate. Interest is paid annually. The bonds mature in 12 years. If your required rate of return is 8 percent, what is the value of a bond to you?
    (The solution can be found on page 201.)

Concept Check

1. What two factors determine an investor's required rate of return?
2. How does the required rate of return affect a bond's value?

In the preceding Walmart illustration, the interest payments were assumed to be paid annually. However, companies typically pay interest to bondholders semiannually. For example, Walmart actually pays a total of $45.50 per year, but disburses the interest semi-annually ($22.75 each June 15 and December 15).

Several steps are involved in adapting equation (7-2b) for semiannual interest payments.[3] First, thinking in terms of *periods* instead of years, a bond with a life of n years paying interest semiannually has a life of $2n$ periods. In other words, a 4-year bond ($n = 4$) that remits its interest on a semiannual basis actually makes 8 payments. Although the number of periods has doubled, the *dollar* amount of interest being sent to the investors for each period and the bondholders' required rate of return are half of the equivalent annual figures. I_t becomes $I_t/2$ and r_b is changed to $r_b/2$; thus, for semiannual compounding, equation (7-2b) becomes

$$V_b = \frac{\$I_1/2}{\left(1 + \frac{r_b}{2}\right)^1} + \frac{\$I_2/2}{\left(1 + \frac{r_b}{2}\right)^2} + \frac{\$I_3/2}{\left(1 + \frac{r_b}{2}\right)^3} + \cdots + \frac{\$I_n/2}{\left(1 + \frac{r_b}{2}\right)^{2n}} + \frac{\$M}{\left(1 + \frac{r_b}{2}\right)^{2n}} \qquad (7\text{-}3)$$

We can now compute the value of the Walmart bonds, recognizing that interest is being paid semiannually. We simply change the number of periods from 4 years to 8 semiannual periods and the required rate of return from 2.48 percent annually to 1.24 percent per semiannual period and divide interest payment by 2 to get $22.75. The value of the bond would now be $1,078.36.

This solution can be found using a calculator as shown in the margin or a spreadsheet that would look as follows:

CALCULATOR SOLUTION

Data Input	Function Key
$2n \rightarrow 2 \times 4 \rightarrow 8$	N
$2.48 \div 2 \rightarrow 1.24$	I/Y
$22.75	+/− PMT
1000	+/− FV

Function Key	Answer
CPT	
PV	1,078.36

	A	B	C	D	E
1	Required rate of return	Rate	1.24%		
2	Years left to maturity	Nper	8		
3	Annual interest payment	Pmt	−22.75		
4	Future value	FV	−1,000		
5	Present value	PV	$1,078.36		
6					
7		Equation:			
8		=PV(Rate,Nper,Pmt,FV) = PV(C1,C2,C3,C4)			
9					
10					
11					

[3]The logic for calculating the value of a bond that pays interest semiannually is similar to the material presented in Chapter 5, where compound interest with nonannual periods was discussed.

DID YOU GET IT?

COMPUTING A BOND'S VALUE

The LaFiesta bond with a 6 percent coupon rate pays $60 in interest per year ($60 = 0.06 coupon rate × $1,000 par value). Thus, you would receive $60 per year for 12 years plus the $1,000 in par value in year 12. Assuming an 8 percent required rate of return, the value of the bond would be $849.28.

CALCULATOR SOLUTION

Data Input	Function Key
8	I/Y
12	N
60	+/– PMT
1,000	+/– FV

Function Key	Answer
CPT	
PV	849.28

If an investor owns a bond that pays $60 in interest each year for 12 years, she would earn exactly her required rate of return of 8 percent if she paid $849.28 today.

Concept Check

1. How do semiannual interest payments affect the asset valuation equation?

Now that we know how to value a bond, we will next examine a bondholder's rate of return from investing in a bond, or what is called bond yields.

Bond Yields

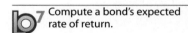 Compute a bond's expected rate of return.

There are two calculations used to measure the rate of return a bondholder receives from owning a bond: the yield to maturity and the current yield.

Yield to Maturity

Theoretically, each bondholder could have a different required rate of return for a particular bond. However, the financial manager is interested only in the expected rate of return that is implied by the market prices of the firm's bonds, or what we call the yield to maturity.

To measure the bondholder's **expected rate of return**, $\bar{r}_b$, we would find the *discount rate that equates the present value of the future cash flows (interest and maturity value) with the current market price of the bond.*[4] It is also the *rate of return the investor will earn if the bond is held to maturity*, thus the name **yield to maturity**. So, when referring to bonds, the terms *expected rate of return* and *yield to maturity* are often used interchangeably.

To illustrate this concept, consider the Brister Corporation's bonds, which are selling for $1,100. The bonds carry a coupon interest rate of 9 percent and mature in 10 years. (Remember, the coupon rate determines the interest payment—coupon rate × par value.)

To determine the expected rate of return ($\bar{r}_b$) implicit in the current market price, we need to find the rate that discounts the anticipated cash flows back to a present value of $1,100, the current market price (P_0) for the bond.

expected rate of return (1) the discount rate that equates the present value of the future cash flows (interest and maturity value) of a bond with its current market price. It is the rate of return an investor will earn if the bond is held to maturity. (2) The rate of return the investor expects to receive on an investment by paying the existing market price of the security.

yield to maturity The rate of return a bondholder will receive if the bond is held to maturity. (It is equivalent to the expected rate of return.)

---

[4]When we speak of computing an expected rate of return, we are not describing the situation very accurately. Expected rates of return are ex ante (before the fact) and are based on "expected and unobservable future cash flows" and, therefore, can only be "estimated."

Data Input	Function Key
10	N
1100	+/− PV
90	PMT
1000	FV

Function Key	Answer
CPT	
I/Y	7.54

The expected return for the Brister Corporation bondholders is 7.54 percent, which can be found as presented in the margin by using the TI BA II Plus calculator, or by using a computer spreadsheet, as follows:

	A	B	C	D	E
1	Years left to maturity	Nper	10		
2	Annual interest payment	Pmt	90		
3	Present value	PV	−1,100		
4	Future value	FV	1,000		
5	Required rate of return	Rate	7.54%		
6					
7		Equation:			
8		=RATE(Nper,Pmt,PV,FV) = RATE(C1,C2,C3,C4)			
9					
10					

Current Yield

current yield the ratio of a bond's annual interest payment to its market price.

The **current yield** on a bond refers to the *ratio of the annual interest payment to the bond's current market price*. If, for example, we have a bond with an 8 percent coupon interest rate, a par value of $1,000, and a market price of $700, it would have a current yield of 11.4 percent:

$$\text{Current yield} = \frac{\text{annual interest payment}}{\text{current market price of the bond}} \tag{7-4}$$

In our example

$$\text{Current yield} = \frac{0.08 \times \$1,000}{\$700} = \frac{\$80}{\$700} = 0.114 = 11.4\%$$

We should understand that the current yield, although frequently quoted in the popular press, is an incomplete picture of the expected rate of return from holding a bond. The current yield indicates the cash income that results from holding a bond in a given year, but it fails to recognize the capital gain or loss that will occur if the bond is held to maturity. As such, it is not an accurate measure of the bondholder's expected rate of return.

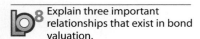 Explain three important relationships that exist in bond valuation.

Bond Valuation: Three Important Relationships

We have now learned to find the value of a bond (V_b), given (1) the amount of interest payments (I_t), (2) the maturity value (M), (3) the length of time to maturity (n periods), and (4) the investor's required rate of return, r_b. We also know how to compute the expected rate of return ($\overline{r}_b$), which also happens to be the current interest rate on the bond, given (1) the current market value (P_0), (2) the amount of interest payments (I_t), (3) the maturity value (M), and (4) the length of time to maturity (n periods). We now have the basics. But let's go further in our understanding of bond valuation by studying several important relationships:

1. The value of a bond is inversely related to changes in the investor's present required rate of return. In other words, as interest rates increase (decrease), the value of the bond decreases (increases).

    To illustrate, assume that an investor's required rate of return for a given bond is 12 percent. The bond has a par value of $1,000 and annual interest payments of $120, indicating a 12 percent coupon interest rate ($120 ÷ $1,000 = 12%). Assuming a 5-year maturity date, the bond would be worth $1,000, computed as follows:

$$V_b = \frac{\$I_1}{(1 + r_b)^1} + \cdots + \frac{\$I_n}{(1 + r_b)^n} + \frac{\$M}{(1 + r_b)^n}$$

CAN YOU DO IT?
COMPUTING THE YIELD TO MATURITY AND CURRENT YIELD

The Argon Corporation bonds are selling for $925. They have a 5 percent coupon interest rate paid annually and mature in 8 years. What is the yield to maturity for the bonds if an investor buys them at the $925 market price? What is the current yield?

(The solution can be found on page 204.)

In our example

$$V_b = \frac{\$120}{(1 + 0.12)^1} + \frac{\$120}{(1 + 0.12)^2} + \frac{\$120}{(1 + 0.12)^3} + \frac{\$120}{(1 + 0.12)^4} + \frac{\$120}{(1 + 0.12)^5} + \frac{\$1,000}{(1 + 0.12)^5}$$

Using a calculator, we find the value of the bond to be $1,000.

CALCULATOR SOLUTION

Data Input	Function Key
12	I/Y
5	N
120	+/− PMT
1,000	+/− FV

Function Key	Answer
CPT	
PV	1,000

If, however, the investors' required rate of return increases from 12 percent to 15 percent, the value of the bond would decrease to $899.44, computed as follows:

CALCULATOR SOLUTION

Data Input	Function Key
15	I/Y
5	N
120	+/− PMT
1,000	+/− FV

Function Key	Answer
CPT	
PV	899.44

On the other hand, if the investor's required rate of return decreases to 9 percent, the bond would increase in value to $1,116.69.

CALCULATOR SOLUTION

Data Input	Function Key
9	I/Y
5	N
120	+/− PMT
1,000	+/− FV

Function Key	Answer
CPT	
PV	1,116.69

This inverse relationship between the investor's required rate of return and the value of a bond is presented in Figure 7-3. Clearly, as investors demand a higher rate of return, the value of a bond decreases: The higher rate of return can be achieved only by paying less for the bond. Conversely, a lower required rate of return yields a higher market value for the bond.

DID YOU GET IT?

COMPUTING THE YIELD TO MATURITY AND CURRENT YIELD

The Argon bonds pay $50 in interest per year ($50 = 0.05 coupon rate × $1,000 par value) for the duration of the bond, or for 8 years. The investor will then receive $1,000 at the bond's maturity. Given a market price of $925, the yield to maturity would be 6.2 percent.

CALCULATOR SOLUTION

Data Input	Function Key
8	N
925	PV
50	+/− PMT
1,000	+/− FV

Function Key	Answer
CPT	
I/Y	6.22

$$\text{Current yield} = \frac{\text{annual interest payment}}{\text{current market price of the bond}}$$

$$= \frac{\$50}{\$925} = 0.0541 = 5.41\%$$

If an investor paid $925 for a bond that pays $50 in interest each year for 8 years, along with the $1,000 par value in the eighth year, he would earn exactly 6.2 percent on the investment.

Changes in bond prices represent an element of uncertainty for the bond investor. If the current interest rate (required rate of return) changes, the price of a bond also fluctuates. An increase in interest rates causes the bondholder to incur a loss in market value. Because future interest rates and the resulting bond value cannot be predicted with certainty, a bond investor is exposed to the *risk of changing values as interest rates vary*. This risk has come to be known as **interest rate risk**.

interest rate risk the variability in a bond's value caused by changing interest rates.

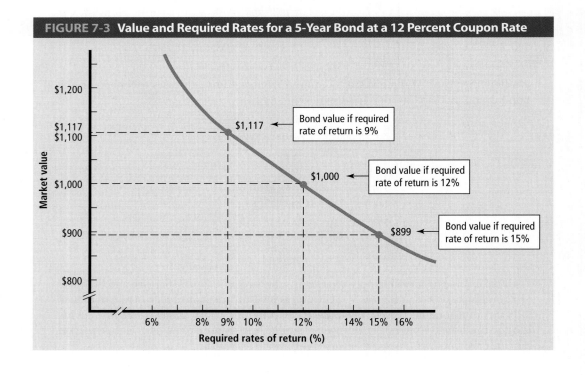

FIGURE 7-3   Value and Required Rates for a 5-Year Bond at a 12 Percent Coupon Rate

2. The market value of a bond will be less than the par value if the required rate of return of investors is above the coupon interest rate; but it will be valued above par value if the required rate of return of investors is below the coupon interest rate.

Using the previous example, we observed that

♦ The bond has a *market value* of $1,000, equal to the par, or maturity, value, when the required rate of return demanded by investors equals the 12 percent coupon interest rate. In other words, if

> *required rate = coupon rate*, then *market value = par value*
> 12%   =   12%,   then $1,000 = $1,000

♦ When the required rate is 15 percent, which exceeds the 12 percent coupon rate, the market value of the bond falls below par value to $899.44; that is, if

> *required rate > coupon rate*, then *market value < par value*
> 15%   >   12%,   then $899.44 < $1,000

In this case the *bond sells at a discount below par value*; thus, it is called a **discount bond**.

discount bond a bond that sells at a discount, or below par value.

♦ When the required rate is 9 percent, or less than the 12 percent coupon rate, the market value, $1,116.69, exceeds the bond's par value. In this instance, if

> *required rate < coupon rate*, then *market value > par value*
> 9%   <   12%,   then $1,116.69 > $1,000

The *bond is now selling at a premium above par value*; thus, it is a **premium bond**.

premium bond a bond that is selling above its par value.

3. Long-term bonds have greater interest rate risk than do short-term bonds.

As already noted, a change in current interest rates (the required rate of return) causes an inverse change in the market value of a bond. However, the impact on value is greater for long-term bonds than it is for short-term bonds.

In Figure 7-3 we observed the effect of interest rate changes on a 5-year bond paying a 12 percent coupon interest rate. What if the bond did not mature until 10 years from today instead of 5 years? Would the changes in market value be the same? Absolutely not. The changes in value would be more significant for the 10-year bond. For example, what if the current interest rates increase from 9 percent to 12 percent and then to 15 percent? In this case, a 10-year bond's value would drop more sharply than a 5-year bond's value would. The values for both the 5-year and the 10-year bonds are shown here.

	MARKET VALUE FOR A 12% COUPON-RATE BOND MATURING IN	
REQUIRED RATE	5 YEARS	10 YEARS
9%	$1,116.69	$1,192.53
12%	1,000.00	1,000.00
15%	899.44	849.44

The reason long-term bond prices fluctuate more than short-term bond prices in response to interest rate changes is simple. Assume an investor bought a 10-year bond yielding a 12 percent interest rate. If the current interest rate for bonds of similar risk increased to 15 percent, the investor would be locked into the lower rate for 10 years. If, on the other hand, a shorter term bond had been purchased—say, one maturing in 2 years—the investor would have to accept the lower return for only 2 years and not the full 10 years. At the end of year 2, the investor would receive the maturity value of $1,000 and could buy a bond offering the higher 15 percent rate for the remaining 8 years. Thus, interest rate risk is determined, at least in part, by the length of time an investor is required to commit to an investment.

FIGURE 7-4 The Market Values of a 5-Year and a 10-Year Bond at Different Required Rates of Return

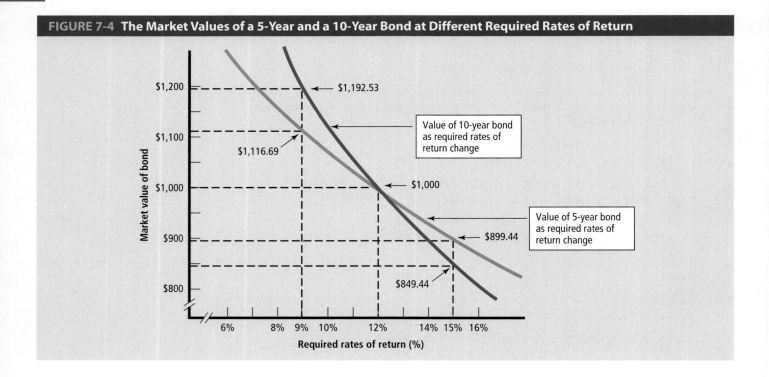

Using these values and the required rates, we can graph the changes in values for the two bonds relative to different interest rates. These comparisons are provided in Figure 7-4. The figure clearly illustrates that the price of a long-term bond (say, 10 years) is more responsive or sensitive to interest rate changes than the price of a short-term bond (say, 5 years). However, the holder of a long-term bond can take some comfort from the fact that long-term interest rates are usually not as volatile as short-term rates. If the short-term rate changed 1 percentage point, for example, it would not be unusual for the long-term rate to change only 0.3 percentage points.

Concept Check

1. Why does a bond sell at a discount when the coupon rate is lower than the required rate of return and vice versa?

2. As interest rates increase, why does the price of a long-term bond decrease more than a short-term bond?

Summary

Distinguish between different kinds of bonds.

Understanding how to compute the value of a security underlies much of what we do in finance. Only if we know what matters to our investors can we maximize the firm's value.

There is a variety of types of bonds, including:

Debentures	Eurobonds
Subordinated debentures	Convertible bonds
Mortgage bonds	

Explain the more popular features of bonds.

Some of the more popular terms and characteristics used to describe bonds include the following:

Claims on assets and income	Call provision
Par value	Indenture
Coupon interest rate	Bond ratings
Maturity	

Value is defined differently depending on the context. But for us, value is the present value of future cash flows expected to be received from an investment, discounted at the investor's required rate of return.

Three basic factors determine an asset's value: (1) the amount and timing of future cash flows, (2) the riskiness of the cash flows, and (3) the investor's attitude about the risk.

The valuation process can be described as follows: It is assigning value to an asset by calculating the present value of its expected future cash flows using the investor's required rate of return as the discount rate. The investor's required rate of return, r, equals the risk-free rate of interest plus a risk premium to compensate the investor for assuming risk.

The value of a bond is the present value of both future interest to be received and the par or maturity value of the bond.

To measure the bondholder's expected rate of return, we find the discount rate that equates the present value of the future cash flows (interest and maturity value) with the current market price of the bond. The expected rate of return for a bond is also the rate of return the investor will earn if the bond is held to maturity, or the yield to maturity. We may also compute the current yield as the annual interest payment divided by the bond's current market price, but this is not an accurate measure of a bondholder's expected rate of return.

Certain key relationships exist in bond valuation, these being:

1. A decrease in interest rates (the required rates of return) will cause the value of a bond to increase; by contrast, an interest rate increase will cause a decrease in value. The change in value caused by changing interest rates is called interest rate risk.

2. If the required rate of return (current interest rate):
   a. Equals the coupon interest rate, the bond will sell at par, or maturity value.
   b. Exceeds the bond's coupon rate, the bond will sell below par value, or at a discount.
   c. Is less than the bond's coupon rate, the bond will sell above par value, or at a premium.

3. A bondholder owning a long-term bond is exposed to greater interest rate risk than one owning a short-term bond.

 3 Define the term *value* as used for several different purposes.

 4 Explain the factors that determine value.

 5 Describe the basic process for valuing assets.

 6 Estimate the value of a bond.

 7 Compute a bond's expected rate of return.

 8 Explain three important relationships that exist in bond valuation.

Key Terms

Bond 189	High-yield bond 194
Book value 194	Indenture 193
Callable bond (redeemable bond) 192	Interest rate risk 204
Call protection period 192	Intrinsic, or economic, value 195
Convertible bond 190	Junk bond 194
Coupon interest rate 192	Liquidation value 195
Current yield 202	Market value 195
Debenture 189	Maturity 192
Discount bond 205	Mortgage bond 190
Efficient market 195	Par value 192
Eurobond 190	Premium bond 205
Expected rate of return 201	Subordinated debenture 190
Fair value 195	Yield to maturity 201
Fixed-rate bond 192	Zero coupon bond 192

Review Questions

All Review Questions and Study Problems are available in MyFinanceLab.

7-1. Distinguish between debentures and mortgage bonds.

7-2. Define (a) Eurobonds, (b) zero coupon bonds, and (c) junk bonds.

7-3. Describe the bondholder's claim on the firm's assets and income.

7-4. a. How does a bond's par value differ from its market value?

   b. Explain the difference between a bond's coupon interest rate, current yield, and required rate of return.

7-5. What factors determine a bond's rating? Why is the rating important to the firm's manager?

7-6. What are the basic differences between book value, liquidation value, market value, and intrinsic value?

7-7. What is a general definition of the intrinsic value of an asset?

7-8. Explain the three factors that determine the intrinsic, or economic, value of an asset.

7-9. Explain the relationship between the required rate of return and the value of a security.

7-10. Define the expected rate of return to bondholders.

Self-Test Problems

(The solution to the following problems are found at the end of the chapter.)

ST-1. (*Bond valuation*) Trico bonds have an annual coupon rate of 8 percent and a par value of $1,000 and will mature in 20 years. If you require a return of 7 percent, what price would you be willing to pay for the bond? What happens if you pay *more* for the bond? What happens if you pay *less* for the bond?

ST-2. (*Bond valuation*) Sunn Co.'s bonds, maturing in 7 years, pay 8 percent interest on a $1,000 face value. However, interest is paid semiannually. If your required rate of return is 10 percent, what is the value of the bond? How would your answer change if the interest were paid annually?

ST-3. (*Bondholders' expected rate of return*) Sharp Co. bonds are selling in the market for $1,045. These 15-year bonds pay 7 percent interest annually on a $1,000 par value. If they are purchased at the market price, what is the expected rate of return?

Study Problems

7-1. (*Bond valuation*) You own a 20-year, $1,000 par value bond paying 7 percent interest annually. The market price of the bond is $875, and your required rate of return is 10 percent.

    a. Compute the bond's expected rate of return.
    b. Determine the value of the bond to you, given your required rate of return.
    c. Should you sell the bond or continue to own it?

7-2. (*Bond valuation*) Calculate the value of a bond that will mature in 14 years and has a $1,000 face value. The annual coupon interest rate is 7 percent, and the investor's required rate of return is 10 percent.

7-3. (*Bond valuation*) At the beginning of the year, you bought a $1,000 par value corporate bond with a 6 percent annual coupon rate and a 10-year maturity date. When you bought the bond, it had an expected yield to maturity of 8 percent. Today the bond sells for $1,060.

    a. What did you pay for the bond?
    b. If you sold the bond at the end of the year, what would be your one-period return on the investment?

7-4. (*Bond valuation*) Shelly Inc. bonds have a 10 percent coupon rate. The interest is paid semiannually, and the bonds mature in 8 years. Their par value is $1,000. If your required rate of return is 8 percent, what is the value of the bond? What is the value if the interest is paid annually?

7-5. (*Bond relationship*) Crawford Inc. has two bond issues outstanding, both paying the same annual interest of $85, called Series A and Series B. Series A has a maturity of 12 years, whereas Series B has a maturity of 1 year.

    a. What would be the value of each of these bonds when the going interest rate is (1) 5 percent, (2) 8 percent, and (3) 12 percent? Assume that there is only one more interest payment to be made on the Series B bonds.
    b. Why does the longer-term (12-year) bond fluctuate more when interest rates change than does the shorter-term (1-year) bond?

7-6. (*Bondholders' expected rate of return*) The market price is $900 for a 10-year bond ($1,000 par value) that pays 8 percent interest (4 percent semiannually). What is the bond's expected rate of return?

7-7. (*Bondholders' expected rate of return*) You own a bond that has a par value of $1,000 and matures in 5 years. It pays a 9 percent annual coupon rate. The bond currently sells for $1,200. What is the bond's expected rate of return?

7-8. (*Bond valuation*) ExxonMobil 20-year bonds pay 9 percent interest annually on a $1,000 par value. If bonds sell at $945, what is the bonds' expected rate of return?

7-9. (*Bondholders' expected rate of return*) Zenith Co.'s bonds mature in 12 years and pay 7 percent interest annually. If you purchase the bonds for $1,150, what is your expected rate of return?

7-10. (*Bond valuation*) National Steel 15-year, $1,000 par value bonds pay 8 percent interest annually. The market price of the bonds is $1,085, and your required rate of return is 10 percent.

    a. Compute the bond's expected rate of return.
    b. Determine the value of the bond to you, given your required rate of return.
    c. Should you purchase the bond?

7-11. (*Bond valuation*) You own a bond that pays $100 in annual interest, with a $1,000 par value. It matures in 15 years. Your required rate of return is 12 percent.

    a. Calculate the value of the bond.
    b. How does the value change if your required rate of return (1) increases to 15 percent or (2) decreases to 8 percent?
    c. Explain the implications of your answers in part b as they relate to interest rate risk, premium bonds, and discount bonds.
    d. Assume that the bond matures in 5 years instead of 15 years. Recompute your answers in part b.
    e. Explain the implications of your answers in part d as they relate to interest rate risk, premium bonds, and discount bonds.

7-12. (*Bond valuation*) New Generation Public Utilities issued a bond with a $1,000 par value that pays $80 in annual interest. It matures in 20 years. Your required rate of return is 7 percent.

    a. Calculate the value of the bond.
    b. How does the value change if your required rate of return (1) increases to 10 percent or (2) decreases to 6 percent?
    c. Explain the implications of your answers in part b as they relate to interest rate risk, premium bonds, and discount bonds.
    d. Assume that the bond matures in 10 years instead of 20 years. Recompute your answers in part b.
    e. Explain the implications of your answers in part d as they relate to interest rate risk, premium bonds, and discount bonds.

7-13. (*Bond valuation—zero coupon*) The Logos Corporation is planning on issuing bonds that pay no interest but can be converted into $1,000 at maturity, 7 years from their purchase. To price these bonds competitively with other bonds of equal risk, it is determined that they should yield 9 percent, compounded annually. At what price should the Logos Corporation sell these bonds?

7-14. (*Bond valuation*) You are examining three bonds with a par value of $1,000 (you receive $1,000 at maturity) and are concerned with what would happen to their market value if interest rates (or the market discount rate) changed. The three bonds are

    Bond A—a bond with 3 years left to maturity that has a 10 percent annual coupon interest rate, but the interest is paid semiannually.
    Bond B—a bond with 7 years left to maturity that has a 10 percent annual coupon interest rate, but the interest is paid semiannually.
    Bond C—a bond with 20 years left to maturity that has a 10 percent annual coupon interest rate, but the interest is paid semiannually.

What would be the value of these bonds if the market discount rate were

    a. 10 percent per year compounded semiannually?
    b. 4 percent per year compounded semiannually?
    c. 16 percent per year compounded semiannually?
    d. What observations can you make about these results?

7-15. (*Yield to maturity*) Assume the market price of a 5-year bond for Margaret Inc. is $900, and it has a par value of $1000. The bond has an annual interest rate of 6 percent that is paid semi-annually. What is the yield to maturity of the bond?

7-16. (*Current yield*) Assume you have a bond with a semiannual interest payment of $35, a par value of $1000, and a current market price of $780. What is the current yield of the bond?

7-17. (*Yield to maturity*) An 8-year bond for Katy Corporation has a market price of $700 and a par value of $1,000. If the bond has an annual interest rate of 6 percent, but pays interest semiannually, what is the bond's yield to maturity?

7-18. (*Expected rate of return*) Assume you own a bond with a market value of $820 that matures in 7 years. The par value of the bond is $1,000. Interest payments of $30 are paid semiannually. What is your expected rate of return on the bond?

7-19. (*Yield to maturity*) You own a 10-year bond that pays 6 percent interest annually. The par value of the bond is $1,000 and the market price of the bond is $900. What is the yield to maturity of the bond?

7-20. (*Bondholders' expected rate of return*) You purchased a bond for $1,100. The bond has a coupon rate of 8 percent, which is paid semiannually. It matures in 7 years and has a par value of $1,000. What is your expected rate of return?

Mini Case

Here are data on $1,000 par value bonds issued by Microsoft, Ford, and Xerox at the end of 2008. Assume you are thinking about buying these bonds as of January 2009. Answer the following questions:

a. Calculate the values of the bonds if your required rates of return are as follows: Microsoft, 6 percent; Ford, 15 percent; Xerox, 10 percent; where

	MICROSOFT	FORD	XEROX
Coupon interest rate	5.25%	7.125%	8.0%
Years to maturity	30	25	16

b. At the end of 2008, the bonds were selling for the following amounts:

Microsoft $1,009.00
Ford $ 610.00
Xerox $ 805.00

What were the expected rates of return for each bond?

c. How would the value of the bonds change if (1) your required rate of return (r_b) increased 2 percentage points or (2) decreased 2 percentage points?

d. Explain the implications of your answers in part b in terms of interest rate risk, premium bonds, and discount bonds.

e. Should you buy the bonds? Explain.

Self-Test Solutions

SS-1.

$$\text{Value } (V_b) = \frac{\$80}{(1.07)^1} + \frac{\$80}{(1.07)^2} + \cdots + \frac{\$80}{(1.07)^{20}} + \frac{\$1000}{(1.07)^{20}}$$

Using a financial calculator, we find the value of the bond to be $1,105.94:

CALCULATOR SOLUTION	
Data Input	Function Key
7	I/Y
20	N
80	+/− PMT
1,000	+/− FV
Function Key	Answer
CPT	
PV	1,105.94

If you pay more for the bond, your required rate of return will not be satisfied. In other words, by paying an amount for the bond that exceeds $1,105.94, the expected rate of return for the bond is less than the required rate of return. If you have the opportunity to pay less for the bond, the expected rate of return exceeds the 7 percent required rate of return.

SS-2. If interest is paid semiannually:

$$\text{Value } (V_b) = \frac{\$40}{(1.05)^1} + \cdots + \frac{\$40}{(1.05)^{14}} + \frac{\$1,000}{(1.05)^{14}}$$

The value of the bond would be $901.01:

CALCULATOR SOLUTION

Data Input	Function Key	
5	I/Y	
14	N	
40	+/−	PMT
1,000	+/−	FV

Function Key	Answer
CPT	
PV	901.01

If interest is paid annually:

$$\text{Value } (V_b) = \frac{\$80}{(1.10)^1} + \cdots + \frac{\$80}{(1.10)^7} + \frac{\$1,000}{(1.10)^7}$$

The value of the bond would be $902.63:

CALCULATOR SOLUTION

Data Input	Function Key	
10	I/Y	
7	N	
80	+/−	PMT
1,000	+/−	FV

Function Key	Answer
CPT	
PV	902.63

SS-3. Finding the bond's yield to maturity, the expected rate of return is based on the following equation:

$$\$1,045 = \frac{\$70}{(1 + \bar{r}_b)^1} + \cdots + \frac{\$70}{(1 + \bar{r}_b)^{15}} + \frac{\$1,000}{(1 + \bar{r}_b)^{15}}$$

Using a financial calculator, we find the yield to maturity to be 6.52 percent:

CALCULATOR SOLUTION

Data Input	Function Key	
15	N	
70	+/−	PMT
1000	+/−	FV
1045	PV	

Function Key	Answer
CPT	
I/Y	6.52

Chapter 8

The Valuation and Characteristics of Stock

Learning Objectives

After reading this chapter, you should be able to:

 Identify the basic characteristics of preferred stock.

 Value preferred stock.

 Identify the basic characteristics of common stock.

Value common stock.

Calculate a stock's expected rate of return.

Some companies believe that a good name can be their most important asset—and actually boost the stock price. For example, a print ad by United Technologies Corp. looked deceptively like an assembly diagram for a model helicopter. Study it more closely, however, and you'll notice that the color schematic of UTC's Sikorsky S-92 copter is embedded with messages aimed at Wall Street.

Text near the engine trumpets 40 percent lower maintenance costs than comparable helicopters and a "health and usage system" that ensures the S-92 "always operates at peak performance." Next to a view of the cockpit, you learn that the thermal imaging system lets rescuers find people they can't see. Other text notes fuel efficiency that allows "more rescues per gallon" and paint with few compounds that harm the environment. "You don't have to understand everything we do to profit from it," crows the tagline. The underlying theme: UTC is a great investment because it is a leader in innovation and eco-friendly technologies that help the bottom line.

More research went into crafting those messages than you might imagine. The $49 billion Hartford conglomerate has long been frustrated that the strengths of its individual brands may be well known, but as for the publicly traded parent, investor surveys showed "most view us as some sleepy Northeast company," says UTC Communications Vice-President Nancy T. Lintner.

So UTC turned to a tiny consulting firm named Communications Consulting Worldwide, led by sociologist Pamela Cohen and former Ernst & Young strategist Jonathan Low, pioneers in the nascent study of how public perceptions affect a company's stock price. A CCW team spent months processing a bewildering amount of assorted data UTC had amassed over the years. It included studies tracking consumer perceptions of its brands, employee satisfaction, views of stock analysts and investors, corporate press releases, thousands of newspaper and magazine articles, and two years' worth of UTC financial information and daily stock movements. After feeding the data into an elaborate computer model, Cohen and Low concluded that 27 percent of UTC's stock market value was attributable to intangibles like its reputation.

The duo determined the way to drive up the stock was to make investors more aware of UTC's environmental responsibility, innovation, and employee training—points the company had not stressed publicly. To make sure investors got the message, UTC plastered the Sikorsky S-92 ads and others like it featuring an Otis elevator, a Pratt & Whitney jet engine, and a hybrid bus with UTC Power fuel cells, on four commuter train stations in Connecticut towns with high concentrations of financiers. "The work we did with CCW guided the development of our ad strategy," says Lintner. "We're very happy with the results."

Many investment pros scoff at suggestions they can be influenced by image manipulation. And to most CEOs, corporate image is not something to fret about—at least, not until a crisis erupts, like an options scandal, employee class action, or ecological disaster. Even when execs try to be proactive, it's often by gut. Want to be viewed as a good corporate citizen? Order up a PR blitz on your charity work or efforts to go green. Eager to land on a magazine's most-admired list? Gin up a strategy to game the selection process.

But a more sophisticated understanding of the power of perception is starting to take hold among savvy corporations. More and more are finding that the way in which the outside world expects a company to behave and perform can be its most important asset. Indeed, a company's reputation for being able to deliver growth, attract top talent, and avoid ethical mishaps can account for much of the 30 percent to 70 percent gap between the book value of most companies and their market capitalizations. And while the value of a reputation is vastly less tangible than property, revenue, or cash, more experts are arguing it is possible not only to quantify it but even to predict how image changes in specific areas will harm or hurt the share price.

Of course, spin alone can't create a lasting public image. A company's message must be grounded in reality, and its reputation is built over years. And if there is a negative image based on a poor record of reliability, safety, or labor relations, "please don't hire a PR company to fix it," says strategy professor Phil Rosenzweig of Switzerland's International Institute for Management Development. "Correct the underlying problem first." The biggest driver of a company's reputation and stock performance is, after all, its financial results, notes Rosenzweig, author of *The Halo Effect*, a book that details how quickly reputations can turn.

Regardless of our conclusion about the merits of image management, the fact remains that managers care deeply about their company's stock price, frequently believing that their stock is undervalued. In this chapter, we will be studying the basic characteristics of stock, both preferred and common stock. We will then examine how stocks are valued and how we can determine the market's rate of return for a given stock.

In Chapter 7, we developed a general concept about valuation, and economic value was defined as the present value of the expected future cash flows generated by an asset. We then applied that concept to valuing bonds.

Source: Adapted from "What Price Reputation?" *Business Week*, July 9, 2007, http://www.businessweek .com/magazine/content/07_28/b4042050.htm, accessed June 30, 2009.

We continue our study of valuation in this chapter, but we now give our attention to valuing stocks, both preferred stock and common stock. As already noted at the outset of our study of finance and on several occasions since, the financial manager's objective should be to maximize the value of the firm's common stock. Thus, we need to understand what determines stock value. Also, only with an understanding of valuation can we compute a firm's cost of capital, a concept essential to making effective capital investment decisions—an issue to be discussed in Chapter 9.

Preferred Stock

L.O.1
Identify the basic characteristics of preferred stock.

preferred stock a hybrid security with characteristics of both common stock and bonds. Preferred stock is similar to common stock in that it has no fixed maturity date, the nonpayment of dividends does not bring on bankruptcy, and dividends are not deductible for tax purposes. Preferred stock is similar to bonds in that dividends are limited in amount.

Preferred stock is often referred to as a *hybrid security* because it has *many characteristics of both common stock and bonds*. Preferred stock is similar to common stock in that (1) it has no fixed maturity date, (2) if the firm fails to pay dividends, it does not bring on bankruptcy, and (3) dividends are not deductible for tax purposes. On the other hand, preferred stock is similar to bonds in that dividends are fixed in amount.

The amount of the preferred stock dividend is generally fixed either as a dollar amount or as a percentage of the par value. For example, Georgia Pacific has preferred stock outstanding that pays an annual dividend of $53, whereas AT&T has some 6⅜ percent preferred stock outstanding. The AT&T preferred stock has a par value of $25; hence, each share pays 6.375 percent × $25, or $1.59 in dividends annually.

To begin, we first discuss several features associated with almost all preferred stock. Then we take a brief look at methods of retiring preferred stock. We close by learning how to value preferred stock.

The Characteristics of Preferred Stock

Although each issue of preferred stock is unique, a number of characteristics are common to almost all issues. Some of these more frequent traits include

- Multiple series of preferred stock
- Preferred stock's claim on assets and income
- Cumulative dividends
- Protective provisions
- Convertibility
- Retirement provisions

All these features are presented in the discussion that follows.

Multiple Series   If a company desires, it can issue more than one series of preferred stock, and each series can have different characteristics. In fact, it is quite common for firms that issue preferred stock to issue more than one series. These issues can be differentiated in that some are convertible into common stock and others are not, and they have varying protective provisions in the event of bankruptcy. For instance, the Xerox Corporation has a Series B and Series C preferred stock.

Claim on Assets and Income   Preferred stock has priority over common stock with regard to claims on assets in the case of bankruptcy. The preferred stock claim is honored after that of bonds and before that of common stock. Multiple issues of preferred stock may be given an order of priority. Preferred stock also has a claim on income before common stock. That is, the firm must pay its preferred stock dividends before it pays common stock dividends. Thus, in terms of risk, preferred stock is safer than common stock because it has a prior claim on assets and income. However, it is riskier than long-term debt because its claims on assets and income come after those of debt, such as bonds.

REMEMBER YOUR PRINCIPLES

Principle Valuing preferred stock relies on three of our principles presented in Chapter 1, namely:

Principle 1: Cash Flow Is What Matters.

Principle 2: Money Has a Time Value.

Principle 3: Risk Requires a Reward.

Determining the economic worth, or value, of an asset always relies on these three principles. Without them, we would have no basis for explaining value. With them, we can know that the amount and timing of cash, not earnings, drives value. Also, we must be rewarded for taking risk; otherwise, we will not invest.

Cumulative Dividends   Most preferred stocks carry a **cumulative feature** that *requires all past, unpaid preferred stock dividends be paid before any common stock dividends are declared.* The purpose is to provide some degree of protection for the preferred shareholder.

cumulative feature a requirement that all past, unpaid preferred stock dividends be paid before any common stock dividends are declared.

Protective Provisions   In addition to the cumulative feature, protective provisions are common to preferred stock. These **protective provisions** generally *allow for voting rights in the event of nonpayment of dividends, or they restrict the payment of common stock dividends if the preferred stock payments are not met or if the firm is in financial difficulty.* For example, consider the stocks of Tenneco Corporation and Reynolds Metals. The Tenneco preferred stock has a protective provision that provides preferred stockholders with voting rights whenever six quarterly dividends are in arrears. At that point the preferred shareholders are given the power to elect a majority of the board of directors. The Reynolds Metals preferred stock includes a protective provision that precludes the payment of common stock dividends during any period in which the preferred stock payments are in default. Both provisions offer preferred stockholders protection beyond that provided by the cumulative provision and further reduce their risk. Because of these protective provisions, preferred stockholders do not require as high a rate of return. That is, they will accept a lower dividend payment.

protective provisions provisions for preferred stock that protect the investor's interest. The provisions generally allow for voting in the event of nonpayment of dividends, or they restrict the payment of common stock dividends if sinking-fund payments are not met or if the firm is in financial difficulty.

Convertibility   Much of the preferred stock that is issued today is **convertible preferred stock**; that is, *at the discretion of the holder, the stock can be converted into a predetermined number of shares of common stock.* In fact, today about one-third of all preferred stock issued has a convertibility feature. The convertibility feature is, of course, desirable to the investor and, thus, reduces the cost of the preferred stock to the issuer.

convertible preferred stock preferred shares that can be converted into a predetermined number of shares of common stock, if investors so choose.

Retirement Provisions   Although preferred stock does not have a set maturity date associated with it, issuing firms generally provide for some method of retiring the stock, usually in the form of a call provision or a sinking fund. A **call provision** *entitles a company to repurchase its preferred stock from holders at stated prices over a given time period.* In fact, the Securities and Exchange Commission discourages firms from issuing preferred stock without some call provision. For example, Wyeth, a large pharmaceutical and health care products company, published the following news release:

call provision a provision that entitles the corporation to repurchase its preferred stock from investors at stated prices over specified periods.

> **Madison, N.J., April 23, 2009**—Wyeth (NYSE: WYE) announced today that it will fully redeem all of its outstanding Convertible Preferred Stock, effective on July 15, 2009 (the "Redemption Date"). As of April 22, 2009, there were 8,896 shares of Convertible Preferred Stock outstanding.
>
> The redemption price for each share of Convertible Preferred Stock is $60.08, which includes an amount equal to all accrued but unpaid dividends up to, and including, the Redemption Date.

The call feature on preferred stock usually requires buyers to pay an initial premium of approximately 10 percent above the par value or issuing price of the preferred stock. Then, over time, the call premium generally decreases. By setting the initial call price above the initial issue price and allowing it to decline slowly over time, the firm protects the investor from an early call that carries no premium. A call provision also allows the issuing firm to plan the retirement of its preferred stock at predetermined prices.

A **sinking-fund provision** *requires the firm to periodically set aside an amount of money for the retirement of its preferred stock.* This money is then used to purchase the preferred stock in the open market or to call the stock, whichever method is cheaper. For instance, the Xerox Corporation has two preferred stock issues, one that has a 7-year sinking-fund provision and another with a 17-year sinking-fund provision.

sinking-fund provision a protective provision that requires the firm periodically to set aside an amount of money for the retirement of its preferred stock. This money is then used to purchase the preferred stock in the open market or through the use of the call provision, whichever method is cheaper.

Valuing Preferred Stock

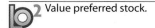
Value preferred stock.

As already explained, the owner of preferred stock generally receives a constant dividend from the investment in each period. In addition, most preferred stocks are perpetuities (nonmaturing). In this instance, finding the value (present value) of preferred stock, (V_{ps}), with a level cash-flow stream continuing indefinitely, may best be explained by an example.

EXAMPLE 8.1

Consider Xerox's Series C preferred stock issue. In similar fashion to valuing bonds in Chapter 7, we use a three-step valuation procedure.

STEP 1 Estimate the amount and timing of the receipt of the future cash flows the preferred stock is expected to provide. Xerox's preferred stock pays an annual dividend of $6.25. The shares do not have a maturity date; that is, they are a perpetuity.

STEP 2 Evaluate the riskiness of the preferred stock's future dividends and determine the investor's required rate of return. The investor's required rate of return is assumed to equal 5 percent for the Xerox preferred stock.[1]

STEP 3 Calculate the economic, or intrinsic, value of the Xerox share of preferred stock, which is the present value of the expected dividends discounted at the investor's required rate of return. The valuation model for a share of preferred stock, V_{ps}, is therefore defined as follows:

$$V_{ps} = \frac{\text{dividend in year 1}}{(1 + \text{required rate of return})^1}$$

$$+ \frac{\text{dividend in year 2}}{(1 + \text{required rate of return})^2}$$

$$+ \cdots + \frac{\text{dividend in infinity}}{(1 + \text{required rate of return})^\infty}$$

$$= \frac{D_1}{(1 + r_{ps})^1} + \frac{D_2}{(1 + r_{ps})^2} + \cdots + \frac{D_\infty}{(1 + r_{ps})^\infty}$$

(8-1)

Notice that equation (8-1) is a restatement in a slightly different form of equation (7-1) in Chapter 7. Recall that equation (7-1) states that the value of an asset is the present value of future cash flows to be received by the investor.

Because the dividends in each period are equal for preferred stock, equation (8-1) can be reduced to the following relationship:[2]

$$V_{ps} = \frac{\text{annual dividend}}{\text{required rate of return}} = \frac{D}{r_{ps}}$$

(8-2)

---

[1] In Chapter 6, we learned about measuring an investor's required rate of return.

[2] To verify this result, we begin with equation (8-1):

$$V_{ps} = \frac{D_1}{(1 + r_{ps})^1} + \frac{D_2}{(1 + r_{ps})^2} + \cdots + \frac{D_n}{(1 + r_{ps})^n}$$

If we multiply both sides of this equation by $(1 + r_{ps})$, we have

$$V_{ps}(1 + r_{ps}) = D_1 + \frac{D_2}{(1 + r_{ps})} + \cdots + \frac{D_n}{(1 + r_{ps})^{n-1}}$$

(8-1i)

Subtracting (8-1) from (8-1i) yields

$$V_{ps}(1 + r_{ps} - 1) = D_1 - \frac{D_n}{(1 + r_{ps})^n}$$

(8-1ii)

As n approaches infinity, $D_n/(1 + r_{ps})^n$ approaches zero. Consequently,

$$V_{ps} r_{ps} = D_1 \text{ and } V_{ps} = \frac{D_1}{r_{ps}}$$

(8-1iii)

Because $D_1 = D_2 = \cdots = D_n$, we need not designate the year. Therefore,

$$V_{ps} = \frac{D}{r_{ps}}$$

(8-2)

FINANCE AT WORK

READING A STOCK QUOTE IN THE WALL STREET JOURNAL

Following is a section of the *Wall Street Journal* that gives the quotes on July 29, 2009, for some of the stocks traded on the New York Stock Exchange that day.

The stocks listed include familiar companies—such as General Dynamic, General Electric (GE), and General Mills—that are listed in the *Wall Street Journal* on a daily basis.

To help us understand how we read the quotes, consider General Electric.

- The 52-week *high* column shows General Electric stock reached a high of 30.39 ($30.39) during the past year.
- The 52-week *low* column shows that General Electric sold at a low of 5.73 ($5.73) during the past year.

- The *stock* (General Electric) and *div* column give the corporation's name and the amount of dividend that General Electric paid its stockholders in the last year; $0.40 per share.
- *Yld*% (3.3) is the stock's dividend yield—the amount of the dividend divided by the day's closing price (0.40 ÷ 12.26).
- *PE* (9) gives the current market price (12.26) divided by the firm's earnings per share.
- The amount of General Electric stock traded on July 29, 2009, is represented in the *Volume* column, or 76,116,275.
- The previous day's closing price is subtracted from the closing price (*close*) of $12.26 for July 29, 2009, for a net change (*Net Chg*) of −0.26.

| 52 WEEKS | | | | | | | |
HI	LO	STOCK (DIV)	YLD%	PE	VOLUME	CLOSE	NET CHG
94.41	35.28	General Dynamics	2.8	9	3,427,486	54.55	0.81
30.39	5.73	General Electric 0.40	3.3	9	76,116,275	12.26	−0.26
20.52	6.40	General Maritime 2.00	22.4	12	979,772	8.94	−0.28
72.01	46.37	General Mills 1.88	3.2	16	1,633,649	59.08	
16.68	1.84	General Steel Holdings			568,207	4.75	−0.23
38.74	10.37	Genesco		16	262,004	20.23	−0.41

(Notice the large differences between the 52-week high and low prices. This gives us a small glimpse of the significance of the stock market declines in 2008.)

Note: You can also see stock quotes on the *Wall Street Journal* website at http://online.wsj.com/mdc/public/page/2_3024-NYSE.html?mod=mdc_uss_pglnk.

Equation (8-2) represents the present value of an infinite stream of cash flows, when the cash flows are the same each year. We can determine the value of the Xerox preferred stock, using equation (8-2), as follows:

$$V_{ps} = \frac{D}{r_p} = \frac{\$6.25}{0.05} = \$125.00$$

In summary, the value of a preferred stock is the present value of all future dividends. But because most preferred stocks are nonmaturing—the dividends continue to infinity—we rely on a shortcut for finding value as represented by equation (8-2).

Concept Check

1. What features of preferred stock are different from bonds?
2. What provisions are available to protect a preferred stockholder?
3. What cash flows associated with preferred stock are included in the valuation model equation (8-1)? Why is the valuation model simplified in equation (8-2)?

CAN YOU DO IT?

VALUING PREFERRED STOCK

If a preferred stock pays 4 percent on its par, or stated, value of $100, and your required rate of return is 7 percent, what is the stock worth to you?

(The solution can be found on page 218.)

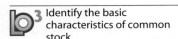

3 Identify the basic characteristics of common stock.

common stock shares that represent the ownership in a corporation.

Common Stock

Common stock is *a certificate that indicates ownership in a corporation*. In effect, bondholders and preferred stockholders can be viewed as creditors, whereas the common stockholders are the true owners of the firm. Common stock does not have a maturity date but exists as long as the firm does. Common stock also does not have an upper limit on its dividend payments. Dividend payments must be declared each period (usually quarterly) by the firm's board of directors. In the event of bankruptcy, the common stockholders, as owners of the corporation, will not receive any payment until the firm's creditors, including the bondholders and preferred shareholders, have been paid. Next we look at several characteristics of common stock. Then we focus on valuing common stock.

The Characteristics of Common Stock

We now examine common stock's claim on income and assets, its limited liability feature, and holders' voting and preemptive rights.

Claim on Income As the owners of a creditors, the common shareholders have the right to the residual income after creditors and preferred stockholders have been paid. This income may be paid directly to the shareholders in the form of dividends or retained within the firm and reinvested in the business. Although it is obvious the shareholder benefits immediately from the distribution of income in the form of dividends, the reinvestment of earnings also benefits the shareholder. Plowing back earnings into the firm should result in an increase in the value of the firm, its earning power, future dividends, and, ultimately, an increase in the value of the stock. In effect, residual income is distributed directly to shareholders in the form of dividends or indirectly in the form of capital gains (value increases) on their common stock.

The right to residual income has advantages and disadvantages for the common stockholder. The advantage is that the potential return is limitless. Once the claims of the senior securities, such as bonds and preferred stock, have been satisfied, the remaining income flows to the common stockholders in the form of dividends or capital gains. The disadvantage is that if the bond and preferred stock claims on income totally absorb earnings, common shareholders receive nothing. In years when earnings fall, it is the common shareholders who suffer first.

Claim on Assets Just as common stock has a residual claim on income, it also has a residual claim on assets in the case of liquidation. Unfortunately, when bankruptcy does occur, the claims of the common shareholders generally go unsatisfied because debt holders and preferred stockholders have first and second claims on the assets. This residual claim on assets adds to the risk of common stock. Thus, although common stocks have historically

FINANCE AT WORK

DOES STOCK BY ANY OTHER NAME SMELL AS SWEET?

All publicly traded stocks have ticker symbols, or abbreviations used to identify them. During 2005–2006, Harley-Davidson Inc.'s investor-relations personnel thought about changing their firm's stock ticker symbol, HDI. It wasn't exactly evocative of the motorcycle maker's image, and there was something better available: HOG (biker-slang for a Harley motorcycle). Interestingly, after Harley-Davidson adopted the new symbol in mid-August 2006, its shares gained nearly 16 percent in 5 weeks, compared with about 4 percent for the Standard & Poor's 500 Index.

It wasn't the first time a stock had risen after adopting a catchy ticker symbol. Counterintuitive as it may seem, research suggests that companies with clever symbols do better than other companies. Any suggestion of a cause-and-effect relationship may be hokum, but tickers that make investors chuckle— think Sotheby's BID, Advanced Medical Optics Inc.'s EYE, or PORK for Premium Standard Farms Inc.—also may make them richer, at least for a time. In one study, researchers at Princeton University found that companies with pronounceable symbols do better soon after an IPO than companies with symbols that can't be said as a word. In another study, researchers found that a portfolio of stocks with clever ticker symbols returned 23.6 percent compounded annually during the years 1990–2004, compared with 12.3 percent for a hypothetical index of all NYSE and Nasdaq stocks. The clever stocks included such well-known stocks as Anheuser Busch Cos. (BUD) and Southwest Airlines Co. (LUV), along with companies eventually delisted or acquired, such as Grand Havana Enterprises Inc. (PUFF) and Lion Country Safari (GRRR).

Some companies are more deliberate in aligning their ticker symbol with their brand. Yum Brands Inc., which runs restaurant chains including KFC, Pizza Hut, and Long John Silver's, actually changed its name in 2002, in part, to reflect its ticker symbol, YUM. The company, formerly known as Tricon Global Restaurants Inc., is trying to attract individual investors by advertising its name and ticker symbol at events such as the Kentucky Derby.

"It's easy for people to remember and puts a smile on their face," said Virginia Ferguson, a Yum spokeswoman. With a share price of $53.01, the stock is up about 230 percent from its 1997 debut price of $16, adjusted for splits, and has risen 68 percent since the name change to Yum Brands.

Michael Cooper, an associate professor of finance at the University of Utah, who has studied investor behavior, said that both papers were "intriguing," but that he would need to see further study before accepting the results.

The researchers themselves say it probably wouldn't behoove investors to make decisions based on their studies. "We certainly don't recommend that people make trading decisions based on our findings," said one researcher. "Rather, our findings suggest that economic models should take psychological factors into account if they are designed to faithfully capture how the markets operate in practice."

Source: Adapted from Jennifer Valentino, "Does Stock by Any Other Name Smell as Sweet?" *Wall Street Journal*, September 28, 2006, P. C1.

---

provided a large return, averaging 10 percent annually since the late 1920s, there is also a higher risk associated with common stock.

Limited Liability   Although the common shareholders are the actual owners of the corporation, their *liability in the case of bankruptcy is limited to the amount of their investment*. The advantage is that investors who might not otherwise invest their funds in the firm become willing to do so. This **limited liability** feature aids the firm in raising funds.

limited liability a protective provision whereby the investor is not liable for more than the amount he or she has invested in the firm.

Voting Rights   The common stock shareholders are entitled to elect the board of directors and are, in general, the only security holders given a vote. Common shareholders have the right not only to elect the board of directors but also to approve any change in the corporate charter. A typical change might involve the authorization to issue new stock or to accept a merger proposal. Voting for directors and charter changes occurs at the corporation's annual meeting. Although shareholders can vote in person, the majority generally vote by proxy. A **proxy** *gives a designated party the temporary power of attorney to vote for the signee at the corporation's annual meeting*. The firm's management generally solicits proxy votes, and, if the shareholders are satisfied with the firm's performance, has little problem securing them. However, in times of financial distress or when managerial takeovers are threatened, **proxy fights**—*battles between rival groups for proxy votes*—occur.

proxy a means of voting in which a designated party is provided with the temporary power of attorney to vote for the signee at the corporation's annual meeting.

proxy fight a battle between rival groups for proxy votes in order to control the decisions made in a stockholders' meeting.

Although each share of common stock carries the same number of votes, the voting procedure is not always the same from company to company. The two procedures commonly used are majority and cumulative voting. Under **majority voting**, *each share of stock allows the*

majority voting voting in which each share of stock allows the shareholder one vote, and each position on the board of directors is voted on separately. As a result, a majority of shares has the power to elect the entire board of directors.

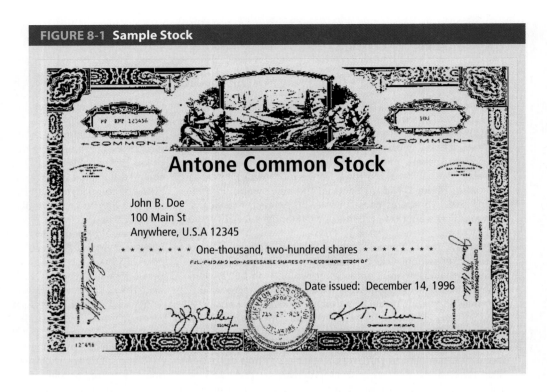

FIGURE 8-1 Sample Stock

Antone Common Stock

John B. Doe
100 Main St
Anywhere, U.S.A 12345

* * * * * * * * One-thousand, two-hundred shares * * * * * * * *

FULL-PAID AND NON-ASSESSABLE SHARES OF THE COMMON STOCK OF

Date issued: December 14, 1996

shareholder one vote, and each position on the board of directors is voted on separately. Because each member of the board of directors is elected by a simple majority, a majority of shares has the power to elect the entire board of directors.

With **cumulative voting**, *each share of stock allows the stockholder a number of votes equal to the number of directors being elected.* The shareholder can then cast all of his or her votes for a single candidate or split them among the various candidates. The advantage of a cumulative voting procedure is that it gives minority shareholders the power to elect a director.

In theory, the shareholders pick the corporate board of directors, generally through proxy voting, and the board of directors, in turn, picks the management. In reality, shareholders are offered a slate of nominees selected by management from which to choose. The end result is that management effectively selects the directors, who then may have more allegiance to the managers than to the shareholders. This sets up the potential for agency problems in which a divergence of interests between managers and shareholders is allowed to exist, with the board of directors not monitoring the managers on behalf of the shareholders as they should.

cumulative voting voting in which each share of stock allows the shareholder a number of votes equal to the number of directors being elected. The shareholder can then cast all of his or her votes for a single candidate or split them among the various candidates.

Preemptive Rights   The **preemptive right** *entitles the common shareholder to maintain a proportionate share of ownership in the firm.* When new shares are issued, common shareholders have the first right of refusal. If a shareholder owns 25 percent of the corporation's stock, then he or she is entitled to purchase 25 percent of the new shares. *Certificates issued to the shareholders giving them an option to purchase a stated number of new shares of stock at a specified price during a 2- to 10-week period* are called **rights**. These rights can be exercised (generally at a price set by management below the common stock's current market price), allowed to expire, or sold in the open market.

preemptive right the right entitling the common shareholder to maintain his or her proportionate share of ownership in the firm.

right a certificate issued to common stockholders giving them an option to purchase a stated number of new shares at a specified price during a 2- to 10-week period.

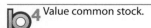4 Value common stock.

Valuing Common Stock

Like bonds and preferred stock, a common stock's value is equal to the present value of all future cash flows—dividends in this case—expected to be received by the stockholder. However, in contrast to preferred stock dividends, common stock does not provide the investor with a predetermined, constant dividend. For common stock, the dividend is based on the profitability of the firm and its decision to pay dividends or to retain the profits for reinvestment. As a consequence, dividend streams tend to increase with the growth in corporate earnings. Thus, the growth of future dividends is a prime distinguishing feature of common stock.

The Growth Factor in Valuing Common Stock What is meant by the term *growth* when used in the context of valuing common stock? A company can grow in a variety of ways. It can become larger by borrowing money to invest in new projects. Likewise, it can issue new stock for expansion. Managers can also acquire another company to merge with the existing firm, which would increase the firm's assets. Although it can accurately be said that the firm has grown, the original stockholders may or may not participate in this growth. Growth is realized through the infusion of new capital. The firm size clearly increases, but unless the original investors increase their investment in the firm, they will own a smaller portion of the expanded business.

Another means of growing is **internal growth**, which requires that *managers retain some or all of the firm's profits for reinvestment in the firm*, resulting in the growth of future earnings and, hopefully, the value of the common stock. This process underlies the essence of potential growth for the firm's current stockholders and is the only relevant growth for our purposes of valuing a firm's common shares.[3]

internal growth a firm's growth rate resulting from reinvesting the company's profits rather than distributing them as dividends. The growth rate is a function of the amount retained and the return earned on the retained funds.

EXAMPLE 8.2

To illustrate the nature of internal growth, assume that the return on equity for PepsiCo is 16 percent.[4] If PepsiCo decides to pay all the profits out in dividends to its stockholders, the firm will experience no growth internally. It might become larger by borrowing more money or issuing new stock, but internal growth will come only through the retention of profits. If, on the other hand, PepsiCo retains all of the profits, the stockholders' investment in the firm would grow by the amount of profits retained, or by 16 percent. If, however, PepsiCo keeps only 50 percent of the profits for reinvestment, the common shareholders' investment would increase only by half of the 16 percent return on equity, or by 8 percent. We can express this relationship by the following equation:

$$g = ROE \times pr$$

where g = the growth rate of future earnings and the growth in the common stockholders' investment in the firm

ROE = the return on equity (net income/common book value)

pr = *the company's percentage of profits retained*, called the **profit-retention rate**[5]

profit-retention rate the company's percentage of profits retained.

Therefore, if only 25 percent of the profits were retained by PepsiCo, we would expect the common stockholders' investment in the firm and the value of the stock price to increase, or grow, by 4 percent; that is,

$$g = 16\% \times 0.25 = 4\%$$

In summary, common stockholders frequently rely on an increase in the stock price as a source of return. If the company is retaining a portion of its earnings for reinvestment, future profits and dividends should grow. This growth should be reflected by an increase in the market price of the common stock in future periods. Therefore, both types of return (dividends and price appreciation) must be recognized in valuing common stock.

---

[3]We are not arguing that the existing common stockholders never benefit from the use of external financing; however, such benefit is nominal if capital markets are efficient.

[4]The return on equity is the accounting rate of return on the common shareholders' investment in the company and is computed as follows:

$$\text{Return on equity} = \frac{\text{net income}}{(\text{common stock} + \text{retained earnings})}$$

[5]The retention rate is also equal to (1 − the percentage of profits paid out in dividends). *The percentage of profits paid out in dividends* is often called the **dividend-payout ratio**.

dividend-payout ratio dividends as a percentage of earnings.

CAUTIONARY TALE

FORGETTING PRINCIPLE 4—MARKET PRICES ARE GENERALLY RIGHT

Principle 4 tells us that Market Prices Are Generally Right. But there are always investors who think they can outsmart the market by statistical analysis. Jason Zweig describes some of the more "creative," or should we say foolish, attempts to beat the market.

The Super Bowl market indicator holds that stocks will do well after a team from the old National Football League wins the Super Bowl. The Pittsburgh Steelers, an original NFL team, won this year, and the market is up as well. Unfortunately, the losing Arizona Cardinals also are an old NFL team.

The "Sell in May and go away" rule advises investors to get out of the market after April and get back in after October. With the market up 17 percent since April 30 [less than 10 weeks], that rule isn't looking so good at this point.

Meanwhile, dozens—probably hundreds—of Web sites hawk "proprietary trading tools" and analytical "models" based on factors with cryptic names like McMillan oscillators or floors and ceilings.

There is no end to such rules. But there isn't much sense to most of them either. An entertaining new book, *Nerds on Wall Street*, by

the veteran quantitative money manager David Leinweber, dissects the shoddy thinking that underlies most of these techniques.

The stock market generates such vast quantities of information that, if you plow through enough of it for long enough, you can always find some relationship that appears to generate spectacular returns—by coincidence alone. This sham is known as "data mining."

Every year, billions of dollars pour into data-mined investing strategies. No one knows if these techniques will work in the real world. Their results are hypothetical—based on "back-testing," or a simulation of what would have happened if the manager had actually used these techniques in the past, typically without incurring any fees, trading costs or taxes.

Those assumptions are completely unrealistic, of course. But data-mined numbers can be so irresistible that, as Mr. Leinweber puts it, "they are one of the leading causes of the evaporation of money. . . ."

Source: Adapted from Jason Zweig, "Data Mining Isn't a Good Bet For Stock-Market Predictions," *Wall Street Journal*, August 8–9, 2009, p. C1.

Dividend Valuation Model The value of a common stock when defining value as the present value of future dividends relies on the same basic equation that we used with preferred stock [equation (8-1)], with the exception that we are using the required rate of return of common stockholders, r_{cs}. That is,

$$V_{cs} = \frac{D_1}{(1 + r_{cs})^1} + \frac{D_2}{(1 + r_{cs})^2} + \cdots + \frac{D_n}{(1 + r_{cs})^n} + \cdots + \frac{D_\infty}{(1 + r_{cs})^\infty} \qquad (8\text{-}3)$$

If you turn back to Chapter 7 and compare equation (7-1) with equation (8-3), you will notice that equation (8-3) is merely a restatement of equation (7-1). Recall that equation (7-1), which is the basis for our work in valuing securities, states that the value of an asset is the present value of future cash flows to be received by the investor. Equation (8-3) simply applies equation (7-1) to valuing common stock.

Equation (8-3) indicates that we are discounting the dividend at the end of the first year, D_1, back 1 year; the dividend in the second year, D_2, back 2 years; the dividend in the nth year back n years; and the dividend in infinity back an infinite number of years. The required rate of return is r_{cs}. In using equation (8-3), note that the value of the stock is established

CAN YOU DO IT?

MEASURING JOHNSON & JOHNSON'S GROWTH RATE

In 2008, Johnson & Johnson had a return on equity of 19.47 percent, as computed to the right. The firm's earnings per share was $4.63 and it paid $1.87 in dividends per share. If these relationships hold in the future, what will be the firm's internal growth rate?

(The solution can be found on page 224.)

$$\frac{\text{Return on}}{\text{equity (ROE)}} = \frac{\text{net income}}{\text{common stock + retained earnings}}$$

$$= \frac{\$12,849}{\$66,499}$$

$$= 19.47\%$$

at the beginning of the year, say January 1, 2010. The most recent past dividend, D_0, would have been paid the previous day, December 31, 2009. Thus, if we purchased the stock on January 1, the first dividend would be received in 12 months, on December 31, 2010, which is represented by D_1.

Fortunately, equation (8-3) can be reduced to a much more manageable form if dividends grow each year at a constant rate, g. The constant-growth, common-stock valuation equation can be presented as follows:[6]

$$\text{Common stock value} = \frac{\text{dividend in year 1}}{\text{required rate of return} - \text{growth rate}} \qquad (8\text{-}4)$$

$$V_{cs} = \frac{D_1}{r_{cs} - g}$$

In other words, the intrinsic value (present value) of a share of common stock whose dividends grow at a constant annual rate can be calculated using equation (8-4). Although the interpretation of this equation might not be intuitively obvious, simply remember that it solves for the present value of the future dividend stream growing at a rate, g, to infinity, assuming that r_{cs} is greater than g.

EXAMPLE 8.3

Consider the valuation of a share of common stock that paid a $2 dividend at the end of last year and is expected to pay a cash dividend every year from now to infinity. Each year the dividends are expected to grow at a rate of 10 percent. Based on an assessment of the riskiness of the common stock, the investor's required rate of return is 15 percent. Using this information, we would compute the value of the common stock as follows:

1. Because the $2 dividend was paid last year, we must compute the next dividend to be received, that is, D_1, where

$$D_1 = D_0 (1 + g)$$

$$= \$2(1 + 0.10)$$

$$= \$2.20$$

---

[6]When common stock dividends grow at a constant rate of g every year, we can express the dividend in any year in terms of the dividend paid at the end of the previous year, D_0. For example, the expected dividend year 1 hence is simply $D_0(1 + g)$. Likewise, the dividend at the end of t years is $D_0(1 + g)^t$. Using this notation, the common-stock valuation equation in (8-3) can be rewritten as follows:

$$V_{cs} = \frac{D_0 (1 + r_{cs})^1}{(1 + g)^1} + \frac{D_0 (1 + g)^2}{(1 + r_{cs})^2} + \cdots + \frac{D_0 (1 + g)^n}{(1 + r_{cs})^n} + \cdots + \frac{D_0 (1 + g)^\infty}{(1 + r_{cs})^\infty} \qquad (8\text{-}3\text{i})$$

If both sides of equation (8-3i) are multiplied by $(1 + r_{cs})/(1 + g)$ and then equation (8-4) is subtracted from the product, the result is

$$\frac{V_{cs} (1 + r_{cs})}{1 + g} - V_{cs} = D_0 - \frac{D_0 (1 + g)^\infty}{(1 + r_{cs})^\infty} \qquad (8\text{-}3\text{ii})$$

If $r_{cs} > g$, which normally should hold, $[D_0(1 + g)(1 + r_{cs}^\infty]$ approaches zero. As a result,

$$\frac{V_{cs} (1 + r_{cs})}{1 + g} - V_{cs} = D_0$$

$$V_{cs} \left(\frac{1 + r_{cs}}{1 + g}\right) - V_{cs} \left(\frac{1 + g}{1 + g}\right) = D_0$$

$$V_{cs} \left[\frac{(1 + r_{cs}) - (1 + g)}{1 + g}\right] = D_0 \qquad (8\text{-}3\text{iii})$$

$$V_{cs} (r_{cs} - g) = D_0 (1 + g)$$

$$V_{cs} = \frac{D_1}{r_{cs} - g}$$

DID YOU GET IT?
MEASURING JOHNSON & JOHNSON'S GROWTH RATE

To compute Johnson & Johnson's internal growth rate, we must know (1) the firm's return on equity, and (2) what percentage of the earnings are being retained and reinvested in the business—that is, used to grow the business.

The return on equity was computed to be 19.47 percent. We then calculate the percentage of the profits that is being retained as follows:

$$\text{Percentage of profits retained} = 1 - \frac{\text{dividends per share}}{\text{earnings per share}}$$

$$= 1 - \frac{\$1.87}{\$4.63}$$

$$= 1 - 0.404$$

$$= 0.596 = 59.6\%$$

Thus, Johnson & Johnson is paying out 40.4 percent of its earnings, which means it is retaining 59.6 percent.

Then we compute the internal growth rate as follows:

$$\text{Internal growth rate} = \text{return on equity} \times \text{percentage of earnings retained}$$

$$= 19.47\% \times 59.6\%$$

$$= 11.6\%$$

The ability of a firm to grow is critical to its future, but only if the firm has attractive opportunities in which to invest. Also, there must be a way to finance the growth, which can occur by borrowing more, issuing stock, or not distributing the profits to the owners (not paying dividends). The last option is called internal growth. Johnson & Johnson was able to grow internally by almost 12 percent by earning 19.47 percent on the equity's investment and retaining about 60 percent of the profits in the business.

2. Now, using equation (8-4),

$$V_{cs} = \frac{D_1}{r_{cs} - g}$$

$$= \frac{\$2.20}{0.15 - 0.10}$$

$$= \$44$$

We have argued that the value of a common stock is equal to the present value of all future dividends, which is without question a fundamental premise of finance. In practice, however, managers, along with many security analysts, often talk about the relationship between stock value and earnings, rather than dividends. We would encourage you to be very cautious in using earnings to value a stock. Even though it may be a popular practice,

CAN YOU DO IT?
CALCULATING COMMON STOCK VALUE

The Abraham Corporation paid $1.32 in dividends per share *last year*. The firm's projected growth rate is 6 percent for the foreseeable future. If the investor's required rate of return for a firm with Abraham's level of risk is 10 percent, what is the value of the stock?
(The solution can be found on page 225.)

significant available evidence suggests that investors look to the cash flows generated by the firm, not the earnings, for value. A firm's value truly is the present value of the cash flows it produces.

Concept Check

1. What features of common stock indicate ownership in the corporation versus preferred stock or bonds?
2. In what two ways does a shareholder benefit from ownership?
3. How does internal growth versus the infusion of new capital affect the original shareholders?
4. Describe the process for common stock valuation.

> ### REMEMBER YOUR PRINCIPLES
> **Principle** Valuing common stock is no different from valuing preferred stock; only the pattern of the cash flows changes. Thus, the valuation of common stock relies on the same three principles developed in Chapter 1 that were used in valuing preferred stock:
>
> **Principle 1: Cash Flow Is What Matters.**
> **Principle 2: Money Has a Time Value.**
> **Principle 3: Risk Requires a Reward.**
>
> Determining the economic worth, or value, of an asset always relies on these three principles. Without them, we would have no basis for explaining value. With them, we can know that the amount and timing of cash, not earnings, drives value. Also, we must be rewarded for taking risk; otherwise, we will not invest.

The Expected Rate of Return of Stockholders

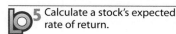 **5** Calculate a stock's expected rate of return.

As stated in Chapter 7, the expected rate of return, or yield to maturity, on a bond is the return the bondholder expects to receive on the investment by paying the existing market price for the security. This rate of return is of interest to the financial manager because it tells the manager about investors' expectations. The same can be said for the financial manager needing to know the expected rate of return of the firm's stockholders, which is the topic of this section.

The Expected Rate of Return of Preferred Stockholders

To compute the expected rate of return of preferred stockholders, we use the valuation equation for preferred stock. Earlier, equation (8-2) specified the value of a preferred stock, V_{ps}, as

$$V_{ps} = \frac{\text{annual dividend}}{\text{required rate of return}} = \frac{D}{r_{ps}}$$

Solving equation (8-2) for r_{ps}, we have

$$r_{ps} = \frac{\text{annual dividend}}{\text{preferred stock value}} = \frac{D}{V_{ps}} \tag{8-5}$$

DID YOU GET IT?
CALCULATING COMMON STOCK VALUE

Abraham's stock value would be $35:

$$\text{Value} = \frac{\text{dividend year 1}}{\text{required rate of return} - \text{growth rate}}$$

$$= \frac{\$1.32 \times (1 + .06)}{0.10 - 0.06} = \frac{\$1.40}{0.04} = \$35$$

So the value of a common stock, much like preferred stock, is the present value of all future dividends. However, unlike preferred stock, common stock dividends are assumed to increase as the firm's profits increase. So the dividend is growing over time. And with a bit of calculus—keep the faith, baby—we can find the stock value by taking the dividend that is expected to be received at the end of the coming year and dividing it by the investor's required rate of return less the assumed constant growth rate. When we do, we have the present value of the dividends, which is the value of the stock.

Thus, the *required* rate of return of preferred stockholders simply equals the stock's annual dividend divided by the stock's intrinsic value. We can also use this equation to solve for a preferred stock's *expected* rate of return, $\bar{r}_{ps}$, as follows:[7]

$$\bar{r}_{ps} = \frac{\text{annual dividend}}{\text{preferred stock market price}} = \frac{D}{P_{ps}} \qquad (8\text{-}6)$$

Note that we have merely substituted the current market price, P_{ps}, for the intrinsic value, V_{ps}. The expected rate of return, $\bar{r}_{ps}$, therefore, equals the annual dividend relative to the price the stock is currently selling for, P_{ps}. Thus, the **expected rate of return**, $\bar{r}_{ps}$, *is the rate of return the investor can expect to earn from the investment if it is bought at the current market price.*

For example, if the present market price of the preferred stock is $50, and it pays a $3.64 annual dividend, the expected rate of return implicit in the present market price is

$$\bar{r}_{ps} = \frac{D}{P_{ps}} = \frac{\$3.64}{\$50} = 7.28\%$$

Therefore, investors (who pay $50 per share for a preferred security that is paying $3.64 in annual dividends) are expecting a 7.28 percent rate of return.

The Expected Rate of Return of Common Stockholders

The valuation equation for common stock was defined earlier in equation (8-3) as

$$\text{Common stock value} = \frac{\text{dividend in year 1}}{(1 + \text{required rate of return})^1}$$
$$+ \frac{\text{dividend in year 2}}{(1 + \text{required rate of return})^2}$$
$$+ \cdots + \frac{\text{dividend in year infinity}}{(1 + \text{required rate of return})^\infty}$$

$$V_{cs} = \frac{D_1}{(1 + r_{cs})^1} + \frac{D_2}{(1 + r_{cs})^2} + \cdots + \frac{D_\infty}{(1 + r_{cs})^\infty}$$

Owing to the difficulty of discounting to infinity, we made the key assumption that the dividends, D_t, increase at a constant annual compound growth rate of g. If this assumption is valid, equation (8-4) was shown to be equivalent to

$$\text{Common stock value} = \frac{\text{dividend in year 1}}{\text{required rate of return} - \text{growth rate}}$$

$$V_{cs} = \frac{D_1}{r_{cs} - g}$$

Thus, V_{cs} represents the maximum value that investors having a required rate of return of r_{cs} would pay for a security having an anticipated dividend in year 1 of D_1 that is expected to grow in future years at rate g. Solving equation (8-4) for r_{cs}, we can compute the common stockholders' required rate of return as follows:[8]

$$r_{cs} = \frac{D_1}{V_{cs}} + g \qquad (8\text{-}7)$$

dividend yield   annual growth rate

CAN YOU DO IT?

COMPUTING THE EXPECTED RATE OF RETURN

Calculate the expected rate of return for the two following stocks:

Preferred stock: The stock is selling for $80 and pays a 5 percent dividend on its $100 par or stated value.

Common stock: The stock paid a dividend of $4 last year and is expected to increase each year at a 5 percent growth rate. The stock sells for $75.

(The solution can be found below.)

According to this equation, the required rate of return is equal to the dividend yield plus a growth factor. Although the growth rate, g, applies to the growth in the company's dividends, given our assumptions, the stock's value can also be expected to increase at the same rate. For this reason, g represents the annual percentage growth in the stock value. In other words, the required rate of return of investors is satisfied by their receiving dividends *and* capital gains, as reflected by the expected percentage growth rate in the stock price.

As was done for preferred stock earlier, we may revise equation (8-7) to measure a common stock's *expected* rate of return, $\bar{r}_{cs}$. Replacing the intrinsic value, V_{cs}, in equation (8-7) with the stock's current market price, P_{cs}, we may express the stock's expected rate of return as follows:

$$\bar{r}_{cs} = \frac{\text{dividend in year 1}}{\text{market price}} + \text{growth rate} = \frac{D_1}{P_{cs}} + g \qquad (8\text{-}8)$$

Historically, most of the returns on stocks come from price appreciation, or capital gains, with a smaller part of the return coming from dividends, with 2008–2009 being the exception. The Standard & Poor's 500 Index, for example, returned a 10 percent annual return

DID YOU GET IT?

COMPUTING THE EXPECTED RATE OF RETURN

Preferred stock:

$$\text{Expected return} = \frac{\text{dividend}}{\text{stock price}} = \frac{\$5}{\$80} = 0.0625 \text{ or } 6.25\%$$

Common stock:

$$\text{Expected return} = \frac{\text{dividend in year 1}}{\text{stock price}} + \text{growth rate}$$

$$= \frac{\$4 \times (1 + 0.05)}{\$75} + 5\% = \frac{\$4.20}{\$75} + 5\%$$

$$= 5.6\% + 5\% = 10.6\%$$

At this point, we are not concerned what the value of the stock is to us. Instead, we want to know what rate of return we could expect if we buy a common stock at the current market price. So the price is given, and we are finding the corresponding expected return based on the current market price. We can then ask ourselves if the expected rate of return is acceptable, given the amount of risk we would be assuming.

on average since 1926. But the dividend yield (dividend ÷ stock price) accounted for only about 2–3 percent of the return. The remaining 7–8 percent resulted from price appreciation.

As a final note, we should understand that the *expected* rate of return implied by a given market price equals the *required* rate of return for investors at the margin. For these investors, the expected rate of return is just equal to their required rate of return and, therefore, they are willing to pay the current market price for the security. These investors' required rate of return is of particular significance to the financial manager because it represents the cost of new financing to the firm.

Concept Check

1. In computing the required rate of return for common stock, why should the growth factor be added to the dividend yield?

2. How does an efficient market affect the required and expected rates of return?

Summary

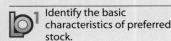

Identify the basic characteristics of preferred stock.

Valuation is an important process in financial management. An understanding of valuation, both the concepts and procedures, supports the financial officer's objective of maximizing the value of the firm.

Preferred stock has no fixed maturity date, and the dividends are fixed in amount. Some of the more common characteristics of preferred stock include the following:

- There are multiple classes of preferred stock.
- Preferred stock has a priority claim on assets and income over common stock.
- Any dividends, if not paid as promised, must be paid before any common stock dividends may be paid; that is, they are cumulative.
- Protective provisions are included in the contract with the shareholder to reduce the investor's risk.
- Some preferred stocks are convertible into common stock shares.

In addition, there are provisions frequently used to retire an issue of preferred stock, such as the ability of the firm to call its preferred stock or to use a sinking-fund provision.

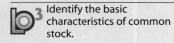

Value preferred stock.

Value is the present value of future cash flows discounted at the investor's required rate of return. Although the valuation of any security entails the same basic principles, the procedures used in each situation vary. For example, we learned in Chapter 7 that valuing a bond involves calculating the present value of the future interest to be received plus the present value of the principal returned to the investor at the maturity of the bond.

For securities with cash flows that are constant in each year but with no specified maturity, such as preferred stock, the present value equals the dollar amount of the annual dividend divided by the investor's required rate of return; that is,

$$\text{Preferred stock value} = \frac{\text{annual dividend}}{\text{required rate of return}}$$

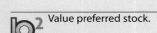

Identify the basic characteristics of common stock.

Common stock involves ownership in the corporation. In effect, bondholders and preferred stockholders can be viewed as creditors, whereas common stockholders are the owners of the firm. Common stock does not have a maturity date but exists as long as the firm does. Nor does common stock have an upper limit on its dividend payments. Dividend payments must be declared by the firm's board of directors before they are issued. In the event of bankruptcy, the common stockholders, as owners of the corporation, cannot exercise claims on assets until the firm's creditors, including its bondholders and preferred shareholders, have been satisfied. However, common stockholders' liability is limited to the amount of their investment.

The common stockholders are entitled to elect the firm's board of directors and are, in general, the only security holders given a vote. Common shareholders also have the right to approve any change in the company's corporate charter. Although each share of stock carries the same number of votes, the voting procedure is not always the same from company to company.

The preemptive right entitles the common shareholder to maintain a proportionate share of ownership in the firm.

When future dividends are expected to increase at a constant growth rate, the value of the common stock may be given by the following equation:

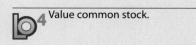

Value common stock.

$$\text{Common stock value} = \frac{\text{dividend in year 1}}{\text{required rate of return} - \text{growth rate}}$$

Growth here relates to *internal* growth only—growth achieved by retaining part of the firm's profits and reinvesting them in the firm—as opposed to growth achieved by issuing new stock or acquiring another firm.

Growth in and of itself does not mean that a firm is creating value for its stockholders. Only if profits are reinvested at a rate of return greater than the investor's required rate of return will growth result in increased stockholder value.

The expected rate of return on a security is the required rate of return of investors who are willing to pay the present market price for the security, but no more. This rate of return is important to the financial manager because it equals the required rate of return of the firm's investors.

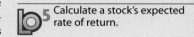

Calculate a stock's expected rate of return.

The expected rate of return for preferred stock is computed as follows:

$$\text{Expected return, preferred stock} = \frac{\text{annual dividend}}{\text{market price}}$$

The expected rate of return for common stock is calculated as follows:

$$\text{Expected return, common stock} = \frac{\text{dividend in year 1}}{\text{market price}} + \text{growth rate}$$

Key Terms

Call provision   215

Common stock   218

Convertible preferred stock   215

Cumulative feature   215

Cumulative voting   220

Dividend-payout ratio   221

Expected rate of return   226

Internal growth   221

Limited liability   219

Majority voting   219

Preemptive right   220

Preferred stock   214

Profit-retention rate   221

Protective provisions   215

Proxy   219

Proxy fight   219

Right   220

Sinking-fund provision   215

Review Questions

All Review Questions and Study Problems are available in MyFinanceLab.

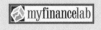

8-1. Why is preferred stock referred to as a hybrid security? It is often said to combine the worst features of common stock and bonds. What is meant by this statement?

8-2. Because preferred stock dividends in arrears must be paid before common stock dividends, should they be considered a liability and appear on the right-hand side of the balance sheet?

8-3. Why would a preferred stockholder want the stock to have a cumulative dividend feature and protective provisions?

8-4. Why is preferred stock frequently convertible? Why is it callable?

8-5. Compare valuing preferred stock and common stock.

8-6. Define investors' expected rate of return.

8-7. State how investors' expected rate of return is computed.

8-8. The common stockholders receive two types of return from their investment. What are they?

Self-Test Problems

(The solutions to the following problems are found at the end of the chapter.)

ST-1. (*Preferred stock valuation*) What is the value of a preferred stock when the dividend rate is 16 percent on a $100 par value? The appropriate discount rate for a stock of this risk level is 12 percent.

ST-2. (*Preferred stockholder expected return*) You own 250 shares of Dalton Resources preferred stock, which currently sells for $38.50 per share and pays annual dividends of $3.25 per share.

    a. What is your expected return?

    b. If you require an 8 percent return, given the current price, should you sell or buy more stock?

ST-3. (*Preferred stock valuation*) The preferred stock of Armlo pays a $2.75 dividend. What is the value of the stock if your required return is 9 percent?

ST-4. (*Common stock valuation*) Crosby Corporation common stock paid $1.32 in dividends last year and is expected to grow indefinitely at an annual 7 percent rate. What is the value of the stock if you require an 11 percent return?

ST-5. (*Common stockholder expected return*) Blackburn & Smith common stock currently sells for $23 per share. The company's executives anticipate a constant growth rate of 10.5 percent and an end-of-year dividend of $2.50.

    a. What is your expected rate of return?

    b. If you require a 17 percent return, should you purchase the stock?

Study Problems

8-1. (*Preferred stock expected return*) You are planning to purchase 100 shares of preferred stock and must choose between Stock A and Stock B. Stock A pays an annual dividend of $4.50 and is currently selling for $35. Stock B pays an annual dividend of $4.25 and is selling for $36. If your required return is 12 percent, which stock should you choose?

8-2. (*Measuring growth*) The Fisayo Corporation wants to achieve a steady 7 percent growth rate. If it can achieve a 12 percent return on equity, what percentage of earnings must Fisayo retain for investment purposes?

8-3. (*Common stock valuation*) Dalton Inc. has an 11.5 percent return on equity and retains 55 percent of its earnings for reinvestment purposes. It recently paid a dividend of $3.25 and the stock is currently selling for $40.

    a. What is the growth rate for Dalton Inc.?

    b. What is the expected return for Dalton's stock?

    c. If you require a 13 percent return, should you invest in the firm?

8-4. (*Common stock valuation*) Bates Inc. pays a dividend of $1 and is currently selling for $32.50. If investors require a 12 percent return on their investment from buying Bates stock, what growth rate would Bates Inc. have to provide the investors?

8-5. (*Preferred stock valuation*) What is the value of a preferred stock when the dividend rate is 14 percent on a $100 par value? The appropriate discount rate for a stock of this risk level is 12 percent.

8-6. (*Preferred stockholder expected return*) Solitron preferred stock is selling for $42.16 per share and pays $1.95 in dividends. What is your expected rate of return if you purchase the security at the market price?

8-7. (*Preferred stockholder expected return*) You own 200 shares of Somner Resources preferred stock, which currently sells for $40 per share and pays annual dividends of $3.40 per share.

    a. What is your expected return?

    b. If you require an 8 percent return, given the current price, should you sell or buy more stock?

8-8. (*Common stock valuation*) You intend to purchase Marigo common stock at $50 per share, hold it 1 year, and then sell it after a dividend of $6 is paid. How much will the stock price have to appreciate for you to satisfy your required rate of return of 15 percent?

8-9. (*Common stockholder expected return*) Made-It common stock currently sells for $22.50 per share. The company's executives anticipate a constant growth rate of 10 percent and an end-of-year dividend of $2.

    a. What is your expected rate of return if you buy the stock for $22.50?

    b. If you require a 17 percent return, should you purchase the stock?

8-10. (*Common stock valuation*) Header Motor Inc. paid a $3.50 dividend last year. At a constant growth rate of 5 percent, what is the value of the common stock if the investors require a 20 percent rate of return?

8-11. (*Measuring growth*) Given that a firm's return on equity is 18 percent and management plans to retain 40 percent of earnings for investment purposes, what will be the firm's growth rate?

8-12. (*Common stockholder expected return*) The common stock of Zaldi Co. is selling for $32.84 per share. The stock recently paid dividends of $2.94 per share and has a projected constant growth rate of 9.5 percent. If you purchase the stock at the market price, what is your expected rate of return?

8-13. (*Common stock valuation*) Honeywag common stock is expected to pay $1.85 in dividends next year, and the market price is projected to be $42.50 per share by year-end. If investors require a rate of return of 11 percent, what is the current value of the stock?

8-14. (*Common stockholder expected return*) The market price for Hobart common stock is $43 per share. The price at the end of 1 year is expected to be $48, and dividends for next year should be $2.84. What is the expected rate of return?

8-15. (*Preferred stock valuation*) Pioneer preferred stock is selling for $33 per share in the market and pays a $3.60 annual dividend.

    a. What is the expected rate of return on the stock?

    b. If an investor's required rate of return is 10 percent, what is the value of the stock for that investor?

    c. Should the investor acquire the stock?

8-16. (*Common stock valuation*) The common stock of NCP paid $1.32 in dividends last year. Dividends are expected to grow at an 8 percent annual rate for an indefinite number of years.

    a. If NCP's current market price is $23.50 per share, what is the stock's expected rate of return?

    b. If your required rate of return is 10.5 percent, what is the value of the stock for you?

    c. Should you make the investment?

8-17. (*Preferred stock valuation*) Calculate the value of a preferred stock that pays a dividend of $6 per share if your required rate of return is 12 percent.

8-18. (*Measuring growth*) Pepperdine Inc.'s return on equity is 16 percent, and the management plans to retain 60 percent of earnings for investment purposes. What will be the firm's growth rate?

8-19. (*Preferred stock expected return*) You are planning to purchase 100 shares of preferred stock and must choose between stock in Kristen Corporation and Titus Corporation. Your required rate of return is 9 percent. If the stock in Kristen pays a dividend of $2 and is selling for $23 and the stock in Titus pays a dividend of $3.25 and is selling for $31, which stock should you choose?

8-20. (*Preferred stockholder expected return*) You own 150 shares of James Corporation preferred stock at a market price of $22 per share. James pays dividends of $1.55. What is your expected rate of return? If you have a required rate of return of 9 percent, should you buy more stock?

8-21. (*Preferred stock expected return*) You are considering the purchase of 150 shares of preferred stock. Your required return is 11 percent. If the stock is currently selling for $40 and pays a dividend of $5.25, should you purchase the stock?

8-22. (*Common stockholder expected return*) If you purchased 125 shares of common stock that pays an end-of-year dividend of $3, what is your expected rate of return if you purchased the stock for $30 per share? Assume the stock is expected to have a constant growth rate of 7 percent.

8-23. (*Preferred stockholder expected return*) You are considering the purchase of Davis stock at a market price of $36.72 per share. Assume the stock pays an annual dividend of $2.33. What would be your expected return? Should you purchase the stock if your required return is 8 percent?

8-24. (*Common stockholder expected return*) Daisy executives anticipate a growth rate of 12 percent for the company's common stock. The stock is currently selling for $42.65 per share and pays an end-of-year dividend of $1.45. What is your expected rate of return if you purchase the stock for its current market price of $42.65?

Mini Case

You have finally saved $10,000 and are ready to make your first investment. You have the three following alternatives for investing that money:

- Capital Cities ABC, Inc. bonds with a par value of $1,000, that pays an 8.75 percent on its par value in interest, sells for $1,314, and matures in 12 years.
- Southwest Bancorp preferred stock paying a dividend of $2.50 and selling for $25.50.
- Emerson Electric common stock selling for $36.75, with a par value of $5. The stock recently paid a $1.32 dividend and the firm's earnings per share has increased from $1.49 to $3.06 in the past five years. The firm expects to grow at the same rate for the foreseeable future.

Your required rates of return for these investments are 6 percent for the bond, 7 percent for the preferred stock, and 15 percent for the common stock. Using this information, answer the following questions.

    a. Calculate the value of each investment based on your required rate of return.
    b. Which investment would you select? Why?
    c. Assume Emerson Electric's managers expect an earnings downturn and a resulting decrease in growth of 3 percent. How does this affect your answers to parts a and b?
    d. What required rates of return would make you indifferent to all three options?

Self-Test Solutions

SS-1. Value $(V_{ps}) = \dfrac{0.16 \times \$100}{0.12}$

$$= \frac{\$16}{0.12}$$

$$= \$133.33$$

SS-2. a. Expected return $= \dfrac{\text{dividend}}{\text{market price}} = \dfrac{\$3.25}{\$38.50} = 0.0844 = 8.44\%$

    b. Given your 8 percent required rate of return, the stock is worth $40.62 to you:

$$\text{Value} = \frac{\text{dividend}}{\text{required rate of return}} = \frac{\$3.25}{0.08} = \$40.63$$

Because the expected rate of return (8.44%) is greater than your required rate of return (8%) or because the current market price ($38.50) is less than $40.63, the stock is undervalued and you should buy.

SS-3. Value $(V_{ps}) = \dfrac{\text{dividend}}{\text{required rate of return}} = \dfrac{\$2.75}{0.09} = \$30.56$

SS-4. Value $(V_{cs}) = \dfrac{\text{last year dividend }(1 + \text{growth rate})}{\text{required rate of return} - \text{growth rate}}$

$$= \frac{\$1.32(1.07)}{0.11 - 0.07}$$

$$= \$35.31$$

SS-5. a. Expected rate of return $(\bar{r}_{cs}) = \dfrac{\text{dividend in year 1}}{\text{market price}} + \text{growth rate}$

$$\bar{r}_{cs} = \frac{\$2.50}{\$23.00} + 0.105 = 0.2137$$

$$\bar{r}_{cs} = 21.37\%$$

b. $V_{cs} = \dfrac{\$2.50}{0.17 - 0.105} = \$38.46$

The expected rate of return exceeds your required rate of return, which means that the value of the security to you is greater than the current market price. Thus, you should buy the stock.

Chapter 9

The Cost of Capital

Learning Objectives

After reading this chapter, you should be able to:

 Describe the concepts underlying the firm's cost of capital (technically, its weighted average cost of capital) and the purpose for its calculation.

 Calculate the after-tax cost of debt, preferred stock, and common equity.

 Calculate a firm's weighted average cost of capital.

 Describe the procedure used by PepsiCo to estimate the cost of capital for a multidivisional firm.

 Use the cost of capital to evaluate new investment opportunities.

 Calculate equivalent interest rates for different countries.

On November 4, 2008, ExxonMobil Corp. (XOM) announced the biggest quarterly and annual earnings for any U.S. company, ever! The earnings were $4.83 billion for the third quarter of 2008. But is ExxonMobil creating value for its shareholders? The key to answering this question rests not just on the level of the firm's earnings but also on (i) how large an investment has been made in the company in order to produce these earnings and (ii) how risky the firm's investors perceive the company's investments to be. In other words, we need to know two things: What *rate* of return did the company earn on its invested capital, and what is the *market's required rate of return* on that invested capital (the company's cost of capital)?

The firm's cost of capital provides an estimate of just how much return the firm's combined investors expect from the company. Estimating a firm's cost of capital is very intuitive in theory but can be somewhat tedious in practice. In theory, what is required is the following: One, identifying all of the firm's sources of capital and their relative importance (that is, what fraction of the firm's invested capital comes from each source). Two, estimating the market's required rate of return for each source of capital the firm uses. Three, calculating an average of the required rates of return for each source of capital where the required rate of return for each source has been weighted by its contribution to the total capital invested in the firm.

The cost of capital is not only important when evaluating the company's overall performance, but is also used when evaluating individual investment decisions made by the firm. For example, when ExxonMobil is considering the development of a new oil production property in Nigeria, the company needs to estimate just how much return is needed to justify the investment. Similarly, when it is considering a chemical plant in Southeast Asia or Louisiana, the company's analysts need a benchmark return to compare to the investment's expected return. The cost of capital provides this benchmark.

Not to hold you in suspense any longer, ExxonMobil Corp. earned a whopping 36 percent rate of return on the firm's book assets and a 15 percent rate of return on the market value of the firm's investments. Given that the firm had to earn less than 10 percent to satisfy all of its investors (both equity and debt), it created a lot of value for its investors even in the midst of a worsening financial crisis. In this chapter, we investigate how to estimate the cost of funds to the firm. We will refer to the combined cost of borrowed money and money invested in the company by the firm's stockholders as the weighted average cost of capital or simply the firm's cost of capital.

Having studied the connection between risk and investor required rates of return (Chapter 6) and specifically, investor required rates of return for bondholders and stockholders in Chapters 7 and 8, we are now ready to consider required rates of return for the firm as a whole. That is, just as the individuals that lend the firm money (bondholders) and those that invest in its stock have their individual required rates of return, we can also think about a combined required rate of return for the firm as a whole. This required rate of return for the firm is a blend of the required rates of return of all investors that we will estimate using a weighted average of the individual rates of return called the firm's **weighted average cost of capital** or simply the firm's cost of capital. Just like any cost of doing business, the firm must earn at least this cost if it is to create value for its owners.

In this chapter, we discuss the fundamental determinants of a firm's cost of capital and the rationale for its calculation and use. This entails developing the logic for estimating the cost of debt capital, preferred stock, and common stock. Chapter 12 takes up consideration of the impact of the firm's financing mix on the cost of capital.

> **weighted average cost of capital** a composite of the individual costs of financing incurred by each capital source. A firm's weighted cost of capital is a function of (1) the individual costs of capital, and (2) the capital structure mix.

The Cost of Capital: Key Definitions and Concepts

 Describe the concepts underlying the firm's cost of capital (technically, its weighted average cost of capital) and the purpose for its calculation.

Opportunity Costs, Required Rates of Return, and the Cost of Capital

The firm's cost of capital is sometimes referred to as the firm's opportunity cost of capital. The term *opportunity cost* comes from the study of economics and is defined as the cost of making a choice in terms of the next best opportunity that is foregone. For example, the opportunity cost of taking a part-time job at Starbucks (SBUX) is the lost wages from the on-campus job you would have taken otherwise. Similarly, when a firm chooses to invest money it has raised from investors, it is in essence deciding not to return the money to the investors. Thus, the opportunity cost of investing the money is the cost the firm incurs by keeping the money and not returning it to the investors which is the firm's cost of capital.

CAN YOU DO IT?

DETERMINING HOW FLOTATION COSTS AFFECT THE COST OF CAPITAL

McDonald's Corporation sold a portion of its ownership interest in its rapidly growing fast-food Mexican restaurant Chipotle in January of 2006 for $22.00 per share. If the investor's required rate of return on these shares was 18 percent, and McDonald's incurred transaction costs totaling $2.00 per share, what was the cost of capital to McDonald's after adjusting for the effects of the transaction costs?
   (The solution can be found on page 237.)

Is the investor's required rate of return the same thing as the cost of capital? Not exactly. Two factors drive a wedge between the investor's required rate of return and the cost of capital to the firm.

1. **Taxes.** When a firm borrows money to finance the purchase of an asset, the interest expense is deductible for federal income tax calculations. Consider a firm that borrows at 9 percent and then deducts its interest expense from its revenues before paying taxes at a rate of 34 percent. For each dollar of interest it pays, the firm reduces its taxes by $0.34. Consequently, the actual cost of borrowing to the firm is only 5.94% [0.09 − (0.34 × 0.09) = 0.09(1 − 0.34) = 0.0594, or 5.94%].

2. **Transaction costs.** Here we are referring to the costs the firm incurs *when it raises funds by issuing a particular type of security.* As you learned in Chapter 2, these are sometimes called flotation costs. For example, if a firm sells new shares for $25 per share but incurs transaction costs of $5 per share, then the cost of capital for the new common equity is increased. Assume that the investor's required rate of return is 15 percent for each $25 share; then 0.15 × $25 = $3.75 must be earned each year to satisfy the investor's required return. However, the firm has only $20 to invest, so the cost of capital (k) is calculated as the rate of return that must be earned on the $20 net proceeds that will produce a return of $3.75; that is,

$$\$20k = \$25 \times 0.15 = \$3.75$$

$$k = \frac{\$3.75}{\$20.00} = 0.1875, \text{ or } 18.75\%$$

We will have more to say about both these considerations when we discuss the costs of the individual sources of capital to the firm shortly.

The Firm's Financial Policy and the Cost of Capital

financial policy the firm's policies regarding the sources of financing it plans to use and the particular mix (proportions) in which they will be used.

A firm's **financial policy**—that is, *the policies regarding the sources of finances it plans to use and the particular mix (proportions) in which they will be used*—governs its use of debt and equity financing. The particular mixture of debt and equity that the firm uses can impact the firm's cost of capital. However, in this chapter, we assume that the firm maintains a fixed financial policy that is reflected in a fixed debt–equity ratio. Determining the target mix of debt and equity financing is the subject of Chapter 12.

Concept Check

1. How is an investor's required rate of return related to an opportunity cost?
2. How do flotation costs impact the firm's cost of capital?

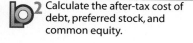

Calculate the after-tax cost of debt, preferred stock, and common equity.

Determining the Costs of the Individual Sources of Capital

In order to attract new investors, companies have created a wide variety of financing instruments or securities. In this chapter, we stick to three basic types: debt, preferred stock, and common stock. In calculating the respective cost of financing using each of these types of securities, we estimate the investor's required rate of return after properly adjusting for any transaction or flotation costs. In addition, because we will be discounting after-tax cash flows, we adjust our cost of capital for the effects of corporate taxes. In summary, the cost of a particular source of capital is equal to the investor's required rate of return after adjusting for the effects of both flotation costs and corporate taxes.

The Cost of Debt

In Chapter 7 we learned that the value of a bond can be described in terms of the present value of the bond's future interest and principal payments. For example, if the bond has three years until maturity and pays interest annually, its value can be expressed as follows:

$$\begin{aligned}\text{Bond price} = \frac{\text{interest paid in year 1}}{\left(1 + \begin{array}{c}\text{bondholder's required}\\\text{rate of return }(r_d)\end{array}\right)^1} + \frac{\text{interest paid in year 2}}{\left(1 + \begin{array}{c}\text{bondholder's required}\\\text{rate of return }(r_d)\end{array}\right)^2}\\[2ex] + \frac{\text{interest paid in year 3}}{\left(1 + \begin{array}{c}\text{bondholder's required}\\\text{rate of return }(r_d)\end{array}\right)^3} + \frac{\text{principal}}{\left(1 + \begin{array}{c}\text{bondholder's required}\\\text{rate of return }(r_d)\end{array}\right)^3}\end{aligned} \tag{9-1}$$

In Chapter 7, we used the above bond price equation to estimate the bondholder's required rate of return. This required rate of return is commonly referred to as the bond's yield to maturity.

Since firms must pay flotation costs when they sell bonds, the net proceeds per bond received by the firm is less than the market price of the bond. Consequently, the cost of debt capital (k_d) is higher than the bondholder's required rate of return and is calculated using equation (9-2) as follows:

$$\begin{aligned}\text{Net proceeds per bond} = \frac{\text{interest paid in year 1}}{\left(1 + \begin{array}{c}\text{cost of debt}\\\text{capital or }k_d\end{array}\right)^1} + \frac{\text{interest paid in year 2}}{\left(1 + \begin{array}{c}\text{cost of debt}\\\text{capital or }k_d\end{array}\right)^2}\\[2ex] + \frac{\text{interest paid in year 3}}{\left(1 + \begin{array}{c}\text{cost of debt}\\\text{capital or }k_d\end{array}\right)^3} + \frac{\text{principal}}{\left(1 + \begin{array}{c}\text{cost of debt}\\\text{capital or }k_d\end{array}\right)^3}\end{aligned} \tag{9-2}$$

Note that the adjustment for flotation costs simply involves replacing the market price of the bond with the net proceeds per bond received by the firm after paying these costs. The result of this adjustment is that the discount rate that solves equation (9-2) is now the firm's cost of debt financing before adjusting for the effect of corporate taxes—that is, the before-tax cost of debt (k_d). The final adjustment we make is to account for the fact that interest is tax deductible. Thus, the after-tax cost of debt capital is simply the before-tax cost of debt (k_d) times one minus the corporate tax rate.

DID YOU GET IT?
DETERMINING HOW FLOTATION COSTS AFFECT THE COST OF CAPITAL

If the required rate of return on the shares was 18 percent, and the shares sold for $22.00 with $2.00 in transaction costs incurred per share, then the cost of equity capital for Chipotle Mexican Grill is found by grossing up the investor's required rate of return as follows:

$$\text{Cost of equity capital} = \frac{\text{investor's required rate of return}}{(1 - \text{\% flotation costs})} = \frac{18\%}{1 - \left(\dfrac{\$2.00}{\$22.00}\right)} = 19.80\%$$

Incidentally, although the shares were sold to the public for $22.00 per share, they doubled to $44.00 by the end of the day after being traded in the secondary market.

Synopticom Inc. plans a bond issue for the near future and wants to estimate its current cost of debt capital. After talking with the firm's investment banker, the firm's chief financial officer has determined that a 20-year maturity bond with a $1,000 face value and 8 percent coupon (paying 8% × $1,000 = $80 per year in interest) can be sold to investors for $908.32. As we illustrated earlier in Chapter 7, equation (9-1) can be generalized to solve for the investor's required rate of return (r_d) for a 20-year bond. In this instance the bond pays 20 annual interest payments of $80 plus a $1,000 principal amount in the 20th year; that is,

$$\$908.32 = \frac{\$80}{(1 + r_d)^1} + \frac{\$80}{(1 + r_d)^2} + \frac{\$80}{(1 + r_d)^3} + \cdots + \frac{\$80}{(1 + r_d)^{19}} + \frac{\$80 + \$1,000}{(1 + r_d)^{20}}$$

In this case, Synopticom's creditors require a 9 percent rate of return. The cost of capital to the firm is higher than 9 percent, however, because the firm will have to pay flotation costs of $58.32 per bond when it issues the securities. The flotation costs reduce the net proceeds to Synopticom to $850. Substituting into equation (9-2), we find that the before-tax cost of capital for the bond issue (k_d) is 9.73 percent, that is,

$$\$850.00 = \frac{\$80}{(1 + k_d)^1} + \frac{\$80}{(1 + k_d)^2} + \frac{\$80}{(1 + k_d)^3} + \cdots + \frac{\$80}{(1 + k_d)^{19}} + \frac{\$80 + \$1,000}{(1 + k_d)^{20}}$$

Once again, we can solve equation (9-2) using a financial calculator, as we illustrate in the margin.

One final adjustment is necessary to obtain the firm's after-tax cost of debt capital. Assuming that Synopticom is in the 34 percent corporate income tax (T_c) bracket, we estimate the after-tax cost of debt capital as follows:

$$\text{After-tax cost of debt} = \text{before-tax cost of debt} \times \left(1 - \frac{\text{corporate}}{\text{tax rate}} \right)$$

$$= 9.73\%(1 - 0.34) = 6.422\%$$

CALCULATOR SOLUTION

Data Input	Function Key
20	N
−850	PV
80	PMT
1000	FV

Function Key	Answer
CPT I/Y	9.73

The Cost of Preferred Stock

You may recall from Chapter 8 that the price of a share of preferred stock is equal to the present value of the constant stream of preferred stock dividends, i.e.,

$$\text{Price of a share of preferred stock} = \frac{\text{preferred stock dividend}}{\text{required rate of return of the preferred stockholder } (r_{ps})} \tag{9-3}$$

If we can observe the price of the share of preferred stock and we know the preferred stock dividend, we can calculate the preferred stockholder's required rate of return as follows:

$$\text{Required rate of return of the preferred stockholder } (r_{ps}) = \frac{\text{preferred stock dividend}}{\text{price of a share of preferred stock}} \tag{9-4}$$

Once again, because flotation costs are usually incurred when new preferred shares are sold, the investor's required rate of return is less than the cost of preferred capital to the firm. To calculate the cost of preferred stock, we must adjust the required rate of return to reflect these flotation costs. We replace the price of a preferred share in equation (9-4) with the net proceeds per share from the sale of new preferred shares. The resulting formula can be used to calculate the cost of preferred stock to the firm.

$$\text{Cost of preferred stock } (k_{ps}) = \frac{\text{preferred stock dividend}}{\text{net proceeds per preferred share}} \tag{9-5}$$

Note that the net proceeds per share are equal to the price per share of preferred stock minus flotation cost per share of newly issued preferred stock.

What about corporate taxes? In the case of preferred stock, no tax adjustment must be made because, unlike interest payments, preferred dividends are not tax deductible.

EXAMPLE 9.2

El Paso Edison has issued preferred stock that pays an annual dividend of $4.25 per share. On November 23, 2009, the stock closed at $58.50. Assume that if the firm were to sell an issue of preferred stock with the same characteristics as its outstanding issue, it would incur flotation costs of $1.375 per share and the shares would sell for their November 23, 2009, closing price. What is El Paso Edison's cost of preferred stock?

Substituting into equation (9-5), we get the following cost of preferred stock for El Paso Edison:

$$k_{ps} = \frac{\$4.25}{(\$58.50 - \$1.375)} = 0.0744, \text{ or } 7.44\%$$

Note that there is no adjustment for taxes because preferred dividends are not tax deductible—that is, preferred dividends are paid after corporate taxes, unlike bond interest, which is paid with before-tax dollars.

The Cost of Common Equity

Common equity is unique in two respects. First, the cost of common equity is more difficult to estimate than the cost of debt or cost of preferred stock because the common stockholder's required rate of return is not observable. For example, there is no stated coupon rate or set dividend payment they receive. This results from the fact that common stockholders are the residual owners of the firm, which means that their return is equal to what is left of the firm's earnings after paying the firm's bondholders their contractually set interest and principal payments and the preferred stockholders their promised dividends. Second, common equity can be obtained either from the retention and reinvestment of firm earnings or through the sale of new shares. The costs associated with each of these sources are different from one another because the firm does not incur any flotation costs when it retains earnings, but it does incur costs when it sells new common shares.

We discuss two methods for estimating the common stockholder's required rate of return, which is the foundation for our estimate of the firm's cost of equity capital. These methods are based on the dividend growth model and the capital asset pricing model, which were both discussed in Chapter 8 when we discussed stock valuation.

The Dividend Growth Model

Recall from Chapter 8 that the value of a firm's common stock is equal to the present value of all future dividends. When dividends are expected to grow at a rate g forever, and g is less than the investor's required rate of return, k_{cs}, then the value of a share of common stock, P_{cs}, can be written as

$$P_{cs} = \frac{D_1}{k_{cs} - g} \tag{9-6}$$

where D_1 is the dividend expected to be received by the firm's common shareholders 1 year hence. The expected dividend is simply the current dividend (D_0) multiplied by 1 plus the annual rate of growth in dividends (that is, $D_1 = D_0 (1 + g)$). The investor's required rate of return then is found by solving equation (9-6) for k_{cs}.

$$k_{cs} = \frac{D_1}{P_{cs}} + g \tag{9-7}$$

CAN YOU DO IT?

CALCULATING THE COST OF DEBT FINANCING

General Auto Parts Corporation recently issued a 2-year bond with a face value of $20 million and a coupon rate of 5.5 percent per year (assume interest is paid annually). The subsequent cash flows to General Auto Parts were as follows:

	TODAY	YEAR 1	YEAR 2
Principal	$18 million	($0.00 million)	($20 million)
Interest		($0.99 million)	($0.99 million)
Total	$18 million	($0.99 million)	($20.99 million)

What was the cost of capital to General Auto Parts for the debt issue?
    (The solution can be found on page 241.)

CAN YOU DO IT?

CALCULATING THE COST OF PREFERRED STOCK FINANCING

Carson Enterprises recently issued $25 million in preferred stock at a price of $2.50 per share. The preferred shares carry a 10 percent dividend, or $0.25 per share (assume that it is paid annually). After paying all the fees and costs associated with the preferred issue the firm realized $2.25 per share issued.
    What was the cost of capital to Carson Enterprises from the preferred stock issue?
    (The solution can be found on page 241.)

Note that k_{cs} is the investor's required rate of return for investing in the firm's stock. It also serves as our estimate of the cost of equity capital, where new equity capital is obtained by retaining a part of the firm's current-period earnings. Recall that common equity financing can come from one of two sources: the retention of earnings or the sale of new common shares. When the firm retains earnings, it doesn't incur any flotation costs; thus, the investor's required rate of return is the same as the firm's cost of new equity capital in this instance.

If the firm issues new shares to raise equity capital, then it incurs flotation costs. Once again we adjust the investor's required rate of return for flotation costs by substituting the net proceeds per share, NP_{cs}, for the stock price, P_{cs}, in equation (9-7) to estimate the cost of new common stock, k_{ncs}.

$$k_{ncs} = \frac{D_1}{NP_{cs}} + g \tag{9-8}$$

EXAMPLE 9.3

The Talbot Corporation's common shareholders anticipate receiving a $2.20 per share dividend next year, based on the fact that they received $2 last year and expect dividends to grow 10 percent next year. Furthermore, analysts predict that dividends will continue to grow at a rate of 10 percent into the foreseeable future. Given that the firm's stock is trading for $50 per share, we can calculate the investor's required rate of return (and the cost of retained earnings) as follows:

$$k_{cs} = \frac{D_1}{P_{cs}} + g = \frac{\$2.20}{\$50.00} + 0.10 = 0.144, \text{ or } 14.4\%$$

DID YOU GET IT?

CALCULATING THE COST OF DEBT FINANCING

General Auto Parts Corporation receives $18 million from the sale of the bonds (after paying flotation costs) and is required to make principal plus interest payments at the end of the next 2 years. The total cash flows (both the inflow and the outflows) are summarized below:

	TODAY	YEAR 1	YEAR 2
Principal	$18 million	($0.00 million)	($20 million)
Interest		($0.99 million)	($0.99 million)
Total	$18 million	($0.99 million)	($20.99 million)

We can estimate the before-tax cost of capital from the bond issue by solving for k_d in the following bond valuation equation:

$$\text{Net bond proceeds}_{today} = \frac{\text{interest paid in year 1}}{(1 + k_d)^1} + \frac{\text{interest paid in year 2}}{(1 + k_d)^2} + \frac{\text{principal paid in year 2}}{(1 + k_d)^2}$$

$$\$18,000,000 = \frac{\$990,000}{(1 + k_d)^1} + \frac{\$990,000}{(1 + k_d)^2} + \frac{\$20,000,000}{(1 + k_d)^2}$$

$$k_d = 10.77\%$$

DID YOU GET IT?

CALCULATING THE COST OF PREFERRED STOCK FINANCING

Carson Enterprises sold its shares of preferred stock for net proceeds of $2.25 a share, and each share entitles the holder to a $0.25 cash dividend every year. Because the dividend payment is constant for all future years, we can calculate the cost of capital raised by the sale of preferred stock (k_{ps}) as follows:

$$\text{Cost of preferred stock } (k_{ps}) = \frac{\text{preferred stock dividend}}{\text{net proceeds per preferred share}} = \frac{\$0.25}{\$2.25} = 11.11\%$$

Should Talbot decide to issue new common stock, then it would incur a cost of $7.50 per share, or 15 percent of the current stock price. The resulting cost of new common equity capital would be

$$k_{ncs} = \frac{D_1}{NP_{cs}} + g = \frac{\$2.20}{\$50 - \$7.50} + 0.10 = 0.1518, \text{ or } 15.18\%$$

Thus, Talbot faces two costs of capital with respect to common equity. If it uses retained earnings, then the cost of capital to the firm is 14.4 percent, and if it issues new common stock, the corresponding cost is 15.18 percent. This difference will prove to be important later when we calculate the overall or weighted average cost of capital for the firm.

Issues in Implementing the Dividend Growth Model

The principal advantage of the dividend growth model as a basis for calculating the firm's cost of capital as it relates to common stock is the model's simplicity. To estimate an investor's required rate of return, the analyst needs only to observe the current dividend and stock price and to estimate the rate of growth in future dividends. The primary drawback relates to the applicability or appropriateness of the valuation model. That is, the dividend growth model is based on the fundamental assumption that dividends are expected to grow at a constant rate g forever. To avoid this assumption, analysts frequently utilize more complex valuation models in which dividends are expected to grow for, say, 5 years at one rate and then grow at a lower rate from year 6 forward. We do not consider these more complex models here.

Even if the constant growth rate assumption is acceptable, we must arrive at an estimate of that growth rate. We could estimate the rate of growth in historical dividends ourselves or go to published sources of growth rate expectations. Investment advisory services such as Value Line provide their own analysts' estimates of earnings growth rates (generally spanning up to 5 years), and the Institutional Brokers' Estimate System (I/B/E/S) collects and publishes earnings per share forecasts made by more than 1,000 analysts for a broad list of stocks. These estimates are helpful but still require the careful judgment of an analyst in their use because they relate to earnings (not dividends) and extend only 5 years into the future (not forever, as required by the dividend growth model). Nonetheless, these estimates provide a useful guide to making your initial dividend growth rate estimate.

The Capital Asset Pricing Model

Recall from Chapter 6 that the capital asset pricing model (CAPM) provides a basis for determining the investor's expected or required rate of return from investing in a firm's common stock. The model depends on three things:

1. The risk-free rate, r_f
2. The systematic risk of the common stock's returns relative to the market as a whole, or the stock's beta coefficient, β
3. The market-risk premium, which is equal to the difference in the expected rate of return for the market as a whole, that is, the expected rate of return for the "average security" minus the risk-free rate, or in symbols, $r_m - r_f$

Using the CAPM, the investor's required rate of return can be written as follows:

$$k_c = r_f + \beta(r_m - r_f) \tag{9-9}$$

EXAMPLE 9.4

Talbot Corporation's common stock has a beta coefficient of 1.40. Furthermore, the risk-free rate is currently 3.75 percent, and the expected rate of return on the market portfolio of all risky assets is 12 percent. Using the CAPM from equation (9-9), we can estimate Talbot's cost of equity as follows:

$$k_c = r_f + \beta(r_m - r_f)$$
$$= 0.0375 + 1.4(0.12 - 0.0375) = 0.153, \text{ or } 15.3\%$$

Note that the required rate of return we have estimated is the cost of retained earnings because no transaction costs are considered.

Issues in Implementing the CAPM

The CAPM approach has two primary advantages when it comes to calculating a firm's cost of capital as it relates to common stock. First, the model is simple and easy to understand and implement. The model variables are readily available from public sources, with the possible exception of beta coefficients for small firms and/or privately held firms. Second, because the model does not rely on dividends or any assumption about the growth rate in dividends, it can be applied to companies that do not currently pay dividends or are not expected to experience a constant rate of growth in dividends.

CAN YOU DO IT?

CALCULATING THE COST OF NEW COMMON STOCK USING THE DIVIDEND GROWTH MODEL

In March of 2010, the Mayze Corporation sold an issue of common stock in a public offering. The shares sold for $100 per share. Mayze's dividend in 2009 was $8 per share, and analysts expect that the firm's earnings and dividends will grow at a rate of 6 percent per year for the foreseeable future. What is the common stock investor's required rate of return (and the cost of retained earnings)?

Although the shares sold for $100 per share, Mayze received net proceeds from the issue of only $95 per share. The difference represents the flotation cost paid to the investment banker.

What is your estimate of the cost of new equity for Mayze using the dividend growth model?

(The solution can be found on page 245.)

CAN YOU DO IT?

CALCULATING THE COST OF COMMON STOCK USING THE CAPM

The Mayze Corporation issued common stock in March 2010, for $100 per share. However, before the issue was made, the firm's chief financial officer (CFO) asked one of his financial analysts to estimate the cost of the common stock financing using the CAPM. The analyst looked on Yahoo! Finance and got an estimate of 0.90 for the firm's beta coefficient. She also consulted online sources to get the current yield on a 10-year U.S. Treasury bond, which was 5.5 percent. The final estimate she needed to complete her calculation of the cost of equity using the CAPM was the market-risk premium, or the difference in the expected rate of return on all equity securities and the rate of return on the 10-year U.S. Treasury bond. After a bit of research she decided that the risk premium should be based on a 12 percent expected rate of return for the market portfolio and the 5.5 percent rate on the Treasury bond.

What is your estimate of the cost of common stock for Mayze using the CAPM?

(The solution can be found on page 245.)

Of course, using the CAPM requires that we obtain estimates of each of the three model variables—r_f, β, and $(r_m - r_f)$. Let's consider each in turn. First, the analyst has a wide range of U.S. government securities on which to base an estimate of the risk-free rate (r_f). Treasury securities with maturities from 30 days to 20 years are readily available. Unfortunately, the CAPM offers no guidance about the appropriate choice. In fact, the model itself assumes that there is but one risk-free rate, and it corresponds to a one-period return (the length of the period is not specified, however). Consequently, we are left to our own judgment about which maturity we should use to represent the risk-free rate. For applications of the cost of capital involving long-term capital expenditure decisions, it seems reasonable to select a risk-free rate of comparable maturity. So, if we are calculating the cost of capital to be used as the basis for evaluating investments that will provide returns over the next 20 years, it seems appropriate to use a risk-free rate corresponding to a U.S. Treasury bond of comparable maturity.

Second, estimates of security beta (β) coefficients are available from a wide variety of investment advisory services, including Merrill Lynch and Value Line, among others. Alternatively, we could collect historical stock market returns for the company of interest as well as a general market index (such as the Standard and Poor's 500 Index) and estimate the stock's beta as the slope of the relationship between the two return series—as we did in Chapter 6. However, because beta estimates are widely available for a large majority of publicly traded firms, analysts frequently rely on published sources for betas.

Finally, estimating the market-risk premium can be accomplished by looking at the history of stock returns and the premium earned over (under) the risk-free rate of interest. In Chapter 6, we reported a summary of the historical returns earned on risk-free securities and common stocks in Figure 6-2. We saw that on average over the past 70 years, common stocks have earned a premium of roughly 5.5 percent over long-term government bonds. Thus, for our purposes, we will utilize this estimate of the market-risk premium ($r_m - r_f$) when estimating the investor's required rate of return on equity using the CAPM.

FINANCE AT WORK

IPOS: SHOULD A FIRM GO PUBLIC?

When a privately owned company decides to distribute its shares to the general public, it goes through a process known as an initial public offering (IPO). There are a number of advantages to having a firm's shares traded in the public equity market, including the following:

- **New capital is raised.** When the firm sells its shares to the public, it acquires new capital that can be invested in the firm.
- **The firm's owners gain liquidity of their share holdings.** Publicly traded shares are more easily bought and sold, so the owners can more easily liquidate all or part of their investment in the firm.
- **The firm gains future access to the public capital market.** Once a firm has raised capital in the public markets, it is easier to go back a second and third time.
- **Being a publicly traded firm can benefit the firm's business.** Public firms tend to enjoy a higher profile than their privately held counterparts. This may make it easier to make sales and attract vendors to supply goods and services to the firm.

However, all is not rosy as a publicly held firm. There are a number of potential disadvantages, including the following:

- **Reporting requirements can be onerous.** Publicly held firms are required to file periodic reports with the Securities and Exchange Commission (SEC). This is not only onerous in terms of the time and effort required, but also some business owners feel they must reveal information to their competitors that could be potentially damaging.

- **The private equity investors now must share any new wealth with the new public investors.** Once the firm is a publicly held company, the new shareholders share on an equal footing with the company founders the good (and bad) fortune of the firm.
- **The private equity investors lose a degree of control over the organization.** Outsiders gain voting control over the firm to the extent that they own its shares.
- **An IPO is expensive.** A typical firm may spend 15 to 25 percent of the money raised on expenses directly connected to the IPO. This cost is increased further if we consider the cost of lost management time and disruption of business associated with the IPO process.
- **Exit of the company's owners is usually limited.** The company's founders may want to sell their shares through the IPO, but this is not allowed for an extended period of time following the IPO. Therefore, this is not usually a good mechanism for cashing out the company founders.
- **Everyone involved faces legal liability.** The IPO participants are jointly and severally liable for each others' actions. This means that they can be sued for any omissions from the IPO's prospectus should the market valuation fall below the IPO offering price.

Carefully weighing the financial consequences of each of these advantages and disadvantages can provide a company's owners (and managers) with some basis for answering the question of whether they want to become a public corporation.

Other Sources: Professor Ivo Welch's Web site: welch.som.yale.edu provides a wealth of information concerning IPOs.

In addition to the historical average market-risk premium, we can also utilize surveys of professional economists' opinions regarding future premiums.[1] For example, in a survey conducted in 1998 by Yale economist Ivo Welch, the median 30-year market-risk premium for all survey participants was 7 percent. When the survey was repeated in 2000, the corresponding market-risk premium had fallen to 5 percent. These results suggest two things. First, the market-risk premium is not fixed. It varies through time with the general business cycle. In addition, it appears that using a market-risk premium somewhere between 5 percent and 7 percent is reasonable when estimating the cost of capital using the capital asset pricing model.

Concept Check

1. Define the cost of debt, preferred equity, and common equity financing.
2. The cost of common equity financing is more difficult to estimate than the costs of debt and preferred equity. Explain why.
3. What is the dividend growth model, and how is it used to estimate the cost of common equity financing?
4. Describe the capital asset pricing model and how it can be used to estimate the cost of common equity financing.
5. What practical problems are encountered in using the CAPM to estimate common equity capital cost?

[1] The results reported here come from Ivo Welch, "Views of Financial Economists on the Equity Premium and on Professional Controversies," *Journal of Business* 73–74 (October 2000): pp. 501–537; and Ivo Welch, "The Equity Premium Consensus Forecast Revisited," Cowles Foundation Discussion Paper No. 1325 (September 2001).

The Weighted Average Cost of Capital

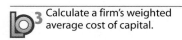

Calculate a firm's weighted average cost of capital.

Now that we have calculated the individual costs of capital for each of the sources of financing the firm might use, we turn to the combination of these capital costs into a single weighted average cost of capital. To estimate the weighted average cost of capital, we need to know the cost of each of the sources of capital used and the capital structure mix. We use the term **capital structure** to refer to *the proportions of each source of financing used by the firm*. Although a firm's capital structure can be quite complex, we focus our examples on the three basic sources of capital: bonds, preferred stock, and common equity.

capital structure the mix of long-term sources of funds used by the firm. This is also called the firm's capitalization. The relative total (percentage) of each type of fund is emphasized.

In words, we calculate the weighted average cost of capital for a firm that uses only debt and common equity using the following equation:

$$\begin{matrix}\text{Weighted} \\ \text{average cost} \\ \text{of capital}\end{matrix} = \begin{pmatrix}\text{after-tax} \\ \text{cost of} \\ \text{debt}\end{pmatrix} \times \begin{matrix}\text{proportion} \\ \text{of debt} \\ \text{financing}\end{matrix} + \begin{pmatrix}\text{cost of} \\ \text{equity}\end{pmatrix} \times \begin{matrix}\text{proportion} \\ \text{of equity} \\ \text{financing}\end{matrix} \qquad (9\text{-}10)$$

For example, if a firm borrows money at 6 percent after taxes, pays 10 percent for equity, and raises its capital in equal proportions from debt and equity, its weighted average cost of capital is 8 percent—that is,

Weighted average cost of capital $= [0.06 \times 0.5] + [0.10 \times 0.5] = 0.08$ or 8%

In practice, the calculation of the cost of capital is more complex than this example. For one thing, firms often have multiple debt issues with different required rates of return, and they also use preferred equity as well as common equity financing. Furthermore, when common equity capital is raised, it is sometimes the result of retaining and reinvesting the firm's earnings and, at other times, it involves a new stock offering. Of course, in the case of retained earnings, the firm does not incur the costs associated with selling new common stock. This means that equity from retained earnings is less costly than a new stock offering. In the examples that follow, we address each of these complications.

DID YOU GET IT?

CALCULATING THE COST OF NEW COMMON STOCK USING THE DIVIDEND GROWTH MODEL

We can estimate the cost of equity capital using the dividend growth model by substituting into the following equation:

$$\text{Cost of new common stock } (k_{ncs}) = \frac{\text{expected dividend next year } (D_1)}{\text{net proceeds per share } (NP_{cs})} + \text{dividend growth rate } (g) = \frac{\$8.00}{\$95.00} + 0.06 = 14.42\%$$

DID YOU GET IT?

CALCULATING THE COST OF COMMON STOCK USING THE CAPM

The CAPM can be used to estimate the investor's required rate of return as follows:

$$\begin{matrix}\text{Cost of} \\ \text{common equity}(k_{cs})\end{matrix} = \begin{pmatrix}\text{risk-free} \\ \text{rate of interest } (r_f)\end{pmatrix} + \begin{pmatrix}\text{Mayze's beta} \\ \text{coefficient } (\beta)\end{pmatrix} \times \left[\begin{pmatrix}\text{expected market} \\ \text{rate of return } (r_m)\end{pmatrix} - \begin{pmatrix}\text{risk-free} \\ \text{rate of interest } (r_f)\end{pmatrix}\right]$$

Making the appropriate substitutions, we get the following estimate of the investor's required rate of return using the CAPM model:

Cost of common equity $(k_{cs}) = 0.055 + 0.90 \times (0.12 - 0.055) = 0.1135$ or 11.35%

Capital Structure Weights

The reason we calculate a cost of capital is that it enables us to evaluate one or more of the firm's investment opportunities. Remember that the cost of capital should reflect the riskiness of the project being evaluated, so a firm should calculate multiple costs of capital when it makes investments in multiple divisions or business units having different risk characteristics. Thus, for the calculated cost of capital to be meaningful, it must correspond directly to the riskiness of the particular project being analyzed. That is, in theory the cost of capital should reflect the particular way in which the funds are raised (the capital structure used) and the systemic risk characteristics of the project. Consequently, the correct way to calculate capital structure weights is to use the actual dollar amounts of the various sources of capital actually used by the firm.[2]

In practice, *the mixture of financing sources used by a firm will vary from year to year.* For this reason, many firms find it expedient to use target capital structure proportions when calculating the firm's weighted average cost of capital. For example, a firm might use its target mix of 40 percent debt and 60 percent equity to calculate its weighted average cost of capital even though, in that particular year, it raised the majority of its financing requirements by borrowing. Similarly, it would continue to use the target proportions in the subsequent year, when it might raise the majority of its financing needs by reinvesting earnings or issuing new stock.

Calculating the Weighted Average Cost of Capital

The weighted average cost of capital, k_{wacc}, is simply a weighted average of all the capital costs incurred by the firm. Table 9-1 illustrates the procedure used to estimate k_{wacc} for a firm that has debt, preferred stock, and common equity in its target capital structure mix. Two possible scenarios are described in the two panels. First, in Panel A the firm is able to finance all of its target capital structure requirements for common equity using retained earnings. Second, in Panel B the firm must use a new equity offering to raise the equity capital it requires. For example, if the firm has set a 75 percent target for equity financing and has current earnings of $750,000, then it can raise up to $750,000/0.75 = $1,000,000 in new financing before it has to sell new equity. For $1,000,000 or less in capital spending, the firm's weighted average cost of capital would be calculated using the cost of equity from retained earnings (following Panel A of Table 9-1). For more than $1,000,000 in new capital, the cost of capital would rise to reflect the impact of the higher cost of using new common stock (following Panel B of Table 9-1).

TABLE 9-1 Calculating the Weighted Average Cost of Capital

PANEL A: COMMON EQUITY RAISED BY RETAINED EARNINGS

Source of Capital	Weights	Capital Structure × Cost of Capital	= Product
Bonds	w_d	$k_d(1 - T_c)$	$w_d \times k_d(1 - T_c)$
Preferred stock	w_{ps}	k_{ps}	$w_{ps} \times k_{ps}$
Common equity			
Retained earnings	w_{cs}	k_{cs}	$w_{cs} \times k_{cs}$
Sum =	100%	Sum =	k_{wacc}

PANEL B: COMMON EQUITY RAISED BY SELLING NEW COMMON STOCK

Source of Capital	Weights	Capital Structure × Cost of Capital	= Product
Bonds	w_d	$k_d(1 - T_c)$	$w_d \times k_d(1 - T_c)$
Preferred stock	w_{ps}	k_{ps}	$w_{ps} \times k_{ps}$
Common equity			
Common stock	w_{ncs}	k_{ncs}	$w_{ncs} \times k_{ncs}$
Sum =	100%	Sum =	k_{wacc}

[2]There are instances when we will want to calculate the cost of capital for the firm as a whole. In this case, the appropriate weights to use are based on the market value of the various capital sources used by the firm. Market values rather than book values properly reflect the sources of financing used by a firm at any particular point in time. However, when a firm is privately owned, it is not possible to get market values of its securities, and book values are often used.

EXAMPLE 9.5

Ash Inc.'s capital structure and estimated capital costs are found in Table 9-2. Note that the sum of the capital structure weights must equal 100 percent if we have properly accounted for all sources of financing and in the correct amounts. For example, Ash plans to invest a total of $3 million in common equity to fund a $5 million investment. Because Ash has earnings equal to the $3,000,000 it needs in new equity financing, the entire amount of new equity will be raised by retaining earnings.

We calculate the weighted average cost of capital following the procedure described in Panel A of Table 9-1 and using the information found in Table 9-2. The resulting calculations are found in Panel A of Table 9-3, in which Ash Inc.'s weighted average cost of capital for up to $5,000,000 in new financing is found to be 12.7 percent.

If Ash needs more than $5,000,000, it will not have any retained earnings to provide the additional equity capital. Thus, to maintain its desired 60 percent equity financing proportion, Ash will now have to issue common stock that costs 18 percent.

Panel B of Table 9-3 contains the calculation of Ash's weighted average cost of capital for more than $5,000,000. The resulting cost is 13.9 percent.

In practice, many firms calculate only one cost of capital, using a cost of equity capital that ignores the transaction costs associated with raising new equity capital. In essence, they would use the capital cost calculated for Ash in Panel A of Table 9-3, regardless of the level of new financing for the year. Although this is technically incorrect, it is an understandable practice given the inexactness of the estimates of equity capital cost and the relatively small differences that result from the adjustment.

TABLE 9-2 Capital Structure and Capital Costs for Ash Inc.

Source of Capital	Amount of Funds Raised ($)	Percentage of Total	After-Tax Cost of Capital
Bonds	1,750,000	35%	7%
Preferred stock	250,000	5%	13%
Retained earnings	3,000,000	60%	16%
Total	5,000,000	100%	

TABLE 9-3 The Weighted Average Cost of Capital for Ash Inc.

PANEL A: COST OF CAPITAL FOR $0 TO $5,000,000 IN NEW CAPITAL			
	Capital Structure		
Source of Capital	Weights	Cost of Capital	Product
Bonds	35%	7%	2.45%
Preferred stock	5%	13%	0.65%
Retained earnings	60%	16%	9.60%
Total	100%	$k_{wacc} =$	12.70%

PANEL B: COST OF CAPITAL FOR MORE THAN $5,000,000			
	Capital Structure		
Source of Capital	Weights	Cost of Capital	Product
Bonds	35%	7%	2.45%
Preferred stock	5%	13%	0.65%
New common stock	60%	18%	10.80%
Total	100%	$k_{wacc} =$	13.90%

CAUTIONARY TALE

FORGETTING PRINCIPLE 3: RISK REQUIRES A REWARD

What happens to a firm's cost of capital when the capital market that the firm depends on for financing simply stops working? Investment banking firm Goldman Sachs discovered the answer to this question the hard way. In 2008, as potential lenders became very nervous about the future of the economy, the credit markets from which Goldman Sachs borrowed money on a regular basis simply stopped functioning. The effect of this shutdown was that Goldman Sachs no longer had access to cheap short-term debt financing. And this meant the firm was at greater risk of financial distress. This high risk of firm failure caused its equity holders to demand a much higher rate of return and thus, Goldman Sachs's cost of equity financing skyrocketed.

Ultimately, faced with a crisis, Goldman arranged for a $10 billion loan from the U.S. Government's Troubled Asset Relief Fund (TARP) and obtained a $5 billion equity investment from famed investor Warren Buffett. The combined effects of these actions stabilized the firm's financial situation and lowered the firm's cost of capital dramatically. Goldman Sachs and Morgan Stanley are the only two large investment banking firms to survive the financial crisis.

So what can Goldman Sachs learn from this experience? Debt financing, and in particular short-term debt financing, may offer higher returns in the short run, but this use of financial leverage comes with a significant increase in risk to the equity holders, and this translates to higher costs of equity financing for the firm.

Concept Check

1. A firm's capital structure and its target capital structure proportions are important determinants of a firm's weighted average cost of capital. Explain.
2. Explain in words the calculation of a firm's weighted average cost of capital. What exactly are we averaging and what do the weights represent?

 4 Describe the procedure used by PepsiCo to estimate the cost of capital for a multidivisional firm.

Calculating Divisional Costs of Capital: PepsiCo Inc.

If a firm operates in multiple industries, each with its own particular risk characteristics, should it use different capital costs for each division? **Principle 1** suggests that the financial manager should recognize these risk differences in estimating the cost of capital to use in each division. This is exactly what PepsiCo did before February 1997, when it was operating in three basic industries.

CAN YOU DO IT?

CALCULATING THE WEIGHTED AVERAGE COST OF CAPITAL

In the fall of 2009, Grey Manufacturing was considering a major expansion of its manufacturing operations. The firm has sufficient land to accommodate the doubling of its operations, which will cost $200 million. To raise the needed funds Grey's management has decided to simply mimic the firm's present capital structure as follows:

SOURCE OF CAPITAL	AMOUNT OF FUNDS RAISED ($)	PERCENTAGE OF TOTAL	AFTER-TAX COST OF CAPITAL*
Debt	$ 80,000,000	40%	5.20%
Common stock	120,000,000	60%	14.50%
Total	$200,000,000	100%	

What is your estimate of Grey's weighted average cost of capital?

*You may assume that these after-tax costs of capital have been appropriately adjusted for any transaction costs incurred when raising the funds.

(The solution can be found on page 250.)

FINANCE AT WORK

THE PILLSBURY COMPANY ADOPTS EVA WITH A GRASSROOTS EDUCATION PROGRAM

A key determinant of the success of any incentive-based program is employee buy-in. If employees simply view a new performance measurement and reward system as "just another" reporting requirement, the program will have little impact on their behavior and, consequently, little effect on the firm's operating performance. In addition, if a firm's employees do not understand the measurement system, it is very likely that it will be distrusted and may even have counterproductive effects on the firm's performance.

So how do you instill in your employees the notion that your performance measurement and reward system does indeed lead to the desired result? Pillsbury took a unique approach to the problem by using a simulation exercise in which the value of applying the principles of Economic Value Added (EVA®) could be learned by simulating the operations of a hypothetical factory. Employees used the simulation to follow the value-creation process from the factory's revenue, to net operating profit after taxes, to the weighted average cost of capital. The results were gratifying. One Pillsbury manager noted, "you saw the lights go on in people's eyes" as employees realized, "Oh, this really does impact my work environment."

Briggs and Stratton used a similar training program to instill the basic principles of EVA in its employees. Its business-simulation

example was even more basic than the Pillsbury factory. Briggs and Stratton used a convenience store's operations to teach line workers the importance of controlling waste, utilizing assets fully, and managing profit margins. Stern Stewart and Company, which coined the term *EVA*, has also developed a training tool, the EVA Training Tutor.™ The EVA Training Tutor addresses four basic issues using CD-ROM technology:

- Why is creating shareholder wealth an important corporate and investor goal?
- What is the best way to measure wealth and business success?
- Which business strategies have created wealth, and which have failed?
- What can you do to create wealth and increase the stock price of your company?

The educational programs described briefly here are examples of how major corporations are seeing the need to improve the financial literacy of their employees to make the most of their human and capital resources.

Sources: Adapted from George Donnelly, "Grassroots EVA," CFO.com (May 1, 2000), www.cfo.com and The EVA Training Tutor™ (Stern Stewart and Company).

PepsiCo went to great lengths to estimate the cost of capital for each of its three major operating divisions (restaurants, snack foods, and beverages).[3] We briefly summarize the basic elements of the calculations involved in these estimates, including the cost of debt financing, the cost of common equity, the target capital structure weights, and the weighted average cost of capital.

Table 9-4 contains the estimates of the after-tax cost of debt for each of PepsiCo's three divisions and assuming a 38 percent tax rate. Table 9-5 contains the estimates of the cost of

TABLE 9-4 Estimating PepsiCo's Cost of Debt

	Pretax Cost of Debt	×	(1 − Tax Rate)	=	After-Tax Cost of Debt
Restaurants	8.93%	×	0.62	=	5.54%
Snack foods	8.43%	×	0.62	=	5.23%
Beverages	8.51%	×	0.62	=	5.28%

TABLE 9-5 The Cost of Equity Capital for PepsiCo's Operating Divisions

	Risk-Free Rate	+	Beta	×	(Expected Market Return − Risk-Free Rate)	=	Cost of Equity
Restaurants	7.28%	+	1.17	×	(11.48% − 7.28%)	=	12.19%
Snack foods	7.28%	+	1.02	×	(11.48% − 7.28%)	=	11.56%
Beverages	7.28%	+	1.07	×	(11.48% − 7.28%)	=	11.77%

[3]PepsiCo spun off its restaurants division in February 1997. However, the example used here was based on the company before the spin-off.

DID YOU GET IT?

CALCULATING THE WEIGHTED AVERAGE COST OF CAPITAL

The weighted average cost of capital (WACC) for Grey Manufacturing can be calculated using the following table:

SOURCE OF CAPITAL	PERCENTAGE OF TOTAL CAPITAL	AFTER-TAX COST OF CAPITAL	PRODUCT
Debt	40%	5.20%	2.0800%
Common stock	60%	14.50%	8.7000%
		WACC =	10.7800%

Consequently, we estimate Grey's WACC to be 10.78%.

TABLE 9-6 PepsiCo's Weighted Average Cost of Capital for Each of Its Operating Divisions

	Cost of Equity Times the Target Equity Ratio	+	After-Tax Cost of Debt Times the Target Debt Ratio	=	Weighted Average Cost of Capital
Restaurants	(12.19%)(0.70)	+	(5.54%)(0.30)	=	10.20%
Snack foods	(11.56%)(0.80)	+	(5.23%)(0.20)	=	10.29%
Beverages	(11.77%)(0.74)	+	(5.28%)(0.26)	=	10.08%

---

equity capital for each of PepsiCo's three operating divisions using the CAPM. We will not explain the intricacies of their method for estimating divisional betas, except to say that they make use of beta estimates for a number of competitor firms from each of the operating divisions, which involves making appropriate adjustments for differences in the use of financial leverage across the competitor firms used in the analysis.[4]

The weighted average cost of capital for each of the divisions is estimated in Table 9-6 using the capital costs estimated in Tables 9-4 and 9-5 and using PepsiCo's target capital structure weights for each operating division. Note that the weighted average costs of capital for all three divisions fall within a very narrow range, between 10.08 percent and 10.29 percent.

Concept Check

1. Why should firms that own and operate multiple businesses with very different risk characteristics use business-specific or divisional costs of capital?
2. Describe the process used to estimate the divisional costs of capital for PepsiCo.

Table 9-7 contains a summary of the formulas you need to estimate the weighted average cost of capital. If divisional costs of capital are to be estimated, then we must apply these formulas individually to each division because the opportunity costs of capital sources and the financing mix (proportions) used can differ, as we have just seen in the PepsiCo example.

---

[4]This method of using betas from comparable firms is sometimes referred to as the pure play method, because the analyst seeks independent beta estimates for firms engaged in only one business (i.e., restaurants or beverages). The betas for these pure play companies are then used to estimate the beta for a business or division.

TABLE 9-7 A Summary of Cost of Capital Formulas

1. The After-Tax Cost of Debt, $k_d(1 - T_c)$

   a) Calculate the before-tax cost of debt, k_d, as follows:

   $$\text{Net proceeds }(NP_d) = \frac{\text{interest (year 1)}}{(1 + \text{cost of debt capital }(k_d))^1} + \frac{\text{interest (year 2)}}{(1 + k_d)^2} + \frac{\text{principal}}{(1 + k_d)^2} \qquad (9\text{-}2)$$

   b) Calculate the after-tax cost of debt as follows:

   after-tax cost of debt $= k_d(1 - T_c)$

   where T_c is the corporate tax rate.

2. The Cost of Preferred Stock, k_{ps}

   $$k_{ps} = \frac{\text{preferred stock dividend}}{\text{net proceeds per share of preferred stock }(NP_{ps})} \qquad (9\text{-}5)$$

   where NP_{ps} is the net proceeds per share of new preferred stock sold after flotation costs.

3. The Cost of Common Equity

   a) Method 1: dividend growth model

   Calculate the cost of internal common equity (retained earnings), k_{cs}, as follows:

   $$k_{cs} = \frac{D_1}{P_{cs}} + g \qquad (9\text{-}7)$$

   where D_1 is the expected dividend for the next year, P_{cs} is the current price of the firm's common stock, and g is the rate of growth in dividends per year.

   Calculate the cost of external common equity (new stock offering), k_{ncs}, as follows:

   $$k_{ncs} = \frac{D_1}{NP_{cs}} + g \qquad (9\text{-}8)$$

   where NP_{cs} is the net proceeds to the firm after flotation costs per share of stock sold.

   b) Method 2: capital asset pricing model, k_c

   $$k_c = r_f + \beta(r_m - r_f) \qquad (9\text{-}9)$$

   where the risk-free rate is k_{rf}; the systemic risk of the common stock's returns relative to the market as a whole, or the stock's beta coefficient, is β; and the market-risk premium, which is equal to the difference in the expected rate of return for the market as a whole (i.e., the expected rate of return for the "average security") minus the risk-free rate, is $k_m - k_{rf}$.

4. The Weighted Average Cost of Capital

   $$\begin{pmatrix}\text{Weighted}\\\text{average cost}\\\text{of capital}\end{pmatrix} = \begin{pmatrix}\text{after-tax}\\\text{cost of}\times\begin{array}{c}\text{proportion}\\\text{of debt}\\\text{financing}\end{array}\\\text{debt}\end{pmatrix} + \begin{pmatrix}\text{cost of}\\\text{equity}\times\begin{array}{c}\text{proportion}\\\text{of equity}\\\text{financing}\end{array}\end{pmatrix} \qquad (9\text{-}10)$$

Note that we are simply calculating a weighted average of the costs of each of the firm's sources of capital where the weights reflect the firm's relative use of each source.

Using a Firm's Cost of Capital to Evaluate New Capital Investments

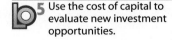

5 Use the cost of capital to evaluate new investment opportunities.

If a firm has traditionally used a single cost of capital for all projects undertaken within each of several operating divisions (or companies) with very different risk characteristics, then the company will likely encounter resistance from the high-risk divisions if it changes to a divisional cost of capital structure. Consider the case of the hypothetical firm Global Energy, whose divisional costs of capital are illustrated in Figure 9-1. Global Energy is an integrated oil company that engages in a wide range of hydrocarbon-related businesses, including exploration and development, pipelines, and refining. Each of these businesses has its unique set of risks. In Figure 9-1 we see that the overall, or enterprise-wide, cost of capital for Global Energy is 11 percent, reflecting an average of the firm's divisional costs of capital, ranging from a low of 8 percent for pipelines up to 18 percent for exploration and development.

At present Global Energy is using a cost of capital of 11 percent to evaluate its new investment proposals from all three operating divisions. This means that exploration and

FINANCE AT WORK

WEIGHTED AVERAGE COSTS OF CAPITAL ESTIMATES: 1993–2005

The value-based management consulting firm Stern Stewart estimates the WACC for the 1,000 largest U.S. firms each year as part of its analysis of their performance. In the 2004 performance review (based on 2003 data) the average WACC across all 1,000 firms was 7.5%, and the median was 7.4%. The maximum WACC was 14% compared to a minimum of only 4.2%. The following list contains the WACC estimates for a sample of well-known firms for 5-year intervals spanning 1993–2005:

COMPANY NAME	2005	2003	1998	1993
Walmart Stores	5.8%	6.2%	6.6%	7.5%
Coca-Cola Co.	5.9%	6.4%	6.6%	7.6%
ExxonMobil Corp.	6.1%	7.0%	7.3%	8.0%
General Electric Co.	6.9%	7.3%	7.7%	8.6%
American Express	8.6%	8.0%	8.4%	9.5%
Procter & Gamble Co.	7.2%	7.4%	8.2%	9.1%
United Parcel Service Inc.	7.4%	7.8%	8.1%	9.2%
Johnson & Johnson	7.8%	8.2%	8.4%	9.3%
Lilly (Eli) & Co.	7.6%	8.0%	8.4%	9.5%
Merck & Co.	7.6%	8.0%	8.5%	9.6%
Amgen Inc.	9.6%	10.0%	10.4%	11.4%
Dell Computer Corp.	10.3%	10.8%	11.1%	11.9%
Hewlett-Packard	10.1%	10.8%	11.4%	12.1%
International Business Machines Corp.	10.8%	11.3%	11.7%	12.8%
Cisco Systems Inc.	12.0%	12.2%	13.0%	14.0%
Microsoft Corp.	11.7%	11.8%	12.5%	13.6%
Intel Corp.	13.2%	13.7%	14.0%	14.8%
Average	8.7%	9.1%	9.5%	10.5%
Aaa Corporate Bond Yield	4.8%	5.63%	6.23%	7.00%
Average WACC - Aaa Bond Yield	3.9%	3.48%	3.31%	3.50%

The average WACC across this sample of firms declines over the period from 12.5 percent down to 9.1 percent. This decline is attributable to the general decline in interest rates (note that the Aaa corporate bond yield declined from 7 percent in 1993 down to 4.8 in 2005 such that the spread of WACC over the Aaa bond yield is relatively flat).

In addition, the WACC estimates are consistent across the period, with Walmart exhibiting the lowest WACC and Intel Corp. the highest.

Source: WACC estimates were taken from the Stern Stewart Annual Performance Ranking for 2006.

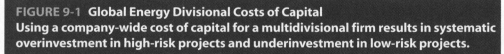

FIGURE 9-1 Global Energy Divisional Costs of Capital
Using a company-wide cost of capital for a multidivisional firm results in systematic overinvestment in high-risk projects and underinvestment in low-risk projects.

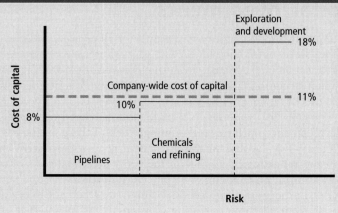

development projects earning as little as 11 percent are being accepted even though the capital market dictates that projects of this risk should earn 18 percent. Thus, Global Energy overinvests in high-risk projects. Similarly, the company will underinvest in its two lower-risk divisions, where the company-wide cost of capital is used.

Now consider the prospect of moving to division costs of capital and the implications this might have for the three divisions. Specifically, the managers of the exploration and development division are likely to see this as an adverse move for them because it will surely cut the level of new investment capital flowing into their operations. In contrast, the managers of the remaining two divisions will see the change as good news because, under the company-wide cost of capital system, they have been rejecting projects earning more than their market-based costs of capital (8 percent and 10 percent for pipelines and refining, respectively) but less than the company's 11 percent cost of capital.

Concept Check

1. What are the implications for a firm's capital investment decisions of using a company-wide cost of capital when the firm has multiple operating divisions that each have unique risk attributes and capital costs?

2. If a firm has decided to move from a situation in which it uses a company-wide cost of capital to divisional costs of capital, what problems is it likely to encounter?

Finance and the Multinational Firm: Why Do Interest Rates Differ Between Countries?[5]

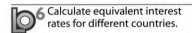

6 Calculate equivalent interest rates for different countries.

If borrowers and lenders can freely obtain money in one country and invest it in another, why are interest rates not the same the world over? Stated somewhat differently, if capital markets are fully integrated and money flows to the highest rate of interest, it would seem that the forces of competition would make interest rates the same for a borrower with a given amount of risk.

Let's consider a hypothetical example to see how this might work. Assume that a U.S. firm can borrow 1,000 yen in Japan for 5 percent interest, paying back 1,050 yen in 1 year. Alternatively, the U.S. firm can borrow an equivalent amount in the United States and pay 15.5 percent interest. Why the big difference? Is capital 10.5 percent cheaper in Japan, and if so, why don't U.S. firms simply switch to the Japanese capital market for their funds? The answer, as we will now illustrate, lies in the differences in the anticipated rates of inflation for Japan versus the United States.

Although it was not obvious in the preceding example, we assumed a zero rate of inflation for the Japanese economy and a 10 percent rate of inflation for the U.S. economy.

CAN YOU DO IT?

EVALUATING INTEREST RATE PARITY ACROSS COUNTRIES

The rate of interest on a 1-year Treasury bill was 5 percent at the end of 2007, and the corresponding rate of interest on a 1-year note issued by the Brazilian government was 18 percent. The international Fisher effect states that the real rate of interest is the same in both countries.

If the real rate is equal to 2 percent, what are the rates of inflation in the two countries? What is the ratio of 1 plus the nominal rates of interest in the two countries? What is the corresponding ratio of 1 plus the rate of inflation in the two countries?

(The solution can be found on page 255.)

[5]This section is from W. Carl Kester and Timothy A. Luehrman, "What Makes You Think U.S. Capital Is So Expensive?" *Journal of Applied Corporate Finance* (Summer 1992): pp. 29–41. Reprinted with permission.

DID YOU GET IT?
EVALUATING INTEREST RATE PARITY ACROSS COUNTRIES

The international Fisher theory of interest rate parity states that the real rate of interest should be the same across countries but nominal rates across countries will differ as a result of differential rates of anticipated inflation. Thus, for the U.S.–Brazil example, we estimate the ratio of 1 plus the nominal rates of interest as follows (where the U.S. is in the numerator):

$$\frac{(1 + 0.05)}{(1 + 0.18)} = 0.8898$$

Using the Fisher model to estimate the rates of inflation impounded in the nominal rates of interest for the United States and Brazil, and where the real rate is assumed to be 2 percent in both countries, we get estimated inflation for the United States equal to 2.94 percent and 15.69 percent for Brazil. The ratio of 1 plus these two rates of inflation then equals:

$$\frac{(1 + 0.0294)}{(1 + 0.1569)} = 0.8898$$

With a zero anticipated rate of inflation, the nominal rate of interest in Japan (the rate we see quoted in the financial press) is equal to the real rate of 5 percent.[6] Under these assumptions, the nominal rate in the United States can be calculated using the Fisher model as follows:

$$\text{U.S. nominal rate of interest} = (1 + \text{real rate, U.S.})(1 + \text{inflation rate, U.S.}) - 1$$

$$= (1.05)(1.10) - 1 = 0.155, \text{ or } 15.5\%$$

To understand the reason for the different interest rates in Japan and the United States, we must extend the Fisher model to its international counterpart.

Rearranging terms, we get the following relationship between nominal interest rates in the domestic and foreign country and the differences in anticipated inflation in the two countries:

$$r_{n,b} - r_{n,f} = i_b - i_f \tag{9-11}$$

Economists have formalized the relationship between interest rates of different countries in the interest rate parity theorem. This theorem is as follows:

$$\frac{(1 + r_{n,b})}{(1 + r_{n,f})} = \frac{E_1}{E_0} \tag{9-12}$$

where $r_{n,b}$ is the domestic one-period rate of interest, $r_{n,f}$ is the corresponding rate of interest in a foreign country, E_0 and E_1 are the exchange rates corresponding to the current period (i.e., the spot exchange rate) and one period hence (i.e., the one-period forward exchange rate).

Thus, differences in observed nominal rates of interest should equal differences in the expected rates of inflation between the two countries. This means that when we compare the interest rates for similar loans in two countries and they are not the same, we should immediately suspect that the expected rates of inflation for the two economies differ by an amount roughly equal to the interest rate differential.

To illustrate, let's consider the previous example, in which the domestic one-period interest rate ($r_{n,b}$) is 15.5 percent, the Japanese rate of interest ($r_{n,f}$) is 5 percent, the spot exchange ratio (E_0) is \$1 to 1 yen, and the forward exchange rate (E_1) is \$1.10 to 1 yen. Substituting into equation (9-12) produces the following result:

$$\frac{(1 + 0.155)}{(1 + 0.05)} = \frac{1.1}{1} = 1.10$$

---

[6] The real rate of interest is simply the rate of interest that is earned where the expected rate of inflation is zero.

The key thing to note here is that nominal interest rates are tied to exchange rates, and, as we learned earlier, differences in nominal rates of interest are tied to expected rates of inflation.

Why would we expect the interest rate parity relationship to hold? The answer lies in the fact that there are investors who stand ready to engage in arbitrage (trading) to enforce this relationship (within the bounds of transaction costs). Formally, we rely on the fundamental dictum of an efficient market (the law of one price). Very simply, the exchange-adjusted prices of identical loans must be within transaction costs of equality or the opportunity exists for traders to buy the low-cost loan and sell the higher-priced loan for a profit.

Summary

In Chapter 6 we learned about the connection between risk and investor required rates of return. Moreover, in Chapters 7 and 8 we calculated investor required rates of return for bondholders and stockholders. In Chapter 9 we combined these individual costs of funds from borrowed and owners into a single cost of capital for the firm as a whole. This required rate of return for the firm is a blend of the required rates of return of all investors that we will estimate using a weighted average of the individual rates of return called the firm's weighted average cost of capital or simply the firm's cost of capital. Just like any cost of doing business, the firm must earn at least this cost if it is to create value for its owners.

 Describe the concepts underlying the firm's cost of capital (technically, its weighted average cost of capital) and the purpose for its calculation.

The investor's required rate of return must be adjusted for the flotation costs incurred in selling new securities to get an estimate of the firm's cost of capital. For debt or bonds the after-tax cost of capital is calculated as follows:

 Calculate the after-tax cost of debt, preferred stock, and common equity.

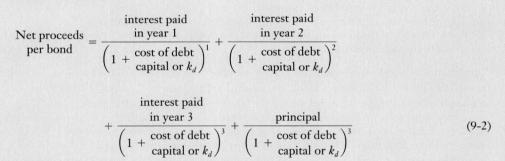

$$\text{Net proceeds per bond} = \frac{\text{interest paid in year 1}}{\left(1 + \frac{\text{cost of debt capital or } k_d}{}\right)^1} + \frac{\text{interest paid in year 2}}{\left(1 + \frac{\text{cost of debt capital or } k_d}{}\right)^2}$$

$$+ \frac{\text{interest paid in year 3}}{\left(1 + \frac{\text{cost of debt capital or } k_d}{}\right)^3} + \frac{\text{principal}}{\left(1 + \frac{\text{cost of debt capital or } k_d}{}\right)^3} \qquad (9\text{-}2)$$

After solving equation (9-2) for the cost of debt, k_d, we adjust this before-tax cost of financing to an after-tax cost by multiplying it by one minus the corporate tax rate.

The cost of preferred stock financing (k_{ps}) is calculated as follows:

$$\text{Cost of preferred stock } (k_{ps}) = \frac{\text{preferred stock dividend}}{\text{net proceeds per preferred share}} \qquad (9\text{-}5)$$

The after-tax cost of common equity can be calculated in one of two ways. The first involves the use of the dividend growth model of stock valuation introduced in Chapter 7, i.e.,

$$\text{Cost of common stock } (k_{cs}) = \frac{\text{common stock dividend for year 1 } (D_1)}{\text{price of common stock}}$$

$$+ \frac{\text{growth rate}}{\text{in dividends } (g)} \qquad (9\text{-}8)$$

The second method for estimating the cost of common equity involves the use of the capital asset pricing model (CAPM), which we first discussed in Chapter 6. There we learned that the CAPM provides a basis for evaluating investors' required rates of return on common equity, r_m, using three variables:

1. The risk-free rate, r_f
2. The systematic risk of the common stock's returns relative to the market as a whole, or the stock's beta coefficient, β

3. The market-risk premium, which is equal to the difference in the expected rate of return for the market as a whole—that is, the expected rate of return for the "average security" minus the risk-free rate, $r_m - r_f$

The CAPM is written as follows:

$$k_c = r_f + \beta(r_m - r_f) \tag{9-9}$$

3 Calculate a firm's weighted average cost of capital.

We found that all of the variables on the right side of equation (9-9) could be obtained from public sources for larger, publicly traded firms. However, for privately held firms, the CAPM is more difficult to apply in the estimation of investor-required rates of return.

The firm's weighted average cost of capital, k_{wacc}, can be defined as follows:

$$k_{wacc} = w_d k_d (1 - T_c) + w_{ps} k_{ps} + w_{cs} k_{cs} + w_{ncs} k_{ncs} \tag{9-10}$$

where the terms in equation (9-10) are defined as follows:

k_{wacc} = the weighted average cost of capital
w_d = the weight associated with debt financing (i.e., proportion of the total capital that is financed using debt)
w_{ps} = the weight associated with preferred stock financing (i.e., the proportion of the total capital that is financed using preferred stock)
w_{cs} = the weight associated with common stock financing resulting from the retention of firm earnings (i.e., the proportion of the total capital that is financed by retaining and reinvesting earnings)
w_{ncs} = the weight associated with new common stock financing (i.e., the proportion of the total capital that is financed through the sale of common stock)
k_d = the cost of debt financing
k_{ps} = the cost of preferred stock financing
k_{cs} = the cost of common stock financing through the retention of earnings
k_{ncs} = the cost of common stock financing through the sale of a new issue of common stock
T_c = the corporate tax rate

Note that the w terms represent the market value weights associated with the firm's use of each of its sources of financing. We are calculating a weighted average of the costs of each of the firm's sources of capital where the weights reflect the firm's relative use of each source.

The weights used to calculate k_{wacc} should theoretically reflect the market values of each capital source as a fraction of the total market value of all capital sources (i.e., the market value of the firm). However, the analyst frequently finds the use of market value weights is impractical, either because the firm's securities are not publicly traded or because all capital sources are not used in proportion to their makeup of the firm's target capital structure in every financing episode. In these instances, we found that the weights should be the firm's long-term target financial mix.

4 Describe the procedure used by PepsiCo to estimate the cost of capital for a multidivisional firm.

The firm's weighted average cost of capital will reflect the operating or business risk of the firm's present set of investments and the financial risk attendant upon the way in which those assets are financed. Therefore, this cost of capital estimate is useful only for evaluating new investment opportunities that have similar business and financial risks. Remember that the primary determinant of the cost of capital for a particular investment is the risk of the investment itself, not the source of the capital. Multidivisional firms such as PepsiCo resolve this problem by calculating a different cost of capital for each of their major operating divisions.

5 Use the cost of capital to evaluate new investment opportunities.

If borrowers and lenders can freely choose where they borrow and lend money, why aren't interest rates the same all over the world? The answer lies in differences in the anticipated rates of inflation between countries. In fact, the international Fisher effect states that the differences in the rates of interest charged for the same loan in two different countries is equal to the difference in the anticipated rates of inflation in the countries. So, rates of interest are equal around the world only after we account for differences in rates of inflation between countries. Of course, the international Fisher effect does not hold exactly due to political and other risk considerations that can serve to restrict capital flow between countries. However, the Fisher effect does provide a useful starting point for understanding why there are differences in interest rates throughout the world.

6 Calculate equivalent interest rates for different countries.

Key Terms

Capital structure   245

Financial policy   236

Weighted average cost
of capital   235

Review Questions

All Review Questions and Study Problems are available in MyFinanceLab.

9-1. Define the term *cost of capital*.

9-2. Why do we calculate a firm's weighted average cost of capital?

9-3. In computing the cost of capital, which sources of capital do we consider?

9-4. How does a firm's tax rate affect its cost of capital? What is the effect of the flotation costs associated with a new security issue?

9-5. a. Distinguish between internal common equity and new common stock.

   b. Why is a cost associated with internal common equity?

   c. Describe the two approaches that could be used in computing the cost of common equity.

9-6. What might we expect to see in practice in the relative costs of different sources of capital?

Self-Test Problems

(The solutions to the following problems are provided at the end of the chapter.)

ST-1. (*Individual or component costs of capital*) Compute the cost for the following sources of financing:

   a. A $1,000 par value bond with a market price of $970 and a coupon interest rate of 10 percent. Flotation costs for a new issue would be approximately 5 percent. The bonds mature in 10 years and the corporate tax rate is 34 percent.

   b. A preferred stock selling for $100 with an annual dividend payment of $8. The flotation cost will be $9 per share. The company's marginal tax rate is 30 percent.

   c. Retained earnings totaling $4.8 million. The price of the common stock is $75 per share, and the dividend per share was $9.80 last year. The dividend is not expected to change in the future.

   d. New common stock when the most recent dividend was $2.80. The company's dividends per share should continue to increase at an 8 percent growth rate into the indefinite future. The market price of the stock is currently $53; however, flotation costs of $6 per share are expected if the new stock is issued.

ST-2. (*Weighted average cost of capital*) The capital structure for the Carion Corporation is provided here. The company plans to maintain its debt structure in the future. If the firm has a 5.5 percent after-tax cost of debt, a 13.5 percent cost of preferred stock, and an 18 percent cost of common stock, what is the firm's weighted average cost of capital?

CAPITAL STRUCTURE ($000)	
Bonds	$1,083
Preferred stock	268
Common stock	3,681
	$5,032

ST-3. (*Weighted average cost of capital*) ABBC Inc. operates a very successful chain of yogurt and coffee shops spread across the southwestern part of the United States and needs to raise funds for its planned expansion into the Northwest. The firm's balance sheet at the close of 2009 appeared as follows:

Cash	$ 2,010,000		
Accounts receivable	4,580,000		
Inventories	1,540,000	Long-term debt	$ 8,141,000
Net property, plant, and equipment	32,575,000	Common equity	32,564,000
Total assets	$40,705,000	Total debt and equity	$40,705,000

At present the firm's common stock is selling for a price equal to 2.5 times its book value, and the firm's bonds are selling at par. The company's management estimates that the market requires an

18 percent return on its common stock, the firm's bonds command a yield to maturity of 8 percent, and the firm faces a tax rate of 35 percent. At the end of the previous year ABBC's common stock was selling for a price of 2.5 times its book value, and its bonds were trading near their par value.

a. What does ABBC's capital structure look like?

b. What is ABBC's weighted average cost of capital?

c. If ABBC's stock price were to rise such that it sold at 3.5 times book value and the cost of equity fell to 15 percent, what would the firm's weighted average cost of capital be (assuming the cost of debt and tax rate do not change)?

ST-4. (*Divisional costs of capital and investment decisions*) Belton Oil and Gas Inc. is a Houston-based independent oil and gas firm. In the past Belton's managers have used a single firmwide cost of capital of 13 percent to evaluate new investments. However, the firm has long recognized that its exploration and production division is significantly more risky than the pipeline and transportation division. In fact, comparable firms to Belton's E&P division have equity betas of about 1.7, whereas distribution companies typically have equity betas of only 0.8. Given the importance of getting the cost of capital estimate as close to correct as possible, the firm's chief financial officer has asked you to prepare cost of capital estimates for each of the two divisions. The requisite information needed to accomplish your task is contained here:

◆ The cost of debt financing is 7 percent before taxes of 35 percent. However, if the E&P division were to borrow based on its projects alone, the cost of debt would probably be 9 percent, and the pipeline division could borrow at 5.5 percent. You may assume these costs of debt are after any flotation costs the firm might incur.

◆ The risk-free rate of interest on long-term U.S. Treasury bonds is currently 4.8 percent, and the market-risk premium has averaged 7.3 percent over the past several years.

◆ The E&P division adheres to a target debt ratio of 10 percent, whereas the pipeline division utilizes 40 percent borrowed funds.

◆ The firm has sufficient internally generated funds such that no new stock will have to be sold to raise equity financing.

a. Estimate the divisional costs of capital for the E&P and pipeline divisions.

b. What are the implications of using a company-wide cost of capital to evaluate new investment proposals in light of the differences in the costs of capital you estimated previously?

Study Problems

9-1. (*Individual or component costs of capital*) Compute the cost of the following:

a. A bond that has $1,000 par value (face value) and a contract or coupon interest rate of 11 percent. A new issue would have a flotation cost of 5 percent of the $1,125 market value. The bonds mature in 10 years. The firm's average tax rate is 30 percent and its marginal tax rate is 34 percent.

b. A new common stock issue that paid a $1.80 dividend last year. The par value of the stock is $15, and earnings per share have grown at a rate of 7 percent per year. This growth rate is expected to continue into the foreseeable future. The company maintains a constant dividend–earnings ratio of 30 percent. The price of this stock is now $27.50, but 5 percent flotation costs are anticipated.

c. Internal common equity when the current market price of the common stock is $43. The expected dividend this coming year should be $3.50, increasing thereafter at a 7 percent annual growth rate. The corporation's tax rate is 34 percent.

d. A preferred stock paying a 9 percent dividend on a $150 par value. If a new issue is offered, flotation costs will be 12 percent of the current price of $175.

e. A bond selling to yield 12 percent after flotation costs, but before adjusting for the marginal corporate tax rate of 34 percent. In other words, 12 percent is the rate that equates the net proceeds from the bond with the present value of the future cash flows (principal and interest).

9-2. (*Cost of equity*) Salte Corporation is issuing new common stock at a market price of $27. Dividends last year were $1.45 and are expected to grow at an annual rate of 6 percent forever. Flotation costs will be 6 percent of market price. What is Salte's cost of equity?

9-3. (*Cost of debt*) Belton is issuing a $1,000 par value bond that pays 7 percent annual interest and matures in 15 years. Investors are willing to pay $958 for the bond. Flotation costs will be 11 percent of market value. The company is in an 18 percent tax bracket. What will be the firm's after-tax cost of debt on the bond?

9-4. (*Cost of preferred stock*) The preferred stock of Julian Industries sells for $36 and pays $3.00 in dividends. The net price of the security after issuance costs is $32.50. What is the cost of capital for the preferred stock?

9-5. (*Cost of debt*) The Zephyr Corporation is contemplating a new investment to be financed 33 percent from debt. The firm could sell new $1,000 par value bonds at a net price of $945. The coupon interest rate is 12 percent, and the bonds would mature in 15 years. If the company is in a 34 percent tax bracket, what is the after-tax cost of capital to Zephyr for bonds?

9-6. (*Cost of preferred stock*) Your firm is planning to issue preferred stock. The stock sells for $115; however, if new stock is issued, the company would receive only $98. The par value of the stock is $100, and the dividend rate is 14 percent. What is the cost of capital for the stock to your firm?

9-7. (*Cost of internal equity*) Pathos Co.'s common stock is currently selling for $23.80. Dividends paid last year were $0.70. Flotation costs on issuing stock will be 10 percent of market price. The dividends and earnings per share are projected to have an annual growth rate of 15 percent. What is the cost of internal common equity for Pathos?

9-8. (*Cost of equity*) The common stock for the Bestsold Corporation sells for $58. If a new issue is sold, the flotation costs are estimated to be 8 percent. The company pays 50 percent of its earnings in dividends, and a $4 dividend was recently paid. Earnings per share 5 years ago were $5. Earnings are expected to continue to grow at the same annual rate in the future as during the past 5 years. The firm's marginal tax rate is 34 percent. Calculate the cost of (a) internal common equity and (b) external common equity.

9-9. (*Cost of debt*) Sincere Stationery Corporation needs to raise $500,000 to improve its manufacturing plant. It has decided to issue a $1,000 par value bond with a 14 percent annual coupon rate and a 10-year maturity. The investors require a 9 percent rate of return.

    a. Compute the market value of the bonds.

    b. What will the net price be if flotation costs are 10.5 percent of the market price?

    c. How many bonds will the firm have to issue to receive the needed funds?

    d. What is the firm's after-tax cost of debt if its average tax rate is 25 percent and its marginal tax rate is 34 percent?

9-10. (*Cost of debt*)

    a. Rework problem 9-9 as follows: Assume an 8 percent coupon rate. What effect does changing the coupon rate have on the firm's after-tax cost of capital?

    b. Why is there a change?

9-11. (*Divisional costs of capital*) LPT Inc. is an integrated oil company headquartered in Dallas, Texas. The company has three operating divisions: oil exploration and production (commonly referred to as E&P), pipelines, and refining. Historically, LPT did not spend a great deal of time thinking about the opportunity costs of capital for each of its divisions and used a company-wide weighted average cost of capital of 14 percent for all new capital investment projects. Recent changes in its businesses have made it abundantly clear to LPT's management that this is not a reasonable approach. For example, investors demand a much higher expected rate of return for exploration and production ventures than for pipeline investments. Although LPT's management agrees, in principle at least, that different operating divisions should face an opportunity cost of capital that reflects their individual risk characteristics, they are not in agreement about whether a move toward divisional costs of capital is a good idea based on practical considerations.

    a. Pete Jennings is the chief operating officer for the E&P division, and he is concerned that going to a system of divisional costs of capital may restrain his ability to undertake very promising exploration opportunities. He argues that the firm really should be concerned about finding those opportunities that offer the highest possible rate of return on invested capital. Pete contends that using the firm's scarce capital to take on the most promising projects would lead to the greatest increase in shareholder value. Do you agree with Pete? Why or why not?

    b. The pipeline division manager, Donna Selma, has long argued that charging her division the company-wide cost of capital of 14 percent severely penalizes her opportunities to increase shareholder value. Do you agree with Donna? Explain.

9-12. (*Weighted average cost of capital*) Crawford Enterprises is a publicly held company located in Arnold, Kansas. The firm began as a small tool and die shop but grew over its 35-year life to become a leading supplier of metal fabrication equipment used in the farm tractor industry. At the close of 2009 the firm's balance sheet appeared as follows:

Cash	$ 540,000		
Accounts receivable	4,580,000		
Inventories	7,400,000	Long-term debt	$12,590,000
Net property, plant, and equipment	18,955,000	Common equity	18,885,000
Total assets	$31,475,000	Total debt and equity	$31,475,000

At present the firm's common stock is selling for a price equal to its book value, and the firm's bonds are selling at par. Crawford's managers estimate that the market requires a 15 percent return on its common stock, the firm's bonds command a yield to maturity of 8 percent, and the firm faces a tax rate of 34 percent.

a. What is Crawford's weighted average cost of capital?

b. If Crawford's stock price were to rise such that it sold at 1.5 times book value, causing the cost of equity to fall to 13 percent, what would the firm's cost of capital be (assuming the cost of debt and tax rate do not change)?

9-13. (*Divisional costs of capital and investment decisions*) In May of this year Newcastle Mfg. Company's capital investment review committee received two major investment proposals. One of the proposals was put forth by the firm's domestic manufacturing division, and the other came from the firm's distribution company. Both proposals promise internal rates of return equal to approximately 12 percent. In the past Newcastle has used a single firmwide cost of capital to evaluate new investments. However, managers have long recognized that the manufacturing division is significantly more risky than the distribution division. In fact, comparable firms in the manufacturing division have equity betas of about 1.6, whereas distribution companies typically have equity betas of only 1.1. Given the size of the two proposals, Newcastle's management feels it can undertake only one, so it wants to be sure that it is taking on the more promising investment. Given the importance of getting the cost of capital estimate as close to correct as possible, the firm's chief financial officer has asked you to prepare cost of capital estimates for each of the two divisions. The requisite information needed to accomplish your task is contained here:

◆ The cost of debt financing is 8 percent before taxes of 35 percent. You may assume this cost of debt is after any flotation costs the firm might incur.

◆ The risk-free rate of interest on long-term U.S. Treasury bonds is currently 4.8 percent, and the market-risk premium has averaged 7.3 percent over the past several years.

◆ Both divisions adhere to target debt ratios of 40 percent.

◆ The firm has sufficient internally generated funds such that no new stock will have to be sold to raise equity financing.

a. Estimate the divisional costs of capital for the manufacturing and distribution divisions.

b. Which of the two projects should the firm undertake (assuming it cannot do both due to labor and other nonfinancial restraints)? Discuss.

Mini Case

The balance sheet that follows indicates the capital structure for Nealon Inc. Flotation costs are (a) 15 percent of market value for a new bond issue, and (b) $2.01 per share for preferred stock. The dividends for common stock were $2.50 last year and are projected to have an annual growth rate of 6 percent. The firm is in a 34 percent tax bracket. What is the weighted average cost of capital if the firm's finances are in the following proportions?

TYPE OF FINANCING	PERCENTAGE OF FUTURE FINANCING
Bonds (8%, $1,000 par, 16-year maturity)	38%
Preferred stock (5,000 shares outstanding, $50 par, $1.50 dividend)	15%
Common equity	47%
Total	100%

a. Market prices are $1,035 for bonds, $19 for preferred stock, and $35 for common stock. There will be sufficient internal common equity funding (i.e., retained earnings) available such that the firm does not plan to issue new common stock. Calculate the firm's weighted average cost of capital.

b. In part a we assumed that Nealon would have sufficient retained earnings such that it would not need to sell additional common stock to finance its new investments. Consider the situation now, when Nealon's retained earnings anticipated for the coming year are expected to fall short of the equity requirement of 47 percent of new capital raised. Consequently, the firm foresees the possibility that new common shares will have to be issued. To facilitate the sale of shares, Nealon's investment banker has advised management that they should expect a price discount of approximately 7 percent, or $2.45 per share. Under these terms, the new shares should provide net proceeds of about $32.55. What is Nealon's cost of equity capital when new shares are sold, and what is the weighted average cost of the added funds involved in the issuance of new shares?

Self-Test Solutions

The following notations are used in this group of problems:

k_d = the before-tax cost of debt

k_{ps} = the cost of preferred stock

k_{cs} = the cost of internal common equity

k_{ncs} = the cost of new common stock

T_c = the marginal tax rate

D_t = the dollar dividend per share, where D_0 is the most recently paid dividend and D_1 is the forthcoming dividend

P_0 = the market price of a security

NP_0 = the value of security less any flotation costs incurred in issuing the security

SS-1.

a. $$\$921.50 = \sum_{t=1}^{n} \frac{\$100}{(1 + k_d)^t} + \frac{\$1,000}{(1 + k_d)^{10}}$$

RATE	VALUE
11%	$940.90
k_d%	$921.50
12%	$887.00

$$\$19.40$$
$$\$53.90$$

$$k_d = 0.11 + \left(\frac{\$19.40}{\$53.90}\right)0.01 = 0.1136 = 11.36\%$$

$$k_{d(1-t)} = 11.36\%(1 - 0.34) = 7.50\%$$

b. $$k_{ps} = \frac{D}{NP_0}$$

$$k_{ps} = \frac{\$8}{\$100 - \$9} = 0.0879 = 8.79\%$$

c. $$k_{cs} = \frac{D_1}{P_0} + g$$

$$k_{cs} = \frac{\$9.80}{\$75} + 0\% = 0.1307 = 13.07\%$$

d. $$k_{ncs} = \frac{D_1}{NP_0} + g$$

$$k_{ncs} = \frac{\$2.80(1 + 0.08)}{\$53 - \$6} + 0.08 = 0.1443 = 14.43\%$$

SS-2.

Carion Corporation—Weighted Cost of Capital

	CAPITAL STRUCTURE	WEIGHTS	INDIVIDUAL COSTS	WEIGHTED COSTS
Bonds	$1,083	0.2152	5.5%	1.18%
Preferred stock	268	0.0533	13.5%	0.72%
Common stock	3,681	0.7315	18.0%	13.17%
	$5,032	1.0000		15.07%

SS-3. Given:

Cash	$ 2,010,000		
Accounts receivable	4,580,000		
Inventories	1,540,000	Long-term debt	$ 8,141,000
Net property, plant, and equipment	32,575,000	Common equity	32,564,000
Total assets	$40,705,000	Total debt and equity	$40,705,000
Cost of debt financing	8%		
Cost of equity	18%		
Tax rate	35%		
Market-to-book ratio	2.50		

a. *What does ABBC's capital structure look like?* Note that because the market-to-book ratio (market value of equity to book value of equity) is 2.5, the market value of the firm's equity is $2.5 \times \$32,564,000$, or $81,410,000. The market value of debt is assumed to equal its book value. Thus,

COMPONENT	MARKET VALUE BALANCE SHEET	PROPORTION	AFTER-TAX COST	PRODUCT
Long-term debt	$ 8,141,000	9%	4.88%	0.44%
Common equity	81,410,000	91%	18.00%	16.38%
	$89,551,000			16.82%

b. *What is ABBC's weighted average cost of capital?* Based on the above calculations, the answer is 16.8 percent.

c. *If ABBC's stock price were to rise such that it sold at 3.5 times book value and the cost of equity fell to 15 percent, what would the firm's weighted average cost of capital be (assuming the cost of debt and tax rate do not change)?*

Cost of debt financing	8%
Cost of equity	15%
Tax rate	35%
Market-to-book ratio	3.50

COMPONENT	MARKET VALUE BALANCE SHEET	PROPORTION	AFTER-TAX COST	PRODUCT
Long-term debt	$ 8,141,000	7%	5.20%	0.36%
Common equity	113,974,000	93%	15.00%	13.95%
	$122,115,000			14.31%

SS-4. Given:

	E&P DIVISION	PIPELINE DIVISION
Equity beta	1.7	0.8
Tax rate	35.0%	35.0%
Cost of debt	9.0%	5.5%
Debt ratio	10.0%	40.0%
Risk-free rate	4.8%	
Market-risk premium	7.3%	

a.

EXPLORATION AND DEVELOPMENT DIVISION			
COMPONENT	PROPORTION	AFTER-TAX COST	PRODUCT
Debt	10.0%	5.9%	0.6%
Equity	90.0%	17.2%	15.5%
			16.1%

PIPELINE DIVISION			
COMPONENT	PROPORTION	AFTER-TAX COST	PRODUCT
Debt	40.0%	3.6%	1.4%
Equity	60.0%	10.6%	6.4%
			7.8%

b. The very dramatic differences in the two divisional cost of capital estimates underscore the importance of carefully analyzing the capital costs that correspond as closely as possible to the riskiness of the use for which the funds are being requested. For example, using a 13 percent cost of capital for the firm as a whole leads to accepting E&P projects that fall well below the true cost of raising funds for these types of investments (16.1 percent). Similarly, using the 13 percent company-wide cost of capital will result in the rejection of value-enhancing investments that earn in excess of the 7.8 percent cost of capital that is appropriate to the pipeline division.

Chapter 10

Capital-Budgeting Techniques and Practice

Learning Objectives

After reading this chapter, you should be able to:

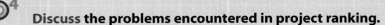

Discuss the difficulty encountered in finding profitable projects in competitive markets and the importance of the search.

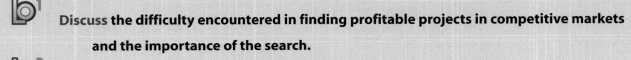

Determine whether a new project should be accepted or rejected using the payback period, the net present value, the profitability index, and the internal rate of return.

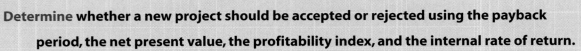

Explain how the capital-budgeting decision process changes when a dollar limit is placed on the capital budget.

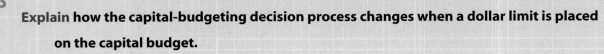

Discuss the problems encountered in project ranking.

Explain the importance of ethical considerations in capital-budgeting decisions.

Discuss the trends in the use of different capital-budgeting criteria.

Explain how foreign markets provide opportunities for finding new capital-budgeting projects.

Back in 1955, the Walt Disney Company changed the face of entertainment when it opened Disneyland, its first theme park in Anaheim, California, at a cost of $17.5 million. Since then Disney has opened theme parks in Orlando, Florida; Tokyo, Japan; Paris, France, and in September 2005, 香港迪士尼樂園, or Hong Kong Disneyland, was opened. This $3.5 billion project, with much of that money provided by the Hong Kong government, was opened in the hopes of reaching what has largely been an untapped Chinese market. For Disney, a market this size was simply too large to pass up.

Hong Kong Disneyland opened spectacularly, with more than 250,000 annual flowering plants, 15,000 canopy trees, plenty of rides and attractions, and, as its centerpiece, Sleeping Beauty's castle, complete with its trademark blue-pointed turret. To boost visitors, more attractions, including the Pirates of the Caribbean, It's a Small World, Peter Pan's Flight, Big Thunder Mountain Railroad, and the Haunted Mansion, were all added. Still, Hong Kong Disneyland cannot be termed a success, steadily losing money since it opened.

For Disney, keeping its theme parks and resorts division healthy is extremely important because this division accounts for over one-quarter of the company's revenues. Certainly, there are opportunities for Disney in China; with a population of 1.26 billion people, it accounts for 20 percent of the entire world's total population and Hong Kong Disneyland was supposed to provide Disney with a foothold in the potentially lucrative market in China. While Hong Kong Disneyland has not lived up to Disney's expectations, Disney has not given up and in 2009 a proposal by Disney to build Shanghai Disneyland, scheduled to open by 2014, received approval from the central government. Learning from its mistakes in Hong Kong, Disney's new proposed park would be much larger and easier for Chinese families to visit.

To say the least, with an investment of close to $6 billion, the outcome of this decision will have a major effect on Disney's future. Whether this was a good or bad decision, only time will tell. The question we will ask in this chapter is: How did Disney go about making this decision to enter the Chinese market and build Hong Kong Disneyland and, after losing money on its Hong Kong venture, how did it go about making the decision to build Shanghai Disneyland? The answer is that the company did it using the decision criteria we will examine in this chapter.

This chapter is actually the first of two chapters dealing with the process of decision making with respect to making investments in fixed assets—that is, should a proposed project be accepted or rejected? We will refer to this process as capital budgeting. In this chapter we will look at the methods used to evaluate new projects. In deciding whether to accept a new project, we will focus on free cash flows. Free cash flows represent the benefits generated from accepting a capital-budgeting proposal. We will assume we know what level of free cash flows is generated by a project and will work on determining whether that project should be accepted. In the following chapter, we will examine what a free cash flow is and how we measure it. We will also look at how risk enters into this process.

Finding Profitable Projects

 Discuss the difficulty encountered in finding profitable projects in competitive markets and the importance of the search.

Without question it is easier to *evaluate profitable projects or investments in fixed assets, a process referred to as* **capital budgeting**, than it is to find them. In competitive markets, generating ideas for profitable projects is extremely difficult. The competition is brisk for new profitable projects, and once they have been uncovered, competitors generally rush in, pushing down prices and profits. For this reason a firm must have a systematic strategy for generating capital-budgeting projects based on these ideas. Without this flow of new projects and ideas, the firm cannot grow or even survive for long. Instead, it will be forced to live off the profits from existing projects with limited lives. So where do these ideas come from for new products, or for ways to improve existing products or make them more profitable? The answer is from inside the firm—from everywhere inside the firm, in fact.

capital budgeting the process of decision making with respect to investments made in fixed assets—that is, should a proposed project be accepted or rejected.

Typically, a firm has a research and development (R&D) department that searches for ways of improving existing products or finding new products. These ideas may come from within the R&D department or may be based on referral ideas from executives, sales personnel, anyone in the firm, or even customers. For example, at Ford Motor Company before the 1990s, ideas for product improvements had typically been generated in Ford's R&D department. Unfortunately, this strategy was not enough to keep Ford from losing much of its market share to Japanese competitors. In an attempt to cut costs and improve product quality, Ford moved from strict reliance on an R&D department to seeking the input of employees at all levels for new ideas. Bonuses are now provided to workers for their cost-cutting suggestions, and assembly-line personnel who can see the production process from a hands-on point of view are now brought into the hunt for new projects. The effect on Ford has been positive and it helped Ford avoid the bankruptcy problems that befell GM and Chrysler. Although not all suggested projects prove to be profitable, many new ideas generated from within the firm turn out to be good ones.

Another way an existing product can be applied to a new market is illustrated by Kimberly-Clark, the manufacturer of Huggies disposable diapers. The company took its existing diaper product line, made the diapers more waterproof, and began marketing them as disposable swim pants called Little Swimmers. Sara Lee Hosiery boosted its market by expanding its offerings to appeal to more customers and more customer needs. For example, Sara Lee Hosiery introduced Sheer Energy pantyhose for support, Just My Size pantyhose aimed at larger-women sizes, and Silken Mist pantyhose in shades better suited for African American women.

Big investments such as these go a long way toward determining the future of the company, but they don't always work as planned. Just look at Burger King's development of its new french fries. It looked like a slam dunk great idea. Burger King took an uncooked french fry and coated it with a layer of starch that made it crunchier and kept it hot longer. The company spent over $70 million on the new fries, and even gave away 15 million orders on a "Free Fryday." Unfortunately, the product didn't go down with consumers, and Burger King was left to eat the loss. Given the size of the investment we're talking about, you can see why such a decision is so important.

Concept Check

1. Why is it so difficult to find an exceptionally profitable project?
2. Why is the search for new profitable projects so important?

CAUTIONARY TALE

FORGETTING PRINCIPLE 3: RISK REQUIRES A REWARD AND PRINCIPLE 4: MARKET PRICES ARE GENERALLY RIGHT

In the world of investing, you win some, you lose some. A common misconception is that high-risk investments always provide high returns. In fact, there are no guarantees. That's why consistently high returns paid year in and year out from a fund known for its exclusivity and its double-digit rates of return should have given investors pause.

In December of 2008 an investor in the fund, quoted in *Time* magazine, wrote, "All we knew was that my wife's entire family had been in the fund for decades and lived well on the returns, which ranged from 15% to 22%. It was all very secretive and tough to get into, which, looking back, was a brilliant strategy to lure suckers."

The fund in question is the one we now know as the Ponzi scheme orchestrated by Bernard "Bernie" Madoff. A Ponzi scheme is an investment that pays returns to investors from the money they originally invested along with money provided by new investors, rather than any profits earned. A Ponzi scheme is destined to collapse because the payments made exceed any earnings from the investment. Madoff's scam is considered to be the biggest Wall Street fraud ever attempted. Prosecutors estimate the size of the scam as somewhere between $50 billion to $54.8 billion.

In efficient markets, high returns are extremely difficult to achieve in good and bad years. Harry Markopolos, who once worked for one of Madoff's competitors, long suspected that Madoff's returns were simply too good to be true and wrote letters for at least a decade to the Securities and Exchange Commission trying to persuade them to investigate Madoff. As Markopolos observed, one thing that we know from efficient markets is that if an investment promises a return that looks too good to be true, it probably is.

Source: Robert Chew, "How I Got Screwed by Bernie Madoff," *Time*, December 15, 2008, http://www.time.com/time/business/article/0,8599,1866398,00.html.

Capital-Budgeting Decision Criteria

As we explained, when deciding whether to accept a new project, we focus on cash flows because cash flows represent the benefits generated from accepting a capital-budgeting proposal. In this chapter we assume a given cash flow is generated by a project and work on determining whether that project should be accepted.

We consider four commonly used criteria for determining the acceptability of investment proposals. The first one is the least sophisticated in that it does not incorporate the time value of money into its calculations; the other three do take it into account. For the time being, the problem of incorporating risk into the capital-budgeting decision is ignored. This issue is examined in Chapter 11. In addition, we assume that the appropriate discount rate, required rate of return, or cost of capital is given.

The Payback Period

The **payback period** is the *number of years needed to recover the initial cash outlay related to an investment*. Because this criterion measures how quickly the project will return its original investment, it deals with free cash flows, which measure the true timing of the benefits, rather than accounting profits. Unfortunately, it also ignores the time value of money and does not discount these free cash flows back to the present. Rather, the accept/reject criterion centers on whether the project's payback period is less than or equal to the firm's maximum desired payback period. For example, if a firm's maximum desired payback period is 3 years, and an investment proposal requires an initial cash outlay of $10,000 and yields the following set of annual cash flows, what is its payback period? Should the project be accepted?

YEAR	FREE CASH FLOW
1	$2,000
2	4,000
3	3,000
4	3,000
5	9,000

In this case, after 3 years the firm will have recaptured $9,000 on an initial investment of $10,000, leaving $1,000 of the initial investment to be recouped. During the fourth year $3,000 will be returned from this investment, and, assuming it will flow into the firm at a constant rate over the year, it will take one-third of the year ($1,000/$3,000) to recapture the remaining $1,000. Thus, the payback period on this project is 3⅓ years, which is more than the desired payback period. Using the payback period criterion, the firm would reject this project without even considering the $9,000 cash flow in year 5.

Although the payback period is used frequently, it does have some rather obvious drawbacks that are best demonstrated through the use of an example. Consider two investment projects, A and B, which involve an initial cash outlay of $10,000 each and produce the annual cash flows shown in Table 10-1. Both projects have a payback period of 2 years; therefore, in terms of the payback criterion both are equally acceptable. However, if we had our

TABLE 10-1	**Payback Period Example**	
	PROJECTS	
	A	**B**
Initial cash outlay	−$10,000	−$10,000
Annual free cash inflows		
Year 1	$ 6,000	$ 5,000
2	4,000	5,000
3	3,000	0
4	2,000	0
5	1,000	0

choice, it is clear we would select A over B, for at least two reasons. First, regardless of what happens after the payback period, project A returns more of our initial investment to us faster within the payback period ($6,000 in year 1 versus $5,000). Thus, because there is a time value of money, the cash flows occurring within the payback period should not be weighted equally, as they are. In addition, all cash flows that occur after the payback period are ignored. This violates the principle that investors desire more in the way of benefits rather than less—a principle that is difficult to deny, especially when we are talking about money. Finally, the choice of the maximum desired payback period is arbitrary. That is, there is no good reason why the firm should accept projects that have payback periods less than or equal to 3 years rather than 4 years.

Although these deficiencies limit the value of the payback period as a tool for investment evaluation, the payback period has several positive features. First, it deals with cash flows, as opposed to accounting profits, and therefore focuses on the true timing of the project's benefits and costs, even though it does not adjust the cash flows for the time value of money. Second, it is easy to visualize, quickly understood, and easy to calculate. Third, the payback period may make sense for the capital-constrained firm, that is, the firm that needs funds and is having problems raising additional money. These firms need cash flows early on to allow them to continue in business and to take advantage of future investments. Finally, although the payback period has serious deficiencies, it is often used as a rough screening device to eliminate projects whose returns do not materialize until later years. This method emphasizes the earliest returns, which in all likelihood are less uncertain, and provides for the liquidity needs of the firm. Although its advantages are certainly significant, its disadvantages severely limit its value as a discriminating capital-budgeting criterion.

Discounted Payback Period   To deal with the criticism that the payback period ignores the time value of money, some firms use the discounted payback period approach. The **discounted payback period** method is similar to the traditional payback period except that it uses discounted free cash flows rather than actual undiscounted free cash flows in calculating the payback period. The discounted payback period is defined as *the number of years needed to recover the initial cash outlay from the discounted free cash flows*. The accept-reject criterion then becomes whether the project's discounted payback period is less than or equal to the firm's maximum desired discounted payback period. Using the assumption that the required rate of return on projects A and B illustrated in Table 10-1 is 17 percent, the discounted cash flows from these projects are given in Table 10-2. On project A, after three years, only $74 of the initial outlay remains to be recaptured, whereas year 4 brings in a discounted free cash flow of $1,068. Thus, if the $1,068 comes in a constant rate over the year, it will take about 7/100s of the year ($74/$1,068) to recapture the remaining $74. The discounted payback period for project A is 3.07 years, calculated as follows:

$$\text{discounted payback period}_A = 3.0 + \$74/\$1{,}068 = 3.07 \text{ years}$$

If project A's discounted payback period was less than the firm's maximum desired discounted payback period, then project A would be accepted. Project B, however, does not have a discounted payback period because it never fully recovers the project's initial cash outlay, and thus should be rejected. The major problem with the discounted payback period comes in setting the firm's maximum desired discounted payback period. This is an arbitrary decision that affects which projects are accepted and which ones are rejected. In addition, cash flows that occur after the discounted payback period are not included in the analysis. Thus, although the discounted payback period is superior to the traditional payback period, in that it accounts for the time value of money in its calculations, its use is limited by the arbitrariness of the process used to select the maximum desired payback period. Moreover, as we will soon see, the net present value criterion is theoretically superior and no more difficult to calculate.

The Net Present Value

The **net present value (*NPV*)** of an investment proposal is equal to the *present value of its annual free cash flows less the investment's initial outlay*. The net present value can be expressed as follows:

discounted payback period the number of years it takes to recapture a project's initial outlay using discounted cash flows.

net present value (*NPV*) the present value of an investment's annual free cash flows less the investment's initial outlay.

TABLE 10-2 Discounted Payback, Period Example Using a 17 Percent Required Rate of Return

PROJECT A

Year	Undiscounted Free Cash Flows	Discounted Free Cash Flows at 17%	Cumulative Discounted Free Cash Flows
0	−$10,000	−$10,000	−$10,000
1	6,000	5,130	−4,870
2	4,000	2,924	−1,946
3	3,000	1,872	−74
4	2,000	1,068	994
5	1,000	456	1,450

PROJECT B

Year	Undiscounted Free Cash Flows	Discounted Free Cash Flows at 17%	Cumulative Discounted Free Cash Flows
0	−$10,000	−$10,000	−$10,000
1	5,000	4,275	−5,725
2	5,000	3,655	−2,070
3	0	0	−2,070
4	0	0	−2,070
5	0	0	−2,070

NPV = (present value of all the future annual free cash flows) − (the initial cash outlay)

$$= \frac{FCF_1}{(1+k)^1} + \frac{FCF_2}{(1+k)^2} + \cdots + \frac{FCF_n}{(1+k)^n} - IO \qquad (10\text{-}1)$$

where FCF_t = the annual free cash flow in time period t (this can take on either positive or negative values)

k = the firm's required rate of return or cost of capital[1]

IO = the initial cash outlay

n = the project's expected life

If any of the future free cash flows ($FCFs$) are cash outflows rather than inflows, say for example that there is another large investment in year 2 that results in the FCF_2 being negative, then the FCF_2 would take on a negative sign when calculating the project's net present value. In effect, the NPV can be thought of as the present value of the benefits minus the present value of the costs,

$$NPV = PV_{\text{benefits}} - PV_{\text{costs}}$$

A project's NPV measures the net value of the investment proposal in terms of today's dollars. Because all cash flows are discounted back to the present, comparing the difference between the present value of the annual cash flows and the investment outlay recognizes the time value of money. The difference between the present value of the annual cash flows and the initial outlay determines the net value of the investment proposal. Whenever the project's NPV is greater than or equal to zero, we will accept the project; whenever the NPV is negative, we will reject the project. If the project's NPV is zero, then it returns the required rate of return and should be accepted. This accept/reject criterion is represented as follows:

$NPV \geq 0.0$: accept

$NPV < 0.0$: reject

REMEMBER YOUR PRINCIPLES

Principle The final three capital-budgeting criteria all incorporate **Principle 2: Money Has a Time Value** in their calculations. If we are to make rational business decisions, we must recognize that money has a time value. In examining the following three capital-budgeting techniques, you will notice that this principle is the driving force behind each of them.

---

[1]The required rate of return or cost of capital is the rate of return necessary to justify raising funds to finance the project or, alternatively, the rate of return necessary to maintain the firm's current market price per share. These terms were defined in detail in Chapter 9.

Realize, however, that the worth of the *NPV* calculation is a function of the accuracy of the cash flow predictions.

The following example illustrates the use of *NPV* as a capital-budgeting criterion.

EXAMPLE 10.1

Ski-Doo is considering new machinery that would reduce manufacturing costs associated with its Mach Z snowmobile for which the free cash flows are shown in Table 10-3. If the firm has a 12 percent required rate of return, the present value of the free cash flow is $47,675, as calculated in Table 10-4. Subtracting the $40,000 initial outlay leaves an *NPV* of $7,675. Because this value is greater than zero, the *NPV* criterion indicates that the project should be accepted.

The *NPV* criterion is the capital-budgeting decision tool we find most favorable for several reasons. First of all, it deals with free cash flows rather than accounting profits. In this regard it is sensitive to the true timing of the benefits resulting from the project. Moreover, recognizing the time value of money allows the benefits and costs to be compared in a logical manner. Finally, because projects are accepted only if a positive *NPV* is associated with them, the acceptance of a project using this criterion will increase the value of the firm, which is consistent with the goal of maximizing the shareholders' wealth.

The disadvantage of the *NPV* method stems from the need for detailed, long-term forecasts of the free cash flows accruing from the project's acceptance. Despite this drawback, the *NPV* is the most theoretically correct criterion that we will examine. The following example provides an additional illustration of its application.

TABLE 10-3 Ski-Doo's Investment in New Machinery and Its Associated Free Cash Flows

	Free Cash Flow
Initial outlay	−$40,000
Inflow year 1	15,000
Inflow year 2	14,000
Inflow year 3	13,000
Inflow year 4	12,000
Inflow year 5	11,000

CALCULATOR SOLUTION (USING A TEXAS INSTRUMENTS BA II PLUS):

Data and Key Input	Display
CF ; −40,000; ENTER	CF0 = −40,000.
↓ ; 15,000; ENTER	C01 = 15,000.
↓ ; 1; ENTER	F01 = 1.00
↓ ; 14,000; ENTER	C02 = 14,000.
↓ ; 1; ENTER	F02 = 1.00
↓ ; 13,000; ENTER	C03 = 13,000.
↓ ; 1; ENTER	F03 = 1.00
↓ ; 12,000; ENTER	C04 = 12,000.
↓ ; 1; ENTER	F04 = 1.00
↓ ; 11,000; ENTER	C05 = 11,000.
↓ ; 1; ENTER	F05 = 1.00
NPV	I = 0.00
12; ENTER	I = 12.00
↓ ; CPT	NPV = 7,675.

TABLE 10-4 Calculating the *NPV* of Ski-Doo's Investment in New Machinery

	PRESENT VALUE				
	Free Cash Flow	×	Factor at 12 Percent	=	Present Value
Inflow year 1	$15,000	×	$\dfrac{1}{(1 + 0.12)^1}$	=	$ 13,393
Inflow year 2	14,000	×	$\dfrac{1}{(1 + 0.12)^2}$	=	11,161
Inflow year 3	13,000	×	$\dfrac{1}{(1 + 0.12)^3}$	=	9,253
Inflow year 4	12,000	×	$\dfrac{1}{(1 + 0.12)^4}$	=	7,626
Inflow year 5	11,000	×	$\dfrac{1}{(1 + 0.12)^5}$	=	6,242
Present value of free cash flows					$ 47,675
Initial outlay					−40,000
Net present value					$ 7,675

EXAMPLE 10.2

A firm is considering the purchase of a new computer system, which will cost $30,000 initially, to aid in credit billing and inventory management. The free cash flows resulting from this project are provided below:

	FREE CASH FLOW
Initial outlay	−$30,000
Inflow year 1	15,000
Inflow year 2	15,000
Inflow year 3	15,000

The required rate of return demanded by the firm is 10 percent. To determine the system's *NPV*, the 3-year $15,000 cash flow annuity is first discounted back to the present at 10 percent. The present value of the $15,000 annuity can be found using a calculator (as is done the margin), or by using the relationship from equation (5-4),

$$PV = PMT \left[\frac{1 - \frac{1}{(1 + k)^n}}{k} \right].$$ Using the mathematical relationship we get:

$$PV = \$15,000 \left[\frac{1 - \frac{1}{(1 + 0.10)^3}}{0.10} \right] = \$15,000 \ (2.4869) = \$37,303$$

Seeing that the cash inflows have been discounted back to the present, they can now be compared with the initial outlay because both of the flows are now stated in terms of today's dollars. Subtracting the initial outlay ($30,000) from the present value of the cash inflows ($37,303), we find that the system's *NPV* is $7,303. Because the *NPV* on this project is positive, the project should be accepted.

CALCULATOR SOLUTION
STEP 1
Calculate payment value of inflows

Data Input	Function key
3	N
10	I/Y
−15,000	PMT
0	FV

Function Key	Answer
CPT	
PV	37,303

STEP 2
Subtract initial outlay from present value of inflows
$ 37,303
−30,000
$ 7,303

Using Spreadsheets to Calculate the Net Present Value

Although we can calculate the *NPV* by hand or with a financial calculator, it is more commonly done with the help of a spreadsheet. Just as with the keystroke calculations on a financial calculator, a spreadsheet can make easy work of *NPV* calculations. The only real glitch here is that in Excel, along with most other spreadsheets, the =*NPV* function only calculates the present value of only the future cash flows and ignores the initial outlay in its *NPV* calculations. Sounds strange? Well, it is. It is essentially just a carryforward of an error in one of the first spreadsheets. That means that the actual *NPV* is the Excel-calculated *NPV*, minus the initial outlay:

Actual *NPV* = Excel-calculated *NPV* − initial outlay

This can be input into a spreadsheet cell as:

=*NPV*(rate,inflow 1,inflow 2, . . . inflow 29)-initial outlay

CAN YOU DO IT?

DETERMINING THE *NPV* OF A PROJECT

Determine the *NPV* for a new project that costs $7,000, is expected to produce 10 years' worth of annual free cash flows of $1,000 per year, and has a required rate of return of 5 percent.
   (The solution can be found on page 273.)

Looking back at the Ski-Doo example in Table 10-3, we can use a spreadsheet to calculate the net present value of the investment in machinery as long as we remember to subtract the initial outlay in order to get the correct number.

	A	B	C	D	E
2	**Spreadsheets and NPV – the Ski-Doo Example**				
3					
4	Looking at the example in Table 10-3, given a 12 percent				
5	discount rate and the following after-tax cash flows, the				
6	Net Present Value could be calculated as follows:				
7					
8			rate (*k*) =	12%	
9					
10			Year	Cash Flow	
11			Initial Outlay	($40.000)	
12			1	$15.000	
13			2	$14.000	
14			3	$13.000	
15			4	$12.000	
16			5	$11.000	
17					
18		NPV =	$7,674.63		
19					
20	Excel formula: =NPV(rate,inflow1,inflow2, …,inflow29)				
21					
22	Again, from the Excel NPV calculation we must then				
23	subtract out the initial outlay in order to calculate the				
24	actual NPV.				
25					
26					
27					

Entered value in cell c18: =NPV(D8,D12:D16)−40000

The Profitability Index (Benefit–Cost Ratio)

profitability index (*PI*) or benefit–cost ratio the ratio of the present value of an investment's future free cash flows to the investment's initial outlay.

The **profitability index (*PI*), or benefit–cost ratio**, is the *ratio of the present value of the future free cash flows to the initial outlay*. Although the *NPV* investment criterion gives a measure of the absolute dollar desirability of a project, the profitability index provides a relative measure of an investment proposal's desirability—that is, the ratio of the present value of its future net benefits to its initial cost. The profitability index can be expressed as follows:

$$PI = \frac{\text{present value of all the future annual free cash flows}}{\text{initial cash outlay}}$$

$$= \frac{\dfrac{FCF_1}{(1 + k)^1} + \dfrac{FCF_2}{(1 + k)^2} + \cdots + \dfrac{FCF_n}{(1 + k)^n}}{IO} \tag{10-2}$$

where FCF_t = the annual free cash flow in time period t (this can take on either positive or negative values)

k = the firm's required rate of return or cost of capital

IO = the initial cash outlay

n = the project's expected life

The decision criterion is to accept the project if the *PI* is greater than or equal to 1.00 and to reject the project if the *PI* is less than 1.00.

$PI \geq 1.0$: accept
$PI < 1.0$: reject

Looking closely at this criterion, we see that it yields the same accept/reject decision as the *NPV* criterion. Whenever the present value of the project's free cash flows is greater than the initial cash outlay, the project's *NPV* will be positive, signaling a decision to accept. When this is true, then the project's *PI* will also be greater than 1 because the present value

DID YOU GET IT?

DETERMINING THE *NPV* OF A PROJECT

You were asked to determine the *NPV* for a project with an initial outlay of $7,000 and free cash flows in years 1 through 10 of $1,000, given a 5 percent required rate of return.

> *NPV* = (present value of all future free cash flows) − (initial outlay)

1. **Using the Mathematical Formulas.**

    STEP 1 Determine the present value of the future cash flows.

    Substituting these example values in equation (5-4), we find

    $$PV = \$1,000 \left[\frac{1 - \dfrac{1}{(1 + 0.05)^{10}}}{0.05} \right]$$

    = $1,000 [(1 − 1/1.62889463)/0.05]

    = $1,000 [(1 − 0.61391325)/0.05]

    = $1,000 (7.72173493) = $7,721.73

    STEP 2 Subtract the initial outlay from the present value of the free cash flows.

    $7,721.73
    − $7,000.00
     $ 721.73

2. **Using a Financial Calculator.**

    STEP 1 Determine the present value of the future cash flows.

Data Input	Function Key
10	N
5	I/Y
−1,000	PMT
0	FV

Function Key	Answer
CPT	
PV	7,721.73

STEP 2 Subtract the initial outlay from present value of the free cash flows.

$7,721.73
− $7,000.00
 $ 721.73

Alternatively, you could use the CF button on your calculator (using a TI BA II Plus).

Data and Key Input	Display
CF ; 2nd ; CE/C	CF0 = 0. (this clears out any past cash flows)
−7,000; ENTER	CF0 = −7,000.
↓ ; 1,000; ENTER	C01 = 1,000.
↓ ; 10; ENTER	F01 = 10.00
NPV	I = 0.
5; ENTER	I = 5.00
↓	NPV = 0.
CPT	NPV = 721.73

of the free cash flows (the *PI*'s numerator) is greater than the initial outlay (the *PI*'s denominator). Thus, these two decision criteria will always yield the same decision, although they will not necessarily rank acceptable projects in the same order. This problem of conflicting ranking is dealt with at a later point.

Because the *NPV* and *PI* criteria are essentially the same, they have the same advantages over the other criteria examined. Both employ free cash flows, recognize the timing of the cash flows, and are consistent with the goal of maximizing shareholders' wealth. The major disadvantage of the *PI* criterion, similar to the *NPV* criterion, is that it requires long, detailed free cash flow forecasts.

EXAMPLE 10.3

A firm with a 10 percent required rate of return is considering investing in a new machine with an expected life of 6 years. The free cash flows resulting from this investment are given in Table 10-5. Discounting the project's future net free cash flows back to the present yields a present value of $53,682; dividing this value by the initial outlay of $50,000 yields a profitability index of 1.0736, as shown in Table 10-6. This tells us that the present value of the future benefits accruing from this project is 1.0736 times the level of the initial outlay. Because the profitability index is greater than 1.0, the project should be accepted.

TABLE 10-5   The Free Cash Flows Associated with an Investment in New Machinery

	Free Cash Flow
Initial outlay	−$50,000
Inflow year 1	15,000
Inflow year 2	8,000
Inflow year 3	10,000
Inflow year 4	12,000
Inflow year 5	14,000
Inflow year 6	16,000

TABLE 10-6   Calculating the *PI* of an Investment in New Machinery

	Free Cash Flow	×	Present Value Factor at 10 Percent	=	Present Value
Inflow year 1	15,000	×	$\dfrac{1}{(1 + .10)^1}$	=	13,636
Inflow year 2	8,000	×	$\dfrac{1}{(1 + .10)^2}$	=	6,612
Inflow year 3	10,000	×	$\dfrac{1}{(1 + .10)^3}$	=	7,513
Inflow year 4	12,000	×	$\dfrac{1}{(1 + .10)^4}$	=	8,196
Inflow year 5	14,000	×	$\dfrac{1}{(1 + .10)^5}$	=	8,693
Inflow year 6	16,000	×	$\dfrac{1}{(1 + .10)^6}$	=	9,032

$$PI = \frac{\dfrac{FCF_1}{(1 + k)^1} + \dfrac{FCF_2}{(1 + k)^2} + \cdots + \dfrac{FCF_n}{(1 + k)^n}}{IO}$$

$$= \frac{\$13,636 + \$6,612 + \$7,513 + \$8,196 + \$8,693 + \$9,032}{\$50,000}$$

$$= \frac{\$53,682}{\$50,000}$$

$$= 1.0736$$

The Internal Rate of Return

internal rate of return (*IRR*) the rate of return that the project earns. For computational purposes, the internal rate of return is defined as the discount rate that equates the present value of the project's free cash flows with the project's initial cash outlay.

The **internal rate of return (*IRR*)** attempts to answer the question, what rate of return does this project earn? For computational purposes, the internal rate of return is defined as *the discount rate that equates the present value of the project's free cash flows with the project's initial cash outlay*. Mathematically, the internal rate of return is defined as the value *IRR* in the following equation:

IRR = the rate of return that equates the present value of the project's free cash flows with the initial outlay

$$IO = \frac{FCF_1}{(1 + IRR\,\%)^1} + \frac{FCF_2}{(1 + IRR\,\%)^2} + \cdots + \frac{FCF_n}{(1 + IRR\,\%)^n} \qquad (10\text{-}3)$$

where FCF_t = the annual free cash flow in time period t (this can take on either positive or negative values)

IO = the initial cash outlay

n = the project's expected life

IRR = the project's internal rate of return

In effect, the *IRR* is analogous to the concept of the yield to maturity for bonds, which was examined in Chapter 7. In other words, a project's *IRR* is simply the rate of return that the project earns.

The decision criterion is to accept the project if the *IRR* is greater than or equal to the firm's required rate of return. We reject the project if its *IRR* is less than the required rate of return. This accept/reject criterion can be stated as

IRR ≥ firm's required rate of return or cost of capital: accept
IRR < firm's required rate of return or cost of capital: reject

If the *IRR* on a project is equal to the firm's required rate of return, then the project should be accepted because the firm is earning the rate that its shareholders are demanding. By contrast, accepting a project with an *IRR* below the investors' required rate of return will decrease the firm's stock price.

If the *NPV* is positive, then the *IRR* must be greater than the required rate of return, *k*. Thus, all the discounted cash flow criteria are consistent and will result in similar accept/reject decisions. One disadvantage of the *IRR* relative to the *NPV* deals with the implied reinvestment rate assumptions made by these two methods. The *NPV* assumes that cash flows over the life of the project are reinvested back in projects that earn the required rate of return. That is, if we have a mining project with a 10-year expected life that produces a $100,000 cash flow at the end of the second year, the *NPV* technique assumes that this $100,000 is reinvested over years 3 though 10 at the required rate of return. The use of the *IRR*, however, implies that cash flows over the life of the project can be reinvested at the *IRR*. Thus, if the mining project we just looked at has a 40 percent *IRR*, the use of the *IRR* implies that the $100,000 cash flow that is received at the end of year 2 could be reinvested at 40 percent over the remaining life of the project. In effect, *the NPV method implicitly assumes that cash flows over the life of the project can be reinvested at the project's required rate of return, whereas the use of the IRR method implies that these cash flows could be reinvested at the IRR.* The better assumption is the one made by the *NPV*—that the cash flows can be reinvested at the required rate of return because they can either be (1) returned in the form of dividends to shareholders, who demand the required rate of return on their investments, or (2) reinvested in a new investment project. If these cash flows are invested in a new project, then they are simply substituting for external funding on which the required rate of return is again demanded. Thus, the opportunity cost of these funds is the required rate of return.

The bottom line of all this is that the *NPV* method makes the best reinvestment rate assumption, and, as such, is superior to the *IRR* method. Why should we care which method is used if both methods result in similar accept/reject decisions? The answer, as we will see, is that although they may result in the same accept/reject decision, they may rank projects differently in terms of desirability.

Computing the *IRR* with a Financial Calculator   With today's calculators, determining an *IRR* is merely a matter of a few keystrokes. In Chapter 5, whenever we were solving time value of money problems for *i*, we were really solving for the *IRR*. For instance, in Chapter 5 when we solved for the rate at which $100 must be compounded annually for it to grow to $179.10 in 10 years, we were actually solving for that problem's *IRR*. Thus, with financial calculators we need only input the initial outlay, the cash flows, and their timing and then input the function key "I/Y" or the "IRR" button to calculate the *IRR*. On some calculators it is necessary to press the compute key, CPT, before pressing the function key to be calculated.

Computing the *IRR* with a Spreadsheet   Calculating the *IRR* using a spreadsheet is extremely simple. Once the cash flows have been entered on the spreadsheet, all you need to do is input the Excel *IRR* function into a spreadsheet cell and let the spreadsheet do the calculations for you. Of course, at least one of the cash flows must be positive and at least one must be negative. The *IRR* function to be input into a spreadsheet cell is: **=IRR(values)**, where "values" is simply the range of cells in which the cash flows including the initial outlay are stored.

	A	B	C	D	E
1					
2		**Spreadsheets and the IRR**			
3					
4	Three investment proposals being examined have the following				
5	cash flows:				
6					
7	Year	Project A	Project B	Project C	
8	Initial Outlay	($10.000)	($10.000)	($10.000)	
9	1	3.362	0	1.000	
10	2	3.362	0	3.000	
11	3	3.362	0	6.000	
12	4	3.362	13.605	7.000	
13					
14	IRR=	13.001%	8.000%	19.040%	
15					
16	Excel Formula: =IRR(values)				
17					
18	where:				
19	values =	the range of cells where the cash flows are stored.			
20		Note: There must be at least one positive and one			
21		negative cash flow.			

Entered value in cell B14:=IRR(B8:B12)
Entered value in cell C14:=IRR(C8:C12)
Entered value in cell D14:=IRR(D8:D12)

Computing the *IRR* for Uneven Cash Flows with a Financial Calculator   Solving for the *IRR* when the cash flows are uneven is quite simple with a calculator: One need only key in the initial cash outlay, the cash flows, and their timing and press the "IRR" button. Let's take a look at how you might solve a problem with uneven cash flows using a financial calculator. Every calculator works a bit differently, so you'll want to be familiar with how to input data into yours, but that being said, they all work essentially the same way. As you'd expect, you will enter all the cash flows, then solve for the project's *IRR*. With a Texas Instruments BA II Plus calculator, you begin by hitting the CF button. Then, CFo indicates the initial outlay, which you'll want to give a negative value; C01 is the first free cash flow; and F01 is the number of years in which the first free cash flow appears. Thus, if the free cash flows in years 1, 2, and 3 are all $1,000, then F01 = 3. C02 then becomes the second free cash flow, and F02 is the number of years in which the second free cash flow appears. You'll notice that you move between the different cash flows using the down arrow (↓) located on the top row of your calculator. Once you have inputted the initial outlay and all the free cash flows, you then calculate the project's *IRR* by hitting the "IRR" button followed by "CPT," the compute button. Let's look at a quick example. Consider the following investment proposal:

Initial outlay	−$5,000
FCF in year 1	2,000
FCF in year 2	2,000
FCF in year 3	3,000

CALCULATOR SOLUTION
(USING A TI BA II PLUS):

Data and Key Input	Display
CF ;−5,000; ENTER	CFo = −5,000.00
↓ 2,000; ENTER	C01 = 2,000.00
↓ 2; ENTER	F01 = 2.00
↓ 3,000; ENTER	C02 = 3,000.00
↓ 1; ENTER	F02 = 1.00
IRR ; CPT	IRR = 17.50%

CAN YOU DO IT?

DETERMINING THE *IRR* OF A PROJECT

Determine the *IRR* for a new project that costs $5,019 and is expected to produce 10 years' worth of annual free cash flows of $1,000 per year.

(The solution can be found on page 277.)

EXAMPLE 10.4

Consider the following investment proposal:

Initial outlay	−$10,010
FCF in year 1	1,000
FCF in year 2	3,000
FCF in year 3	6,000
FCF in year 4	7,000

**CALCULATOR SOLUTION
(USING A TI BA II PLUS)**

Data and Key Input	Display
CF ; −10,010; ENTER	CF0 = −10,010.00
↓ 1,000; ENTER	C01 = 1,000.00
↓ 1; ENTER	F01 = 1.00
↓ 3,000; ENTER	C02 = 3,000.00
↓ 1; ENTER	F02 = 1.00
↓ 6,000; ENTER	C03 = 6,000.00
↓ 1; ENTER	F03 = 1.00
↓ 7,000; ENTER	C04 = 7,000.00
↓ 1; ENTER	F04 = 1.00
IRR ; CPT	IRR = 19.00%

Viewing the *NPV–IRR* Relationship: The Net Present Value Profile

Perhaps the easiest way to understand the relationship between the *IRR* and the *NPV* value is to view it graphically through the use of a **net present value profile**. A net present value profile is simply *a graph showing how a project's NPV changes as the discount rate changes*. To graph a project's net present value profile, you simply need to determine the project's *NPV*, first using a 0 percent discount rate, then slowly increasing the discount rate until a representative curve has been plotted. How does the *IRR* enter into the net present value profile? The *IRR* is the discount rate at which the *NPV* is zero.

Let's look at an example of a project that involves an after-tax initial outlay of $105,517 with free cash flows expected to be $30,000 per year over the project's 5-year life.

net present value profile a graph showing how a project's *NPV* changes as the discount rate changes.

DID YOU GET IT?

DETERMINING THE *IRR* OF A PROJECT

You were asked to determine the *IRR* for a project with an initial outlay of $5,019 and free cash flows in years 1 through 10 of $1,000.

1. **Using a Financial Calculator.** Substituting in a financial calculator, we are solving for *i*.

Data Input	Function Key
10	N
−5,019	PV
1,000	PMT
0	FV

Function Key	Answer
CPT	
I/Y	15

Alternatively, you could use the CF button on your calculator (using a TI BA II Plus):

Data and Key Input	Display
CF ; −5,019; ENTER	CF0 = −5,019.
↓ ; 1,000; ENTER	C01 = 1,000.
↓ ; 10; ENTER	F01 = 10.00
IRR; CPT	IRR = 15

2. **Using Excel.** Using Excel, the *IRR* could be calculated using the = **IRR** function.

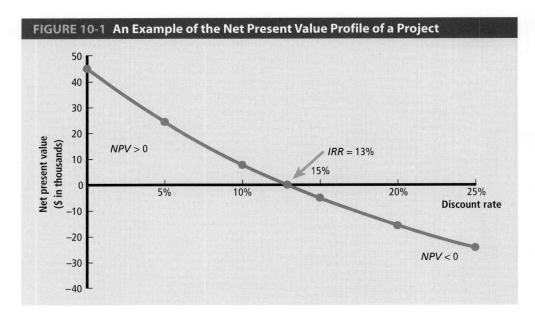

FIGURE 10-1   An Example of the Net Present Value Profile of a Project

Calculating the *NPV* of this project at several different discount rates results in the following:

Discount Rate	Project's *NPV*
0%	$44,483
5%	$24,367
10%	$ 8,207
13%	$ 0
15%	−$ 4,952
20%	−$15,798
25%	−$24,839

Plotting these values yields the net present value profile in Figure 10-1.

Where is the *IRR* in this figure? Recall that the *IRR* is the discount rate that equates the present value of the inflows with the present value of the outflows; thus, the *IRR* is the point at which the *NPV* is equal to zero—in this case, 13 percent. This is exactly the process that we use in computing the *IRR* for a series of uneven cash flows—we simply calculate the project's *NPV* using different discount rates and the discount rate that makes the *NPV* equal to zero is the project's *IRR*.

From the net present value profile you can easily see how a project's *NPV* varies inversely with the discount rate—as the discount rate is raised, the *NPV* drops. By analyzing a project's net present value profile, you can also see how sensitive the project is to your selection of the discount rate. The more sensitive the *NPV* is to the discount rate, the more important it is that you use the correct one in your calculations.

Complications with the *IRR*: Multiple Rates of Return

Although any project can have only one *NPV* and one *PI*, a single project under certain circumstances can have more than one *IRR*. The reason for this can be traced to the calculations involved in determining the *IRR*. Equation (10-3) states that the *IRR* is the discount rate that equates the present value of the project's future net cash flows with the project's initial outlay:

$$IO = \frac{FCF_1}{(1 + IRR)^1} + \frac{FCF_2}{(1 + IRR)^2} + \cdots + \frac{FCF_n}{(1 + IRR)^n} \tag{10-3}$$

However, because equation (10-3) is a polynomial of a degree *n*, it has *n* solutions. Now if the initial outlay (*IO*) is the only negative cash flow and all the annual free cash flows (*FCF*) are positive, then all but one of these *n* solutions is either a negative or imaginary number and there is no problem. But problems occur when there are sign reversals in the cash flow stream; in fact, there can be as many solutions as there are sign reversals. A normal, or "conventional,"

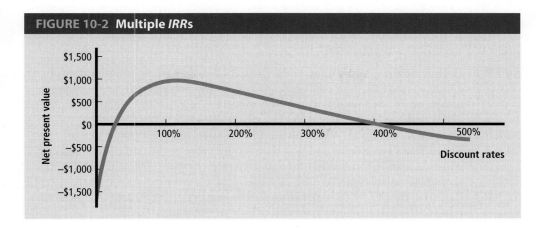

FIGURE 10-2 Multiple *IRR*s

pattern with a negative initial outlay and positive annual free cash flows after that (−, +, +, +, . . . , +) has only one sign reversal, hence, only one positive *IRR*. However, an "unconventional" pattern with more than one sign reversal can have more than one *IRR*.

	FREE CASH FLOW
Initial outlay	−$ 1,600
Year 1 free cash flow	+$10,000
Year 2 free cash flow	−$10,000

In this pattern of cash flows, there are two sign reversals: one from −$1,600 to +$10,000 and one from +$10,000 to −$10,000, so there can be as many as two positive *IRR*s that will make the present value of the free cash flows equal to the initial outlay. In fact, two internal rates of return solve this problem: 25 percent and 400 percent. Graphically, what we are solving for is the discount rate that makes the project's *NPV* equal to zero. As Figure 10-2 illustrates, this occurs twice.

Which solution is correct? The answer is that neither solution is valid. Although each fits the definition of *IRR*, neither provides any insight into the true project returns. In summary, when there is more than one sign reversal in the cash flow stream, the possibility of multiple *IRR*s exists, and the normal interpretation of the *IRR* loses its meaning. In this case, try the *NPV* criterion instead.

The Modified Internal Rate of Return (*MIRR*)[2]

Problems with multiple rates of return and the reinvestment rate assumption make the *NPV* superior to the *IRR* as a capital-budgeting technique. However, because of the ease of interpretation, the *IRR* is preferred by many practitioners. Recently, a new technique, the modified internal rate of return (*MIRR*), has gained popularity as an alternative to the *IRR* method because it avoids multiple *IRR*s and allows the decision maker to directly specify the appropriate reinvestment rate. As a result, the *MIRR* provides the decision maker with the intuitive appeal of the *IRR* coupled with an improved reinvestment rate assumption.

Is this really a problem? The answer is yes. One of the problems of the *IRR* is that it creates unrealistic expectations both for the corporation and for its shareholders. For example, the consulting firm McKinsey & Company examined one firm that approved 23 major projects over 5 years based on average *IRR*s of 77 percent.[3] However, when McKinsey adjusted the reinvestment rate on these projects to the firm's required rate of return, this return rate fell to 16 percent. The ranking of the projects also changed with the top-ranked project falling to the 10th most attractive project. Moreover, the returns on the highest-ranked projects with *IRR*s of 800, 150, and 130 percent dropped to 15, 23, and 22 percent, respectively, once the reinvestment rate was adjusted downward.

---

[2]This section is relatively complex and can be omitted without loss of continuity.
[3]John C. Kellecher and Justin J. MacCormack, "Internal Rate of Return: A Cautionary Tale," *McKinsey Quarterly*, September 24, 2004, pp. 1–4.

The driving force behind the *MIRR* is the assumption that all free cash flows over the life of the project are reinvested at the required rate of return until the termination of the project. Thus, to calculate the *MIRR*, we:

STEP 1 Determine the present value of the project's free cash *out*flows. We do this by discounting all the free cash *out*flows back to the present at the required rate of return. If the initial outlay is the only free cash *out*flow, then the initial outlay is the present value of the free cash *out*flows.

STEP 2 Determine the future value of the project's free cash *in*flows. Take all the annual free cash *in*flows and find their future value at the end of the project's life, compounded forward at the required rate of return. We will call this the project's *terminal value*, or *TV*.

STEP 3 Calculate the *MIRR*. The *MIRR* is the discount rate that equates the present value of the free cash outflows with the project's terminal value.[4]

Mathematically, the modified internal rate of return is defined as the value of *MIRR* in the following equation:

$$PV_{\text{outflows}} = \frac{TV_{\text{inflows}}}{(1 + MIRR)^n} \tag{10-4}$$

where PV_{outflows} = the present value of the project's free cash *out*flows
TV_{inflows} = the project's terminal value, calculated by taking all the annual free cash *in*flows and finding their future value at the end of the project's life, compounded forward at the required rate of return
n = the project's expected life
$MIRR$ = the project's modified internal rate of return

EXAMPLE 10.5   **Calculating the *MIRR***

Let's look at an example of a project with a 3-year life and a required rate of return of 10 percent assuming the following cash flows are associated with it:

	FREE CASH FLOWS
Initial outlay	−$6,000
Year 1	2,000
Year 2	$3,000
Year 3	4,000

The calculation of the *MIRR* can be viewed as a three-step process, which is also shown graphically in Figure 10-3.

STEP 1 Determine the present value of the project's free cash *out*flows. In this case, the only *out*flow is the initial outlay of $6,000, which is already at the present; thus, it becomes the present value of the cash *out*flows.

STEP 2 Determine the terminal value of the project's free cash *in*flows. To do this, we merely use the project's required rate of return to calculate the future value of the project's three cash *in*flows at the termination of the project. In this case, the *terminal value* becomes $9,720.

STEP 3 Determine the discount rate that equates the present value of the *terminal value* and the present value of the project's cash *out*flows. Thus, the *MIRR* is calculated to be 17.446 percent.

---

[4]You will notice that we differentiate between annual cash inflows and annual cash outflows, compounding all the inflows to the end of the project and bringing all the outflows back to the present as part of the present value of the cost. Although there are alternative definitions of the *MIRR*, this is the most widely accepted definition.

FIGURE 10-3 Calculating the *MIRR*

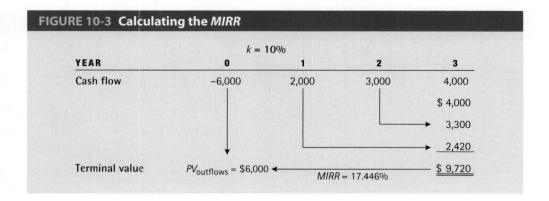

For our example, the calculations are as follows:

$$\$6,000 = \frac{TV_{inflows}}{(1 + MIRR)^n}$$

$$\$6,000 = \frac{\$2,000(1 + 0.10)^2 + \$3,000(1 + 0.10)^1 + \$4,000(1 + 0.10)^0}{(1 + MIRR)^3}$$

$$\$6,000 = \frac{\$2,420 + \$3,300 + \$4,000}{(1 + MIRR)^3}$$

$$\$6,000 = \frac{\$9,720}{(1 + MIRR)^3}$$

$$MIRR = 17.45\%$$

Thus, the *MIRR* for this project (17.45% percent) is less than its *IRR*, which comes out to 20.614 percent. In this case, it only makes sense that the *IRR* should be greater than the *MIRR*, because the *IRR* implicitly assumes intermediate cash *in*flows to grow at the *IRR* rather than the required rate of return.

In terms of decision rules, if the project's *MIRR* is greater than or equal to the project's required rate of return, then the project should be accepted; if not, it should be rejected:

MIRR ≥ required rate of return: accept
MIRR < required rate of return: reject

Because of the frequent use of the *IRR* in the real world as a decision-making tool and its limiting reinvestment rate assumption, the *MIRR* has become increasingly popular as an alternative decision-making tool.

Using Spreadsheets to Calculate the *MIRR*

As with other financial calculations using a spreadsheet, calculating the *MIRR* is extremely simple. The only difference between this calculation and that of the traditional *IRR* is that with a spreadsheet you also have the option of specifying both a *financing rate* and a *reinvestment rate*. The financing rate refers to the rate at which you borrow the money needed for the investment, whereas the reinvestment rate is the rate at which you reinvest the cash flows. Generally, it is assumed that these two values are one and the same. Thus, we enter the value of k, the appropriate discount rate, for both of these values. Once the cash flows have been entered on the spreadsheet, all you need to do is input the Excel *MIRR* function into a spreadsheet cell and let the spreadsheet do the calculations for you. Of course, as with the *IRR* calculation, at least one of the cash flows must be positive and at least one must be negative. The *MIRR* function to be input into a spreadsheet cell is: **=MIRR(values,finance rate,reinvestment rate)**, where values is simply the range of cells where the cash flows are stored, and k is entered for both the finance rate and the reinvestment rate.

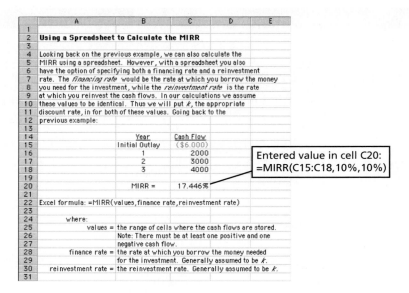

Concept Check

1. Provide an intuitive definition of an internal rate of return for a project.
2. What does a net present value profile tell you, and how is it constructed?
3. What is the difference between the *IRR* and the *MIRR*?
4. Why do the net present value and profitability index always yield the same accept or reject decision for any project?

3 Explain how the capital-budgeting decision process changes when a dollar limit is placed on the capital budget.

capital rationing placing a limit on the dollar size of the capital budget.

Capital Rationing

The use of our capital-budgeting decision rules developed in this chapter implies that the size of the capital budget is determined by the availability of acceptable investment proposals. However, a firm may *place a limit on the dollar size of the capital budget*. This situation is called **capital rationing**. As we will see, examining capital rationing not only better enables us to deal with complexities of the real world but also serves to demonstrate the superiority of the *NPV* method over the *IRR* method for capital budgeting. It is always somewhat uncomfortable to deal with problems associated with capital rationing because, under rationing, projects with positive net present values are rejected. This is a situation that violates the firm's goal of shareholder wealth maximization. However, in the real world, capital rationing does exist, and managers must deal with it. Often when firms impose capital constraints, they are recognizing that they do not have the ability to profitably handle more than a certain number of new and/or large projects.

Using the *IRR* as the firm's decision rule, a firm accepts all projects with an *IRR* greater than the firm's required rate of return. This rule is illustrated in Figure 10-4, where projects A through E would be chosen. However, when capital rationing is imposed, the dollar size of the total investment is limited by the budget constraint. In Figure 10-4, the budget constraint of $*X* precludes the acceptance of an attractive investment, project E. This situation obviously contradicts prior decision rules. Moreover, choosing the projects with the highest *IRR* is complicated by the fact that some projects are indivisible. For example, it may be illogical to recommend that half of project D be undertaken.

The Rationale for Capital Rationing

In general, three principal reasons are given for imposing a capital-rationing constraint. First, managers may think market conditions are temporarily adverse. In the period surrounding the downturn in the economy in the late 2000s, this reason was frequently given.

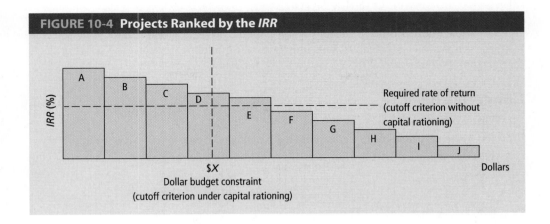

FIGURE 10-4 Projects Ranked by the *IRR*

At that time stock prices were depressed, which made the cost of funding projects high. Second, there may be a shortage of qualified managers to direct new projects; this can happen when projects are of a highly technical nature. Third, there may be intangible considerations. For example, managers may simply fear debt, wishing to avoid interest payments at any cost. Or perhaps the firm wants to limit the issuance of common stock to maintain a stable dividend policy.

So what is capital rationing's effect on the firm? In brief, the effect is negative. To what degree it is negative depends on the severity of the rationing. If the rationing is minor and short-lived, the firm's share price will not suffer to any great extent. In this case, capital rationing can probably be excused, although it should be noted that any capital-rationing action that rejects projects with positive *NPV*s is contrary to the firm's goal of maximization of shareholders' wealth. If the capital rationing is a result of the firm's decision to limit dramatically the number of new projects or to use only internally generated funds for projects, then this policy will eventually have a significantly negative effect on the firm's share price. For example, a lower share price will eventually result from lost competitive advantage if, because of a decision to arbitrarily limit its capital budget, a firm fails to upgrade its products and manufacturing processes.

Capital Rationing and Project Selection

If a firm decides to impose a capital constraint on its investment projects, the appropriate decision criterion is to select the set of projects with the highest *NPV* subject to the capital constraint. In effect, it should select the projects that increase shareholders' wealth the most. This guideline may preclude merely taking the highest-ranked projects in terms of the *PI* or the *IRR*. If the projects shown in Figure 10-4 are divisible, the last project accepted will be only partially accepted. Although partial acceptance may be possible, as we have said, in some cases, the indivisibility of most capital investments prevents it. For example, purchasing half a sales outlet or half a truck is impossible.

Consider a firm with a budget constraint of $1 million and five indivisible projects available to it, as given in Table 10-7. If the highest-ranked projects were taken, projects A and B would be taken first. At that point there would not be enough funds available to take on

TABLE 10-7 Capital Rationing: Choosing among Five Indivisible Projects

Project	Initial Outlay	Profitability Index	Net Present Value
A	$200,000	2.4	$280,000
B	200,000	2.3	260,000
C	800,000	1.7	560,000
D	300,000	1.3	90,000
E	300,000	1.2	60,000

project C; hence, projects D and E would be taken on. However, a higher total *NPV* is provided by the combination of projects A and C. Thus, projects A and C should be selected from the set of projects available. This illustrates our guideline: to select the set of projects that maximizes the firm's *NPV*.

Concept Check

1. What is capital rationing?
2. How might capital rationing conflict with the goal of maximizing shareholders' wealth?
3. What are mutually exclusive projects? How might they complicate the capital-budgeting process?

LO4 Discuss the problems encountered in project ranking.

mutually exclusive projects projects that, if undertaken, would serve the same purpose. Thus, accepting one will necessarily mean rejecting the others.

Ranking Mutually Exclusive Projects

In the past, we have proposed that all projects with a positive *NPV*, a *PI* greater than 1.0, or an *IRR* greater than the required rate of return be accepted, assuming there is no capital rationing. However, this acceptance is not always possible. In some cases, when two projects are judged acceptable by the discounted cash flow criteria, it may be necessary to select only one of them because they are mutually exclusive. **Mutually exclusive projects** *are projects that, if undertaken, would serve the same purpose.* For example, a company considering the installation of a computer system might evaluate three or four systems, all of which have positive *NPV*s. However, the acceptance of one system automatically means rejection of the others. In general, to deal with mutually exclusive projects, we simply rank them by means of the discounted cash flow criteria and select the project with the highest ranking. On occasion, however, problems of conflicting ranking may arise. As we will see, in general, the *NPV* method is the preferred decision-making tool because it leads to the selection of the project that increases shareholder wealth the most.

When dealing with mutually exclusive projects, there are three general types of ranking problems: the size-disparity problem, the time-disparity problem, and the unequal-lives problem. Each involves the possibility of conflict in the ranks yielded by the various discounted cash flow, capital-budgeting criteria. As noted previously, when one discounted cash flow criterion gives an accept signal, they will all give an accept signal, but they will not necessarily rank all projects in the same order. In most cases this disparity is not critical; however, for mutually exclusive projects the ranking order is important.

The Size-Disparity Problem

The size-disparity problem occurs when mutually exclusive projects of unequal size are examined. This problem is most easily clarified with an example.

EXAMPLE 10.6

Suppose a firm is considering two mutually exclusive projects, A and B; both have required rates of return of 10 percent. Project A involves a $200 initial outlay and a cash inflow of $300 at the end of 1 year, whereas project B involves an initial outlay of $1,500 and a cash inflow of $1,900 at the end of 1 year. The net present values, profitability indexes, and internal rates of return for these projects are given in Table 10-8.

In this case, if the *NPV* criterion is used, project B should be accepted; whereas if the *PI* or *IRR* criterion is used, project A should be chosen. The question now becomes, which project is better? The answer depends on whether capital rationing exists. Without capital rationing, project B is better because it provides the largest increase in shareholders' wealth; that is, it has a larger *NPV*. If there is a capital constraint, the problem then focuses on what can be done with the additional $1,300 that is freed up if project A is chosen (costing $200, as opposed to $1,500). If the firm can earn more on project A plus the project financed with the additional $1,300 than it can on project B, then project A and the marginal project should be accepted. In effect, we are attempting to select the set of projects that maximize the firm's *NPV*. Thus, if the marginal project has an *NPV* greater than $154.55 ($227.28 − $72.73), selecting it plus project A with an *NPV* of $72.73 will provide an *NPV* greater than $227.28, the *NPV* for project B.

TABLE 10-8 **The Size-Disparity Ranking Problem**		
PROJECT A:		
		$k = 10\%$
YEARS	**0**	**1**
Cash Flow	−200	300
$NPV = \$72.73$		
$PI = 1.36$		
$IRR = 50\%$		
PROJECT B:		
		$k = 10\%$
YEARS	**0**	**1**
Cash Flow	−1,500	1,900
$NPV = \$227.28$		
$PI = 1.15$		
$IRR = 27\%$		

In summary, whenever the size-disparity problem results in conflicting rankings between mutually exclusive projects, the project with the largest *NPV* will be selected, provided there is no capital rationing. When capital rationing exists, the firm should select the set of projects with the largest *NPV*.

The Time-Disparity Problem

The time-disparity problem and the conflicting rankings that accompany it result from the differing reinvestment assumptions made by the net present value and internal rate of return decision criteria. The *NPV* criterion assumes that cash flows over the life of the project can be reinvested at the required rate of return or cost of capital, whereas the *IRR* criterion implicitly assumes that the cash flows over the life of the project can be reinvested at the *IRR*. One possible solution to this problem is to use the *MIRR* method introduced earlier. As you recall, this method allows you to explicitly state the rate at which cash flows over the life of the project will be reinvested. Again, this problem may be illustrated through the use of an example.

EXAMPLE 10.7

Suppose a firm with a required rate of return or cost of capital of 10 percent and with no capital constraint is considering the two mutually exclusive projects illustrated in Table 10-9. The *NPV* and *PI* indicate that project A is the better of the two, whereas the *IRR* indicates that project B is the better. Project B receives its cash flows earlier than project A, and the different assumptions made about how these flows can be reinvested result in the difference in rankings. Which criterion would be followed depends on which reinvestment assumption is used. The *NPV* criterion is preferred in this case because it makes the most acceptable assumption for the wealth-maximizing firm. It is certainly the most conservative assumption that can be made, because the required rate of return is the lowest possible reinvestment rate. Moreover, as we have already noted, the *NPV* method maximizes the value of the firm and the shareholders' wealth.

TABLE 10-9 **The Time-Disparity Ranking Problem**				
PROJECT A:				
		$k = 10\%$		
YEARS	**0**	**1**	**2**	**3**
Cash Flow	−1000	100	200	2000
$NPV = \$758.83$				
$PI = 1.759$				
$IRR = 35\%$				
PROJECT B:				
		$k = 10\%$		
YEARS	**0**	**1**	**2**	**3**
Cash Flow	−1000	650	650	650
$NPV = \$616.45$				
$PI = 1.616$				
$IRR = 43\%$				

The Unequal-Lives Problem

The final ranking problem to be examined asks whether it is appropriate to compare mutually exclusive projects with different life spans. The incomparability of projects with different lives arises because future, profitable investment proposals will be precluded without ever having been considered. For example, let's say you own an older hotel on some prime beachfront property on Hilton Head Island, and you're considering either remodeling the hotel, which will extend its life by 5 years, or tearing it down and building a new hotel that has an expected life of 10 years. Either way you're going to make money because beachfront property is exactly where everyone would like to stay. But clearly, you can't do both.

Is it fair to compare the *NPV*s on these two projects? No. Why not? Because if you accept the 10-year project, you will not only be rejecting the 5-year project but also the chance to do something else profitable with the property in years 5 through 10. In effect, if the project with the shorter life were taken, at its termination you could either remodel again or rebuild and receive additional benefits, whereas accepting the project with the longer life would exclude this possibility, which is not included in the analysis. The key question thus becomes: Does today's investment decision include all future profitable investment proposals in its analysis? If not, the projects are not comparable.

EXAMPLE 10.8

Suppose a firm with a 10 percent required rate of return must replace an aging machine and is considering two replacement machines, one with a three-year life and one with a six-year life. The relevant cash flow information for these projects is given in Figure 10-5.

Examining the discounted cash flow criteria, we find that the net present value and profitability index criteria indicate that project B is the better project, whereas the internal rate of return favors project A. This ranking inconsistency is caused by the different life spans of the projects being compared. In this case, the decision is a difficult one because the projects are not comparable.

There are several methods to deal with this situation. The first option is to assume that the cash inflows from the shorter-lived investment will be reinvested at the required rate of return until the termination of the longer-lived asset. Although this approach is the simplest because it merely involves calculating the net present value, it actually ignores the problem at hand—the possibility of undertaking another replacement oppor-

FIGURE 10-5 Unequal Lives Ranking Problem

PROJECT A:

$k = 10\%$

YEARS	0	1	2	3
Cash Flows	−1,000	500	500	500

NPV = $243.43
PI = 1.243
IRR = 23.4%

PROJECT B:

$k = 10\%$

YEARS	0	1	2	3	4	5	6
Cash Flows	−1,000	300	300	300	300	300	300

NPV = $306.58
PI = 1.307
IRR = 19.9%

tunity with a positive net present value. Thus, the proper solution involves projecting reinvestment opportunities into the future—that is, making assumptions about possible future investment opportunities. Unfortunately, whereas the first method is too simplistic to be of any value, the second is extremely difficult, requiring extensive cash flow forecasts. The final technique for confronting the problem is to assume that the firm's reinvestment opportunities in the future will be similar to its current ones. The two most common ways of doing this are by creating a replacement chain to equalize the life spans of projects or by calculating the equivalent annual annuity (*EAA* of the projects). Using a replacement chain, the present example would call for the creation of a two-chain cycle for project A; that is, we assume that project A can be replaced with a similar investment at the end of 3 years. Thus, project A would be viewed as two A projects occurring back to back, as illustrated in Figure 10-6. The first project begins with a $1,000 outflow in year 0, or the beginning of year 1. The second project would have an initial outlay of $1,000 at the beginning of year 4, or end of year 3, followed by $500 cash flows in years 4 through 6. As a result, in year 3 there would be a $500 inflow associated with the first project along with a $1,000 outflow associated with repeating the project, resulting in a net cash flow in year 3 of −$500. The net present value on this replacement chain is $426.32, which can be compared with project B's net present value. Therefore, project A should be accepted because the net present value of its replacement chain is greater than the net present value of project B.

One problem with replacement chains is that, depending on the life of each project, it can be quite difficult to come up with equivalent lives. For example, if the two projects

FIGURE 10-6 Replacement Chain Illustration: Two Project A's Back to Back

$k = 10\%$

YEARS	0	1	2	3	4	5	6
Cash Flows	−1,000	500	500	−500	500	500	500

NPV = $426.32

equivalent annual annuity (*EAA*) an annuity cash flow that yields the same present value as the project's *NPV*.

had 7- and 13-year lives, because the lowest common denominator is $7 \times 13 = 91$, a 91-year replacement chain would be needed to establish equivalent lives. In this case, it is easier to determine the project's **equivalent annual annuity (*EAA*)**. A project's *EAA* is simply *an annuity cash flow that yields the same present value as the project's NPV*. To calculate an *EAA*, we need only calculate a project's *NPV* and then determine what annual annuity (PMT on your financial calculator) it is equal to. This can be done in two steps as follows:

STEP 1 Calculate the project's *NPV*. In Figure 10-5 we determined that project A had an *NPV* of $243.43, whereas project B had an *NPV* of $306.58.

STEP 2 Calculate the *EAA*. The *EAA* is determined by using the *NPV* as the project's present value (PV), the number of years in the project as (N), the required rate of return as (I/Y), entering a 0 for the future value (FV), and solving for the annual annuity (PMT). This determines the level of an annuity cash flow that would produce the same *NPV* as the project. For project A the calculations are:

CALCULATOR SOLUTION

Date Input	Function Key
3	N
10	I/Y
−243.43	PV
0	FV

Function Key	Answer
CPT	
PMT	97.89

For project B, the calculations are:

CALCULATOR SOLUTION

Data Input	Function Key
6	N
10	I/Y
−306.58	PV
0	FV

Function Key	Answer
CPT	
PMT	70.39

How do we interpret the *EAA*? For a project with an *n*-year life, it tells us what the dollar value is of an *n*-year annual annuity that would provide the same *NPV* as the project. Thus, for project A, it means that a 3-year annuity of $97.89 with a discount rate of 10 percent would produce a net present value the same as project A's net present value, which is $243.43. We can now compare the equivalent annual annuities directly to determine which project is better. We can do this because we now have found the level of annual annuity that produces an *NPV* equivalent to the project's *NPV*. Thus, because they are both annual annuities, they are comparable.

Concept Check

1. What are the three general types of ranking problems?

ETHICS IN FINANCIAL MANAGEMENT

THE FINANCIAL DOWNSIDE OF POOR ETHICAL BEHAVIOR

As we discussed in Chapter 1, ethics and trust are essential elements of the business world. Knowing the inevitable outcome—for truth does percolate—why do bright and experienced people ignore it? For even if the truth is known only within the confines of the company, it will get out. Circumstances beyond even the best manager's control take over once the chance has passed to act on the moment of truth. Consider the following cases:

Dow Corning didn't deserve its bankruptcy or the multibillion-dollar settlements for its silicone implants because the science didn't support the alleged damages. However, there was a moment of truth when those implants, placed on a blotter, left a stain. The company could have disclosed the possible leakage, researched the risk, and warned doctors and patients. Given the congressional testimony on the implants, many women would have chosen them despite the risk. Instead, they sued because they were not warned.

Beech-Nut's crisis was a chemical concoction instead of apple juice in its baby food products. Executives there ignored an in-house chemist who tried to tell them they were selling adulterated products.

Kidder-Peabody fell despite warnings from employees about a glitch in its accounting system that was reporting bond swaps as sales and income.

In 2004, Merck removed one of the world's best-selling painkillers from the market after a study showed Vioxx caused an increased risk of serious cardiovascular events, such as stroke and heart attack. Producing Vioxx wasn't Merck's problem, its problem was that, according to an editorial in the *New England Journal of Medicine*, Merck was alleged to have withheld data and information that would affect conclusions drawn in an earlier study that appeared in the *New England Journal of Medicine*

in 2000. Now, Merck faces thousands of lawsuits, and studies continue to deliver bad news about the drug. In fact, in one case, a jury awarded $51 million to a retired FBI agent who suffered a heart attack after taking the drug.

As a now-infamous memo reveals, Ford and Firestone did not feel obligated to reveal to the U.S. Transportation Department that certain tires were being recalled in overseas markets. The companies should have realized that it was not a question of whether the recall would be reported, but by whom.

These cases all have several things in common. First, their moments of truth came and went while the companies took no action. Second, employees who raised the issue were ignored or, in some cases, fired. Third, there were lawyers along for the ride, as they were with Ford and Firestone.

Never rely on a lawyer in these moments of truth. Lawyers are legal experts but are not particularly good at controlling damage. They shouldn't make business decisions; managers should. More importantly, moments of truth require managers with strong ethics who will do more than the law requires.

Do businesses ever face a moment of truth wisely? One example is Foxy brand lettuce, which in 2006, shortly after E. coli-contaminated spinach was linked to three deaths, recalled all its lettuce after they discovered irrigation water on their farms tested positive for the bacterium. Although their lettuce was not found to be carrying any bacterium, they did everything possible to protect the public and, as a result, have very loyal customers.

Source: Kevin Kingsbury, "Corporate News: Merck Settles Claims Over Vioxx Ads," *Wall Street Journal*, May 21, 2008, page B3; "Manager's Journal: Ford-Firestone Lesson: Heed the Moment of Truth," *Wall Street Journal*, September 11, 2000, page A44; "Foxy's lettuce recalled after E. coli scare," *USA Today*, October 9, 2006, page A10; and Joe Queenan, "Juice Men—Ethics and the Beech-Nut Sentences," *Barron's*, June 20, 1988, page 14.

Ethics in Capital Budgeting

 5 Explain the importance of ethical considerations in capital-budgeting decisions.

Although it may not seem obvious, ethics play a role in capital budgeting. Firestone and Ford, Merck, Dow Corning, and Beech-Nut provide examples of how ethical rules have been violated in the past and what the consequences can be. The most damaging event a business can experience is a loss of the public's confidence in the business's ethical standards. In making capital-budgeting decisions, we must be aware of this and that ethical behavior is doing the right thing and is the right thing to do. The "Ethics in Financial Management" article, The Financial Downside of Poor Ethical Behavior, explains how important it is for firms to not only tell the truth but also make sure that consumers have all the facts they need.

A Glance at Actual Capital-Budgeting Practices

 6 Discuss the trends in the use of different capital-budgeting criteria.

During the past 40 years, the popularity of each of the capital-budgeting methods has shifted rather dramatically. In the 1960s, the payback period method dominated capital budgeting. Through the 1970s and 1980s, the *IRR* and the *NPV* techniques slowly gained popularity and are used by the majority of major corporations today.

Interestingly, a recent survey of 392 CFOs by John Graham and Campbell Harvey of Duke University found that 74.9 percent of CFOs always or almost always use net present value and 75.7 percent always or almost always use the internal rate of return.[5] The payback period was also found to be very popular; 56.7 percent indicated that they always or almost always use the payback period. The profitability index was found to be considerably less popular; only 11.9 percent of the CFOs surveyed indicated that they always or almost always use it. Moreover, the survey found that in firms headed by older CEOs and those without an MBA, the use of the payback period was more common.

The survey also found that large firms are significantly more likely to use *NPV* to evaluate capital-budgeting projects than are small firms. On the other hand, when it comes to capital budgeting, small firms use the payback period almost as frequently as they use *NPV* and *IRR*. Apart from the survey, one of the reasons commonly given for the use of the payback period approach is that it makes sense for the capital-constrained firm. However, the survey didn't find any evidence of this being the case.

Without taking on new projects, a company simply wouldn't continue to exist. For example, Polaroid's inability to come up with a product to replace its instant camera resulted in that company going under in 2001. Finding new profitable projects and correctly evaluating them are central to a firm's continued existence—and that's what capital budgeting is all about. In fact, much of what is done within a business involves the capital-budgeting process. Many times it's referred to as strategic planning, but it generally involves capital-budgeting decisions. For example, you may be involved in market research dealing with a proposed new product or its marketing plan, or be analyzing its costs—these are all part of the capital-budgeting process. Once all this information has been gathered, it is analyzed using the techniques and tools that we have presented in this chapter. Actually, almost any business decision can be analyzed using the framework we presented here. That's because the *NPV* method "values" the project under consideration. That is, it looks at the present value of its benefits relative to the present value of its costs, and if the present value of the benefits outweighs the costs, the project is accepted. That's a pretty good decision rule, and it can be applied to any decision a business faces.

Concept Check

1. What capital-budgeting criteria seem to be used most frequently in the real world? Why do you think this is so?

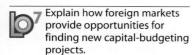

Explain how foreign markets provide opportunities for finding new capital-budgeting projects.

Finance and the Multinational Firm: Capital Budgeting

Without question, the key to success in capital budgeting is to identify good projects, and for many companies these good projects are overseas. Just look at the success that Coca-Cola has had in the international markets. More than 80 percent of its beverage profits come from foreign markets, and the company earns more in Japan than in the United States. Likewise, ExxonMobil earns over half its profits from abroad and is involved in gas and oil exploration projects in West Africa, the Caspian Sea, Russia, the Gulf of Mexico, and South America.

But how do you enter these markets initially? One approach that has been used successfully is through international joint ventures or strategic alliances. Under these arrangements two or more corporations merge their skills and resources on a specific project, trading things such as technology and access to marketing channels. For example, Northwest Airlines and KLM Royal Dutch Airlines entered into a joint venture that provides Northwest

[5]John R. Graham and Campbell R. Harvey, "The Theory and Practice of Corporate Finance: Evidence from the Field," *Journal of Financial Economics* 60, 1–2 (May/June 2001), 187–243.

with routes to Europe where KLM has a strong presence, and provides KLM with routes in the U.S. and Asia where Northwest is well established.

Similarly, U.S. oil giant Armco formed a joint venture with Mitsubishi to sell Armco's lightweight plastics in Japan. Georgia-Pacific and Canfor Japan Corporation have a joint venture in which Georgia-Pacific gained access to Canfor's marketing expertise in Japan to sell pulp and paper products there. Likewise, H. J. Heinz Co. announced a joint venture with an Indonesian firm to gain access to its Indonesian marketing channels. Joint ventures also provide a way to get around trade barriers. For example, India and Mexico require joint ventures for entry into their markets. As a result, U.S. firms such as Apple Computer and Hewlett-Packard have been forced to enter into Mexican joint ventures in order to be allowed to ship their products into Mexico.

What is the alternative to not looking abroad for projects? It is losing out on potential revenues. Keep in mind that firms such as Xerox, Hewlett-Packard, Dow Chemical, IBM, and Gillette all earn more than 50 percent of their profits from sales abroad. International boundaries no longer apply in finance.

Concept Check

1. What methods do corporations use to enter international markets?

Summary

The process of capital budgeting involves decision making with respect to investments in fixed assets. Before a profitable project can be adopted, it must be identified or found. Unfortunately, coming up with ideas for new products, for ways to improve existing products, or for ways to make existing products more profitable is extremely difficult. In general, the best source of ideas for new, potentially profitable products is within the firm.

Discuss the difficulty encountered in finding profitable projects in competitive markets and the importance of the search.

We examine four commonly used criteria for determining the acceptance or rejection of capital-budgeting proposals. The first method, the payback period, does not incorporate the time value of money into its calculations. However, the net present value, profitability index, and internal rate of return methods do account for the time value of money. These methods are summarized in Table 10-10 on pages 292–293.

Determine whether a new project should be accepted or rejected using the payback period, the net present value, the profitability index, and the internal rate of return.

There are several complications related to the capital-budgeting process. First, we examined capital rationing and the problems it can create by imposing a limit on the dollar size of the capital budget. Although capital rationing does not, in general, maximize shareholders' wealth, it does exist. The goal of maximizing shareholders' wealth remains, but it is now subject to a budget constraint.

Explain how the capital-budgeting decision process changes when a dollar limit is placed on the capital budget.

There are a number of problems associated with evaluating mutually exclusive projects. Mutually exclusive projects occur when different investments, if undertaken, would serve the same purpose. In general, to deal with mutually exclusive projects, we rank them by means of the discounted cash flow criteria and select the project with the highest ranking. Conflicting rankings can arise because of the projects' size disparities, time disparities, and unequal lives. The incomparability of projects with different life spans is not simply a result of the different life spans; rather, it arises because future profitable investment proposals will be rejected without being included in the initial analysis. Replacement chains and equivalent annual annuities can solve this problem.

Discuss the problems encountered in project ranking.

Ethics and ethical decisions continuously crop up in capital budgeting. Just as with all other areas of finance, violating ethical considerations results in a loss of public confidence, which can have a significant negative effect on shareholder wealth.

Explain the importance of ethical considerations in capital-budgeting decisions.

Over the past 40 years, the discounted capital-budgeting techniques have continued to gain in popularity and today dominate in the decision-making process.

Discuss the trends in the use of different capital-budgeting criteria.

The international markets provide another source for finding good capital-budgeting projects. In fact, many times a new project simply involves taking an existing product and selling it in a foreign market. Joint ventures and strategic alliances have been successfully used to enter foreign markets.

Explain how foreign markets provide opportunities for finding new capital-budgeting projects.

TABLE 10-10 Capital-Budgeting Methods: A Summary

1A. Payback period = number of years required to recapture the initial investment

Accept if payback period ≤ maximum acceptable payback period
Reject if payback period > maximum acceptable payback period

Advantages:
- Uses free cash flows.
- Is easy to calculate and understand.
- Benefits the capital-constrained firm.
- May be used as rough screening device.

Disadvantages:
- Ignores the time value of money.
- Ignores cash flows occurring after the payback period.
- Selection of the maximum acceptable payback period is arbitrary.

1B. Discounted payback period = the number of years needed to recover the initial cash outlay from the *discounted net cash flows*

Accept if discounted payback ≤ maximum acceptable discounted payback period
Reject if discounted payback > maximum acceptable discounted payback period

Advantages:
- Uses cash flows.
- Is easy to calculate and understand.
- Considers time value of money.

Disadvantages:
- Ignores cash flows occurring after the payback period.
- Selection of the maximum acceptable discounted payback period is arbitrary.

2. Net present value = present value of the annual free cash flows less the investment's initial outlay

NPV = present value of all the future annual free cash flows − the initial cash outlay

$$= \frac{FCF_1}{(1+k)^1} + \frac{FCF_2}{(1+k)^2} + \cdots + \frac{FCF_n}{(1+k)^n} - IO$$

where FCF_t = the annual free cash flow in time period t (this can take on either positive or negative values)
k = the required rate of return or the cost of capital
IO = the initial cash outlay
n = the project's expected life

Accept if $NPV \geq 0.0$
Reject if $NPV < 0.0$

Advantages:
- Uses free cash flows.
- Recognizes the time value of money.
- Is consistent with the firm's goal of shareholder wealth maximization.

Disadvantages:
- Requires detailed long-term forecasts of a project's cash flows.

3. Profitability index = the ratio of the present value of the future free cash flows to the initial outlay.

$$PI = \frac{\text{present value of all the future annual free cash flows}}{\text{initial cash outlay}}$$

$$= \frac{\frac{FCF_1}{(1+k)^1} + \frac{FCF_2}{(1+k)^2} + \cdots + \frac{FCF_n}{(1+k)^n}}{IO}$$

Accept if $PI \geq 1.0$
Reject if $PI < 1.0$

Advantages:
- Uses free cash flows.
- Recognizes the time value of money.
- Is consistent with the firm's goal of shareholder wealth maximization.

Disadvantages:
- Requires detailed long-term forecasts of a project's cash flows.

4A. Internal rate of return = the discount rate that equates the present value of the project's future free cash flows with the project's initial outlay

IRR = the rate of return that equates the present value of the project's free cash flows with the initial outlay

$$IO = \frac{FCF_1}{(1+IRR\%)^1} + \frac{FCF_2}{(1+IRR\%)^2} + \cdots + \frac{FCF_n}{(1+IRR\%)^n}$$

where IRR = the project's internal rate of return

Accept if $IRR \geq$ required rate of return
Reject if $IRR <$ required rate of return

Advantages:
- Uses free cash flows.
- Recognizes the time value of money.
- Is, in general, consistent with the firm's goal of shareholder wealth maximization.

Disadvantages:
- Requires detailed long-term forecasts of a project's cash flows.
- Possibility of multiple *IRR*s.
- Assumes cash flows over the life of the project can be reinvested at the *IRR*.

4B. Modified internal rate of return = the rate of return that equates the present value of the cash outflows with the terminal value of the cash inflows

$$PV_{outflows} = \frac{TV_{inflows}}{(1 + MIRR)^n}$$

where $PV_{outflows}$ = the present value of the project's free cash outflows
$TV_{inflows}$ = the project's terminal value, calculated by taking all the annual free cash inflows and finding their future value at the end of the project's life, compounded forward at the required rate of return
$MIRR$ = the project's modified internal rate of return

Accept if $MIRR \geq$ required rate of return
Reject if $MIRR <$ required rate of return

Advantages:
- Uses free cash flows.
- Recognizes the time value of money.
- Is consistent with the firm's goal of shareholder wealth maximization.
- Allows reinvestment rate to be directly specified.

Disadvantages:
- Requires detailed long-term cash flow forecasts.

Key Terms

Capital budgeting 265

Capital rationing 282

Discounted payback period 268

Equivalent annual annuity (*EAA*) 288

Internal rate of return (*IRR*) 274

Mutually exclusive projects 284

Net present value (*NPV*) 268

Net present value profile 277

Payback period 267

Profitability index (*PI*) or benefit–cost ratio 272

Review Questions

All Review Questions and Study Problems are available in MyFinanceLab.

10-1. Why is capital budgeting such an important process? Why are capital-budgeting errors so costly?

10-2. What are the disadvantages of using the payback period as a capital-budgeting technique? What are its advantages? Why is it so frequently used?

10-3. In some countries, the expropriation (seizure) of foreign investments is a common practice. If you were considering an investment in one of those countries, would the use of the payback period criterion seem more reasonable than it otherwise might? Why or why not?

10-4. Briefly compare and contrast the *NPV*, *PI*, and *IRR* criteria. What are the advantages and disadvantages of using each of these methods?

10-5. What are mutually exclusive projects? Why might the existence of mutually exclusive projects cause problems in the implementation of the discounted cash flow capital-budgeting criteria?

10-6. What are common reasons for capital rationing? Is capital rationing rational?

10-7. How should managers compare two mutually exclusive projects of unequal size? Should the approach change if capital rationing is a factor?

10-8. What causes the time-disparity ranking problem? What reinvestment rate assumptions are associated with the *NPV* and *IRR* capital-budgeting criteria?

10-9. When might two mutually exclusive projects having unequal lives be incomparable? How should managers deal with this problem?

Self-Test Problem

(The solution to this problem is provided at the end of this chapter.)

ST-1. You are considering buying a machine that will require an initial outlay of $54,200. The machine has an expected life of 5 years and will generate free cash flows to the company as a whole of $20,608 at the end of each year over its 5-year life. In addition to the $20,608 cash flow from operations during the fifth and final year, there will be an additional free cash inflow of $13,200 at the end of the fifth year associated with the salvage value of the machine, making the cash flow in year 5 equal to $33,808. Thus, the cash flows associated with this project look like this:

	CASH FLOW
Initial outlay	−$54,200
Inflow year 1	20,608
Inflow year 2	20,608
Inflow year 3	20,608
Inflow year 4	20,608
Inflow year 5	33,808

Given a required rate of return of 15 percent, calculate the following:

a. Payback period   b. *NPV*   c. *PI*   d. *IRR*

Should this project be accepted?

Study Problems

10-1. (*IRR calculation*) Determine the *IRR* on the following projects:

a. An initial outlay of $10,000 resulting in a single free cash flow of $17,182 after 8 years
b. An initial outlay of $10,000 resulting in a single free cash flow of $48,077 after 10 years
c. An initial outlay of $10,000 resulting in a single free cash flow of $114,943 after 20 years
d. An initial outlay of $10,000 resulting in a single free cash flow of $13,680 after 3 years

10-2. (*IRR calculation*) Determine the *IRR* on the following projects:

a. An initial outlay of $10,000 resulting in a free cash flow of $1,993 at the end of each year for the next 10 years
b. An initial outlay of $10,000 resulting in a free cash flow of $2,054 at the end of each year for the next 20 years
c. An initial outlay of $10,000 resulting in a free cash flow of $1,193 at the end of each year for the next 12 years
d. An initial outlay of $10,000 resulting in a free cash flow of $2,843 at the end of each year for the next 5 years

10-3. (*IRR calculation*) Determine to the nearest percent the *IRR* on the following projects:

a. An initial outlay of $10,000 resulting in a free cash flow of $2,000 at the end of year 1, $5,000 at the end of year 2, and $8,000 at the end of year 3
b. An initial outlay of $10,000 resulting in a free cash flow of $8,000 at the end of year 1, $5,000 at the end of year 2, and $2,000 at the end of year 3
c. An initial outlay of $10,000 resulting in a free cash flow of $2,000 at the end of years 1 through 5 and $5,000 at the end of year 6

10-4. (*NPV, PI, and IRR calculations*) Fijisawa Inc. is considering a major expansion of its product line and has estimated the following cash flows associated with such an expansion. The initial outlay would be $1,950,000, and the project would generate incremental free cash flows of $450,000 per year for 6 years. The appropriate required rate of return is 9 percent.

a. Calculate the *NPV*.
b. Calculate the *PI*.
c. Calculate the *IRR*.
d. Should this project be accepted?

10-5. (*Payback period, NPV, PI, and IRR calculations*) You are considering a project with an initial cash outlay of $80,000 and expected free cash flows of $20,000 at the end of each year for 6 years. The required rate of return for this project is 10 percent.

a. What is the project's payback period?

   b. What is the project's *NPV*?

   c. What is the project's *PI*?

   d. What is the project's *IRR*?

10-6. (*NPV, PI, and IRR calculations*) You are considering two independent projects, project A and project B. The initial cash outlay associated with project A is $50,000, and the initial cash outlay associated with project B is $70,000. The required rate of return on both projects is 12 percent. The expected annual free cash inflows from each project are as follows:

	PROJECT A	PROJECT B
Initial outlay	−$50,000	−$70,000
Inflow year 1	12,000	13,000
Inflow year 2	12,000	13,000
Inflow year 3	12,000	13,000
Inflow year 4	12,000	13,000
Inflow year 5	12,000	13,000
Inflow year 6	12,000	13,000

Calculate the *NPV*, *PI*, and *IRR* for each project and indicate if the project should be accepted.

10-7. (*Payback period calculations*) You are considering three independent projects, project A, project B, and project C. Given the following cash flow information, calculate the payback period for each.

	PROJECT A	PROJECT B	PROJECT C
Initial outlay	−$1,000	−$10,000	−$5,000
Inflow year 1	600	5,000	1,000
Inflow year 2	300	3,000	1,000
Inflow year 3	200	3,000	2,000
Inflow year 4	100	3,000	2,000
Inflow year 5	500	3,000	2,000

If you require a 3-year payback before an investment can be accepted, which project(s) would be accepted?

10-8. (*NPV with varying required rates of return*) Gubanich Sportswear is considering building a new factory to produce aluminum baseball bats. This project would require an initial cash outlay of $5,000,000 and will generate annual free cash inflows of $1,000,000 per year for 8 years. Calculate the project's *NPV* given:

   a. A required rate of return of 9 percent

   b. A required rate of return of 11 percent

   c. A required rate of return of 13 percent

   d. A required rate of return of 15 percent

10-9. (*IRR calculations*) Given the following free cash flows, determine the *IRR* for the three independent projects A, B, and C.

	PROJECT A	PROJECT B	PROJECT C
Initial outlay	−$50,000	−$100,000	−$450,000
Cash inflows:			
Year 1	$10,000	$125,000	$200,000
Year 2	15,000	25,000	200,000
Year 3	20,000	25,000	200,000
Year 4	25,000	25,000	—
Year 5	30,000	25,000	—

10-10. (*NPV with varying required rates of return*) Big Steve's, a maker of swizzle sticks, is considering the purchase of a new plastic stamping machine. This investment requires an initial outlay of $100,000 and will generate free cash inflows of $18,000 per year for 10 years.

   a. If the required rate of return is 10 percent, what is the project's *NPV*?

   b. If the required rate of return is 15 percent, what is the project's *NPV*?

   c. Would the project be accepted under part a or b?

   d. What is the project's *IRR*?

10-11. (*Mutually exclusive projects*) Nanotech, Inc. currently has a production electronics facility and it is cost prohibitive to expand this production facility. Nanotech is deciding between the following four contracts:

	CONTRACT'S *NPV*	USE OF PRODUCTION FACILITY
A	$100 million	100%
B	$90 million	80%
C	$60 million	60%
D	$50 million	40%

Which project or projects should they accept?

10-12. (*IRR with uneven cash flows*) The Tiffin Barker Corporation is considering introducing a new currency verifier that has the ability to identify counterfeit dollar bills. The required rate of return on this project is 12 percent. What is the *IRR* on this project if it is expected to produce the following cash flows?

Initial outlay	−$927,917
FCF in year 1	200,000
FCF in year 2	300,000
FCF in year 3	300,000
FCF in year 4	200,000
FCF in year 5	200,000
FCF in year 6	160,000

10-13. (*NPV calculation*) Calculate the *NPV* given the following cash flows if the appropriate required rate of return is 10%.

YEAR	CASH FLOWS
0	−$60,000
1	20,000
2	20,000
3	10,000
4	10,000
5	30,000
6	30,000

Should the project be accepted?

10-14. (*NPV calculation*) Calculate the *NPV* given the following cash flows if the appropriate required rate of return is 10%.

YEAR	CASH FLOWS
0	−$70,000
1	30,000
2	30,000
3	30,000
4	−30,000
5	30,000
6	30,000

Should the project be accepted?

10-15. (*MIRR calculation*) Calculate the *MIRR* given the following cash flows if the appropriate required rate of return is 10% (use this as the reinvestment rate).

YEAR	CASH FLOWS
0	−$50,000
1	25,000
2	25,000
3	25,000
4	−25,000
5	25,000
6	25,000

Should the project be accepted?

10-16. (*PI calculation*) Calculate the *PI* given the following cash flows if the appropriate required rate of return is 10%.

YEAR	CASH FLOWS
0	−$55,000
1	10,000
2	10,000
3	10,000
4	10,000
5	10,000
6	10,000

Should the project be accepted? Without calculating the *NPV*, do you think it would be positive or negative? Why?

10-17. (*Discounted payback period*) Gio's Restaurants is considering a project with the following expected cash flows:

YEAR	PROJECT CASH FLOW
0	−$150 million
1	90 million
2	70 million
3	90 million
4	100 million

If the project's appropriate discount is 12 percent, what is the project's discounted payback?

10-18. (*Discounted payback period*) You are considering a project with the following cash flows:

YEAR	PROJECT CASH FLOW
0	−$50,000
1	20,000
2	20,000
3	20,000
4	20,000

If the appropriate discount rate is 10 percent, what is the project's discounted payback period?

10-19. (*Mutually exclusive projects and NPV*) You have been assigned the task of evaluating two mutually exclusive projects with the following projected cash flows:

YEAR	PROJECT A CASH FLOW	PROJECT B CASH FLOW
0	−$100,000	−$100,000
1	33,000	0
2	33,000	0
3	33,000	0
4	33,000	0
5	33,000	220,000

If the appropriate discount rate on these projects is 10 percent, which would be chosen and why?

10-20. (*IRR*) Jella Cosmetics is considering a project that costs $800,000, and is expected to last for 10 years and produce future cash flows of $175,000 per year. If the appropriate discount rate for this project is 12 percent, what is the project's *IRR*?

10-21. (*IRR*) Your investment advisor has offered you an investment that will provide you with one cash flow of $10,000 at the end of 20 years if you pay premiums of $200 per year at the end of each year for 20 years. Find the internal rate of return on this investment.

10-22. (*IRR, payback, and calculating a missing cash flow*) Mode Publishing is considering a new printing facility that will involve a large initial outlay and then result in a series of positive cash flows for four years. The estimated cash flows are associated with this project are:

YEAR	PROJECT CASH FLOW
0 (initial outlay)	?
1	$800 million
2	400 million
3	300 million
4	500 million

If you know that the project has a regular payback of 2.5 years, what is the project's internal rate of return?

10-23. (*Discounted payback period*) Sheinhardt Wig Company is considering a project that has the following cash flows:

YEAR	PROJECT CASH FLOW
0	−$100,000
1	20,000
2	60,000
3	70,000
4	50,000
5	40,000

If the appropriate discount rate is 10 percent, what is the project's discounted payback?

10-24. (*IRR of uneven cash flow stream*) Microwave Oven Programming, Inc. is considering the construction of a new plant. The plant will have an initial cash outlay of $7 million, and will produce cash flows of $3 million at the end of year 1, $4 million at the end of year 2, and $2 million at the end of years 3 through 5. What is the internal rate of return on this new plant?

10-25. (*MIRR*) Dunder Mifflin Paper Company is considering purchasing a new stamping machine that costs $400,000. This new machine will produce cash inflows of $150,000 each year at the end of years 1 through 5, then at the end of year 7 there will be a cash *out*flow of $200,000. The company has a weighted average cost of capital of 12 percent (use this as the reinvestment rate). What is the MIRR of the investment?

10-26. (*MIRR calculation*) Artie's Wrestling Stuff is considering building a new plant. This plant would require an initial cash outlay of $8 million and will generate annual free cash inflows of $2 million per year for 8 years. Calculate the project's *MIRR* given:

    a. A required rate of return of 10 percent
    b. A required rate of return of 12 percent
    c. A required rate of return of 14 percent

10-27. (*Size-disparity problem*) The D. Dorner Farms Corporation is considering purchasing one of two fertilizer-herbicides for the upcoming year. The more expensive of the two is better and will produce a higher yield. Assume these projects are mutually exclusive and that the required rate of return is 10 percent. Given the following free cash flows:

	PROJECT A	PROJECT B
Initial outlay	−$500	−$5,000
Inflow year 1	700	6,000

    a. Calculate the *NPV* of each project.
    b. Calculate the *PI* of each project.
    c. Calculate the *IRR* of each project.
    d. If there is no capital-rationing constraint, which project should be selected? If there is a capital-rationing constraint, how should the decision be made?

10-28. (*Time-disparity problem*) The State Spartan Corporation is considering two mutually exclusive projects. The free cash flows associated with those projects are as follows:

	PROJECT A	PROJECT B
Initial outlay	−$50,000	−$50,000
Inflow year 1	15,625	0
Inflow year 2	15,625	0
Inflow year 3	15,625	0
Inflow year 4	15,625	0
Inflow year 5	15,625	100,000

The required rate of return on these projects is 10 percent.

    a. What is each project's payback period?
    b. What is each project's *NPV*?
    c. What is each project's *IRR*?
    d. What has caused the ranking conflict?
    e. Which project should be accepted? Why?

10-29. (*Capital rationing*) The Cowboy Hat Company of Stillwater, Oklahoma, is considering seven capital investment proposals for which the total funds available are limited to a maximum of $12 million. The projects are independent and have the following costs and profitability indexes associated with them:

PROJECT	COST	PROFITABILITY INDEX
A	$4,000,000	1.18
B	3,000,000	1.08
C	5,000,000	1.33
D	6,000,000	1.31
E	4,000,000	1.19
F	6,000,000	1.20
G	4,000,000	1.18

    a. Under strict capital rationing, which projects should be selected?
    b. What problems are there with capital rationing?

Mini Case

Your first assignment in your new position as assistant financial analyst at Caledonia Products is to evaluate two new capital-budgeting proposals. Because this is your first assignment, you have been asked not only to provide a recommendation but also to respond to a number of questions aimed at assessing your understanding of the capital-budgeting process. This is a standard procedure for all new financial analysts at Caledonia, and it will serve to determine whether you are moved directly into the capital-budgeting analysis department or are provided with remedial training. The memorandum you received outlining your assignment follows.

    To: The New Financial Analysts
    From: Mr. V. Morrison, CEO, Caledonia Products
    Re: Capital-Budgeting Analysis

Provide an evaluation of two proposed projects, both with 5-year expected lives and identical initial outlays of $110,000. Both of these projects involve additions to Caledonia's highly successful Avalon product line, and as a result, the required rate of return on both projects has been established at 12 percent. The expected free cash flows from each project are as follows:

	PROJECT A	PROJECT B
Initial outlay	−$110,000	−$110,000
Inflow year 1	20,000	40,000
Inflow year 2	30,000	40,000
Inflow year 3	40,000	40,000
Inflow year 4	50,000	40,000
Inflow year 5	70,000	40,000

In evaluating these projects, please respond to the following questions:

a. Why is the capital-budgeting process so important?
b. Why is it difficult to find exceptionally profitable projects?
c. What is the payback period on each project? If Caledonia imposes a 3-year maximum acceptable payback period, which of these projects should be accepted?
d. What are the criticisms of the payback period?
e. Determine the *NPV* for each of these projects. Should they be accepted?
f. Describe the logic behind the *NPV*.
g. Determine the *PI* for each of these projects. Should they be accepted?
h. Would you expect the *NPV* and *PI* methods to give consistent accept/reject decisions? Why or why not?
i. What would happen to the *NPV* and *PI* for each project if the required rate of return increased? If the required rate of return decreased?
j. Determine the *IRR* for each project. Should they be accepted?
k. How does a change in the required rate of return affect the project's internal rate of return?
l. What reinvestment rate assumptions are implicitly made by the *NPV* and *IRR* methods? Which one is better?

You have also been asked for your views on three unrelated sets of projects. Each set of projects involves two mutually exclusive projects. These projects follow.

m. Caledonia is considering two investments with 1-year lives. The more expensive of the two is the better and will produce more savings. Assume these projects are mutually exclusive and that the required rate of return is 10 percent. Given the following free cash flows:

	PROJECT A	PROJECT B
Initial outlay	−$195,000	−$1,200,000
Inflow year 1	240,000	1,650,000

1. Calculate the *NPV* for each project.
2. Calculate the *PI* for each project.
3. Calculate the *IRR* for each project.
4. If there is no capital-rationing constraint, which project should be selected? If there is a capital-rationing constraint, how should the decision be made?

n. Caledonia is considering two additional mutually exclusive projects. The free cash flows associated with these projects are as follows:

	PROJECT A	PROJECT B
Initial outlay	−$10,000	−$100,000
Inflow year 1	32,000	0
Inflow year 2	32,000	0
Inflow year 3	32,000	0
Inflow year 4	32,000	0
Inflow year 5	32,000	200,000

The required rate of return on these projects is 11 percent.
1. What is each project's payback period?
2. What is each project's *NPV*?
3. What is each project's *IRR*?
4. What has caused the ranking conflict?
5. Which project should be accepted? Why?

Self-Test Solution

SS-1.

a. Payback period $= \dfrac{\$54,200}{\$20,608} = 2.630$ years

b. NPV = present value of all the future annual free cash flows − the initial cash outlay

$$= \frac{FCF_1}{(1+k)^1} + \frac{FCF_2}{(1+k)^2} + \cdots + \frac{FCF_n}{(1+k)^n} - IO$$

$$= \$20,608(2.855) + \$33,808(0.497) - \$54,200$$

$$= \$58,836 + \$16,803 - \$54,200$$

$$= \$21,439$$

c. $PI = \dfrac{\text{present value of all the future annual free cash flows}}{\text{initial cash outlay}}$

$$= \frac{\dfrac{FCF_1}{(1+k)^1} + \dfrac{FCF_2}{(1+k)^2} + \cdots + \dfrac{FCF_n}{(1+k)^n}}{IO}$$

$$= \frac{\$75,639}{\$54,200}$$

$$= 1.396$$

d. Using your financial calculator:

**CALCULATOR SOLUTION
(USING A TI BA II PLUS):**

Data and Key Input	Display
CF ; −54,200; ENTER	CF0 = −54,200.
↓ ; 20,608; ENTER	C01 = 20,608.
↓ ; 4; ENTER	F01 = 4.00
↓ ; 33,808; ENTER	C02 = 33,808.
↓ ; 1; ENTER	F02 = 1.00
NPV	I = 0.00
15;	I = 15.00
↓ ; CPT	NPV = 21,444.
IRR ; CPT	IRR = 29.5907

Chapter 11

Cash Flows and Other Topics in Capital Budgeting

Learning Objectives

After reading this chapter, you should be able to:

 Identify guidelines by which we measure cash flows.

 Explain how a project's benefits and costs—that is, its free cash flows—are calculated.

 Explain the importance of options, or flexibility, in capital budgeting.

 Explain what the appropriate measure of risk is for capital-budgeting purposes.

 Determine the acceptability of a new project using the risk-adjusted discount method of adjusting for risk.

Explain the use of simulation for imitating the performance of a project under evaluation.

Explain why a multinational firm faces a more difficult time estimating cash flows along with increased risks.

In 2001, when Toyota introduced the first-generation model of its gas-electric hybrid car, the Prius, it seemed more like a little science experiment than real competition for the auto industry. In fact, in 2004, General Motors vice-chairman Bob Lutz dismissed hybrids as "an interesting curiosity." But that's all changed. As gas prices climbed to over $4 a gallon in 2008, suddenly the gas-electric hybrid car seemed to be the way to go. In fact, from its humble beginnings in 2001 through February 2009 Toyota sold more than 700,000 Prius in the U.S., making up over half of the Prius worldwide market.

How did Toyota gain leadership in the gas-electric hybrid car market? It started with its capital-budgeting decision to enter the gas-electric hybrid car market with the Prius and a very large investment—in excess of $1 billion. This action vaulted Toyota into the lead and could leave Toyota in great shape for the future if JPMorgan is right in their 2009 forecast. They predict that the global market for hybrids will grow more than 23-fold and that hybrid cars will account for nearly one in five cars sold in the United States by 2020.

Still, according to most analysts, Toyota has yet to make a dime on the Prius. In fact, when the Prius first came out, Toyota had it priced so that it was losing about $3,000 on each car it sold. Finally in 2008, Toyota announced they were actually making money on the Prius, but in spite of that announcement, it is widely believed by analysts that the automaker is really just breaking even at best.

Toyota's decision to introduce the Prius and enter the hybrid car market was a difficult one. Would it simply move Toyota customers from one Toyota car to another, or would it bring new customers to Toyota? Was this a chance to gain a foothold on the new technology of the future, or were hybrid cars simply a fad?

Where is Toyota going next? In 2009, Toyota continued to move the hybrid technology to its other cars and lines, announcing three new offerings including the launch of the Lexus HS250h. In addition, Toyota announced that it was investing heavily in a joint battery project with Panasonic and it plans to sell an all-electric car by 2012. How did Toyota make the decision to go ahead with the Prius and the all-electric car? It used the basic capital-budgeting techniques described in the previous chapter. But even before it could apply those techniques, Toyota had to come up with the cash flow forecasts and adjust for the risks associated with these projects. That's what we'll be looking at in this chapter.

This chapter continues our discussion of decision-making rules for deciding when to invest in new projects. First, we examine what a relevant cash flow is and how to calculate it. We then turn our attention to the problem of capital budgeting under uncertainty. When we discussed capital-budgeting techniques in the preceding chapter, we implicitly assumed the level of risk associated with each investment proposal was the same. In this chapter we lift that assumption and examine various ways in which risk can be incorporated into the capital-budgeting decision.

Guidelines for Capital Budgeting

 Identify guidelines by which we measure cash flows.

To evaluate investment proposals, we must first set guidelines by which we measure the value of each proposal. In effect, we are deciding what is and what isn't a relevant cash flow.

Use Free Cash Flows Rather than Accounting Profits

We use free cash flows, not accounting profits, as our measurement. The firm receives and is able to reinvest free cash flows, whereas accounting profits are shown when they are earned rather than when the money is actually in hand. Unfortunately, a firm's accounting profits and free cash flows may not be timed to occur together. For example, capital expenses, such as vehicles and plant and equipment, are depreciated over several years, with their annual depreciation subtracted from profits. Free cash flows correctly reflect the timing of benefits and costs—that is, when the money is received, when it can be reinvested, and when it must be paid out.

Think Incrementally

Unfortunately, calculating free cash flows from a project may not be enough. Decision makers must ask, *What new free cash flows will the company as a whole receive if the company takes on a given project?* What if the company does not take on the project? Interestingly, we may find that not all cash flows a firm expects from an investment proposal are incremental in nature.

incremental after-tax free cash flows the funds that the firm receives and is able to reinvest, as opposed to accounting profits, which are shown when they are earned rather than when the money is actually in hand.

When measuring free cash flows, however, the trick is to think incrementally. In doing so, we will see that only **incremental after-tax free cash flows** matter. As such, our guiding rule in deciding if a free cash flow is incremental is to look at the company with, versus without, the new project. As you will see in the upcoming sections, this may be easier said than done.

Beware of Cash Flows Diverted from Existing Products

> ### REMEMBER YOUR PRINCIPLES
>
> **Principle** If we are to make intelligent capital-budgeting decisions, we must accurately measure the timing of a project's benefits and costs, that is, when we receive money and when it leaves our hands. **Principle 1: Cash Flow Is What Matters** speaks directly to this. Remember, it is cash inflows that can be reinvested and cash outflows that involve paying out money.

Assume for a moment that we are managers of a firm considering a new product line that might compete with one of our existing products and possibly reduce its sales. In determining the free cash flows associated with the proposed project, we should consider only the incremental sales brought to the company as a whole. New-product sales achieved at the cost of losing sales of other products in our line are not considered a benefit. For example, when Quaker Oats introduced Cap'n Crunch's Cozmic Crunch, the product competed directly with the company's Cap'n Crunch and Crunch Berries cereals. (In fact Cozmic Crunch was almost identical to Crunch Berries, with the shapes changed to stars and moons, along with a packet of orange space dust that turns milk green.) Quaker meant to target the market niche held by Post Fruity Pebbles, but there was no question that sales recorded by Cozmic Crunch bit into—literally cannibalized—Quaker's existing product line.

Remember that we are interested only in the sales dollars to the firm if the project is accepted, as opposed to what the sales dollars would be if the project were rejected. Just moving sales from one product line to a new product line does not bring anything new into the company. But if sales are captured from competitors or if sales that would have been lost to new competing products are retained, then these are relevant incremental free cash flows.

Look for Incidental or Synergistic Effects

Although in some cases a new project may take sales away from a firm's current projects, in other cases a new effort might actually bring new sales to the existing line.

For example, in November 2010, GM's Chevrolet division is scheduled to introduce the Chevy Volt, an electric car that allows you to drive 40 miles before a recharge is needed. If you're still on the road and the battery runs out, a small gas-powered engine kicks in to give you a driving range of 640 miles on a single tank of gas. For years, GM was criticized for not keeping pace with the rest of the automotive industry, a sad fact that contributed to its bankruptcy in 2009. Its cars remained fuel inefficient and GM's reputation for innovation was nonexistent. GM hopes that introducing the Chevy Volt will send a message to car buyers that GM is back on track and has something new to offer—that the Volt will bring curious customers to showrooms, and those customers will in turn, either buy a Volt or another GM product. This is called a *synergistic* effect. The cash flow comes from any GM sale that would not have occurred if a customer had not visited a GM showroom to see a Volt. Synergistic effects are quite common in the business world.

If you owned a convenience store and were considering adding gas pumps, would you evaluate the project looking only at cash flows from the sale of gas? No. You would look at any new sales to any part of your business that the new gas pumps brought in. No doubt the additional traffic that the gas pumps bring in would increase your convenience-store sales. As such, these cash flows would be considered in evaluating whether or not to install the gas pumps. In effect, you should look at any change in cash flow to the company as a whole that results from the project being evaluated.

Work in Working-Capital Requirements

Many times a new project involves an additional investment in working capital. This may take the form of new inventory to stock a sales outlet, an additional investment in accounts receivable resulting from additional credit sales, or an increased investment in cash to operate cash registers, and more. Working-capital requirements are considered a free cash flow even though they do not leave the company. Generally, working-capital requirements are tied up over the life of the project. When the project terminates, there is usually an offsetting cash inflow as the working capital is recovered, although this offset is not perfect because of the time value of money.

Consider Incremental Expenses

Just as cash inflows from a new project are measured on an incremental basis, expenses, or cash outflows, should also be measured on an incremental basis. For example, if introducing a new product line necessitates training the sales staff, the after-tax cash flow associated with the training program must be considered a cash outflow and charged against the project. Likewise, if accepting a new project dictates that a production facility be reengineered, the cash flows associated with that capital investment should be charged against the project, and they will then be depreciated over the life of the project. Again, any incremental after-tax cash flow affecting the company as a whole is a relevant cash flow, whether it is flowing in or flowing out.

Remember That Sunk Costs Are Not Incremental Cash Flows

Only cash flows that are affected by the decision making at the moment are relevant in capital budgeting. The manager asks two questions: (1) Will this cash flow occur if the project is accepted? (2) Will this cash flow occur if the project is rejected? Yes to the first question and no to the second equals an incremental cash flow. For example, let's assume you are considering introducing a new taste treat called Puddin' in a Shoe. You would like to do some test-marketing before production. If you are considering the decision to test-market and have not yet done so, the costs associated with the test-marketing are relevant cash flows. Conversely, if you have already test-marketed, the cash flows involved in test-marketing are no longer relevant to the project's evaluation. It's a matter of timing. Regardless of what you might decide about future production, the cash flows allocated to the marketing test have already occurred. Cash flows that have already taken place are often referred to as "sunk costs" because they have been sunk into the project and cannot be undone. As a rule, any cash flows that are not affected by the accept/reject criterion should not be included in capital-budgeting analysis.

Account for Opportunity Costs

Now we will focus on the cash flows that are lost because a given project consumes scarce resources that would have produced cash flows if that project had been rejected. This is the opportunity cost of doing business. For example, a product consumes valuable floor space in a production facility. Although the cash flow is not obvious, the real question remains: What else could be done with this space? The space could have been rented out, or another product could have been stored there. The key point is that opportunity-cost cash flows should reflect the net cash flows that would have been received if the project under consideration were rejected. Again, we are analyzing the cash flows to the company as a whole, with or without the project.

Decide If Overhead Costs Are Truly Incremental Cash Flows

Although we certainly want to include any incremental cash flows resulting in changes from overhead expenses such as utilities and salaries, we also want to make sure that these are truly incremental cash flows. Many times, overhead expenses—heat, light, rent—occur whether a given project is accepted or rejected. There is often not a single, specific project to which these expenses can be allocated. Thus, the question is not whether the project benefits from the overhead costs a firm spends but whether they are incremental cash flows associated with the project and relevant to capital budgeting.

Ignore Interest Payments and Financing Flows

To evaluate new projects and determine cash flows, we must separate the investment decision from the financing decision. Interest payments and other financing cash flows that might

FINANCE AT WORK

UNIVERSAL STUDIOS

A major capital-budgeting decision led Universal Studios to build its Islands of Adventure theme park. The purpose of this $2.6 billion investment by Universal was to get first crack at the tourist's dollar in Orlando, Florida. Although this capital-budgeting decision may, on the surface, seem like a relatively simple decision, forecasting the expected cash flows associated with the theme park was, in fact, quite complicated.

To begin with, Universal was introducing a product that competed directly with itself. The original Universal Studios Park features rides such as "Hollywood Rip, Ride, Rockit" and "Jimmy Neutron's Nicktoon Blast," while Islands of Adventure would feature "The Incredible Hulk Coaster" and "Dudley Do-Right's Ripsaw Falls." Were there enough tourist dollars to support both theme parks, or would the new Islands of Adventure park simply cannibalize ticket sales from the older Universal Studios Park? In addition, what would happen when Disney countered with a new park of its own?

In the case of Universal's Islands of Adventure, we could ask what would happen to attendance at the original Universal Studios Park if the new park were not opened versus what the attendance would be with the new park? In addition, would tourist traffic through the Islands of Adventure lead to additional sales and viewership of NBC Universal television and movies?

From Universal's point of view, the objective may actually have been threefold: to increase its share of the tourist market; to keep from losing market share as tourists look for the latest in technological rides and entertainment; and to promote NBC Universal's ventures such as television and movies. However, for companies in very competitive markets, the evolution and introduction of new products may serve more to preserve market share than to expand it. Certainly, that's the case in the computer market, where Apple introduces upgraded models that continually render current models obsolete. The bottom line here is that, with respect to estimating cash flows, things are many times more complicated than they first appear. As such, we have to dig deep to understand how a firm's free cash flows are affected by the decision at hand.

result from raising funds to finance a project should not be considered incremental cash flows. If accepting a project means we have to raise new funds by issuing bonds, the interest charges associated with raising funds are not a relevant cash outflow. Why? Because when we discount the incremental cash flows back to the present at the required rate of return, we are implicitly accounting for the cost of raising funds to finance the new project. In essence, the required rate of return reflects the cost of the funds needed to support the project. Managers first determine the desirability of the project and then determine how best to finance it.

Concept Check

1. What is an incremental cash flow? What is a sunk cost? Why must you account for opportunity costs?

2. If Ford introduces a new auto line, might some of the cash flows from that new car line be diverted from existing product lines? How should you deal with this?

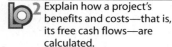
2 Explain how a project's benefits and costs—that is, its free cash flows—are calculated.

An Overview of the Calculations of a Project's Free Cash Flows

As we have explained, in measuring cash flows, we will focus our attention on the difference in the firm's after-tax free cash flows *with* versus *without* the project—the project's *free cash flows*. The worth of our decision depends on the accuracy of our cash flow estimates. For this reason, we first examined the question of which cash flows are relevant. Now we will see that, in general, a project's free cash flows will fall into one of three categories: (1) the initial outlay, (2) the annual free cash flows over the project's life, and (3) the terminal free cash flow. Once we have taken a look at these categories, we will take on the task of measuring these free cash flows.

What Goes Into the Initial Outlay

initial outlay the immediate cash outflow necessary to purchase the asset and put it in operating order.

The **initial outlay** is the *immediate cash outflow necessary to purchase the asset and put it in operating order*. This amount includes (1) the cost of purchasing the asset and getting it operational, including the purchase price, shipping and installation, and any training costs for employees who will be operating the equipment, and (2) any increases in working-capital requirements. The working capital includes any increases in current assets, less any increase in accounts payable. If we are considering a new sales outlet, there might be additional cash flows associated with making a net investment in working capital in the form of increased accounts receivable, inventory, and cash necessary to operate the outlet. Although these cash flows are not included in the cost of the asset or even shown as an expense on the income statement, they must be included in our analysis. The after-tax cost of expense items incurred as a result of the new investment must also be included as cash outflows—for example, any training expenses that would not have been incurred otherwise.

Finally, if the investment decision is a replacement decision, the cash inflow associated with the selling price of the old asset, in addition to any tax effects resulting from its sale, must be included. It should be stressed that the incremental nature of the cash flow is of great importance. In many cases, if the project is not accepted, then status quo for the firm will simply not continue. Thus, we must be realistic in estimating what the cash flows to the company would be if the new project were not accepted.

In a replacement decision, the initial outlay is equal to the cost of the new asset, less the amount we received from selling the old asset. Typically, when the old asset is sold there will be a gain or loss from the sale, which means we will have to pay taxes if there is a gain from the sale or a reduction of taxes if there is a loss. Thus the initial outlay is calculated as follows:

$$\begin{matrix} \text{Initial} \\ \text{outlay} \end{matrix} = \begin{matrix} \text{cost of} \\ \text{new asset} \end{matrix} - \begin{matrix} \text{sales price} \\ \text{of the old asset} \end{matrix} +/- \begin{matrix} \text{taxes recovered or paid} \\ \text{from a loss or gain on the} \\ \text{sale of the old asset} \end{matrix}$$

So we need to state the sale of the old asset on an after-tax basis. When it comes to the taxes, there are three possible situations that can result:

1. The old asset is sold for a price above the depreciated value. Here the difference between the old machine's selling price and its depreciated value is considered a taxable gain and is taxed at the marginal corporate tax rate. If, for example, the old machine was originally purchased for $15,000, had a book value of $10,000, and was sold for $17,000, assuming the firm's marginal corporate tax rate is 34 percent, the taxes due from the gain would be ($17,000 − $10,000) × (0.34), or $2,380.

2. The old asset is sold for its depreciated value. In this case, no taxes result, because there is neither a gain nor a loss in the asset's sale.

3. The old asset is sold for less than its depreciated value. In this case, the difference between the depreciated book value and the salvage value of the asset is a taxable loss and can be used to offset capital gains and thus results in a tax savings. For example, if the depreciated book value of the asset is $10,000 and it is sold for $7,000, we have a $3,000 loss. Assuming the firm's marginal corporate tax rate is 34 percent, the cash inflow from the tax savings is ($10,000 − $7,000) × (0.34), or $1,020.

What Goes Into the Annual Free Cash Flows over the Project's Life

Annual free cash flows come from operating cash flows (that is, what you've made as a result of taking on the project), changes in working capital, and any capital spending that might take place. In our calculations we'll begin with our pro forma statements and work from there. We will have to make adjustments for interest, depreciation, and working capital, along with any capital expenditures that might occur.

Before we look at the calculations, let's look at the types of adjustments that we're going to have to make to go from operating cash flows to free cash flows. To do this we'll have to make adjustments for:

♦ **Depreciation and taxes**   Depreciation is a non–cash flow expense. It occurs because you bought a fixed asset (for example, you built a plant) in an earlier period, and now, through depreciation, you're expensing it over time—but depreciation does not involve a cash flow.

That means the firm's net income understates cash flows by this amount. Therefore, we'll want to compensate for this by adding depreciation back into our measure of accounting income when calculating cash flows.

Although depreciation expense is a non-cash expense, it does affect cash flow because it is a tax-deductible expense. The higher the depreciation expense, the lower the firm's profits, which results in lower taxes.

There are a number of different methods for computing depreciation expense. For instance, we could use the Accelerated Cost Recovery System (ACRS) provided by the IRS. However, for our purposes, we will use a simplified straight-line method, where we calculate annual depreciation by taking the project's initial depreciable value and dividing by its depreciable life as follows:

$$\text{Annual depreciation using the simplified straight-line method} = \frac{\text{initial depreciable value}}{\text{depreciable life}}$$

The initial depreciable value is equal to the cost of the asset plus any expenses necessary to get the new asset into operating order.

This is not how depreciation would actually be calculated. The reason we have simplified the calculation is to allow you to focus directly on what should and should not be included in the cash flow calculations. Moreover, because the tax laws change rather frequently, we are more interested in recognizing the tax implications of depreciation than in understanding the specific depreciation provisions of the current tax laws.

♦ **Interest expenses**   There's no question that if you take on a new project, you'll have to pay for it somehow—either through internally generated cash or, say, by selling new stocks or bonds. In other words, there's a cost to that money. We recognize this principle when we discount future cash flows back to the present at the required rate of return. Remember, the project's required rate of return is the rate of return that it must earn to justify your taking on the project. It recognizes the risk of the project and the fact that there is an opportunity cost of money. If we discounted the future cash flows back to the present and also subtracted out interest expenses, then we would have double counted the cost of money—accounting for the cost of money once when we subtracted out interest expenses and once when we discounted the cash flows back to the present. Therefore, we want to make sure that cash flows are not lowered by financing costs such as interest payments. That means we'll want to make sure that financing flows (interest expense) are not included.

♦ **Changes in net working capital**   As we have explained, many projects require an increased investment in working capital. For example, some of the new sales may be credit sales resulting in an increased investment in accounts receivable. Also, in order to produce and sell the product, the firm may have to increase its investment in inventory. On the other hand, some of this increased working-capital investment may be financed by an increase in accounts payable. Because all these potential changes are changes in assets and liabilities, they don't affect accounting income. Thus, if this project brings with it a positive change in net working capital, then it means money is going to be tied up in increased working capital, and this would be a cash outflow. That means we'll have to make sure we account for any changes in working capital that might occur.

♦ **Changes in capital spending**   From an accounting perspective, the cash flow associated with the purchase of a fixed asset is not an expense. For example, when Marriott spends $50 million on building a new hotel resort, although there is a significant cash outflow, there is no accompanying expense. Instead, the $50 million cash outflow creates an annual depreciation expense over the life of the hotel. We'll want to make sure we include any changes in capital spending such as this in our cash flow calculations.

What Goes Into the Terminal Cash Flow

The terminal cash flow is associated with the project's termination and includes the annual free cash flow and salvage value of the project plus or minus any taxable gains or losses associated with its sale. Under the current tax laws, in most cases there will be tax payments associated with the salvage value at termination. This is because the current laws allow all projects to be depreciated to zero. So, if a project has a book value of zero at termination and a positive salvage value, then that salvage value will be taxed. The tax effects associated with the salvage value of the project at termination are determined exactly like the tax effects on the sale of the old machine associated with the initial outlay. The salvage value proceeds are compared with the depreciated value, in this case zero, to determine the tax.

In addition to the salvage value, there may be a cash outlay associated with the project termination. For example, at the close of a strip-mining operation, the mine must be refilled in an ecologically acceptable manner.

Now let's put this all together and measure the project's free cash flows.

Calculating the Free Cash Flows

Free cash flow calculations can be broken down into three basic parts: cash flows from operations, cash flows associated with working-capital requirements, and capital-spending cash flows. Let's begin our discussion by looking at how to measure cash flows from operations and then move on to discuss measuring cash flows from working-capital requirements and capital spending.

STEP 1 *Measure the project's change in the firm's after-tax operating cash flows.* An easy way to calculate operating cash flows is to take the information provided on the firm's projected income statement and simply convert the accounting information into cash flow information. To do this we take advantage of the fact that the difference between the change in sales and the change in costs should be equal to the change in earnings before interest and taxes (EBIT) plus depreciation.

Under this method, the calculation of a project's operating cash flow involves three steps. First, we determine the company's *earnings before interest and taxes (EBIT)* with and without this project. Second, we subtract out the change in taxes. Keep in mind that in calculating the change in taxes, we will ignore any interest expenses. Third, we adjust this value for the fact that depreciation, a non–cash flow item, has been subtracted out in the calculation of EBIT. We do this by adding back depreciation. Thus, operating cash flows are calculated as follows:

Operating cash flows = change in earnings before interest and taxes (EBIT)
− change in taxes
+ change in depreciation

EXAMPLE 11.1

Let's look at an example to show the calculation of operating cash flows. Assume that a new project will annually generate additional revenues of $1,000,000 and additional fixed and variable costs of $500,000, while increasing depreciation by $150,000 per year. In addition, let's assume that the firm's marginal tax rate is 34 percent. Given this, the firm's net profit after tax or net income can be calculated as:

Revenue	$1,000,000
− Cash fixed and variable costs	500,000
− Depreciation	150,000
= EBIT	$ 350,000
− Taxes (34%)	119,000
= Net income	$ 231,000

Operating cash flows = change in earnings before interest and taxes
− change in taxes + change in depreciation
= $350,000 − $119,000 + $150,000 = $381,000

STEP 2 *Calculate the cash flows from the change in the firm's net working capital.* As we mentioned earlier in this chapter, many times a new project will involve additional investment in working capital—perhaps new inventory to stock a new sales outlet or simply additional investment in accounts receivable. There also may be some spontaneous short-term financing—for example, increases in accounts payable—that result from the new project. Thus, the change in net working capital is the additional investment in current assets minus any additional short-term liabilities that were generated.

STEP 3 *Calculate the cash flows from the change in the firm's capital spending.* Although there is generally a large cash outflow associated with a project's initial outlay, there may also be additional capital-spending requirements over the life of the project. For example, you may know ahead of time that the plant will need some minor retooling in the second year of the project in order to keep the project abreast of new technological changes that are expected to take place. In effect, we will look at the company with and without the new project, and any changes in capital spending that occur are relevant.

STEP 4 *Putting it together: calculating a project's free cash flows.* Thus, a project's free cash flows are:

Project's free cash flows = change in earnings before interest and taxes (EBIT)
− change in taxes
+ change in depreciation
− change in net working capital
− change in capital spending

To estimate the changes in EBIT, taxes, depreciation, net working capital, and capital spending we start with estimates of how many units we expect to sell, what the costs—both fixed and variable—will be, what the selling price will be, and what the required capital investment will be. From there we can put together a pro forma statement that should provide us with the data we need to estimate the project's free cash flows. However, you must keep in mind that our capital-budgeting decision will only be as good as our estimates of the costs and future demand associated with the project. In fact, most capital-budgeting decisions that turn out to be bad decisions are not so because of using a bad decision rule but because the estimates of future demand and costs were inaccurate. Let's look at an example.

EXAMPLE 11.2

You are considering expanding your product line that currently consists of Lee's Press-on Nails to take advantage of the fitness craze. The new product you are considering introducing is "Press-on Abs." You feel you can sell 100,000 of these per year for 4 years (after which time this project is expected to shut down because forecasters predict looking healthy will no longer be in vogue, and looking like a couch potato will). The Press-on Abs would sell for $6.00 each, with variable costs of $3.00 for each one produced. Annual fixed costs associated with production would be $90,000. In addition, there would be a $200,000 initial capital expenditure associated with the purchase of new production equipment. It is assumed that this initial expenditure will be depreciated, using the simplified straight-line method, down to zero over 4 years. The project will also require a one-time initial investment of $30,000 in net working capital associated with the inventory. Finally, assume that the firm's marginal tax rate is 34 percent.

INITIAL OUTLAY

Let's begin by estimating the initial outlay. In this example, the initial outlay is the $200,000 initial capital expenditure plus the investment of $30,000 in net working capital, for a total of $230,000.

TABLE 11-1 Calculating the Annual Change in Earnings Before Interest and Taxes for the Press-on Abs Project

Δ Sales (100,000 units at $6.00/unit)	$ 600,000
Less: Δ Variable costs (variable cost $3.00/unit)	$ 300,000
Less: Δ Fixed costs	$ 90,000
Equals: EBITDA (assuming amortization is 0)	$ 210,000
Less: Δ Depreciation ($200,000/4 years)	$ 50,000
Equals: Δ EBIT	$ 160,000
Less: Δ Taxes: (taxed at 34%)	$ 54,400
Equals: Δ Net income	$ 105,600

ANNUAL FREE CASH FLOWS

Table 11-1 calculates the annual change in earnings before interest and taxes. This calculation begins with the change in sales (Δ Sales) and subtracts the change in fixed and variable costs in addition to the change in depreciation, to arrive at the change in earnings before interest and taxes (Δ EBIT). Depreciation is calculated using the simplified straight-line method, which is simply the depreciable value of the asset ($200,000 divided by the asset's expected life of 4 years). Taxes are then calculated assuming a 34 percent marginal tax rate. Once we have calculated EBIT and taxes, we don't need to go any further, because these are the only two values from the income statement that we need. In addition, in this example there is not any annual increase in working capital associated with the project under consideration. Also notice that we have ignored any interest payments and financing flows that might have occurred. As mentioned earlier, when we discount the free cash flows back to the present at the required rate of return, we are implicitly accounting for the cost of the funds needed to support the project.

The project's annual *change in operating cash flow* is calculated in Table 11-2.

Remember: **The project's annual *free cash flow* is simply the *change in operating cash flow* less any *change in net working capital* and less any *change in capital spending*.** In this example there are no changes in net working capital and capital spending over the life of the project. This is not the case for all projects that you will consider. For example, on a project where sales increase annually, it is likely that working capital will also increase each year to support a larger inventory and a higher level of accounts receivable. Similarly, on some projects the capital expenditures may be spread out over several years. The point here is that what we are trying to do is look at the firm with this project and without this project and measure the change in cash flows other than any interest payments and financing flows that might occur.

TERMINAL CASH FLOW

For this project, the terminal cash flow is quite simple. The only unusual cash flow at the project's termination is the recapture of the net working capital associated with the project. In effect, the investment in inventory of $30,000 is liquidated when the project is shut down in 4 years. Keep in mind that in calculating free cash flow we subtract out the

TABLE 11-2 Calculating the Annual Change in Operating Cash Flow, Press-on Abs Project

Δ Earnings before interest and taxes (EBIT)	$160,000
Minus: Δ Taxes	$ 54,400
Plus: Δ Depreciation	$ 50,000
Equals: Δ Operating cash flow	$155,600

TABLE 11-3 Calculating the Terminal Free Cash Flow, Press-on Abs Project

Δ Earnings before interest and taxes (EBIT)	$160,000
Minus: Δ Taxes	$ 54,400
Plus: Δ Depreciation	$ 50,000
Minus: Δ Net working capital	($ 30,000)
Equals: Δ Free cash flow	$185,600

FIGURE 11-1 Free Cash Flow Diagram for Press-on Abs

YEAR	0	1	2	3	4
Cash Flow	−$230,000	155,600	155,600	155,600	185,600

change in net working capital, but because the change in net working capital is negative (we are reducing our investment in inventory), we are subtracting a negative number, which has the effect of adding it back in. Thus, working capital was a negative cash flow when the project began and we invested in inventory, but at termination it becomes a positive offsetting cash flow when the inventory was liquidated. The calculation of the terminal free cash flow is illustrated in Table 11-3.

If we were to construct a free cash flow diagram from this example (Figure 11-1), it would have an initial outlay of $230,000, the free cash flows during years 1 through 3 would be $155,600, and the free cash flow in the terminal year would be $185,600.

A Comprehensive Example: Calculating Free Cash Flows

Now let's put what we know about capital budgeting together and look at a capital-budgeting decision for a firm in the 34 percent marginal tax bracket with a 15 percent required rate of return or cost of capital. The project we are considering involves the introduction of a new electric scooter line by Raymobile. Our first task is that of estimating cash flows which is the focus of this section. This project is expected to last 5 years and then, because this is somewhat of a fad product, be terminated. Thus, our first task becomes that of estimating the initial outlay, the annual free cash flows, and the terminal free cash flow. Given the information in Table 11-4, we want to determine the free cash flows associated with the project. Once we have that, we can easily calculate the project's net present value, the profitability index, and the internal rate of return and apply the appropriate decision criteria.

To determine the differential annual free cash flows, we first need to determine the annual change in operating cash flow. To do this we will take the change in EBIT, subtract out the change in taxes, and then add in the change in depreciation. This is shown in Sec-

CAN YOU DO IT?

CALCULATING OPERATING CASH FLOWS

Assume that a new project will generate revenues of $300,000 annually, and the annual cash expenses, including both fixed and variable costs, will be $190,000 per year. Depreciation will be $20,000 per year. In addition, the firm's marginal tax rate is 40 percent. Calculate the operating cash flows.

(The solution can be found on page 313.)

DID YOU GET IT?

CALCULATING OPERATING CASH FLOWS

You were asked to determine the operating cash flows for a project. Operating cash flows are calculated as:

Operating cash flows = change in earnings before interest and taxes (EBIT)
− change in taxes
+ change in depreciation

STEP 1 Calculate the change in EBIT

Revenue	$300,000
−Cash fixed and variable expenses	190,000
−Depreciation	20,000
=EBIT	$ 90,000

STEP 2 Calculate taxes by multiplying the increase in EBIT times the marginal tax rate of 40 percent

Change in EBIT	$90,000
Times: Taxes (40%)	= 36,000

STEP 3 Calculate operating cash flows

Operating cash flows = change in earnings before interest and taxes (EBIT)
− change in taxes
+ change in depreciation
= $90,000 − $36,000 + $20,000 = $74,000

The operating cash flows of $74,000 then become an input to the calculation of the free cash flows.

TABLE 11-4 Raymobile Scooter Line Capital-Budgeting Example

Cost of new plant and equipment	$9,700,000
Shipping and installation costs	$ 300,000
Unit sales	

YEAR	UNITS SOLD
1	50,000
2	100,000
3	100,000
4	70,000
5	50,000

Sales price per unit	$150/unit in years 1 through 4, $130/unit in year 5
Variable cost per unit	$80/unit
Annual fixed costs	$500,000 in years 1–5
Working-capital requirements	There will be an initial working-capital requirement of $100,000 just to get production started. Then, for each year, the *total* investment in net working capital will be equal to 10 percent of the dollar value of sales for that year. Thus, the investment in working capital will increase during years 1 and 2, then decrease in year 4. Finally, all working capital will be liquidated at the termination of the project at the end of year 5.
The depreciation method	We use the simplified straight-line method over 5 years. It is assumed that the plant and equipment will have no salvage value after 5 years. Thus, annual depreciation is $2,000,000/year for 5 years.

tion II of Table 11-5. We first determine what the change in sales revenue will be by multiplying the units sold times the sale price. From the change in sales revenue, we subtract out variable costs, which are $80 per unit. Then, the change in fixed costs is subtracted out, and the result is earnings before interest, taxes, depreciation, and amortization (EBITDA).

TABLE 11-5 Calculating the Free Cash Flow for Raymobile Scooters

YEAR	0	1	2	3	4	5
Section I. Calculate the Change in EBIT, Taxes, and Depreciation (This Becomes an Input in the Calculation of Operating Cash Flow in Section II)						
Units sold		50,000	100,000	100,000	70,000	50,000
Sales price		$150	$150	$150	$150	$130
Sales revenue		$7,500,000	$15,000,000	$15,000,000	$10,500,000	$6,500,000
Less: Variable costs		4,000,000	8,000,000	8,000,000	5,600,000	4,000,000
Less: Fixed costs		500,000	500,000	500,000	500,000	500,000
Equals: EBITDA		$3,000,000	$ 6,500,000	$ 6,500,000	$ 4,400,000	$2,000,000
Less: Depreciation (amortization is assumed to be 0)		2,000,000	2,000,000	2,000,000	2,000,000	2,000,000
Equals: EBIT		$1,000,000	$ 4,500,000	$ 4,500,000	$ 2,400,000	0
Taxes (@34%)		340,000	1,530,000	1,530,000	816,000	0
Section II. Calculate Operating Cash Flow (This Becomes an Input in the Calculation of Free Cash Flow in Section IV)						
Operating cash flow:						
EBIT		$1,000,000	$ 4,500,000	$ 4,500,000	$ 2,400,000	$ 0
Minus: Taxes		340,000	1,530,000	1,530,000	816,000	0
Plus: Depreciation		2,000,000	2,000,000	2,000,000	2,000,000	2,000,000
Equals: Operating cash flows		$2,660,000	$ 4,970,000	$ 4,970,000	$ 3,584,000	$2,000,000
Section III. Calculate the Net Working Capital (This Becomes an Input in the Calculation of Free Cash Flow in Section IV)						
Change in net working capital:						
Revenue		$7,500,000	$15,000,000	$15,000,000	$10,500,000	$6,500,000
Initial working-capital requirement	$100,000					
Net working-capital needs		750,000	1,500,000	1,500,000	1,050,000	650,000
Liquidation of working capital						650,000
Change in working capital	100,000	650,000	750,000	0	(450,000)	(1,050,000)
Section IV. Calculate Free Cash Flow (Using Information Calculated in Sections II and III, in Addition to the Change in Capital Spending)						
Free cash flow:						
Operating cash flow		$2,660,000	$ 4,970,000	$ 4,970,000	$ 3,584,000	$2,000,000
Minus: Change in net working capital	$ 100,000	650,000	750,000	0	(450,000)	(1,050,000)
Minus: Change in capital spending	10,000,000	0	0	0	0	0
Equals: Free cash flow	$(10,100,000)	$2,010,000	$ 4,220,000	$ 4,970,000	$ 4,034,000	$3,050,000

Subtracting the change in depreciation and amortization, which in this case is assumed to be zero, from EBITDA then leaves us with the change in earnings before interest and taxes (EBIT). From the change in EBIT, we can then calculate the change in taxes, which are assumed to be 34 percent of EBIT.

Using the calculations provided in Section I of Table 11-5, we then calculate the operating cash flow in Section II of Table 11-5. As you recall, the operating cash flow is simply EBIT minus taxes, plus depreciation.

To calculate the annual free cash flows from this project, we subtract the change in net working capital and the change in capital spending from operating cash flow. Thus, the first step becomes determining the change in net working capital, which is shown in Section III of Table 11-5. The change in net working capital generally includes both increases in inventory and increases in accounts receivable that naturally occur as sales increase from the introduction of the new product line. Some of the increase in accounts receivable may be offset by increases in accounts payable, but, in general, most new projects involve some type of increase in net working capital. In this example, there is an initial working capital requirement of $100,000. In addition, for each year the total investment in net working capital will be equal to 10 percent of sales for each year. Thus, the investment in working capital for

CAN YOU DO IT?

CALCULATING FREE CASH FLOWS

Hurley's Hidden Snacks is introducing a new product and has an expected change in EBIT of $800,000. Hurley's Hidden Snacks has a 40 percent marginal tax rate. This project will also produce $100,000 of depreciation per year. In addition, this project will also cause the following changes in year 1:

	WITHOUT THE PROJECT	WITH THE PROJECT
Accounts receivable	$35,000	$63,000
Inventory	65,000	70,000
Accounts payable	70,000	90,000

What is the project's free cash flow in year 1?
   (The solution can be found on page 316.)

FIGURE 11-2 Free Cash Flow Diagram for the Raymobile Scooter Line

	$r = 15\%$					
YEAR	0	1	2	3	4	5
Cash Flow	−$10,100,000	2,010,000	4,220,000	4,970,000	4,034,000	3,050,000

year 1 is $750,000 (because sales are estimated to be $7,500,000). Working capital will already be at $100,000, so the change in net working capital will be $650,000. Net working capital will continue to increase during years 1 and 2, then decrease in year 4. Finally, all working capital is liquidated at the termination of the project at the end of year 5.

With the operating cash flow and the change in net working capital already calculated, the calculation of the project's free cash flow becomes easy. All that is missing is the change in capital spending, which in this example will simply be the $9,700,000 for plant and equipment plus the $300,000 for shipping and installation. Thus, the change in capital spending becomes $10,000,000. We then need merely to take operating cash flow and subtract from it both the change in net working capital and the change in capital spending. This is done in Section IV of Table 11-5 with the annual free cash flows given in the last row in that table. A free cash flow diagram for this project is provided in Figure 11-2.

Concept Check

1. In general, a project's cash flows will fall into one of three categories. What are these categories?
2. What is a free cash flow? How do we calculate it?
3. Although depreciation is not a cash flow item, it plays an important role in the calculation of cash flows. How does depreciation affect a project's cash flows?

Options in Capital Budgeting

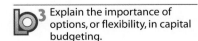
3 Explain the importance of options, or flexibility, in capital budgeting.

The use of discounted cash flow decision criteria, such as the *NPV* method, provides an excellent framework within which to evaluate projects. However, what happens if the project being analyzed has the potential to be modified after some future uncertainty has been resolved? For example, if a project that had an expected life of 10 years turns out to be better than anticipated, it may be expanded or continued past 10 years, perhaps going on for 20 years. On the other hand, if its cash flows do not meet expectations, it may not last a full 10 years and be scaled back, abandoned, or sold. In addition, suppose the project were

DID YOU GET IT?

CALCULATING FREE CASH FLOWS

You were asked to determine the free cash flows in year 1 for a new product being introduced by Hurley's Hidden Snacks.

STEP 1 Calculate the change in net working capital.

The change in net working capital equals the increase in accounts receivable and inventory less the increase in accounts payable = $28,000 + $5,000 − $20,000 = $13,000.

STEP 2 Calculate the change in free cash flows.

Project's free cash flows = change in earnings before interest and taxes (EBIT)
- change in taxes
+ change in depreciation
- change in net working capital
- change in capital spending
= $800,000 − ($800,000 × .40) + $100,000 − $13,000 − $0 = $567,000

The project's free cash flows represent the "Cash Flow Is What Matters" that we discussed in **Principle 1**.

---

delayed for a year or two. This flexibility is something that the *NPV* and our other decision-making criteria have difficulty dealing with. In fact, the *NPV* may actually understate the value of the project if the future opportunities associated with modifying it have a positive value. It is this value of flexibility that we will be examining using options.

Three of the most common option types that can add value to a capital-budgeting project are (1) the option to delay a project until the future cash flows are more favorable—this option is common when the firm has exclusive rights, perhaps a patent, to a product or technology; (2) the option to expand a project, perhaps in size or even to develop new products that would not have otherwise been feasible; and (3) the option to abandon a project if the future cash flows fall short of expectations.

The Option to Delay a Project

There is no question that the estimated cash flows associated with a project can change over time. In fact, as a result of changing expected cash flows, a project that currently has a negative net present value may have a positive net present value in the future. Let's take another look at the gas-electric hybrid car market we examined in the introduction to this chapter. This time, let's assume that you've developed a high-voltage, nickel-metal hydride battery that can be used to increase the mileage on hybrid cars to up to 150 miles per gallon. However, as you examine the costs of producing this new battery, you realize that it is still relatively expensive to manufacture and that, given the costs, the market for a car using this battery is quite small right now. Does that mean that the rights to the high-voltage, nickel-metal hydride battery have no value? No, they have value because you may be able to improve on this technology in the future and make the battery even more efficient and less expensive. They also have value because oil prices might rise even further, which would lead to a bigger market for super-fuel-efficient cars. In effect, the ability to delay this project with the hope that technological and market conditions will change, making this project profitable, lends value to the project.

Another example of the option to delay a project until the future cash flows are more favorable involves a firm that owns the oil rights to some oil-rich land and is considering an oil-drilling project. Suppose after all of the costs and the expected oil output are considered, the project has a negative net present value. Does that mean the firm should give away its oil rights or that those oil rights have no value? Certainly not. There is a chance that in the future oil prices could rise to the point that this negative *NPV* project could become a positive *NPV* project. It is this ability to delay development that provides value. Thus, the value in this seemingly negative *NPV* project is provided by the option to delay the project until the future cash flows are more favorable.

The Option to Expand a Project

Just as we saw with the option to delay a project, the estimated cash flows associated with a project can change over time, making it valuable to expand a project. Again, this flexibility to adjust production to demand has value. For example, a firm might deliberately build a production plant with excess capacity so that if the product has more-than-anticipated demand, the firm can simply increase production. Alternatively, taking on this project might provide the firm with a foothold in a new industry and lead to other products that would not have otherwise been feasible. This reasoning has led many firms to expand into e-businesses, hoping to gain know-how and expertise that will lead to other profitable projects down the line. It also provides some of the rationale for research and development expenditures to explore new markets.

Let's go back to our example of the gas-electric hybrid car and examine the option to expand that project. One of the reasons that most of the major automobile firms are introducing gas-electric hybrid cars is that they feel that if gas prices keep moving beyond the $2 to $3 per gallon price, these hybrids may become the future of the industry, and the only way to gain the know-how and expertise to produce a hybrid is to do it. As the cost of technology declines and the demand increases—perhaps pushed on by increases in gas prices—then the companies will be ready to expand into full-fledged production. This strategy becomes clear when you look at Honda, which first introduced the Insight in 2000, and Toyota, which introduced the Prius in 2001.

When hybrids were first introduced, analysts estimated that Honda was losing about $8,000 on each Insight it sold, whereas Toyota was losing about $3,000 per car, but both firms hoped to break even in a few years. Still, these projects made sense because they allowed these automakers to gain the technological and production expertise to profitably produce a gas-electric hybrid car. And, as mentioned in the chapter introduction, with predictions that hybrids will account for nearly one out of five cars sold in the United States by 2020, it is a big market they're looking at. Moreover, the technology Honda and Toyota developed with the Insight and Prius may have profitable applications for other cars or in other areas. In effect, it is the option of expanding production in the future that brings value to this project.

The Option to Abandon a Project

The option to abandon a project as the estimated cash flows associated with it change over time also has value. Again, it is this flexibility to adjust to new information that provides the value. For example, a project's sales in the first year or two might not live up to expectations, with the project being barely profitable. The firm might then decide to liquidate the project and sell the plant and all of the equipment. That liquidated value may be more than the value of keeping the project going.

Again, let's go back to our example of the gas-electric hybrid car and, this time, examine the option to abandon that project. If after a few years the cost of gas falls dramatically while the cost of technology remains high, the gas-electric hybrid car might not become profitable. At that point the manufacturer might decide to abandon the project and sell the technology, including all the patent rights to it. In effect, the original project, the gas-electric hybrid car, may not be of value, but the technology that has been developed might be. As a result, the value of abandoning the project and selling the technology might be more than the value of keeping the project running. Again, it is the value of flexibility associated with the possibility of modifying the project in the future—in this case abandoning the project—that can produce positive value.

Options in Capital Budgeting: The Bottom Line

Because of the potential to be modified in the future after some future uncertainty has been resolved, we may find that a project with a negative net present value based upon its expected free cash flows is a "good" project and should be accepted. This demonstrates the value of options. In addition, we may find that a project with a positive net present value may be of more value if its acceptance is delayed. Options also explain the logic that drives firms to take on negative *NPV* projects that allow them to enter new markets. The option to abandon a project explains why firms hire employees on a temporary basis rather than permanently, why they lease rather than buy equipment, and why they enter into contracts with suppliers on an annual basis rather than long term.

Concept Check

1. Give an example of an option to delay a project. Why might this be of value?
2. Give an example of an option to expand a project. Why might this be of value?
3. Give an example of an option to abandon a project. Why might this be of value?

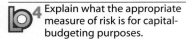
4 Explain what the appropriate measure of risk is for capital-budgeting purposes.

Risk and the Investment Decision

Up to this point we have ignored risk in capital budgeting; that is, we have discounted expected cash flows back to the present and ignored any uncertainty that there might be surrounding that estimate. In reality the future cash flows associated with the introduction of a new sales outlet or a new product are estimates of what is *expected* to happen in the future, not necessarily what will happen. For example, when Coca-Cola decided to replace Classic Coke with "New Coke," you can bet that the expected cash flows it based its decision on were nothing like the cash flows it realized. As a result, it didn't take Coca-Cola long to reintroduce Classic Coke. Other famous failures that didn't produce the cash flows that were expected include Bic disposable underwear, Thirsty Dog! beef-flavored bottled water for dogs, and Coors Rocky Mountain Spring Water. The cash flows we have discounted back to the present so far have only been our best estimate of the expected future cash flows. A cash flow diagram based on the possible outcomes of an investment proposal rather than the expected values of these outcomes appears in Figure 11-3.

In this section, we assume that we do not know beforehand what cash flows will actually result from a new project. However, we do have expectations concerning the possible outcomes and are able to assign probabilities to these outcomes. Stated another way, although we do not know what the cash flows resulting from the acceptance of a new project will be, we can formulate the probability distributions from which the flows will be drawn. As we learned in Chapter 6, risk occurs when there is some question about the future outcome of an event.

In the remainder of this chapter, we assume that although future cash flows are not known with certainty, the probability distribution from which they are derived can be estimated. Also, because we have illustrated that the dispersion of possible outcomes reflects risk, we are prepared to use a measure of dispersion, or variability, later in the chapter when we quantify risk.

In the pages that follow, remember that there are only two basic issues that we address: (1) What is risk in terms of capital-budgeting decisions, and how should it be measured? and (2) How should risk be incorporated into a capital-budgeting analysis?

What Measure of Risk Is Relevant in Capital Budgeting?

Before we begin our discussion of how to adjust for risk, it is important to determine just what type of risk we are to adjust for. In capital budgeting, a project's risk can be looked at

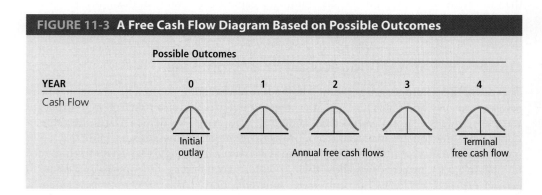

FIGURE 11-3 A Free Cash Flow Diagram Based on Possible Outcomes

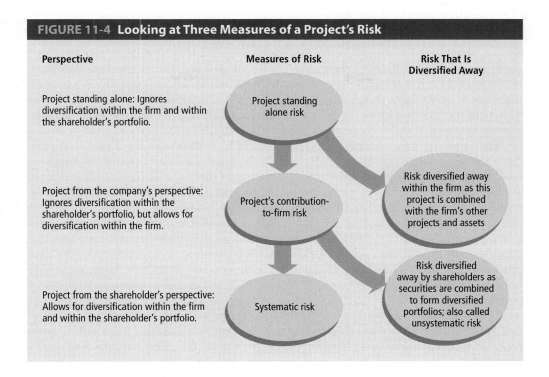

FIGURE 11-4 Looking at Three Measures of a Project's Risk

on three levels. First, there is the **project standing alone risk**, which is a *project's risk ignoring the fact that much of this risk will be diversified away*. Second, we have the project's **contribution-to-firm risk**, which is the *amount of risk that the project contributes to the firm as a whole; this measure considers the fact that some of the project's risk will be diversified away as the project is combined with the firm's other projects and assets, but it ignores the effects of the diversification of the firm's shareholders*. Finally, there is **systematic risk**, which is the *risk of the project from the viewpoint of a well-diversified shareholder; this measure takes into account that some of a project's risk will be diversified away as the project is combined with the firm's other projects, and, in addition, some of the remaining risk will be diversified away by shareholders as they combine this stock with other stocks in their portfolios*. Graphically, this is shown in Figure 11-4.

Should we be interested in the project standing alone risk? The answer is no. Perhaps the easiest way to understand why not is to look at an example. Let's take the case of research and development projects at Johnson & Johnson. Each year Johnson & Johnson takes on hundreds of new R&D projects, knowing that they have only about a 10 percent probability of being successful. If they are successful, the profits can be enormous; if they fail, the investment is lost. If the company has only one project, and it is an R&D project, the company would have a 90 percent chance of failure. Thus, if we look at these R&D projects individually and measure their stand-alone risk, we would have to judge them to be enormously risky. However, if we consider the effect of the diversification that comes about from taking on several hundred independent R&D projects a year, all with a 10 percent chance of success, we can see that each R&D project does not add much risk to Johnson & Johnson. In short, because much of a project's risk is diversified away within the firm, the project standing alone risk is an inappropriate measure of the meaningful level of risk of a capital-budgeting project.

Should we be interested in the project's contribution-to-firm risk? Once again, at least in theory, the answer is no, provided investors are well diversified and there are no bankruptcy costs. From our earlier discussion of risk in Chapter 6, we saw that as shareholders, if we combined an individual security with other securities to form a diversified portfolio, much of the risk of the individual security would be diversified away. In short, all that affects the shareholders is the systematic risk of the project and, as such, it is all that is theoretically relevant for capital budgeting.

project standing alone risk a project's risk ignoring the fact that much of this risk will be diversified away.

contribution-to-firm risk the amount of risk that the project contributes to the firm as a whole; this measure considers the fact that some of the project's risk will be diversified away as the project is combined with the firm's other projects and assets, but ignores the effects of diversification of the firm's shareholders.

systematic risk the risk of the project from the viewpoint of a well-diversified shareholder; this measure takes into account that some of a project's risk will be diversified away as the project is combined with the firm's other projects, and, in addition, some of the remaining risk will be diversified away by shareholders as they combine this stock with other stocks in their portfolios.

Measuring Risk for Capital-Budgeting Purposes with a Dose of Reality—Is Systematic Risk All There Is?

According to the capital asset pricing model (CAPM) we discussed in Chapter 6, systematic risk is the only relevant risk for capital-budgeting purposes. However, reality complicates this somewhat. In many instances a firm will have undiversified shareholders, including owners of small corporations. Because they are not diversified, for those shareholders the relevant measure of risk is the project's contribution-to-firm risk.

The possibility of bankruptcy also affects our view of what measure of risk is relevant. As you recall in developing the CAPM, we made the assumption that bankruptcy costs were zero. Because the project's contribution-to-firm risk reflects risk that the firm faces, that is, the risk that may lead to bankruptcy, this may be an appropriate measure of risk: Quite obviously, there is a cost associated with bankruptcy. First, if a firm fails, its assets, in general, cannot be sold for their true economic value. Moreover, the amount of money actually available for distribution to stockholders is further reduced by liquidation and legal fees that must be paid. Finally, the opportunity cost associated with the delays related to the legal process further reduces the funds available to the shareholder. Therefore, because costs are associated with bankruptcy, reducing the chance of a bankruptcy has a very real value associated with it.

The indirect costs of bankruptcy also affect other areas of the firm, including production, sales, and the quality and efficiency of management. For example, firms with a higher probability of bankruptcy may have a more difficult time recruiting and retaining quality managers because jobs with that firm are viewed as being less secure. Suppliers may be less willing to sell to the firm on credit. Finally, customers may lose confidence and fear that the firm is cutting corners in terms of quality, and/or will not be around to honor a warranty or supply spare parts for products in the future. As a result, as the probability of bankruptcy increases, an eventual bankruptcy can become self-fulfilling as potential customers and suppliers flee. The end result is that because a project's contribution-to-firm risk affects the probability of bankruptcy for the firm, it may be a relevant risk measure for capital budgeting.

Finally, problems in measuring a project's systematic risk make its implementation extremely difficult. It is much easier talking about a project's systematic risk than measuring it.

Given all this, what risk measure do we use? The answer is that we will give consideration to both systematic risk and contribution-to-firm risk measures. We know in theory systematic risk is correct. We also know that bankruptcy costs and undiversified shareholders violate the assumptions of the theory, which makes the concept of a project's contribution-to-firm risk a relevant measure. Still, the concept of systematic risk holds value for capital-budgeting decisions because that is the risk that shareholders are compensated for assuming. Therefore, we will concern ourselves with both the project's contribution-to-firm risk and the project's systematic risk and not try to make any specific allocation of importance between the two for capital-budgeting purposes.

Concept Check

1. In terms of capital budgeting, a project's risk can be looked at on three levels. What are they and what are the measures of risk?
2. Is a project's standing alone risk the appropriate level of risk for capital budgeting? Why or why not?
3. What is systematic risk?
4. What problems are associated with using systematic risk as the measure for risk in capital budgeting?

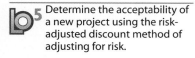
Determine the acceptability of a new project using the risk-adjusted discount method of adjusting for risk.

Incorporating Risk Into Capital Budgeting

Because different investment projects do in fact contain different levels of risk, let's now look at the risk-adjusted discount rate, which is based on the notion that investors require higher rates of return on more risky projects.

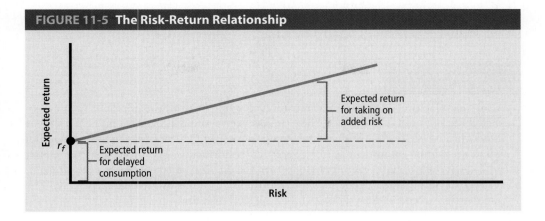

FIGURE 11-5 The Risk-Return Relationship

Risk-Adjusted Discount Rates

The use of **risk-adjusted discount rates** is based on the concept that investors demand higher returns for more risky projects. This is the basic principle behind **Principle 3** and the CAPM and is illustrated graphically in Figure 11-5.

As we know from **Principle 3**, the expected rate of return on any investment should include compensation for delaying consumption equal to the risk-free rate of return, plus compensation for any risk taken on. Under the risk-adjusted discount rate approach, if the risk associated with the investment is greater than the risk involved in a typical endeavor, the discount rate is adjusted upward to compensate for this added risk. Once the firm determines the appropriate required rate of return for a project with a given level of risk, the cash flows are discounted back to the present at the risk-adjusted discount rate. Then the normal capital-budgeting criteria are applied, except in the case of the *IRR*. For the *IRR*, the hurdle rate with which the project's *IRR* is compared now becomes the risk-adjusted discount rate. Expressed mathematically, the *NPV* using the risk-adjusted discount rate becomes

risk-adjusted discount rate a method of risk adjustment when the risk associated with the investment is greater than the risk involved in a typical endeavor. Using this method, the discount rate is adjusted upward to compensate for this added risk.

> **REMEMBER YOUR PRINCIPLES**
> All the methods used to compensate for risk in capital budgeting find their roots in **Principle 3: Risk Requires a Reward**. In fact, the risk-adjusted discount method puts this concept directly into play.

$$\mathrm{NPV} = \left[\begin{array}{l} \text{present value of all the} \\ \text{future annual free cash} \\ \text{flows discounted back} \\ \text{to present at the risk-adjusted} \\ \text{rate of return} \end{array}\right] - \left[\begin{array}{l} \text{the initial cash outlay} \end{array}\right] \quad (11\text{-}1)$$

$$= \frac{FCF_1}{(1 + k^*)^1} + \frac{FCF_2}{(1 + k^*)^2} + \cdots + \frac{FCF_n}{(1 + k^*)^n} - IO$$

where FCF_t = the annual free cash flow expected in time period t

IO = the initial cash outlay

k^* = the risk-adjusted discount rate

n = the project's expected life

The logic behind the risk-adjusted discount rate stems from the idea that if the level of risk associated with a project is different from that of the typical project, then managers must incorporate the shareholders' probable reaction to this new endeavor into the decision-making process. For example, if the project has more risk than a typical project, then a higher required rate of return should apply. Otherwise, marginal projects will lower the firm's share price—that is, reduce shareholders' wealth. This will occur as the market raises its required rate of return on the firm to reflect the addition of the more risky project, because the incremental cash flows resulting from it might not be large enough to offset this risk. By the same logic, if the project has less than normal risk, a reduction in the required rate of return is appropriate. Thus, the risk-adjusted discount method attempts to apply more stringent standards—that is, require a higher rate of return—to projects that will increase the firm's risk level.

> ### EXAMPLE 11.3
>
> A toy manufacturer is considering introducing a line of fishing equipment with an expected life of 5 years. In the past, the firm has been quite conservative in its investment in new products, sticking primarily to standard toys. In this context, the introduction of a line of fishing equipment is considered an abnormally risky project. Management thinks that the normal required rate of return for the firm of 10 percent is not sufficient. Instead, the minimum acceptable rate of return on this project should be 15 percent. The initial outlay would be $110,000, and the expected cash flows are as follows:
>
> | YEAR | EXPECTED FREE CASH FLOW |
> |------|------------------------|
> | 1 | $30,000 |
> | 2 | 30,000 |
> | 3 | 30,000 |
> | 4 | 30,000 |
> | 5 | 30,000 |
>
> Discounting this annuity back to the present at 15 percent makes the present value of the future free cash flows $100,560. Because the initial outlay on this project is $110,000, the *NPV* becomes −$9,435, and the project should be rejected. If the normal required rate of return of 10 percent had been used as the discount rate, the project would have been accepted with a *NPV* of $3,724.

In practice, when the risk-adjusted discount rate is used, projects are generally grouped according to purpose, or risk class; then the discount rate preassigned to that purpose or risk class is used. For example, a firm with a required rate of return of 12 percent might use the following rate-of-return categorization:

PROJECT	REQUIRED RATE OF RETURN (%)
Replacement decision	12
Modification or expansion of existing product line	15
Project unrelated to current operations	18
Research and development operations	25

The purpose of this categorization of projects is to make their evaluation easier, but it also introduces a sense of arbitrariness into the calculations that makes the evaluation less meaningful. The trade-offs involved in the preceding classification are obvious: Time and effort are minimized but only at the cost of precision.

Measuring a Project's Systematic Risk

When we initially talked about systematic risk or the beta, we were talking about measuring it for the entire firm. As you recall, although we could estimate a firm's beta using historical data, we did not have complete confidence in our results. As we will see, estimating the appropriate level of systematic risk for a single project is even more fraught with difficulties. To truly understand what it is we are trying to do and the difficulties we will encounter, let's step back a bit and examine systematic risk and the risk adjustment for a project.

What we are trying to do is use the CAPM to determine the level of risk and the appropriate risk–return trade-offs for a particular project. We then take the expected return on this project and compare it to the required return suggested by the CAPM to determine whether the project should be accepted. If the project appears to be a typical one for the firm, using the CAPM to determine the appropriate risk–return trade-offs and then judging the project against them may be a warranted approach. But if the project is not a typical project, what do we do? Historical data generally do not exist for a new project. In fact, for some capital investments—for example, a truck or a new building—historical data would not have much meaning. What we need to do is make the best of a bad situation. We either (1) fake it—that is, use historical accounting data, if available, to substitute for historical price data in estimating systematic risk—or (2) attempt to find a substitute firm in the same industry as the capital-budgeting project and use the substitute firm's estimated systematic risk as a proxy for the project's systematic risk.

Using Accounting Data to Estimate a Project's Beta

When we are dealing with a project that is identical to the firm's other projects, we need only estimate the level of systematic risk for the firm and use that estimate as a proxy for the project's risk. Unfortunately, when projects are not typical of the firm, this approach does not work. For example, when Altria, which owns Philip Morris, the tobacco company, and Ste. Michelle Wine Estates, introduces a new dessert wine, this new product most likely carries with it a different level of systematic risk than what is typical for Altria as a whole.

To get a better approximation of the systematic risk level on this project, it would be great if we could estimate the level of systematic risk for the wine division and use that as a proxy for the project's systematic risk. Unfortunately, historical stock price data are available only for the company as a whole, and as you recall, historical stock return data are generally used to estimate a firm's beta. Thus, we are forced to use accounting return data rather than historical stock return data for the division to estimate the division's systematic risk. To estimate a project's beta using accounting data we need only run a time-series regression of the division's return on assets (net income/total assets) on the market index (the S&P 500). The regression coefficient from this equation would be the project's accounting beta and would serve as an approximation for the project's true beta, or measure of systematic risk. Alternatively, a multiple regression model based on accounting data could be developed to explain betas. The results of this model could then be applied to firms that are not publicly traded to estimate their betas.

How good is the accounting beta technique? It certainly is not as good as a direct calculation of the beta. In fact, the correlation between the accounting beta and the beta calculated on historical stock return data is only about 0.6. However, better luck has been experienced with multiple regression models used to predict betas. Unfortunately, in many cases there may not be any realistic alternative to the calculation of the accounting beta. Because adjusting for a project's risk is so important, the accounting beta method is much preferred to doing nothing.

The Pure Play Method for Estimating Beta

Whereas the accounting beta method attempts to directly estimate a project's or division's beta, the **pure play method** attempts to identify publicly traded firms that are engaged solely in the same business as the project or division. Once the proxy or pure play firm is identified, its systematic risk is determined and then used as a proxy for the project's or division's level of systematic risk. What we are doing is *looking for a publicly traded firm with a project like ours and using that firm's required rate of return to judge our project.* In doing so we are presuming that the systematic risk and the capital structure of the proxy firm are identical to those of the project.

pure play method a method for estimating a project's or division's beta that attempts to identify publicly traded firms engaged solely in the same business as the project or division.

In using the pure play method it should be noted that a firm's capital structure is reflected in its beta. When the capital structure of the proxy firm is different from that of the project's firm, some adjustment must be made for this difference. Although not a perfect approach, it does provide some insights about the level of systematic risk a project might have.

Concept Check

1. What is the most commonly used method for incorporating risk into the capital-budgeting decision? How is this technique related to Principle 3?

2. Describe two methods for estimating a project's systematic risk.

LO6 Explain the use of simulation for imitating the performance of a project under evaluation.

simulation a method for dealing with risk where the performance of the project under evaluation is estimated by randomly selecting observations from each of the distributions that affect the outcome of the project and continuing with this process until a representative record of the project's probable outcome is assembled.

Examining a Project's Risk through Simulation

Simulation: Explained and Illustrated

Another method for evaluating risk in the investment decision is through the use of **simulation**. The risk-adjusted discount rate approach provided us with a single value for the risk-adjusted *NPV*, whereas a simulation approach gives us a probability distribution for the investment's *NPV* or *IRR*. Simulation *involves the process of imitating the performance of the project under evaluation. This is done by randomly selecting observations from each of the distributions that affect the outcome of the project and continuing with this process until a representative record of the project's probable outcome is assembled.*

The easiest way to develop an understanding of the computer simulation process is to follow through an example simulation for an investment project evaluation. Suppose a chemical producer is considering an extension to its processing plant. The simulation process is portrayed in Figure 11-6. First, the probability distributions are determined for all the factors that affect the project's returns. In this case, let us assume there are nine such variables:

1. Market size
2. Selling price
3. Market growth rate
4. Share of market (which results in physical sales volume)
5. Investment required
6. Residual value of investment
7. Operating costs
8. Fixed costs
9. Useful life of facilities

Then the computer randomly selects one observation from each of the probability distributions, according to its chance of actually occurring in the future. These nine observations are combined, and an *NPV* or *IRR* figure is calculated. This process is repeated as many times as desired, until a representative distribution of possible future outcomes is assembled. Thus, the inputs to a simulation include all the principal factors affecting the project's profitability, and the simulation output is a probability distribution of net present values or internal rates of return for the project. The decision maker bases the decision on the full range of possible outcomes. The project is accepted if the decision maker feels that enough of the distribution lies above the normal cutoff criteria (*NPV* ≥ 0 or *IRR* ≥ required rate of return).

Suppose the output from the simulation of a chemical producer's project is as shown in Figure 11-7. This output provides the decision maker with the probability of different outcomes occurring in addition to the range of possible outcomes. Sometimes called **scenario analysis**, it *identifies the range of possible outcomes under the worst, best, and most likely cases.* The firm's management then examines the distribution to determine the project's level of risk and makes the appropriate decisions.

You'll notice that although the simulation approach helps us to determine the amount of total risk a project has, it does not differentiate between systematic and unsystematic risk. However, it does provide important insights about the total risk level of a given investment project. Now we will look briefly at how the simulation approach can be used to perform sensitivity analysis.

scenario analysis a simulation approach for gauging a project's risk under the worst, best, and most likely outcomes. The firm's management examines the distribution of the outcomes to determine the project's level of risk and then makes the appropriate adjustment.

FIGURE 11-6 Capital-Budgeting Simulation

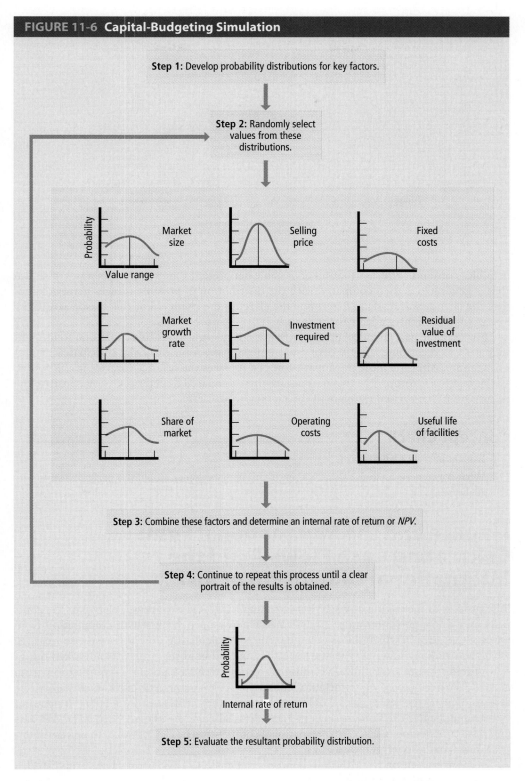

Step 1: Develop probability distributions for key factors.

Step 2: Randomly select values from these distributions.

Market size

Selling price

Fixed costs

Market growth rate

Investment required

Residual value of investment

Share of market

Operating costs

Useful life of facilities

Step 3: Combine these factors and determine an internal rate of return or *NPV.*

Step 4: Continue to repeat this process until a clear portrait of the results is obtained.

Internal rate of return

Step 5: Evaluate the resultant probability distribution.

Conducting a Sensitivity Analysis through Simulation

Sensitivity analysis involves *determining how the distribution of possible net present values or internal rates of return for a particular project is affected by a change in one particular input variable.* This is done by changing the value of one input variable while holding all other input

sensitivity analysis a method for dealing with risk where the change in the distribution of possible net present values or internal rates of return for a particular project resulting from a change in one particular input variable is calculated. This is done by changing the value of one input variable while holding all other input variables constant.

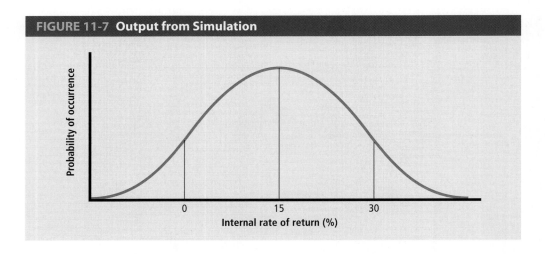

FIGURE 11-7 Output from Simulation

variables constant. The distribution of possible net present values or internal rates of return that is generated is then compared with the distribution of possible returns generated before the change was made to determine the effect of the change. For this reason sensitivity analysis is commonly called *what-if analysis*.

For example, the chemical producer that is considering a possible expansion to its plant may wish to determine the effect of a more pessimistic forecast of the anticipated market growth rate. After the more pessimistic forecast replaces the original forecast in the model, the simulation is rerun. The two outputs are then compared to determine how sensitive the results are to the revised estimate of the market growth rate.

Concept Check

1. Explain how simulations work.
2. What is a scenario analysis? What is a sensitivity analysis? When would you perform a sensitivity analysis?

Explain why a multinational firm faces a more difficult time estimating cash flows along with increased risks.

Finance and the Multinational Firm: Calculating Cash Flows Amid the International Dimension of Risk

The process of measuring a project's incremental, after-tax cash flows relative to the company as a whole gets a bit more complicated when we are dealing with competition from abroad. One area in which this is certainly true is in calculating the right base case—that is, what the firm's incremental after-tax cash flows would be if the project is not taken on. In determining future cash flows we must always be aware of potential competition from abroad. We need only look to the auto industry to see that competition from abroad can be serious. During the 1970s, who would have thought that firms such as Toyota, Honda, and Nissan could enter the U.S. markets and actually challenge the likes of Ford and GM? The end result of opening markets to international competition has led not only to increased opportunities but also to increased risks.

Just as competition from around the world can challenge U.S. firms, U.S. firms can also move into international markets. For example, Yum! Brands (YUM), the parent firm for KFC, Long John Silver's, Pizza Hut, and Taco Bell, has been registering with its operating profits from China increases of an average of 30% per year for the past 10 years. Yum! Brands is also looking to other parts of the world and in 2008 it launched its first Taco Bell in Dubai. The store opened to wild success with patrons waiting over four hours to taste a Gordita Supreme.

Along with all the benefits from going multinational come the risks. One of the major risks involves currency fluctuations. For example, Toyota lowered the base prices on its

Prius in order to remain competitive with the price of Honda's hybrid, the Insight, worried that pricing the Prius several thousand dollars above the Insight's price might result in lost sales. Unfortunately for Toyota, by mid-2009, the Japanese yen was trading at around 96 yen per U.S. dollar, down from 122 yen per U.S. dollar just two years earlier. What does this mean for Toyota? It means that Toyota received only 79 percent as many yen on each Prius it sells in the United States. Because Toyota pays its workers in yen and its material costs are in yen, this wiped out any profits Toyota might have made on the Prius.

Concept Check

1. In what ways does the process of measuring the incremental after-tax cash flows to the company as a whole get a bit more complicated when we are dealing with competition from abroad?
2. What new risks does a firm face when it enters the international markets?

Summary

In this chapter, we examined the measurement of the incremental cash flows associated with a firm's investment proposals and methods used to evaluate those proposals. Relying on **Principle 1: Cash Flow Is What Matters** we focused only on the incremental, or differential, after-tax cash flows attributed to an investment proposal. Care is taken to beware of cash flows diverted from existing products, look for incidental or synergistic effects, consider working-capital requirements, consider incremental expenses, ignore sunk costs, account for opportunity costs, examine overhead costs carefully, and ignore interest payments and financing flows.

 Identify guidelines by which we measure cash flows.

To measure a project's benefits, we use the project's free cash flows:

Project's free cash flows = project's change in operating cash flows
 − change in net working capital
 − change in capital spending

 Explain how a project's benefits and costs—that is, its free cash flows—are calculated.

We can rewrite this, inserting our calculation for the project's change in operating cash flows, to get

Project's free cash flows = change in earnings before interest and taxes
 − change in taxes
 + change in depreciation
 − change in net working capital
 − change in capital spending

 Explain the importance of options, or flexibility, in capital budgeting.

Options, or flexibility, can make it worthwhile to pursue projects that would otherwise be rejected or make projects undertaken more valuable. Three of the most common types of options that can add value to a capital-budgeting project are (1) the option to delay a project until the future cash flows are more favorable (this option is common when the firm has an exclusive right, perhaps a patent, to a product or technology); (2) the option to expand a project, perhaps in size or even to introduce new products that would not have otherwise been feasible; and (3) the option to abandon a project if its future cash flows fall short of expectations.

 Explain what the appropriate measure of risk is for capital-budgeting purposes.

There are three types of capital-budgeting risk: the project standing alone risk, the project's contribution-to-firm risk, and the project's systematic risk. In theory, systematic risk is the appropriate risk measure, but bankruptcy costs and the issue of undiversified shareholders also give weight to considering a project's contribution-to-firm risk as the appropriate risk measure. Both measures of risk are valid, and we avoid making any specific allocation of the importance between the two.

The risk-adjusted discount rate relies on **Principle 3: Risk Requires a Reward** and involves an upward adjustment of the discount rate to compensate for risk. This method is based on the concept that investors demand higher returns for riskier projects. Thus, projects are evaluated using the appropriate, or risk-adjusted, discount rate.

 Determine the acceptability of a new project using the risk-adjusted discount method of adjusting for risk.

The simulation method is used to provide information about the location and shape of the distribution of possible outcomes of the project. Decisions can be based directly on this method or used as an input to make decisions using the risk-adjusted discount rate method.

 Explain the use of simulation for imitating the performance of a project under evaluation.

The process of measuring the free cash flows to the company as a whole becomes more complicated when we are dealing with competition from abroad. One area in which this is certainly true is in calculating the right base case—that is, what the firm's free cash flows would be if the project is not taken on. Another complication involves the risks associated with currency fluctuations.

 Explain why a multinational firm faces a more difficult time estimating cash flows along with increased risks.

Key Terms

Contribution-to-firm risk   319

Incremental after-tax free cash flows   304

Initial outlay   306

Project standing alone risk   319

Pure play method   323

Risk-adjusted discount rate   321

Scenario analysis   324

Sensitivity analysis   325

Simulation   324

Systematic risk   319

Review Questions

All Review Questions and Study Problems are available in MyFinanceLab.

11-1. Why do we focus on cash flows rather than accounting profits in making our capital-budgeting decisions? Why are we interested only in incremental cash flows rather than total cash flows?

11-2. If depreciation is not a cash flow expense, does it affect the level of cash flows from a project in any way? Why?

11-3. If a project requires an additional investment in working capital, how should this be treated when calculating the project's cash flows?

11-4. How do sunk costs affect the determination of cash flows associated with an investment proposal?

11-5. In the preceding chapter we examined the payback period capital-budgeting criterion. Often this capital-budgeting criterion is used as a risk-screening device. Explain the rationale behind its use.

11-6. Use the concept of real options to explain why large restaurant chains often introduce new concept restaurants that have negative *NPV*s.

11-7. Explain how simulation works. What is the value in using a simulation approach?

Self-Test Problem

(The solution to this problem is provided at the end of the chapter.)

ST-1. The Easterwood Corporation, a firm in the 34 percent marginal tax bracket with a 15 percent required rate of return or cost of capital, is considering a new project. The project involves the introduction of a new product. The project is expected to last 5 years and then, because this is somewhat of a fad product, be terminated. Given the following information, determine the free cash flows associated with the project, the project's net present value, the profitability index, and the internal rate of return. Apply the appropriate decision criteria.

Cost of new plant and equipment	$20,900,000
Shipping and installation costs	$ 300,000
Unit sales	

YEAR	UNITS SOLD
1	100,000
2	130,000
3	160,000
4	100,000
5	60,000

Sales price per unit	$500/unit in years 1 through 4, $380/unit in year 5
Variable cost per unit	$260/unit
Annual fixed costs	$300,000 per year in years 1–5
Working-capital requirements	There will be an initial working-capital requirement of $500,000 just to get production started. For each year, the total investment in net working capital will be equal to 10 percent of the dollar value of sales for that year. Thus, the investment in working capital will increase during years 1 through 3, then decrease in year 4. Finally, all working capital is liquidated at the termination of the project at the end of year 5.
The depreciation method	Use the simplified straight-line method over 5 years. Assume that the plant and equipment will have no salvage value after 5 years.

Study Problems

11-1. (*Capital gains tax*) The J. Harris Corporation is considering selling one of its old assembly machines. The machine, purchased for $30,000 5 years ago, had an expected life of 10 years and an expected salvage value of zero. Assume Harris uses simplified straight-line depreciation (depreciation of $3,000 per year) and could sell this old machine for $35,000. Also assume Harris has a 34 percent marginal tax rate.

    a. What would be the taxes associated with this sale?
    b. If the old machine were sold for $25,000, what would be the taxes associated with this sale?
    c. If the old machine were sold for $15,000, what would be the taxes associated with this sale?
    d. If the old machine were sold for $12,000, what would be the taxes associated with this sale?

11-2. (*Relevant cash flows*) Captins' Cereal is considering introducing a variation of its current breakfast cereal, Crunch Stuff. The new cereal will be similar to the old with the exception that it will contain sugarcoated marshmallows shaped in the form of stars and called Crunch Stuff n' Stars. It is estimated that the sales for the new cereal will be $25 million; however, 20 percent of those sales will be former Crunch Stuff customers who have switched to Crunch Stuff n' Stars but who would not have switched if the new product had not been introduced. What is the relevant sales level to consider when deciding whether to introduce Crunch Stuff n' Stars?

11-3. (*Calculating free cash flows*) Racin' Scooters is introducing a new product and has an expected change in EBIT of $475,000. Racin' Scooters has a 34 percent marginal tax rate. The project will also produce $100,000 of depreciation per year. In addition, the project will also cause the following changes in year 1:

	WITHOUT THE PROJECT	WITH THE PROJECT
Accounts receivable	$45,000	$63,000
Inventory	65,000	80,000
Accounts payable	70,000	94,000

What is the project's free cash flow in year 1?

11-4. (*Calculating free cash flows*) Spartan Stores is expanding operations with the introduction of a new distribution center. Not only will sales increase, but investment in inventory will decline due to increased efficiencies in getting inventory to showrooms. As a result of this new distribution center, Spartan expects a change in EBIT of $900,000. While inventory is expected to drop from $90,000 to $70,000, accounts receivables are expected to climb as a result of increased credit sales from $80,000 to $110,000. In addition, accounts payable are expected to increase from $65,000 to $80,000. This project will also produce $300,000 of depreciation per year and Spartan Stores is in the 34 percent marginal tax rate. What is the project's free cash flow in year 1?

11-5. (*Calculating operating cash flows*) Assume that a new project will annually generate revenues of $2,000,000. Cash expenses including both fixed and variable costs will be $800,000, and depreciation will increase by $200,000 per year. In addition, let's assume that the firm's marginal tax rate is 34 percent. Calculate the operating cash flows.

11-6. (*Consideration of sunk and opportunity costs*) Hewlett-Packard has designed a new type of printer that produce professional quality photos. These new printers took 2 years to develop with research and development running at $10 million after taxes over that period. Now all that's left is an investment of $22 million after taxes in new production equipment. It is expected that this new product line will bring in free cash flows of $5 million per year for each of the next 10 years. In addition, if Hewlett-Packard goes ahead with the new line of printers, the current production facility for the old printers that are to be replaced with this new line could be sold to a competitor, generating $3 million after tax.

    a. How should the $10 million of research and development be treated?
    b. How should the $3 million from the sale of the existing production facility for the old printers be treated?
    c. Given the information above, what are the cash flows associated with the new printers?

11-7. (*Calculating free cash flows*) Presently, Solartech Skateboards is considering expanding its product line to include gas-powered skateboards; however, it is questionable how well they will be received by skateboarders. While you feel there is a 60 percent chance you will sell 10,000 of these per year for 10 years (after which time this project is expected to shut down because solar-powered skateboards will become more popular), you also recognize that there is a 20 percent chance that you will only sell 3,000 and also a 20 percent chance you will sell 13,000. The gas skateboards would sell for $100 each and have a variable cost of $40 each. Regardless of how many you sell, the annual fixed costs associated with production would be $160,000. In addition, there would be a $1,000,000 initial expenditure associated with the purchase of new production equipment. It is assumed that this initial expenditure will be depreciated using the simplified straight-line method down to zero over 10 years. Because of the number of stores that will need inventory, the working capital requirements are the same regardless of the level of sales, and this project will require a one-time initial investment of $50,000 in net working capital, and that working-capital investment will be recovered when the project is shut down. Finally, assume that the firm's marginal tax rate is 34 percent.

    a. What is the initial outlay associated with the project?

    b. What are the annual free cash flows associated with the project for years 1 through 9 under each sales forecast? What is the expected annual free cash flows for years 1 through 9?

    c. What is the terminal cash flow in year 10 (that is, what is the free cash flow in year 10 plus any additional cash flows associated with the termination of the project)?

    d. Using the expected free cash flows, what is the project's *NPV* given a 10 percent required rate of return? What would the project's *NPV* be if they sold 10,000 skateboards?

11-8. (*Calculating free cash flows*) You are considering new elliptical trainers and you feel you can sell 5,000 of these per year for 5 years (after which time this project is expected to shut down when it is learned that being fit is unhealthy). The elliptical trainers would sell for $1,000 each and have a variable cost of $500 each. The annual fixed costs associated with production would be $1,000,000. In addition, there would be a $5,000,000 initial expenditure associated with the purchase of new production equipment. It is assumed that this initial expenditure will be depreciated using the simplified straight-line method down to zero over 5 years. This project will also require a one-time initial investment of $1,000,000 in net working capital associated with inventory, and that working-capital investment will be recovered when the project is shut down. Finally, assume that the firm's marginal tax rate is 34 percent.

    a. What is the initial outlay associated with this project?

    b. What are the annual free cash flows associated with this project for years 1 through 4?

    c. What is the terminal cash flow in year 5 (that is, what is the free cash flow in year 5 plus any additional cash flows associated with the termination of the project)?

    d. What is the project's *NPV* given a 10 percent required rate of return?

11-9. (*New project analysis*) The Chung Chemical Corporation is considering the purchase of a chemical analysis machine. Although the machine being considered will result in an increase in earnings before interest and taxes of $35,000 per year, it has a purchase price of $100,000, and it would cost an additional $5,000 to properly install the machine. In addition, to properly operate the machine, inventory must be increased by $5,000. This machine has an expected life of 10 years, after which it will have no salvage value. Also, assume simplified straight-line depreciation and that this machine is being depreciated down to zero, a 34 percent marginal tax rate, and a required rate of return of 15 percent.

    a. What is the initial outlay associated with this project?

    b. What are the annual after-tax cash flows associated with this project for years 1 through 9?

    c. What is the terminal cash flow in year 10 (what is the annual after-tax cash flow in year 10 plus any additional cash flows associated with the termination of the project)?

    d. Should this machine be purchased?

11-10. (*New project analysis*) Raymobile Motors is considering the purchase of a new production machine for $500,000. The purchase of this machine will result in an increase in earnings before interest and taxes of $150,000 per year. To operate this machine properly, workers would have to go through a brief training session that would cost $25,000 after taxes. It would cost $5,000 to install the machine properly. Also, because the machine is extremely efficient, its purchase would necessitate an increase in inventory of $30,000. This machine has an expected life of 10 years, after which it will have no salvage value. Assume simplified straight-line depreciation and that this machine is being depreciated down to zero, a 34 percent marginal tax rate, and a required rate of return of 15 percent.

    a. What is the initial outlay associated with this project?

    b. What are the annual after-tax cash flows associated with this project for years 1 through 9?

c. What is the terminal cash flow in year 10 (what is the annual after-tax cash flow in year 10 plus any additional cash flows associated with the termination of the project)?

d. Should the machine be purchased?

11-11. (*New project analysis*) Garcia's Truckin' Inc. is considering the purchase of a new production machine for $200,000. The purchase of this machine will result in an increase in earnings before interest and taxes of $50,000 per year. To operate the machine properly, workers would have to go through a brief training session that would cost $5,000 after taxes. It would cost $5,000 to install the machine properly. Also, because this machine is extremely efficient, its purchase would necessitate an increase in inventory of $20,000. This machine has an expected life of 10 years, after which it will have no salvage value. Finally, to purchase the new machine, it appears that the firm would have to borrow $100,000 at 8 percent interest from its local bank, resulting in additional interest payments of $8,000 per year. Assume simplified straight-line depreciation and that the machine is being depreciated down to zero, a 34 percent marginal tax rate, and a required rate of return of 10 percent.

a. What is the initial outlay associated with this project?

b. What are the annual after-tax cash flows associated with this project for years 1 through 9?

c. What is the terminal cash flow in year 10 (what is the annual after-tax cash flow in year 10 plus any additional cash flows associated with the termination of the project)?

d. Should the machine be purchased?

11-12. (*Comprehensive problem*) Traid Winds Corporation, a firm in the 34 percent marginal tax bracket with a 15 percent required rate of return or cost of capital, is considering a new project. This project involves the introduction of a new product. The project is expected to last 5 years and then, because this is somewhat of a fad product, be terminated. Given the following information, determine the free cash flows associated with the project, the project's net present value, the profitability index, and the internal rate of return. Apply the appropriate decision criteria.

Cost of new plant and equipment	$14,800,000	
Shipping and installation costs	$ 200,000	
Unit sales		
	YEAR	UNITS SOLD
	1	70,000
	2	120,000
	3	120,000
	4	80,000
	5	70,000
Sales price per unit	$300/unit in years 1 through 4, $250/unit in year 5	
Variable cost per unit	$140/unit	
Annual fixed costs	$700,000 per year in years 1–5	
Working-capital requirements	There will be an initial working-capital requirement of $200,000 just to get production started. For each year, the total investment in net working capital will be equal to 10 percent of the dollar value of sales for that year. Thus, the investment in working capital will increase during years 1 and 2, then decrease in year 4. Finally, all working capital is liquidated at the termination of the project at the end of year 5.	
The depreciation method	Use the simplified straight-line method over 5 years. Assume that the plant and equipment will have no salvage value after 5 years.	

11-13. (*Comprehensive problem*) The Shome Corporation, a firm in the 34 percent marginal tax bracket with a 15 percent required rate of return or cost of capital, is considering a new project. The project involves the introduction of a new product. This project is expected to last 5 years and then, because this is somewhat of a fad product, be terminated. Given the following information, determine the free cash flows associated with the project, the project's net present value, the profitability index, and the internal rate of return. Apply the appropriate decision criteria.

Cost of new plant and equipment	$6,900,000
Shipping and installation costs	$ 100,000
Unit sales	

YEAR	UNITS SOLD
1	80,000
2	100,000
3	120,000
4	70,000
5	70,000

Sales price per unit	$250/unit in years 1 through 4, $200/unit in year 5
Variable cost per unit	$130/units
Annual fixed costs	$300,000 per year in years 1–5
Working-capital requirements	There will be an initial working-capital requirement of $100,000 just to get production started. For each year, the total investment in net working capital will be equal to 10 percent of the dollar value of sales for that year. Thus, the investment in working capital will increase during years 1 through 3, then decrease in year 4. Finally, all working capital is liquidated at the termination of the project at the end of year 5.
The depreciation method	Use the simplified straight-line method over 5 years. Assume that the plant and equipment will have no salvage value after 5 years.

11-14. (*Risk-adjusted NPV*) The Hokie Corporation is considering two mutually exclusive projects. Both require an initial outlay of $10,000 and will operate for 5 years. Project A will produce expected cash flows of $5,000 per year for years 1 through 5, whereas project B will produce expected cash flows of $6,000 per year for years 1 through 5. Because project B is the riskier of the two projects, the management of Hokie Corporation has decided to apply a required rate of return of 15 percent to its evaluation but only a 12 percent required rate of return to project A. Determine each project's risk-adjusted net present value.

11-15. (*Risk-adjusted discount rates and risk classes*) The G. Wolfe Corporation is examining two capital-budgeting projects with 5-year lives. The first, project A, is a replacement project; the second, project B, is a project unrelated to current operations. The G. Wolfe Corporation uses the risk-adjusted discount rate method and groups projects according to purpose, and then it uses a required rate of return or discount rate that has been preassigned to that purpose or risk class. The expected cash flows for these projects are given here:

	PROJECT A	PROJECT B
Initial investment	−$250,000	−$400,000
Cash inflows:		
Year 1	$130,000	$135,000
Year 2	40,000	135,000
Year 3	50,000	135,000
Year 4	90,000	135,000
Year 5	130,000	135,000

The purpose/risk classes and preassigned required rates of return are as follows:

PURPOSE	REQUIRED RATE OF RETURN
Replacement decision	12%
Modification or expansion of existing product line	15
Project unrelated to current operations	18
Research and development operations	20

Determine each project's risk-adjusted net present value.

11-16. (*Real options*) Hurricane Katrina brought unprecedented destruction to New Orleans and the Mississippi gulf coast in 2005. Notably, the burgeoning casino gambling industry along the Mississippi coast was virtually wiped out overnight. GCC Corporation owns one of the oldest casinos in the Biloxi, MS area, and its casino was damaged but not destroyed by the tidal surge from the storm. The reason was that it had located several blocks back from the beach on higher ground. However, since the competitor casinos were completely destroyed and will have to rebuild from scratch, GCC believes that they are likely to have a number of good opportunities. You have been hired to provide GCC with strategic advice. What have you learned about real options that will help you develop a strategy for GCC?

11-17. (*Real options and capital budgeting*) You have come up with a great idea for a Tex-Mex-Thai fusion restaurant. After doing a financial analysis of this venture you estimate that the initial outlay will be $6 million. You also estimate that there is a 50 percent chance that this new restaurant will be well received and will produce annual cash flows of $800,000 per year forever (a perpetuity), while there is a 50 percent chance of it producing a cash flow of only $200,000 per year forever (a perpetuity) if it isn't received well.

   a. What is the *NPV* of the restaurant if the required rate of return you use to discount the project cash flows is 10 percent?
   b. What are the real options that this analysis may be ignoring?
   c. Explain why the project may be worthwhile taking even though you have just estimated that its *NPV* is negative.

11-18. (*Real options and capital budgeting*) Go-Power Batteries has developed a high-voltage nickel-metal hydride battery that can be used to power a hybrid automobile. They can sell the technology immediately to Toyota for $10 million, or alternatively, Go-Power Batteries can invest $50 million in a plant and produce the batteries for itself and sell them. Unfortunately, given the current size of the market for hybrids, the present value of the cash flows from such a plant would only be $40 million, implying that the plant has a negative expected *NPV* of −$10 million. What are the real options that are being ignored in this analysis? Can you come up with a compelling reason why Go-Power should keep the technology rather than sell it to Toyota?

Mini Case

It's been 2 months since you took a position as an assistant financial analyst at Caledonia Products. Although your boss has been pleased with your work, he is still a bit hesitant about unleashing you without supervision. Your next assignment involves both the calculation of the cash flows associated with a new investment under consideration and the evaluation of several mutually exclusive projects. Given your lack of tenure at Caledonia, you have been asked not only to provide a recommendation but also to respond to a number of questions aimed at judging your understanding of the capital-budgeting process. The memorandum you received outlining your assignment follows:

>To: The Assistant Financial Analyst
>From: Mr. V. Morrison, CEO, Caledonia Products
>Re: Cash Flow Analysis and Capital Rationing

We are considering the introduction of a new product. Currently we are in the 34 percent marginal tax bracket with a 15 percent required rate of return or cost of capital. This project is expected to last 5 years and then, because this is somewhat of a fad product, be terminated. The following information describes the new project:

Cost of new plant and equipment	$ 7,900,000
Shipping and installation costs	$ 100,000
Unit sales	

YEAR	UNITS SOLD
1	70,000
2	120,000
3	140,000
4	80,000
5	60,000

Sales price per unit	$300/unit in years 1 through 4, $260/unit in year 5
Variable cost per unit	$180/unit
Annual fixed costs	$200,000 per year in years 1–5
Working-capital requirements	There will be an initial working-capital requirement of $100,000 just to get production started. For each year, the total investment in net working capital will be equal to 10 percent of the dollar value of sales for that year. Thus, the investment in working capital will increase during years 1 through 3, then decrease in year 4. Finally, all working capital is liquidated at the termination of the project at the end of year 5.
The depreciation method	Use the simplified straight-line method over 5 years. Assume that the plant and equipment will have no salvage value after 5 years.

a. Should Caledonia focus on cash flows or accounting profits in making its capital-budgeting decisions? Should the company be interested in incremental cash flows, incremental profits, total free cash flows, or total profits?

b. How does depreciation affect free cash flows?

c. How do sunk costs affect the determination of cash flows?

d. What is the project's initial outlay?

e. What are the differential cash flows over the project's life?

f. What is the terminal cash flow?

g. Draw a cash flow diagram for this project.

h. What is its net present value?

i. What is its internal rate of return?

j. Should the project be accepted? Why or why not?

k. In capital budgeting, risk can be measured from three perspectives. What are those three measures of a project's risk?

l. According to the CAPM, which measurement of a project's risk is relevant? What complications does reality introduce into the CAPM view of risk, and what does that mean for our view of the relevant measure of a project's risk?

m. Explain how simulation works. What is the value in using a simulation approach?

n. What is sensitivity analysis and what is its purpose?

Self-Test Solution

SS-1.

YEAR	0	1	2	3	4	5
SECTION I. CALCULATE THE CHANGE IN EBIT, TAXES, AND DEPRECIATION						
(THIS BECOMES AN INPUT IN THE CALCULATION OF OPERATING CASH FLOW IN SECTION II)						
Units sold		100,000	130,000	160,000	100,000	60,000
Sales price		$ 500	$ 500	$ 500	$ 500	$ 380
Sales revenue		$ 50,000,000	$ 65,000,000	$80,000,000	$50,000,000	$22,800,000
Less: Variable costs		26,000,000	33,800,000	41,600,000	26,000,000	15,600,000
Less: Fixed costs		$ 300,000	$ 300,000	$ 300,000	$ 300,000	$ 300,000
Equals: EBITDA (assuming amortization is O)		$ 23,700,000	$ 30,900,000	$38,100,000	$23,700,000	$ 6,900,000
Less: Depreciation		$ 4,240,000	$ 4,240,000	$ 4,240,000	$ 4,240,000	$ 4,240,000
Equals: EBIT		$ 19,460,000	$ 26,660,000	$33,860,000	$19,460,000	$ 2,660,000
Taxes (@ 34%)		$ 6,616,400	$ 9,064,400	$11,512,400	$ 6,616,400	$ 904,400
SECTION II. CALCULATE OPERATING CASH FLOW						
(THIS BECOMES AN INPUT IN THE CALCULATION OF FREE CASH FLOW IN SECTION IV)						
Operating cash flow:						
EBIT		$ 19,460,000	$ 26,660,000	$33,860,000	$19,460,000	$ 2,660,000
Minus: Taxes		$ 6,616,400	$ 9,064,400	$11,512,400	$ 6,616,400	$ 904,400
Plus: Depreciation		$ 4,240,000	$ 4,240,000	$ 4,240,000	$ 4,240,000	$ 4,240,000
Equals: Operating cash flow		$ 17,083,600	$ 21,835,600	$26,587,600	$17,083,600	$ 5,995,600
SECTION III. CALCULATE THE NET WORKING CAPITAL						
(THIS BECOMES AN INPUT IN THE CALCULATION OF FREE CASH FLOW IN SECTION IV)						
Change in net working capital:						
Revenue		$ 50,000,000	$ 65,000,000	$80,000,000	$50,000,000	$22,800,000
Initial working-capital requirement	$ 500,000					
Net working-capital needs		$ 5,000,000	$ 6,500,000	$ 8,000,000	$ 5,000,000	$ 2,280,000
Liquidation of working capital						$ 2,280,000
Change in working capital	$ 500,000	$ 4,500,000	$ 1,500,000	$ 1,500,000	($ 3,000,000)	($ 5,000,000)
SECTION IV. CALCULATE FREE CASH FLOW						
(USING INFORMATION CALCULATED IN SECTIONS II AND III, IN ADDITION TO CHANGE IN CAPITAL SPENDING)						
Free cash flow:						
Operating cash flow		$ 17,083,600	$ 21,835,600	$26,587,600	$17,083,600	$ 5,995,600
Minus: Change in net working capital	$ 500,000	$ 4,500,000	$ 1,500,000	$ 1,500,000	($ 3,000,000)	($ 5,000,000)
Minus: Change in capital spending	$21,200,000	0	0	0	0	0
Equals: Free cash flow	($21,700,000)	$ 12,583,600	$ 20,335,600	$25,087,600	$20,083,600	$10,995,600

NPV = $38,064,020; Accept project; NPV is positive

PI = 2.75; Accept project; PI is greater than 1.0

IRR = 73.6%; Accept project; IRR is greater than the required rate of return.

Chapter 12

Determining the Financing Mix

Learning Objectives

After reading this chapter, you should be able to:

 Understand the difference between business risk and financial risk.

 Use the technique of break-even analysis in a variety of analytical settings.

 Distinguish among the financial concepts of operating leverage, financial leverage, and combined leverage.

 Understand the concept of an optimal capital structure.

Understand and be able to graph the moderate position on capital structure importance.

Incorporate the concepts of agency costs and free cash flow into a discussion on capital structure management.

Use the basic tools of capital structure management.

When a firm needs funds to support its investment plans, it typically raises them internally by reinvesting all or part of its earnings. This process of reinvesting firm earnings is tantamount to increasing the investment of the firm's common shareholders in the firm because the earnings represent what is left for the common stockholders after everyone else has been paid. However, occasionally firms find that they need to raise funds externally from the capital markets either because they do not have sufficient earnings to reinvest or they want to rebalance their capital structures. Historically, when firms tried to raise external sources of funds, they had to go to the public capital market where they sold bonds or stocks with the help of investment bankers to a diverse group of investors.

However, external financing is no longer limited to public capital markets. Today, private equity firms raise billions of dollars through the sale of limited partnership interests and then use the proceeds to invest in other firms. In fact, the total amount of private equity now exceeds $180 billion. Private equity funds are not for everyone, however. They tend to focus their investments in turnaround situations, in which the promised returns are very high and the need for funds is brief. Nonetheless, there's a new kid on the block when it comes to raising money externally.

Earlier chapters allowed us to develop an understanding of how financial assets are valued in the marketplace. Drawing on the tenets of valuation theory, we presented various approaches to measuring the cost of funds to the business organization. This chapter presents concepts that relate to the valuation process and the cost of capital; it also discusses the crucial problem of planning the firm's financing mix.

The cost of capital provides a direct link between the formulation of the firm's asset structure and its financial structure. This is illustrated in Figure 12-1. Recall that the cost of capital is a basic input to the time-adjusted, capital-budgeting models. Therefore, it affects the capital-budgeting, or asset-selection, process. The cost of capital is affected, in turn, by the composition of the right-hand side of the firm's balance sheet—that is, its financial structure.

This chapter examines tools that can be useful aids to the financial manager in determining the firm's proper financial structure. First, we review the notion of risk from the perspective of the firm's shareholders as it relates to the potential volatility in shareholder earnings. Corporate CEOs and boards of directors are very sensitive to the earnings numbers they report to Wall Street, so it behooves the financial manager to understand fully how the firm's capital structure affects the variability of earnings.

Next, we turn to a discussion of capital structure theory and the basic tools of capital structure management. Actual capital structure practices are also placed in perspective. We close with a discussion involving the multinational firm and its relationship to both the business-risk concept and global sales opportunities.

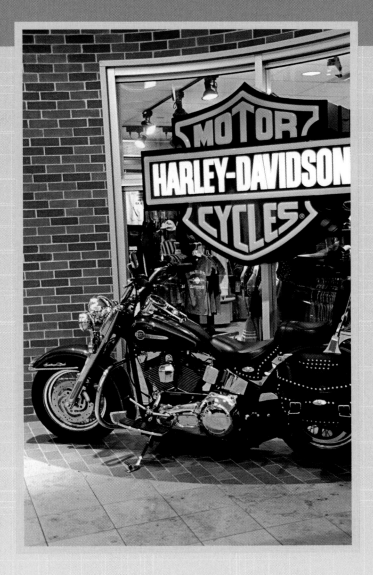

What is it about the nature of business that causes changes in sales revenues to translate into larger variations in net income and, finally, the earnings available to the common shareholders? It would be a good planning tool for management to be able to decompose such fluctuations into those policies associated with the operating side of the business and those policies associated with the financing side of the business.

Harley-Davidson Inc. has had a rather moderate exposure to financial risk in the management of its funds' sources. Harley has about 8,500 employees and sales revenues of $3.36 billion and, for reporting year 2001, ranked 466th among the *Fortune* 500. Even though the overall economy was slow, Harley improved to a ranking of 392nd for 2002 within this same set of 500 companies. For 2001, Harley generated $698.2 million in earnings before interest and taxes (EBIT) and incurred an interest expense of $24.8 million. This put its times interest-earned ratio at 28.2 times ($698.2 million/$24.8 million) for 2001. So in an adverse economic year, Harley's EBIT could slip to about 1/28th of its 2001 amount and the firm would still be able to pay its contractual debt obligations. This is a very safe interest coverage ratio. By the way, the times-interest-earned ratio is defined as earnings before interest and taxes divided by interest expense (refer to the glossary at the back of this text).

If you understand the material and analytical processes in this chapter, you will be able to make positive contributions to company strategies that deal with the firm's financing mix. You will be able to formulate a defensible answer to the question, Should we finance our next capital project with a new issue of bonds or a new issue of common stock? You can also help a lot of firms avoid making serious financial errors, the consequences of which can last for several years.

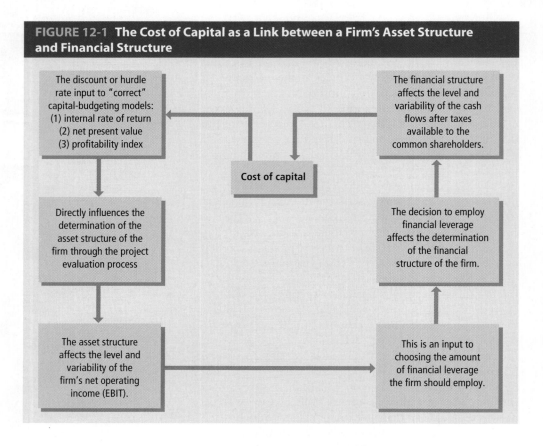

FIGURE 12-1 The Cost of Capital as a Link between a Firm's Asset Structure and Financial Structure

¹ Understand the difference between business risk and financial risk.

Business and Financial Risk

If investors are surprised by lower-than-expected corporate earnings, this can lead to a downward revision in their expectations of the firm's future prospects and, consequently, reduce the firm's common stock price. Thus, corporate executives and their boards of directors pay close attention to the earnings that they report to Wall Street. For this reason the financial analyst needs to understand the sources of volatility in firm earnings per share.

In this section we separate the variation in the firm's income stream into one of three sources:

1. **Choice of business line**—the variation in firm earnings that arises out of the natural volatility in revenues attributable to the industry in which it operates. For example, if the firm operates in a highly volatile industry in which revenues fluctuate with the business cycle, then the firm's earnings will be more volatile than another firm that operates in an industry that is less sensitive to the business cycle. We will refer to this source of variation in firm earnings as **business risk**.

2. **Choice of an operating cost structure**—the volatility in the firm's operating earnings that results from the firm's cost structure,[1] that is, the mix of fixed and variable operating costs the firm pays to do business. Greater fixed operating costs (versus variable costs) increase the variability in operating earnings in response to changes in revenues. The firm's mixture of fixed versus variable operating costs is largely determined

business risk the relative dispersion or variability in the firm's expected earnings before interest and taxes (EBIT). The nature of the firm's operations causes its business risk. This type of risk is affected by the firm's cost structure, product demand characteristics, and intra-industry competitive position. In capital structure theory, business risk is distinguished from financial risk. Compare **financial risk**.

---

[1]Recall that the term EBIT is the acronym for earnings before interest and taxes. If what accountants call *other income* and *other expenses* are equal to zero, then EBIT is equal to net operating income. For our purposes we use these two terms interchangeably.

by the industry in which the firm operates. For example, automobile manufacturing requires that large investments be made in plant and equipment. This results in high fixed operating costs regardless of the level of plant operations. We will refer to this source of variation in the firm earnings as operating risk.

3. **Choice of a capital structure**—the source of variation in the firm's earnings that results from its use of sources of financing that require a fixed return, such as debt financing. We will refer to this source of variation in earnings as financial risk.

We now spend some time developing an understanding of all three of these sources of volatility in firm earnings.

Concept Check

1. Why do managers care about the volatility of their firms' earnings?
2. What are the three determinants of the volatility of a firm's earnings?

Business Risk

The amount of business risk the firm decides to take on is most critical at the time the business is started. However, because business risk can affect the volatility of a firm's revenues, it can affect the firm's earnings per share. Thus, it behooves us to spend a little time discussing the sources of business risk. We identify four basic determinants of a firm's business risk:

1. **The stability of the domestic economy.**   Firms that operate in more volatile economies, such as those of developing nations, are subject to swings in revenues that are much more severe than those that operate within developed countries. For example, a chain of clothing stores operating within the United States faces a less volatile revenue stream than, say, a chain located in Nigeria or even Brazil.

2. **The exposure to, and stability of, foreign economies.**   In today's global economy more and more firms produce and sell their products in multiple countries. This means that it is not only the natural volatility of the firm's home country that drives the volatility of the firm's revenues but also that of the countries in which its goods and services are produced and sold.

3. **Sensitivity to the business cycle.**   Some industries are more sensitive to the business cycle than others. For example, the sales of consumer durable goods such as automobiles, housing, and appliances tend to be more sensitive to swings in the business cycle than necessities such as food and clothing.

4. **Competitive pressures in the firm's industry.**   Here we refer to the forces of other firms within the firm's marketplace that provide the same (or close substitute) products and services. Greater competitive pressures will force the firm to make price concessions sooner and deeper than would otherwise be the case.

Although business risk is obviously a critical determinant of earnings volatility, for the balance of this chapter we will assume that the firm's business risk is fixed, or given. This will allow us to focus on operating and financial risks, over which managers have more control.

Operating Risk

Operating risk increases when the firm incurs more fixed versus variable costs. Fixed costs do not vary with the firm's revenues, but variable costs, as the name implies, do rise and fall with revenues. A key tool for evaluating operating risk is break-even analysis. Therefore, we open our discussion of operating risk by defining the break-even chart.

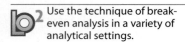

Use the technique of break-even analysis in a variety of analytical settings.

Break-Even Analysis

Both small and large organizations utilize the break-even analysis tool for two reasons: It is based on straightforward assumptions, and companies have found that the information gained from the break-even model is beneficial in decision-making situations. A break-even analysis is used to determine the "break-even" quantity of the firm's output. What is meant by the break-even quantity of output? It is that quantity of output, denominated in units, that results in an EBIT equal to zero. In other words, a break-even analysis enables the financial officer (1) to determine the quantity of output that must be sold to cover all operating costs, as distinct from financial costs, and (2) to calculate the EBIT that will be achieved at various output levels.

Essential Elements of the Break-Even Model

To implement the break-even model, we must separate the production costs of the company into two mutually exclusive categories: fixed costs and variable costs. You will recall from your study of basic economics that in the long run all costs are variable. The break-even analysis, therefore, is a short-run concept.

fixed costs costs that do not vary in total dollar amount as sales volume or quantity of output changes. Also called **indirect costs**.

indirect costs see **fixed costs**.

Fixed Costs   **Fixed costs**, also referred to as **indirect costs**, *do not vary with either the firm's sales or output*. As the production volume increases, the fixed cost *per unit* of product falls, because the firm's total fixed costs are spread over larger and larger quantities of output. Figure 12-2 graphs the behavior of total fixed costs with respect to the company's relevant range of output. This total is shown to be unaffected by the quantity of product that is manufactured and sold. Over some other relevant output range, the amount of total fixed costs might be higher or lower for the same company.

In a manufacturing setting, some specific examples of fixed costs are

1. Administrative salaries
2. Depreciation
3. Insurance
4. Lump sums spent on intermittent advertising programs
5. Property taxes
6. Rent

variable costs costs that are fixed per unit of output but vary in total as output changes. Also called **direct costs**.

direct costs see **variable costs**.

Variable Costs   **Variable costs** are sometimes referred to as **direct costs**. Variable costs *per unit vary as output changes*. Total variable costs are computed by taking the variable cost per unit and multiplying it by the total quantity produced and sold. The break-even model assumes proportionality between total variable costs and sales. Thus, if sales rise by 10 percent, it is assumed that variable costs will rise by 10 percent. Notice that if zero units of the

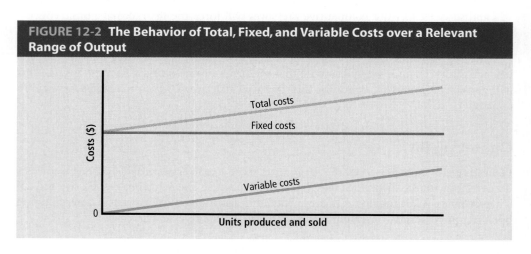

FIGURE 12-2 The Behavior of Total, Fixed, and Variable Costs over a Relevant Range of Output

product are manufactured, then variable costs are zero, but fixed costs are greater than zero. This implies that some contribution to the coverage of fixed costs occurs as long as the selling price per unit exceeds the variable costs per unit. This helps explain why some firms will operate a plant even when sales are temporarily depressed—that is, to try to cover fixed costs.

Some examples of variable costs include

1. Direct labor
2. Direct materials
3. Energy costs (fuel, electricity, natural gas) associated with production
4. Freight costs for products leaving the plant
5. Packaging
6. Sales commissions

Figure 12-2 also graphs total costs with respect to the company's relevant range of output. Total cost is simply the sum of the firm's fixed and variable costs.

More on the Behavior of Costs   No one really believes that *all* costs behave as neatly as we have illustrated the fixed and variable costs in Figure 12-2. Nor does any law or accounting principle dictate that a certain element of the firm's total costs always will be classified as fixed or variable. This depends on each firm's specific circumstances. In one firm, energy costs may be predominantly fixed, whereas in another they may vary with output.[2]

Furthermore, some costs may be fixed for a while, then rise sharply to a higher level as a higher output is reached, remain fixed, and then rise again with further increases in production. Such costs may be termed either *semivariable* or *semifixed*. The label is your choice because both are used in practice. An example might be the salaries paid to production supervisors. Should output be cut back by 15 percent for a short period, the organization is not likely to lay off 15 percent of its supervisors. Similarly, the percentage commissions paid to salespeople are often incrementally stepped up the more they sell. This sort of cost behavior is shown in Figure 12-3.

To implement the break-even model and deal with such a complex cost structure, the financial manager must (1) identify the most relevant output range for planning purposes and then (2) approximate the cost effect of semivariable items over this range by segregating a portion of them to fixed costs and a portion to variable costs. In the actual business setting this procedure is not fun. It is not unusual for the analyst who deals with the figures to spend considerably more time allocating costs to fixed and variable categories than doing the actual break-even calculations.

Total Revenue and Volume of Output   Besides fixed and variable costs, the essential elements of the break-even model include total revenue from sales and volume of output.

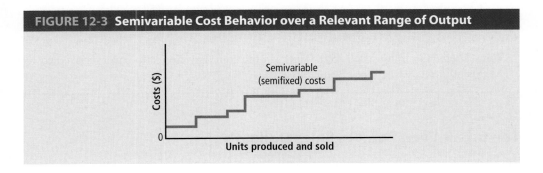

FIGURE 12-3 Semivariable Cost Behavior over a Relevant Range of Output

[2]In a greenhouse operation, in which plants are grown (manufactured) under strictly controlled temperatures, heat costs will tend to be fixed whether the building is full or only half-full of seedlings. In a metal stamping operation, in which levers are being produced, there is no need to heat the plant to as high a temperature when the machines are stopped and the workers are not there. In this latter case, the heat costs will tend to be variable.

total revenue total sales dollars.

volume of output a firm's level of operations expressed either in sales dollars or as units of output.

Total revenue means *total sales dollars* and is equal to the selling price per unit multiplied by the quantity sold. The **volume of output** refers to the *firm's level of operations* and may be *indicated either as a unit quantity or as sales dollars.*

Finding the Break-Even Point

Finding the break-even point in terms of units of production can be accomplished in several ways. All approaches require the essential elements of the break-even model just described. The break-even model is a simple adaptation of the firm's income statement expressed in the following analytical format:

$$\text{Sales} - (\text{total variable cost} + \text{total fixed cost}) = \text{profit} \tag{12-1}$$

On a units-of-production basis, it is necessary to introduce (1) the price at which each unit is sold and (2) the variable cost per unit of output. Because the profit item studied in a break-even analysis is EBIT, we use this acronym instead of the word *profit*. In terms of units, the income statement shown in equation (12-1) becomes the break-even model by setting EBIT equal to zero:

$$\left(\begin{array}{c}\text{Sales price}\\\text{per unit}\end{array}\right) \times \left(\begin{array}{c}\text{units}\\\text{sold}\end{array}\right) - \left[\left(\begin{array}{c}\text{variable cost}\\\text{per unit}\end{array}\right) \times \left(\begin{array}{c}\text{units}\\\text{sold}\end{array}\right) + \left(\begin{array}{c}\text{total fixed}\\\text{cost}\end{array}\right)\right] = \text{EBIT} = \$0 \tag{12-2}$$

Our task now becomes finding the number of units that must be produced and sold in order to satisfy equation (12-2)—that is, to arrive at EBIT = $0. This can be done by simply solving equation (12-2) for the number of units sold that make EBIT = 0.

Specifically, the break-even number of units sold is found to equal:

$$\begin{array}{c}\text{Break-even}\\\text{level of}\\\text{units}\end{array} = \dfrac{\text{total fixed cost}}{\left(\begin{array}{c}\text{sales price}\\\text{per unit}\end{array} - \begin{array}{c}\text{variable cost}\\\text{per unit}\end{array}\right)} \tag{12-3}$$

EXAMPLE 12.1

Even though Pierce Grain Company manufactures several different products, it has observed over a lengthy period that its product mix is rather constant. This allows management to conduct its financial planning by using a "normal" sales price per unit and a "normal" variable cost per unit. The "normal" sales price and variable cost per unit are calculated from the constant product mix. It is like assuming that the product mix is one big product. The selling price is $10 and the variable cost is $6. Total fixed costs for the firm are $100,000 per year. What is the break-even point in units produced and sold for the company during the coming year?

Substituting into equation (12-3), we calculate Pierce's break-even quantity as follows:

$$\text{Break-even level of units} = \dfrac{\$100,000}{(\$10.00 - \$6.00)} = 25,000 \text{ units}$$

Thus, Pierce Grain must sell 25,000 units in the coming year just to cover its fixed costs. At this point, its EBIT will be equal to zero.

The Break-Even Point in Sales Dollars

For the multiproduct firm, it is convenient to compute the break-even point in terms of sales dollars rather than units sold. Sales, in effect, become a common denominator associated with a particular product mix. Furthermore, an outside analyst might not have access to internal unit cost data. He or she may, however, be able to obtain annual reports for the firm. If the analyst can separate the firm's total costs as identified from its annual reports into their

CAN YOU DO IT?

ANALYZING THE BREAK-EVEN SALES LEVEL

Creighton Manufacturing Company assembles brake controllers used to upgrade the brake systems of vintage automobiles that are being restored. The firm's revenues for the past year were $20 million, on which the firm had earnings before interest and taxes (EBIT) of $10 million. Fixed expenses were $2 million. Variable costs were of $8 million, or 40 percent of the firm's revenues. What do you estimate the firms break-even level of revenues to be based on its current cost structure?

(The solution can be found on page 344.)

TABLE 12-1 Income Statement for Pierce Grain Company	
Sales	$300,000
Less: Total variable costs	180,000
Revenue before fixed costs	$120,000
Less: Total fixed costs	100,000
EBIT	$ 20,000

fixed and variable components, he or she can calculate a general break-even point in sales dollars.

We illustrate this procedure using Pierce Grain Company's cost structure. Suppose that the reported financial information is arranged in the format shown in Table 12-1. We refer to this type of financial statement as an *analytical income statement*. This distinguishes it from audited income statements published, for example, in the annual reports of public corporations. If we are aware of the simple mathematical relationships on which cost-volume-profit analysis is based, we can use Table 12-1 to find the break-even point in sales dollars for Pierce Grain Company.

We can solve for the break-even level of revenues (as opposed to units sold) using equation (12-4) as follows:

$$\text{Break-even level of revenues} = \frac{\text{total fixed costs}}{\left(1 - \dfrac{\text{variable costs}}{\text{revenues}}\right)} \tag{12-4}$$

In the Pierce Grain Company example the ratio of the firm's variable costs ($180,000) to revenues ($300,000) is $180,000/$300,000, or 0.60, and is assumed to be constant for all revenue levels. Consequently, we can use equation (12-4) to solve for Pierce's break-even level of revenues as follows:

$$\text{Break-even level of revenues} = \frac{\$100,000}{\left(1 - \dfrac{\$180,000}{\$300,000}\right)} = \$250,000$$

Concept Check

1. Distinguish among fixed costs, variable costs, and semivariable costs.
2. When is it useful or sometimes necessary to compute the break-even point in terms of sales dollars rather than units of output?

Operating Leverage

When a firm has fixed operating costs, then it is subject to the effects of **operating leverage**. Moreover, the operating leverage increases the sensitivity of the firm's operating income to changes in sales.

 3 Distinguish among the financial concepts of operating leverage, financial leverage, and combined leverage.

operating leverage the incurring of fixed operating costs in a firm's income stream.

DID YOU GET IT?
ANALYZING THE BREAK-EVEN SALES LEVEL

Creighton Manufacturing Company has fixed operating costs of $2 million and pays variable costs equal to $8 million/$20 million = 40 percent. Therefore, using equation (12-4), we can solve for the firm's break-even sales level as follows:

$$\text{Break-even level of revenues} = \frac{\$2,000,000}{\left(1 - \frac{\$8,000,000}{\$20,000,000}\right)} = \$3,333,333$$

TABLE 12-2 How Operating Leverage Affects EBIT: An Increase in Pierce Grain Company's Sales

Item	Base Sales Level, t	Forecast Sales Level, $t+1$	Percentage Change
Sales	$300,000	$360,000	+20%
Less: Total variable costs	180,000	216,000	
Revenue before fixed costs	$120,000	$144,000	
Less: Total fixed costs	100,000	100,000	
EBIT	$ 20,000	$ 44,000	+120%

For example, highly leveraged firms will see their incomes rise sharply when their sales rise. By contrast, firms with less leverage will see less-sharp rises in their incomes when their sales rise. To illustrate how this works, consider the Pierce Grain Company example. The firm's current sales are equal to $300,000, as found in Table 12-2. If Pierce's sales were to rise by 20 percent, up to $360,000, we calculate that the firm's EBIT would rise from $20,000 to $44,000. Note in the last column of Table 12-2 that we calculate the percent change in both revenues and EBIT. Revenues increase by just 20 percent, but the EBIT increases by a whopping 120 percent. The reason for this difference is the effect of operating leverage. If Pierce had no operating leverage (that is, all of its operating costs were variable), then the increase in EBIT would have been 20 percent, just like revenues. Note also that if Pierce had experienced a 20 percent decline in revenues, it would have experienced a 120 percent decline in EBIT, as the numbers in Table 12-3 illustrate. Clearly, a higher operating leverage means higher volatility in EBIT!

So, what does this all mean for the management team at Pierce Grain? Is there something they can or should do in response to having high operating leverage? Yes, there is. Recognizing that firm operating earnings will be very sensitive to changes in firm revenues

CAN YOU DO IT?
ANALYZING THE EFFECTS OF OPERATING LEVERAGE

JGC Electronics operates in a very cyclical business environment such that it is not uncommon for the firm's sales to increase or decrease by 20 percent or more from year to year. Moreover, the firm has made a substantial investment in plant and equipment. The company's high fixed operating expenses associated with the plant and equipment make the firm's earnings before interest and taxes (EBIT) very sensitive to changes in revenues. In fact, if revenues were to rise by 20 percent, the firm's managers estimate that EBIT would rise by 40 percent. If JGC's revenues were to fall by 20 percent from their current level of $10 million, what percentage decline in EBIT would you anticipate for the firm?

(The solution can be found on page 345.)

TABLE 12-3 How Operating Leverage Affects EBIT: A Decrease in Pierce Grain Company's Sales

Item	Base Sales Level, t	Forecast Sales Level, $t+1$	Percentage Change
Sales	$300,000	$240,000	−20%
Less: Total variable costs	180,000	144,000	
Revenue before fixed costs	$120,000	$ 96,000	
Less: Total fixed costs	100,000	100,000	
EBIT	$ 20,000	$ −4,000	−120%

should make management very wary about using lots of financial leverage that carries with it fixed principal and interest payments. Moreover, with highly variable operating earnings, Pierce's management will probably want to hold a safety net of cash and marketable securities to help the firm weather any periods when revenues falls below the break-even level.

Before we complete this discussion of operating leverage and move on to the subject of financial leverage, ask yourself, "Which type of leverage is more under the control of management?" You will probably (and correctly) come to the conclusion that the firm's managers have less control over the operating cost structure and almost complete control over its financial structure. What the firm actually produces, for example, will determine to a significant degree the division between fixed and variable costs. However, there is more room for substitution among the various sources of financial capital than there is among the labor and real capital inputs that enable the firm to meet its production requirements. Thus, you can anticipate more arguments over the choice of the firm's financial structure than operating structure.

Concept Check

1. When is operating leverage present in the firm's cost structure? What condition is necessary for operating leverage not to be present in the firm's cost structure?
2. What is the effect of operating leverage on the volatility of a firm's EBIT?

DID YOU GET IT?

ANALYZING THE EFFECTS OF OPERATING LEVERAGE

At its current level of sales, JGC anticipates that any percentage change in revenues will result in double that percentage change in EBIT. Thus, a decline in revenues by 20 percent would be expected to result in a decline in EBIT of 40 percent. Recall, however, that this relationship between percentage changes in revenues and EBIT changes as the level of revenue changes.

CAN YOU DO IT?

ANALYZING THE EFFECTS OF FINANCIAL LEVERAGE

JGC Electronics currently uses no financial leverage in its capital structure. Should the firm's earnings before interest and taxes (EBIT) increase by 20 percent, what percentage change would you expect in JGC's earnings per share?

(The solution can be found on page 346.)

DID YOU GET IT?

ANALYZING THE EFFECTS OF FINANCIAL LEVERAGE

Because JGC uses no financial leverage, there is *no* magnification effect of the percent change in EBIT on earnings per share. Therefore, a 20 percent increase in EBIT would lead to an equal 20 percent increase in the firm's earnings per share.

Financial Leverage

financial leverage the use of securities bearing a fixed (limited) rate of return to finance a portion of a firm's assets. Financial leverage can arise from the use of either debt or preferred stock financing. The use of financial leverage exposes the firm to financial risk.

Financial leverage means *financing a portion of the firm's assets with securities bearing a fixed (limited) rate of return* in hopes of increasing the ultimate return to the common stockholders. The decision to use debt or preferred stock in the financial structure of the corporation means that those who own the common shares of the firm are exposed to financial risk. Any given level of variability in EBIT is magnified by the firm's use of financial leverage, and such additional variability is embodied in the variability of earnings available to the common stockholder and earnings per share.

Let's now focus on the responsiveness of the company's earnings per share to changes in its EBIT. (We are *not* saying that earnings per share is the appropriate criterion for all financing decisions. In fact, the weakness of such a contention is examined later. Rather, the use of financial leverage produces a certain type of *effect* on earnings per share.)

Let us assume that Pierce Grain Company is in the process of getting started as a going concern. The firm's potential owners have estimated that $200,000 is needed to purchase the necessary assets to conduct the business. Three possible financing plans have been identified for raising the $200,000; they are presented in Table 12-4. In plan A no financial risk is assumed: The entire $200,000 is raised by selling 2,000 common shares for $100 per share. In plan B a moderate amount of financial risk is assumed: 25 percent of the assets are financed with a debt issue that carries an 8 percent annual interest rate. Plan C would use the most financial leverage: 40 percent of the assets would be financed with a debt issue costing 8 percent.

Table 12-5 presents the impact of financial leverage on earnings per share associated with each fund-raising alternative. If EBIT should increase from $20,000 to $40,000, then earnings per share would rise by 100 percent under plan A. The same change in EBIT would result in an earnings-per-share rise of 125 percent under plan B, and 147 percent under plan C. In plans B and C, the 100 percent increase in EBIT (from $20,000 to $40,000) is magnified

TABLE 12-4	Possible Capital Structures for Pierce Grain Company		
PLAN A: 0% DEBT			
		Total debt	$ 0
		Common equity	200,000[a]
Total assets	$200,000	Total liabilities and equity	$200,000
PLAN B: 25% DEBT AT 8% INTEREST RATE			
		Total debt	$ 50,000
		Common equity	150,000[b]
Total assets	$200,000	Total liabilities and equity	$200,000
PLAN C: 40% DEBT AT 8% INTEREST RATE			
		Total debt	$ 80,000
		Common equity	120,000[c]
Total assets	$200,000	Total liabilities and equity	$200,000

[a]2,000 common shares outstanding. [b]1,500 common shares outstanding. [c]1,200 common shares outstanding.

TABLE 12-5 An Analysis of Financial Leverage at Different EBIT Levels: Pierce Grain Company

(1)	(2)	(3) = (1) − (2)	(4) = (3) × 0.5	(5) = (3) − (4)	(6)
EBIT	Interest	EBT	Taxes	Net Income to Common Shareholders	Earnings Per Share
PLAN A: 0% DEBT; $200,000 COMMON EQUITY; 2,000 SHARES					
$ 0	$ 0	$ 0	$ 0	$ 0	$ 0
100% { 20,000	0	20,000	10,000	10,000	5.00 } 100%
40,000	0	40,000	20,000	20,000	10.00
60,000	0	60,000	30,000	30,000	15.00
80,000	0	80,000	40,000	40,000	20.00
PLAN B: 25% DEBT; 8% INTEREST RATE; $150,000 COMMON EQUITY; 1,500 SHARES					
$ 0	$4,000	$(4,000)	$(2,000)[a]	$(2,000)	$(1.33)
100% { 20,000	4,000	16,000	8,000	8,000	5.33 } 125%
40,000	4,000	36,000	18,000	18,000	12.00
60,000	4,000	56,000	28,000	28,000	18.67
80,000	4,000	76,000	38,000	38,000	25.33
PLAN C: 40% DEBT; 8% INTEREST RATE; $120,000 COMMON EQUITY; 1,200 SHARES					
$ 0	$6,400	$(6,400)	$(3,200)[a]	$(3,200)	$(2.67)
100% { 20,000	6,400	13,600	6,800	6,800	5.67 } 147%
40,000	6,400	33,600	16,800	16,800	14.00
60,000	6,400	53,600	26,800	26,800	22.33
80,000	6,400	73,600	36,800	36,800	30.67

[a]The negative tax bill recognizes the credit arising from the carryback and carryforward provision of the tax code.

to a greater-than-100-percent increase in earnings per share. The firm is employing financial leverage and exposing its owners to financial risk when the following situation exists:

$$\frac{\text{percentage change in earnings per share}}{\text{percentage change in EBIT}} > 1.00$$

As we have illustrated using the Pierce Grain Company example, the greater the firm's use of financial leverage, the greater will be the ratio of the percent change in earnings per share divided by the corresponding percent change in EBIT. To reiterate, this means that the use of financial leverage *magnifies* the effect of changes in EBIT on earnings per share. If, for example, the aforementioned ratio were 2, then a 20 percent change in EBIT (either positive or negative) would lead to a 40 percent change in earnings per share. For a firm that had even more financial leverage in its capital structure, the ratio might be 3, such that a 20 percent change in EBIT would lead to a 60 percent change in earnings per share.

CAN YOU DO IT?
ANALYZING THE COMBINED EFFECTS OF OPERATING AND FINANCIAL LEVERAGE

Peterson Timber Company operates saw mills throughout the redwood areas of the Pacific Northwest. The firm's current level of revenues, EBIT, and earnings per share are $10 million, $4 million, and $1.00 per share, respectively. Peterson's CFO recently forecasted the firm's revenues and profits for next year and estimated that total revenues will grow to $12 million, EBIT will rise to $5.2 million, and earnings per share will be $1.60 a share. Analyze the effects of operating, financial, and combined leverage for Peterson.

(The solution can be found on page 348.)

DID YOU GET IT?
ANALYZING THE COMBINED EFFECTS OF OPERATING AND FINANCIAL LEVERAGE

Peterson's CFO estimates that firm's revenues will increase by 20 percent, EBIT will increase by 30 percent, and earnings per share will rise 60 percent. Consequently, Peterson's operating leverage produces an increase in EBIT that is 1.5 times the 20 percent increase in sales, and earnings per share increase by 60 percent, which is twice the percent change in EBIT that is 30 percent. Once again, we see that operating and financial leverage interact in a multiplicative fashion. That is, the percent increase in earnings per share is 2 times the increase in EBIT, which is 1.5 times the increase in sales. The net result is that the percent increase in earnings per share is equal to $1.5 \times 2 = 3$ times the percent increase in sales. Consequently, the 20 percent increase in sales results in a 3×20 percent = 60 percent increase in earnings per share.

Concept Check

1. What creates financial leverage in a firm's capital structure?

2. How does financial leverage affect the volatility of firm earnings in response to changes in EBIT?

3. If the ratio of the percent change in earnings per share to the corresponding percent change in EBIT were 2, what percent change in earnings would you expect to follow a 15 percent decline in EBIT?

Combining Operating and Financial Leverage

Operating leverage causes changes in sales revenues to lead to even greater changes in EBIT. Additionally, changes in EBIT due to financial leverage translate into larger variations in both earnings per share (EPS) and the net income available to the common shareholders (NI), if the firm chooses to use financial leverage. It should be no surprise, then, to find out that combining operating and financial leverage causes rather large variations in earnings per share. This entire process is visually displayed in Figure 12-4.

Because the risk associated with possible earnings per share is affected by the use of combined, or total, leverage, it is useful to quantify the effect. To illustrate, we refer once more to Pierce Grain Company. The cost structure identified for Pierce Grain in our discussion of break-even analysis still holds. Furthermore, assume that plan B, which carried a 25 percent debt ratio, was chosen to finance the company's assets. Turn your attention to Table 12-6 to see how the effects of operating and financial leverage are combined.

In Table 12-6 an increase in output for Pierce Grain from 30,000 to 36,000 units is analyzed. This increase represents a 20 percent rise in sales revenues. From our earlier discussion of operating leverage and the data in Table 12-6, we can see that this 20 percent increase in sales is magnified into a 120 percent rise in EBIT. Moreover, the 120 percent rise in EBIT induces a change in earnings per share and earnings available to the common shareholders of 150 percent. The upshot of the analysis is that the modest 20 percent rise in sales has been magnified to produce a 150 percent change in earnings per share.

Pierce Grain's use of both operating and financial leverage will cause any percentage change in sales (from the specific base level) to be magnified by a factor of 7.50 when the

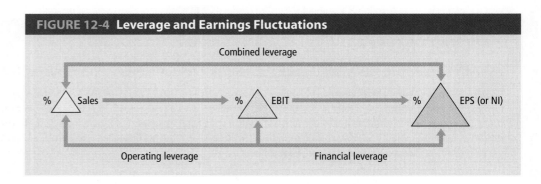

FIGURE 12-4 Leverage and Earnings Fluctuations

TABLE 12-6 The Combined-Leverage Effect on Pierce Grain Company's Earnings per Share

Item	Base Sales Level, t	Forecast Sales Level, $t+1$	Percentage Change
Sales	$300,000	$360,000	+20%
Less: Total variable costs	180,000	216,000	
Revenue before fixed costs	$120,000	$144,000	
Less: Total fixed costs	100,000	100,000	
EBIT	$ 20,000	$ 44,000	+120%
Less: Interest expense	4,000	4,000	
Earnings before taxes (EBT)	$ 16,000	$ 40,000	
Less: Taxes at 50%	8,000	20,000	
Net income	$ 8,000	$ 20,000	+150%
Less: Preferred dividends	0	0	
Earnings available to common shareholders (EAC)	$ 8,000	$ 20,000	+150%
Number of common shares	1,500	1,500	
Earnings per share (EPS)	$ 5.33	$ 13.33	+150%

effect on earnings per share is computed. A 10 percent change in sales, for example, will result in a 75 percent change in earnings per share.

The total risk exposure the firm assumes can be managed by combining operating and financial leverage in different degrees. Knowing the various leverage measures will help you determine the proper level of overall risk that should be accepted. For example, if a high degree of business risk is inherent in the specific line of commercial activity, then a low amount of financial risk will minimize additional earnings fluctuations stemming from changes in the firm's sales. Conversely, the firm that by its very nature incurs a low level of fixed operating costs might choose to use a high degree of financial leverage in the hope of increasing earnings per share and the rate of return on its common equity.

Concept Check

1. How do operating and financial leverage interact to affect the volatility of a firm's earnings per share?

2. If a firm's operating and financial leverage are such that a 10 percent change in sales revenue produced a 20 percent change in EBIT, and a 10 percent change in EBIT led to a 20 percent change in earnings per share, what percentage change in earnings would you expect should revenues decline by 25 percent?

FINANCE AT WORK

WHEN FINANCIAL LEVERAGE PROVES TO BE TOO MUCH TO HANDLE

The financial crisis that began in 2007 and the ensuing economic slowdown had a heavy toll on U.S. automakers. General Motors (GM), once the largest automaker in the world, found itself drowning in more debt than it could afford. So, facing the prospect of not being able to honor its financial obligations the company approached its creditors with an offer to restructure its debt. The offer included the following for each dollar of debt owed: $0.08 in cash, $0.16 in unsecured debt, plus a 90% stake in the automaker. With about $28 billion in debt to bondholders,

the GM offer translated into $2.2 billion in cash, $4.3 billion in unsecured debt plus a stake in the restructured firm. Although the terms may sound extreme for the firm's bondholders, they were even harsher on the current stockholders who went from owning 100% of the firm's equity down to only 10%! Of course, if the firm were to declare bankruptcy the common stockholders would likely be wiped out completely.

Source: Reuters UK, http://uk.reuters.com/article/businessNews/idUKTRE52T6ZZ20090331, accessed April 2, 2009.

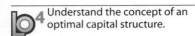

4 Understand the concept of an optimal capital structure.

financial structure the mix of all funds sources that appears on the right-hand side of the balance sheet.

capital structure the mix of interest bearing short- and long-term debt plus equity funds used by the firm.

Planning the Financing Mix

It is now time to consider the determination of the appropriate financing mix for the firm. A complete listing of the sources of financing a firm has used to finance its assets is found in the right-hand side of the firm's balance sheet. We will refer to this list of all sources of financing as the firm's **financial structure**. For example, in Table 12-7 we see a balance sheet for a firm that has $300 in assets that have been financed using a mixture of sources of financing that consists of $80 in current liabilities (debts that must be repaid within a period of one year or less), $70 in long-term debt, $50 in preferred stock, and finally $100 in common equity.

Note that some of the firm's current liabilities arise naturally as the firm carries out its day-to-day operations. We are referring to accounts payable and accrued expenses. For example, when the firm orders additional items of inventory its suppliers automatically extend credit to the firm which appears on the balance sheet as accounts payable. Moreover, the firm accrues interest and other expenses continually over time but pays it only periodically, (e.g., semi-annually). These accrued expenses then represent a liability of the firm that also arises naturally as the firm carries out its day-to-day business. Since accounts payable and accrued expense items arise automatically in response to the events that create them, these liabilities are not the ones we are directly concerned about in this chapter. Specifically, we are interested in that part of the firm's financial structure that requires the discretionary management by the firm. We refer to this as the firm's **capital structure**. In Table 12-7 the financial structure consists of all $300 of liabilities and owners' equity found on the right-hand side of the balance sheet whereas the capital structure excludes accounts payable and accrued expenses and totals $275.

The relationship between a firm's financial structure and capital structure can be expressed in equation form as follows:

$$\text{financial structure} = \left(\begin{array}{c} \text{non-interest-} \\ \text{bearing liabilities} \end{array} \right) + \left(\begin{array}{c} \text{capital} \\ \text{structure} \end{array} \right) \qquad (12\text{-}5)$$

accounts payable		short-term debt
accrued expenses		long-term debt
		preferred stock
		common equity

Note that we refer to accounts payable and accrued expenses as non-interest-bearing liabilities. The reason for this is that there is no explicit interest expense associated with these liabilities. An explicit interest expense would be something like the interest you pay on a bank loan. When a firm purchases items of inventory on credit, the credit terms simply say that the amount of the purchase must be paid within a specific time interval such as 30 days.

TABLE 12-7 Distinguishing Between a Firm's Financial Structure and Its Capital Structure

Current assets	$ 100	Accounts payable	$ 10	
Fixed assets	200	Accrued expenses	15	
Total assets	$ 300	Short-term debt	50	
		Current portion of long-term debt	5	Financial structure
		Current liabilities	$ 80	
		Long-term debt	70	Capital structure
		Preferred equity	50	
		Common equity	100	
		Total liabilities and owners' equity	$300	

CAUTIONARY TALE

FORGETTING PRINCIPLE 3: RISK REQUIRES A REWARD

In 2008, we learned that when faced with a severe economic downturn, even the smartest of the Wall Street investment bankers can be done in. As 2008 dawned, there were five major independent investment banks. Now, there are only two (Goldman Sachs and Morgan Stanley). So what did them in? The answer, very simply, is the excessive use of financial leverage.

Leverage can be a double-edged sword. In booming times, using leverage helped the investment banks increase their rates of return significantly. Of course, higher returns entail higher risk. And these banks—Bear Stearns, Lehman Brothers, and Merrill Lynch—were in effect exposing themselves to two types of risk: First, they were faced with the risk that their investments might not earn more than the costs to finance them. For example, if the rate of return the banks earned on their assets dropped below the rate they were paying for financing, then the shortfall in earnings came out of the stockholders' return. Second, the investment banks were borrowing funds using short-term loans called commercial paper and then investing this borrowed money in long-term investments. This meant that they continuously faced a refinancing risk as they needed to continually issue and re-issue commercial paper.

When the commercial paper market shut down as a result of the financial crisis in 2008, this left the investment banks without a source of financing, forcing them to sell their long-term investments at distressed prices. The result was that Bear Stearns, Lehman Brothers, and Merrill Lynch all found themselves unable to continue their operations. Merrill Lynch was bought by Bank of America, Bear Stearns was purchased by JPMorgan, and Lehman declared bankruptcy and the British investment banking firm Barclays purchased many of its assets.

Consequently, the supplier is providing 30 days of credit to the firm without specifying a rate of interest. The supplier is aware of the fact that they are supplying credit and surely will incorporate some interest cost in the price terms for the items. The important point, however, is that this interest is hidden and not explicitly stated so accounts payable and accrued expenses do not give rise to interest expense to the firm.

The design of a prudent capital structure requires that we address two questions:

1. **Debt maturity composition**—what mix of short-term and long-term debt should the firm use?
2. **Debt-equity composition**—what mix of debt and equity should the firm use?

The primary influence on the debt maturity composition of the firm's capital structure (short- versus long-term debt) is the nature of the assets owned by the firm. Firms that are heavily committed to investments in fixed assets that are expected to produce cash flow over many years generally favor long-term debt to the extent that they borrow. Firms that tend to invest more heavily in assets that produce relatively short-lived cash flows tend to finance more heavily using short-term debt.

The focus of this chapter is on answering the question noted previously—this process is usually called *capital structure management*.

A firm's capital structure should mix the permanent sources of funds used by the firm in a manner that will maximize the company's common stock price, or, put differently, *minimize the firm's composite cost of capital*. We can call this proper mix of fund sources the **optimal capital structure**.

Table 12-7 looks at equation (12-5) in terms of a balance sheet. It helps us visualize the overriding problem of capital structure management. The sources of funds that give rise to financing fixed costs (long-term debt and preferred equity) must be combined with common equity in the proportions most suitable to the investment marketplace. If that mix can be found, then holding all other factors constant, the firm's common stock price will be maximized.

Obviously, taking on excessive financial risk can put the firm into bankruptcy proceedings. But using too little financial leverage results in an undervaluation of the firm's shares. The financial manager must know how to find the area of optimum financial leverage use—this will enhance share value, all other considerations being held constant.

The rest of this chapter covers three main areas. First, we briefly discuss the theory of capital structure. Second, we examine the basic tools of capital structure management. We conclude with a real-world look at actual capital structure management.

optimal capital structure the capital structure that minimizes the firm's composite cost of capital (maximizes the common stock price) for raising a given amount of funds.

Concept Check

1. What is the objective of capital structure management?
2. What is the key attribute that defines a firm's optimal capital structure?

A Quick Look at Capital Structure Theory

In this section of the chapter we address the theoretical underpinnings as to why a firm's capital structure is important to the firm's common stockholders. To do this we first discuss a world in which capital structure is unimportant—that is, where the particular mix of debt and equity in the firm's capital structure has no effect on the value of the firm or its cost of capital (Chapter 9). The reason we do this is to make it very clear why capital structure matters and to help us make prudent decisions about its composition. The heart of the argument about the importance of capital structure is found in the following question:

Can the Firm Affect Its Overall Cost of Funds, Either Favorably or Unfavorably, by Varying the Mixture of Financing Sources Used?

This controversy has taken many elegant forms in the finance literature and tends to appeal more to academics than financial practitioners. To emphasize the ingredients of capital structure theory that have practical applications for business financial management, we will pursue an intuitive, or nonmathematical, approach to reach a better understanding of the underpinnings of this cost of capital, or capital structure, argument.

The Importance of Capital Structure

It makes economic sense for the firm to strive to minimize the cost of using financial capital. Both capital costs and other costs, such as manufacturing costs, share a common characteristic in that they potentially reduce the size of the cash dividend that could be paid to common stockholders.

Independence Position

Two Nobel Prize–winning financial economists, Franco Modigliani and Merton Miller (hereafter MM), analyzed the importance of the capital structure decision within the context of a very restrictive set of assumptions about the world in which businesses operate. Specifically, MM assumed that a firm's investment policies (i.e., the set of investments it would undertake) and dividend policy (the amount of the firm's earnings paid to stockholders in dividends) were fixed such that they are not influenced by the firm's capital structure decision. They then demonstrated, under a set of assumptions, that the firm's capital structure mix did not affect the firm's cost of capital or the value of the firm's common equity. This position is sometimes referred to as capital structure independence since the value of the firm is independent of how it has been financed (i.e., its capital structure). Some of the key assumptions underlying the MM independence proposition include the following:

1. Corporate income is not subject to taxation.
2. Capital structures consist only of stocks and bonds.
3. Investors make homogeneous forecasts of net operating income (what we earlier called EBIT).
4. Stocks and bonds are traded in perfect or efficient markets.

In this market setting, the answer to the question, "Can the firm affect its overall cost of funds, either favorably or unfavorably, by varying the mixture of financing sources used?" is no.

To summarize, the Modigliani and Miller hypothesis, or the MM view, puts forth that within the perfect economic world previously described, the total market value of the firm's outstanding securities will be *unaffected* by the manner in which the right-hand side of the balance sheet is arranged. This means the sum of the market value of outstanding common stock plus outstanding debt will always be the same regardless of how much or how little

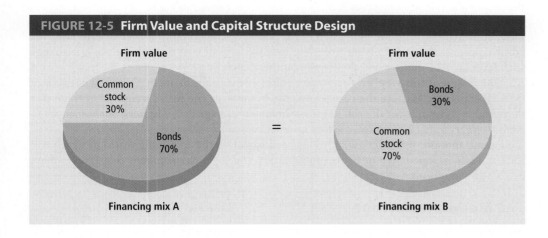

FIGURE 12-5 Firm Value and Capital Structure Design

debt is actually used by the company. This MM view is sometimes called the *independence hypothesis*, as firm value is independent of capital structure design.

The crux of this position on financing choice is illustrated in Figure 12-5. Here the firm's asset mix (the left-hand side of the balance sheet) is held constant. All that is different is the way the assets are financed. Under financing mix A, the firm funds 30 percent of its assets with common stock and the other 70 percent with bonds. Under financing mix B, the firm reverses this mix and funds 70 percent of the assets with common stock and only 30 percent with bonds. From our earlier discussions we know that financing mix A is the more heavily leveraged plan.

Notice, however, that the size of the "pies" in Figure 12-5 are exactly the same. The pie represents firm value—the total market value of the firm's outstanding securities. Thus, the total firm value associated with financing mix A equals that associated with financing mix B. Firm value is *independent* of the actual financing mix that has been chosen.

This implication is taken further in Figure 12-6 where we see that the firm's overall cost of capital, k_{wacc}, is unaffected by an increased use of financial leverage. If more debt is used

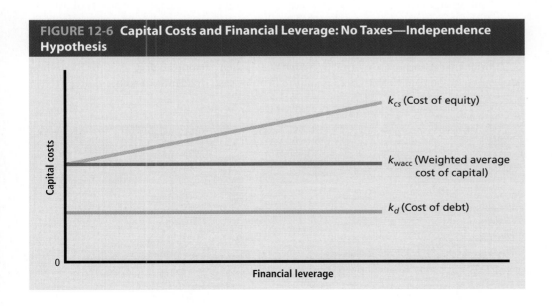

FIGURE 12-6 Capital Costs and Financial Leverage: No Taxes—Independence Hypothesis

with a cost of k_d in the capital structure, the cost of common equity, k_{cs}, will rise at the same rate additional earnings are generated. This will keep the composite cost of capital to the corporation unchanged. Furthermore, because the overall cost of capital does not change with leverage use, neither will the firm's common stock price.

The lesson of this view on financing choices is that debt financing is not as cheap as it first appears to be because the composite cost of funds or the firm's weighted average cost of capital is constant over the full range of financial leverage use. *The stark implication for financial officers is that one capital structure is just as good as any other.*

Recall, though, the strict assumptions used to define the economic world in which this theory was developed. We next turn to a market and legal environment that relaxes these extreme assumptions.

The Moderate Position

We turn now to a more moderate description of the relationship between the firm's cost of capital and its capital structure that has wide appeal to both business practitioners and academics. This moderate view is based on the relaxation of two of the very restrictive assumptions underlying the MM independence theory:

1. **Interest expense is tax deductible**—when a firm incurs debt on which it pays interest that interest is tax deductible, which reduces the cost of debt to the firm by an amount equal to the reduced taxes the firm must pay. This constitutes an advantage of using debt financing rather than equity since the dividends paid to stockholders are not tax deductible.

2. **Debt financing increases the risk of default**—since the interest and principal payments associated with borrowing must be paid in accordance with the debt contract, the firm faces the risk of being forced into bankruptcy if it fails to meet its contractual interest and principal payment obligations. This constitutes a disadvantage of using debt financing, for using more debt leads to an increased likelihood of financial distress. Financial distress, in turn, forces the firm to incur added costs and may even lead to bankruptcy which could result in the total destruction of the value of the common shares of the firm.

Combining the plus of interest tax deductibility with the minus of added risk of financial distress provides the conceptual basis for designing a prudent capital structure.

The Benefits of Financial Leverage—Interest Tax Savings   Table 12-8 illustrates this important element of the U.S. system of corporate taxation. We assume that Skip's Camper Manufacturing Company has an expected level of earnings before interest and taxes (EBIT) of $2 million and faces a corporate tax rate (made simple for example purposes) of 50 percent. Two financing plans are analyzed. The first is an unleveraged capital structure. The other assumes that Skip's Camper has $8 million of bonds outstanding that carry an interest rate of 6 percent per year.

Notice that if corporate income were *not* taxed, then earnings before taxes of $2 million per year could be paid to shareholders in the form of cash dividends or to bond investors in

TABLE 12-8 Skip's Camper Cash Flows to All Investors—The Case of Taxes		
	Unleveraged Capital Structure	Leveraged Capital Structure
Expected level of net operating income	$2,000,000	$2,000,000
Less: Interest expense	0	480,000
Earnings before taxes	$2,000,000	$1,520,000
Less: Taxes at 50%	1,000,000	760,000
Earnings available to common stockholders	$1,000,000	$ 760,000
Expected payments to all security holders	$1,000,000	$1,240,000

the form of interest payments, or any combination of the two. This means that the *sum* of the cash flows that Skip's Camper could pay to its contributors of debt or equity is *not* affected by its financing mix.

When corporate income is taxed by the government and bond interest is a tax deductible expense, however, the sum of the cash flows earned for all contributors of financial capital is affected by the firm's financing mix. Table 12-8 illustrates this point.

If Skip's Camper chooses the leveraged capital structure, the total payments to equity and debt holders will be $240,000 *greater* than under the all-common-equity capitalization. Where does this $240,000 come from? The answer is that the government's take, through taxes collected, is lower by that amount. This *difference, which flows to* Skip's Camper *security holders*, is called the **tax shield** on debt. In general, it may be calculated by equation (12-6), where r_d is the interest rate paid or interest tax savings on the debt, M is the principal amount of the debt, and T_c is the firm's marginal tax rate:

tax shield the reduction in taxes due to the tax deductibility of interest expense.

$$\text{Tax shield} = r_d(M)(T_c) \tag{12-6}$$

The moderate position on the importance of capital structure presumes that the tax shield must have value in the marketplace. Accordingly, this tax benefit will increase the total market value of the firm's outstanding securities relative to the all-equity financing mix. Note that in this case financial leverage does affect firm value. Because the cost of capital is just the other side of the valuation coin, financial leverage also affects the firm's composite cost of capital. Can the firm increase firm value indefinitely and lower its cost of capital continuously by using more and more financial leverage? Common sense would tell us no! So would most financial managers and academicians. The acknowledgment of bankruptcy costs provides one possible rationale.

The Likelihood of Firm Failure   The probability that the firm will be unable to meet the financial obligations identified in its debt contracts increases as more debt is employed. The highest costs would be incurred if the firm actually went into bankruptcy proceedings. Here, assets would be liquidated and often at distressed sale prices. If these assets do sell for something less than their perceived market values, both equity investors and debt holders could suffer losses. Other problems accompany bankruptcy proceedings. Additional lawyers and accountants have to be hired and paid. Managers must spend time preparing lengthy reports for those involved in the legal action. Moreover, all this distracts the firm's management from the efficient running of the business, and this causes missed opportunities and lost value.

Milder forms of financial distress also have their costs, as we have discussed. As the firm's financial condition weakens, creditors may take action to restrict normal business activity. Suppliers may not deliver materials on credit. Profitable capital investments may have to be forgone, and dividend payments may even be interrupted. At some point the expected cost of default will be large enough to outweigh the tax shield advantage of debt financing. The firm will turn to other sources of financing, mainly common equity (retained earnings).

The Moderate View: The Saucer-Shaped Cost-of-Capital Curve

 5 Understand and be able to graph the moderate position on capital structure importance.

This moderate view of the relationship between financing mix and the firm's cost of capital is depicted in Figure 12-7. The result is a saucer-shaped (or U-shaped) weighted-average-cost-of-capital curve, k_{wacc}. The firm's average cost of equity, k_{cs}, is seen to rise as the firm uses more debt financing. For a while the firm can borrow funds at a relatively low after-tax cost of debt, k_d. Even though the cost of equity is rising, it does not rise at a fast enough rate to offset the use of the less-expensive debt financing. Thus, between points 0 and A on the financial-leverage axis, the average cost of capital declines, and stock price rises.

Eventually, however, the threat of financial distress causes the cost of debt to rise. In Figure 12-7 this increase in the cost of debt shows up in the after-tax average-cost-of-debt

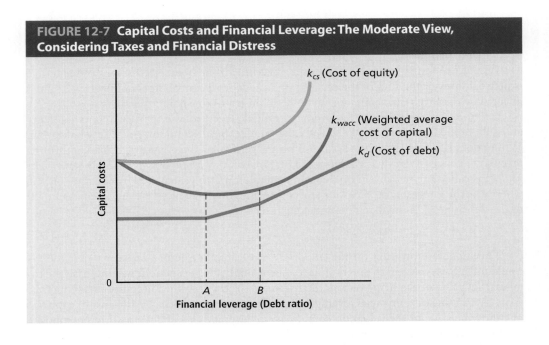

FIGURE 12-7 **Capital Costs and Financial Leverage: The Moderate View, Considering Taxes and Financial Distress**

optimal range of financial leverage the range of various capital structure combinations that yield the lowest overall cost of capital for the firm.

debt capacity the maximum proportion of debt that the firm can include in its capital structure and still maintain its lowest composite cost of capital.

curve, k_d, at point A. Between points A and B, mixing debt and equity funds produces an average cost of capital that is (relatively) flat. The firm's **optimal range of financial leverage** lies between points A and B. *All capital structures between these two points are optimal because they produce the lowest composite cost of capital.* As we said earlier in this chapter, finding this optimal range of financing mixes is the objective of capital structure management.

Point B signifies the firm's debt capacity. **Debt capacity** is the *maximum proportion of debt the firm can include in its capital structure and still maintain its lowest composite cost of capital.* Beyond point B, additional fixed-charge capital can be attracted only at very costly interest rates. At the same time, this excessive use of financial leverage would cause the firm's cost of equity to rise at a faster rate than it did previously. The composite cost of capital would then rise quite rapidly, and the firm's stock price would decline.

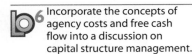 Incorporate the concepts of agency costs and free cash flow into a discussion on capital structure management.

Firm Value and Agency Costs

In Chapter 1 we mentioned the notion of agency problems. Recall that agency problems give rise to agency costs, which tend to occur in business organizations because the owners of the firm do not run the business, managers do. Thus, the firm's managers can properly be thought of as agents of the firm's stockholders. To ensure that agent-managers act in the stockholders' best interests requires that (1) they have proper incentives to do so and (2) their decisions are monitored. The incentives usually take the form of executive compensation plans and perquisites (or "perks"). The perquisites, though, might be a bloated support staff, country club memberships, luxurious corporate planes, or other amenities. Monitoring this requires that certain costs be borne by the stockholders, such as (1) bonding the managers, (2) auditing financial statements, (3) structuring the organization in unique ways that limit managerial decisions, and (4) reviewing the costs and benefits of management perquisites. This list is indicative, not exhaustive. The main point is that monitoring costs are ultimately covered by the owners of the company—its common stockholders.

FIGURE 12-8 The Agency Costs of Debt: Trade-Offs

No protective bond covenants	Many protective bond covenants
High interest rates	Low interest rates
Low monitoring costs	High monitoring costs
No lost operating efficiencies	Many lost operating efficiencies

Capital structure management also gives rise to agency costs. Agency problems stem from conflicts of interest, and capital structure management gives rise to a natural conflict between stockholders and bondholders. For example, if acting in the stockholders' best interests causes managers to invest in extremely risky projects, existing investors in the firm's bonds could logically take a dim view of such an investment policy. This is because changing the risk structure of the firm's assets would change the business-risk exposure of the firm. This could lead to a downward revision of the bond rating the firm currently enjoys. A lowered bond rating, in turn, would lower the current market value of the firm's bonds. Clearly, bondholders would be unhappy with this result.

To reduce this conflict of interest, the creditors (bond investors) and stockholders may agree to include several protective covenants in the bond contract. These bond covenants were discussed in more detail in Chapter 7, but essentially they may be thought of as restrictions on managerial decision making. Typical covenants restrict the payment of cash dividends on common stock, limit the acquisition or sale of assets, or limit further debt financing. To make sure managers comply with the protective covenants means that monitoring costs are incurred. Like all monitoring costs, they are borne by common stockholders. Furthermore, like many costs, they involve the analysis of an important trade-off.

Figure 12-8 displays some of the trade-offs involved with the use of protective bond covenants. Note (in the left panel of Figure 12-8) that the firm might be able to sell bonds that carry no protective covenants only by incurring very high interest rates. With no protective covenants, there are no associated monitoring costs. Also, there are no lost operating efficiencies, such as being able to move quickly to acquire a particular company in the acquisitions market. Conversely, restrictive covenants could reduce the explicit cost of the debt contract, but this would involve incurring significant monitoring costs and losing some operating efficiencies (which also translates into higher costs). When the debt issue is first sold, then a trade-off will be made.

Next, we have to consider the presence of monitoring costs at low and higher levels of leverage. When the firm operates at a low debt-to-equity ratio, there is little need for creditors to insist on a long list of bond covenants. The financial risk is just not there to require that type of activity. The firm will likewise benefit from low explicit interest rates when leverage is low. When the debt-to-equity ratio is high, however, it is logical for creditors to demand a great deal of monitoring. This increase in agency costs will raise the implicit cost (the true total cost) of debt financing. It seems logical, then, to suggest that monitoring costs will rise as the firm's use of financial leverage increases. Just as the likelihood of firm failure (financial distress) raises a company's overall cost of capital (k_{wacc}), so do agency costs. On the other side of the coin, this means that total firm value (the total market value of the firm's securities) will be *lower* because of agency costs. Taken together, the agency costs and the costs associated with financial distress argue in favor of the concept of an *optimal* capital structure for the individual firm.

Agency Costs, Free Cash Flow, and Capital Structure

In 1986, Professor Michael C. Jensen further extended the concept of agency costs into the area of capital structure management. The contribution revolves around a concept that Jensen labels "free cash flow," which he defines as follows:

> Free cash flow is cash flow in excess of that required to fund all projects that have positive net present values when discounted at the relevant cost of capital.[3]

Jensen then proposed that substantial free cash flow can lead to misbehavior by managers and poor decisions that are not in the best interests of the firm's common stockholders. In other words, managers have an incentive to hold onto the free cash flow and have "fun" with it, rather than "disgorge" it, say, in the form of higher cash dividend payments.

But all is not lost. This leads to what Jensen calls his "control hypothesis" for using debt. This means that by leveraging up (taking on debt), the firm's shareholders will enjoy increased control over their management team. For example, if the firm issues new debt and uses the proceeds to retire outstanding common stock, then managers are obligated to pay out cash to service the debt—this simultaneously reduces the amount of free cash flow available to them to have fun with.

We can also refer to this motive for financial leverage use as the "threat hypothesis." Managers work under the threat of financial failure; therefore, according to the "free cash flow theory of capital structure," they work more efficiently. This is supposed to reduce the agency costs of free cash flow, which will in turn be recognized by the marketplace in the form of greater returns on the common stock.

Note that the free cash flow theory of capital structure does not give a theoretical solution to the question of just how much financial leverage is enough. Nor does it suggest how much leverage is too much. It is a way of thinking about why shareholders and their boards of directors might use more debt to control managerial behavior and decisions. The basic decision tools of capital structure management still have to be utilized. They are presented later in this chapter.

REMEMBER YOUR PRINCIPLES

The discussions on agency costs, free cash flow, and the control hypothesis for debt creation return us to **Principle 5: Conflicts of Interest Cause Agency Problems.** The control hypothesis put forth by Jensen suggests that managers will work harder for shareholder interests when they have to "sweat it out" to meet contractual interest payments on debt securities. But we also learned that managers and bond investors can have a conflict that leads to agency costs associated with using debt capital. Thus, the theoretical benefits that flow from minimizing the agency costs of free cash flow by using more debt will cease when the rising agency costs of debt exactly offset those benefits. You can see how very difficult it is, then, for financial managers to identify precisely their true optimal capital structure.

Managerial Implications

Where does our examination of capital structure theory leave us? The upshot is that determining the firm's financing mix is centrally important to the financial manager because the firm's stockholders are affected by capital structure decisions. At the very least, and before bankruptcy costs and agency costs become detrimental, the tax shield effect will cause the shares of a leveraged firm to sell at a higher price than they would if the company had avoided debt financing. Because both the risk of failure and agency costs accompany the excessive use of leverage, the financial manager must exercise caution in the use of fixed-charge capital. This problem of searching for the optimal range of financial leverage is our next task.

You have now developed a workable knowledge of capital structure theory. This makes you better equipped to search for your firm's optimal capital structure. Several tools are available to help you in this search process and simultaneously help you make prudent financing choices. These tools are decision oriented. They help us answer the question, "The next time we need $20 million, should we issue common stock or sell long-term bonds?"

---

[3]Michael C. Jensen, "Agency Costs of Free Cash Flow, Corporate Finance, and Takeovers," *American Economic Review* 76 (May 1986), pp. 323–29.

Concept Check

1. What is the basic controversy surrounding capital structure theory?
2. Who are MM and what did they have to say about capital structure?
3. Explain the independence hypothesis as it relates to capital structure management.
4. Explain the moderate view of the relationship between a firm's financing mix and its average cost of capital.
5. How do agency costs and free cash flow relate to capital structure management?

The Basic Tools of Capital Structure Management

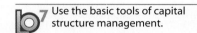
Use the basic tools of capital structure management.

We will review two basic tools that are commonly used in the evaluation of capital structure decisions. The first is the EBIT-EPS chart, which provides a way to visualize the effects of alternative capital structures on both the level and volatility of the firm's earnings per share (EPS). The second tool we review entails the analysis of the capital structures of comparable firms through the use of financial leverage ratios. Here we use ratios to standardize capital structure information as we did when we discussed financial ratios in Chapter 4 so that we can compare the capital structures of similar firms.

EBIT-EPS Analysis

EXAMPLE 12.2

Assume that plan B presented earlier in Table 12-4 is the existing capital structure for the Pierce Grain Company. Furthermore, the asset structure of the firm is such that EBIT is expected to be $20,000 per year for a very long time. A capital investment is available to Pierce Grain that will cost $50,000. Acquisition of this asset is expected to raise the projected EBIT level to $30,000 permanently. The firm can raise the needed cash by (1) selling 500 shares of common stock at $100 each or (2) selling new bonds that will net the firm $50,000 and carry an interest rate of 8.5 percent. These capital structures and corresponding EPS amounts are summarized in Table 12-9.

At the projected EBIT level of $30,000, the EPS for the common stock and debt alternatives are $6.50 and $7.25, respectively. Both are considerably above the $5.33 that would occur if the new project were rejected and the additional financial capital were not raised. Based on a criterion of selecting the financing plan that will provide the highest EPS, the bond alternative is favored. But what if the basic business risk to which the firm is exposed causes the EBIT level to vary over a considerable range? Can we be sure that the bond alternative will *always* have the higher EPS associated with it? The answer, of course, is no. When the EBIT level is subject to uncertainty, a graphic analysis of the proposed financing plans can provide useful information to the financial manager.

Before we launch into an analysis of the relationship between earnings per share (EPS) and EBIT for alternative capital structures, we need to remind ourselves why this is important. Specifically, in light of our discussions of capital structure theory you might ask, "Why should the firm's owners care about the effects of the capital structure on earnings per share (EPS)?" One possible response to this question is that corporate CEOs and boards of directors are very sensitive to the earnings numbers they report to Wall Street. The reason we offered earlier for this sensitivity relates to the perception of investors that the level of a firm's reported EPS signals important information about the firm's future prospects. For example, when a firm announces that its earnings will fall short of analyst expectations, this often triggers a revision in investor expectations regarding the future earnings prospects

TABLE 12-9 Analyzing Pierce Grain Company's Financing Choices

PART A: CAPITAL STRUCTURES

Existing Capital Structure		With New Common Stock Financing		With New Debt Financing	
Long-term debt at 8%	$ 50,000	Long-term debt at 8%	$ 50,000	Long-term debt at 8%	$ 50,000
Common stock	150,000	Common stock	200,000	Long-term debt at 8.5%	50,000
				Common stock	150,000
Total liabilities and equity	$200,000	Total liabilities and equity	$250,000	Total liabilities and equity	$250,000
Common shares outstanding	1,500	Common shares outstanding	2,000	Common shares outstanding	1,500

PART B: PROJECTED EPS LEVELS

	Existing Capital Structure	With New Common Stock Financing	With New Debt Financing
EBIT	$20,000	$30,000	$30,000
Less: Interest expense	4,000	4,000	8,250
Earnings before taxes (EBT)	$16,000	$26,000	$21,750
Less: Taxes at 50%	8,000	13,000	10,875
Net income	$ 8,000	$13,000	$10,875
Less: Preferred dividends	0	0	0
Earnings available to common shareholders	$ 8,000	$13,000	$10,875
EPS	$ 5.33	$ 6.50	$ 7.25

for the firm. This downward revision, in turn, results in a drop in the firm's stock price. Thus, corporate executives are very aware of the importance investors attach to earnings and take this information into account when considering the design of the firm's capital structure.

Graphic Analysis   The EBIT-EPS analysis chart allows the decision maker to visualize the impact of different financing plans on EPS over a range of EBIT levels. The relationship between EPS and EBIT is linear. All we need to construct the chart is two points for each alternative. Part B of Table 12-9 already provides us with one of these points. The answer to the following question for each choice gives us the second point: At what EBIT level will the EPS for the plan be exactly zero? If the EBIT level *just covers* the plan's financing costs (on a before-tax basis), then EPS will be zero. For the stock plan, an EPS of zero is associated with an EBIT of $4,000. The $4,000 is the interest expense incurred under the existing capital structure. If the bond plan is elected, the interest costs will be the present $4,000 plus $4,250 per year arising from the new debt issue. An EBIT level of $8,250, then, is necessary to provide a zero EPS with the bond plan.

The EBIT-EPS analysis chart representing the financing choices available to the Pierce Grain Company is shown as Figure 12-9. EBIT is charted on the horizontal axis and EPS on the vertical axis. The intercepts on the horizontal axis represent the before-tax equivalent financing charges related to each plan. The straight lines for each plan tell us the EPS amounts that will occur at different EBIT amounts.

Notice that the bond-plan line has a *steeper slope* than the stock-plan line. This ensures that the lines for each financing choice will *intersect*. Above the intersection point, the EPS for the plan with greater leverage will exceed that for the plan with lesser leverage. The intersection point, circled in Figure 12-9, occurs at an EBIT level of $21,000 and produces EPS of $4.25 for each plan. When EBIT is $30,000, notice that the bond plan produces EPS of $7.25, and the stock plan, $6.50. Below the intersection point, the EPS with the stock plan will *exceed* that of the more highly leveraged bond plan. The steeper slope

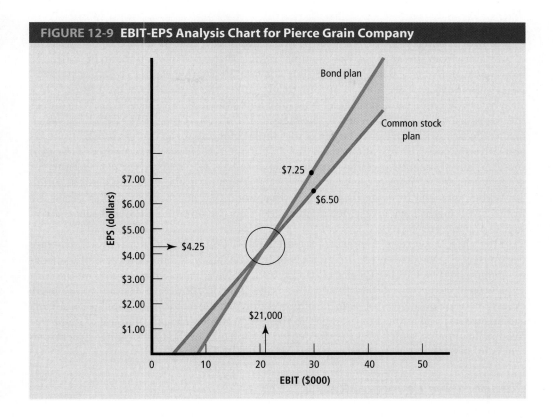

FIGURE 12-9 **EBIT-EPS Analysis Chart for Pierce Grain Company**

of the bond-plan line indicates that with greater leverage, EPS is more sensitive to EBIT changes.

Computing Indifference Points   The point of intersection in Figure 12-9 is called the **EBIT-EPS indifference point**. It identifies the *EBIT level at which the EPS will be the same regardless of the financing plan chosen by the financial manager*. This indifference point, sometimes called the break-even point, has major implications for financial planning. At EBIT amounts in excess of the EBIT indifference level, the more heavily leveraged financing plan will generate a higher EPS. At EBIT amounts below the EBIT indifference level, the financing plan involving less leverage will generate a higher EPS. It is important, then, to know the EBIT indifference level.

EBIT-EPS indifference point the level of earnings before interest and taxes (EBIT) that will equate earnings per share (EPS) between two different financing plans.

We can find it graphically, as in Figure 12-9. At times it may be more efficient, though, to calculate the indifference point directly. This can be done by using the following equation:

EPS: STOCK PLAN   **EPS: BOND PLAN**

$$\frac{(\text{EBIT} - I)(1 - T_c) - P}{S_s} = \frac{(\text{EBIT} - I)(1 - T_c) - P}{S_b} \tag{12-7}$$

where S_s and S_b are the number of common shares outstanding under the stock and bond plans, respectively; I is interest expense; T_c is the firm's income tax rate; and P is preferred dividends paid. In the present case, P is zero because there is no preferred stock outstanding. If preferred stock is associated with one of the financing alternatives, keep in mind that the preferred dividends, P, are not tax deductible. Equation (12-7) does take this fact into consideration.

For the present example, we calculate the indifference level of EBIT as

$$\frac{(\text{EBIT} - \$4,000)(1 - 0.5) - 0}{2,000} = \frac{(\text{EBIT} - \$8,250)(1 - 0.5) - 0}{1,500}$$

When the expression above is solved for EBIT, we obtain \$21,000. If EBIT turns out to be \$21,000, then EPS will be \$4.25 under both plans.

A Word of Caution   Okay, now we know that using more financial leverage *may* provide higher firm earnings if EBIT is above the break-even point. But this is not all that we need to take away from this analysis. For example, assume that EBIT is expected to be above the break-even point 99.9 percent of the time for two alternative capital structure policies. Does this mean that we should automatically select the higher leverage option? The answer, as you might have suspected, is no, and here's the logic for this answer. The higher the firm's use of financial leverage, the steeper the slope of the EBIT-EPS line, which means the firm will experience larger swings in EPS for any given change in EBIT. CEOs and corporate boards care about these swings for the reason we noted earlier. That is, if the firm fails to meet its earnings expectations, investors may revise their expectations for the firm's future earnings prospects downward, at which point the share price might suffer. So, higher financial leverage increases the likelihood that an unanticipated swing in the firm's EBIT might have a very detrimental effect on the reported EPS, and this is a real source of concern.

How then are we to interpret and use the EBIT-EPS chart to analyze capital structure design issues? The answer, like many tools of financial analysis, entails the use of managerial judgment. The EBIT-EPS chart is simply a tool that can be used to learn about the consequences of using more or less financial leverage. The decision as to whether to use more or less financial leverage must be made after weighing all the factors that impinge on a firm's capital structure decision. For example, in the next section we look at the use of comparative financial ratios, which indicate the degree of similarity of the firm's capital structure to others in its same industry, or peer group.

Comparative Leverage Ratios

In Chapter 4 we explored the overall usefulness of financial ratio analysis. Leverage ratios, one of the categories of financial ratios, are identified in that chapter. We emphasize here that the computation of leverage ratios is one of the basic tools of capital structure management.

Two types of leverage ratios must be computed when a financing decision faces the firm. We call these *balance-sheet leverage ratios* and *coverage ratios*. The firm's balance sheet supplies inputs for computing the balance-sheet leverage ratios. In various forms these balance-sheet metrics compare the firm's use of funds supplied by creditors with those supplied by owners.

Inputs to the coverage ratios generally come from the firm's income statement. At times the external analyst may have to refer to balance-sheet information to construct some of these needed estimates. On a privately placed debt issue, for example, some fraction of the current portion of the firm's long-term debt might have to be used as an estimate of that issue's sinking fund. Coverage ratios provide estimates of the firm's ability to service its financing contracts. High coverage ratios, compared with a standard, imply unused debt capacity.

In reality, we know that EBIT might be expected to vary over a considerable range of outcomes. For this reason the coverage ratios should be calculated several times, each at a different level of EBIT. If this is accomplished over all possible values of EBIT, a probability distribution for each coverage ratio can be constructed. This provides the financial manager with much more information than simply calculating the coverage ratios based on the expected value of EBIT.

Industry Norms

The comparative leverage ratios have utility only if they can be compared with some standard. Generally, corporate financial analysts, investment bankers, commercial bank loan officers, and bond-rating agencies rely on industry classes to compute "normal" ratios. Although industry groupings may actually contain firms whose basic business-risk exposure differs widely, the practice is entrenched in American business behavior. At the very least, then, the financial officer must be interested in industry standards because almost everybody else is.

Capital structure ratios tend to differ among industry classes. For example, random samplings of the common equity ratios of large retail firms seem to differ statistically from those of major steel producers. The major steel producers use financial leverage to a lesser degree than do the large retail organizations. On the whole, firms operating in the *same* industry tend to exhibit capital structure ratios that cluster around a central value that we call a norm. The degree of business risk varies from industry to industry as well. As a consequence, the capital structure norms vary from industry to industry.

This is not to say that all companies in the industry will maintain leverage ratios "close" to the norm. For instance, firms that are very profitable might display high coverage ratios and high balance-sheet leverage ratios. The moderately profitable firm, though, might find such a posture unduly risky. Here the usefulness of industry-normal leverage ratios is clear. If the firm chooses to deviate substantially from the accepted values for the key ratios, it must have a sound reason.

Concept Check

1. Explain the meaning of the EBIT-EPS indifference point.
2. How are various leverage ratios and industry norms used in capital structure management?

A Glance at Actual Capital Structure Management

We now examine some opinions and practices of financial executives that reinforce the importance of capital structure management.

Figure 12-10 reports a portion of the results of a survey of 392 corporate executives about the factors they considered to be either important or very important in deciding whether to use debt in their firm's capital structure. Specifically, we report the top 10

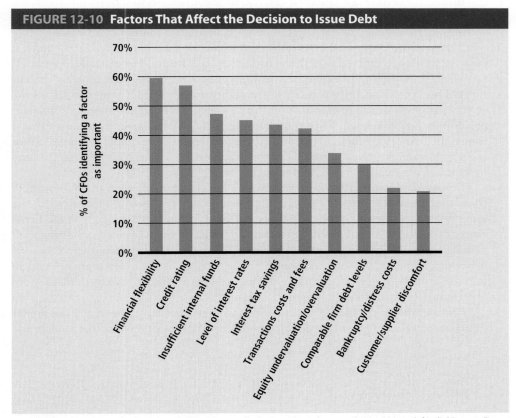

FIGURE 12-10 Factors That Affect the Decision to Issue Debt

Source: John Graham and Campbell Harvey, "How do CFOs make capital budgeting and capital structure decisions?," *Journal of Applied Corporate Finance,* Volume 15, Number 1, Spring 2002, 8–23. (Used with permission)

factors that the corporate executives as a group felt were most important factors influencing the decision to issue debt.

These 10 factors provide some practical guidance to the financial manager who is wrestling with capital structure design and management issues. Let's briefly consider each factor to see why it is relevant.

Financial Flexibility   When a firm needs to raise additional funds, its bargaining position is better if it has options or choices. For example, firms that have used very little debt in the past will find it easier to borrow or sell new shares of stock than firms that have borrowed heavily.

Credit Rating   Dropping a notch in the rating system leads to an increase in the firm's borrowing costs, so managers like to avoid this if at all possible.[4] Moreover, sometimes firms have contractual provisions inserted into some of their other debt agreements that require the firm to maintain a particular credit rating. For example, Enron's bankruptcy was triggered by the firm dropping one credit rating, which put the firm below investment-grade status. The firm had billions of dollars in outstanding debt that contained a covenant requiring them to maintain a BBB or higher rating.

Insufficient Internal Funds   It has long been known that firms tend to follow a priority list when raising new funds that has been referred to as a "pecking order." The order in which firms typically finance their operations begins with internally generated profits, followed by debt financing, and, finally, by issuing new equity.

Level of Interest Rates   Other things being the same, firms prefer to borrow when they feel interest rates are low relative to their expectations. For example, when interest rates are historically very low, a CFO may feel more inclined to enter into long-term debt agreements. However, there is little evidence that a CFO, or anyone for that matter, has any talent for knowing when rates are low and about to rise, or high and about to fall. Nonetheless, all that is required for this factor to be considered important is a strong opinion about the future path of interest rates.

Interest Tax Savings   Interest expense, unlike dividends paid to shareholders, is a tax-deductible expense. This tax-savings feature serves as a subsidy to corporate borrowing and makes debt appear cheap relative to alternative sources of financing.

Transaction Costs and Fees   When a firm chooses between debt and equity, it faces very different costs of issuing the two types of securities. For example, debt holders receive interest and principal payments as prescribed in the debt contract (indenture). This type of security is relatively straightforward, and its value hinges on the creditworthiness of the firm. However, when a firm issues equity, there are no rules prescribing how much will be paid back to the buyers of the stock. This means that it can be much more costly to entice an investor to become a stockholder than to entice them to loan money to the firm. Thus, the differentially higher costs of issuing equity make it less attractive as a source of financing.

Equity Undervaluation/Overvaluation   Earlier we mentioned that CFOs often try to time their debt offerings to take advantage of abnormally low interest rates. The same holds true for equity offerings. For example, if the CFO thinks that the firm's shares of stock are undervalued, he or she will want to borrow money rather than sell new shares and risk the price of the shares falling further. Once again, there is no evidence that corporate executives are any better at forecasting their own share prices than they are at predicting the future of interest rates, but they only have to think they are good at it to believe it is an important factor.

Comparable Firm Debt Levels   Firms in similar businesses tend to have similar capital structures. This is made doubly important by virtue of the fact that lenders and

---

[4]We discussed bond ratings in Chapter 7.

FINANCE AT WORK

CAPITAL STRUCTURES AROUND THE WORLD

The use of debt financing by firms is influenced by many factors, and one of them apparently is the home country of the firm. To illustrate, consider the listing of median leverage ratios (total debt divided by the market value of the firm) by country provided below.*

COUNTRY	LEVERAGE RATIO
South Korea	70%
Pakistan	49%
Brazil	47%
Thailand	46%
India	40%
Japan	33%
China	33%
France	28%
Belgium	26%
Mexico	26%
Chile	21%
Germany	17%
United Kingdom	16%
United States	16%
Greece	10%

The highest leverage ratio is observed in South Korea where the leverage ratio is close to 70%, while the lowest is only 10%, observed in Greece. The median leverage ratio in the United States is only 16%, which may seem quite low. However, this is the result of the fact that these ratios are based on the market values of the firms rather than their book value.

What kind of factors might encourage the use of debt in different countries? One factor that researchers found is that firms that operate in countries where the legal systems provide better protection for financial claimants tend to use less total debt, and the debt they use tends to be of a longer-term maturity. In addition, as you might expect, the tax policy of the country that the firm operates within also plays a role in the level of debt that a firm uses.

*The market value of the firm is defined to be the market value of common equity plus the book values of preferred stock and total debt.

Source: Joseph P. H. Fan, Sheridan Titman, and Garry J. Twite, "An International Comparison of Capital Structure and Debt Maturity Choices" (October 2008). AFA 2005 Philadelphia Meetings available at SSRN: http://ssrn.com/abstract=423483.

---

credit-rating agencies often compare a firm's debt ratios to those of comparable firms when deciding credit terms and ratings.

Bankruptcy/Distress Costs   The more debt a firm has used in the past, the higher the likelihood is that the firm will at some point face financial distress and possibly fail. This risk forms the basis for the firm's credit rating.

Customer/Supplier Discomfort   An important source of financial distress brought on by the use of debt financing comes in the form of pressures from both the firm's customers (who fear that financial distress may interrupt their source of supply) and the firm's suppliers (who fear that financial distress may interrupt an important source of demand for their goods and services). The latter is compounded further if the supplier has provided the firm with trade credit, which is at risk if the firm fails.

After reading through the discussion of each of the 10 factors, you are probably beginning to think that capital structure management is more art than science. In other words, there simply is no magic formula that you can use to solve for the optimal capital structure. However, you should be gaining an appreciation for the basic considerations that go into the judgment call that the CFOs ultimately must make and that drives the capital structure of firms. Furthermore, selected comments from financial executives point to the widespread use of target debt ratios.

Concept Check

1. Identify several factors that influence the decision to issue debt.
2. Why is capital structure design both an art and a science?

Summary

Understand the difference between business risk and financial risk.

Use the technique of break-even analysis in a variety of analytical settings.

Distinguish among the financial concepts of operating leverage, financial leverage, and combined leverage.

Understand the concept of an optimal capital structure.

Understand and be able to graph the moderate position on capital structure importance.

Incorporate the concepts of agency costs and free cash flow into a discussion on capital structure management.

Use the basic tools of capital structure management.

In this chapter we studied the process of arriving at an appropriate financial structure for the firm, and we examined tools that can assist the financial manager in this task. We are concerned with assessing the variability in the firm's residual earnings stream (either earnings per share or earnings available to the common shareholders) as a result of the use of operating and financial leverage. This assessment builds on the tenets of break-even analysis.

We then dealt with the design of the firm's financing mix, emphasizing the management of the firm's permanent sources of funds—that is, its capital structure. The objective of capital structure management is to arrange the company's sources of funds so that its common stock price is maximized.

A break-even analysis permits the financial manager to determine the quantity of output or the level of sales that will result in an EBIT level of zero. This means the firm has neither a profit nor a loss before any tax considerations. The effect of price changes, cost structure changes, or volume changes on profits (EBIT) can be studied. But to do so it is necessary to first classify the firm's costs as fixed or variable. Not all costs fit neatly into one of these two categories. Over short planning horizons, though, the preponderance of costs can be assigned to either the fixed or variable classification. Once the cost structure has been identified, the break-even point can be found.

Operating leverage is the responsiveness of the firm's EBIT to changes in sales revenues. It arises from the firm's use of fixed operating costs. When fixed operating costs are present in the company's cost structure, increases in sales are magnified into even greater changes in EBIT. But leverage is a two-edged sword. For example, when sales decrease by some percentage, the negative impact on EBIT is again even larger.

A firm employs financial leverage when it finances a portion of its assets with securities bearing a fixed rate of return. The presence of debt and/or preferred stock in the company's financial structure means that it is using financial leverage. When financial leverage is used, changes in EBIT translate into larger changes in earnings per share. Very simply, the firm's use of financial leverage makes its earnings per share more sensitive to changes in EBIT higher. All other things being equal, the more fixed-charge securities the firm employs in its financial structure, the greater its financial leverage. Clearly, EBIT can rise or fall. If it falls, and financial leverage is used, the firm's shareholders endure negative changes in earnings per share that are larger than the relative decline in EBIT. Again, leverage is a two-edged sword.

Can the firm affect its composite cost of capital by altering its financing mix? Attempts to answer this question have surrounded capital structure theory for over 3 decades. Those taking extreme positions say that the firm's stock price is either unaffected or continually affected as the firm infinitely increases its reliance on leverage. However, in the real world, interest expense is tax deductible, and market imperfections operate to restrict the amount of fixed-income obligations a firm can issue. Consequently, most financial officers and financial academics subscribe to the concept of an optimal capital structure. The optimal capital structure minimizes the firm's composite cost of capital. Searching for a proper range of financial leverage, then, is an important financial management activity.

Another type of agency cost is related to "free cash flow." Managers, for example, have an incentive to hold onto free cash flow and enjoy it, rather than pay it out in the form of higher cash dividend payments. This conflict between managers and stockholders leads to the concept of the *free cash flow theory of capital structure*. This same theory is also known as the *control hypothesis* and the *threat hypothesis*. The ultimate resolution of these agency costs affects the specific form of the firm's capital structure.

The decision to use debt financing in the firm's capital structure causes two types of financial-leverage effects. The first is the added variability in the earnings-per-share stream that accompanies the use of fixed-charge securities. The second financial-leverage effect relates to the level of earnings per share (EPS) at a given EBIT under a specific capital structure. Via an EBIT-EPS analysis, the decision maker can inspect the impact of alternative financing plans on EPS over a full range of EBIT levels.

A second tool of capital structure management is the calculation of comparative leverage ratios. Comparing these ratios with industry standards enables the financial officer to determine if the firm's key ratios are in line with accepted practice.

CFO indicate that several factors influence the decision to issue debt. The top two are the firm's financial flexibility and its credit rating. If the firm has the flexibility to choose either debt or equity, then it is in a better financial position. Maintaining the firm's credit rating reflects the CFO's recognition that interest costs vary inversely with the firm's credit rating. If the firm has AA credit, then dropping to A or lower will drive up the firm's cost of borrowing.

Key Terms

Business risk   338

Capital structure   350

Debt capacity   356

Direct costs   340

EBIT-EPS indifference point   361

Financial leverage   346

Financial structure   350

Fixed costs   340

Indirect costs   340

Operating leverage   343

Optimal capital structure   351

Optimal range of financial leverage   356

Tax shield   355

Total revenue   342

Variable costs   340

Volume of output   342

Review Questions

All Review Questions and Study Problems are available in MyFinanceLab.

12-1. Distinguish between business risk and financial risk. What gives rise to, or causes, each type of risk?

12-2. Define the term *financial leverage*. Does the firm use financial leverage if preferred stock is present in its capital structure?

12-3. Define the term *operating leverage*. What type of effect occurs when the firm uses operating leverage?

12-4. A manager in your firm decides to employ a break-even analysis. Of what shortcomings should this manager be aware?

12-5. A break-even analysis assumes linear revenue and cost functions. In reality, these linear functions deviate over large output and sales levels. Why?

12-6. Define the following terms:
   a. Financial structure
   b. Capital structure
   c. Optimal capital structure
   d. Debt capacity

12-7. What is the primary weakness of using EBIT-EPS analysis as a financing decision tool?

12-8. What is the objective of capital structure management?

12-9. Why might firms whose sales levels change drastically over time choose to use debt only sparingly in their capital structures?

12-10. What does the term *independence hypothesis* mean as it applies to capital structure theory?

12-11. Many CFOs believe that the firm's composite cost of capital is saucer-shaped or U-shaped. What does this mean?

12-12. Define the EBIT-EPS indifference point.

12-13. Explain how industry norms might be used by the financial manager in the design of the company's financing mix.

12-14. Define the term *free cash flow*.

12-15. What is meant by the *free cash flow theory of capital structure*?

12-16. In almost every instance, what funds source do managers use first?

Self-Test Problem

(The solution to the following problem is provided at the end of the chapter.)

ST-1. (*Fixed costs and the break-even point*) Bonaventure Manufacturing expects to earn $210,000 next year after taxes. Sales will be $4 million. The firm's single plant is located on the outskirts of Olean, New York. The firm manufactures a combined bookshelf and desk unit used extensively in college dormitories. These units sell for $200 each and have a variable cost per unit of $150. Bonaventure experiences a 30 percent tax rate.
   a. What are the firm's fixed costs expected to be next year?
   b. Calculate the firm's break-even point in both units and dollars.

Study Problems

12-1. (*Leverage analysis*) You have developed the following income statement for the Hugo Boss Corporation. It represents the most recent year's operations, which ended yesterday.

Sales	$ 50,439,375
Variable costs	(25,137,000)
Revenue before fixed costs	$ 25,302,375
Fixed costs	(10,143,000)
EBIT	$ 15,159,375
Interest expense	(1,488,375)
Earnings before taxes	$ 13,671,000
Taxes at 50%	(6,835,500)
Net income	$ 6,835,500

Your supervisor in the controller's office has just handed you a memorandum asking for written responses to the following questions:

    a. What is the firm's break-even point in sales dollars?

    b. If sales should increase by 30 percent, by what percent would earnings before taxes (and net income) increase?

12-2. (*EBIT-EPS analysis*) Two inventive entrepreneurs have interested a group of venture capitalists in backing a new business project. The proposed plan would consist of a series of international retail outlets to distribute and service a full line of ingenious home garden tools. The stores would be located in high-traffic cities in Latin America such as Panama City, Bogotá, São Paulo, and Buenos Aires. Two financing plans have been proposed by the entrepreneurs. Plan A is an all-common-equity structure. Five million dollars would be raised by selling 160,000 shares of common stock. Plan B would involve the use of long-term debt financing. Three million dollars would be raised by marketing bonds with an effective interest rate of 14 percent. Under the alternative, another $2 million would be raised by selling 64,000 shares of common stock. With both plans, $5 million is needed to launch the new firm's operations. The debt funds raised under plan B are considered to have no fixed maturity date, because this portion of financial leverage is thought to be a permanent part of the company's capital structure. The two promising entrepreneurs have decided to use a 35 percent tax rate in their analysis, and they have hired you on a consulting basis to do the following:

    a. Find the EBIT indifference level associated with the two financing proposals.

    b. Prepare income statements for the two plans that proves EPS will be the same regardless of the plan chosen at the EBIT level found in part a.

12-3. (*Break-even point and operating leverage*) Footwear Inc. manufactures a complete line of men's and women's dress shoes for independent merchants. The average selling price of its finished product is $85 per pair. The variable cost for this same pair of shoes is $58. Footwear Inc. incurs fixed costs of $170,000 per year.

    a. What is the break-even point in pairs of shoes for the company?

    b. What is the dollar sales volume the firm must achieve to reach the break-even point?

    c. What would be the firm's profit or loss at the following units of production sold: 7,000 pairs of shoes? 9,000 pairs of shoes? 15,000 pairs of shoes?

12-4. (*Break-even point and selling price*) Parks Castings Inc. will manufacture and sell 200,000 units next year. Fixed costs will total $300,000, and variable costs will be 60 percent of sales.

    a. The firm wants to achieve a level of earnings before interest and taxes of $250,000. What selling price per unit is necessary to achieve this result?

    b. Set up an analytical income statement to verify your solution to part a.

12-5. (*Operating leverage*) Rocky Mount Metals Company manufactures an assortment of wood-burning stoves. The average selling price for the various units is $500. The associated variable cost is $350 per unit. Fixed costs for the firm average $180,000 annually.

    a. What is the break-even point in units for the company?

    b. What is the dollar sales volume the firm must achieve to reach the break-even point?

c. What is the degree of operating leverage for a production and sales level of 5,000 units for the firm? (Calculate to three decimal places.)

d. What will be the projected effect on earnings before interest and taxes if the firm's sales level should increase by 20 percent from the volume noted in part c?

12-6. (*EBIT-EPS analysis*) A group of retired college professors has decided to form a small manufacturing corporation. The company will produce a full line of traditional office furniture. Two financing plans have been proposed by the investors. Plan A is an all-common-equity alternative. Under this agreement, 1 million common shares will be sold to net the firm $20 per share. Plan B involves the use of financial leverage. A debt issue with a 20-year maturity period will be privately placed. The debt issue will carry an interest rate of 10 percent, and the principal borrowed will amount to $6 million. The corporate tax rate is 50 percent.

a. Find the EBIT indifference level associated with the two financing proposals.

b. Prepare an analytical income statement that proves EPS will be the same regardless of the plan chosen at the EBIT level found in part a.

c. Prepare an EBIT-EPS analysis chart for this situation.

d. If a detailed financial analysis projects that long-term EBIT will always be close to $2.4 million annually, which plan will provide for the higher EPS?

12-7. (*Assessing leverage use*) Some financial data for three corporations are displayed here.

MEASURE	FIRM A	FIRM B	FIRM C	INDUSTRY NORM
Debt ratio	20%	25%	40%	20%
Times interest covered	8 times	10 times	7 times	9 times
Price–earnings ratio	9 times	11 times	6 times	10 times

a. Which firm appears to be excessively leveraged?

b. Which firm appears to be employing financial leverage to the most appropriate degree?

c. What explanation can you provide for the higher price–earnings ratio enjoyed by firm B as compared with firm A?

Mini Case

1. Imagine that you were hired recently as a financial analyst for a relatively new, highly leveraged ski manufacturer located in the foothills of Colorado's Rocky Mountains. Your firm manufactures only one product, a state-of-the-art snow ski. The company has been operating up to this point without much quantitative knowledge of the business and financial risks it faces.

Ski season just ended, however, so the president of the company has started to focus more on the financial aspects of managing the business. He has set up a meeting for next week with the CFO, Maria Sanchez, to discuss matters such as the business and financial risks faced by the company. Accordingly, Maria has asked you to prepare an analysis to assist her in her discussions with the president.

As a first step in your work, you compiled the following information regarding the cost structure of the company:

Output level	80,000 units
Operating assets	$4,000,000
Operating asset turnover	8 times
Return on operating assets	32%
Degree of operating leverage	6 times
Interest expense	$600,000
Tax rate	35%

As the next step, you need to determine the break-even point in units of output for the company. One of your strong points has been that you always prepare supporting work papers, which show how you arrived at your conclusions. You know Maria would like to see these work papers to facilitate her review of your work. Therefore, you will have the information you require to prepare an analytical income statement for the company. You are sure that Maria would also like to see this statement. In addition, you know that you need it to be able to answer the following questions. You also know Maria expects you to prepare, in a format that is presentable to the president, answers to the following questions to serve as a basis for her discussions with the president.

   a. What is the firm's break-even point in sales dollars?

   b. If sales should increase by 30 percent (as the president expects), by what percentage would EBT (earnings before taxes) and net income increase?

   c. Prepare another income statement, this time to verify the calculations from part b.

2. Camping USA Inc. has only been operating for 2 years in the outskirts of Albuquerque, New Mexico, and is a new manufacturer of a top-of-the-line camping tent. You are starting an internship as assistant to the chief financial officer of the company, and the owner and CEO, Tom Charles, has decided that this is the right time to know more about the business and financial risks his company must deal with. For this, the CFO has asked you to prepare an analysis to support him in his next meeting with Tom Charles a week from today.

To make the required calculations, you have put together the following data regarding the cost structure of the company:

Output level	120,000 units
Operating assets	$6,000,000
Operating asset turnover	12 times
Return on operating assets	48%
Degree of operating leverage	10 times
Interest expense	$720,000
Tax rate	42%

The CFO has instructed you to first determine the break-even point in units of output for the company. He requires that you prepare supporting documents, which demonstrate how you arrived at your conclusion and can facilitate his review of your work. Accordingly, you are required to have the information needed to prepare an analytical income statement for the company to be presented to the CFO. In a format that is acceptable for a meeting discussion with the CEO, you also need to prepare answers to the following questions:

   a. What is the firm's break-even point in sales dollars?

   b. If sales should increase by 40 percent, by what percentage would EBT (earnings before taxes) and net income increase?

   c. Prepare another income statement, this time to verify the calculations from part b.

Self-Test Solution

SS-1.

a.
$$[(P \cdot Q) - [(V \cdot Q) + F]](1 - 0.3) = \$210{,}000$$
$$[(\$4{,}000{,}000) - (\$3{,}000{,}000) - F](0.7) = \$210{,}000$$
$$(\$1{,}000{,}000 - F)(0.7) = \$210{,}000$$
$$\$700{,}000 - 0.7F = \$210{,}000$$
$$0.7F = \$490{,}000$$
$$F = \underline{\$700{,}000}$$

Fixed costs next year, then, are expected to be $700,000.

b. $Q_B = \dfrac{F}{P - V} = \dfrac{\$700{,}000}{\$50} = \underline{14{,}000}$ units

$S = \dfrac{F}{1 - \dfrac{VC}{S}} = \dfrac{\$700{,}000}{1 - 0.75} = \dfrac{\$700{,}000}{0.25} = \underline{\$2{,}800{,}000}$

The firm will break even (EBIT = 0) when it sells 14,000 units. With a selling price of $200 per unit, the break-even sales level is $2,800,000.

Chapter 13

Dividend Policy and Internal Financing

Learning Objectives

After reading this chapter, you should be able to:

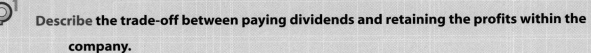

1. **Describe** the trade-off between paying dividends and retaining the profits within the company.

2. **Explain** the relationship between a corporation's dividend policy and the market price of its common stock.

3. **Describe** practical considerations that may be important to the firm's dividend policy.

4. **Distinguish** among the types of dividend policies corporations frequently use.

5. **Specify** the procedures a company follows in administering the dividend payment.

6. **Describe** why and how a firm might pay noncash dividends (stock dividends and stock splits) instead of cash dividends.

7. **Explain** the purpose and procedures related to stock repurchases.

Corporations distribute cash back to their owners (the stockholders) either as cash dividends or by repurchasing shares of stock in the open market. Even in the economic downturn following the financial crisis that began in 2007, many firms continue to announce repurchase programs. For example, in October 2008 Gilead Sciences (GILD), a biotechnology company, announced plans to repurchase $3 billion of its shares and trucking firm Celadon Group (CLDN) announced its intention to repurchase 2 million of its approximately 22 million shares. But none of these programs rivals Microsoft Corporation (MSFT), which announced on September 22, 2008, its plans to increase its cash dividend by 18 percent and to repurchase up to $40 billion in company shares over the period ending September 30, 2013. This new repurchase program follows the completion of a previous $40 billion in share repurchases. In fact, combining dividends and share repurchases Microsoft has distributed $115 billion to shareholders over the five-year period just ended.

Why should an investor care about a firm's cash distributions? The answer, very simply, is that these cash distributions represent the *return on* the investment made by the stockholders. As such these distributions are tangible evidence of the value created by the firm for its owners. But not all companies distribute cash either as dividends or share repurchases. Microsoft, for example, did not distribute any cash during the early years of the company's life when it was growing rapidly and needed all its internally generated earnings to support its growth. Similarly, rapidly growing technology giant Google Inc. (GOOG) earned $7.8 billion from its operations in 2008 and had a cash plus marketable securities balance of over $15 billion but paid no cash dividends. So why did Google's stock price hover around $363 on April 3, 2009, if they were not distributing any cash? The answer is that it is the investor's expectation that at some point in the future the firm will begin distributing cash just as Microsoft has done.

So it is the anticipated dividends and share repurchases that are the cash flow (Principle 1) that underlies stock valuation.

Because the goal of a firm should be to maximize the value, or price, of the firm's common stock, the success or failure of managerial decisions can be evaluated only in light of their impact on the price. We observed that the company's investment (Chapters 10 and 11) and financing decisions (Chapter 12) can increase the value of the firm. As we look at the firm's policies regarding dividends and internal financing (how much of the company's financing comes from cash flows generated internally), we return to the same basic question: Can managers influence the price of the firm's stock, in this case through its dividend policies? After addressing this important question, we then look at the practical side of the question: What practices do managers commonly follow when making decisions about paying or not paying a dividend to the firm's stockholders? We conclude with a discussion of the multinational firm that chooses to follow a policy of low dividend payments but is confronted, then, with the prospect of exploring international markets for high net present value projects.

Key Terms

 Describe the trade-off between paying dividends and retaining the profits within the company.

Before taking up the particular issues relating to dividend policy, we must understand several key terms and interrelationships.

A firm's dividend policy includes two basic components. First, the **dividend payout ratio** indicates the *amount of dividends paid relative to the company's earnings*. For instance, if the dividend per share is $2, and the earnings per share are $4, the payout ratio is 50 percent ($2/$4). The second component is the stability of the dividends over time. As you will learn later in the chapter, dividend stability can be almost as important to the investor as the amount of dividends received.

dividend payout ratio the amount of dividends relative to the company's net income or earnings per share.

In formulating a dividend policy, the financial manager faces trade-offs. Assuming that management has already decided how much to invest and has chosen its debt–equity mix for financing the firm's investments, the decision to pay a large dividend means simultaneously deciding to retain less of the firm's profits; this in turn results in a greater reliance on external equity financing. Conversely, given the firm's investment and financing decisions, a small dividend payment corresponds to high profit retention, making it less necessary to generate funds externally. These trade-offs, which are fundamental to our discussion, are illustrated in Figure 13-1.

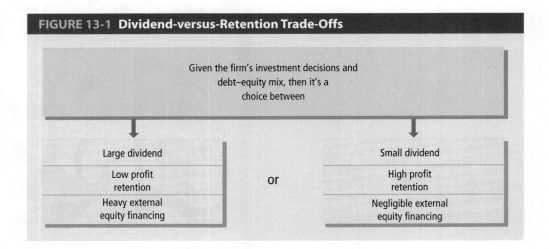

FIGURE 13-1 Dividend-versus-Retention Trade-Offs

Concept Check

1. Provide a financial executive with a useful definition of the term *dividend payout ratio*.
2. How does the firm's actual dividend policy affect its need for externally generated financial capital?

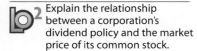

2 Explain the relationship between a corporation's dividend policy and the market price of its common stock.

Does a Firm's Dividend Policy Affect the Company's Stock Price?

What is a sound rationale or motivation for dividend payments? Put another way, given the firm's capital-budgeting and borrowing decisions, what is the effect of the firm's dividend policies on the stock price? *Does a high dividend payment decrease a stock's value, increase it, or make no real difference?*

At first glance, we might reasonably conclude that a firm's dividend policy is important. We have already (in Chapter 8) pointed out that the value of a stock is equal to the present value of its expected future dividends. Why else do so many companies pay dividends, and why else is a page in the *Wall Street Journal* devoted to dividend announcements? How can we not conclude that dividend policies are important?

Three Basic Views

Some would argue that the amount of a dividend is irrelevant and any time spent on the decision is a waste of energy. Others contend that a high dividend results in a high stock price. Still others take the view that dividends actually hurt the value of the dividend-paying stocks.

Before we delve into the various theories, or "views," on the dividend policy question, we need to be very careful about the conditions under which we pose the question. Specifically, we begin with the basic assumption that the firm plans to undertake all positive *NPV* investment opportunities *regardless* of whether it pays dividends or not. This is critical because if we allow the decision to pay a dividend to interfere with the firm's decision to undertake a good investment, then the policy obviously matters to the firm's stockholders. So, assuming that the firm will make the right set of investment decisions, why might the company's dividend policy matter?

View 1: A Firm's Dividend Policy Is Irrelevant   Much of the controversy about the dividend issue is based in time-honored disagreements between the academic and professional communities. Experienced practitioners tend to believe that stock prices change as a result of dividend announcements and, therefore, see dividends as important. Professors often argue that the seemingly apparent relationship between dividends and stock prices may be an illusion.

The notion that dividends are not important rests on two preconditions. First, we must assume that the firm's investment and borrowing decisions have already been made and that these decisions will not be altered by the amount of any dividend payments. Second, **perfect capital markets** must exist, which means that *(1) investors can buy and sell stocks without incurring any transaction costs, such as brokerage commissions; (2) companies can issue stocks without any cost of doing so; (3) there are no corporate or personal taxes; (4) complete information about the firm is readily available; (5) there are no conflicts of interest between managers and stockholders; and (6) financial distress and bankruptcy costs are nonexistent.*

The first assumption—that the firm has already made its investment and financing decisions—simply keeps us from confusing the issues. We want to know the effect of dividend decisions on a stand-alone basis, without mixing in other decisions. The second assumption, that of perfect markets, also allows us to study the effect of dividend decisions in isolation, much as a physicist studies motion in a vacuum to avoid the influence of friction.

Given these assumptions, the effect of a dividend decision on share price may be stated unequivocally: *There is no relationship between dividend policy and stock value.* One dividend policy is as good as another. In the aggregate, investors are concerned only with *total* returns from investment decisions; they are indifferent to whether these returns come from capital gains or dividend income. They also recognize that the dividend decision is really a choice of financing strategy. That is, to finance growth, the firm (a) may choose to issue stock, allowing internally generated funds (profits) to be used to pay dividends, or (b) may use internally generated funds to finance its growth, paying less in dividends but not having to issue stock. In the first case, shareholders receive dividend income; in the second case, the value of their stocks should increase. Thus, the nature of the return is the only difference; total returns should be about the same.

View 2: High Dividends Increase Stock Values   The belief that a firm's dividend policy is unimportant implicitly assumes that an investor is indifferent about whether the increased income comes through capital gains (stock price increase) or comes through dividends. However, dividends are more predictable than capital gains. Managers can control dividends, but they cannot dictate the price of the stock. Investors are less certain of receiving income from capital gains than from dividends. The incremental risk associated with capital gains relative to dividend income implies a higher required rate for discounting a dollar of capital gains than for discounting a dollar of dividends. In other words, we would value a dollar of expected dividends more highly than a dollar of expected capital gains. We might, for example, require a 14 percent rate of return for a stock that pays its entire return from dividends, but a 20 percent return for a high-growth stock that pays no dividends. This view, which says *dividends are more certain than capital gains*, has been called the **bird-in-the-hand dividend theory**.

The position that dividends are less risky than capital gains, and should, therefore, be valued differently, is not without its critics. If we hold to our basic decision not to let the firm's dividend policy influence its investment and capital-mix decisions, the company's operating cash flows, in both expected amount and variability, are unaffected by its dividend policy. Because the dividend policy has no impact on the volatility of the company's overall cash flows, it has no impact on the riskiness of the firm.

Increasing a firm's dividend does not reduce the basic riskiness of the stock; rather, if a dividend payment requires managers to issue new stock, it only transfers risk *and* ownership from the current owners to new owners. We would have to acknowledge that the current investors who receive the dividend trade an uncertain capital gain for a "safe" asset (the cash dividend). However, if risk reduction is the only goal, the investor could have kept the money in the bank and not bought the stock in the first place.

View 3: Low Dividends Increase Stock Values   The third view of how dividends affect stock price argues that dividends actually hurt the investors. This belief has largely been based on the difference in the tax treatment of dividends versus capital gains. Contrary to

perfect capital markets an assumption that allows one to study the effect of dividend decisions in isolation. It assumes that (1) investors can buy and sell stocks without incurring any transaction costs, such as brokerage commissions; (2) companies can issue stocks without any cost of doing so; (3) there are no corporate or personal taxes; (4) complete information about the firm is readily available; (5) there are no conflicts of interest between management and stockholders; and (6) financial distress and bankruptcy costs are nonexistent.

bird-in-the-hand dividend theory the view that dividends are more certain than capital gains.

the perfect-markets assumption of no taxes, most investors do pay income taxes. For these taxpayers, the objective is to maximize the *after-tax* return on an investment relative to the risk assumed. This is done by *minimizing* the effective tax rate on the income and, whenever possible, by *deferring* the payment of taxes.

Like most tax code complexities, Congress over the years has changed whether capital gains are taxed at a lower or similar rate to "earned income." Think of a water faucet being randomly turned on and then off. From 1987 through 1992, no federal tax advantage was provided for capital gains income relative to dividend income. A revision in the tax code that took effect beginning in 1993 did provide a preference for capital gains income. Then the Taxpayer Relief Act of 1997 made the difference (preference) even more favorable for capital gains as opposed to cash dividend income. For some taxpayers, if a minimum holding period had been reached, the tax rate applied to capital gains was reduced to 20 percent from the previous level of 28 percent. But wait: In 2003, Congress again felt the need to change the tax code as it pertained to both dividend income and capital gains income. On May 28, President Bush signed into law the Jobs and Growth Tax Relief Reconciliation Act. Part of the impetus for this act was the recession that commenced in 2001 and the slow rate of job creation that followed that recession.

In a nutshell, this 2003 act lowered the top tax rate on dividend income to 15 percent from a previous top rate of 38.6 percent and also lowered the top rate paid on realized long-term capital gains to the same 15 percent from a previous 20 percent. Thus, you can see that the so-called investment playing field was (mostly) leveled for dividend income relative to qualifying capital gains.

Actually, a different benefit exists for capital gains returns relative to dividend income. Taxes on dividend income are paid when the dividend is received, whereas taxes on price appreciation (capital gains) are deferred until the stock is actually sold. Thus, when it comes to tax considerations, many investors prefer the retention of a firm's earnings—in expectation of a later capital gain—as opposed to the near-term payment of cash dividends. Again, if earnings are retained within the firm, hopefully the stock price increases, but the increase is not taxed until the stock is sold.

Although the majority of investors are subject to taxes, certain investment companies, trusts, and pension plans are not when it comes to their dividend income. Also, for tax purposes, a corporation can generally exclude 70 percent of the dividend income it receives from another corporation. In these cases, investors will prefer dividends over capital gains.

To summarize, when it comes to taxes, we want to maximize our *after*-tax return, as opposed to our *before*-tax return. Investors try to defer taxes whenever possible. Stocks that allow tax deferral (low dividends–high capital gains) will possibly sell at a premium relative to stocks that require current taxation (high dividends–low capital gains). This suggests that a policy of paying low or no dividends will result in a higher stock price. That is, high dividends hurt investors, whereas low dividends and high retention help investors. This is the logic of the advocates of the low-dividend policy. It does presume that the firm's management has a roster of positive net present value projects that will put the dollars retained to productive use. However, as pointed out, the 2003 act lowered the taxes on dividends to such a great extent that this logic can now be reasonably questioned.

Improving Our Thinking

We have now looked at three views on dividend policy. Which is right? The argument that dividends are irrelevant is difficult to refute, given the perfect-market assumptions. However, in the real world, it is not always easy to feel comfortable with such an argument. Conversely, the high-dividend philosophy, which measures risk by how we split the firm's cash flows between dividends and retained earnings, is not particularly appealing when studied carefully. The third view, which is essentially a tax argument against high dividends, is persuasive. Even today, although the preferential tax rate for capital gains is limited, the "deferral advantage" of capital gains is still alive and well. However, if low dividends are so advantageous and generous dividends are so hurtful, why do companies continue to pay dividends? It is difficult to believe that managers would forgo such an easy opportunity to benefit their stockholders. What are we missing?

The need to find the missing elements in our "dividend puzzle" has not been ignored. When we need to better understand an issue or phenomenon, we can either improve our thinking or gather more evidence about the topic. Scholars and practitioners have taken both approaches. Although no single definitive answer has yet been found that is acceptable to all, several plausible explanations have been developed. Some of the more popular explanations include (1) the residual dividend theory, (2) the clientele effect, (3) the information effect, (4) agency costs, and (5) the expectations theory.

The Residual Dividend Theory   In perfect markets, there are no costs to the firm when it issues new securities. However, in reality the process is quite expensive, and the flotation costs associated with a new offering may be as much as 20 percent of the dollar issue size. Thus, if managers choose to issue stock rather than retain profits to finance new investments, a larger amount of securities is required to finance the investment. For example, if $30 million is needed to finance the investment, more than $30 million will have to be issued to offset the flotation costs. This means, very simply, that new equity capital raised through the sale of common stock will be more expensive than capital raised via retained earnings.

In effect, flotation costs eliminate our indifference by using internal capital versus issuing new common stock. Given these costs, *dividends should be paid only if the firm's profits are not completely used for investment purposes.* That is, only "residual earnings" should be paid out. This policy is called the **residual dividend theory**.

Given the existence of flotation costs, the firm's dividend policy should therefore be as follows:

residual dividend theory a theory that a company's dividend payment should equal the cash left after financing all the investments that have positive net present values.

1. Accept an investment if the *NPV* is positive; that is, if the expected rate of return exceeds the cost of capital.

2. Finance the equity portion of new investments *first* by using internally generated funds. Only after this capital is fully utilized should the firm issue new common shares.

3. If any internally generated funds still remain after making all acceptable investments, pay dividends to the investors. However, if all of the internal capital is needed to finance acceptable investments, pay no dividends.

Thus, dividend policy is influenced by (1) the company's investment opportunities and (2) the availability of internally generated capital. Dividends are then paid *only* after all acceptable investments have been financed. According to this concept, a dividend policy is totally passive in nature and can't affect the market price of the common stock.

Now, let us consider a dose of corporate reality.

The Clientele Effect   What if the investors do not like the dividend policy chosen by managers? In perfect markets, in which we incur no costs when buying or selling stock, there is no problem. Investors can simply satisfy their personal income preferences by purchasing or selling securities when the dividends they receive do not satisfy their current needs. In other words, if an investor does not view the dividends received in any given year to be sufficient, he or she can simply sell a portion of stock, thereby "creating a dividend." In addition, if the dividend is larger than the investor desired, he or she can simply purchase stock with the "excess cash" created by the dividend.

However, once we remove the assumption of perfect markets, we find that buying or selling stock is not cost free. Brokerage fees are incurred, ranging from approximately 1 percent to 10 percent. Even more costly is the fact that the investor who buys the stock with cash received from a dividend will have to pay taxes before reinvesting the cash. And when a stock is bought or sold, it must first be reevaluated. This can be time consuming and costly for investors. Finally, some institutional investors, such as investors in university endowment funds, are precluded from selling stock.

As a result of these considerations, investors may not be too inclined to buy stocks that require them to "create" a dividend stream more suitable to their purposes. Rather, if investors do in fact have a preference between dividends and capital gains, we could expect them to invest in firms that have a dividend policy consistent with these preferences. They would, in essence, "sort themselves out" by buying stocks that satisfy their preferences for dividends and capital gains. For example, individuals and institutions that need current income would be drawn to companies that have high dividend payouts. Other investors, such as wealthy individuals, would much prefer to avoid taxes by holding securities that offer no or small dividend income but large capital gains. In other words, there would be a **clientele effect**: *Firms draw a given clientele, depending upon their stated dividend policy.*

The possibility that clienteles of investors exist might lead us to believe that the firm's dividend policy matters. However, unless there is a greater aggregate demand for a particular policy than the market can satisfy, one policy is as good as the other. The clientele effect only warns firms to avoid making capricious changes in their dividend policy. Moreover, given that the firm's investment decisions are already made, the level of the dividend is still unimportant. The change in the policy matters only when it requires clientele to shift to another company.

The Information Effect   An investor in a world of perfect markets would argue with considerable persuasion that a firm's value is determined strictly by its investment and financing decisions and that its dividend policy has no impact on value. Yet we know from experience that a large, unexpected change in dividends can have a significant impact on the stock price. For instance, in November 1990, Occidental Petroleum cut its dividend from $2 to $1. In response, the firm's stock price went from about $32 to $17. How can we suggest that dividend policy matters little, when we can cite numerous such examples?

Despite such "evidence," some experts claim we are not looking at the real cause and effect. It may be that investors use a change in dividend policy as a *signal* about the firm's financial condition, especially its earning power. Thus, a dividend increase that is larger than expected might signal to investors that managers expect significantly higher earnings in the future. Conversely, a dividend decrease, or even a less-than-expected increase, might signal that managers are forecasting less-favorable future earnings.

Likewise, some claim that managers frequently have inside information about the firm that cannot be made available to investors. This *difference in accessibility to information*, called **information asymmetry**, *they believe, can result in a lower or higher stock price than would otherwise occur.*

Dividends may, therefore, be important as a communication tool because managers may have no other credible way to inform investors about future earnings, or at least no convincing way that is less costly.

Agency Costs   Conflicts often exist between stockholders and a firm's management. As a result, the stock price of a company owned by investors who are separate from management may be less than the stock price of a closely held firm. This potential difference in price is the *cost of the conflict to the owners*, which has come to be called **agency costs**.

Recognizing the possible problem, managers, acting independently or at the insistence of the firm's board of directors, frequently take action to minimize agency costs. Such action, which in itself is costly, includes auditing by independent accountants, assigning supervisory functions to the company's board of directors, creating covenants in lending agreements that restrict managerial powers, and providing incentive compensation plans for managers that help "bond" them with the owners.

A firm's dividend policy may be perceived by owners as a tool to minimize agency costs. Assuming that the payment of a dividend requires managers to issue stock to finance new investments, new investors will be attracted to the company only if they are convinced that the capital will be used profitably. Thus, the payment of dividends indirectly results in a closer monitoring of management's investment activities. In this case, dividends may make a meaningful contribution to the value of the firm.

The Expectations Theory   A common thread through much of our discussion of dividend policy, particularly as it relates to information effects, is the word *expected*. We should not overlook the significance of this word when we are making any financial decision within the

---

clientele effect the belief that individuals and institutions that need current income will invest in companies that have high dividend payouts. Other investors prefer to avoid taxes by holding securities that offer only small dividend income but large capital gains. Thus, we have a "clientele" of investors.

information asymmetry the difference in accessibility to information between managers and investors, which may result in a lower stock price than would be true in conditions of certainty.

agency costs the costs, such as a reduced stock price, associated with potential conflict between managers and investors when these two groups are not the same.

firm. *No matter what the decision area, how the market price responds to a firm's actions is not determined entirely by the action itself; it is also affected by investors' expectations about the ultimate decision to be made by management.* This concept or idea is called the **expectations theory**.

For example, as the time approaches for managers to announce the amount of the firm's next dividend, investors form expectations about how much that dividend will be. These expectations are based on several factors related to the firm, such as past dividend decisions, current and expected earnings, investment strategies, and financing decisions. Investors also consider such things as the condition of the general economy, the strength or weakness of the industry at the time, and possible changes in government policies.

When the actual dividend decision is announced, the investor compares the actual decision with the expected decision. If the amount of the dividend is as expected, even if it represents an increase from prior years, the market price of the stock will remain unchanged. However, if the dividend is higher or lower than expected, investors will reassess their perceptions of the firm. In short, an actual decision about the firm's dividend policy is not likely to be terribly significant unless it departs from investors' expectations. But if there is a difference between actual and expected dividends, we will more than likely see a movement in the stock price.

expectations theory the concept that, no matter what the decision area, how the market price responds to management's actions is not determined entirely by the action itself; it is also affected by investors' expectations about the ultimate decision to be made by management.

What Are We to Conclude?

A firm must develop a dividend policy regardless, so here are some of the things we have learned about the relevance of a firm's dividend policy.

1. As a firm's investment opportunities increase, its dividend payout ratio should decrease. In other words, an inverse relationship should exist between the amount of money a firm invests with expected rates of return that exceed the cost of capital (positive *NPV*s) and the dividends it remits investors. Because of flotation costs, internally generated equity financing is preferable to selling stock (in terms of the wealth of the current common shareholders).

2. The firm's dividend policy appears to be important; however, appearances can be deceptive. The real issue is the firm's *expected* earning power, and investors will use the dividend payment as a source of information about these earnings. The dividend may carry greater weight than a statement by management that earnings will be increasing or decreasing. (Actions speak louder than words.)

3. If dividends influence the stock price, this is probably based on the investor's desire to minimize or defer taxes and on the fact that dividends can minimize agency costs.

4. If the expectations theory has merit, which we believe it does, the firm should avoid surprising investors when it comes to its dividend decision.

5. The firm's dividend policy should effectively be treated as a *long-term residual*. Rather than project investment requirements for a single year, managers should anticipate financing needs for several years. If internal funds remain after the firm has undertaken all acceptable investments, dividends should be paid. Conversely, if over the long term the entire amount of internally generated capital is needed for reinvestment in the company, then no dividend should be paid.

In setting a firm's dividend policy, financial managers must work in the messy world of reality. This means that our theories do not provide an equation that perfectly explains the key relationships. However, they give us a more complete view of the world, which can only help us make better decisions.

Concept Check _____

1. Summarize the position that a dividend policy may be irrelevant with regard to the firm's stock price.
2. What is meant by the bird-in-the-hand dividend theory?
3. Why are cash dividend payments thought to be more certain than capital gains?
4. How might personal taxes affect both the firm's dividend policy and its share price?
5. Distinguish between the residual dividend theory and the clientele effect.

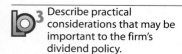

3 Describe practical considerations that may be important to the firm's dividend policy.

The Dividend Decision in Practice

There are a number of practical considerations that will have an impact on a firm's decision to pay dividends. Some of the more obvious ones include the following.

Legal Restrictions

Certain legal restrictions can limit the amount of dividends a firm may pay. These legal constraints fall into two categories. First, *statutory restrictions* may prevent a company from paying dividends. Although the specific limitations vary by state, generally a corporation may not pay a dividend (1) if the firm's liabilities exceed its assets, (2) if the amount of the dividend exceeds the firm's accumulated profits (retained earnings), and (3) if the dividend is being paid from capital invested in the firm.

The second type of legal restriction is unique to each firm and results from the restrictions in debt and preferred stock contracts. To minimize their risk, investors frequently impose restrictive provisions on managers as a condition to their investment in the company. These constraints might include the provision that dividends may not be declared before the debt is repaid. Also, the corporation might be required to maintain a given amount of working capital. Preferred stockholders might stipulate that common dividends may not be paid when any preferred dividends are delinquent.

Liquidity Constraints

Contrary to common opinion, the mere fact that a company shows a large amount of retained earnings in its balance sheet does not indicate that cash is available for the payment of dividends. The firm's liquid assets, including its cash, are basically independent of its retained earnings account. Generally, retained earnings are either reinvested in the company within a short period or used to pay maturing debt. Thus, a firm can be extremely profitable and still be *cash poor*. Because dividends are paid with cash, *and not with retained earnings*, the firm must have cash available for the dividends to be paid. Hence, the firm's liquidity position has a direct bearing on its ability to pay dividends.

Earnings Predictability

A company's dividend payout ratio depends to some extent on the predictability of a firm's profits over time. If its earnings fluctuate significantly, the firm's managers know they cannot necessarily rely on internally generated funds to meet its future needs. As a result, when profits *are* realized, the firm is likely to retain larger amounts to ensure that money is available when needed. Conversely, a firm with a stable earnings trend will typically pay out a larger portion of its earnings in dividends. This company has less concern about the availability of profits to meet its future capital requirements.

Maintaining Ownership Control

For many large corporations, control through the ownership of common stock is not an important issue. However, for many small and medium-sized companies, maintaining voting control is a high priority. If the current common stockholders are unable to participate in a new offering, issuing new stock is unattractive, in that the control of the current stockholder is diluted. The owners might prefer that managers finance new investments with debt and retained earnings rather than issue new common stock. This firm's growth is then constrained by the amount of debt capital available to it and by the company's ability to generate profits.

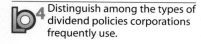

4 Distinguish among the types of dividend policies corporations frequently use.

Alternative Dividend Policies

Regardless of a firm's long-term dividend policy, most firms choose one of several year-to-year dividend payment patterns.

1. **A constant dividend payout ratio.**   Under this policy, the *percentage of earnings paid out in dividends is held constant*. Although the dividend-to-earnings ratio is stable, the dollar amount of the dividend naturally fluctuates from year to year as profits vary.

2. **A stable dollar dividend per share.**   This policy *maintains a relatively stable dollar dividend over time*. An increase in the dollar dividend usually does not occur until management is convinced that the higher dividend level can be maintained in the future. Conversely, a lower dollar dividend will not be paid until the evidence clearly indicates that a continuation of the current dividend cannot be supported.

3. **A small, regular dividend plus a year-end extra.**   A corporation following this policy *pays a small, regular dollar dividend plus a year-end extra dividend in prosperous years*. The extra dividend is declared toward the end of the fiscal year after the company's profits for the period can be estimated. The objective is *to avoid the connotation of a permanent dividend being paid*. However, this purpose may be defeated if *recurring* extra dividends come to be expected by investors.

constant dividend payout ratio a dividend payment policy in which the percentage of earnings paid out in dividends is held constant. The dollar amount fluctuates from year to year as profits vary.

stable dollar dividend per share a dividend policy that maintains a relatively stable dollar dividend per share over time.

small, regular dividend plus a year-end extra a corporate policy of paying a small regular dollar dividend plus a year-end extra dividend in prosperous years to avoid the connotation of a permanent dividend.

Concept Check

1. Identify some practical considerations that affect a firm's payout policy.
2. Identify and explain three different dividend policies. *Hint:* One of these is a constant dividend payout ratio.

Dividend Payment Procedures

 Specify the procedures a company follows in administering the dividend payment.

After the firm's dividend policy has been structured, several procedural details must be arranged. For instance, how frequently are dividend payments to be made? If a stockholder sells the shares during the year, who is entitled to the dividend? To answer these questions, we need to understand dividend payment procedures.

Generally, companies pay dividends quarterly. For example, on February 6, 2009, General Electric (GE) announced that it would pay a quarterly dividend of $0.31 per quarter to its shareholders for 2009. The annual dividend then would be 4 × $0.31 = $1.24 per share.

The final approval of a dividend payment comes from the company's board of directors. For example, the announcement or **declaration date** for General Electric's dividend was February 6, 2009, that holders of record as of February 23 would receive the dividend on the April 27 **payment date**. The **date of record**, February 23, designates when the stock transfer books are to be closed. Investors shown to own the stock on this date receive the dividend. If a notification of a transfer is recorded subsequent to February 23, the new owner is not entitled to the dividend. However, a problem could develop if the stock were sold on February 22, one day prior to the record date. Time would not permit the sale to be reflected on the stockholder list by the date of record. To address this problem, stock brokerage companies have uniformly terminated the right of ownership to the dividend two working days before the record date such that the **ex-dividend date** for the GE dividend is February 19 (note that in this instance February 23 was a Monday so the ex-dividend date was set two business days prior, which was February 19). The dividend declaration and payment process can be summarized as follows:

declaration date the date upon which a dividend is formally declared by the board of directors.

payment date the date on which the company mails a dividend check to each investor of record.

date of record the date at which the stock transfer books are to be closed for determining the investors to receive the next dividend payment.

ex-dividend date the date upon which stock brokerage companies have uniformly decided to terminate the right of ownership to the dividend, which is two days prior to the date of record.

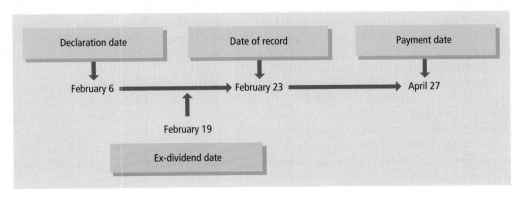

Concept Check _____

1. What is the typical frequency with which cash dividends are paid to investors?

2. Distinguish among the (a) declaration date, (b) date of record, and (c) ex-dividend date.

6 Describe why and how a firm might pay noncash dividends (stock dividends and stock splits) instead of cash dividends.

Stock Dividends and Stock Splits

A stock dividend entails the distribution of additional shares of stock in lieu of a cash payment. A stock split involves exchanging more (or less in the case of a "reverse" split) shares of stock for the firm's outstanding shares. In both cases the number of common shares outstanding changes but the firm's investments and future earnings prospects do not. In essence, the ownership pie is simply cut into more pieces (or fewer pieces in the case of a reverse split).

stock split a stock dividend exceeding 25 percent of the number of shares currently outstanding.

stock dividend a distribution of shares of up to 25 percent of the number of shares currently outstanding, issued on a pro rata basis to the current stockholders.

The only difference between a stock dividend and a stock split relates to their respective accounting treatments. Both represent a proportionate distribution of additional shares to the current stockholders. However, *for accounting purposes* the **stock split** has been defined as a *stock dividend exceeding 25 percent*. Thus, a **stock dividend** is conventionally defined as a *distribution of shares up to 25 percent of the number of shares currently outstanding.*

Although stock dividends and splits occur far less frequently than cash dividends, a significant number of companies choose to use these share distributions either with or in lieu of cash dividends. The extent of stock splits and stock dividends over the years can be made clear by a little price comparison. In 1926, a ticket to the movies cost 25¢—and even much less in the rural communities. At the same time, the average share price on the New York Stock Exchange was $35. Today, if we want to go to a new movie, we pay $7 or more. However, the average share price is still about $35. The relatively constant share price is the result of the shares being split over and over again. We can only conclude that investors apparently like it that way. But why do they, if no economic benefit results to the investor from doing so?

Proponents of stock dividends and splits frequently maintain that stockholders receive a key benefit because the price of the stock will not fall precisely in proportion to the share increase. For a two-for-one split, the price of the stock might not decrease a full 50 percent, so the stockholder is left with a higher total value. There are two reasons for this disequilibrium. First, many financial executives believe that an optimal price range exists. Within this range, the total market value of the common stockholders is thought to be maximized. As the price exceeds this range, fewer investors can purchase the stock, thereby restraining demand for the shares. Consequently, downward pressure is placed on its price. For example, Apple (AAPL) has engaged in multiple stock splits each time its share price rose above $100. It had 2-for-1 splits in 1987, 2000, and 2005. Rumors abounded in 2007 prior to the onset of the current recession that the company would split again as its stock price passed $160 in October of that year.

The second explanation relates to the *informational content* of the dividend-split announcement. Stock dividends and splits have generally been associated with companies with growing earnings. The announcement of a stock dividend or split has therefore been perceived as favorable news. The empirical evidence, however, fails to verify these conclusions. Most studies indicate that investors are perceptive in identifying the true meaning of such a distribution. If the stock dividend or split is not accompanied by a positive trend in earnings and increases in cash dividends, price increases surrounding the stock dividend or split are insignificant. Therefore, we should be suspicious of the assertion that a stock dividend or split can help increase investors' net worth.

A second reason for stock dividends or splits is the conservation of corporate cash. If a company is encountering cash problems, it may substitute a stock dividend for a cash dividend. However, as before, investors will probably look beyond the dividend to ascertain the underlying reason for conserving cash. If the stock dividend is an effort to conserve cash for attractive investment opportunities, shareholders might bid up the stock price. If the move to conserve cash relates to financial difficulties within the firm, the market price will most likely react adversely.

Concept Check

1. What is the difference between a stock split and a stock dividend?
2. What managerial logic might lie behind a stock split or a stock dividend?

Stock Repurchases

Explain the purpose and procedures related to stock repurchases.

A **stock repurchase (stock buyback)** occurs when a *firm repurchases its own stock. This results in a reduction in the number of shares outstanding.* For well over 3 decades, corporations have been actively repurchasing their own equity securities. In the introduction we noted that Microsoft Corporation (MSFT) announced on September 22, 2008, that it planned to repurchase up to $40 billion in company shares over the period ending September 30, 2013. This new repurchase program follows the completion of a previous $40 billion in share repurchases. Note the use of the word *plan* in the announcement. This is important for it provides Microsoft leeway as to whether it carries out the planned repurchases in light of the uncertainties faced in the economic downturn that began with the financial crisis of 2007. However, uncertain economic times did not influence Walmart (WMT), which announced on June 5, 2009, that it planned to repurchase $15 billion of its shares. This follows a period of five years during which time the firm repurchased approximately $21 billion of shares.

stock repurchase (stock buyback) the repurchase of common stock by the issuing firm for any of a variety of reasons, resulting in reduction of shares outstanding.

Also, if you were to look at the balance sheet of almost any publicly held firm, you would see that the firm's treasury stock—the amount paid for repurchasing its own stock—is oftentimes severalfold the total amount originally invested by the stockholders. This situation is not unusual for many large companies. Several reasons have been given for stock repurchases. The benefits include:

1. A means for providing an internal investment opportunity
2. An approach for modifying the firm's capital structure
3. A favorable impact on earnings per share
4. The elimination of a minority ownership group of stockholders
5. The minimization of the dilution in earnings per share associated with mergers
6. The reduction in the firm's costs associated with servicing small stockholders

Also, from the shareholders' perspective, a stock repurchase, as opposed to a cash dividend, has a potential tax advantage.

A Share Repurchase as a Dividend Decision

Clearly, the payment of a common stock dividend is the conventional method for distributing a firm's profits to its owners. However, it need not be the only way. Another approach is to repurchase the firm's stock. The concept may best be explained by an example.

EXAMPLE 13.1

Telink Inc. is planning to pay $4 million ($4 per share) in dividends to its common stockholders. The following earnings and market price information is provided for Telink:

Net income	$7,500,000
Number of shares	1,000,000
Earnings per share	$7.50
Price–earnings ratio	8
Expected market price per share after dividend payment	$60

In a recent meeting, several board members, who are also major stockholders, question the need for a dividend payment. They maintain that they do not need the income, so why not allow the firm to retain the funds for future investments? In response, managers contend that the available investments are not sufficiently profitable to justify retention of the income. That is, the investors' required rates of return exceed the expected rates of return that could be earned with the additional $4 million in investments.

Because managers oppose the idea of retaining the profits for investment purposes, one of the firm's directors has suggested that the $4 million be used to repurchase the company's stock. In this way, the value of the stock should increase. This result can be demonstrated as follows:

1. Assume that shares are repurchased by the firm at the $60 market price (ex-dividend price) plus the contemplated $4 dividend per share, or for $64 per share.
2. Given a $64 price, 62,500 shares would be repurchased ($4 million ÷ $64 price).
3. If net income is not reduced but the number of shares declines as a result of the share repurchase, earnings per share would increase from $7.50 to $8, computed as follows:

$$\text{Earnings per share} = \text{net income/outstanding shares}$$
$$\text{(before repurchase)} = \$7,500,000/1,000,000$$
$$= \$7.50$$
$$\text{(after repurchase)} = \$7,500,000/(1,000,000 - 62,500)$$
$$= \$8$$

4. Assuming that the price–earnings ratio remains at 8, the new price after the repurchase would be $64, up from $60, where the increase exactly equals the amount of the forgone dividend.

In this example, Telink's stockholders are essentially provided the same value, whether a dividend is paid or stock is repurchased. If managers pay a dividend, the investor will have a stock valued at $60 plus $4 received from the dividend. Conversely, if stock is repurchased in lieu of the dividend, the stock will be worth $64. These results were based on assuming (1) the stock is being repurchased at the exact $64 price, (2) the $7,500,000 net income is unaffected by the repurchase, and (3) the price–earnings ratio of 8 does not change after the repurchase. Given these assumptions, however, the stock repurchase serves as a perfect substitute for the dividend payment to the stockholders.

The Investor's Choice

Given the choice between a stock repurchase and a dividend payment, which should an investor prefer? If there are no taxes, no commissions when buying and selling stock, and no informational content assigned to a dividend, the investor should be indifferent with regard to the choices. For example, if the investor wants cash flow and the stock he owns does not pay a dividend, he can create a dividend by simply selling a portion of his shares. Note that these sales will not necessarily deplete the value of his investment as the value of the firm's shares should be growing because the firm's earnings are not being paid in dividends but are being reinvested.

There are certainly drawbacks related to repurchasing stock that investors should care about. First, the firm may have to pay too high a price for the repurchased stock, which is to the detriment of the remaining stockholders. If a relatively large number of shares are being bought, the price may be bid up too high, only to fall after the repurchase operation. Second, as a result of the repurchase, the market may perceive the riskiness of the corporation as increasing, which would lower the price–earnings ratio and the value of the stock.

A Financing or Investment Decision?

Repurchasing stock when the firm has excess cash can be regarded as a dividend decision. However, a stock repurchase can also be viewed as a financing decision. By issuing debt and

FINANCE AT WORK

COMPANIES INCREASINGLY USE SHARE REPURCHASES TO DISTRIBUTE CASH TO THEIR STOCKHOLDERS

There has been a fundamental shift away from paying dividends and toward the buyback of company shares of stock. This change is at least partially due to changes in the U.S. tax code, which charges an additional 15% tax on dividends paid out to shareholders (before the Bush administration, this tax was as high as the graduated income tax—in some cases exceeding 35% on the federal level alone).

Evidence supporting the growth in share repurchases is found in the fact that the firms in the Standard & Poor's 500 repurchased $349 billion of their shares in 2005 alone. In fact, firms spent 73% more on buybacks than they did on dividends. On average, stock repurchases represented 61% of company earnings and dividends were only 32%. Clearly, there is a strong preference for share repurchases.*

Obviously firms are finding share repurchases a preferred way to distribute cash, but is this always best for the investor? Asked somewhat differently, are there reasons to prefer dividends over share repurchases? The answer is yes. For example, investors who need cash from their investments to live on may prefer dividends rather than being forced to sell shares and incur brokerage fees. Also, there's something comforting about receiving a regular check in the mail and not having to worry so much about fluctuations in the value of your shares from day to day.

Some companies now recognize the varied interests of their stockholders and attempt to blend share repurchases with cash dividends. For example, Home Depot has paid out about 65% of its earnings in a mix of share repurchases and dividend payments. For example, for the year ended January 29, 2006, the firm reported total net income of $5.838 billion, paid $0.857 billion in dividends and repurchased $2.626 billion in company shares. This represents a total distribution of 59.7% of company earnings with 45% being distributed via share repurchase and 14.7% via dividends.**

*Matt Krantz, "More companies go for stock buybacks," *USA Today* (March 23, 2006).

**http://finance.yahoo.com/q/cf?s=HD&annual.

Source: Leslie Schism, "Many Companies Use Excess Cash to Repurchase Their Shares," September 2, 1993, the *Wall Street Journal*, Eastern edition. Copyright by Dow Jones & Co. Inc. Reproduced with permission of Dow Jones & Co. Inc.

then repurchasing stock, a firm can immediately alter its debt–equity mix toward a higher proportion of debt. Essentially, rather than choose how to distribute cash to the stockholders, managers are using stock repurchases as a means to change the corporation's capital structure.

In addition to dividend and financing decisions, many managers consider a stock repurchase to be an investment decision. When equity prices are depressed in the marketplace, they may view the firm's own stock as being materially undervalued and therefore a good investment opportunity. Although this may be a wise move, the decision cannot and should not be viewed in the context of an investment decision. Buying its own stock cannot provide expected returns as other investments do. No company can survive, much less prosper, by investing only in its own stock.

Practical Considerations—The Stock Repurchase Procedure

If management intends to repurchase a block of the firm's outstanding shares, it should make this information public. All investors should be given the opportunity to work with complete information. They should be told the purpose of the repurchase, as well as the method to be used to acquire the stock.

Three methods for stock repurchase are available. First, the shares can be bought in the open market. Here the firm acquires the stock through a stockbroker at the going market price. This approach can put upward pressure on the stock price. Also, commissions must be paid to the stockbrokers as a fee for their services.

The second method is to make a tender offer to the firm's shareholders. A **tender offer** is a *formal offer by the company to buy a specified number of shares at a predetermined and stated price. The tender price is set above the current market price in order to attract sellers.* A tender offer is best when a relatively large number of shares are to be bought because the company's intentions are clearly known and each shareholder has the opportunity to sell the stock at the tendered price.

tender offer a formal offer by the company to buy a specified number of shares at a predetermined and stated price. The tender price is set above the current market price in order to attract sellers.

The third and final method for repurchasing stock entails the purchase of the stock from one or more major stockholders. These purchases are made on a negotiated basis. Care should be taken to ensure a fair and equitable price. Otherwise, the remaining stockholders may be hurt as a result of the sale.

Concept Check

1. Identify three reasons why a firm might buy back its own common stock shares.
2. What financial relationships must hold for a stock repurchase to be a perfect substitute for a cash dividend payment to stockholders?
3. Within the context of a stock repurchase, what is meant by a tender offer?

Summary

 Describe the trade-off between paying dividends and retaining the profits within the company.

A company's dividend decision has an immediate impact on the firm's financial mix. If the dividend payment is increased, fewer funds are available internally for financing investments. Consequently, if additional equity capital is needed, the company has to issue new common stock.

In perfect markets, the choice between paying or not paying a dividend does not matter. However, when we realize that in the real world there are costs of issuing stock, we have a preference to use internal equity to finance our investment opportunities. Here the dividend decision is simply a residual factor, in which the dividend payment should equal the remaining internal capital after the firm finances all of its investments.

 Explain the relationship between a corporation's dividend policy and the market price of its common stock.

Other market imperfections that may cause a company's dividend policy to affect the firm's stock price include (1) the deferred tax benefit of capital gains, (2) agency costs, (3) the clientele effect, and (4) the informational content of a given policy.

Other practical considerations that may affect a firm's dividend payment decision include

- Legal restrictions
- The firm's liquidity position
- The company's accessibility to capital markets
- The stability of the firm's earnings
- The desire of investors to maintain control of the company

In practice, managers have generally followed one of three dividend policies:

- A constant dividend payout ratio, whereby the percentage of dividends to earnings is held constant
- A stable dollar dividend per share, whereby a relatively stable dollar dividend is maintained over time
- A small, regular dividend plus a year-end extra, whereby the firm pays a small, regular dollar dividend plus a year-end extra dividend in prosperous years

 Describe practical considerations that may be important to the firm's dividend policy.

 Distinguish among the types of dividend policies corporations frequently use.

Of the three dividend policies, the stable dollar dividend is by far the most common. The Jobs and Growth Tax Relief Reconciliation Act of 2003 reduced the top tax rate on dividend income to 15 percent and placed the top tax rate on realized long-term capital gains at this same 15 percent rate. This helped level the investment landscape for dividend income relative to qualifying capital gains. Taxes paid on capital gains, however, are still deferred until realized, but dividend income is taxed in the year that it is received by the investing taxpayer.

 Specify the procedures a company follows in administering the dividend payment.

Generally, companies pay dividends on a quarterly basis. The final approval of a dividend payment comes from the board of directors. The critical dates in this process are as follows:

- Declaration date—the date when the dividend is formally declared by the board of directors
- Date of record—the date when the stock-transfer books are closed to determine who owns the stock

- Ex-dividend date—two working days before the date of record, after which the right to receive the dividend no longer goes with the stock
- Payment date—the date the dividend check is mailed to the stockholders

Stock dividends and stock splits have been used by corporations either in lieu of or to supplement cash dividends. At present, no empirical evidence identifies a relationship between stock dividends and splits and the market price of the stock. Yet a stock dividend or split could conceivably be used to keep the stock price within an optimal trading range. Also, if investors perceive that the stock dividend contains favorable information about the firm's operations, the price of the stock could increase.

As an alternative to paying a dividend, the firm can repurchase stock. In perfect markets, an investor would be indifferent between receiving a dividend or a share repurchase. The investor could simply create a dividend stream by selling stock when income is needed. If, however, market imperfections exist, the investor may have a preference for one of the two methods of distributing the corporate income.

A stock repurchase can also be viewed as a financing decision. By issuing debt and then repurchasing stock, a firm can immediately alter its debt–equity mix toward a higher proportion of debt. Also, many managers consider a stock repurchase an investment decision—buying the stock when they believe it to be undervalued.

 Describe why and how a firm might pay noncash dividends (stock dividends and stock splits) instead of cash dividends.

 Explain the purpose and procedures related to stock repurchases.

Key Terms

Agency costs   378

Bird-in-the-hand dividend theory   375

Clientele effect   378

Constant dividend payout ratio   381

Date of record   381

Declaration date   381

Dividend payout ratio   373

Ex-dividend date   381

Expectations theory   379

Information asymmetry   378

Payment date   381

Perfect capital markets   375

Residual dividend theory   377

Small, regular dividend plus a year-end extra   381

Stable dollar dividend per share   381

Stock dividend   382

Stock repurchase (stock buyback)   383

Stock split   382

Tender offer   385

Review Questions

All Review Questions and Study Problems are available in MyFinanceLab.

13-1. What is meant by the term *dividend payout ratio*?

13-2. Explain the trade-off between retaining internally generated funds and paying cash dividends.

13-3. a. What are the assumptions of a perfect market?

  b. What effect does a dividend policy have on the share price in a perfect market?

13-4. What is the impact of flotation costs on the financing decision?

13-5. a. What is the *residual dividend theory*?

  b. Why is this theory operational only in the long term?

13-6. Why might investors prefer capital gains to the same amount of dividend income?

13-7. What legal restrictions may limit the amount of dividends to be paid?

13-8. How does a firm's liquidity position affect the payment of dividends?

13-9. How can ownership control constrain the growth of a firm?

13-10. a. Why is a stable dollar dividend policy popular from the viewpoint of the corporation?

  b. Is it also popular with investors? Why?

13-11. Explain what a dividend's declaration date, date of record, and ex-dividend date are.

13-12. What are the advantages of a stock split or dividend over a cash dividend?

13-13. Why would a firm repurchase its own stock?

Self-Test Problems

(Solutions to these problems are found at the end of the chapter.)

ST-1. (*Dividend growth rate*) Schulz Inc. maintains a constant dividend payout ratio of 35 percent. Earnings per share last year were $8.20 and are expected to grow indefinitely at a rate of 12 percent. What will be the dividend per share this year? In 5 years?

ST-2. (*Stock split*) The debt and equity section of the Robson Corporation balance sheet is shown here. The current market price of the common shares is $20. Reconstruct the financial statement assuming that (a) a 15 percent stock dividend is issued and (b) a two-for-one stock split is declared.

Debt	$1,800,000
Common equity	
Par ($2; 100,000 shares)	200,000
Paid-in capital	400,000
Retained earnings	900,000
	$3,300,000

Study Problems

13-1. (*Dividend policies*) Final earnings estimates for Chilean Health Spa & Fitness Center have been prepared for the CFO of the company and are shown in the following table. The firm has 7,500,000 shares of common stock outstanding. As assistant to the CFO, you are asked to determine the yearly dividend per share to be paid depending on the following possible policies:

a. A stable dollar dividend targeted at 40 percent of earnings over a 5-year period
b. A small, regular dividend of $0.60 per share plus a year-end extra when the profits in any year exceed $20,000,000. The year-end extra dividend will equal 50 percent of profits exceeding $20,000,000.
c. A constant dividend payout ratio of 40 percent

YEAR	PROFITS AFTER TAXES
1	$18,000,000
2	21,000,000
3	19,000,000
4	23,000,000
5	25,000,000

13-2. (*Flotation costs and issue size*) Your firm needs to raise $10 million. Assuming that flotation costs are expected to be $15 per share, and that the market price of the stock is $120, how many shares would have to be issued? What is the dollar size of the issue?

13-3. (*Flotation costs and issue size*) If the flotation costs for a common stock issue are 18 percent, how large must the issue be so that the firm will net $5,800,000? If the stock sells for $85 per share, how many shares must be issued?

13-4. (*Repurchase of stock*) The Dunn Corporation is planning to pay dividends of $500,000. There are 250,000 shares outstanding, and earnings per share are $5. The stock should sell for $50 after the ex-dividend date. If, instead of paying a dividend, the firm decides to repurchase stock,

a. What should be the repurchase price?
b. How many shares should be repurchased?
c. What if the repurchase price is set below or above your suggested price in part a?
d. If you own 100 shares, would you prefer that the company pay the dividend or repurchase stock?

13-5. (*Flotation costs and issue size*) D. Butler Inc. needs to raise $14 million. Assuming that the market price of the firm's stock is $95, and flotation costs are 10 percent of the market price, how many shares would have to be issued? What is the dollar size of the issue?

Mini Case

The following article appeared in the July 2, 1995, issue of the *Dallas Morning News*. In the article, Scott Burns, the author, makes the case for the importance of dividends.

Let us now praise the lowly dividend.

Insignificant to some. Small potatoes to others. An irksome sign of tax liability to many. However characterized, dividends are experiencing yet another round of defamation on Wall Street.

Why pay out dividends, the current argument goes, when a dollar of dividend can be retained as a dollar of book value that the market will value at two, three, or four dollars? With the average stock now selling at more than three times book value, investors should prefer companies that retain earnings rather than pay them out, even if they do nothing more with the money than repurchase shares.

The New Wisdom

Instead, the New Wisdom says, the investor should go for companies that retain earnings, reinvest them, and try to maximize shareholder value. Dividends should be avoided in the pursuit of long-term capital gains.

The only problem with this reasoning is that we've heard it before. And always at market tops.
- We heard it in the late 1960s as stock prices soared and dividend yields fell.
- We heard it again in the early 1970s as investors fixated on the "Nifty Fifty" and analysts calmly projected that with growth companies yielding 1 percent or less, the most important part of the return was the certainty of 20 percent annual earnings growth.
- And we're hearing it now, with stock prices hitting new highs each day. The Standard Poor's 500 Index, for instance, is up 19.7 percent since December 31, the equivalent of more than 7 years of dividends at the current yield of 2.6 percent.

Tilting the Yield

Significantly, we didn't hear that dividends were irrelevant in the late 1970s, as stock valuations moved to new lows. At that time, portfolio managers talked about "yield tilt"—running a portfolio with a bias toward dividend return to offset some of the risk of continuing stock market decline. Indeed, many of the best performing funds in the late 1970s were equity-income funds, the funds that seek above-average dividend income.

You can understand how much dividends contribute to long-term returns by taking a look at the performance of a major index, with and without dividend reinvestment. If you had invested $10,000 in the S&P's 500 Index in January 1982 and taken all dividends in cash, your original investment would have grown to $37,475 by the end of 1994.

It doesn't get much better than that.

The gain clocks a compound annual return of 10.7 percent, and a total gain of $27,475. During the same period you would have collected an additional $14,244 in dividends.

Not a trivial sum, either.

In other words, during one of the biggest bull markets in history, unreinvested dividend income accounted for more than one-third of your total return.

If you had reinvested those dividends in additional stock, the final score would have been even better: $60,303. The appreciation of your original investment would have been $27,475, and the growth from reinvested dividends would have been $22,828. Nearly half—45 percent—of your total return came from reinvested dividends. And this happened during a stellar period of rising stock prices.

Now consider the same investment during a period of misery. If you had invested $10,000 in the S&P's 500 Index stocks in January 1968, your investment would have grown to only $14,073 over the next 13 years, a gain of only $4,073. During much of that time, the value of your original investment would have been less than $10,000. Dividends during the period would have totaled $7,088—substantially more than stock appreciation. Reinvested, the same dividends would have grown to \$9,705, helping your original investment grow to \$23,778.

In a period of major ups and downs that many investors don't like to remember, dividends accounted for 70 percent of total return (see the accompanying table).

We could fiddle with these figures any number of ways. We could reduce the value of dividends by calculating income taxes. We could raise it by starting with the Dow Jones industrial average stocks, which tend to have higher dividends. But the point here is very simple: Whether you spend them or reinvest them, dividends are always an important part of the return on common stock.

Source: Scott Burns, "Those Lowly Dividends," *Dallas Morning News*, July 2, 1995, p. 1H. Reprinted with permission of the *Dallas Morning Star*.

A Close Look at Dividends in Two Markets

ANATOMY OF THE BULL MARKET, 1982 TO 1994		
Original investment		\$ 10,000
Gain on original investment		\$ 27,475
Total dividends	\$14,244	
Gain on reinvested dividends	\$ 8,584	
Total gain from dividends		\$22,828
Total		\$60,303
Compound annualized return equals 14.8%; 45% from dividends.		

ANATOMY OF A BEAR MARKET, 1968 TO 1980		
Original investment		\$10,000
Gain on original investment		\$ 4,073
Total dividends	\$ 7,088	
Gain on reinvested dividends	\$ 2,617	
Total gain from dividends		\$ 9,705
Total		\$23,778
Compound annualized return equals 6.9%; 70% from dividends		

Source: Franklin/Templeton Group Hypothetical Illustration Program.

Based on your reading of this chapter, evaluate what Burns is saying. Do you agree or disagree with him? Why?

Self-Test Solutions

SS-1.

$$\text{Dividend per share} = 35\% \times \$8.20$$
$$= \$2.87$$

Dividends:

$$1 \text{ year} = \$2.87(1 + 0.12)$$
$$= \$3.21$$
$$5 \text{ years} = \$2.87(1 + 0.12)^5$$
$$= \$2.87(1.762)$$
$$= \$5.06$$

SS-2.

a. If a 15 percent stock dividend is issued, the financial statement would appear as follows:

Debt	$1,800,000
Common equity	
Par ($2 par; 115,000 shares)	230,000
Paid-in capital	670,000
Retained earnings	600,000
	$3,300,000

b. A two-for-one split would result in a 100 percent increase in the number of shares. Because the total par value remains at $200,000, the new par value per share is $1 ($200,000/200,000 shares). The new financial statement would be as follows:

Debt	$1,800,000
Common equity	
Par ($1 par; 200,000 shares)	200,000
Paid-in capital	400,000
Retained earnings	900,000
	$3,300,000

Chapter 14

Short-Term Financial Planning

Learning Objectives

 Use the percent of sales method to forecast the financing requirements of a firm.

 Describe the limitations of the percent of sales forecast method.

 Prepare a cash budget and use it to evaluate the amount and timing of a firm's financing needs.

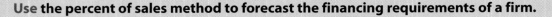

Forecasting is an integral part of the planning process, yet there are countless examples of when our ability to predict the future is not very good.

In the summer of 2008, the price of a gallon of gas was about $4.00 in most parts of the country. If you were a financial manager in July 2008 working on the financial plans for the coming year at the United Parcel Service (UPS), this volatility in the price of fuel would cause you significant headaches. Fuel costs are a major component of the operating expenses of UPS so the future price of a gallon of gasoline is a critical element of the financial forecast. If you were to find yourself engaged in the same planning process in April 2009 when the price of gasoline was about $2.00 a gallon, the future cost would no doubt be quite different than back in July 2008.

If forecasting the future is so difficult and plans are built on forecasts, why do firms engage in planning efforts? Obviously, they do, but why? The answer, oddly enough, does not lie in the accuracy of the firm's projections, for planning offers its greatest value when the future is the most uncertain. The value of planning is derived out of the process itself. That is, by thinking about what the future might be like, the firm builds contingency plans that can improve its ability to respond to adverse events and take advantage of opportunities that arise.

Chapter 14 has two primary objectives:

◆ First, it will help you gain an appreciation for the role forecasting plays in the firm's financial planning process. Basically, forecasts of future sales revenues and their associated expenses give the firm the information it needs to project its future financing needs.

◆ Second, this chapter provides an overview of the basic elements of a financial plan: the cash budget, pro forma (planned) income statement, and pro forma balance sheet.

Pro forma financial statements give us a useful tool for analyzing the effects of the firm's forecasts and planned activities on its financial performance, as well as its needs for financing. In addition, pro forma statements can be used as a benchmark or standard to compare against actual operating results. Used in this way, pro forma statements are an instrument for monitoring and controlling the firm's progress throughout the planning period. For example, after the first energy crisis of the 1970s, the price of crude oil rose from $2.00 to more than $20.00 per barrel. Many thought that the price would rise above $50.00. Then in 1986, the price dropped to only $10.00 per barrel, and the $50.00 price looked like a foolish dream. However, in 2008, the price of a barrel of oil rose to $140.00 and then dropped into the $70–80 range by 2009. What's next, will the price continue to rise or will it drop again as it did in an earlier crisis?

Financial Forecasting

Use the percent of sales method to forecast the financing requirements of a firm.

Financial forecasting is the process of attempting to estimate a firm's future financing requirements. The basic steps involved in predicting those financing needs are the following:

STEP 1 Project the firm's sales revenues and expenses over the planning period.

STEP 2 Estimate the levels of investment in current and fixed assets that are needed to support the sales forecast.

STEP 3 Determine the firm's financing needs throughout the planning period that are required to fund its assets.

The Sales Forecast

The key ingredient in the firm's planning process is the sales forecast. This projection is generally derived using information from a number of sources. At a minimum, the sales forecast for the coming year reflects (1) any past trend in sales that is expected to carry through into the new year and (2) the influence of any anticipated events that might materially affect that trend.[1] An example of the latter is the initiation of a major advertising campaign or a change in the firm's pricing policy.

Forecasting Financial Variables

Traditional financial forecasting takes the sales forecast as a given and projects its impact on the firm's various expenses, assets, and liabilities. The most commonly used method for making these projections is the percent of sales method.

---

[1]A complete discussion of forecast methodologies is outside the scope of this book. The interested reader will find a large number of books on business forecasting with a simple web search.

The Percent of Sales Method of Financial Forecasting

The **percent of sales method** involves *estimating the level of an expense, asset, or liability for a future period as a percentage of the sales forecast.* The percentage used can come from the most recent financial statement item as a percentage of current sales, from an average computed over several years, from the judgment of the analyst, or from some combination of these sources.

Table 14-1 presents a complete example that uses the percent of sales method of financial forecasting for Drew Inc. In this example each item in the firm's balance sheet that varies with sales is converted to a percentage of 2010 sales, which was $10 million. The forecast of the new balance for each item is then calculated by multiplying this percentage times the $12 million in projected sales for the 2011 planning period. This method offers a relatively low-cost and easy-to-use way to estimate the firm's future financing needs.

Note that in the example in Table 14-1, both current and fixed assets are assumed to vary with the level of sales. This means that the firm does not have sufficient productive capacity to absorb a projected increase in sales. Thus, if sales were to rise by $1, fixed assets would rise by $0.40, or 40 percent of the projected increase in sales. If instead the fixed assets the firm currently owns are sufficient to support the projected level of sales, then the assets will not be converted to a percentage of sales and will be projected to remain unchanged for the period being forecast.

Also, note that accounts payable and accrued expenses are the only liabilities allowed to vary with sales. Both these liability accounts might reasonably be expected to rise and fall with the level of firm sales, hence, the use of the percent of sales forecast. Because these two

---

TABLE 14-1   Using the Percent of Sales Method to Forecast Drew Inc.'s Financing Requirements for 2011

	A	B	C	D	E	F	G	H	I
1	Drew Inc.						Drew Inc.		
2	Income Statement for 2010						Pro forma Income Statement for 2011		
3					% of 2010 Sales			Calculation	
4							Sales growth rate =	20%	
5	Sales		$ 10,000,000				Sales	$10 million x (1+.20) =	$ 12,000,000
6	Net Income		$ 500,000	[$500,000 /$10,000,000 =	5.0%		Net Income	$12 million x .05 =	$ 600,000
7									
8									
9									
10	Drew Inc.						Drew Inc.		
11	Balance Sheet for 2010						Pro forma Balance Sheet for 2011		
12					% of 2010 Sales			Calculation	
13									
14	Current assets		$ 2,000,000	[$2m /$10m] =	20.0%		Current assets	.20 x$12m =	$ 2,400,000
15	Net fixed assets		4,000,000	[$4m /$10m] =	40.0%		Net fixed assets	.40 x$12m =	$ 4,800,000
16	Total		$ 6,000,000				Total		$ 7,200,000
17									
18	Accounts payable		$ 1,000,000	[$1m /$10 m] =	10.0%		Accounts payable	.10 x$12m =	$ 1,200,000
19	Accrued expenses		1,000,000	[$1m /$10m] =	10.0%		Accrued expenses	.10 x$12m =	1,200,000
20	Notes payable		500,000		NA*		Notes payable	No change	500,000
21	Current Liabilities		$ 2,500,000				Current Liabilities		$ 2,900,000
22	Long-term debt		2,000,000		NA*		Long-term debt	No change	$ 2,000,000
23	Total Liabilities		$ 4,500,000				Total Liabilities		$ 4,900,000
24	Common stock (par)		100,000		NA*		Common stock (par)	No change	100,000
25	Paid-in capital		200,000		NA*		Paid-in capital	No change	200,000
26	Retained earnings		1,200,000				Retained earnings	Calculation*	1,500,000
27	Common Equity		$ 1,500,000				Common Equity		1,800,000
28	Total		$ 6,000,000				Total Financing Provided		$ 6,700,000
29							Discretionary Financing Needed (Plug)*		$ 500,000
30							Total Financing Needed = Total Assets		$ 7,200,000
31									
32	*Not applicable. These account balances do not vary with sales.								
33-35	bProjected retained earnings for 2011 equals $1,500,000 which is equal to the 2010 level of retained earnings of $1,200,000 plus net income of $600,000 less common dividends equal to 50% of projected net income or $300,000.								
36-37	cDiscretionary financing needed (DFN) for 2011 is a "plug figure" that equals the difference in the firm's projected total financing requirements or total assets equal to $7,200,000 and total financing provided which is $6,700,000. In this scenario DFN is $500,000.								
38									

categories of current liabilities normally vary directly with the level of sales, they are often referred to as sources of **spontaneous financing**. Included in spontaneous financing are *trade credit and other accounts payable that arise spontaneously in the firm's day-to-day operations.* Chapter 15, which discusses working-capital management, has more to say about these forms of financing. Notes payable, long-term debt, common stock, and paid-in capital are not assumed to vary directly with the level of firm sales. These sources of financing are termed **discretionary financing**, *which requires an explicit decision on the part of the firm's management every time funds are raised. An example is a bank note that requires that negotiations be undertaken and an agreement signed setting forth the terms and conditions for the financing.* Finally, note that the level of retained earnings does vary with estimated sales. The predicted change in the level of retained earnings equals the estimated after-tax profits (projected net income) equal to 5 percent of sales, or $600,000, less the common stock dividends of $300,000.

In the Drew Inc. example found in Table 14-1, we estimate that firm sales will increase from $10 million to $12 million, which will cause the firm's need for total assets to rise to $7.2 million. These assets will then be financed by $4.9 million in existing liabilities plus spontaneous liabilities; $1.8 million in owner funds, which includes the $300,000 in retained earnings from next year's sales; and finally, $500,000 in discretionary financing, which can be raised by issuing notes payable, selling bonds, offering an issue of stock, or some combination of these sources.

In summary, we can estimate the firm's discretionary financing needs (*DFN*), using the percent of sales method of financial forecasting, by following a four-step procedure:

STEP 1 Convert each asset and liability account that varies directly with firm sales to a percentage of the current year's sales.

> **EXAMPLE 14.1**   **Expressing Current Assets as a Percentage of Sales**
>
> $$\frac{\text{Current assets}}{\text{sales}} = \frac{\$2M}{\$10M} = 0.2 \text{ or } 20\%$$

STEP 2 Project the level of each asset and liability account in the balance sheet using its percentage of sales multiplied by projected sales or by leaving the account balance unchanged when the account does not vary with the level of sales.

> **EXAMPLE 14.2**   **Predicting Current Assets**
>
> $$\text{Projected current assets} = \text{projected sales} \times \frac{\text{current assets}}{\text{sales}} = \$12M \times 0.2 = \$2.4M$$

STEP 3 Project the addition to retained earnings available to help finance the firm's operations. This equals projected net income for the period less planned common stock dividends.

> **EXAMPLE 14.3**   **Predicting Additional Retained Earnings**
>
> $$\begin{array}{l}\text{Projected addition} \\ \text{to retained earnings}\end{array} = \text{projected sales} \times \frac{\text{net income}}{\text{sales}} \times \left(1 - \frac{\text{cash dividends}}{\text{net income}}\right)$$
>
> $$= \$12M \times 0.05 \times (1 - 0.5) = \$300,000$$

STEP 4 Project the firm's *DFN* as the projected level of total assets less projected liabilities and owners' equity.

spontaneous financing the trade credit and other accounts payable that arise spontaneously in the firm's day-to-day operations.

discretionary financing sources of financing that require an explicit decision on the part of the firm's management every time funds are raised. An example is a bank note that requires that negotiations be undertaken and an agreement signed setting forth the terms and conditions of the financing.

> ### EXAMPLE 14.4   Predicting Discretionary Financing Needs
>
> Discretionary financing needed
>
> $$= \text{projected total assets} - \text{projected total liabilities} - \text{projected owners' equity}$$
>
> $$= \$7.2\text{M} - \$4.9\text{M} - \$1.8\text{M} = \$500{,}000$$

Analyzing the Effects of Profitability and Dividend Policy on *DFN*

Projecting discretionary financing needed, we can quickly and easily evaluate the sensitivity of our projected financing requirements to changes in key variables. For example, using the information from the preceding example, we evaluate the effect of net profit margins (*NPMs*) equal to 1 percent, 5 percent, and 10 percent in combination with dividend payout ratios of 30 percent, 50 percent, and 70 percent, as follows:

Discretionary Financing Needed for Various Net Profit Margins and Dividend Payout Ratios

NET PROFIT MARGIN	DIVIDEND PAYOUT RATIOS = DIVIDENDS ÷ NET INCOME		
	30%	50%	70%
1%	$716,000	$740,000	$764,000
5%	380,000	500,000	620,000
10%	(40,000)	200,000	440,000

If these *NPMs* are reasonable estimates of the possible ranges of values the firm might experience, and if the firm is considering dividend payouts ranging from 30 percent to 70 percent, then we estimate that the firm's financing requirements will range from ($40,000), which represents a surplus of $40,000, to a situation in which it would need to acquire $764,000. Lower *NPMs* mean higher needs for discretionary financing. Also, higher dividend payout percentages, other things remaining constant, lead to a need for more discretionary financing. This is a direct result of the fact that a high-dividend-paying firm retains less of its earnings.

Analyzing the Effects of Sales Growth on a Firm's *DFN*

In Figure 14-1 we analyzed the *DFN* for Drew Inc., whose sales were expected to grow from $10 million to $12 million during the coming year. Recall that the 20 percent expected in-

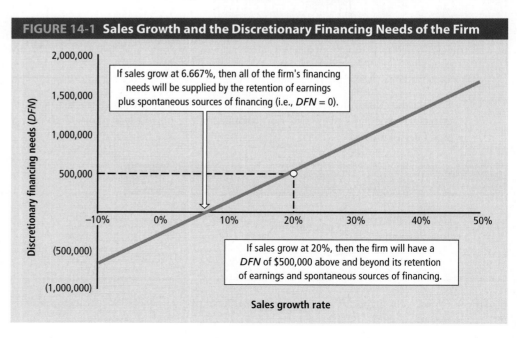

FIGURE 14-1 Sales Growth and the Discretionary Financing Needs of the Firm

CAN YOU DO IT?
PERCENT OF SALES FORECASTING

The CFO for Madrigal Plumbing Supplies Inc. is developing financial plans for next year when he estimates that his sales will reach $10 million. During the 4 years the firm has been in business, its inventories have represented approximately 15% of its revenues. What would you estimate the firm's needs for inventories to be next year (using the percent of sales forecast method)? If Madrigal has economies of scale, would you expect its inventory needs to be more than, the same as, or less than the percent of sales forecast?

(The solution can be found on page 398.)

crease in sales led to an increase in the firm's needs for discretionary financing in the amount of $500,000. We referred to this added financing requirement as the firm's *DFN* because all these funds must be raised from sources, such as bank borrowing or a new equity issue, that require that management exercise its discretion in selecting the source. In this section we want to investigate how a firm's *DFN* varies with different rates of anticipated sales growth.

Table 14-2 expands on the financial forecast found in Table 14-1. Specifically, we use the same assumptions and prediction methods that underlie Table 14-1 but apply them to sales growth rates of 0 percent, 20 percent, and 40 percent. The *DFN* for these sales growth rates ranges from ($250,000) to $1,250,000. When *DFN* is negative, this means that the firm has more money than it needs to finance the assets used to generate the projected sales.

TABLE 14-2 Discretionary Financing Needs (*DFN*) and the Growth Rate in Sales

	A	B	C	D	E	F	G	H	I	J	K
1	Drew Inc.						Drew Inc.				
2	Income Statement for 2010						Pro forma Income Statement for 2011				
3					% of 2010 Sales						
4								Alternative Growth Rates in Sales	0%	20%	40%
5	Sales		$ 10,000,000				Sales		$ 10,000,000	$ 12,000,000	$ 14,000,000
6	Net Income		$ 500,000	$500,000/$10,000,000 =	5.0%		Net Income		$ 500,000	$ 600,000	$ 700,000
7											
8											
9	Drew Inc.						Drew Inc.				
10	Balance Sheet for 2010						Pro forma Balance Sheet for 2011				
11					% of 2010 Sales			Calculation			
12											
13	Current assets		$ 2,000,000	[$2m /$10m] =	20.0%		Current assets	.20 x$12m =	$ 2,000,000	$ 2,400,000	$ 2,800,000
14	Net fixed assets		4,000,000	[$4m /$10m] =	40.0%		Net fixed assets	.40 x$12m =	4,000,000	$ 4,800,000	$ 5,600,000
15	Total		$ 6,000,000				Total		$ 6,000,000	$ 7,200,000	$ 8,400,000
16											
17	Accounts payable		$ 1,000,000	[$1m /$10 m] =	10.0%		Accounts payable	.10 x$12m =	$ 1,000,000	$ 1,200,000	$ 1,400,000
18	Accrued expenses		1,000,000	[$1m /$10m] =	10.0%		Accrued expenses	.10 x$12m =	1,000,000	1,200,000	1,400,000
19	Notes payable		500,000		NA*		Notes payable	No change	500,000	500,000	500,000
20	Current Liabilities		$ 2,500,000				Current Liabilities		$ 2,500,000	$ 2,900,000	$ 3,300,000
21	Long-term debt		2,000,000		NA*		Long-term debt	No change	2,000,000	2,000,000	2,000,000
22	Total Liabilities		$ 4,500,000				Total Liabilities		$ 4,500,000	$ 4,900,000	$ 5,300,000
23	Common stock (par)		100,000		NA*		Common stock (par)	No change	$ 100,000	$ 100,000	$ 100,000
24	Paid-in capital		200,000		NA*		Paid-in capital	No change	200,000	200,000	200,000
25	Retained earnings		1,200,000				Retained earnings	Calculation[b]	1,450,000	1,500,000	1,550,000
26	Common Equity		$ 1,500,000				Common Equity		$ 1,750,000	$ 1,800,000	$ 1,850,000
27	Total		$ 6,000,000				Total Financing Provided		$ 6,250,000	$ 6,700,000	$ 7,150,000
28							Discretionary Financing Needed (Plug)*		$ (250,000)	$ 500,000	$ 1,250,000
29							Total Financing Needed = Total Assets		$ 6,000,000	$ 7,200,000	$ 8,400,000
30											
31	*Not applicable. These account balances do not vary with sales.										
32-33	[b]Projected retained earnings for 2011 based on the 20% growth rate scenario is $1,500,000 and is calculated as follows: The 2010 retained earnings of $1,200,000 added to 2011 projected net income of $600,000 less common dividends of $300,000. Note that dividends are assumed to be 50% or net income, so dividends vary across the three scenarios.										
34-35	[c]Discretionary financing needed (DFN) for 2011 and the 20% growth rate scenario is a "plug figure" that equals the difference in the firm's projected total financing requirements or total assets of $7,200,000 and total financing provided of $6,700,000. In this scenario DFN is $500,000.										
38											

DID YOU GET IT?

PERCENT OF SALES FORECASTING

Madrigal projects that its inventories will be 15% of revenues such that its projected inventory needs for next year will be the following:

$$0.15 \times \$10 \text{ million} = \$1,500,000$$

If Madrigal faces economies of scale, then its inventory needs will be less than the $1,500,000 predicted using the percent of sales method. When economies of scale are present, the firm's inventory needs do not increase proportionately with sales (nor do they decrease proportionately).

Alternatively, when *DFN* is positive, this means that the firm must raise additional funds in this amount, by either borrowing or issuing stock. We can calculate *DFN* using the following relationship:

$$DFN = \begin{matrix} \text{predicted change} \\ \text{in total assets} \end{matrix} - \begin{matrix} \text{predicted change} \\ \text{in spontaneous liabilities} \end{matrix} - \begin{matrix} \text{predicted change} \\ \text{in retained earnings} \end{matrix} \quad (14\text{-}1)$$

Notice that in defining *DFN* we consider only changes in spontaneous liabilities, which you will recall are those liabilities that arise more or less automatically in the course of doing business (examples include accrued expenses and accounts payable). In Table 14-1 the only liabilities that are allowed to change with sales are spontaneous liabilities, so we can calculate the change in spontaneous liabilities simply by comparing total liabilities at the current sales level with total liabilities for the predicted sales level.

Equation (14-1) can be used to estimate the *DFN* numbers found in Table 14-2. For example, when sales are expected to grow at a rate of 10 percent (that is, *g* equals 10 percent), *DFN* can be calculated as follows:

$$DFN(g = 10\%) = (\$6,600,000 - \$6,000,000) - (\$4,700,000 - \$4,500,000)$$
$$- (\$1,475,000 - \$1,200,000) = \$125,000$$

external financing needs that portion of a firm's requirements for financing that exceeds its sources of internal financing (i.e., the retention of earnings) plus spontaneous sources of financing (e.g., trade credit).

Sometimes analysts prefer to calculate a firm's **external financing needs** (*EFN*), which include *all the firm's needs for financing beyond the funds provided internally through the retention of earnings*. Thus,

$$EFN = \text{predicted change in total assets} - \text{change in retained earnings} \quad (14\text{-}2)$$

For an anticipated growth in sales of 10 percent, *EFN* equals $325,000. The difference between *EFN* and *DFN* equals the $200,000 in added spontaneous financing that the firm anticipates receiving when its sales rise from $10 million to $11 million. We prefer to use the *DFN* concept because it focuses the analyst's attention on the amount of funds that the firm must actively seek to meet the firm's financing requirements.

Figure 14-1 contains a graphic representation of the relationship between growth rates for sales and *DFN*. The straight line in the graph depicts the level of *DFN* for each of the different rates of growth in firm sales. For example, if sales grow by 20 percent, then the firm projects a *DFN* of $500,000, which must be raised externally by borrowing or a new equity offering. Note that when sales grow at 6.667 percent, the firm's *DFN* will be exactly zero. For firms that have limited sources of external financing or choose to grow through internal financing plus spontaneous financing, it is important that they be able to estimate the sales growth rate that they can "afford," which in this case is 6.667 percent.

Concept Check

1. If we cannot predict the future perfectly, then why do firms engage in financial forecasting?
2. Why are sales forecasts so important to developing a firm's financial plans?
3. What is the percent of sales method of financial forecasting?
4. What are some examples of spontaneous and discretionary sources of financing?
5. What is the distinction between discretionary financing needs (*DFN*) and external financing needs (*EFN*)?

Limitations of the Percent of Sales Forecasting Method

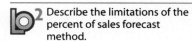

2 Describe the limitations of the percent of sales forecast method.

The percent of sales method of financial forecasting provides reasonable estimates of a firm's financing requirements only when asset requirements and financing sources can be accurately forecast as a constant percent of sales. For example, predicting inventories for 2010 using the percent of sales method involves the following equation.

$$\text{Predicted inventories for 2010} = \left(\frac{\text{inventories for 2009}}{\text{sales for 2009}}\right) \times \text{predicted sales for 2010}$$

Figure 14-2A depicts this predictive relationship. Note that the percent of sales predictive model is simply a straight line that passes through the origin (that is, has a zero intercept). There are some fairly common instances in which this type of relationship fails to describe the relationship between an asset category and sales. Two such examples involve assets for which there are scale economies and assets that must be purchased in discrete quantities ("lumpy assets").

Economies of scale are sometimes realized from investing in certain types of assets. For example, a new computer system is likely to support a firm's operations over a wide range of firm sales. This means that these assets do not increase in direct proportion to sales. Figure 14-2B reflects one instance in which the firm realizes economies of scale from its investment in inventory. Note that inventories as a percentage of sales decline from 120 percent of sales, or $120 when sales are $100, to 30 percent of sales, or $300 when sales equal $1,000. This reflects the fact that there is a fixed component of inventories (in this case $100) that the firm must have on hand regardless of the level of sales, plus a variable component (20 percent of sales). In this instance the predictive equation for inventories is as follows:

$$\text{Inventories}_t = a + b\,\text{sales}_t$$

In this example, a (the intercept[2] of the inventories equation) is equal to 100 and b (the slope in the equation) is 0.20.

Figure 14-2C is an example of *lumpy assets*, that is, assets that must be purchased in large, nondivisible components. For example, if the firm spends $500 on plant and equipment, it can produce up to $100 in sales per year. If it spends another $500 (for a total of $1,000), then it can support sales of $200 to $300 per year, and so forth. Note that when a block of assets is purchased, it creates excess capacity until sales grow to the point at which the capacity is fully used. The result is a step function like the one depicted in Figure 14-2C. Thus, if the firm does not expect sales to exceed the current capacity of its plant and equipment, there would be no projected need for added plant and equipment capacity.

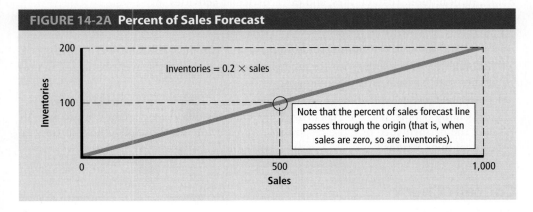

FIGURE 14-2A Percent of Sales Forecast

[2]Economies of scale are evidenced by the nonzero intercept value. However, scale economies can also result in nonlinear relationships between sales and a particular asset category. Later, when we discuss cash management, we will find that one popular cash management model predicts a nonlinear relationship between the optimal cash balance and the level of cash transactions.

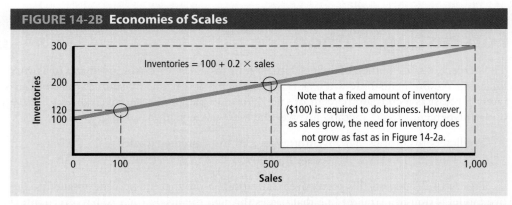

FIGURE 14-2B **Economies of Scales**

Inventories = 100 + 0.2 × sales

Note that a fixed amount of inventory ($100) is required to do business. However, as sales grow, the need for inventory does not grow as fast as in Figure 14-2a.

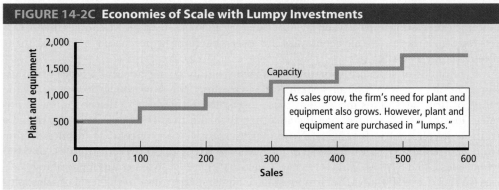

FIGURE 14-2C **Economies of Scale with Lumpy Investments**

Capacity

As sales grow, the firm's need for plant and equipment also grows. However, plant and equipment are purchased in "lumps."

3 Prepare a cash budget and use it to evaluate the amount and timing of a firm's financing needs.

Constructing and Using a Cash Budget

The cash budget, like the pro forma income statement and pro forma balance sheet, is an essential tool of financial planning. The cash budget contains a detailed listing of planned cash inflows and outflows for each year of the planning period.

Budget Functions

budget an itemized forecast of a company's expected revenues and expenses for a future period.

A **budget** is simply *a forecast of future events*. For example, students preparing for final exams make use of time budgets to help them allocate their limited preparation time among their courses. Students also must budget their financial resources among competing uses, such as books, tuition, food, rent, clothes, and extracurricular activities.

Budgets perform three basic functions for a firm.

◆ First, they indicate the amount and timing of the firm's needs for future financing.
◆ Second, they provide the basis for taking corrective action in the event budgeted figures do not match actual or realized figures.
◆ Third, budgets provide the basis for performance evaluation and control. Plans are carried out by people, and budgets provide benchmarks that management can use to evaluate the performance of those responsible for carrying out those plans and, in turn, to control their actions.

Concept Check

1. What, in words, is the fundamental relationship (equation) used in making percent of sales forecasts?
2. Under what circumstances does a firm violate the basic relationship underlying the percent of sales forecast method?

ETHICS IN FINANCIAL MANAGEMENT

TO BRIBE OR NOT TO BRIBE

The pressure to "get the forecast right" can be tremendous, and these pressures can lead managers to engage in practices (especially in underdeveloped countries) of offering bribes and payoffs to public officials because they are considered the norm in business transactions. This raises a perplexing ethical question. If paying bribes is not considered unethical in a foreign country, should you consider it unethical to make these payments?

This situation provides an example of an ethical issue that gave rise to legislation. The Foreign Corrupt Practices Act of 1977 (as amended in the Omnibus Trade and Competitiveness Act of 1988) established criminal penalties for making payments to foreign officials, political parties, or candidates in order to obtain or retain business. Ethical problems are frequently areas just outside the boundaries of current legislation and often lead to the passage of new legislation.

Consider the following question: If you were involved in negotiating an important business deal in a foreign country and the success or failure of the deal hinged on whether you paid a local government official to help you consummate the deal, would you authorize the payment? Assume that the form of the payment is such that you do not expect to be caught and punished; for example, your company agrees to purchase supplies from a family member of the government official at a price slightly above the competitive price. Can you see any pitfalls related to such a deal?

The Cash Budget

The **cash budget** represents a *detailed plan of future cash flows* and is composed of four elements: cash receipts, cash disbursements, net change in cash for the period, and new financing needed.

> **cash budget** a detailed plan of future cash flows. This budget is composed of four elements: cash receipts, cash disbursements, net change in cash for the period, and new financing needed.

EXAMPLE 14.5   Constructing a Cash Budget

To demonstrate the construction and use of the cash budget, consider Salco Furniture Company Inc., a regional distributor of household furniture. Salco is in the process of preparing a monthly cash budget for the upcoming 6 months (January through June 2011). The company's sales are highly seasonal, peaking in the months of March through May. Roughly 30 percent of Salco's sales are collected 1 month after the sale, 50 percent 2 months after the sale, and the remainder during the third month following the sale.

Salco attempts to pace its purchases with its forecast of future sales. Purchases generally equal 75 percent of sales and are made 2 months in advance of anticipated sales. Payments are made in the month following purchases. For example, June sales are estimated at $100,000; thus, April purchases are 0.75 × $100,000 = $75,000. Correspondingly, payments for purchases in May equal $75,000. Wages, salaries, rent, and other cash expenses are recorded in Table 14-3, which shows Salco's cash budget for the 6-month period ended in June 2011. Additional expenditures are recorded in the cash budget related to the purchase of equipment in the amount of $14,000 during February and the repayment of a $12,000 loan in May. In June, Salco will pay $7,500 interest on its $150,000 in long-term debt for the period of January to June 2011. Interest on the $12,000 short-term note repaid in May for the period January through May equals $600 and is paid in May.

Salco currently has a cash balance of $20,000 and wants to maintain a minimum balance of $10,000. Additional borrowing necessary to maintain that minimum balance is estimated in the final section of Table 14-3. Borrowing takes place at the beginning of the month in which the funds are needed. Interest on the borrowed funds equals 12 percent per annum, or 1 percent per month, and is paid in the month following the one in which funds are borrowed. Thus, interest on funds borrowed in January will be paid in February equal to 1 percent of the loan amount outstanding during January.

ETHICS IN FINANCIAL MANAGEMENT

BEING HONEST ABOUT THE UNCERTAINTY OF THE FUTURE

Put yourself in the shoes of Ben Tolbert, who is the CFO of Bonajet Enterprises. Ben's CEO is scheduled to meet with a group of outside analysts tomorrow to discuss the firm's financial forecast for the last quarter of the year. Ben's analysis suggests that there is a very real prospect that the coming quarter's results could be very disappointing. How would you handle Ben's dilemma?

As Ben looks over a draft of the report he must submit to the company CEO, he becomes increasingly concerned. Although the forecast is below initial expectations, this is not what worries Ben. The problem is that some of the basic assumptions underlying his prediction might not come true. If this is the case, then the company's performance for the last quarter of the year will

be dramatically below its annual forecast. The result would be a potentially severe reaction in the investment community, causing a downward adjustment of unknown proportions in the firm's stock price.

Bonajet's CEO is a no-nonsense guy who really doesn't like to see his CFO hedge his predictions, so Ben is under pressure to decide whether to ignore the downside prospects or make them known to his CEO. Complicating matters is the fact that the worst-case scenario would probably give rise to a reorganization of Bonajet that would lead to substantial layoffs of its workforce. Here is Ben's dilemma: What should he tell the CEO in their meeting tomorrow morning?

The financing-needed line in Salco's cash budget determines that the firm's cumulative short-term borrowing will be $36,350 in February, $65,874 in March, $86,633 in April, and $97,599 in May. In June the firm will be able to reduce its borrowing to $79,875. Note that the cash budget indicates not only the amount of financing needed during the period but also when the funds will be needed.

Concept Check

1. What is a cash budget?
2. How is a cash budget used in financial planning?

TABLE 14-3 Salco Furniture Co. Inc. Cash Budget for the 6 Months Ended June 30, 2011

	A	B	C	D	E	F	G	H	I	J	K	L
		October	November	December	January	February	March	April	May	June	July	August
1												
2	Worksheet											
3	Sales (forecasted)	55,000	62,000	50,000	60,000	75,000	88,000	100,000	110,000	100,000	80,000	75,000
4	Purchases (75% of sales in 2 months)			56,250	66,000	75,000	82,500	75,000	60,000	56,250		
5												
6	Cash Receipts											
7	Collections:											
8	First Month after sale (30%)				15,000	18,000	22,500	26,400	30,000	33,000		
9	Second Month after sale (50%)				31,000	25,000	30,000	37,500	44,000	50,000		
10	Third Month after sale (20%)				11,000	12,400	10,000	12,000	15,000	17,600		
11	Total Cash Receipts				57,000	55,400	62,500	75,900	89,000	100,600		
12												
13	Cash Disbursements											
14	Payments (one-month lag of purchases from row 4)				56,250	66,000	75,000	82,500	75,000	60,000		
15	Wages and Salaries				3,000	10,000	7,000	8,000	6,000	4,000		
16	Rent				4,000	4,000	4,000	4,000	4,000	4,000		
17	Other Expenses				1,000	500	1,200	1,500	1,500	1,200		
18	Interest expense on existing debt*								600	7,500		
19	Taxes						4,460			5,200		
20	Purchase of Equipment					14,000						
21	Loan Repayment*								12,000			
22	Total Cash Disbursements				64,250	94,500	91,660	96,000	99,100	81,900		
23												
24	Net Change in Cash for the Period				(7,250)	(39,100)	(29,160)	(20,100)	(10,100)	18,700		
25	Plus: Beginning cash balance				20,000	12,750	10,000	10,000	10,000	10,000		
26	Less: Interest on short-term borrowing				0	0	(364)	(659)	(866)	(976)		
27	Equals: Ending cash balance before short-term borrowing				12,750	(26,350)	(19,524)	(10,759)	(966)	27,724		
28												
29	New Financing Needed*				0	36,350	29,524	20,759	10,966	(17,724) *		
30	Ending cash balance				12,750	10,000	10,000	10,000	10,000	10,000		
31	Cumulative borrowing				0	36,350	65,874	86,633	97,599	79,875		
32												
33												
34	*An interest payment of $600 on the $12,000 loan is due in May, and an interest payment of $7500 on the $150,000 long-term debt is due in June.											
35	*The principal amount of the $12,000 loan is also due in May.											
36	*The amount of financing that is required to raise the firm's ending cash balance up to its $10,000 desired cash balance.											
37	*Negative financing needed simply means the firm has excess cash that can be used to retire a part of its short-term borrowing from prior months.											
38												

Summary

This chapter developed the role of forecasting within the context of the firm's financial-planning activities. Forecasts of the firm's sales revenues and related expenses provide the basis for projecting future financing needs. The most popular method for forecasting financial variables is the percent of sales method.

 Use the percent of sales method to forecast the financing requirements of a firm.

The percent of sales method presumes that the asset or liability being forecast is a constant percent of sales for all future levels of sales. There are instances when this assumption is not reasonable and, consequently, the percent of sales method does not provide reasonable predictions. One such instance arises when there are economies of scale in the use of the asset being forecast. For example, the firm may need at least $10 million in inventories to open its doors and operate even for sales as low as $100 million per year. If sales double to $200 million, inventories may only increase to $15 million. Thus, inventories do not increase with sales in a constant proportion. A second situation in which the percent of sales method fails to work properly is when asset purchases are lumpy. That is, if plant capacity must be purchased in, say, $50 million increments, then plant and equipment will not remain a constant percentage of sales.

 Describe the limitations of the percent of sales forecast method.

How serious are these possible problems and should we use the percent of sales method? Even in the face of these problems, the percent of sales method works reasonably well when predicted sales levels do not differ drastically from the level used to calculate the percentage of sales. For example, if the current sales level used in calculating the percentage of sales for inventories is $40 million, then we can feel more comfortable forecasting the level of inventories corresponding to a new sales level of $42 million than when sales are predicted to rise to $60 million.

The cash budget is the primary tool of financial forecasting and planning. It contains a detailed plan of the firm's future cash flow estimates and consists of four elements or segments: cash receipts, cash disbursements, net change in cash for the period, and new financing needed. Once prepared, the cash budget also serves as a tool for monitoring and controlling the firm's operations. By comparing actual cash receipts and disbursements to those in the cash budget, the financial manager can gain an appreciation of how well the firm is performing. In addition, deviations from the plan can serve as an early warning system to signal the onset of financial difficulties ahead.

 Prepare a cash budget and use it to evaluate the amount and timing of a firm's financing needs.

Key Terms

Budget   400

Cash budget   401

Discretionary financing   395

External financing needs   398

Percent of sales method   394

Spontaneous financing   395

Review Questions

All Review Questions and Study Problems are available in MyFinanceLab.

14-1. Discuss the shortcomings of the percent of sales method of financial forecasting.

14-2. What would be the probable effect on a firm's cash position of the following events?

   a. Rapidly rising sales
   b. A delay in the payment of payables
   c. A more liberal credit policy on sales (to the firm's customers)
   d. Holding larger inventories

14-3. A cash budget is usually thought of as a means of planning for future financing needs. Why would a cash budget also be important for a firm that has excess cash on hand?

14-4. Explain why a cash budget would be of particular importance to a firm that experiences seasonal fluctuations in its sales.

Self-Test Problems

(Solutions to these problems are found at the end of the chapter.)

ST-1. (*Financial forecasting*) Use the percent of sales method to prepare a pro forma income statement for Calico Sales Co. Inc. Projected sales for next year equal $4 million. Cost of goods sold equals 70 percent of sales, administrative expense equals $500,000, and depreciation expense is $300,000. Interest expense equals $50,000, and income is taxed at a rate of 40 percent. The firm plans to spend $200,000 during the period to renovate its office facility and will retire $150,000 in notes payable. Finally, selling expense equals 5 percent of sales.

ST-2. (*Cash budget*) Stauffer Inc. has estimated its sales and purchase requirements for the last half of the coming year. Past experience indicates that it will collect 20 percent of its sales in the month of the sale, 50 percent of the remainder 1 month after the sale, and the balance in the second month following the sale. Stauffer prefers to pay for half its purchases in the month of the purchase and the other half in the following month. The labor expense for each month is expected to equal 5 percent of that month's sales, with cash payment being made in the month in which the expense is incurred.

Depreciation expense is $5,000 per month; miscellaneous cash expenses are $4,000 per month and are paid in the month incurred. General and administrative expenses of $50,000 are recognized and paid monthly. A $60,000 truck is to be purchased in August and is to be depreciated on a straight-line basis over 10 years with no expected salvage value. The company also plans to pay a $9,000 cash dividend to its stockholders in July. The company feels that a minimum cash balance of $30,000 should be maintained. Any borrowing will cost 12 percent annually, with interest paid in the month following the month in which the funds are borrowed. Borrowing takes place at the beginning of the month in which the need for funds arises. For example, if during the month of July the firm should need to borrow $24,000 to maintain its $30,000 desired minimum balance, then $24,000 will be taken out on July 1 with interest owed for the entire month of July. Interest for the month of July would then be paid on August 1. Sales and purchase estimates are shown here. Prepare a cash budget for the months of July and August (cash on hand June 30 was $30,000, sales for May and June were $100,000, and purchases were $60,000 for each of these months).

MONTH	SALES	PURCHASES
July	$120,000	$50,000
August	150,000	40,000
September	110,000	30,000

ST-3. (*Forecasting net income*) The chief financial officer of Clairmont Manufacturing Inc. prepares a forecast of net income for the coming year as a starting point for developing financial plans. At the close of 2010, the firm's income statement appeared as follows (in $000):

Income Statement ($000)

FOR THE YEAR ENDED 2010	
Sales	$25,000
Cost of goods sold	(16,250)
Gross profit	8,750
Operating costs	(4,500)
Depreciation expense	(150)
Net operating profit	4,100
Interest expense	(1,580)
Earnings before taxes	2,520
Taxes	(882)
Net income	$ 1,638
Dividends	$ 1,500
Addition to retained earnings	$ 138

The CFO normally uses the most recent income statement to guide her estimate of what the future will bring. For example, she has made the following assumptions and estimates for 2011:

Sales growth rate	15%
COGS/sales	65%
Operating expenses/sales	18%
Depreciation expense ($000)	$ 150
Interest expense ($000)	$1,580
Tax rate	35%
Dividends ($000)	$1,500

Note that these estimates are derived from the 2010 income statement, reflecting the fact that the CFO believes the only real change for the coming year is the level of sales, which she estimates to be 15 percent higher. Of course, cost of goods sold and operating expenses will rise in proportion to the increase in sales following the percent of sales noted earlier.

What do you estimate net income for the firm to be in 2011? If the firm retains its $1,500,000 dividend payment, how much do you estimate the firm will be able to retain in 2011?

Study Problems

14-1. (*Financial forecasting*) Zapatera Enterprises is evaluating its financing requirements for the coming year. The firm has been in business for only 1 year, but its CFO predicts that the firm's operating expenses, current assets, net fixed assets, and current liabilities will remain at their current proportion of sales.

Last year Zapatera had $12 million in sales, and net income of $1.2 million. The firm anticipates that next year's sales will reach $15 million, with net income rising to $2 million. Given its present high rate of growth, the firm retains all its earnings to help defray the cost of new investments.

The firm's balance sheet for 2010 is found below:

Zapatera Enterprises Inc.

BALANCE SHEET		
	12/31/2010	**% OF SALES**
Current assets	$3,000,000	25%
Net fixed assets	6,000,000	50%
Total	$9,000,000	

LIABILITIES AND OWNERS' EQUITY		
Accounts payable	$3,000,000	25%
Long-term debt	2,000,000	NA[a]
Total liabilities	$5,000,000	
Common stock	1,000,000	NA
Paid-in capital	1,800,000	NA
Retained earnings	1,200,000	
Common equity	4,000,000	
Total	$9,000,000	

[a]Not applicable. This figure does not vary directly with sales and is assumed to remain constant for purposes of making next year's forecast of financing requirements.

Estimate Zapatera's financing requirements (i.e., total assets) for 2011 and its discretionary financing needs (*DFN*).

14-2. (*Pro forma accounts receivable balance calculation*) On March 31, 2010, Mike's Bike Shop had outstanding accounts receivable of $17,500. Mike's sales are roughly evenly split between credit and cash sales, with the credit sales collected half in the month after the sale and the remainder 2 months after the sale. Historical and projected sales for the bike shop are given here:

MONTH	SALES	MONTH	SALES
January	$15,000	March	$25,000
February	20,000	April (projected)	30,000

a. Under these circumstances, what should the balance in accounts receivable be at the end of April?

b. How much cash did Mike's realize during April from sales and collections?

14-3. (*Financial forecasting*) Sambonoza Enterprises projects its sales next year to be $4 million and expects to earn 5 percent of that amount after taxes. The firm is currently in the process of projecting its financing needs and has made the following assumptions (projections):

1. Current assets will equal 20 percent of sales, and fixed assets will remain at their current level of $1 million.

2. Common equity is currently $0.8 million, and the firm pays out half its after-tax earnings in dividends.

3. The firm has short-term payables and trade credit that normally equal 10 percent of sales, and it has no long-term debt outstanding.

What are Sambonoza's financing needs for the coming year?

14-4. (*Financial forecasting—percent of sales*) Tulley Appliances Inc. projects next year's sales to be $20 million. Current sales are $15 million, based on current assets of $5 million and fixed assets of $5 million. The firm's net profit margin is 5 percent after taxes. Tulley forecasts that its current assets will rise in direct proportion to the increase in sales, but that its fixed assets will increase by only $100,000. Currently, Tulley has $1.5 million in accounts payable (which vary directly with sales),

$2 million in long-term debt (due in 10 years), and common equity (including $4 million in retained earnings) totaling $6.5 million. Tulley plans to pay $500,000 in common stock dividends next year.

    a. What are Tulley's total financing needs (i.e., total assets) for the coming year?

    b. Given the firm's projections and dividend payments plans, what are its discretionary financing needs?

    c. Based on your projections, and assuming that the $100,000 expansion in fixed assets will occur, what is the largest increase in sales the firm can support without having to resort to the use of discretionary sources of financing?

14-5. (*Pro forma balance sheet construction*) Use the following industry-average ratios to construct a pro forma balance sheet for Phoebe's Cat Foods Inc.

Total asset turnover	1.5 times
Average collection period	
(assume 365-day year)	15 days
Fixed asset turnover	5 times
Inventory turnover	
(based on cost of goods sold)	3 times
Current ratio	2 times
Sales (all on credit)	$3.0 million
Cost of goods sold	75% of sales
Debt ratio	50%

		Current liabilities	
Cash		Long-term debt	
Accounts receivable	_____	Common stock plus	_____
Net fixed assets	$	Retained earnings	$

14-6. (*Cash budget*) The Sharpe Corporation's projected sales for the first 8 months of 2011 are as follows:

January	$190,000	May	$300,000
February	120,000	June	270,000
March	135,000	July	225,000
April	240,000	August	150,000

Of Sharpe's sales, 10 percent is for cash, another 60 percent is collected in the month following the sales, and 30 percent is collected in the second month following sales. November and December sales for 2010 were $220,000 and $175,000, respectively.

Sharpe purchases its raw materials 2 months in advance of its sales. The purchases are equal to 60 percent of the final sales price of Sharpe's products. The supplier is paid 1 month after it makes a delivery. For example, purchases for April sales are made in February, and payment is made in March.

In addition, Sharpe pays $10,000 per month for rent and $20,000 each month for other expenditures. Tax prepayments of $22,500 are made each quarter, beginning in March.

The company's cash balance on December 31, 2010, was $22,000. This is the minimum balance the firm wants to maintain. Any borrowing that is needed to maintain this minimum is paid off in the subsequent month if there is sufficient cash. Interest on short-term loans (12 percent) is paid monthly. Borrowing to meet estimated monthly cash needs takes place at the beginning of the month. Thus, if in the month of April the firm expects to have a need for an additional $60,500, these funds would be borrowed at the beginning of April with interest of $605 (0.12 × 1/12 × $60,500) owed for April and paid at the beginning of May.

    a. Prepare a cash budget for Sharpe covering the first 7 months of 2011.

    b. Sharpe has $200,000 in notes payable due in July that must be repaid or renegotiated for an extension. Will the firm have ample cash to repay the notes?

14-7. (*Percent of sales forecasting*) Which of the following accounts would most likely vary directly with the level of a firm's sales? Discuss each briefly.

	YES	NO		YES	NO
Cash	___	___	Notes payable	___	___
Marketable securities	___	___	Plant and equipment	___	___
Accounts payable	___	___	Inventories	___	___

14-8. (*Financial forecasting—percent of sales*) The balance sheet of the Boyd Trucking Company (BTC) follows:

Boyd Trucking Company Balance Sheet, December 31, 2010 ($ Millions)

Current assets	$10	Accounts payable	$ 5
Net fixed assets	15	Notes payable	0
Total	$25	Bonds payable	10
		Common equity	10
		Total	$25

BTC had sales for the year ended December 31, 2010, of $25 million. The firm follows a policy of paying all net earnings out to its common stockholders in cash dividends. Thus, BTC generates no funds from its earnings that can be used to expand its operations. (Assume that depreciation expense is just equal to the cost of replacing worn-out assets.)

    a. If BTC anticipates sales of $40 million during the coming year, develop a pro forma balance sheet for the firm on December 31, 2011. Assume that current assets vary as a percent of sales, net fixed assets remain unchanged, and accounts payable vary as a percent of sales. Use notes payable as a balancing entry.

    b. How much "new" financing will BTC need next year?

    c. What limitations does the percent of sales forecast method suffer from? Discuss briefly.

14-9. (*Financial forecasting—discretionary financing needs*) The most recent balance sheet for the Armadillo Dog Biscuit Co. Inc. is shown in the following table. The company is about to embark on an advertising campaign, which is expected to raise sales from the current level of $5 million to $7 million by the end of next year. The firm is currently operating at full capacity and will have to increase its investment in both current and fixed assets to support the projected level of new sales. In fact, the firm estimates that both categories of assets will rise in direct proportion to the projected increase in sales.

Armadillo Dog Biscuit Co. Inc. ($ Millions)

	PRESENT LEVEL	PERCENT OF SALES	PROJECTED LEVEL
Current assets	$2.0		
Net fixed assets	3.0		
Total	$5.0		
Accounts payable	$0.5		
Accrued expense	0.5		
Notes payable	—		
Current liabilities	$1.0		
Long-term debt	$2.0		
Common stock	0.5		
Retained earnings	1.5		
Common equity	$2.0		
Total	$5.0		

The firm's net profits were 6 percent of the current year's sales but are expected to rise to 7 percent of next year's sales. To help support its anticipated growth in asset needs next year, the firm has suspended plans to pay cash dividends to its stockholders. In past years a $1.50-per-share dividend has been paid annually. Armadillo's accounts payable and accrued expenses are expected to vary directly with sales. In addition, notes payable will be used to supply the funds needed to finance next year's operations that are not forthcoming from other sources.

    a. Fill in the table and project the firm's needs for discretionary financing. Use notes payable as the balancing entry for future discretionary financing needs.

    b. Compare Armadillo's current ratio and debt ratio (total liabilities ÷ total assets) before the growth in sales and after. What was the effect of the expanded sales on these two dimensions of Armadillo's financial condition?

    c. What difference, if any, would have resulted if Armadillo's sales had risen to $6 million in 1 year and $7 million only after 2 years? Discuss only; no calculations are required.

14-10. (*Forecasting discretionary financing needs*) Fishing Charter Inc. estimates that it invests $0.30 in assets for each dollar of new sales. However, $0.05 in profits are produced by each dollar of additional sales, of which $0.01 can be reinvested in the firm. If sales rise by $500,000 next year from their current level of $5 million, and the ratio of spontaneous liabilities to sales is 15 percent, what will be the firm's need for discretionary financing? (*Hint*: In this situation you do not know what the firm's existing level of assets is, nor do you know how those assets have been financed. Thus, you must estimate the change in financing needs and match this change with the expected changes in spontaneous liabilities, retained earnings, and other sources of discretionary financing.)

14-11. (*Preparation of a cash budget*) Lewis Printing has projected its sales for the first 8 months of 2011 as follows:

January	$100,000	April	$300,000	July	$200,000
February	120,000	May	275,000	August	180,000
March	150,000	June	200,000		

Lewis collects 20 percent of its sales in the month of the sale, 50 percent in the month following the sale, and the remaining 30 percent 2 months following the sale. During November and December of 2010, Lewis's sales were $220,000 and $175,000, respectively.

Lewis purchases raw materials 2 months in advance of its sales. These purchases are equal to 65 percent of its final sales. The supplier is paid 1 month after delivery. Thus, purchases for April sales are made in February and payment is made in March.

In addition, Lewis pays $10,000 per month for rent and $20,000 each month for other expenditures. Tax prepayments of $22,500 are made each quarter beginning in March. The company's cash balance as of December 31, 2010, was $28,000; a minimum balance of $25,000 must be maintained at all times to satisfy the firm's bank line of credit agreement. Lewis has arranged with its bank for short-term credit at an interest rate of 12 percent per annum (1 percent per month) to be paid monthly. Borrowing to meet estimated monthly cash needs takes place at the end of the month, and interest is not paid until the end of the following month. Consequently, if the firm needed to borrow $50,000 during April, then it would pay $500 (= 0.01 × $50,000) in interest during May. Finally, Lewis follows a policy of repaying its outstanding short-term debt in any month in which its cash balance exceeds the minimum desired balance of $25,000.

    a. Lewis needs to know what its cash requirements will be for the next 6 months so that it can renegotiate the terms of its short-term credit agreement with its bank, if necessary. To evaluate this problem, the firm plans to evaluate the impact of a ±20 percent variation in its monthly sales efforts. Prepare a 6-month cash budget for Lewis and use it to evaluate the firm's cash needs.

    b. Lewis has a $20,000 note due in June. Will the firm have sufficient cash to repay the loan?

14-12. (*Forecasting inventories*) Findlay Instruments produces a complete line of medical instruments used by plastic surgeons and has experienced rapid growth over the past 5 years. In an effort to make more accurate predictions of its financing requirements, Findlay is currently attempting to construct a financial-planning model based on the percent of sales forecasting method. However, the firm's chief financial analyst (Sarah Macias) is concerned that the projections for inventories will be seriously in error. She recognizes that the firm has begun to accrue substantial economies of scale in its inventory investment and has documented this fact in the following data and calculations:

YEAR	SALES ($000)	INVENTORY ($000)	% OF SALES
2006	$15,000	$1,150	7.67%
2007	18,000	1,180	6.56%
2008	17,500	1,175	6.71%
2009	20,000	1,200	6.00%
2010	25,000	1,250	5.00%
			Average 6.39%

    a. Plot Findlay's sales and inventories for the past 5 years. What is the relationship between these two variables?

    b. Estimate firm inventories for 2011, when firm sales are projected to reach $30 million. Use the average percentage of sales for the past 5 years, the most recent percentage of sales, and your evaluation of the true relationship between the sales and inventories from part a to make three predictions.

14-13. (*Forecasting net income*) In November of each year the CFO of Barker Electronics begins the financial forecasting process to determine the firm's projected needs for new financing during the coming year. Barker is a small electronics manufacturing company located in Moline, Illinois, which is best known as the home of the John Deere Company. The CFO begins the process with the most recent year's income statement, projects sales growth for the coming year, and then estimates net income and finally the additional earnings he can expect to retain and reinvest in the firm. The firm's income statement for 2010 follows (in $000):

Income Statement ($000)

	YEAR ENDED DECEMBER 31, 2010
Sales	$ 1,500
Cost of goods sold	(1,050)
Gross profit	$ 450
Operating costs	(225)
Depreciation expense	(50)
Net operating profit	$ 175
Interest expense	(10)
Earnings before taxes	$ 165
Taxes	(58)
Net income	$ 107
Dividends	$ 20
Addition to retained earnings	$ 87

The electronics business has been growing rapidly over the past 18 months as the economy recovers, and the CFO estimates that sales will expand by 20 percent in the next year. In addition, he estimates the following relationships between each of the income statement expense items and sales:

COGS/sales	70%
Operating expenses/sales	15%
Depreciation expense ($000)	$50
Interest expense ($000)	$10
Tax rate	35%

Note that for the coming year both depreciation expense and interest expense are projected to remain the same as in 2010.

a. Estimate Barker's net income for 2011 and its addition to retained earnings under the assumption that the firm leaves its dividends paid at the 2010 level.
b. Reevaluate Barker's net income and addition to retained earnings where sales grow at 40 percent over the coming year. However, this scenario requires the addition of new plant and equipment in the amount of $100,000, which increases annual depreciation to $58,000 per year, and interest expense rises to $15,000.

Mini Case

Phillips Petroleum is an integrated oil and gas company with headquarters in Bartlesville, Oklahoma, where it was founded in 1917. The company engages in petroleum exploration and production worldwide. In addition, it engages in natural gas gathering and processing, as well as petroleum refining and marketing primarily in the United States. The company has three operating groups: Exploration and Production, Gas and Gas Liquids, and Downstream Operations, which encompasses Petroleum Products and Chemicals.

In the mid-1980s, Phillips engaged in a major restructuring following two failed takeover attempts, one led by T. Boone Pickins and the other by Carl Ichan.[3] The restructuring resulted in a $4.5 billion plan to exchange a package of cash and debt securities for roughly half the company's shares and to sell $2 billion worth of assets. Phillips's long-term debt increased from $3.4 billion in late 1984 to a peak of $8.6 billion in April 1985.

During 1992, Phillips was able to strengthen its financial structure dramatically. Its subsidiary Phillips Gas Company completed an offering of $345 million of Series A 9.32% cumulative preferred stock. As a result of this action and prior years' debt reductions, the company lowered its long-term

[3]This discussion is based on a story in the *New York Times*, January 7, 1986.

debt-to-capital ratio over the past 5 years from 75 percent to 55 percent. In addition, the firm refinanced over a billion dollars of its debt at reduced rates. A company spokesman said, "Our debt-to-capital ratio is still on the high side, and we'll keep working to bring it down. But the cost of debt is manageable, and we're beyond the point where debt overshadows everything else we do."[4]

Highlights of Phillips's financial condition from 1986 to 1992 are found in the accompanying table. These data reflect the company's financial restructuring following the downsizing and reorganization of Phillips's operations begun in the mid-1980s.

Summary Financial Information for Phillips Petroleum Corporation:
1986 to 1992 (in Millions of Dollars Except for per Share Figures)

	1986	1987	1988	1989	1990	1991	1992
Sales	$10,018.00	$10,917.00	$11,490.00	$12,492.00	$13,975.00	$13,259.00	$12,140.00
Net income	228.00	35.00	650.00	219.00	541.00	98.00	270.00
EPS	0.89	0.06	2.72	0.90	2.18	0.38	1.04
Current assets	2,802.00	2,855.00	3,062.00	2,876.00	3,322.00	2,459.00	2,349.00
Total assets	12,403.00	12,111.00	11,968.00	11,256.00	12,130.00	11,473.00	11,468.00
Current liabilities	2,234.00	2,402.00	2,468.00	2,706.00	2,910.00	2,503.00	2,517.00
Long-term debt	8,175.00	7,887.00	7,387.00	6,418.00	6,505.00	6,113.00	5,894.00
Total liabilities	10,409.00	10,289.00	9,855.00	9,124.00	9,411.00	8,716.00	8,411.00
Preferred stock	270.00	205.00	0.00	0.00	0.00	0.00	359.00
Common equity	1,724.00	1,617.00	2,113.00	2,132.00	2,719.00	2,757.00	2,698.00
Dividends per share	2.02	1.73	1.34	0.00	1.03	1.12	1.12

Source: Phillips annual reports for 1986 to 1992.

Phillips's managers are currently developing its financial plans for the next 5 years and want to develop a forecast of its financing requirements. As a first approximation, they have asked you to develop a model that can be used to make "ballpark" estimates of the firm's financing needs under the proviso that existing relationships found in the firm's financial statements remain the same over the period. Of particular interest is whether Phillips will be able to further reduce its reliance on debt financing. You may assume that Phillips's projected sales (in millions) for 1993 through 1997 are as follows: $13,000; $13,500; $14,000; $14,500; and $15,500.

a. Project net income for 1993 to 1997 using the percent of sales method based on an average of this ratio for 1986 to 1992.
b. Project total assets and current liabilities for 1993 to 1997 using the percent of sales method and your sales projections from part a.
c. Assuming that common equity increases only as a result of the retention of earnings and holding long-term debt and preferred stock equal to its 1992 balances, project Phillips's discretionary financing needs for 1993 to 1997. (Hint: Assume that total assets and current liabilities vary as a percentage of sales as per your answers to part b. In addition, assume that Phillips plans to continue to pay its dividends of $1.12 per share in each of the next 5 years.)

Self-Test Solutions

SS-1.

Calico Sales Co. Inc. Pro Forma Income Statement

Sales		$4,000,000
Cost of goods sold (70%)		(2,800,000)
Gross profit		1,200,000
Operating expense		
Selling expense (5%)	$200,000	
Administrative expense	500,000	
Depreciation expense	300,000	(1,000,000)
Net operating income		200,000
Interest expense		(50,000)
Earnings before taxes		150,000
Taxes (40%)		(60,000)
Net income		$ 90,000

[4]From *SEC Online*, 1992.

Although the office-renovation expenditure and debt retirement are surely cash outflows, they do not enter the income statement directly. These expenditures affect expenses for the period's income statement only through their effect on depreciation and interest expense. A cash budget would indicate the full cash impact of the renovation and debt-retirement expenditures.

SS-2.

	MAY	JUNE	JULY	AUGUST
Sales	$100,000	$100,000	$ 120,000	$ 150,000
Purchases	60,000	60,000	50,000	40,000
Cash receipts:				
Collections from month of sale (20%)	20,000	20,000	24,000	30,000
1 month later (50% of uncollected amount)		40,000	40,000	48,000
2 months later (balance)			40,000	40,000
Total receipts			$ 104,000	$ 118,000
Cash disbursements:				
Payments for purchases—				
From 1 month earlier			$ 30,000	$ 25,000
From current month			$ 25,000	20,000
Total			$ 55,000	$ 45,000
Miscellaneous cash expenses			4,000	4,000
Labor expense (5% of sales)			6,000	7,500
General and administrative expense				
($50,000 per month)			50,000	50,000
Truck purchase			0	60,000
Cash dividends			9,000	—
Total disbursements			$(124,000)	$(166,500)
Net change in cash			(20,000)	(48,500)
Plus: Beginning cash balance			30,000	30,000
Less: Interest on short-term borrowing (1% prior month's borrowing)				(200)
Equals: Ending cash balance—without borrowing			10,000	(18,700)
Financing needed to reach target cash balance			20,000	48,700
Cumulative borrowing			$ 120,000	$ 168,700

SS-3. The projected net income for 2010 is found by first estimating firm sales. For 2011 the CFO anticipates 2010 sales of $25,000,000 will grow by 15 percent to $28,750,000. Deducting cost of goods sold and operating expenses as a proportion of sales, as well as taxes, and the fixed amounts we estimate for depreciation and interest expense, we estimate net income for 2011 to be $2,052,000. Details are provided in the pro forma income statement for 2011 that follows:

Income Statement ($000)

	2010	2011		2010	2011
Sales	$25,000	$28,750	Interest expense	(1,580)	(1,580)
Cost of goods sold	(16,250)	(18,688)	Earnings before taxes	2,520	3,157
Gross profit	8,750	10,062	Taxes	(882)	(1,105)
Operating costs	(4,500)	(5,175)	Net income	$ 1,638	$ 2,052
Depreciation expense	(150)	(150)	Dividends	$ 1,500	$ 1,500
Net operating profit	4,100	4,737	Addition to retained earnings	$ 138	$ 552

Assuming that the firm's dividend payment remains constant at $1,500,000, we estimate that retained earnings will rise by $552,000 in 2011.

Chapter 15

Working-Capital Management

Learning Objectives

After reading this chapter, you should be able to:

 Describe the risk–return trade-off involved in managing a firm's working capital.

 Explain the determinants of net working capital.

 Calculate a firm's cash conversion cycle and interpret its determinants.

 Calculate the effective cost of short-term credit.

 List and describe the basic sources of short-term credit.

Describe the special problems encountered by multinational firms in managing working capital.

Early in its life as a publicly traded firm, the Dell Computer Corporation (DELL) experienced a period of declining sales that produced a serious cash shortfall. At the same time, the company realized that it had to accelerate its growth in order to move from the list of declining, second-tier manufacturers to the list of prospering, top-tier producers, and this required even more cash. The new Dell business model that emerged was designed to better manage the firm's working capital. Specifically, the model sought to lower inventory by 50 percent, improve lead time by 50 percent, reduce assembly costs by 30 percent, and reduce obsolete inventory by 75 percent.

The net result was that inventory dropped because Dell was aligning its inventory with sales and not holding inventories in anticipation of future sales. Furthermore, as its inventory disappeared, the company's profitability grew disproportionately because Dell avoided not only the carrying costs of holding inventories but also the losses associated with obsolete stock. Moreover, Dell was able to save money on purchasing components because the component prices were dropping 3 percent per month.

Because the firm's capital requirements to support its rapidly growing sales did not increase proportionately with sales, the company's financial needs were reduced. All this was brought about by better working-capital management.

Chapter 15 addresses two related topics: It introduces the principles involved in managing a firm's investment in working capital, and it presents a discussion of short-term financing. Traditionally, **working capital** is defined as the *firm's total investment in current assets*. **Net working capital**, on the other hand, is the *difference between the firm's current assets and its current liabilities*.

$$\text{Net working capital} = \text{current assets} - \text{current liabilities} \quad (15\text{-}1)$$

Throughout this chapter, the term *working capital* refers to net working capital. In managing the firm's net working capital, we are also *managing the firm's liquidity*. This entails managing two related aspects of the firm's operations: (1) its investment in current assets, and (2) its use of short-term or current liabilities.

Short-term sources of financing include all forms of financing that have maturities of 1 year or less—that is, current liabilities. There are two major issues involved in analyzing a firm's use of short-term financing: (1) How much short-term financing should the firm use? and (2) What specific sources of short-term financing should the firm select? We use the hedging principle of working-capital management to address the first of these questions. We then address the second issue by considering three basic factors: (1) the effective cost of credit, (2) the availability of credit in the amount needed and for the period that financing is required, and (3) the influence of the use of a particular credit source on the cost and availability of other sources of financing.

Managing Current Assets and Liabilities

 Describe the risk–return trade-off involved in managing a firm's working capital.

working capital a concept traditionally defined as a firm's investment in current assets.

net working capital the difference between the firm's current assets and its current liabilities.

A firm's current assets consist of cash and marketable securities, accounts receivable, inventories, and other assets that the firm's managers expect to be converted to cash within a period of a year or less. Consequently, firms that choose to hold more current assets are, in general, more liquid than firms that do not.

The Risk–Return Trade-Off

Actually firms that want to reduce their risk of illiquidity by holding more current assets do so by investing in larger cash and marketable securities balances. Holding larger cash and marketable securities balances has an unfortunate consequence, however. Because investments in cash and marketable securities earn relatively modest returns when compared with the firm's other investments, the firm that holds larger investments in these assets will reduce its overall rate of return. Thus, the increased liquidity must be traded off against the firm's reduction in return on investment. Managing this trade-off is an important theme of working-capital management.

The firm's use of current versus long-term debt also involves a risk–return trade-off. *Other things remaining the same, the greater the firm's reliance on short-term debt or current liabilities in financing its assets, the greater the risk of illiquidity.* However, the use of current liabilities offers some very real advantages in that they can be less costly than long-term financing, and they provide the firm with a flexible means of financing its fluctuating needs for assets. However, if for some reason the firm has problems raising short-term funds or it should need funds for longer than expected, it can get into real trouble. Thus, a firm can reduce its risk of illiquidity through the use of long-term debt at the expense of a reduction in its return on invested funds. Once again we see that the risk–return trade-off involves an increased risk of illiquidity versus increased profitability.

The Advantages of Current Liabilities: Return

Flexibility   Current liabilities offer the firm a flexible source of financing. They can be used to match the timing of a firm's needs for short-term financing. If, for example, a firm needs funds for a 3-month period during each year to finance a seasonal expansion in inventories, then a 3-month loan can provide substantial cost savings over a long-term loan (even if the interest rate on short-term financing should be higher). The use of long-term debt in this situation involves borrowing for the entire year rather than for the period when the funds are needed, which increases the amount of interest the firm must pay. This brings us to the second advantage generally associated with the use of short-term financing.

Interest Cost   In general, interest rates on short-term debt are lower than on long-term debt for a given borrower. This relationship was introduced in Chapter 2 and is referred to as the term structure of interest rates. For a given firm, the term structure might appear as follows.

LOAN MATURITY	INTEREST RATE
3 months	4.00%
6 months	4.60
1 year	5.30
3 years	5.90
5 years	6.75
10 years	7.50
30 years	8.25

Note that this term structure reflects the rates of interest applicable to a given borrower at a particular time. It would not, for example, describe the rates of interest available to another borrower or even those applicable to the same borrower at a different time.

The Disadvantages of Current Liabilities: Risk

The use of current liabilities, or short-term debt, as opposed to long-term debt subjects the firm to a greater risk of illiquidity for two reasons. First, short-term debt, because of its very nature, must be repaid or rolled over more often, so it increases the possibility that the firm's financial condition might deteriorate to a point at which the needed funds might not be available.[1]

A second disadvantage of short-term debt is the uncertainty of interest costs from year to year. For example, a firm borrowing during a 6-month period each year to finance a seasonal expansion in current assets might incur a different rate of interest each year. This rate reflects the current rate of interest at the time of the loan, as well as the lender's perception of the firm's riskiness. If fixed-rate, long-term debt were used, the interest cost would be stable for the entire period of the loan agreement.

Concept Check

1. How does investing more heavily in current assets while not increasing the firm's current liabilities decrease both the firm's risk and its expected return on its investment?

2. How does the use of current liabilities enhance profitability and also increase the firm's risk of default on its financial obligations?

---

[1]The dangers of such a policy are readily apparent in the experiences of firms that have been forced into bankruptcy. Penn Central, for example, went bankrupt when it had $80 million in short-term debt that it was unable to finance (roll over).

The Appropriate Level of Working Capital

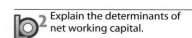

Explain the determinants of net working capital.

Managing the firm's net working capital (its liquidity) involves interrelated decisions regarding its investments in current assets and use of current liabilities. Fortunately, a guiding principle exists that can be used as a benchmark for the firm's working-capital policies: the hedging principle, or principle of self-liquidating debt. This principle provides a guide to the maintenance of a level of liquidity sufficient for the firm to meet its maturing obligations on time.[2]

In Chapter 12 we discussed the firm's financing decision in terms of the choice between debt and equity sources of financing. There is, however, yet another critical dimension of the firm's financing decision. This relates to the maturity structure of the firm's debt. How should the decision be made about whether to use short-term (current debt) or longer-maturity debt? This is one of the fundamental questions addressed in this chapter and one that is critically important to the financial success of the firm.

The Hedging Principles

Very simply, the **hedging principle**, or **principle of self-liquidating debt**, involves *matching the cash flow–generating characteristics of an asset with the maturity of the source of financing used to fund its acquisition*. For example, a seasonal expansion in inventories, according to the hedging principle, should be financed with a short-term loan or current liability. The rationale underlying the rule is straightforward. The funds are needed for a limited period, and when that time has passed, the cash needed to repay the loan will be generated by the sale of the extra inventory items. Obtaining the needed funds from a long-term source (longer than 1 year) would mean that the firm would still have the funds after the inventories they helped finance had been sold. In this case the firm would have "excess" liquidity, which it would either hold in cash or invest in low-yield marketable securities until the seasonal increase in inventories occurs again and the funds are needed. The result of all this would be lower profits.

Consider an example in which a firm purchases a new conveyor belt system, which is expected to produce cash savings to the firm by eliminating the need for two employees and, consequently, their salaries. This amounts to an annual savings of $24,000. The conveyor belt costs $250,000 to install and will last 20 years. If the firm chooses to finance this asset with a 1-year note, then it will not be able to repay the loan from the $24,000 cash flow generated by the asset. In accordance with the hedging principle, the firm should finance the asset with a source of financing that more nearly matches the expected life and cash flow–generating characteristics of the asset. In this case, a 15- to 20-year loan would be more appropriate.

Permanent and Temporary Assets

The notion of maturity matching in the hedging principle can be most easily understood when we think in terms of the distinction between permanent and temporary investments in assets, as opposed to the more traditional fixed and current asset categories. **Permanent investments** in an asset are *investments that the firm expects to hold for a period longer than 1 year*. Note that we are referring to the period the firm plans to hold an investment, not the useful life of the asset. For example, permanent investments are made in the firm's minimum level of current assets, as well as in its fixed assets. **Temporary investments**, by contrast, consist of *current assets that will be liquidated and not replaced within the current year*. Thus, some part of the firm's current assets is permanent and the remainder is temporary. For example, a seasonal increase in level of inventories is a temporary investment: the buildup in inventories that will be eliminated when no longer needed. In contrast, the buildup in inventories to meet a long-term increasing sales trend is a permanent investment.

hedging principle (principle of self-liquidating debt) a working-capital management policy which states that the cash flow–generating characteristics of a firm's investments should be matched with the cash flow requirements of the firm's sources of financing. Very simply, short-lived assets should be financed with short-term sources of financing while long-lived assets should be financed with long-term sources of financing.

permanent investment investments that the firm expects to hold longer than one year. The firm makes permanent investments in fixed and current assets.

temporary investments a firm's investments in current assets that will be liquidated and not replaced within a period of one year or less. Examples include seasonal expansions in inventories and accounts receivable.

---

[2]A value-maximizing approach to the management of the firm's liquidity involves assessing the value of the benefits derived from increasing the firm's investment in liquid assets and weighing them against the added costs to the firm's owners resulting from investing in low-yield current assets. Unfortunately, the benefits derived from increased liquidity relate to the expected costs of bankruptcy to the firm's owners, and these costs are very difficult to measure. Thus, a "valuation" approach to liquidity management exists only in the theoretical realm.

Temporary, Permanent, and Spontaneous Sources of Financing

Because total assets must always equal the sum of temporary, permanent, and spontaneous sources of financing, the hedging approach provides the financial manager with the basis for determining the sources of financing to use at any point.

What constitutes a temporary, permanent, or spontaneous source of financing? Temporary sources of financing consist of current liabilities. Short-term notes payable are the most common example of a temporary source of financing. Examples of notes payable include unsecured bank loans, commercial paper, and loans secured by accounts receivable and inventories. Permanent sources of financing include intermediate-term loans, long-term debt, preferred stock, and common equity.

Spontaneous sources of financing consist of trade credit and other accounts payable that arise *spontaneously* in the firm's day-to-day operations. For example, as the firm acquires materials for its inventories, **trade credit** is often *made available spontaneously or on demand from the firm's suppliers when it orders its supplies or more inventory of products to sell. Trade credit appears on the firm's balance sheet as accounts payable,* and the size of the accounts-payable balance varies directly with the firm's purchases of inventory items. In turn, inventory purchases are related to anticipated sales. Thus, part of the financing needed by the firm is spontaneously provided in the form of trade credit.

In addition to trade credit, wages and salaries payable, accrued interest, and accrued taxes also provide valuable sources of spontaneous financing. These expenses accrue throughout the period until they are paid. For example, if a firm has a wage expense of $10,000 a week and pays its employees monthly, then its employees effectively provide financing equal to $10,000 by the end of the first week following a payday, $20,000 by the end of the second week, and so forth, until the workers are paid. Because these expenses generally arise in direct conjunction with the firm's ongoing operations, they, too, are referred to as spontaneous.

The Hedging Principle: A Graphic Illustration

The hedging principle can now be stated very succinctly: *Asset needs of the firm not financed by spontaneous sources should be financed in accordance with this rule: Permanent-asset investments are financed with permanent sources, and temporary investments are financed with temporary sources.*

The hedging principle is depicted in Figure 15-1 and described in Table 15-1. Total assets are broken down into temporary- and permanent-asset investment categories. The firm's permanent investment in assets is financed by the use of permanent sources of financing (intermediate- and long-term debt, preferred stock, and common equity) or spontaneous sources (trade credit and other accounts payable). For illustration purposes, spontaneous sources of financing are treated as if their amount were fixed. In practice, of

trade credit credit made available by a firm's suppliers in conjunction with the acquisition of materials. Trade credit appears on the balance sheet as accounts payable.

CAUTIONARY TALE

FORGETTING PRINCIPLE 3: RISK REQUIRES A REWARD

An important rule of thumb for financing a firm's assets is something called the hedging principle. Very simply, this principle suggests that the firm's long-term asset investments should be matched with long-term sources of financing such as long-term debt or equity. Similarly, the firm's temporary or short-term assets can be financed using short-term sources of financing. In fact, this principle has been summed up in the maxim "never finance long-term investments using short-term sources of financing."

When firms violate this basic principle, the immediate effect may actually be positive as the firm utilizes lower cost short-term debt to finance its long-term investments. However, at some point, the music stops and the financing merry-go-round stops.

This is exactly what happened with many of the nation's banks during the financial crisis that began in 2007. These firms used short-term borrowing to finance their long-term investments. Moreover, these investments were heavily concentrated in loans and other securities that were tied to real estate. When problems developed in the real estate market that raised concerns about the value of these investments, the firms that were making these investments quickly found that they could no longer get favorable terms on their short-term borrowing.

The important lesson learned here is that matching up the maturity of the sources of financing with the type of investments being financed can be important to your financial health.

FIGURE 15-1 The Hedging Principle Illustrated

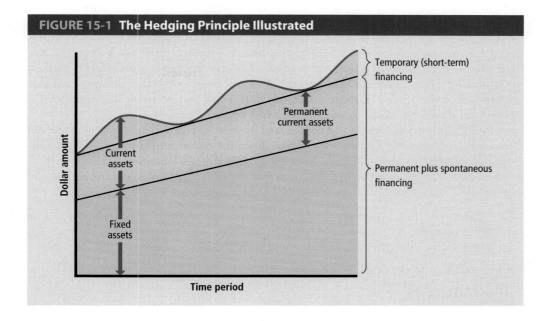

course, spontaneous sources of financing fluctuate with the firm's purchases and its expenditures for wages, salaries, taxes, and other items that are paid on a delayed basis. Its temporary investment in assets is financed with temporary (short-term) debt.

Concept Check

1. What is the hedging principle or principle of self-liquidating debt?
2. What are some examples of permanent and temporary investments in current assets?
3. Is trade credit a permanent, temporary, or spontaneous source of financing? Explain.

TABLE 15-1 The Hedging Principle Applied to Working-Capital Management

A firm's asset needs that are not financed by spontaneous sources of financing should be financed in accordance with the following "matching rule"—permanent-asset investments are financed with permanent sources, and temporary-asset investments are financed with temporary sources of financing.

Classification of a Firm's Investments in Assets	Definitions and Examples	Classification of a Firm's Sources of Financing	Definitions and Examples
Temporary investments	*Definition*: Current assets that will be liquidated and not replaced within the year. *Examples*: Seasonal expansions in inventories and accounts receivable.	Spontaneous financing	*Definition*: Financing that arises more or less automatically in response to the purchase of an asset. *Examples*: Trade credit that accompanies the purchase of inventories and other types of accounts payables created by the purchase of services (for example, wages payable).
		Temporary financing	*Definition*: Current liabilities other than spontaneous sources of financing. *Examples*: Notes payable and revolving credit agreements that must be repaid in a period less than 1 year.
Permanent investments	*Definition*: Current and long-term asset investments that the firm expects to hold for a period longer than 1 year. *Examples*: Minimum levels of inventory and accounts receivable the firm maintains throughout the year as well as its investments in plant and equipment.	Permanent financing	*Definition*: Long-term liabilities not due and payable within the year and equity financing. *Examples*: Term loans, notes, and bonds as well as preferred and common equity.

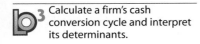

Calculate a firm's cash conversion cycle and interpret its determinants.

The Cash Conversion Cycle

Because firms vary widely with respect to their ability to manage their net working capital, there exists a need for an overall measure of effectiveness. An increasingly popular method for evaluating a firm's effective management of its working capital takes the approach that the firm's objective should be to minimize working capital subject to the constraint that it has sufficient working capital to support the firm's operations.

Minimizing working capital is accomplished by speeding up the collection of cash from sales, increasing inventory turns, and slowing down the disbursement of cash. We can incorporate all of these factors in a single measure called the *cash conversion cycle*.

The cash conversion cycle, or CCC, is simply the sum of days of sales outstanding and days of sales in inventory less days of payables outstanding:

$$\begin{matrix} \text{Cash} \\ \text{conversion} \\ \text{cycle (CCC)} \end{matrix} = \begin{matrix} \text{days of} \\ \text{sales} \\ \text{outstanding (DSO)} \end{matrix} + \begin{matrix} \text{days of} \\ \text{sales in} \\ \text{inventory (DSI)} \end{matrix} - \begin{matrix} \text{days of} \\ \text{payables} \\ \text{outstanding (DPO)} \end{matrix}$$

We calculate days of sales outstanding as follows:

$$\begin{matrix} \text{Days of} \\ \text{sales} \\ \text{outstanding (DSO)} \end{matrix} = \frac{\text{accounts receivable}}{\text{sales}/365} \qquad (15\text{-}2)$$

Recall from Chapter 4 that DSO can also be thought of as the average age of the firm's accounts receivable or the average collection period.

Days of sales in inventory is defined as follows:

$$\begin{matrix} \text{Days of} \\ \text{sales} \\ \text{in inventory (DSI)} \end{matrix} = \frac{\text{inventories}}{\text{cost of goods sold}/365} \qquad (15\text{-}3)$$

Note that DSI can also be thought of as the average age of the firm's inventory; that is, the average number of days that a dollar of inventory is held by the firm.

Days of payables outstanding is defined as follows:

$$\begin{matrix} \text{Days of} \\ \text{payables} \\ \text{outstanding (DPO)} \end{matrix} = \frac{\text{accounts payable}}{\text{cost of goods sold}/365} \qquad (15\text{-}4)$$

This ratio indicates the average age, in days, of the firm's accounts payable.

To illustrate the use of the CCC metric, consider Dell Computer Corporation. In 1989 Dell was a fledgling start-up whose CCC was 121.88 days. By 1998, Dell had reduced this number to −5.6 days. (See Table 15-2.) How, you might ask, does a firm reduce its CCC below zero? The answer is through very aggressive management of its working capital. As Table 15-2 indicates, Dell achieved this phenomenal reduction in CCC primarily through very effective management of inventories (days of sales in inventories dropped from 37.36 in 1995 to 4.65 in 2005) and more favorable trade credit payment practices (days of payables outstanding increased from 40.58 in 1995 to 79.41 in 2005). Specifically, Dell, a direct marketer

CAN YOU DO IT?

COMPUTING THE CASH CONVERSION CYCLE

Harrison Electronics is evaluating its cash conversion cycle and has estimated each of its components as follows:
Days sales outstanding (DSO) = 38 days
Days sales in inventory (DSI) = 41 days
Days payables outstanding (DPO) = 30 days
What is the firm's cash conversion cycle?
(The solution can be found on page 419.)

TABLE 15-2 The Determinants of Dell Computer Corporation's Cash Conversion Cycle for 1995–2005

Cash conversion cycle (CCC) = days of sales outstanding (DSO) + days of sales in inventory (DSI) − days of payables outstanding (DPO)

	1995	1996	1997	1998	1999	2000	2001	2002	2003	2004	2005
Days of sales outstanding (DSO)	50.04	42.48	44.00	49.64	38.69	33.14	26.57	26.66	32.01	32.74	35.59
Days of sales in inventory (DSI)	37.36	15.15	8.92	7.10	7.17	5.79	3.99	9.22	7.75	4.20	4.65
Days of payables outstanding (DPO)	40.58	62.79	62.87	62.34	64.92	62.07	72.87	75.79	79.41	81.46	79.41
Cash conversion cycle (CCC)	46.81	(5.15)	(9.96)	(5.60)	(19.06)	(23.14)	(42.30)	(39.90)	(39.64)	(44.51)	(39.17)

of personal computers, does not build a computer until an order is received. It purchases its supplies using trade credit. This business model results in minimal investment in inventories. Dell has obviously improved its working-capital management practices, as evidenced in Figure 15-2, where we compare Dell with Apple. Obviously both firms follow similar strategies and have been very successful in managing their cash conversion cycle in recent years.

FIGURE 15-2 Cash Conversion Cycles for Apple and Dell: 1995–2005

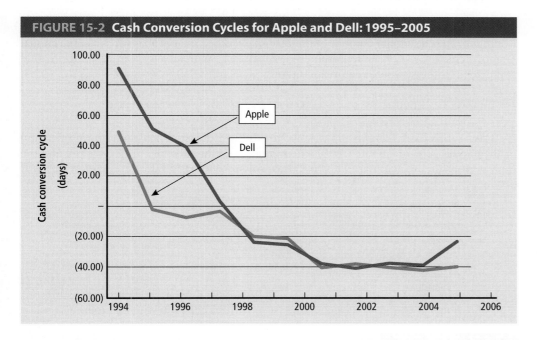

DID YOU GET IT?

COMPUTING THE CASH CONVERSION CYCLE

The cash conversion cycle (CCC) is calculated as follows:

$$
\begin{pmatrix} \text{Cash} \\ \text{conversion} \\ \text{cycle (CCC)} \end{pmatrix} = \begin{pmatrix} \text{days of} \\ \text{sales outstanding} \\ \text{(DSO)} \end{pmatrix} + \begin{pmatrix} \text{days of} \\ \text{sales in inventory} \\ \text{(DSI)} \end{pmatrix} - \begin{pmatrix} \text{days payable} \\ \text{outstanding} \\ \text{(DPO)} \end{pmatrix}
$$

Substituting the following:
Days sales outstanding (DSO) = 38 days
Days sales in inventory (DSI) = 41 days
Days payables outstanding (DPO) = 30 days
What is the firm's cash conversion cycle?

Cash conversion cycle (CCC) = 38 days + 41 days − 30 days = 49 days

We calculate the CCC to be 49 days. Harrison can reduce its cash conversion cycle by reducing DSO (e.g., offering a cash discount for early payment or simply reducing the firm's credit terms) and DSI (e.g., reducing the amount of inventory the firm carries), or by seeking better credit terms that increase its DPO.

Concept Check

1. What three actions can a firm take to minimize its net working capital?
2. Define *days of sales outstanding*, *days of sales in inventory*, and *days of payables outstanding*.

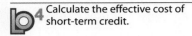
Calculate the effective cost of short-term credit.

Estimating the Cost of Short-Term Credit Using the Approximate Cost-of-Credit Formula

In Chapter 5 when we introduced the time value of money, we first introduced the principles that underlie the computation of the cost of credit. However, we repeat much of that discussion in this chapter because it is critical to gaining an understanding of how to estimate the cost of short-term credit.

The procedure for estimating the cost of short-term credit is a very simple one and relies on the basic interest equation:

$$\text{Interest} = \text{principal} \times \text{rate} \times \text{time} \tag{15-5}$$

where *interest* is the dollar amount of interest on a *principal* that is borrowed at some annual *rate* for a fraction of a year (represented by *time*). For example, a 6-month loan for $1,000 at 8 percent interest would require an interest payment of $40.

$$\text{Interest} = \$1,000 \times 0.08 \times \frac{1}{2} = \$40$$

We use this basic relationship to solve for the cost of a source of short-term financing or the annual percentage rate (*APR*) when the interest amount, the principal sum, and the time period for financing are known. Thus, solving the basic interest equation for *APR* produces[3]

$$APR = \frac{\text{interest}}{\text{principal} \times \text{time}} \tag{15-6}$$

or

$$APR = \frac{\text{interest}}{\text{principal}} \times \frac{1}{\text{time}} \tag{15-7}$$

This equation, called the *APR* calculation, is clarified by the following example.

EXAMPLE 15.1

The SKC Corporation plans to borrow $1,000 for a 90-day period. At maturity the firm will repay the $1,000 principal amount plus $30 interest. The effective annual rate of interest for the loan can be estimated using the *APR* equation, as follows:

$$APR = \frac{\$30}{\$1,000} \times \frac{1}{90/360}$$

$$= 0.03 \times \frac{360}{90} = 0.12 = 12\%$$

The effective annual cost of funds provided by the loan is, therefore, 12 percent.

The simple *APR* calculation does not consider compound interest. To account for the influence of compounding, we can use the following equation:

$$APY = \left(1 + \frac{i}{m}\right)^m - 1 \tag{15-8}$$

[3]For ease of computation, we assume a 30-day month and 360-day year in this chapter.

where EAR is the effective annual rate, i is the nominal rate of interest per year (12 percent in the previous example), and m is the number of compounding periods within a year [$m = 1/time = 1/(90/360) = 4$ in the preceding example]. Thus, the effective rate of interest on the loan in the example problem, considering compounding, is

$$EAR = \left(1 + \frac{0.12}{4}\right)^4 - 1 = 0.126 = 12.6\%$$

Compounding effectively raises the cost of short-term credit. Because the differences between APR and EAR are usually small, we use the simple interest values of APR to compute the cost of short-term credit.

Concept Check

1. What is the fundamental interest equation that underlies the calculation of the approximate cost-of-credit formula?
2. What is the effective annual rate (EAR) and how does it differ from the annual percentage rate (APR)?

Sources of Short-Term Credit

 5 List and describe the basic sources of short-term credit.

Short-term credit sources can be classified into two basic groups: unsecured and secured. **Unsecured loans** include all those *sources that have as their security only the lender's faith in the ability of the borrower to repay the funds when due.* The major sources of unsecured short-term credit include accrued wages and taxes, trade credit, unsecured bank loans, and commercial paper. A **secured loan** involves the *pledge of specific assets as collateral in the event the borrower defaults in payment of principal or interest.* Commercial banks, finance companies, and factors are the primary suppliers of secured credit. The principal sources of collateral include accounts receivable and inventories.

unsecured loans all sources of credit that have as their security only the lender's faith in the borrower's ability to repay the funds when due.

secured loan sources of credit that require security in the form of pledged assets. In the event the borrower defaults in payment of principal or interest, the lender can seize the pledged assets and sell them to settle the debt.

Unsecured Sources: Accrued Wages and Taxes

Because most businesses pay their employees only periodically (weekly, biweekly, or monthly), firms accrue a wages payable account that is, in essence, a loan from their employees. For example, if the wage expense for the Appleton Manufacturing Company is

FINANCE AT WORK

MANAGING WORKING CAPITAL BY TRIMMING RECEIVABLES

LaFarge Corporation is located in Reston, Virginia, and operates in the building materials industry. Last year LaFarge was able to dramatically improve its management of accounts receivable. This improvement is reflected in a decrease in the days of sales outstanding ratio (*DSO*); that is,

$$DSO = \frac{\text{accounts receivable}}{\text{sales}/365}$$

After reviewing this formula, you may recall that we referred to *DSO* in Chapter 4 as the average collection period. The company's success is due in large part to the fact that it ties incentive pay to the return on net assets (*RONA*) as defined here:

$$RONA = \frac{\text{earnings before interest and taxes}}{\text{net assets}}$$

Note that improvements in accounts receivable management that result in a decrease in *DSO* also lead to a reduction in the firm's net assets and a corresponding increase in *RONA*. Of course, this presumes that the reduction in *DSO* does not have an adverse impact on the firm's revenues and, consequently, earnings.

How Did They Do It?

Pete Sacripanti, vice president and controller of LaFarge's Calgary-based construction materials business, credits the firm's improved collections to 12 fundamental steps:[a]

1. **Focusing on customers and collections,** which involves all layers of management and is not just a finance responsibility.
2. **Building a base of preferred customers** that confers a competitive advantage.
3. **Delineating clear ownership of customer accounts** among the sales staff, which prevents passing the buck on delinquent accounts.
4. **Fixing clear guidelines** that govern LaFarge's commitments and responsibilities to customers.
5. **Articulating standard sales terms and conditions,** stipulating terms that are negotiable and those that are never negotiable.
6. **Establishing monthly collection targets by salesperson and division,** with collection targets based on the prior month's sales plus past-due accounts.

7. **Training salespeople on customer profitability,** with particular attention to (1) the link between past-due accounts and increased risk of bad debt write-offs, (2) the volume of business required to recover the cost of bad debts, and (3) higher borrowing costs for the company.
8. **Engaging in regular (weekly) credit and collection meetings** with the sales team, the credit manager, and the general manager.
9. **Encouraging constant "in-your-face" executive management,** featuring weekly status updates of collections by salespeople, including key account information.
10. **Facilitating collections through advance phone calls** to establish expected payment amount and availability and to provide a courier to pick up the payments.
11. **Developing collection skills,** including partial holdback releases; offsetting balances owed for services or equipment; use of construction liens, guarantees, letters of credit, and payment bonds; negotiation techniques for securing extras in lieu of write-offs; and better knowledge of the company's products, its industry, and its customers.
12. **Developing unique value** by building stronger relationships with customers, such as air-miles loyalty programs, engineered solutions, quality assurance, and new-product development.

The key thing to note in this list is that each item represents a managerial action aimed at improving the firm's success in collecting its receivables. The *DSO* metric captures the success of these actions, but it is these 12 steps that actually brought about the improvements.

Measuring Success

LaFarge engaged in a 3-year program aimed at reducing its investment in working capital. The success of the program is most clearly evident in the company's western Canadian construction-materials operation based in Calgary. This unit slashed its working capital by 38 percent to around $36 million while increasing sales by 10 percent to $425 million. The effect on *RONA* was dramatic because the firm simultaneously increased earnings (the numerator of the ratio) and decreased net assets (the denominator).

[a]From S. L. Mintz, "The 1999 Working Capital Survey: Dollars in the Details," *CFO Magazine* (July 1999), p. 58. Used by permission.

$450,000 per week and it pays its employees monthly, then by the end of a 4-week month the firm will owe its employees $1.8 million in wages for services they have already performed during the month. Consequently, the employees finance their own efforts by waiting a full month for payment.

Similarly, firms generally make quarterly income tax payments for their estimated quarterly tax liability. This means that the firm has the use of the tax money it owes based on its quarterly profits through the end of the quarter. In addition, the firm pays sales taxes and withholding (income) taxes for its employees on a deferred basis. The longer the period that the firm holds the tax payments, the greater the amount of financing they provide for the firm.

Note that these sources of financing *rise and fall spontaneously* with the level of the firm's sales. That is, as the firm's sales increase, so do its labor expenses, sales taxes collected, and

CAN YOU DO IT?

THE COST OF SHORT-TERM CREDIT (CONSIDERING COMPOUNDING EFFECTS)

Re-evaluate the cost of short-term credit for Hempstead using the effective annual rate (*EAR*), which incorporates compound interest.

(The solution can be found on page 424.)

income tax. Consequently, these accrued expense items provide the firm with automatic, or spontaneous, sources of financing.

Unsecured Sources: Trade Credit

Trade credit provides one of the most flexible sources of short-term financing available to the firm. We previously noted that trade credit is a primary source of spontaneous, or on-demand, financing. That is, trade credit arises spontaneously with the firm's purchases. To arrange for credit, the firm need only place an order with one of its suppliers. The supplier checks the firm's credit and, if it is good, sends the merchandise. The purchasing firm then pays for the goods in accordance with the supplier's credit terms.

Credit Terms and Cash Discounts   Very often the credit terms offered with trade credit involve a cash discount for early payment. For example, a supplier might offer terms of 2/10, net 30, which means that a 2 percent discount is offered if payment is made within 10 days or the full amount is due in 30 days. Thus, a 2 percent penalty is involved for not paying within 10 days, or for delaying payment from the tenth to the thirtieth day (that is, for 20 days). The effective annual cost of not taking the cash discount can be quite severe. Using a $1 invoice amount, the effective cost of passing up the discount period using the preceding credit terms and our *APR* equation can be estimated.

$$APR = \frac{\$0.02}{\$0.98} \times \frac{1}{20/360} = 0.3673 = 36.73\%$$

Note that the 2 percent cash discount is the *interest* cost of extending the payment period an *additional* 20 days. Note also that the principal amount of the credit is $0.98. This amount constitutes the full principal amount as of the tenth day of the credit period, after which time the cash discount is lost. The effective cost of passing up the 2 percent discount for 20 days is quite expensive: 36.73 percent. Furthermore, once the discount period has passed, there is no reason to pay before the final due date (the thirtieth day). Table 15-3 lists the effective annual cost of a number of alternative credit terms. Note that the cost of trade credit varies directly with the size of the cash discount and inversely with the length of time between the end of the discount period and the final due date.

The Stretching of Trade Credit   Some firms that use trade credit engage in a practice called *stretching of trade accounts*. This practice involves delaying payments beyond the prescribed credit period. For example, a firm might purchase materials under credit terms of 3/10, net 60; however, when faced with a shortage of cash, the firm might delay payment until the eightieth day. Continued violation of trade terms can eventually lead to a loss of

TABLE 15-3 The Rates of Interest on Selected Trade Credit Terms	
Credit Terms	**Effective Rates**
2/10, net 60	14.69%
2/10, net 90	9.18
3/20, net 60	27.84
6/10, net 90	28.72

DID YOU GET IT?
THE COST OF SHORT-TERM CREDIT (CONSIDERING COMPOUNDING EFFECTS)

Using equation (15-8) we can estimate the cost of short-term credit to Hempstead as follows:

$$EAR = \left(1 + \frac{i}{m}\right)^m - 1 = \left(1 + \frac{0.18}{6}\right)^6 - 1 = 0.1941, \text{ or } 19.41\%$$

where i is the nominal annual rate of interest. That is, the cash discount is 3 percent and this gets Hempstead an added 60 days or 1/6th of a year. Therefore, the nominal rate of interest for a year is 6×0.03, or 18 percent. Considering the effects of compound interest, the cost of short-term credit from deferring payment to Hamilton for wiring until the end of the 90-day credit period is 19.41 percent.

---

credit. However, for short periods, and at infrequent intervals, stretching offers the firm an emergency source of short-term credit.

The Advantages of Trade Credit   As a source of short-term financing, trade credit has a number of advantages. First, trade credit is conveniently obtained as a normal part of the firm's operations. Second, no formal agreements are generally involved in extending credit. Furthermore, the amount of credit extended expands and contracts with the needs of the firm; this is why it is classified as a spontaneous, or on-demand, source of financing.

Unsecured Sources: Bank Credit

Commercial banks provide unsecured short-term credit in two basic forms: lines of credit and transaction loans (notes payable). Maturities of both types of loans are usually 1 year or less, with rates of interest depending on the creditworthiness of the borrower and the level of interest rates in the economy as a whole.

line of credit generally an informal agreement or understanding between a borrower and a bank as to the maximum amount of credit the bank will provide the borrower at any one time. Under this type of agreement there is no "legal" commitment on the part of the bank to provide the stated credit.

revolving credit agreement an understanding between the borrower and the bank as to the amount of credit the bank will be legally obligated to provide the borrower.

compensating balance a balance of a given amount that the firm maintains in its demand deposit account. It may be required by either a formal or informal agreement with the firm's commercial bank. Such balances are usually required by the bank (1) on the unused portion of a loan commitment, (2) on the unpaid portion of an outstanding loan, or (3) in exchange for certain services provided by the bank, such as check-clearing or credit information. These balances raise the effective rate of interest paid on borrowed funds.

Line of Credit   A **line of credit** is *generally an informal agreement or understanding between the borrower and the bank about the maximum amount of credit that the bank will provide the borrower at any one time.* Under this type of agreement there is *no legal commitment on the part of the bank to provide the credit.* In a **revolving credit agreement**, which is a variant of this form of financing, a *legal obligation is involved.* The line of credit agreement generally covers a period of 1 year corresponding to the borrower's *fiscal* year. Thus, if the borrower is on a July 31 fiscal year, its lines of credit are based on the same annual period.

Lines of credit generally do not involve fixed rates of interest; instead they state that credit will be extended at $\frac{1}{2}$ *percent over prime* or some other spread over the bank's prime rate.[4] Furthermore, the agreement usually does not spell out the specific use that will be made of the funds beyond a general statement, such as *for working-capital purposes.*

Lines of credit usually require that the borrower maintain a *minimum balance in the bank throughout the loan period*, called a **compensating balance**. This required balance (which can be stated as a percentage of the line of credit or the loan amount) increases the effective cost of the loan to the borrower unless a deposit balance equal to or greater than this balance requirement is maintained in the bank.

The effective cost of short-term bank credit can be estimated using the *APR* equation. Consider the following example.

EXAMPLE 15.2

M&M Beverage Company has a $300,000 line of credit that requires a compensating balance equal to 20 percent of the loan amount. The rate paid on the loan is 10 percent per annum, $200,000 is borrowed for a 6-month period, and the firm does not currently have

---

[4]The *prime rate of interest* is the rate that a bank charges its most creditworthy borrowers.

a deposit with the lending bank. The dollar cost of the loan includes the interest expense and the opportunity cost of maintaining an idle cash balance equal to the 20 percent compensating balance. To accommodate the cost of the compensating-balance requirement, assume that the added funds will have to be borrowed and simply left idle in the firm's checking accounts. Thus, the amount actually borrowed (B) will be larger than the $200,000 needed. In fact, the needed $200,000 will constitute 80 percent of the total borrowed funds because of the 20 percent compensating-balance requirement; hence, $0.80B = \$200,000$, such that $B = \$250,000$. Thus, interest is paid on a $250,000 loan ($\$250,000 \times 0.10 \times \frac{1}{2} = \$12,500$), of which only $200,000 is available for use by the firm.[5] The effective annual cost of credit, therefore, is

$$APR = \frac{\$12,500}{\$200,000} \times \frac{1}{180/360} = 0.125 = 12.5\%$$

In the M&M Beverage Company example, the loan required the payment of principal ($250,000) plus interest ($12,500) at the end of the 6-month loan period. Frequently, bank loans will be made on a discount basis. That is, the loan interest will be deducted from the loan amount before the funds are transferred to the borrower. Extending the M&M Beverage Company example to consider discounted interest involves reducing the loan proceeds ($200,000) in the previous example by the amount of interest for the full 6 months ($12,500). The effective rate of interest on the loan is now

$$APR = \frac{\$12,500}{\$200,000 - \$12,500} \times \frac{1}{180/360}$$
$$= 0.1333 = 13.33\%$$

The effect of discounting interest was to raise the cost of the loan from 12.5 percent to 13.33 percent. This results from the fact that the firm pays interest on the same amount of funds as before ($250,000); however, this time it gets the use of $12,500 less, or $200,000 - \$12,500 = \$187,500$.[6]

Transaction Loans   Still another form of unsecured short-term bank credit can be obtained in the form of a **transaction loan**. Here the loan is *made for a specific purpose*. This is the type of loan that most individuals associate with bank credit and is obtained by signing a promissory note.

An unsecured transaction loan is very similar to a line of credit with regard to its cost, term to maturity, and compensating-balance requirements. In both instances commercial banks often require that the borrower *clean up* its short-term loans for a 30- to 45-day period during the year. This means, very simply, that the borrower must be free of any bank debt for the stated period. The purpose of such a requirement is to ensure that the borrower is not using short-term bank credit to finance a part of its permanent needs for funds.

transaction loan a loan where the proceeds are designated for a specific purpose—for example, a bank loan used to finance the acquisition of a piece of equipment.

---

[5]The same answer would have been obtained by assuming a total loan of $200,000, of which only 80 percent, or $160,000, was available for use by the firm; that is,

$$APR = \frac{\$10,000}{\$160,000} \times \frac{1}{180/360} = 12.5\%$$

Interest is now calculated on the $200,000 loan amount $\left(\$10,000 = \$200,000 \times 0.10 \times \frac{1}{2}\right)$

[6]If M&M needs the use of a full $200,000, then it will have to borrow more than $250,000 to cover both the compensating-balance requirement *and* the discounted interest. In fact, the firm will have to borrow some amount B such that

$$B - 0.2B - \left(0.10 \times \frac{1}{2}\right)B = \$200,000$$
$$0.75B = \$200,000$$
$$B = \frac{\$200,000}{0.75} = \$266,667$$

The cost of credit remains the same at 13.33 percent, as we see here:

$$APR = \frac{\$13,333}{\$266,667 - \$53,333 - \$13,333} \times \frac{1}{180/360}$$
$$= 0.1333 = 13.33\%$$

Unsecured Sources: Commercial Paper

Only the largest and most creditworthy companies are able to use **commercial paper**, which is simply a *short-term promise to pay that is sold in the market for short-term debt securities.*

The maturity of the credit source is generally 6 months or less, although some issues carry 270-day maturities. The interest rate on commercial paper is generally slightly lower ($\frac{1}{2}$ to 1 percent) than the prime rate on commercial bank loans. Also, the interest is usually discounted, although sometimes interest-bearing commercial paper is available.

New issues of commercial paper are either directly placed (sold by the issuing firm directly to the investing public) or dealer placed. A dealer placement involves the use of a commercial paper dealer, who sells the issue for the issuing firm. Many major finance companies, such as General Motors Acceptance Corporation, place their commercial paper directly. The volume of direct versus dealer placements is roughly 4 to 1 in favor of direct placements. Dealers are used primarily by industrial firms that either make only infrequent use of the commercial paper market or, owing to their small size, would have difficulty placing the issue without the help of a dealer.

Commercial Paper as a Source of Short-Term Credit   Several advantages accrue to the user of commercial paper.

1. **Interest rate.**   Commercial paper rates are generally lower than rates on bank loans and comparable sources of short-term financing.
2. **Compensating-balance requirement.**   No minimum balance requirements are associated with commercial paper. However, issuing firms usually find it desirable to maintain line-of-credit agreements sufficient to back up their short-term financing needs in the event that a new issue of commercial paper cannot be sold or an outstanding issue cannot be repaid when due.
3. **Amount of credit.**   Commercial paper offers the firm with very large credit needs a single source for all its short-term financing. Because of loan amount restrictions placed on the banks by the regulatory authorities, obtaining the necessary funds from a commercial bank might require borrowing from a number of institutions.[7]
4. **Prestige.**   Because it is widely recognized that only the most creditworthy borrowers have access to the commercial paper market, its use signifies a firm's credit status.

Using commercial paper for short-term financing, however, involves a very important risk. The commercial paper market is highly impersonal and denies even the most creditworthy borrower any flexibility in terms of repayment. When bank credit is used, the borrower has someone with whom he or she can work out any temporary difficulties that might be encountered in meeting a loan deadline. This flexibility simply does not exist for the user of commercial paper.

Estimating the Cost of Using Commercial Paper   The cost of commercial paper can be estimated using the simple, effective cost-of-credit equation (*APR*). The key points to remember are that commercial paper interest is usually discounted and that if a dealer is used to place the issue, a fee is charged. Even if a dealer is not used, the issuing firm will incur costs associated with preparing and placing the issue, and these costs must be included in estimating the cost of this credit.

EXAMPLE 15.3

The EPG Manufacturing Company uses commercial paper regularly to support its needs for short-term financing. The firm plans to sell $100 million in 270-day-maturity paper, on which it expects to pay discounted interest at a rate of 12 percent per annum

---

[7]Member banks of the Federal Reserve System are limited to 10 percent of their total capital, surplus, and undivided profits when making loans to a single borrower. Thus, when a corporate borrower's needs for financing are very large, it may have to deal with a group of participating banks to raise the needed funds.

($9 million). In addition, EPG expects to incur a cost of approximately $100,000 in dealer placement fees and other expenses of issuing the paper. The effective cost of credit to EPG can be calculated as follows:

$$APR = \frac{\$9,000,000 + \$100,000}{\$100,000,000 - \$100,000 - \$9,000,000} \times \frac{1}{270/360}$$

$$= 0.1335 = 13.35\%$$

where the interest cost is calculated as $\$100,000,000 \times 0.12 \times (270/360) = \$9,000,000$ plus the $100,000 dealer placement fee. Thus, the effective cost of credit to EPG is 13.35 percent.

Secured Sources: Accounts-Receivable Loans

Secured sources of short-term credit have certain assets of the firm pledged as collateral to secure the loan. Upon default of the loan agreement, the lender has first claim to the pledged assets in addition to its claim as a general creditor of the firm. Hence, the secured credit agreement offers an added margin of safety to the lender.

Generally, a firm's receivables are among its most liquid assets. For this reason they are considered by many lenders to be prime collateral for a secured loan. Two basic procedures can be used in arranging for financing based on receivables: pledging and factoring.

Pledging Accounts Receivable   Under the **pledging accounts receivable** arrangement, the *borrower simply pledges accounts receivable as collateral for a loan obtained from either a commercial bank or a finance company*. The amount of the loan is stated as a percentage of the face value of the receivables pledged. If the firm provides the lender with a *general line* on its receivables, then all of the borrower's accounts are pledged as security for the loan. This method of pledging is simple and inexpensive. However, because the lender has no control over the quality of the receivables being pledged, it will set the maximum loan at a relatively low percentage of the total face value of the accounts, generally ranging downward from a maximum of around 75 percent.

> **pledging accounts receivable** a loan the firm obtains from a commercial bank or a finance company using its accounts receivable as collateral.

Still another approach to pledging involves the borrower presenting specific invoices to the lender as collateral for a loan. This method is somewhat more expensive because the lender must assess the creditworthiness of each individual account pledged; however, given this added knowledge, the lender should be willing to increase the loan as a percentage of the face value of the invoices. In this case the loan might reach as high as 85 or 90 percent of the face value of the pledged receivables.

Credit Terms Accounts receivable loans generally carry an interest rate that is 2 to 5 percent higher than the bank's prime lending rate. Finance companies charge an even higher rate. In addition, the lender usually charges a handling fee stated as a percentage of the face value of the receivables processed, which may be as much as 1 to 2 percent of the face value.

> **EXAMPLE 15.4**
>
> The A. B. Good Company sells electrical supplies to building contractors on terms of net 60. The firm's average monthly sales are $100,000; thus, given the firm's 2-month credit terms, its average receivables balance is $200,000. The firm pledges all of its receivables to a local bank, which in turn advances up to 70 percent of the face value of the receivables at 3 percent over prime and charges a 1 percent processing fee on *all* receivables pledged. A. B. Good follows a practice of borrowing the maximum amount possible, and the current prime rate is 10 percent.
>
> The *APR* of using this source of financing for a full year is computed as follows:
>
> $$APR = \frac{\$18,200 + \$12,000}{\$140,000} \times \frac{1}{360/360} = 0.2157 = 21.57\%$$

where the total dollar cost of the loan consists of both the annual interest expense ($0.13 \times 0.70 \times \$200,000 = \$18,200$) and the annual processing fee ($0.01 \times \$100,000 \times 12$ months $= \$12,000$). The amount of credit extended is $0.70 \times \$200,000 = \$140,000$. Note that the processing charge applies to *all* receivables pledged. Thus, the A. B. Good Company pledges $100,000 each month, or $1,200,000 during the year, on which a 1 percent fee must be paid, for a total annual charge of $12,000.

One more point: The lender, in addition to making advances or loans, may be providing certain credit services to the borrower. For example, the lender may provide billing and collection services. The value of these services should be considered in computing the cost of credit. In the preceding example, A. B. Good Company may *save* $10,000 per year in credit department expenses by pledging all of its accounts and letting the lender provide those services. In this case, the cost of short-term credit is only

$$APR = \frac{\$18,200 + \$12,000 - \$10,000}{\$140,000} \times \frac{1}{360/360} = 0.1443 = 14.43\%$$

The Advantages and Disadvantages of Pledging The primary advantage of pledging as a source of short-term credit is the flexibility it provides the borrower. Financing is available on a continuous basis. The new accounts created through credit sales provide the collateral for the financing of new production. Furthermore, the lender may provide credit services that eliminate or at least reduce the need for similar services within the firm. The primary disadvantage associated with this method of financing is its cost, which can be relatively high compared with other sources of short-term credit, owing to the level of the interest rate charged on loans and the processing fee on pledged accounts.

factoring accounts receivable the outright sale of a firm's accounts receivable to another party (the factor) without recourse. The factor, in turn, bears the risk of collection.

factor a firm that, in acquiring the receivables of other firms, bears the risk of collection and, for a fee, services the accounts.

Factoring Accounts Receivable **Factoring accounts receivable** involves the *outright sale of a firm's accounts to a financial institution called a factor*. A **factor** is *a firm that acquires the receivables of other firms*. The factoring institution might be a commercial finance company that engages solely in the factoring of receivables (known as an *old-line factor*) or it might be a commercial bank. The factor, in turn, bears the risk of collection and, for a fee, services the accounts. The fee is stated as a percentage of the face value of all receivables factored (usually 1 to 3 percent).

The factor firm typically does *not* make payment for factored accounts until the accounts have been collected or the credit terms have been met. Should the firm wish to receive immediate payment for its factored accounts, it can borrow from the factor, using the factored accounts as collateral. The maximum loan the firm can obtain is equal to the face value of its factored accounts less the factor's fee (1 to 3 percent) less a reserve (6 to 10 percent) less the interest on the loan. For example, if $100,000 in receivables is factored, carrying 60-day credit terms, a 2 percent factor's fee, a 6 percent reserve, and interest at 1 percent per month on advances, then the maximum loan or advance the firm can receive is computed as follows:

Face amount of receivables factored	$100,000
Less: Fee (0.02 × $100,000)	(2,000)
Reserve (0.06 × $100,000)	(6,000)
Interest (0.01 × $92,000 × 2 months)	(1,840)
Maximum advance	$ 90,160

Note that interest is discounted and calculated based on a maximum amount of funds available for advance ($92,000 = $100,000 − $2,000 − $6,000). Thus, the effective cost of credit can be calculated as follows:

$$APR = \frac{\$1,840 + \$2,000}{\$90,160} \times \frac{1}{60/360}$$

$$= 0.2555 = 25.55\%$$

Secured Sources: Inventory Loans

Inventory loans, or *loans secured by inventories*, provide a second source of security for short-term credit. The amount of the loan that can be obtained depends on both the marketability and perishability of the inventory. Some items, such as raw materials (grains, oil, lumber, and chemicals), are excellent sources of collateral, because they can easily be liquidated. Other items, such as work-in-process inventories, provide very poor collateral because of their lack of marketability.

There are several methods by which inventory can be used to secure short-term financing. These include a floating, or blanket, lien, a chattel mortgage, a field warehouse receipt, and a terminal warehouse receipt.

Under a **floating lien agreement**, *the borrower gives the lender a lien against all of its inventories.* This provides the simplest but least secure form of inventory collateral. The borrowing firm maintains full control of the inventories and continues to sell and replace them as it sees fit. Obviously, this lack of control over the collateral greatly dilutes the value of this type of security to the lender.

Under a **chattel mortgage agreement**, *the inventory is identified* (by serial number or otherwise) *in the security agreement, and the borrower retains title to the inventory but cannot sell the items without the lender's consent.*

Under a **field warehouse agreement**, *inventories used as collateral are physically separated from the firm's other inventories and are placed under the control of a third-party field-warehousing firm.*

A **terminal warehouse agreement** differs from a field warehouse agreement in only one respect. Here *the inventories pledged as collateral are transported to a public warehouse that is physically removed from the borrower's premises.* The lender has an added degree of safety or security because the inventory is totally removed from the borrower's control. Once again the cost of this type of arrangement is increased because the warehouse firm must be paid by the borrower; in addition, the inventory must be transported to and, eventually, from the public warehouse.

inventory loans loans secured by inventories. Examples include floating or blanket lien agreements, chattel mortgage agreements, field-warehouse receipt loans, and terminal-warehouse receipt loans.

floating lien agreement an agreement, generally associated with a loan, whereby the borrower gives the lender a lien against all its inventory.

chattel mortgage agreement a loan agreement in which the lender can increase his or her security interest by having specific items of inventory identified in the loan agreement. The borrower retains title to the inventory but cannot sell the items without the lender's consent.

field warehouse agreement a security agreement in which inventories pledged as collateral are physically separated from the firm's other inventories and placed under the control of a third-party field-warehousing firm.

terminal warehouse agreement a security agreement in which the inventories pledged as collateral are transported to a public warehouse that is physically removed from the borrower's premises. This is the safest (though costly) form of financing secured by inventory.

Concept Check

1. What are some examples of unsecured and secured sources of short-term credit?
2. What is the difference between a line of credit and a revolving credit agreement?
3. What are the types of credit agreements a firm can get that are secured by its accounts receivable as collateral?
4. What are some examples of loans secured by a firm's inventories?

Multinational Working-Capital Management

 Describe the special problems encountered by multinational firms in managing working capital.

The basic principles of working-capital management are the same for multinational and domestic firms. However, because multinationals spend and receive money in different countries, the exchange rate between the firm's home country and each of the countries in which it does business poses an added source of concern when managing working capital.

Multinational firms, by definition, have assets that are denominated or valued in foreign currencies. This means that the multinational will lose value if that foreign currency declines in value vis-á-vis that of the home currency. Technically, the foreign assets of the firm are exposed to exchange-rate risk, the risk that tomorrow's exchange rate will differ from today's rate. However, this risk can be offset by the decline in value of any liability that is also denominated in terms of that foreign currency. Thus, a firm would normally be interested in its net exposed position (exposed assets – exposed liabilities) for each period and in each currency to which the firm has exposure.

If a firm is to manage its foreign-exchange-risk exposure, it needs good measures. There are three popular measures of foreign-exchange risk that can be used: translation exposure, transaction exposure, and economic exposure. *Translation exposure* arises because the foreign operations of multinational corporations have financial accounting statements denominated in the local currency of the country in which the operation is located. For U.S. multinational corporations, the reporting currency for their consolidated financial statements is the dollar, so the assets, liabilities, revenues, and expenses of the foreign operations must be translated into dollars. Furthermore, international transactions often require a payment to be made or received in a foreign currency in the future, so these transactions are exposed to exchange-rate risk, or *transaction risk*. *Economic exposure* exists over the long term because the value of the future cash flows in the reporting currency (that is, the dollar) from foreign operations is exposed to exchange-rate risk. Indeed, the whole stream of future cash flows is exposed. We will discuss these three types of exposures in more detail in Chapter 17.

Summary

Describe the risk–return trade-off involved in managing a firm's working capital.

Working-capital management involves managing the firm's liquidity, which in turn involves managing (1) the firm's investment in current assets and (2) its use of current liabilities. Each of these problems involves risk–return trade-offs. Investing in current assets reduces the firm's risk of illiquidity at the expense of lowering its overall rate of return on its investment in assets. By contrast, the use of long-term sources of financing enhances the firm's liquidity while reducing its rate of return on assets.

Explain the determinants of net working capital.

The hedging principle, or principle of self-liquidating debt, is a benchmark for working-capital decisions. Basically, this principle involves matching the cash flow–generating characteristics of an asset with the maturity of the source of financing used to acquire it.

Calculate a firm's cash conversion cycle and interpret its determinants.

The cash conversion cycle is a key measure of how efficient the firm is in managing its working capital. Specifically, it equals the number of days it takes to collect on credit sales plus the number of days items are in inventory less the number of days that payables are outstanding. The importance of the length of the conversion cycle is that this is the number of days that the firm has its cash tied up in inventories and accounts receivable for which it must provide financing.

The key consideration in selecting a source of short-term financing is the effective cost of credit.

Calculate the effective cost of short-term credit.

The various sources of short-term credit can be categorized into two groups: unsecured and secured. Unsecured credit offers no specific assets as security for the loan agreement. The primary sources include trade credit, lines of credit, unsecured transaction loans from commercial banks, and commercial paper. Secured credit is generally provided to business firms by commercial banks, finance companies, and factors. The most popular sources of security involve the use of accounts receivable and inventories. Loans secured by accounts receivable include pledging agreements, in which a firm pledges its receivables as security for a loan, and factoring agreements, in which the firm sells the receivables to a factor. In a pledging arrangement, the lender retains the right of recourse in the event of default, whereas in factoring, a lender is generally without recourse.

List and describe the basic sources of short-term credit.

Loans secured by inventories can be made using one of several types of security arrangements. Among the most widely used are the floating lien, chattel mortgage, field warehouse agreement, and terminal warehouse agreement. The form of agreement used depends on the type of inventories pledged as collateral and the degree of control the lender wishes to exercise over the collateral.

Describe the special problems encountered by multinational firms in managing working capital.

The problems of working-capital management are fundamentally the same for multinational firms as they are for domestic firms, with some complications. The primary source of complication comes from the fact that the multinational receives and makes payment with foreign currencies. This means that the multinational firm must be concerned not only with having sufficient liquidity but also with the value of its cash and marketable securities in terms of the value of the currencies of the countries in which it does business. Specifically, the multinational firm faces three types of currency exposure risk: translation exposure, transaction exposure, and economic exposure. All three types of currency risk must be managed by the multinational, in addition to the traditional risks of illiquidity.

Key Terms

Chattel mortgage agreement 429

Commercial paper 426

Compensating balance 424

Factor 428

Factoring accounts receivable 428

Field warehouse agreement 429

Review Questions

All Review Questions and Study Problems are available in MyFinanceLab.

15-1. Define and contrast the terms *working capital* and *net working capital*.

15-2. Discuss the risk–return relationship involved in the firm's asset-investment decisions as that relationship pertains to its working-capital management.

15-3. What advantages and disadvantages are generally associated with the use of short-term debt? Discuss.

15-4. Explain what is meant by the statement "The use of current liabilities as opposed to long-term debt subjects the firm to a greater risk of illiquidity."

15-5. Define the hedging principle. How can this principle be used in the management of working capital?

15-6. Define the following terms:

    a. Permanent asset investments
    b. Temporary asset investments
    c. Permanent sources of financing
    d. Temporary sources of financing
    e. Spontaneous sources of financing

15-7. What distinguishes short-term, intermediate-term, and long-term debt?

15-8. What criteria should be used to select a source of short-term credit? Discuss each.

15-9. How can the formula "interest = principle × rate × time" be used to estimate the cost of short-term credit?

15-10. How can we accommodate the effects of compounding in our calculation of the effective cost of short-term credit?

15-11. There are three major sources of unsecured short-term credit other than accrued wages and taxes. List and discuss the distinguishing characteristics of each.

15-12. What is meant by the following trade credit terms: 2/10, net 30? 4/20, net 60? 3/15, net 45?

15-13. Define the following:

    a. Line of credit
    b. Commercial paper
    c. Compensating balance
    d. Prime rate

15-14. List and discuss four advantages of the use of commercial paper.

15-15. What risk is involved in the firm's use of commercial paper as a source of short-term credit? Discuss.

15-16. List and discuss the distinguishing features of the principal sources of secured credit based on a firm's accounts receivable.

Self-Test Problems

(Solutions to these problems are found at the end of the chapter.)

ST-1. (*Analyzing the cost of a commercial paper offering*) The Marilyn Sales Company is a wholesale machine tool broker that has gone through a recent expansion of its activities, resulting in the doubling of its sales. The company has determined that it needs an additional $200 million in short-term funds to finance its peak-season sales during roughly 6 months of the year. Marilyn's treasurer has recommended that the firm use a commercial paper offering to raise the needed funds. Specifically, he has determined that a $200 million offering would require 10 percent interest (paid in advance or discounted) plus a $125,000 placement fee. The paper would carry a 6-month (180-day) maturity. What is the effective cost of credit?

ST-2. (*Analyzing the cost of short-term credit*) The treasurer of the Lights-a-Lot Manufacturing Company is faced with three alternative bank loans. The firm wishes to select the one that minimizes its cost of credit on a $200,000 note that it plans to issue in the next 10 days. Relevant information for the three 1-year loan configurations includes:

   a. An 18 percent rate of interest with interest paid at year-end and no compensating-balance requirement.
   b. A 16 percent rate of interest but carrying a 20 percent compensating-balance requirement. This loan also calls for interest to be paid at year-end.
   c. A 14 percent rate of interest that is discounted, plus a 20 percent compensating-balance requirement.

Analyze the cost of each of these alternatives. You can assume the firm would not normally maintain a bank balance that might be used to meet the 20 percent compensating-balance requirements of alternatives b and c.

ST-3. (*Analyzing the cost of a transaction loan*) The Ace Compost Company of Mart, Texas, has been in the business of converting feedlot manure into garden compost since 1984. The firm has approached the First State Bank of Mart about a short-term loan to help finance the firm's seasonal working-capital needs. Ace's management estimates that it will need a total of $100,000 for a period of 6 months during the coming year. The bank agreed to provide the financing under the following terms: Interest of 10 percent per annum will be paid along with the full principal amount of the loan at maturity. Furthermore, the bank has requested that Ace maintain a 15 percent compensating balance with the bank. Ace has kept an average account balance with the bank of $5,000 over the past year and plans to continue to do so. Consequently, Ace is $10,000 short of the mandatory compensating balance so it will have to borrow an additional $10,000 more than its $100,000 loan needed. What is the effective cost of credit for Ace if it accepts the bank's terms?

Study Problems

15-1. (*Estimating the cost of bank credit*) Paymaster Enterprises has arranged to finance its seasonal working-capital needs with a short-term bank loan. The loan will carry a rate of 12 percent per annum with interest paid in advance (discounted). In addition, Paymaster must maintain a minimum demand deposit with the bank of 10 percent of the loan balance throughout the term of the loan. If Paymaster plans to borrow $100,000 for a period of 3 months, what is the cost of the bank loan?

15-2. (*Estimating the cost of commercial paper*) On February 3, 2010, the Burlington Western Company plans a commercial paper issue of $20 million. The firm has never used commercial paper before but has been assured by the firm placing the issue that it will have no difficulty raising the funds. The commercial paper will carry a 270-day maturity and require interest based on a rate of 11 percent per annum. In addition, the firm will have to pay fees totaling $200,000 to bring the issue to market and place it. What is the effective cost of the commercial paper to Burlington Western?

15-3. (*Cost of trade credit*) Calculate the effective cost of the following trade credit terms when payment is made on the net due date.

   a. 2/10, net 30
   b. 3/15, net 30
   c. 3/15, net 45
   d. 2/15, net 60

15-4. (*Effective annual rate*) Compute the cost of the trade credit terms in problem 15-3 using the compounding formula, or effective annual rate.

15-5. (*Cost of short-term financing*) The R. Morin Construction Company needs to borrow $100,000 to help finance the cost of a new $150,000 hydraulic crane used in the firm's commercial construction business. The crane will pay for itself in 1 year, and the firm is considering the following alternatives for financing its purchase:

Alternative A—The firm's bank has agreed to lend the $100,000 at a rate of 14 percent. Interest would be discounted, and a 15 percent compensating balance would be required. However, the compensating-balance requirement would not be binding on R. Morin because the firm normally maintains a minimum demand deposit (checking account) balance of $25,000 in the bank.

Alternative B—The equipment dealer has agreed to finance the equipment with a 1-year loan. The $100,000 loan would require payment of principal and interest totaling $116,300.

a. Which alternative should R. Morin select?

b. If the bank's compensating-balance requirement were to necessitate idle demand deposits equal to 15 percent of the loan, what effect would this have on the cost of the bank loan alternative?

15-6. (*Cost of short-term bank loan*) On July 1, 2010, the Southwest Forging Corporation arranged for a line of credit with the First National Bank of Dallas. The terms of the agreement call for a $100,000 maximum loan with interest set at 1 percent over prime. In addition, the firm has to maintain a 20 percent compensating balance in its demand deposit account throughout the year. The prime rate is currently 12 percent.

a. If Southwest normally maintains a $20,000 to $30,000 balance in its checking account with FNB of Dallas, what is the effective cost of credit under the line-of-credit agreement when the maximum loan amount is used for a full year?

b. Recompute the effective cost of credit if the firm borrows the compensating balance and the maximum possible amount under the loan agreement. Again, assume the full amount of the loan is outstanding for a whole year.

15-7. (*Cost of commercial paper*) Tri-State Enterprises plans to issue commercial paper for the first time in the firm's 35-year history. The firm plans to issue $500,000 in 180-day maturity notes. The paper will carry a 10½ percent rate with discounted interest and will cost Tri-State $12,000 (paid in advance) to issue.

a. What is the effective cost of credit to Tri-State?

b. What other factors should the company consider in analyzing whether to issue the commercial paper?

15-8. (*Cost of accounts receivable*) Johnson Enterprises Inc. is involved in the manufacture and sale of electronic components used in small AM/FM radios. The firm needs $300,000 to finance an anticipated expansion in receivables due to increased sales. Johnson's credit terms are net 60, and its average monthly credit sales are $200,000. In general, the firm's customers pay within the credit period; thus, the firm's average accounts receivable balance is $400,000. Chuck Idol, Johnson's comptroller, approached the firm's bank with a request for a loan for the $300,000 using the firm's accounts receivable as collateral. The bank offered to make a loan at a rate of 2 percent over prime plus a 1 percent processing charge on all receivables pledged ($200,000 per month). Furthermore, the bank agreed to lend up to 75 percent of the face value of the receivables pledged.

a. Estimate the cost of the receivables loan to Johnson when the firm borrows the $300,000. The prime rate is currently 11 percent.

b. Idol also requested a line of credit for $300,000 from the bank. The bank agreed to grant the necessary line of credit at a rate of 3 percent over prime and required a 15 percent compensating balance. Johnson currently maintains an average demand deposit of $80,000. Estimate the cost of the line of credit to Johnson.

c. Which source of credit should Johnson select? Why?

15-9. (*Cost of factoring*) MDM Inc. is considering factoring its receivables. The firm has credit sales of $400,000 per month and has an average receivables balance of $800,000 with 60-day credit terms. The factor has offered to extend credit equal to 90 percent of the receivables factored less interest on the loan at a rate of 1½ percent per month. The 10 percent difference in the advance and the face value of all receivables factored consists of a 1 percent factoring fee plus a 9 percent reserve, which the factor maintains. In addition, if MDM Inc. decides to factor its receivables, it will sell them all, so that it can reduce its credit department costs by $1,500 a month.

a. What is the cost of borrowing the maximum amount of credit available to MDM Inc. through the factoring agreement?

b. What considerations other than cost should be accounted for by MDM Inc. in determining whether to enter the factoring agreement?

15-10. (*Cost of secured short-term credit*) The Sean-Janeow Import Co. needs $500,000 for the 3-month period ending September 30, 2008. The firm has explored two possible sources of credit.

1. S-J has arranged with its bank for a $500,000 loan secured by its accounts receivable. The bank has agreed to advance S-J 80 percent of the value of its pledged receivables at a rate of

11 percent plus a 1 percent fee based on all receivables pledged. S-J's receivables average a total of $1 million year-round.

2. An insurance company has agreed to lend the $500,000 at a rate of 9 percent per annum, using a loan secured by S-J's inventory of salad oil. A field warehouse agreement would be used, which would cost S-J $2,000 a month.

Which source of credit should S-J select? Explain.

15-11. (*Cost of short-term financing*) You plan to borrow $20,000 from the bank to pay for inventories for a gift shop you have just opened. The bank offers to lend you the money at 10 percent annual interest for the 6 months the funds will be needed.

    a. Calculate the effective rate of interest on the loan.

    b. In addition, the bank requires you to maintain a 15 percent compensating balance in the bank. Because you are just opening your business, you do not have a demand deposit account at the bank that can be used to meet the compensating-balance requirement. This means that you will have to put up 15 percent of the loan amount from your own personal money (which you had planned to use to help finance the business) in a checking account. What is the cost of the loan now?

    c. In addition to the compensating-balance requirement in part b, you are told that interest will be discounted. What is the effective rate of interest on the loan now?

15-12. (*Cost of factoring*) A factor has agreed to lend the JVC Corporation working capital on the following terms: JVC's receivables average $100,000 per month and have a 90-day average collection period. (Note that JVC's credit terms call for payment in 90 days, and accounts receivable average $300,000 because of the 90-day average collection period.) The factor will charge 12 percent interest on any advance (1 percent per month paid in advance) and a 2 percent processing fee on all receivables factored and will maintain a 20 percent reserve. If JVC undertakes the loan, it will reduce its own credit department expenses by $2,000 per month. What is the annual effective rate of interest to JVC on the factoring arrangement? Assume that the maximum advance is taken.

15-13. (*Cost of a short-term bank loan*) Jimmy Hale is the owner and operator of the grain elevator in Brownfield, Texas, where he has lived for most of his 62 years. The rains during the spring have been the best in a decade, and Mr. Hale is expecting a bumper wheat crop. This prompted him to rethink his current financing sources. He now believes he will need an additional $240,000 for the 3-month period ending with the close of the harvest season. After meeting with his banker, Mr. Hale is puzzling over what the additional financing will actually cost. The banker quoted him a rate of 1 percent over prime (which is currently 7 percent) and also requested that the firm increase its current bank balance of $4,000 up to 20 percent of the loan.

    a. If interest and principal are all repaid at the end of the 3-month loan term, what is the annual percentage rate on the loan offer made by Mr. Hale's bank?

    b. If the bank were to offer to lower the rate to prime if interest is discounted, should Mr. Hale accept this alternative?

15-14. (*Cash conversion cycle*) Sims Electric Corp. has been striving for the last five years to improve its management of working capital. Historical data for the firm's sales, accounts receivable, inventories, and accounts payable follow:

	JAN-05	JAN-06	JAN-07	JAN-08	JAN-09
Sales—Net	2,873	3,475	5,296	7,759	12,327
Receivables—Total	411	538	726	903	1,486
Accounts Payable	283	447	466	1,040	1,643
Inventories—Total	220	293	429	251	233

    a. Calculate Sims' days of sales outstanding and days of sales in inventory for each of the five years. What has Sims accomplished in its attempts to better manage its investments in accounts receivable and inventory?

    b. Calculate Sims' cash conversion cycle for each of the five years. Evaluate Sims' overall management of its working capital.

Self-Test Solutions

SS-1. The discounted interest cost of the commercial paper issue is calculated as follows:

Interest expense $= 0.10 \times \$200,000,000 \times 180/360 = \$10,000,000$

The effective cost of credit can now be calculated as follows:

$$APR = \frac{\$10,000,000 + \$125,000}{\$200,000,000 - \$125,000 - \$10,000,000} \times \frac{1}{180/360}$$

$$= 0.1066 = 10.66\%$$

SS-2.

a.

$$APR = \frac{0.18 \times \$200,000}{\$200,000} \times \frac{1}{1}$$

$$= 0.18 = 18\%$$

b.

$$APR = \frac{0.16 \times \$200,000}{\$200,000 - (0.20 \times \$200,000)} \times \frac{1}{1}$$

$$= 0.20 = 20\%$$

c.

$$APR = \frac{0.14 \times \$200,000}{\$200,000 - (0.14 \times \$200,000) - (0.20 \times \$200,000)} \times \frac{1}{1}$$

$$= 0.2121 = 21.21\%$$

Alternative "a" offers the lowest-cost service of financing, although it carries the highest stated rate of interest. The reason for this is that there is no compensating-balance requirement, nor is interest discounted for this alternative.

SS-3. Ace needs $100,000 to finance its seasonal inventory needs for a period of 6 months during the coming year. However, the bank requires a minimum compensating balance of 15 percent of the loan, or $15,000. This is $10,000 larger than Ace's average minimum balance over the past year, so the firm will have to borrow $110,000 to get the funds it needs plus cover the minimum balance requirement. The *APR* for the loan can be calculated as follows:

$$APR = \frac{0.10 \times (\$100,000 + \$10,000) \times 0.5}{\$100,000} \times \frac{1}{0.5} = 0.11, \text{ or } 11\%$$

Chapter 16

Current Asset Management

Learning Objectives

After reading this chapter, you should be able to:

 Understand why a firm holds cash.

 Explain various cash management objectives and decisions.

Describe and analyze the different mechanisms for managing the firm's cash collection and disbursement procedures.

Determine a prudent composition for the firm's marketable-securities portfolio.

 Discuss the determinants of the firm's investment in accounts receivable and learn how decisions regarding changes in credit policy are determined.

Discuss the reasons for carrying inventory and how inventory management decisions are made.

At the end of fiscal year 2008, the Walt Disney Company (DIS) held 4.8 percent of its total assets of approximately $62.5 billion in the form of cash and short-term marketable securities. During 2008, Disney generated sales revenues of $37,843 billion. Based on a 365-day year, this means Disney "produced" $103,679,452 in sales revenues each day. If Disney could have freed up only 1 day's worth of sales and invested it in 3-month U.S. Treasury bills yielding 2.21 percent, the firm's before-tax profits would have jumped by $2,291,316. That is a significant sum, and it demonstrates why firms like to have efficient treasury management departments in place. Shareholders enjoy the added profits that should, in turn, increase the market value of their common stock holdings.

Now, if Disney's managers felt it could bear just a tad more risk, then the freed-up cash might be invested in bank certificates of deposit (CDs) of a similar maturity yielding 2.39 percent to investors. That difference of a mere 18 basis points (2.39% − 2.21%) may not seem like much, but when you put it to work on an investment of over $103 million, it produces a tidy income. Thus, by investing the excess cash in CDs rather than in Treasury bills, Disney's before-tax profits would be $186,622 greater ($2,477,938 − $2,291,316). This might be enough for the firm to hire a new business school graduate or two—just like you.

Managing the cash and the marketable-securities portfolio are important tasks for the financial executive. This chapter teaches you about sophisticated cash management systems and about prudent places to "park" the firm's excess cash balances so they earn a positive rate of return and are liquid at the same time. We also explore sound management techniques that relate to the other asset components of the firm's working capital—accounts receivable and inventory.

436

Chapter 15 provided an introduction and overview of the concept of working-capital management. In this chapter, we explore the management of the asset components of the working-capital equation. Accordingly, we focus on the alternatives available to managers for increasing shareholder wealth with respect to the most important types of current assets: (1) cash, (2) marketable securities, (3) accounts receivable, and (4) inventory. These are listed in order of declining liquidity.

Such alternatives include (1) techniques available to management for favorably influencing cash receipt and disbursement patterns, (2) investments that allow a firm to employ excess cash balances productively, (3) critical decision formulas for determining the appropriate amount of investment in accounts receivable, and (4) methods, such as those pertaining to order quantity and order point issues, for evaluating the most suitable levels of inventory.

These issues are important to the financial manager for several reasons. For example, judicious management of cash and near-cash assets allows the firm to hold the minimum amount of cash necessary to meet the firm's obligations in a timely manner. As a result, the firm is able to take advantage of the opportunity to earn a return on its liquid assets and increase its profitability.

With this in mind, we begin the study of current asset management by exploring the various aspects of the management of cash and marketable securities. Afterward, we analyze the important issues related to the management of accounts receivable and inventory.

Before proceeding to our discussion of cash management, it will be helpful to distinguish among several terms. **Cash** is the *currency and coin the firm has on hand in petty cash drawers, in cash registers, or in checking accounts (demand deposit accounts) at various commercial banks*. **Marketable securities**, also called near cash or near-cash assets, are *security investments that the firm can quickly convert into cash balances*. Generally, firms hold marketable securities with very short maturity periods—less than 1 year. Together, cash and marketable securities constitute the most liquid assets of a firm.

cash currency and coins plus demand deposit accounts.

marketable securities security investments (financial assets) the firm can quickly convert to cash balances. Also known as near cash or near-cash assets.

Why a Company Holds Cash

 Understand why a firm holds cash.

A thorough understanding of why and how a firm holds cash requires an accurate look at how cash flows into and through the enterprise. Figure 16-1 depicts the process of cash generation and disposition in a typical manufacturing setting. The arrows designate the direction of the flow—that is, whether the cash balance increases or decreases.

The Cash Flow Process

The irregular increases in the firm's cash holdings can come from several external sources. Funds can be obtained in the financial markets from the sale of securities such as bonds, preferred stock, and common stock, or the firm can enter into nonmarketable-debt contracts with lenders such as commercial banks. These irregular cash inflows do not occur on a daily basis. The reason is that external financing contracts, or arrangements, usually involve huge sums of money stemming from a major need identified by the company's management, and these needs do not occur every day. For example, a new product might be in the launching process, or a plant expansion might be required to provide added productive capacity.

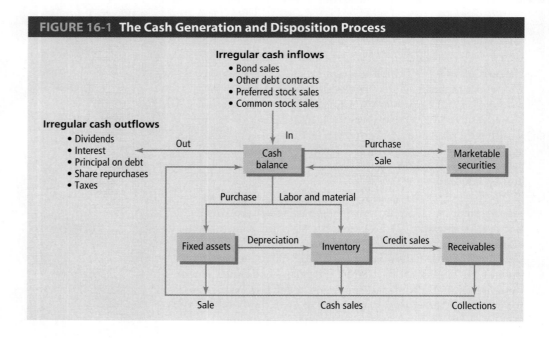

FIGURE 16-1 The Cash Generation and Disposition Process

In most organizations the financial officer responsible for cash management also controls the transactions that affect the firm's investment in marketable securities. As excess cash becomes temporarily available, marketable securities are purchased. By contrast, when cash is in short supply, a portion of the marketable-securities portfolio is liquidated.

Whereas the irregular cash inflows are from external sources, the other main sources of cash arise from internal operations and occur on a more regular basis. Over long periods, the largest receipts come from accounts-receivable collections and, to a lesser extent, from direct cash sales of finished goods. Many manufacturing concerns also generate cash on a regular basis through the liquidation of scrap or obsolete inventory. At various times fixed assets may also be sold, thereby generating some cash inflow.

Apart from the investment of excess cash in near-cash assets, the cash balance experiences reductions for three key reasons. First, on an irregular basis, withdrawals are made to (1) pay cash dividends on preferred and common stock shares, (2) meet interest requirements on debt contracts, (3) repay the principal borrowed from creditors, (4) buy the firm's own shares in the financial markets for use in executive compensation plans or as an alternative to paying a cash dividend, and (5) pay tax bills. Again, by an *irregular basis*, we mean items *not* occurring on a daily or frequent schedule. Second, the company's capital expenditure program designates that fixed assets be acquired at various intervals. Third, inventories are purchased on a regular basis to ensure a steady flow of finished goods rolls off the production line. Note that the arrow linking the investment in fixed assets with the inventory account is labeled *depreciation*. This indicates that a portion of the cost of fixed assets is charged against the products coming off the assembly line. This cost is subsequently recovered through the sale of the finished-goods inventory. This is because the product's selling price will be set by managers to cover all of the costs of production, including depreciation.

Motives for Holding Cash

The influences that affect the firm's cash balance can be classified in terms of the three motives put forth by economist John Maynard Keynes: (1) the transactions motive, (2) the precautionary motive, and (3) the speculative motive.[1]

---

[1]John Maynard Keynes, *The General Theory of Employment, Interest, and Money* (New York: Harcourt Brace Jovanovich, 1936).

The Transactions Motive   Balances held for transaction purposes allow the firm to meet its cash needs that arise in the ordinary course of doing business. In Figure 16-1, cash would be used to meet the irregular outflows as well as the planned acquisition of fixed assets and inventories. The relative amount of cash needed to satisfy transaction requirements is affected by a number of factors, including the industry in which the firm operates. It is well known that utilities can forecast cash receipts quite accurately because of stable demand for their services. Computer software firms, however, have a more difficult time predicting their cash flows. In this industry, new products are brought to market at a rapid pace, thereby making it difficult to project cash flows and balances precisely.

The Precautionary Motive   Precautionary balances serve as a buffer. This motive for holding cash relates to the maintenance of balances used to satisfy possible, but as yet unknown, needs.

The cash flow predictability of the firm has a material influence on this precautionary motive. The airline industry provides a typical illustration. Air passenger carriers are plagued with a high degree of cash flow uncertainty. The weather, rising fuel costs, and continual strikes by operating personnel make cash forecasting difficult for any airline. The upshot of this problem is that because of all of the things that *might* happen, the minimum cash balances desired by air carriers tend to be large.

In actual business practice, the precautionary motive is met to a large extent by the holding of a portfolio of *liquid assets*, not just cash. Notice in Figure 16-1 the two-way flow of funds between the company's holdings of cash and marketable securities. In large corporate organizations, funds may flow either into or out of the marketable-securities portfolio on a daily basis.

The Speculative Motive   Cash is held for speculative purposes in order to take advantage of potential profit-making situations. Construction firms that build private dwellings will, at times, accumulate cash in anticipation of a significant drop in lumber costs. If the price of building supplies does drop, the companies that built up their cash balances stand to profit by purchasing materials in large quantities. This will reduce their cost of goods sold and increase their net profit margins. Generally, the speculative motive is the least important component of a firm's preference for liquidity. The transactions and precautionary motives account for most of the reasons why a company holds cash balances.

Concept Check

1. Describe the typical cash flow cycle for a firm.
2. What are the three motives for holding cash?

Cash Management Objectives and Decisions

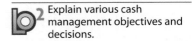 Explain various cash management objectives and decisions.

The Risk–Return Trade-Off

A company-wide cash management program must be concerned with minimizing the firm's risk of insolvency. In the context of cash management, the term **insolvency** describes the *situation in which the firm is unable to meet its maturing liabilities on time*. In such a case the company is *technically insolvent* in that it lacks the necessary liquidity to make prompt payment on its current debt obligations. A firm could avoid this problem by carrying large cash balances to pay the bills that come due.

insolvency the inability to meet interest payments or to repay debt at maturity.

The financial manager must strike an acceptable balance between holding too much cash and too little cash. This is the focal point of the risk–return trade-off. A large cash investment minimizes the chances of insolvency, but it penalizes the company's profitability. A small cash investment frees up excess balances for investment in both marketable securities and longer-lived assets; this enhances profitability and the value of the firm's common shares, but it also increases the chances of the firm running out of cash.

Objectives

The risk–return trade-off can be reduced to two prime objectives for the firm's cash management system.

1. Enough cash must be on hand to meet the disbursal needs that arise in the course of doing business.
2. Investment in idle cash balances must be reduced to a minimum.

Evaluating these objectives and meeting them gives rise to the need for some typical cash management decisions.

Decisions

Two conditions or ideals would allow the firm to operate for extended periods with cash balances near or at zero: (1) a completely accurate forecast of its net cash flows over the planning horizon and (2) perfect synchronization of its cash receipts and disbursements.

Cash flow forecasting is the initial step in any effective cash management program. Given that the firm will, as a matter of necessity, invest in some cash balances, certain types of decisions related to the size of those balances dominate the cash management process. These include decisions that answer the following questions:

1. What can be done to speed up cash collections and slow down or better control cash outflows?
2. What should be the composition of the firm's marketable-securities portfolio?

Concept Check

1. Describe the relationship between the firm's cash management program and the firm's risk of insolvency.
2. What are the fundamental decisions that the financial manager must make with respect to cash management?

3 Describe and analyze the different mechanisms for managing the firm's cash collection and disbursement procedures.

Collection and Disbursement Procedures

The efficiency of the firm's cash management program can be improved by (1) accelerating cash receipts and (2) improving the methods used to disburse cash. In simple terms the firm improves its cash management system by speeding up collections and slowing down disbursements.

Managing the Cash Inflow—Speeding Up Collections

Figure 16-2 illustrates the cash collection system for a firm that does not utilize any advanced methods to enhance the speed of its collections. Note that there are three key events that delay the time it takes the firm to actually get the customer's money. These delays are referred to as **float**.

float the length of time from when a check is written until the actual recipient can draw upon the funds.

◆ First, the customer sends the payment to the firm through the mail. The time required to receive the check is called *mail float*.
◆ Second, the firm processes the check internally to record the account to which the payment belongs and then sends the check on to the firm's bank to begin the process of transferring funds from the customer to the company. The time required to process the check by the company is called *processing float*.
◆ Finally, the company's bank sends the check through the check-clearing system used by banks to actually transfer funds from the customer's account to the firm's account. The time required to accomplish this is referred to as *transit float*.

Speeding up the firm's collection process simply involves reducing the float that enters into the collection process in each of these three ways. The "lockbox" arrangement described

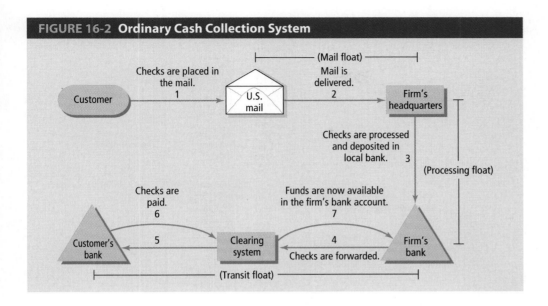

FIGURE 16-2 **Ordinary Cash Collection System**

shortly is probably the most widely used tool for speeding up the collection process and thereby reducing the float.

EXAMPLE 16.1

The positive operating-profit effects that stem from a float reduction can be dramatic when large total revenues are involved. Suppose that we want to estimate the value of a 1-day float reduction for Starbucks Corporation. Starbucks' 2008 sales revenues were reported at $10.383 billion. Let's assume that prudent investment in money-market securities will earn 4 percent annually. We ask, What is the estimated value of a 1-day float reduction to Starbucks? We can calculate this as follows:

$$\frac{\text{Annual revenues}}{\text{days in year}} = 1\text{-day float reduction}$$

which for Starbucks in 2008 was

$$\frac{\$10.383 \text{ billion}}{365} = \$28,446,575$$

Thus, 1 day's freed-up balances for Starbucks will be $28,446,575. Then we find the annual (before-tax) value of the float reduction is

(Sales per day) × (assumed yield) = $28,446,575 × 0.04 = $1,137,863

Profits like these make it worthwhile for the firm and its treasury manager to closely evaluate the cash management services offered by commercial banks—even when the bank fees can also be quite costly. We learn how to make decisions of this nature later in the chapter.

The Lockbox Arrangement

The lockbox system is the most widely used commercial banking service for expediting cash gathering. Banks have offered this service since 1946. Such a system speeds up the conversion of receipts into usable funds by reducing both the mail and processing float of payments. In addition, it is possible to reduce transit float if lockboxes are located near

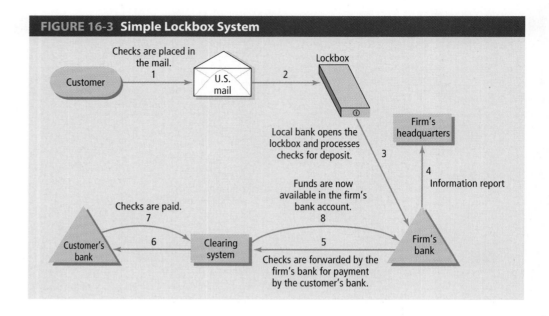

FIGURE 16-3 Simple Lockbox System

Federal Reserve Banks and their branches. For large corporations that receive checks from all parts of the country, float reductions of 2 to 4 days are not unusual.

The lockbox arrangement in Figure 16-3 is based on a simple procedure. The firm's customers are instructed to mail their remittance checks not to company headquarters or regional offices, but to a numbered post office box. The bank that is providing the lockbox service is authorized to open the box, collect the mail, process the checks, and deposit the checks directly into the company's account.

In the introduction to this chapter we calculated the 2008 sales per day for Disney to be in excess of $103 million and assumed the firm could invest its excess cash in marketable securities to yield 2.21 percent annually. If Disney could speed up its cash collections by 4 days, it would be to the firm's advantage. Specifically, the gross annual savings to Disney (apart from operating the lockbox system) would amount to $9.165 million as follows:

$$\begin{array}{ccccc} \text{(Sales per day)} \times & \text{(days of float reduction)} \times & \text{(assumed yield)} & = & \text{gross annual savings} \\ (\$103,679,452) \times & (4) & \times \quad (0.0221) & = & \$9,165,264 \end{array}$$

As you might guess, the prospects for generating revenues of this magnitude are important not only to the firms involved but also to commercial banks that offer lockbox services.

Lockbox services are not free, however. Usually, the bank levies a charge for each check processed through the system. The benefits derived from the acceleration of receipts must exceed the incremental costs of the lockbox system or the firm would be better off without it. Later in this chapter, a straightforward method for assessing the desirability of a specific cash management service, such as the lockbox arrangement, is illustrated.

Managing the Cash Outflow—Slowing Down Disbursements

The objective of managing cash outflows is to increase the company's float by slowing down the disbursement process. This is exactly the opposite of our objective of managing cash collections. There are several tools at the disposal of the cash manager for accomplishing this end, and we describe two here. These are the use of (1) zero balance accounts and (2) payable-through drafts. (See Table 16-1.)

Zero Balance Accounts   Large corporations that operate multiple branches, divisions, or subsidiaries often maintain numerous bank accounts (in different banks) for the pur-

TABLE 16-1 Selected Cash Disbursal Techniques: A Summary

Technique	Objectives	How Accomplished
Zero balance accounts	(1) Achieve better control over cash payments, (2) reduce excess cash balances held in regional banks, and possibly (3) increase disbursing float.	Establish zero balance accounts for all of the firm's disbursing units. These accounts are all in the same concentration bank. Checks are drawn against these accounts, with the balance in each account never exceeding $0. Divisional disbursing authority is thereby maintained at the local level of management.
Payable-through drafts	Achieve effective central-office control over field-authorized payments.	Field office issues drafts rather than checks to settle up payables.

pose of making timely operating disbursements. It does make good business sense for payments for purchased parts that go into, say, an automobile transmission to be made by the Transmission and Chassis Division of the auto manufacturer rather than its central office.

Zero balance accounts (ZBA) *permit centralized control (at the headquarters level) over the firm's cash outflows while maintaining divisional disbursing authority.* Under this system the firm's authorized employees, representing their various divisions, continue to write checks on their individual accounts. Note that the numerous individual disbursing accounts are now *all* located in the same "concentration" bank. Actually these separate accounts contain no funds at all, thus the label, "zero balance."

The firm's authorized agents write their payment checks as usual against their specific accounts. These checks clear through the banking system in the usual way. On a daily basis the checks are presented to the firm's concentration bank (the drawee bank) for payment. As the checks are paid by the bank, negative (debit) balances build up in the proper disbursing accounts. At the end of each day the negative balances are restored to a zero level by means of credits to the ZBAs; a corresponding reduction of funds is then made against the firm's concentration (master) demand deposit account.

Payable-Through Drafts   **Payable-through drafts (PTD)** *are legal instruments that have the physical appearance of ordinary checks but are not drawn on a bank. Instead, payable-through drafts are drawn on and payment is authorized by the issuing firm against its demand deposit account.*

Like checks, the drafts are cleared through the banking system and are presented to the issuing firm's bank. The bank serves as a collection point and passes the drafts on to the firm. The corporate issuer usually has to return by the following business day all drafts it does not wish to cover (pay). Those documents not returned to the bank are automatically paid. The firm inspects the drafts for validity by checking signatures, amounts, and dates. Stop-payment orders can be initiated by the company on any drafts considered inappropriate.

The main purpose of using a payable-through draft system is *to provide for effective control over field payments.* The firm's central office can control payments begun by the regional units because the drafts are reviewed in advance of their final payment. Payable-through drafts, for example, are used extensively in the insurance industry. The claims agent does not typically have check-signing authority against a corporate disbursement account. This agent can issue a draft, however, for quick settlement of a claim.

zero balance accounts (ZBA) a cash management tool that permits centralized control over cash outflow while maintaining divisional disbursing authority. Objectives are (1) to achieve better control over cash payments; (2) to reduce excess cash balances held in regional banks for disbursing purposes; and (3) to increase disbursing float.

payable-through draft (PTD) a legal instrument that has the physical appearance of an ordinary check but is not drawn on a bank. A payable-through draft is drawn on and paid by the issuing firm. The bank serves as a collection point and passes the draft on to the firm.

Concept Check

1. Define *float* and its origins in the cash management process (i.e. mail processing and transit).

2. What is a lockbox arrangement and how does its use reduce a firm's float?

3. Describe the following methods for managing cash outflow: zero balance accounts and payable-through drafts.

Evaluating the Costs of Cash Management Services

A form of break-even analysis can help the financial officer decide whether a particular collection or disbursement service will provide an economic benefit to the firm. The evaluation process involves a very basic relationship in microeconomics:

$$\text{Added costs} = \text{added benefits} \tag{16-1}$$

If equation (16-1) holds exactly, then the firm is no better or worse off for having adopted the given service. We will illustrate this procedure in terms of the desirability of installing an additional lockbox. Equation (16-1) can be restated on a per unit basis as follows:

$$P = (D)(S)(i) \tag{16-2}$$

where P = increases in per check processing cost if the new system is adopted
D = days saved in the collection process (float reduction)
S = average check size in dollars
i = the daily, before-tax opportunity cost (rate of return) of carrying cash

Assume that check processing cost P will rise by $0.18 per check if the lockbox is used. The firm has determined that the average check size, S, that will be mailed to the lockbox location will be $900. If funds are freed up by use of the lockbox, they will be invested in marketable securities yielding an *annual* before-tax return of 6 percent. With these data, it is possible to determine the reduction in check collection time D required to justify the use of the lockbox. That level of D is found to be

$$\$0.18 = (D)(\$900)\left(\frac{0.06}{365}\right)$$

$$1.217 \text{ days} = D$$

Thus, the lockbox is justified if the firm can speed up its collections by *more* than 1.217 days. This same style of analysis can be adapted to analyze the other tools of cash management.

CAN YOU DO IT?

EVALUATING THE COST OF CASH MANAGEMENT SERVICES

Hamilton Inc. is considering the use of a lockbox system for the first time. If the system is adopted, it will increase the firm's check processing cost by $0.20 per check processed. The firm estimates that the average check size sent to the firm is $1,000. Moreover, the firm estimates that it can earn only 1.5% on funds freed up by the lockbox program as a result of the current recession and the willingness of investors to hold short-term risk-free securities that earn very low rates of return. How many days does Hamilton have to save by using the lockbox program to compensate them for the additional $0.20 per check cost of implementing the system?

   (The solution can be found on p. 445.)

Concept Check

1. Describe the use of the break-even concept with respect to the management of cash.
2. How would you estimate the financial benefits of using a lockbox system?

LO 4 Determine a prudent composition for the firm's marketable-securities portfolio.

The Composition of a Marketable-Securities Portfolio

Earlier we described two fundamental decision problems related to cash management. The first related to managing the firm's cash collections and disbursements procedures. The second involved managing the firm's portfolio of marketable securities, which serve as an important source of liquidity for the firm.

DID YOU GET IT?
EVALUATING THE COST OF CASH MANAGEMENT SERVICES

Equation 16-2 defines the per check cost of operating a lockbox system as follows:

$$P = D \times S \times i/365$$

where P = the increase in the per check processing cost under the lockbox system

D = the days saved in the collection process by the initiation of the lockbox system (i.e., the reduction in float)

S = the average check size

i = the before-tax opportunity cost of holding cash such that $i/365$ is the daily opportunity cost

We know that P is $0.20 per check, so we can solve for the days saved in the check collection process needed to justify the system as follows:

$$P = D \times S \times \frac{i}{365}$$
$$\$0.20 = D \times \$1,000 \times 0.015/365$$

Solving for D we get

$$\$0.20 = D \times \$1,000 \times 0.015/365$$

$$D = \frac{\$0.20}{\$1,000 \times 0.015/365} = \frac{\$0.20}{\$1,000 \times 0.015/365} = 4.86 \text{ days}$$

General Selection Criteria

Certain criteria can provide a financial manager with a useful framework for selecting a proper marketable-securities mix. These considerations include evaluating the (1) financial risk, (2) interest rate risk, (3) liquidity, (4) taxability, and (5) yields among different financial assets. The following sections briefly delineate these criteria from the investor's viewpoint.

Financial Risk *Financial risk* here refers to the uncertainty of expected returns from a security attributable to possible changes in the financial capacity of the security issuer to make future payments to the security owner. If the chance of default on the terms of the instrument is high (or low), then the financial risk is said to be high (or low).

Interest Rate Risk *Interest rate risk*, of course, refers to the uncertainty of expected returns from a financial instrument attributable to changes in interest rates. Of particular concern to the corporate treasurer is the price volatility associated with instruments that have long, as opposed to short, terms to maturity. An illustration can help clarify this point.

Suppose the financial officer is weighing the merits of investing temporarily available corporate cash in a new offering of U.S. Treasury obligations that will mature in either 3 years or 20 years from the date of issue. The purchase prices of the 3-year notes or 20-year bonds are at their par values of $1,000 per security. The maturity value of either class of security is equal to par, $1,000, and the coupon rate (stated interest rate) is set at 7 percent, compounded annually.

If after 1 year from the date of purchase prevailing interest rates rise to 9 percent, the market prices of these currently outstanding Treasury securities will fall to bring their yields to maturity in line with what investors could obtain by buying a new issue of a given instrument. The market prices of *both* the 3-year and 20-year obligations will therefore decline. The price of the 20-year instrument will decline by a greater dollar amount, however, than that of the 3-year instrument.

TABLE 16-2 Market Price Effect of Rise in Interest Rates		
Item	Three-Year Instrument	Twenty-Year Instrument
Original price	$1,000.00	$1,000.00
Price after 1 year	964.82	821.10
Decline in price	$ 35.18	$ 178.90

One year from the date of issue, the price obtainable in the marketplace for the original 20-year instrument, which now has 19 years to go to maturity, can be found by computing P as follows:

$$P = \sum_{t=1}^{19} \frac{\$70}{(1 + 0.09)^t} + \frac{\$1,000}{(1 + 0.09)^{19}} = \$821.10$$

where t is the year in which the particular return, either interest or principal amount, is received; $70 is the annual interest payment; and $1,000 is the contractual maturity value of the bond. The rise in interest rates has forced the market price of the bond down to $821.01.

What will happen to the price of the note that has 2 years remaining to maturity? In a similar manner, we can compute its price, P:

$$P = \sum_{t=1}^{2} \frac{\$70}{(1 + 0.09)^t} + \frac{\$1,000}{(1 + 0.09)^2} = \$964.82$$

The market price of the shorter-term note will decline to $964.84. Table 16-2 shows that the market value of the shorter-term security was penalized much less by the given rise in the general level of interest rates.

If we extended the illustration, we would see that, in terms of market price, a 1-year security would be affected less than a 2-year security, a 91-day security less than a 182-day security, and so on. Equity securities would exhibit the largest price changes because of their infinite maturity periods. To hedge against the price volatility caused by interest rate risk, the firm's marketable-securities portfolio will tend to be composed of instruments that mature over short periods.

Liquidity   In the present context of managing the marketable-securities portfolio, *liquidity* refers to the ability to transform a security into cash. Should an unforeseen event require that a significant amount of cash be immediately available, then a sizable portion of the portfolio might have to be sold. The financial manager will want the cash quickly and will not want to accept a large price concession in order to convert the securities. Thus, when choosing the securities for the firm's portfolio, the manager must consider (1) the period needed to sell the security and (2) the likelihood that the security can be sold at or near its prevailing market price.

Taxability   The tax treatment of the income a firm receives from its security investments does not affect the ultimate mix of the marketable-securities portfolio as much as the criteria mentioned earlier. This is because the interest income from most instruments suitable for inclusion in the portfolio is taxable at the federal level. Still, some corporate treasurers seriously evaluate the taxability of interest income and capital gains.

The interest income from only one class of securities escapes the federal income tax. That class of securities is generally referred to as *municipal obligations*, or more simply as *municipals*. Because of the tax-exempt feature of interest income from state and local government securities, municipals sell at lower yields to maturity in the market than securities that pay taxable interest. The after-tax yield on a municipal obligation, however, could be higher than the yield from a non-tax-exempt security. This would depend mainly on the purchasing firm's tax situation.

TABLE 16-3 Comparing After-Tax Yields

	Tax-Exempt Debt Issue (6% Coupon)	Taxable Debt Issue (8% Coupon)
Interest income	$ 60.00	$ 80.00
Income tax (0.34)	0.00	27.20
After-tax interest income	$ 60.00	$ 52.80
After-tax yield	$ 60.00 = 6%	$ 52.80 = 5.28%
	$1,000.00	$1,000.00

Derivation of the equivalent before-tax yield on a taxable debt issue:

$$r = \frac{r^*}{1 - T} = \frac{0.06}{1 - 0.34} = 9.091\%$$

where r = the equivalent before-tax yield
r^* = the after-tax yield on the tax-exempt security
T = the firm's marginal income tax rate

Proof: Interest income ($1,000 × 0.09091)		$ 90.91
Income tax (0.34)		$ 30.91
After-tax interest income		$ 60.00

Consider Table 16-3. A firm is assumed to be analyzing whether to invest in a 1-year tax-free debt issue yielding 6 percent on a $1,000 outlay or a 1-year taxable issue that yields 8 percent on a $1,000 outlay. The firm pays federal taxes at the rate of 34 percent. The yields quoted in the financial press and in the prospectuses that describe debt issues are *before-tax* returns. The actual *after-tax* return enjoyed by the investor depends on his or her tax bracket. Notice that the actual after-tax yield received by the firm is only 5.28 percent on the taxable issue versus 6 percent on the tax-exempt obligation. The lower portion of Table 16-3 shows that the fully taxed bond must yield 9.091 percent to make it comparable with the tax-exempt issue.

Yields　The final selection criterion that we mention is a significant one—the yields that are available on the different financial assets suitable for inclusion in the near-cash portfolio. By now it is probably obvious that the factors of (1) financial risk, (2) interest rate risk, (3) liquidity, and (4) taxability all influence the available yields on financial instruments. The yield criterion involves an evaluation of the risks and benefits inherent in all of these factors. For example, if a given risk is assumed, such as lack of liquidity, a higher yield will be expected on the nonliquid instrument.

Figure 16-4 summarizes our framework for designing the firm's marketable-securities portfolio. The four basic considerations are shown to influence the yields available on securities. The financial manager must focus on the risk–return trade-offs. Coming to grips with these trade-offs will enable the financial manager to determine the proper marketable-securities mix for the company. Let us look now at the marketable securities prominent in firms' near-cash portfolios.

FIGURE 16-4 Designing the Marketable-Securities Portfolio

Considerations →	Influence →	Focus upon →	Determine
Financial risk Interest rate risk Liquidity Taxability	Yields	Risk vs. return preferences	Marketable-securities mix

TABLE 16-4 Features of Selected Money-Market Instruments

Instruments	Denominations	Maturities	Basis	Liquidity	Taxability
U.S. Treasury bills—direct obligations of the U.S. government	$1,000 and increments of $1,000	91 days, 182 days, and 4 weeks	Discount	Excellent secondary market	Exempt from state and local income taxes
Federal agency securities—obligations of corporations and agencies created to effect the federal government's lending programs	Wide variation; from $1,000 to $1 million	5 days (Farm Credit consolidated discount notes) to more than 10 years	Discount or coupon; usually on coupon	Good for issues of "big five" agencies	Generally exempt at local level; FNMA issues are not exempt
Bankers' acceptance—drafts accepted for future payment by commercial banks	No set size; typically range from $25,000 to $1 million	Predominantly from 30 to 180 days	Discount	Good for acceptances of large "money-market" banks	Taxed at all levels of government
Negotiable certificates of deposit—marketable receipts for funds deposited in a bank for a fixed time period	$25,000 to $10 million	1 to 18 months	Accrued interest	Fair to good	Taxed at all levels of government
Commercial paper—short-term unsecured promissory notes	$5,000 to $5 million; $1,000 and $5,000 multiples above the initial offering size are sometimes available.	3 to 270 days	Discount	Poor; no active secondary market in usual sense	Taxed at all levels of government
Repurchase agreements—legal contracts between a borrower (security seller) and lender (security buyer). The borrower will repurchase at the contract price plus an interest charge.	Typical sizes are $500,000 or more.	According to terms of contract	Not applicable	Fixed by the agreement; that is, borrower will repurchase	Taxed at all levels of government
Money-market mutual funds—holders of diversified portfolios of short-term, high-grade debt instruments	Some require an initial investment as small as $1,000.	Shares can be sold at any time.	Net asset value	Good; provided by the fund itself	Taxed at all levels of government

Marketable-Security Alternatives

Money-market securities generally have short-term maturity and are highly marketable. Consequently, they can be quickly liquidated if the firm needs the cash. Table 16-4 summarizes the characteristics of the most widely used money-market securities in terms of five key attributes: (1) the denominations in which securities are available; (2) the maturities that are offered; (3) the basis used (for example, whether the security is sold at a discount or offers coupon interest payments); (4) the liquidity of the instrument, which relates principally to the availability of a secondary market for the security; and (5) taxability of the investment returns.

What type of return can the financial manager expect on a marketable-securities portfolio? This is a reasonable question. Some insight can be obtained by looking at the past, although we must realize that future returns are not guided by past experience. It is also

TABLE 16-5 Annual Yields (Percent) on Selected Three-Month Marketable Securities			
Year	T-Bills	Commercial Paper	CDs
1980	11.51%	12.66%	13.07%
1985	7.48%	7.95%	8.05%
1990	7.51%	8.06%	8.15%
1995	5.51%	5.93%	5.92%
1996	5.01%	5.42%	5.39%
1997	5.06%	5.60%	5.62%
1998	4.78%	5.37%	5.47%
1999	4.64%	5.22%	5.33%
2000	5.82%	6.33%	6.46%
2001	3.40%	3.65%	3.71%
2002	1.61%	1.69%	1.73%
2003	1.01%	1.11%	1.15%
2004	1.03%	1.41%	1.57%
2005	3.15%	3.42%	3.51%
2006	4.73%	5.10%	5.16%
2007	4.36%	4.92%	5.23%
2008 (September)	0.84%	2.17%	4.14%

Source: *Federal Reserve Statistical Release* G.13 (415), various issues, and *Statistical Supplement to the Federal Reserve Bulletin*, November 2008.

useful to have some understanding of how the returns on one type of instrument stack up against another. The behavior of yields on short-term debt instruments over the 1980 to 2008 period is shown in Table 16-5.

Concept Check

1. What are financial risk and interest rate risk?
2. What is meant by the yield structure of marketable securities?

Accounts-Receivable Management

Discuss the determinants of the firm's investment in accounts receivable and learn how decisions regarding changes in credit policy are determined.

We now turn from the most liquid of the firm's current assets (cash and marketable securities) to those that are less liquid—accounts receivable and inventories. All firms by their very nature are involved in selling either goods or services. Although some of these sales will be for cash, a large portion will involve credit. Whenever a sale is made on credit, it increases the firm's accounts receivable. Thus, the importance of how a firm manages its accounts receivable depends on the degree to which the firm sells on credit.

Accounts receivable typically comprise more than 25 percent of a firm's assets. In effect, when we discuss the management of accounts receivable, we are discussing the management of one-quarter of the firm's assets. Moreover, because the cash flows from a sale cannot be invested until the account is collected, the control of receivables takes on added importance in that it affects both the profitability and liquidity of the firm.

The size of the investment in accounts receivable is determined by several factors. First, the percentage of the firm's credit sales to total sales affects the level of accounts receivable held. Although this factor certainly plays a major role in determining a firm's investment in accounts receivable, it generally is not within the control of the financial manager. The nature of the business tends to determine the blend between credit sales and cash sales. A large grocery store tends to sell exclusively on a cash basis, whereas most construction-lumber supply firms make their sales primarily on credit.

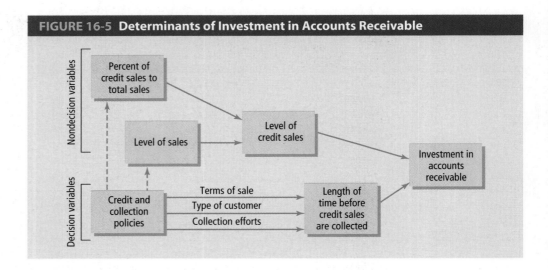

FIGURE 16-5 Determinants of Investment in Accounts Receivable

The level of sales is also a factor in determining the size of the investment in accounts receivable. Very simply, the more sales, the greater the accounts receivable. It is not a decision variable for the financial manager, however.

The final determinants of the level of investment in accounts receivable are the firm's credit and collection policies—more specifically, the terms of sale, the quality of the customer, and the collection efforts. These policies *are* under the control of the financial manager. The terms of sale specify both the time period during which the customer must pay and the terms, such as penalties for late payments or discounts for early payments. The type of credit customer also affects the level of investment in accounts receivable. For example, the acceptance of poorer-credit-risk customers and their subsequent delinquent payments may lead to an increase in accounts receivable. The strength and timing of the collection efforts can affect the period for which past-due accounts remain delinquent, which in turn affects the level of accounts receivable. Collection and credit policy decisions can further affect the level of investment in accounts receivable by causing changes in the sales level and the ratio of credit sales to total sales. The factors that determine the level of investment in accounts receivable are displayed in Figure 16-5.

The Terms of Sale—A Decision Variable

Using the annual percentage rate (*APR*), in Chapter 15 we analyzed the approximate cost of short-term credit from the perspective of the firm that pays for the credit. Likewise we can utilize the *APR* to solve for the rate of return realized on the credit offered by the firm to its own customers.

terms of sale the credit terms identifying the possible discount for early payment.

The **terms of sale** *identify the possible discount for early payment, the discount period, and the total credit period.* They are generally stated in the form *a/b*, net *c*, indicating that the customer can deduct *a* percent if the account is paid within *b* days; otherwise, the account must be paid within *c* days. Thus, for example, trade credit terms of 2/10, net 30, indicate that a 2 percent discount can be taken if the account is paid within 10 days; otherwise it must be paid within 30 days. Failing to take the discount represents a cost to the customer. For instance, if the terms are 2/10, net 30, the annualized opportunity cost of passing up this 2 percent discount in order to withhold payment for an additional 20 days is 36.73 percent. This is determined as follows:

$$\text{Annualized opportunity cost of forgoing the discount} = \frac{a}{1-a} \times \frac{360}{c-b} \qquad (16\text{-}3)$$

Substituting the values from the example, we get

$$36.73\% = \frac{0.02}{1-0.02} \times \frac{360}{30-10}$$

Typically the discount ranges anywhere from $\frac{1}{2}$ to 10 percent, whereas the discount period is generally 10 days and the total credit period varies from 30 to 90 days. Although the terms of credit vary radically from industry to industry, they tend to remain relatively uniform within any particular industry. Moreover, the terms tend to remain relatively constant over time, and they do not appear to be used frequently as a decision variable.

The Type of Customer—A Decision Variable

A second decision variable involves determining the *type of customer* who qualifies for trade credit. Several costs are always associated with extending credit to less-creditworthy customers. First, it is important that the firm be able to identify which of its customers is a poor risk. However, when more time is spent investigating the less-creditworthy customer, the costs of credit investigation increase.

Default costs also vary directly with the quality of the customer. As the customer's credit rating declines, the chance that the account will not be paid on time increases. In the extreme case, payment never occurs. Thus, taking on less-creditworthy customers results in increases in default costs.

Collection costs also increase as the quality of the customer declines. More delinquent accounts force the firm to spend more time and money collecting them. Overall, the decline in customer quality results in increased costs of credit investigation, collection, and default.

In determining whether to grant credit to an individual customer, we are primarily interested in the customer's short-run financial well-being. Thus, its liquidity ratios, other obligations, and overall profitability are the focal point in this analysis. Credit-rating services, such as Dun & Bradstreet, provide information on the financial status, operations, and payment history for most firms. Other possible sources of information include credit bureaus, trade associations, chambers of commerce, competitors, bank references, public financial statements, and, of course, the firm's past relationship with the customer.

One way in which both individuals and firms are often evaluated as credit risks is through the use of credit scoring. **Credit scoring** involves the *numerical evaluation of each applicant.* An applicant receives a score based on his or her answers to a simple set of questions. This score is then evaluated according to a predetermined standard to determine whether credit should be extended. The major advantage of credit scoring is that it is inexpensive and easy to perform. For example, once the standards are set, a computer or clerical worker without any specialized training can easily evaluate any applicant.

credit scoring the numerical evaluation of credit applicants where the score is evaluated relative to a predetermined standard.

The techniques used for constructing credit-scoring indexes range from simply adding up the default rates associated with the answers given to each question, to sophisticated evaluations using multiple discriminant analysis (MDA). MDA is a statistical technique for calculating the appropriate importance to assign each question used in evaluating the applicant.

Finance professor Edward Altman used multiple discriminant analysis to identify businesses that might go bankrupt. In his landmark study, Altman used financial ratios to develop the following index:

$$Z = 3.3\left(\frac{\text{EBIT}}{\text{total assets}}\right) + 1.0\left(\frac{\text{sales}}{\text{total assets}}\right) + 0.06\left(\frac{\text{market value of equity}}{\text{book value of debt}}\right) \\ + 1.4\left(\frac{\text{retained earnings}}{\text{total assets}}\right) + 1.2\left(\frac{\text{working capital}}{\text{total assets}}\right) \tag{16-4}$$

Thus, to use the Altman Z-score model to predict a firm's likelihood of bankruptcy, we substitute the firm's values for each of the predictor variables on the right-hand side of equation (16-4). Altman found that firms that went bankrupt within a year's time tended to have a Z-score below 2.7, whereas firms that did not go bankrupt had Z-scores larger than 2.7.

EXAMPLE 16.2

To see how the credit-scoring model is used, let's consider the credit application of Jamison Electric Corporation. Column D contains the products of the credit-scoring model coefficients found in column B and Jamison's financial attributes found in column C. Adding up all the individual product terms produces a credit score of 2.00. Because this credit score is less than 2.7, we would anticipate that there is a high likelihood that Jamison will become bankrupt sometime during the coming year.[2]

	A	B	C	D
1	Variable	Coefficient	Firm Value	Product
2	EBIT/total assets	3.30	0.10	0.33
3	Sales/total assets	1.00	0.85	0.85
4	Market value of equity/book value of debt	0.06	4.00	0.24
5	Retained earnings/total assets	1.40	0.20	0.28
6	Working capital/total assets	1.20	0.25	0.30
7			Z =	2.00
8				

The Collection Effort—A Decision Variable

The key to maintaining control over the collection of accounts receivable is the fact that the probability of default increases with the age of the account. Thus, eliminating past-due receivables is key. One common way of evaluating the situation is with *ratio analysis*. The financial manager can determine whether accounts receivable are under control by examining the average collection period, the ratio of receivables to assets, the ratio of credit sales to receivables (called the accounts-receivable turnover ratio), and the amount of bad debts relative to sales over time. In addition, the manager can perform what is called an aging of accounts receivable to provide a breakdown in both dollars and percentages of the proportion of receivables that are past due. Comparing the current aging of receivables with past data offers even more control.

Once the delinquent accounts have been identified, the firm's accounts-receivable group makes an effort to collect them. For example, a past-due letter, called a *dunning letter*, is sent if payment is not received on time, followed by an additional dunning letter in a more serious tone if the account becomes 3 weeks past due, followed after 6 weeks by a telephone call. Finally, if the account becomes 12 weeks past due, it might be turned over to a collection agency. Again, a direct trade-off exists between collection expenses and lost goodwill on one hand and noncollection of accounts on the other. This trade-off is always part of making the decision.

 6 Discuss the reasons for carrying inventory and how inventory management decisions are made.

inventory management the control of assets used in the production process or produced to be sold in the normal course of the firm's operations.

Inventory Management

Inventory management involves the *control of the assets that are produced to be sold in the normal course of the firm's operations*. The general categories of inventory include raw-materials inventory, work-in-process inventory, and finished-goods inventory. The importance of inventory management to the firm depends on the extent of its inventory investment. For an average firm, approximately 4.88 percent of all assets are in the form of inventory. However, the percentage varies widely from industry to industry. Thus, the importance of inventory management and control varies from industry to industry also. For example,

---

[2]We should caution the user that the Z-score model is not a perfect predictor (although it was quite good). For example, of 100 firms that actually did go bankrupt over the period of 1 year, Altman found that the model correctly classified 94 firms. Similarly, of 100 firms that did not go bankrupt, the model correctly classified 97 as nonbankrupt.

this activity is much more important in the automotive dealer and service station trade, in which inventories make up 49.72 percent of total assets, than in the hotel business, in which the average investment in inventory is only 1.56 percent of total assets.

Types of Inventory

The purpose of carrying inventories is to uncouple the operations of the firm—that is, to make each function of the business independent of each other function—so that delays or shutdowns in one area do not affect the production and sale of the final product. Because production shutdowns result in increased costs, and because delays in delivery can lose customers, the management and control of inventory are important duties of the financial manager.

Decision making about inventory levels involves a basic trade-off between risk and return. The risk is that if the level of inventory is too low, the various functions of business do not operate independently, and delays in product and customer delivery can result. But a lower level of inventory can also save the firm money and increase returns. Moreover, as the size of inventory increases, storage and handling costs as well as the required return on capital invested in the inventory rise. In short, as the inventory a firm holds is increased, the risk of running out of inventory is lessened, but inventory expenses rise.

Raw-Materials Inventory   **Raw-materials inventory** consists of *basic materials purchased from other firms to be used in the firm's production operations*. These goods may include steel, lumber, petroleum, or manufactured items such as wire, ball bearings, or tires that the firm does not produce itself. Regardless of the specific form of the raw-materials inventory, all manufacturing firms by definition maintain a raw-materials inventory. The purpose is to uncouple the production function from the purchasing function—that is, to make these two functions independent of each other—so delays in the shipment of raw materials do not cause production delays. In the event of a delay, the firm can satisfy its need for raw materials by liquidating its inventory.

raw-materials inventory the basic materials purchased from other firms to be used in the firm's production operations.

Work-in-Process Inventory   **Work-in-process inventory** consists of *partially finished goods requiring additional work before they become finished goods*. The more complex and lengthy the production process, the larger the investment in work-in-process inventory. The purpose of work-in-process inventory is to uncouple the various operations in the production process so that machine failures and work stoppages in one operation will not affect other operations. Assume, for example, there are 10 different production operations, each one involving the piece of work produced in the previous operation. If the machine performing the first production operation breaks down, a firm with no work-in-process inventory will have to shut down all 10 production operations. But if a firm has work-in-process inventory, all remaining 9 operations can continue by drawing the input for the second operation from inventory.

work-in-process inventory partially finished goods requiring additional work before they become finished goods.

Finished-Goods Inventory   **Finished-goods inventory** consists of *goods on which production has been completed but that are not yet sold*. The purpose of a finished-goods inventory is to uncouple the production and sales functions so that it is not necessary to produce the goods before a sale can occur—sales can be made directly out of inventory. In the auto industry, for example, a person would not buy from a dealer who made them wait weeks or months when another dealer could fill the order immediately.

finished-goods inventory goods on which the production has been completed but that are not yet sold.

Stock of Cash   Although we have already discussed cash management at some length, it is worthwhile to mention cash again in the light of inventory management. This is because the *stock of cash* carried by a firm is simply a special type of inventory. In terms of uncoupling the various operations of the firm, the purpose of holding a stock of cash is to make the payment of bills independent of the collection of accounts due. When cash is kept on hand, bills can be paid without prior collection of accounts.

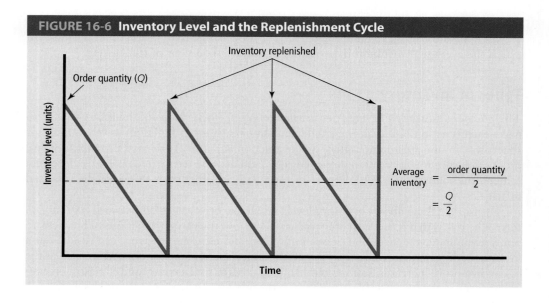

FIGURE 16-6 Inventory Level and the Replenishment Cycle

Inventory Management Techniques

As we explained, the importance of effective inventory management is directly related to the size of the investment in inventory. The effective management of these assets is essential to the goal of maximizing shareholder wealth. To control the investment in inventory, managers must solve two problems: the order quantity problem and the order point problem.

order quantity problem determining the optimal order size for an inventory item given its usage, carrying costs, and ordering costs.

The Order Quantity Problem   The **order quantity problem** involves *determining the optimal order size for an inventory item given its expected usage, carrying costs, and ordering costs.*

The economic order quantity (*EOQ*) model attempts to determine the order size that will minimize total inventory costs. It assumes that

$$\begin{array}{c} \text{Total} \\ \text{inventory costs} \end{array} = \begin{array}{c} \text{total} \\ \text{carrying costs} \end{array} + \begin{array}{c} \text{total} \\ \text{ordering costs} \end{array} \tag{16-5}$$

Assuming the inventory is allowed to fall to zero and then is immediately replenished (this assumption will be lifted when we discuss the order point problem), the average inventory becomes $Q/2$, where Q is inventory order size in units. This can be seen graphically in Figure 16-6.

If the average inventory is $Q/2$ and the carrying cost per unit is C, then carrying costs become

$$\begin{array}{c} \text{Total} \\ \text{carrying costs} \end{array} = \left(\begin{array}{c} \text{number} \\ \text{of orders} \end{array} \right)\left(\begin{array}{c} \text{carrying cost} \\ \text{per order} \end{array} \right)$$

$$= \left(\frac{Q}{2} \right)C \tag{16-6}$$

where Q = the inventory order size in units
 C = the carrying cost per unit

The carrying costs on inventory include the required rate of return on investment in inventory, in addition to warehouse or storage costs, wages for those who operate the warehouse, and costs associated with having too little inventory on hand. Thus, carrying costs include both real cash flows and the opportunity costs associated with having funds tied up in inventory.

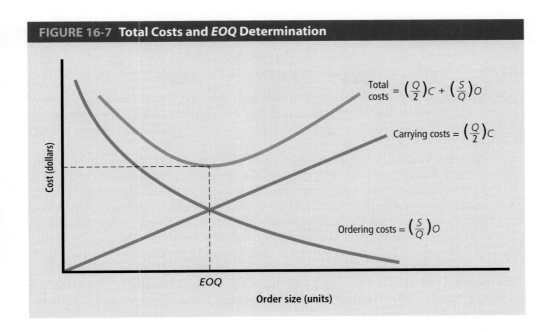

FIGURE 16-7 **Total Costs and *EOQ* Determination**

The ordering costs incurred are equal to the ordering costs per order times the number of orders. If we assume total demand over the planning period is S, and we order in lot sizes of Q, then S/Q represents the number of orders over the planning period. If the ordering cost per order is O, then

$$\text{Total ordering costs} = \left(\begin{array}{c}\text{number}\\\text{of orders}\end{array}\right)\left(\begin{array}{c}\text{ordering cost}\\\text{per order}\end{array}\right) \tag{16-7}$$

$$= \left(\frac{S}{Q}\right)O \tag{16-7a}$$

where S = total demand in units over the planning period
$\qquad O$ = ordering cost per order

Thus, total costs in equation (16-5) become

$$\text{Total costs} = \left(\frac{Q}{2}\right)C + \left(\frac{S}{Q}\right)O \tag{16-8}$$

Figure 16-7 illustrates this equation graphically.

What we are looking for is the order size Q^* that provides the minimum total costs. By manipulating equation (16-8), we find that the optimal value of Q—that is, the economic order quantity (*EOQ*)—is

$$Q^* = \sqrt{\frac{2SO}{C}} \tag{16-9}$$

CAN YOU DO IT?

CALCULATING THE ECONOMIC ORDER QUANTITY

Suppose that a firm expects total demand (S) for its product next year to be 5,000 units. Moreover, to place an order the firm incurs an ordering cost (O) of $200, and the carrying cost per unit (C) is $2. What is the economic order quantity (Q^*) for the company?

(The solution can be found on p. 457.)

Assumptions of the *EOQ* Model   Despite the fact that the *EOQ* model tends to yield quite good results, there are weaknesses associated with several of its assumptions. However, when its assumptions have been dramatically violated, the *EOQ* model can generally be modified to accommodate the situation. The model's assumptions are as follows:

1. **Constant, or uniform, demand.** Although the *EOQ* model assumes constant demand, demand may vary from day to day. If demand is stochastic—that is, not known in advance—the model must be modified through the inclusion of a safety stock.

2. **A constant unit price.**   The inclusion of variable prices resulting from quantity discounts can be handled quite easily through a modification of the original *EOQ* model, and then redefining total costs and solving for the optimum order quantity.

3. **Constant carrying costs.**   Unit carrying costs can vary substantially as the size of the inventory rises, perhaps decreasing because of economies of scale or storage efficiencies or increasing as storage space runs out and new warehouses have to be rented. This situation can be handled through a modification in the original model similar to the one used for variable unit price.

4. **Constant ordering costs.**   Although this assumption is generally valid, its violation can be accommodated by modifying the original *EOQ* model in a manner similar to the one used for variable unit prices.

5. **Instantaneous delivery.**   If delivery is not instantaneous, which is generally the case, the original *EOQ* model must be modified through the inclusion of a safety stock, that is, the inventory held to accommodate any unusually large and unexpected usage during the delivery time.

6. **Independent orders.**   If multiple orders result in cost savings by reducing paperwork and transportation cost, the original *EOQ* model must be further modified. Although this modification is somewhat complicated, special *EOQ* models have been developed to deal with it.

These assumptions illustrate the limitations of the basic *EOQ* model and the ways in which it can be modified to compensate for them. An understanding of the limitations and assumptions of the *EOQ* model provides the financial manager with more of a base for making inventory decisions.

The Order Point Problem   The two most limiting assumptions—those of constant or uniform demand and instantaneous delivery—are dealt with through the inclusion of **safety stock**, which is the *inventory held to accommodate any unusually large and unexpected usage during delivery time*. The *decision about how much safety stock to hold* is generally referred to as the **order point problem**; that is, how low should inventory be depleted before it is reordered?

Two factors that go into the determination of the appropriate order point: (1) the procurement or delivery-time stock and (2) the safety stock desired. Figure 16-8 graphs the process involved in order point determination. We observe that the order point problem can be decomposed into its two components, the **delivery-time stock**—that is, the *inventory needed between the order date and the receipt of the inventory ordered*—and the safety stock. Thus, the order point is reached when inventory falls to a level equal to the delivery-time stock plus the safety stock.

safety stock inventory held to accommodate any unusually large and unexpected usage during delivery time.

order point problem determining how low inventory should be depleted before it is reordered.

delivery-time stock the inventory needed between the order date and the receipt of the inventory ordered.

$$\begin{array}{l}\text{Inventory order point}\\ \text{(order new inventory}\\ \text{when the level of inventory}\\ \text{falls to the level)}\end{array} = \begin{array}{c}\text{delivery-time}\\ \text{stock}\end{array} + \begin{array}{c}\text{safety}\\ \text{stock}\end{array} \qquad (16\text{-}10)$$

As a result of constantly carrying safety stock, the average level of inventory increases. Whereas before the inclusion of safety stock the average level of inventory was equal to *EOQ*/2, now it will be

$$\text{Average inventory} = \frac{EOQ}{2} + \text{safety stock} \qquad (16\text{-}11)$$

FIGURE 16-8 Order Point Determination

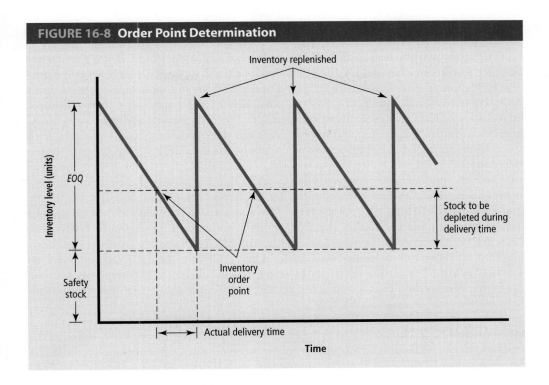

DID YOU GET IT?

CALCULATING THE ECONOMIC ORDER QUANTITY

Equation (16-9) defines the economic order quantity (*EOQ*) relationship:

$$Q^* = \sqrt{\frac{2SO}{C}}$$

where Q^* = the economic order quantity or *EOQ* which minimizes the costs of ordering and holding an inventory

S = the total number of units of inventory the firm will need over the coming year

O = the cost of placing an order

C = the carrying cost per unit of inventory

Substituting into the *EOQ* equation we estimate

$$Q^* = \sqrt{\frac{2 \times 5,000 \times \$200}{\$2}} = \sqrt{1,000,000} = 1,000 \text{ units}$$

Thus, the costs of ordering and carrying an inventory is minimized when we order 1,000 units each time an offer is placed.

In general, several factors simultaneously determine how much delivery-time stock and safety stock should be held. First, the efficiency of the replenishment system affects how much delivery-time stock is needed. Because the delivery-time stock is the expected inventory usage between ordering and receiving inventory, the efficient replenishment of inventory would reduce the need for delivery-time stock.

The uncertainty surrounding both the delivery time and the demand for the product affects the level of safety stock needed. The more certain the patterns of these inflows and outflows from the inventory, the less safety stock required. In effect, if these inflows and outflows are highly predictable, then there is little chance of any stock-out occurring.

However, if they are unpredictable, it becomes necessary to carry additional safety stock to prevent unexpected stock-outs.

The safety margin desired also affects the level of safety stock held. If it is a costly experience to run out of inventory, the safety stock held will be larger than it would be otherwise. If running out of inventory and the subsequent delay in supplying customers result in strong customer dissatisfaction and the possibility of lost future sales, then additional safety stock is necessary. A final determinant is the cost of carrying additional inventory, in terms of both the handling and storage costs and the opportunity cost associated with the investment in additional inventory. Very simply, the greater the costs, the smaller the safety stock.

Over the past decade or so, a different technique aimed at reducing the firm's investment in inventory has been adopted by numerous companies. It is known as the **just-in-time inventory control system**. The aim is to operate with the *lowest average level of inventory possible*. Within the *EOQ* model, the basics are to reduce (1) ordering costs and (2) safety stocks. This is achieved by attempting to receive an almost continuous flow of deliveries of component parts. The result is to actually have about 2 to 4 hours' worth of inventory on hand. In effect, trucks, railroads, and airplanes become the firm's warehouses. This system has spawned a new emphasis on the dual relationship between the firm and its suppliers.

Inflation and *EOQ* Inflation affects the *EOQ* model in two major ways. First, although the *EOQ* model can be modified to assume constant price increases, often major price increases occur only once or twice a year and are announced ahead of time. If this is the case, the *EOQ* model may lose its predictability and may be replaced with **anticipatory buying**—that is, *buying in anticipation of a price increase to secure the goods at a lower cost*. Of course, as with most decisions, there are trade-offs. The costs are the added carrying costs associated with the inventory. The benefits, of course, come from buying at a lower price. The second way inflation affects the *EOQ* model is through increased carrying costs. As inflation pushes interest rates up, the cost of carrying inventory increases. In our *EOQ* model this means that C increases, which results in a decline in Q^*, the optimal economic order quantity.

$$\downarrow Q^* = \sqrt{\frac{2SO}{C\uparrow}}$$

(16-12)

just-in-time inventory control system a production and management system in which inventory is cut down to a minimum through adjustments to the time and physical distance between the various production operations. Under this system the firm keeps a minimum level of inventory on hand, relying upon suppliers to furnish parts "just in time" for them to be assembled.

anticipatory buying buying in anticipation of a price increase to secure goods at a lower cost.

Concept Check

1. Describe the types of inventory that firms have.
2. What is the fundamental objective of the economic order quantity (*EOQ*) formula?
3. What assumptions underlie the *EOQ* formula?

Summary

Understand why a firm holds cash.

As you recall, several of the fundamental principles of financial management relate to the importance of cash and cash flows. In this chapter, we have developed many of the tools that a financial manager needs to manage the firm's cash and other current assets with the overall objective of ensuring that the firm has an appropriate level of liquidity, or net working capital, to carry out the goal of maximizing shareholder wealth.

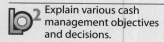

Explain various cash management objectives and decisions.

The firm experiences both regular and irregular cash flows. Once cash is obtained, the firm has three motives for holding cash rather than investing it: to satisfy transactions, precautionary, and speculative liquidity needs. To a certain extent, such needs can be satisfied by holding readily marketable securities rather than cash. A significant challenge of cash management, then, is dealing with the trade-off between the firm's need to have cash on hand to pay liabilities that arise in the course of doing business and the objective of maximizing wealth by minimizing idle cash balances that earn no return.

Various procedures exist to improve the efficiency of a firm's cash management. Such procedures focus on accelerating the firm's cash receipts and improving the methods for disbursing cash. To accelerate cash receipts, significant effort is made to reduce the mail, processing, and transit elements of the float.

On the cash disbursements side, firms try to prolong the time cash stays in their own accounts by increasing the disbursement float through the use of zero balance accounts and payable-through drafts. These methods offer much better central-office control over disbursements. Before any collection or disbursement procedure is introduced, however, a careful analysis should be performed to ensure that expected benefits outweigh the expected costs of such procedures.

Because idle cash earns no return, a financial manager looks for opportunities to invest it until it is required in the operations of the company. A variety of different readily marketable securities, described in the chapter, are available in the market today. The yields on such securities vary depending on four factors: the (1) financial risk, (2) interest rate risk, (3) liquidity, and (4) taxability of the security. By simultaneously taking into account these factors and the desired rate of return, the financial manager is able to determine the most suitable mix of cash and marketable securities for the firm.

When we consider that accounts receivable constitute approximately 25 percent of total assets for the typical firm, the importance of accounts-receivable management becomes even more apparent. The size of a firm's investment in accounts receivable depends on three factors: the percentage of credit sales to total sales, the level of sales, and the credit and collection policies of the firm. The financial manager, however, generally has control only over the terms of the sale, the quality of the customer, and the collection efforts.

Although the level of investment in inventories by the typical firm is less than the investment in accounts receivable, inventory management and control remains an important function of the financial manager because inventories play a significant role in the operations of the firm. The purpose of holding inventory is to make each function of the business independent of the other functions. The primary issues related to inventory management are: (1) How much inventory should be ordered? and (2) When should the order be placed? The *EOQ* model is used to answer the first of these questions. The order point model, which depends on the desired levels of delivery-time stock and safety stock, is applied to answer the second question. The relatively new just-in-time approach to inventory control is growing in popularity as an attempt to obtain additional cost savings by reducing the level of inventory a firm needs to have on hand. Instead of depending solely on its own inventories, the firm relies on its vendors to furnish supplies "just in time" to satisfy the firm's production requirements.

 Describe and analyze the different mechanisms for managing the firm's cash collection and disbursement procedures.

 Determine a prudent composition for the firm's marketable-securities portfolio.

 Discuss the determinants of the firm's investment in accounts receivable and learn how decisions regarding changes in credit policy are determined.

 Discuss the reasons for carrying inventory and how inventory management decisions are made.

Key Terms

Anticipatory buying   458

Cash   437

Credit scoring   451

Delivery-time stock   456

Finished-goods inventory   453

Float   440

Insolvency   439

Inventory management   452

Just-in-time inventory control system   458

Marketable securities   437

Order point problem   456

Order quantity problem   454

Payable-through draft (PTD)   443

Raw-materials inventory   453

Safety stock   456

Terms of sale   450

Work-in-process inventory   453

Zero balance accounts (ZBA)   443

Review Questions

All Review Questions and Study Problems are available in MyFinanceLab.

16-1. What is meant by the cash flow process?

16-2. Identify the principal motives for holding cash and near-cash assets. Explain the purpose of each motive.

16-3. What are the two major objectives of the firm's cash management system?

16-4. What decisions dominate the cash management process?

16-5. Within the context of cash management, what are the key elements of (total) float? Briefly define each element.

16-6. Distinguish between *financial risk* and *interest rate risk* as these terms are commonly used in discussions of cash management.

16-7. What factors determine the size of the investment a firm has in its accounts receivable? Which of these factors are under the control of the financial manager?

16-8. If a credit manager experienced no bad-debt losses over the past year, would this be an indication of proper credit management? Why or why not?

16-9. What are the risk–return trade-offs associated with adopting a more liberal trade credit policy?

16-10. What is the purpose of holding inventory? Name several types of inventory and describe their purpose.

16-11. What are the major assumptions made by the *EOQ* model?

Self-Test Problems

(Solutions to these problems are found at the end of the chapter.)

ST-1. (*Buying and selling marketable securities*) Mountaineer Outfitters has $2 million in excess cash to invest in marketable securities. To buy and sell the securities, however, the firm must pay a transaction fee of $45,000.

    a. Would you recommend purchasing the securities if they yield 12 percent annually and are held for
        1. One month?
        2. Two months?
        3. Three months?
        4. Six months?
        5. One year?
    b. What minimum required yield would the securities have to return for the firm to hold them for 3 months? (What is the break-even yield for a 3-month holding period?)

ST-2. (*EOQ calculations*) Consider the following inventory information and relationships for the F. Beamer Corporation:

    1. Orders can be placed only in multiples of 100 units.
    2. Annual unit usage is 300,000. (Assume a 50-week year in your calculations.)
    3. The carrying cost is 30 percent of the purchase price of the goods.
    4. The purchase price is $10 per unit.
    5. The ordering cost is $50 per order.
    6. The desired safety stock is 1,000 units. (This does not include delivery-time stock.)
    7. Delivery time is 2 weeks.

Given this information,

    a. What is the optimal *EOQ* level?
    b. How many orders will be placed annually?
    c. At what inventory level should a reorder be made?

Study Problems

16-1. (*Buying and selling marketable securities*) Pearl Islands Tour Operator, located in the Pacific Ocean near Panama City, has effectively collected $1,500,000 in excess cash that it plans to invest in marketable securities. The firm will have to pay total transaction costs of $30,000 to buy and sell the securities.

    a. Would you recommend purchasing the securities if they yield 8.25 percent annually and are held for
        1. One month?
        2. Two months?
        3. Three months?
        4. Six months?
        5. One year?
    b. What minimum required yield would the securities have to return for the firm to hold them for 3 months? (What is the break-even yield for a 3-month holding period?)

16-2. (*Cost of services*) As CFO of Portobello Scuba Diving Inc. you are asked to look into the possibility of adopting a lockbox system to expedite cash receipts from clients. Portobello receives check remittances totaling $24 million in a year. The firm records and processes 10,000 checks in the same period. The National Bank of Brazil has informed you that it could provide the service of expediting checks and associated documents through the lockbox system for a unit cost of $0.25 per check. After conducting an analysis, you project that the cash freed up by the adoption of the system can be invested in a portfolio of near-cash assets that will yield an annual before-tax return of 8 percent. The company usually uses a 365-day year in its procedures.

    a. What reduction in check collection time is necessary for Portobello to be neither better nor worse off for having adopted the lockbox system?

    b. How would your solution to part a be affected if Portobello could invest the freed-up balances at an expected annual return of only 4 percent?

    c. What is the logical explanation for the differences in your answers to part a and part b?

16-3. (*Concentration banking*) Byron Sporting Goods operates in Miami, Florida. The firm produces and distributes a full line of athletic equipment on a nationwide basis. The firm currently uses a centralized billing system. Byron Sporting Goods has annual credit sales of $438 million. Austin National Bank has presented an offer to operate a concentration-banking system for the company. Byron already has an established line of credit with Austin. Austin says it will operate the system on a flat-fee basis of $200,000 per year. The analysis done by the bank's cash management services division suggests that 3 days in mail float and 1 day in processing float can be eliminated.

Because Byron borrows almost continuously from Austin National, the value of the float reduction would be applied against the line of credit. The borrowing rate on the line of credit is set at an annual rate of 8 percent. Furthermore, because of the reduction in clerical help, the new system will save the firm $66,000 in processing costs. Byron uses a 365-day year in analyses of this sort. Should Byron accept the bank's offer to install the new system?

16-4. (*Lockbox system*) Penn Steelworks is a distributor of cold-rolled steel products to the automobile industry. All of its sales are on a credit basis, net 30 days. Sales are evenly distributed over its 10 sales regions throughout the United States. Delinquent accounts are no problem. The company has recently undertaken an analysis aimed at improving its cash management procedures. Penn determined that it takes an average of 3.2 days for customers' payments to reach the head office in Pittsburgh from the time they are mailed. It takes another full day in processing time prior to depositing the checks with a local bank. Annual sales average $4.8 million for each regional office. Reasonable investment opportunities can be found that yield 7 percent per year. To alleviate the float problem confronting the firm, the use of a lockbox system in each of the 10 regions is being considered. This would reduce mail float by 1.2 days. One day in processing float would also be eliminated, plus a full day in transit float. The lockbox arrangement would cost each region $250 per month.

    a. What is the opportunity cost to Penn Steelworks of the funds tied up in mailing and processing? Use a 365-day year.

    b. What would the net cost or savings be from use of the proposed cash acceleration technique? Should Penn adopt the system?

16-5. (*Cash receipts acceleration system*) Peggy Pierce Designs Inc. is a vertically integrated, national manufacturer and retailer of women's clothing. Currently, the firm has no coordinated cash management system. A proposal, however, from the First Pennsylvania Bank aimed at speeding up cash collections is being examined by several of Pierce's corporate executives.

The firm currently uses a centralized billing procedure, which requires that all checks be mailed to the Philadelphia head office for processing and eventual deposit. Under this arrangement all the customers' remittance checks take an average of 5 business days to reach the head office. Once in Philadelphia, another 2 days are required to process the checks for ultimate deposit at the First Pennsylvania Bank.

The firm's daily remittances average $1 million. The average check size is $2,000. Pierce Designs currently earns 6 percent annually on its marketable-securities portfolio.

The cash acceleration plan proposed by officers of First Pennsylvania involves both a lockbox system and concentration banking. First Pennsylvania would be the firm's only concentration bank. Lockboxes would be established in (1) San Francisco, (2) Dallas, (3) Chicago, and (4) Philadelphia. This would reduce funds tied up by mail float to 3 days, and processing float will be eliminated. Funds would then be transferred twice each business day by means of automated depository transfer checks from local banks in San Francisco, Dallas, and Chicago to the First Pennsylvania Bank.

Each DTC costs $15. These transfers will occur all 270 business days of the year. Each check processed through the lockbox system will cost $0.18.

    a. What amount of cash balances will be freed up if Peggy Pierce Designs Inc. adopts the system suggested by First Pennsylvania?

    b. What is the opportunity cost of maintaining the current banking setup?

    c. What is the projected annual cost of operating the proposed system?

    d. Should Pierce adopt the new system? Compute the net annual gain or loss associated with adopting the system.

16-6. (*Marketable-securities portfolio*) The Alex Daniel Shoe Manufacturing Company currently pays its employees on a weekly basis. The weekly wage bill is $500,000. This means that on average the firm has accrued wages payable of ($500,000 + $0)/2 = $250,000.

Alex Daniel Jr. works as the firm's senior financial analyst and reports directly to his father, who owns all of the firm's common stock. Alex Daniel Jr. wants to move to a monthly wage-payment system. Employees would be paid at the end of every fourth week. The younger Daniel is fully aware that the labor union representing the company's workers will not permit the monthly payments system to take effect unless the workers are given some type of fringe benefit compensation. A plan has been worked out whereby the firm will make a contribution to the cost of life insurance coverage for each employee. This will cost the firm $35,000 annually. Alex Daniel Jr. expects the firm to earn 7 percent annually on its marketable-securities portfolio.

    a. Based on the projected information, should Daniel Shoe Manufacturing move to the monthly wage-payment system?

    b. What annual rate of return on the marketable-securities portfolio would enable the firm to just break even on this proposal?

16-7. (*Valuing float reduction*) The Cowboy Bottling Company will generate $12 million in credit sales next year. Collection of these credit sales will occur evenly over this period. The firm's employees work 270 days a year. Currently, the firm's processing system ties up 4 days' worth of remittance checks. A recent report from a financial consultant indicated procedures that will enable Cowboy Bottling to reduce processing float by 2 full days. If Cowboy invests the released funds to earn 6 percent, what will be the annual savings?

16-8. (*Accounts-payable policy and cash management*) Bradford Construction Supply Company is suffering from a prolonged decline in new construction in its sales area. In an attempt to improve its cash position, the firm is considering changes in its accounts-payable policy. After careful study, it has determined that the only alternative available is to slow disbursements. Purchases for the coming year are expected to be $37.5 million. Sales will be $65 million, which represents about a 20 percent drop from the current year. Currently, Bradford discounts approximately 25 percent of its payments at 3 percent, 10 days, net 30, and the balance of accounts is paid in 30 days. If Bradford adopts a policy of payment in 45 days or 60 days, how much can the firm gain if the annual opportunity cost of investment is 12 percent? What will be the result if this action causes Bradford Construction suppliers to increase their prices to the company by $\frac{1}{2}$ percent to compensate for the 60-day extended term of payment? In your calculations, use a 365-day year and ignore any compounding effects related to the expected returns.

16-9. (*Interest rate risk*) Two years ago your corporate treasurer purchased for the firm a 20-year bond at its par value of $1,000. The coupon rate on this security is 8 percent. Interest payments are made to bondholders once a year. Currently, bonds of this particular risk class are yielding investors 9 percent. A cash shortage has forced you to instruct your treasurer to liquidate the bond.

    a. At what price will your bond be sold? Assume annual compounding.

    b. What will be the amount of your gain or loss over the original purchase price?

    c. What would be the amount of your gain or loss had the treasurer originally purchased a bond with a 4-year rather than a 20-year maturity? (Assume all characteristics of the bonds are identical except their maturity periods.)

    d. What do we call this type of risk assumed by your corporate treasurer?

16-10. (*Comparison of after-tax yields*) The corporate treasurer of Aggieland Fireworks is considering the purchase of a BBB-rated bond that carries a 9 percent coupon. The BBB-rated security is taxable, and the firm is in the 46 percent marginal tax bracket. The face value of this bond is $1,000.

A financial analyst who reports to the corporate treasurer has alerted him to the fact that a municipal obligation is coming to the market with a $5\frac{1}{2}$ percent coupon. The par value of this security is also $1,000.

a. Which one of the two securities do you recommend the firm purchase? Why?

b. What must the fully taxed bond yield before tax to make it comparable with the municipal offering?

16-11. (*Trade credit discounts*) Determine the effective annualized cost of forgoing the trade credit discount on the following terms:

a. 1/10, net 20

b. 2/10, net 30

c. 3/10, net 30

d. 3/10, net 60

e. 3/10, net 90

f. 5/10, net 60

16-12. (*Altman model*) The following ratios were supplied by six loan applicants. Given this information and the credit-scoring model developed by Altman (equation [16-4]), which loans have a high probability of defaulting next year?

	EBIT ÷ TOTAL ASSETS	SALES ÷ TOTAL ASSETS	MARKET VALUE OF EQUITY ÷ BOOK VALUE OF DEBT	RETAINED EARNINGS ÷ TOTAL ASSETS	WORKING CAPITAL ÷ TOTAL ASSETS
Applicant 1	0.2	0.2	1.2	0.3	0.5
Applicant 2	0.2	0.8	1.0	0.3	0.8
Applicant 3	0.2	0.7	0.6	0.3	0.4
Applicant 4	0.1	0.4	1.2	0.4	0.4
Applicant 5	0.3	0.7	0.5	0.4	0.7
Applicant 6	0.2	0.5	0.5	0.4	0.4

16-13. (*Ratio analysis*) Assuming a 360-day year, calculate what the average investment in inventory would be for a firm, given the following information in each case.

a. The firm has sales of $600,000, a gross profit margin of 10 percent, and an inventory turnover ratio of 6.

b. The firm has a cost-of-goods-sold figure of $480,000 and an average age of inventory of 40 days.

c. The firm has a cost-of-goods-sold figure of $1.15 million and an inventory turnover rate of 5.

d. The firm has a sales figure of $25 million, a gross profit margin of 14 percent, and an average age of inventory of 45 days.

16-14. (*EOQ calculations*) A downtown bookstore is trying to determine the optimal order quantity for a popular novel just printed in paperback. The store feels that the book will sell at four times its hardback figures. It would, therefore, sell approximately 3,000 copies in the next year at a price of $1.50. The store buys the book at a wholesale figure of $1. Costs for carrying the book are estimated at $0.10 a copy per year, and it costs $10 to order more books.

a. Determine the *EOQ*.

b. What would be the total costs for ordering the books 1, 4, 5, 10, and 15 times a year?

c. What questionable assumptions are being made by the *EOQ* model?

16-15. (*Comprehensive EOQ calculations*) Knutson Products Inc. is involved in the production of airplane parts and has the following inventory, carrying, and storage costs:

1. Orders must be placed in round lots of 100 units.

2. Annual unit usage is 250,000. (Assume a 50-week year in your calculations.)

3. The carrying cost is 10 percent of the purchase price.

4. The purchase price is $10 per unit.

5. The ordering cost is $100 per order.

6. The desired safety stock is 5,000 units. (This does not include delivery-time stock.)

7. The delivery time is 1 week.

Given the forgoing information:

a. Determine the optimal *EOQ* level.

b. How many orders will be placed annually?

c. What is the inventory order point? (That is, at what level of inventory should a new order be placed?)

d. What is the average inventory level?

e. What would happen to the *EOQ* if annual unit sales doubled (all other unit costs and safety stocks remaining constant)? What is the elasticity of *EOQ* with respect to sales? (That is, what is the percentage change in *EOQ* divided by the percentage change in sales?)

f. If carrying costs double, what will happen to the *EOQ* level? (Assume the original sales level of 250,000 units.) What is the elasticity of *EOQ* with respect to carrying costs?

g. If the ordering costs double, what will happen to the level of *EOQ*? (Again assume original levels of sales and carrying costs.) What is the elasticity of *EOQ* with respect to ordering costs?

h. If the selling price doubles, what will happen to *EOQ*? What is the elasticity of *EOQ* with respect to selling price?

Mini Case

New Wave Surfing Stuff Inc. is a manufacturer of surfboards and related gear that sells to exclusive surf shops located in several Atlantic and Pacific mainland coastal towns as well as several Hawaiian locations. The company's headquarters are located in Carlsbad, California, a small southern California coastal town. True to form, the company's officers, all veteran surfers, have been somewhat laid back about various critical areas of financial management. With an economic downturn in California adversely affecting their business, however, the officers of the company have decided to focus intently on ways to improve New Wave's cash flows. The CFO, Willy Bonik, has been requested to forgo any more daytime surfing jaunts until he has wrapped up a plan to accelerate New Wave's cash flows.

In an effort to ensure his quick return to the surf, Willy has decided to focus on what he believes is one of the easiest methods of improving New Wave's cash collections, namely, the adoption of a cash receipts acceleration system that includes a lockbox system and concentration banking. Willy is well aware that New Wave's current system leaves much room for improvement. The company's accounts receivable system currently requires that remittances from customers be mailed to the headquarters office for processing and then deposited in the local branch of the Bank of the U.S. Such an arrangement takes a considerable amount of time. The checks take an average of 5 days to reach the Carlsbad headquarters. Then, depending on the surf conditions, processing within the company takes anywhere from 2 to 4 days, with the average from the day of receipt by the company to the day of deposit at the bank being 3 days.

Willy feels pretty certain that such delays are costly. After all, New Wave's average daily collections are $150,000. The average remittance size is $750. If Willy could get these funds into his marketable-securities account more quickly, he could earn an annual rate of 5 percent on them. In addition, if he could arrange for someone else to do the processing, Willy could save $55,000 per year in costs related to clerical staffing.

New Wave's banker was pleased to provide Willy with a proposal for a combination of a lockbox system and a concentration-banking system. Bank of the U.S. would be New Wave's concentration bank. Lockboxes would be established in Honolulu, Newport Beach, and Daytona Beach. Each check processed through the lockbox system would cost New Wave $0.30. This arrangement, however, would reduce mail float by an average 2.5 days. The funds so collected would be transferred twice each day, 270 days a year, from each of the local lockbox banks to Bank of the U.S. Each transfer would cost $0.35. The combination of lockbox system and concentration banking would eliminate the time it takes the company to process cash collections, thereby making the funds available for short-term investment.

a. What would be the average amount of cash made available if New Wave were to adopt the system proposed by Bank of the U.S.?

b. What is the annual opportunity cost of maintaining the current cash collection and deposit system?

c. What is the expected annual cost of the complete system proposed by Bank of the U.S.?

d. What is the net gain or loss that is expected to result from the proposed new system? Should New Wave adopt the new system?

Self-Test Solutions

SS-1.

a. Here we must calculate the dollar value of the estimated return for each holding period and compare it with the transaction fee to determine if a gain can be made by investing in the securities. Those calculations and the resultant recommendations follow.

			RECOMMENDATION
1. $2,000,000 (0.12)($\frac{1}{12}$)	= $ 20,000	<$45,000	No
2. $2,000,000 (0.12)($\frac{2}{12}$)	= $ 40,000	<$45,000	No
3. $2,000,000 (0.12)($\frac{3}{12}$)	= $ 60,000	>$45,000	Yes
4. $2,000,000 (0.12)($\frac{6}{12}$)	= $120,000	>$45,000	Yes
5. $2,000,000 (0.12)($\frac{12}{12}$)	= $240,000	>$45,000	Yes

b. Let (%) be the required yield. With $2 million to invest for 3 months, we have

$$\$2,000,000(\%)(3/12) = \$45,000$$
$$\$2,000,000(\%) = \$180,000$$
$$= \$180,000/\$2,000,000 = 9\%$$

The break-even yield, therefore, is 9 percent.

SS-2.

a. $EOQ = \sqrt{\dfrac{2SO}{C}}$

$= \sqrt{\dfrac{2(300,000)(\$50)}{\$3}}$

= 3,162 units, but because orders must be placed in 100-unit lots, the effective EOQ becomes 3,200 units

b. $\dfrac{\text{total usage}}{EOQ} = \dfrac{300,000}{3,200} = 93.75$ orders per year

c. Inventory order point = delivery-time stock + safety stock

$= \dfrac{2}{50} \times 300,000 + 1,000$

$= 12,000 + 1,000$

$= 13,000$ units

Chapter 17

International Business Finance

Learning Objectives

After reading this chapter, you should be able to:

 Discuss **the internationalization of business.**

 Explain **why foreign exchange rates in two different countries must be in line with each other.**

 Discuss **the concept of interest rate parity.**

 Explain **the purchasing-power parity theory and the law of one price.**

Explain **what exchange rate risk is and how it can be controlled.**

Identify **working-capital management techniques that are useful for international businesses to reduce exchange rate risk and potentially increase profits.**

Explain **how the financing sources available to multinational corporations differ from those available to domestic firms.**

Discuss **the risks involved in direct foreign investment.**

It is generally easier for firms to expand the market for their products rather than develop new products, which is why most large companies look for new markets around the world. That's certainly been the direction that McDonald's (MCD) has taken in recent years. Today, McDonald's operates more than 29,000 restaurants in over 119 countries. The busiest McDonald's restaurant in the world is not in America but thousands of miles away in Pushkin Square in Moscow, Russia. The store serves 30,000 customers a day, as many as on its opening day, January 31, 1990. The menu is essentially the same as in the United States, with the addition of cabbage pie among other traditional Russian food items.

Was this an expensive venture? It certainly was. In fact, the food plants that McDonald's built to supply burgers, fries, and everything else sold there cost more than $60 million. In addition to the costs, there are a number of other factors that make opening an outlet outside of the United States both different and challenging. First, in order to keep the quality consistent with what is served at any McDonald's anywhere in the world, McDonald's spent 6 years putting together a supply chain that would provide the necessary raw materials McDonald's demands. On top of that, there are risks associated with the Russian economy and its currency that are well beyond the scope of the risk exposures in the United States.

These risks all materialized in 1998 when the Russian economy, along with its currency, the ruble, tanked. In the summer of 1998, the Russian economy spun out of control, and in August the entire banking system failed, resulting in a catastrophic decline in the value of the ruble. Because McDonald's sells its Russian burgers for rubles, when it came time to trade the rubles for U.S. dollars, McDonald's Russian outlets were not worth nearly as much as they were the year before. In spite of all this, the Moscow McDonald's has proven to be enormously successful since it opened. In fact, by 2009 there were 127 McDonald's restaurants in 37 Russian cities. McDonald's serves more than 200,000 customers every day in Russia. It all goes to show that not all new investment opportunities require new products; introducing existing products to new international markets can be equally or even more profitable.

This chapter highlights the complications that an international business faces when it deals in multiple currencies. Effective strategies for reducing foreign exchange risk are discussed. Working-capital management and capital structure decisions in the international context are also covered.

The Globalization of Product and Financial Markets

 Discuss the internationalization of business.

To say the least, the market for most products crosses many borders. In fact, some industries and states are highly dependent on the international economy. For example, the electronic consumer products and automobile industries are widely considered to be global industries. Ohio ranks fourth in terms of manufactured exports, and more than half of Ohio workers are employed by firms that depend to some extent on exports.

There has also been a rise in the global level of international portfolio and direct investment. Both direct and portfolio investments in the United States have been increasing faster than U.S. investment overseas. *Direct foreign investment* (DFI) occurs when the **multinational corporation (MNC),** *a corporation with holdings and/or operations in more than one country*, has control over the investment, such as when it builds an offshore manufacturing facility. *Portfolio investment* involves financial assets with maturities greater than 1 year, such as the purchase of foreign stocks and bonds. Total foreign investment in the United States now exceeds such U.S. investment overseas.

multinational corporation (MNC) a corporation with holdings and/or operations in more than one country.

A major reason for direct foreign investment by U.S. companies is the high rates of return obtainable from these investments. And the amount of U.S. direct foreign investment (DFI) abroad is large and growing. Significant amounts of the total assets, sales, and profits of American MNCs are attributable to foreign investments and foreign operations. Direct foreign investment is not limited to American firms. Many European and Japanese firms have operations abroad, too. During the past decade, these firms have been increasing their sales and setting up production facilities abroad, especially in the United States.

Capital flows (portfolio investment) between countries have also been increasing. Many firms, investment companies, and individuals invest in the capital markets in foreign countries. The motivation is twofold: to obtain returns higher than those obtainable in the domestic capital markets and to reduce portfolio risk through international diversification. The increase in world trade and investment activity is reflected in the recent globalization of financial markets. The Eurodollar market is now larger than any domestic financial market, and U.S. companies are increasingly turning to this market for funds. Even companies and public entities that have no overseas presence are beginning to rely on this market for financing.

In addition, most national financial markets are becoming more integrated with global markets because of the rapid increase in the volume of interest rate and currency swaps. (We will discuss currency swaps later in the chapter.) Because of the widespread availability of these swaps, the currency denomination and the source country of financing for many globally integrated companies are dictated by accessibility and relative-cost considerations, regardless of the currency ultimately needed by the firm. Even a *purely domestic firm* that buys all its inputs and sells all its output in its home country is not immune to foreign competition, nor can it totally ignore the workings of the international financial markets.

Concept Check

1. Why do U.S. companies invest overseas?

 Explain why foreign exchange rates in two different countries must be in line with each other.

Exchange Rates

Floating Exchange Rates

floating-rate international currency system a system in which the exchange rates of different currencies are allowed to fluctuate with supply and demand conditions.

Since 1973, a **floating-rate international currency system**, *a system in which exchange rates between different national currencies are allowed to fluctuate with supply and demand conditions*, has been operating. For most currencies, there are no "parity rates" and no "bands" within which the currencies fluctuate.[1] Most major currencies, including the U.S. dollar, fluctuate freely, depending on their values as perceived by the traders in foreign exchange markets. A country's relative economic strengths, its level of exports and imports, the level of monetary activity, and the deficits or surpluses in its balance of payments (BOP) are all important factors that determine exchange rates.[2] Short-term, day-to-day fluctuations in exchange rates are caused by changing supply and demand conditions for different currencies.

The Foreign Exchange Market

The foreign exchange market provides a mechanism for the transfer of purchasing power from one currency to another. This market is not a physical entity like the New York Stock Exchange; it is a network of telephone and computer connections among banks, foreign exchange dealers, and brokers. The market operates simultaneously at three levels. At the first level, customers buy and sell foreign exchange (foreign currency) through their banks. At the second level, banks buy and sell foreign exchange from other banks in the same commercial center. At the last level, banks buy and sell foreign exchange from banks in commercial centers in other countries. Some important commercial centers for foreign exchange trading are New York, London, Zurich, Frankfurt, Hong Kong, Singapore, and Tokyo.

An example illustrates this multilevel trading. A trader in Texas may buy foreign exchange (pounds) from a bank in Houston for payment to a British supplier against some purchase made. The Houston bank, in turn, may purchase the foreign currency (pounds) from a New York bank. The New York bank may buy the pounds from another bank in New York or from a bank in London.

Because this market provides transactions in a continuous manner for a very large volume of sales and purchases, the currency markets are efficient: In other words, it is difficult to make a profit by shopping around from one bank to another. Minute differences in the quotes from different banks are quickly eliminated. Because of constant trading, simultaneous quotes to different buyers in London and New York are likely to be the same.

---

[1]The system of floating rates is referred to as the "floating-rate regime."
[2]The balance of payments for the United States reflects the difference between the import and export of goods (the trade balance) and services. Capital inflows and outflows are tabulated in the capital account.

Two major types of transactions are carried out in the foreign exchange markets: spot transactions and forward transactions, which we explain next.

Spot Exchange Rates

In a typical **spot transaction** *one currency is traded for another currency today*. For example, an American firm might buy foreign currency from its bank and pay for it in dollars. Another type of spot transaction is when an American firm receives foreign currency from abroad and sells the foreign currency to its bank for dollars. *The price of foreign currency in terms of the domestic currency* is the **exchange rate**. The actual exchange rate quotes are expressed in several different ways, as discussed later. To allow time for the transfer of funds, the *value date* when the currencies are actually exchanged is two days after the spot transaction occurs. Four banks could easily be involved in the transactions: the local banks of the buyer and seller of the foreign exchange, and the money-center banks that handle the purchase and sale. Perhaps the buyer or seller will have to move the funds from one of its local banks to another, bringing even more banks into the transaction. A **forward transaction** (as apposed to a spot transaction) entails an agreement today to deliver a specified number of units of a currency on a *future* date in return for a specified number of units of another currency.

In the spot exchange market, contrasted with the over-the-counter market, the quoted exchange rate is typically called a direct quote. A **direct quote** *indicates the number of units of the home currency required to buy one unit of the foreign currency*. That is, in New York the typical exchange rate quote indicates the number of dollars needed to buy one unit of a foreign currency: dollars per pound, dollars per euro, and so on. The spot rates in column 1 of Table 17-1 are the direct exchange quotes taken from the *Wall Street Journal*. Thus, according to Table 17-1, to buy 1 British pound (£1), $1.6288 was needed. To buy Swiss francs and euros, $0.9169 and $1.3939 were needed, respectively.

An **indirect quote** *indicates the number of units of a foreign currency that can be bought for one unit of the home currency*. This reads as pounds per dollar, euros per dollar, and so forth. An indirect quote is the general method used in the over-the-counter market. Exceptions to this rule include British pounds, Australian dollars, and New Zealand dollars, which are quoted via direct quotes for historical reasons. Indirect quotes are given in the last column of Table 17-1 under Currency per U.S. $.

In summary, a direct quote is the dollar/foreign currency rate ($/FC), and an indirect quote is the foreign currency/dollar (FC/$) rate. Therefore, an indirect quote is the reciprocal of a direct quote and vice versa. The following example illustrates the computation of an indirect quote from a given direct quote.

spot transaction a transaction made immediately in the marketplace at the market price.

exchange rate the price of a foreign currency stated in terms of the domestic or home currency.

forward transaction an agreement today to deliver a specified number of units of a currency on a future date in return for a specified number of units of another currency.

direct quote the exchange rate that indicates the number of units of the home currency required to buy one unit of foreign currency.

indirect quote the exchange rate that expresses the number of units of a foreign currency that can be bought for one unit of the home currency.

EXAMPLE 17.1

Suppose you want to compute the indirect quote from the direct quote of the spot rate for pounds given in column 1 of Table 17-1. The direct quote for the U.K. pound is $1.6288. The related indirect quote is calculated as the *reciprocal* of the direct quote as follows:

$$\text{Indirect quote} = \frac{1}{\text{direct quote}}$$

Thus,

$$\frac{1}{\$1.6288} = £0.6139$$

Notice that the previous direct quote and indirect quote are identical to those shown in Table 17-1.

Direct and indirect quotes are useful in conducting international transactions, as the following examples show.

TABLE 17-1 Foreign Exchange Rates Reported July 14, 2009

Key Currency Cross Rates

	Dollar	Euro	Pound	SFranc	Peso	Yen	CdnDlr
			Late New York Trading Tuesday, July 14, 2009				
Canada	1.1358	1.5833	1.8501	1.0415	0.0823	0.0122	....
Japan	93.371	130.15	152.08	85.612	6.7694	....	82.204
Mexico	13.793	19.226	22.466	12.647	....	0.1477	12.143
Switzerland	1.0906	1.5202	1.7764	....	0.0791	0.0117	0.9602
U.K.	0.6139	0.8558	....	0.5629	0.0445	0.0066	0.5405
Euro	0.7174	....	1.1685	0.6578	0.0520	0.0077	0.6316
U.S.	....	1.3939	1.6288	0.9169	0.0725	0.0107	0.8804

Exchange Rates   **July 14, 2009**

Country/currency	U.S. $ Equivalent	Currency per U.S. $	Country/currency	U.S. $ Equivalent	Currency per U.S. $
Americas			*Europe*		
Brazil real	0.5084	1.9670	Euro area euro	1.3939	0.7174
Canada dollar	0.8804	1.1358	Norway krone	0.1544	6.4767
1-mos forward	0.8804	1.1358	Russia ruble‡	0.03104	32.217
3-mos forward	0.8808	1.1353	Sweden krona	0.1262	7.9239
6-mos forward	0.8809	1.1352	Switzerland franc	0.9169	1.0906
Colombia peso	0.0004883	2047.92	1-mos forward	0.9173	1.0902
Mexico peso*	0.0725	13.7931	3-mos forward	0.9181	1.0892
Venezuela b. fuerte	0.46570111	2.1473	6-mos forward	0.9198	1.0872
Asia-Pacific			Turkey lira**	0.6474	1.5447
Australian dollar	0.7897	1.2663	UK pound	1.6288	0.6139
China yuan	0.1464	6.8328	1-mos forward	1.6287	0.6140
Hong Kong dollar	0.1290	7.7504	3-mos forward	1.6285	0.6141
India rupee	0.02046	48.8759	6-mos forward	1.6285	0.6141
Japan yen	0.01071	93.37	*Middle East/Africa*		
1-mos forward	0.010713	93.34	Egypt pound*	0.1790	5.5869
3-mos forward	0.010721	93.27	Israel shekel	0.2528	3.9557
6-mos forward	0.010738	93.13	Saudi Arabia riyal	0.2666	3.7509
New Zealand dollar	0.6352	1.5743	South Africa rand	0.1204	8.3056
Pakistan rupee	0.01213	82.440	UAE dirham	0.2723	3.6724
South Korea won	0.0007718	1295.67			
Vietnam dong	0.00006	17801	*SDR‡*	1.5499	0.6452

*Floating rate
‡Russian Central Bank rate
**Commercial rate
Note: Based on trading among banks of $1 million and more, as quoted at 4 p.m. ET by Thomson Reuters.

Source: *Wall Street Journal,* July 15, 2009, page C2.

EXAMPLE 17.2

An American business must pay 1,000 euros to a German firm on July 14, 2009. How many dollars will be required for this transaction?

$$\$1.3939/€ \times €1,000 = \$1,393.90$$

EXAMPLE 17.3

An American business must pay $2,000 to a U.K. resident on July 14, 2009. How many pounds will the U.K. resident receive?

$$£0.6139/\$ \times \$2,000 = £1,227.80$$

Exchange Rates and Arbitrage

The foreign exchange quotes in two different countries must be in line with each other. If the exchange rate quotations between the London and New York spot exchange markets were *out of line*, then an *enterprising trader could make a profit by buying in the market where the currency was cheaper and selling it in the other*. Such a buy-and-sell strategy would involve a zero net investment of funds and no risk bearing, yet it would provide a sure profit. Such a person is called an **arbitrageur**, and the process of buying and selling in more than one market to make a riskless profit is called arbitrage. Spot exchange markets are efficient in the sense that arbitrage opportunities do not persist for any length of time. That is, the exchange rates between two different markets are quickly brought *in line*, aided by the arbitrage process. **Simple arbitrage** *eliminates exchange rate differentials across the markets for a single currency*, as in the preceding example for the New York and London quotes.

Suppose that London quotes £0.6300/$ instead of £0.6139/$. If you simultaneously bought a pound in London for £0.6300/$ and sold a pound in New York for £0.6139/$, you would have (1) taken a zero net investment position because you bought £1 and sold £1, (2) locked in a sure profit of £0.0161/$ *no matter which way* the pound subsequently moves, and (3) set in motion the forces that will eliminate the different quotes in New York and London. As others in the marketplace learn of your transaction, they will attempt to make the same transaction. The increased demand to buy pounds in London will lead to a higher quote there, and the increased supply of pounds will lead to a lower quote in New York. The workings of the market will produce a new spot rate that lies between £0.6139/$ and £0.6300/$ and is the same in New York and in London.

arbitrageur an individual involved in the process of buying and selling in more than one market to make a riskless profit.

simple arbitrage trading to eliminate exchange rate differentials across the markets for a single currency.

Asked and Bid Rates

Two types of rates are quoted in the spot exchange market: the asked and the bid rates. The **asked rate** is the *rate the bank or the foreign exchange trader "asks" the customer to pay in home currency for foreign currency when the bank is selling and the customer is buying*. The asked rate is also known as the **selling rate** or the *offer rate*. The **bid rate** is *the rate at which the bank buys the foreign currency from the customer by paying in home currency*. The bid rate is also known as the **buying rate**. Note that Table 17-1 contains only the selling, offer, or asked rates, not the buying rate.

The banks sells a unit of foreign currency for more than it pays for it. Therefore, the direct asked quote ($/FC) is greater than the direct bid quote. *The difference between the asked quote and the bid quote* is known as the **bid-asked spread**. When there is a large volume of transactions and the trading is continuous, the spread is small and can be less than 1 percent (0.01) for the major currencies. The spread is much higher for infrequently traded currencies. The spread exists to compensate the banks for holding the risky foreign currency and for providing the service of converting currencies.

asked rate the rate the bank or the foreign exchange trader "asks" the customer to pay in home currency for foreign currency when the bank is selling and the customer is buying. The asked rate is also known as the selling rate or the offer rate.

selling rate the rate the bank or the foreign exchange trader "asks" the customer to pay in home currency for foreign currency when the bank is selling and the customer is buying. The selling rate is also known as the asked rate or the offer rate.

bid rate the rate at which the bank buys the foreign currency from the customer by paying in home currency. The bid rate is also known as the buying rate.

buying rate the rate at which the bank buys the foreign currency from the customer by paying in home currency. The buying rate is also known as the bid rate.

bid-asked spread the difference between the asked quote and the bid quote.

Cross Rates

A **cross rate** is *the computation of an exchange rate for a currency from the exchange rates of two other currencies*. These are given at the top of Table 17-1. The following example illustrates how this works.

cross rate the computation of an exchange rate for a currency from the exchange rates of two other currencies.

CAN YOU DO IT?

USING THE SPOT RATE TO CALCULATE A FOREIGN CURRENCY PAYMENT

An American business must pay the equivalent of $10,000 in United Arab Emirates (UAE) dirhams to a firm in Dubai on July 14, 2009. Using the information in Table 17-1, how many dirhams will the firm in Dubai receive?

(The solution can be found on page 472.)

EXAMPLE 17.4

Taking the dollar/pound and the euro/dollar rates from columns 1 and 2 of Table 17-1, determine the euro/pound and pound/euro exchange rates. We see that

$$(\$/\pounds) \times (€/\$) = (€/\pounds)$$

or

$$1.6288 \times 0.7174 = €1.1685/\pounds$$

Thus, the pound/euro exchange rate is

$$1/1.1685 = \pounds0.8558/€$$

You'll notice that these rates are the same as those given in the top portion of Table 17-1 under Key Currency Cross Rates.

Cross-rate computations make it possible to use quotations in New York to compute the exchange rate between pounds, euros, and other currencies. Arbitrage conditions hold in cross rates, too. For example, the pound exchange rate in euros (the direct quote euros/pound) must be €1.1685/£. The euro exchange rate in London must be £0.8558/€. If the rates were different from the computed cross rates, using quotes from New York, a trader could use three different currencies to lock in arbitrage profits through triangular arbitrage.

Forward Exchange Rates

forward exchange contract a forward contract that requires delivery, at a specified future date, of one currency for a specified amount of another currency.

A **forward exchange contract** *requires delivery, at a specified future date, of one currency for a specified amount of another currency.* The exchange rate for the forward transaction is agreed on today; the actual payment of one currency and the receipt of another currency take place at the future date. For example, a 30-day contract agreed upon March 1 will be delivered March 31. Note that the forward rate is not the same as the spot rate that will prevail in the future. The actual spot rate that will prevail is not known today; only the forward rate is known. The actual spot rate will depend on the market conditions at that time; it may be more or less than today's forward rate. **Exchange rate risk** is the *risk that tomorrow's exchange rate will differ from today's rate.*

exchange rate risk the risk that tomorrow's exchange rate will differ from today's rate.

As indicated earlier, it is extremely unlikely that the future spot rate will be exactly the same as the forward rate quoted today. Assume that you are going to receive a payment denominated in pounds from a British customer in 30 days. If you wait for 30 days and exchange the pounds at the spot rate, you will receive a dollar amount reflecting the exchange rate 30 days hence (that is, the future spot rate). As of today, you have no way of knowing the exact dollar value of your future pound receipts. Consequently, you cannot make precise plans about the use of these dollars. If, conversely, you buy a futures contract, then you

DID YOU GET IT?

USING THE SPOT RATE TO CALCULATE A FOREIGN CURRENCY PAYMENT

On the previous page you were asked to determine how much an American firm had to pay a firm in Dubai in the United Arab Emirates to receive an equivalent of $10,000 in dirhams.

$$3.6724 \text{ dirhams}/\$ \times \$10,000 = 36,724 \text{ dirhams}$$

Any time money changes hands internationally, there is a transaction in the foreign currency markets. Interestingly, the dollar is the most frequently traded currency accounting for over 43% of total trading volume, with the euro coming in second with an 18.5% share.

know the exact dollar value of your future receipts, and you can make precise plans concerning their use. The forward contract, therefore, can reduce your uncertainty about the future. In fact, the major advantage of the forward market is that of risk reduction.

Forward contracts are usually quoted for periods of 30, 90, and 180 days. A contract for any intermediate date can be obtained, usually with the payment of a small premium. Forward contracts for periods longer than 180 days can be obtained by special negotiations with banks. Contracts for periods greater than 1 year can be costly.

Forward rates, like spot rates, are quoted in both direct and indirect form. The direct quotes for the 30-day, 90-day, and 180-day forward contracts on pounds, Swiss francs, Canadian dollars, and Japanese yen are given in the lower half of Table 17-1. The indirect quotes are also indicated. The direct quotes are the dollar/foreign currency rate, and the indirect quotes are the foreign currency/dollar rate similar to the spot exchange quotes.

In Table 17-1 the 1-month forward quote for pounds is $1.6287 per pound. This means that the bank is contractually bound to deliver £1 at this price, and the buyer of the contract is legally obligated to buy it at this price in 30 days. Therefore, this is the price the customer must pay regardless of the actual spot rate prevailing in 30 days. If the spot price of the pound is less than $1.6287, then the customer pays *more* than the spot price. If the spot price is greater than $1.6287, then the customer pays *less* than the spot price.

The forward rate is often quoted at a premium or a discount from the existing spot rate. For example, the 30-day forward rate for the pound may be quoted as a 0.0001 discount (1.6287 forward rate − 1.6288 spot rate). If the British pound is more expensive in the future than it is today, it is said to be selling at a premium relative to the dollar, and the dollar is said to be selling at a discount to the British pound. This premium or discount is also called the **forward-spot differential**.

Notationally, the relationship may be written

$$F - S = \text{premium } (F > S) \text{ or discount } (S > F) \qquad (17\text{-}1)$$

where F = the forward rate, direct quote
   S = the spot rate, direct quote

The premium or discount can also be expressed as an annual percentage rate, computed as follows:

$$\frac{F - S}{S} \times \frac{12}{n} \times 100 = \text{annualized percentage}$$

premium $(F > S)$ or discount $(S > F)$ \qquad (17-2)

where n = the number of months of the forward contract.

forward-spot differential the premium or discount between forward and spot currency exchange rates.

EXAMPLE 17.5

Compute the percent-per-annum discount on the 90-day or 3-month pound.

STEP 1 Identify F, S, and n.

   $F = 1.6285, S = 1.6288, n = 3$ months

STEP 2 Because S is greater than F, we compute the annualized percentage discount:

$$= \frac{1.6285 - 1.6288}{1.6288} \times \frac{12 \text{ months}}{3 \text{ months}} \times 100$$

$$= -0.0737\%$$

The percent-per-annum discount on the 90-day pound is −0.0737% percent.

CAN YOU DO IT?

COMPUTING A PERCENT-PER-ANNUM PREMIUM

Using the information in Table 17-1, compute the percent-per-annum premium on the 90-day (3 month) yen.
(The solution can be found on page 475.)

Exchange Rate Risk

The concept of exchange rate risk applies to all types of international business. The measurement of these risks, and the type of risk, differ among businesses. Let us see how exchange rate risk affects international trade contracts, international portfolio investments, and direct foreign investments.

Exchange Rate Risk in International Trade Contracts   The idea of exchange rate risk in trade contracts is illustrated in the following situations.

Case I An American automobile distributor agrees to buy a car from the manufacturer in Detroit. The distributor agrees to pay $25,000 on delivery of the car, which is expected to be 30 days from today. The car is delivered on the 30th day and the distributor pays $25,000. Notice that from the day this contract was written until the day the car was delivered, the buyer knew the *exact dollar amount* of the liability. There was, in other words, *no uncertainty* about the value of the contract.

Case II An American automobile distributor enters into a contract with a British supplier to buy a car from Britain for £15,350. The amount is payable upon the delivery of the car, 30 days from today. Unfortunately, the exchange rate between British pounds and U.S. dollars may change in the next 30 days. In effect, the American firm is not certain what its future dollar outflow will be 30 days hence. That is, the *dollar value of the contract is uncertain*.

These two examples help illustrate the idea of foreign exchange risk in international trade contracts. In the domestic trade contract (Case I), the exact dollar amount of the future dollar payment is known today with certainty. In the case of the international trade contract (Case II), in which the *contract is written in the foreign currency*, the exact dollar amount of the contract is not known. The variability of the exchange rate causes variability in the future cash flow of the firm.

Exchange rate risk exists when the contract is written in terms of the foreign currency, or *denominated* in foreign currency. There is no direct exchange rate risk if the international trade contract is written in terms of the domestic currency. That is, in Case II, if the contract were written in dollars, the American importer would face *no* direct exchange rate risk. With the contract written in dollars, the British exporter would bear *all* of the exchange rate risk because the British exporter's future pound receipts would be uncertain. That is, the British exporter would receive payment in dollars, which would have to be converted into pounds at an unknown (as of today) pound/dollar exchange rate. In international trade contracts of this type, at least one of the two parties to the contract *always* bears the exchange rate risk.

Certain types of international trade contracts are denominated in a third currency that is different from either the importer's or the exporter's domestic currency. In Case II, the contract might have been denominated in, say, the Hong Kong dollar. With a Hong Kong dollar contract, both the importer and exporter would be subject to exchange rate risk.

Exchange rate risk is not limited to the two-party trade contracts; it exists also in foreign portfolio investments and direct foreign investments.

Exchange Rate Risk in Foreign Portfolio Investments   Let us look at an example of exchange rate risk in the context of portfolio investments. An American investor buys a Hong Kong security. The exact return on the investment in the security is unknown. Thus, the security is a risky investment. The investment return in the holding period of, say, 3 months

---

DID YOU GET IT?
COMPUTING A PERCENT-PER-ANNUM PREMIUM

Compute the percent-per-annum premium on the 90-day yen.

STEP 1 Identify F, S, and n.

$F = \$0.010721/¥$, $S = \$0.01071/¥$, and $n = 3$ months

STEP 2 Because F is greater than S, we compute the annualized percentage premium:

$$\frac{0.010721 - 0.01071}{0.01071} \times \frac{12 \text{ months}}{3 \text{ months}} \times 100 = 0.4108\%$$

The percent-per-annum premium on the 90-day yen is 0.4108 percent.

---

stated in HK\$ could be anything from −2 to +8 percent. In addition, the U.S. dollar/HK\$ exchange rate may depreciate by, say, 4 percent or appreciate by 6 percent during the 3-month period. The return to the American investor in U.S. dollars will, therefore, be in the range of −6 to +14 percent. Hence, the exchange rate fluctuations may increase the riskiness of the investments.

Exchange Rate Risk in Direct Foreign Investment The exchange rate risk of a direct foreign investment (DFI) is more complicated. In a DFI, the parent company invests in assets denominated in a foreign currency. That is, the balance sheet and the income statement of the subsidiary are written in terms of the foreign currency. The parent company, if based in the United States, receives the repatriated (or converted) profit stream from the subsidiary in dollars. Thus, the exchange rate risk concept applies to fluctuations in the dollar value of the assets located abroad as well as to the fluctuations in the home currency–denominated profit stream. Moreover, exchange risk not only affects immediate profits, but it may also affect the future profit stream as well.

Although exchange rate risk can be a serious complication in international business activity, remember the principle of the risk–return trade-off: Traders and corporations find numerous reasons why the returns from international transactions outweigh the risks.

REMEMBER YOUR PRINCIPLES

In international transactions, just as in domestic transactions, the key to value is the timing and amounts of cash flow spent and received. However, economic transactions across international borders add an element of risk because cash flows are denominated in the currency of the country in which business is being transacted. Consequently, the dollar value of the cash flows will depend on the exchange rate that exists at the time the cash changes hands. The fact remains, however, that it's cash spent and received that matters. This is the point of **Principle 1: Cash Flow Is What Matters.**

Concept Check

1. What is a spot transaction? What is a direct quote? An indirect quote?
2. Who is an arbitrageur? How does an arbitrageur make money?
3. What is a forward exchange rate?
4. Describe exchange rate risk in direct foreign investment.

Interest Rate Parity

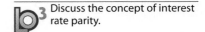 Discuss the concept of interest rate parity.

Interest rates can vary dramatically from country to country. For example, in mid-2009 the 10-year interest rate in Japan was approximately 1.2 percent, while in Australia it was 3.85 percent. The concepts of interest rate parity and purchasing-power parity, which we will introduce shortly, provide the basis for understanding how prices and rates of interest across different countries are related to one another.

interest rate parity (IRP) theory a theory that states that (except for the effects of small transaction costs) the forward premium or discount should be equal and opposite in size to the difference in the national interest rates for securities of the same maturity.

Interest rate parity (IRP) theory can be used to relate differences in the interest rates in two countries to the ratios of spot and forward exchange rates of the two countries' currencies. Specifically, the interest parity condition can stated as follows:

$$\left(1 + \frac{\text{domestic}}{\text{rate of interest}}\right) = \left(\frac{\text{forward exchange rate}}{\text{spot exchange rate}}\right)\left(1 + \frac{\text{foreign}}{\text{rate of interest}}\right) \quad (17\text{-}3)$$

The relationship between domestic and foreign country rates of interest is described by the following relationship (found by dividing both sides of equation (17-3) by one plus the foreign rate of interest):

$$\frac{\text{difference in}}{\text{interest rates}} = \frac{\text{difference between the}}{\text{forward and spot rates}}$$

$$\frac{\left(1 + \dfrac{\text{domestic}}{\text{rate of interest}}\right)}{\left(+ \dfrac{\text{foreign}}{\text{rate of interest}}\right)} = \left(\frac{\text{forward exchange rate}}{\text{spot exchange rate}}\right) \quad (17\text{-}3a)$$

To illustrate, consider the following situation. The six-month risk-free rate of interest in the United States was 2 percent on July 14, 2009. The spot exchange rate between the U.S. dollar and the Japanese yen on this date was 0.01071 and the forward exchange rate for six months hence was 0.010738. According to interest rate parity, what would you expect the six-month risk-free rate of interest to be in Japan? Substituting into equation (17-3) we calculate the following:

$$\left(1 + \frac{\text{U.S. six-month risk-free}}{\text{rate of interest}}\right) = \left(\frac{\text{forward exchange rate}}{\text{spot exchange rate}}\right)\left(1 + \frac{\text{Japanese six-month risk-free}}{\text{rate of interest}}\right)$$

$$(1 + 0.02) = \left(\frac{0.010738}{0.01071}\right)\left(1 + \frac{\text{Japanese six-month risk-free}}{\text{rate of interest}}\right)$$

$$(1 + 0.02) = (1.002614)\left(1 + \frac{\text{Japanese six-month risk-free}}{\text{rate of interest}}\right)$$

Thus, the Japanese six-month risk-free rate of interest = 0.01734 *or* 1.734 percent.

What this means is that you get the same total return whether you change your dollars to yen and invest in the risk-free rate in Japan and then convert them back to dollars, or simply invest your dollars in the U.S. risk-free rate of interest. For example, if you started with $100 and converted it to yen at the spot rate of 0.01071 ¥/$, you'd have 9,337.07 yen. If you invested those yen at 1.734 percent, after six months you'd have ¥9,498.97. Converting this back to dollars at the forward rate you end up with $102.00, the same you would have if you had invested your dollars at the U.S. six month rate of 2 percent.

Concept Check

1. In simple terms, what does the interest rate parity theory mean?

 4 Explain the purchasing-power parity theory and the law of one price.

Purchasing-Power Parity Theory

purchasing-power parity (PPP) theory a theory that states that, in the long run, exchange rates adjust so that the purchasing power of each currency tends to be the same. Thus, exchange rate changes tend to reflect international differences in inflation rates.

Long-run changes in exchange rates are influenced by international differences in inflation rates and the purchasing power of each nation's currency. According to the **purchasing-power parity (PPP) theory**, *in the long run, exchange rates adjust so that the purchasing power of each currency tends to be the same. Thus, exchange rate changes tend to reflect international differences in inflation rates. Countries with high rates of inflation tend to experience declines in the value of their currencies.* Thus, if Britain experiences a 10 percent rate of inflation in a year that Japan experiences only a 6 percent rate, the U.K. currency (the pound) will be expected to decline in value approximately by 3.77 percent $[(1.10/1.06) - 1]$ against the Japanese currency (the yen). More accurately, according to the PPP theory,

$$\text{Expected spot rate} = \text{current spot rate} \times \text{expected difference in inflation rate}$$

$$
\begin{array}{l}
\text{Expected spot rate} \\
\text{domestic currency} \\
\text{per unit of foreign} \\
\text{currency}
\end{array}
=
\begin{array}{l}
\text{current spot rate} \\
\text{domestic currency} \\
\text{per unit of foreign} \\
\text{currency}
\end{array}
\times
\dfrac{1 + \text{expected domestic inflation rate}}{1 + \text{expected foreign inflation rate}}
\qquad (17\text{-}4)
$$

Thus, if the beginning value of the Japanese yen were £0.0066, with a 6 percent inflation rate in Japan and a 10 percent inflation rate in Britain, according to the PPP, the expected value of the Japanese yen at the end of that year will be £0.0066 × [1.10/1.06], or £0.006849.

Again, stated very simply, what does this mean? It means that a dollar should have the same purchasing power anywhere in the world—well, at least on average. Obviously, this is not quite true. However, what the PPP theory tells us is that we should expect, on average, that differences in inflation rates between two countries should be reflected in changes in the exchange rates. In effect, the best forecast of the difference in inflation rates between two countries should also be the best forecast of the change in the spot rate of exchange.

The Law of One Price

Underlying the PPP relationship is the **law of one price**. This law is actually *a proposition that in competitive markets in which there are no transportation costs or barriers to trade, the same goods sold in different countries should sell for the same price if all of the different prices are expressed in terms of the same currency.* The idea is that the worth of a good does not depend on where it is bought or sold. Because inflation will erode the purchasing power of any currency, its exchange rate must adhere to the PPP relationship if the law of one price is to hold over time.

There are enough obvious exceptions to the concept of purchasing-power parity that it may, at first glance, seem difficult to accept. For example, recently a Big Mac cost $2.36 in the United States, and given the then-existing exchange rates, it cost an equivalent of $2.02 in Mexico, $2.70 in Japan, and $3.22 in Germany. On the surface this might appear to violate the PPP theory and the law of one price; however, we must remember that this theory is based on the concept of arbitrage. In the case of a Big Mac, it's pretty hard to imagine buying Big Macs in Mexico for $2.02, shipping them to Germany, and reselling them for $3.22. But for commodities such as gold and other items that are relatively inexpensive to ship and do not have to be consumed immediately, the law of one price holds much better.

law of one price a proposition that in competitive markets in which there are no transportation costs or barriers to trade, the same goods sold in different countries sell for the same price if all the different prices are expressed in terms of the same currency.

The International Fisher Effect

According to the domestic Fisher effect, nominal interest rates reflect the expected inflation rate, a real rate of interest and the product of the real rate of interest and the inflation rate. In other words,

$$
\begin{array}{l}
\text{Nominal} \\
\text{interest rate}
\end{array}
=
\begin{array}{l}
\text{expected} \\
\text{inflation rate}
\end{array}
+
\begin{array}{l}
\text{real rate} \\
\text{of interest}
\end{array}
+
\left(
\begin{array}{l}
\text{expected} \\
\text{inflation rate}
\end{array}
\times
\begin{array}{l}
\text{real rate} \\
\text{of interest}
\end{array}
\right)
\qquad (17\text{-}5)
$$

Although there is mixed empirical support for the international Fisher effect, it is widely thought that, for the major industrial countries, the real rate of interest is about 3 percent when a long-term period is considered. In such a case, with the previous assumption regarding inflation rates, interest rates in Britain and Japan would be (0.10 + 0.03 + 0.003) or 13.3 percent and (0.06 + 0.03 + 0.0018) or 9.18 percent, respectively.

In effect, the international Fisher effect states that the real interest rate should be the same all over the world, with the difference in nominal or stated interest rates simply resulting from the differences in expected inflation rates. As we look at interest rates around the world, this tells us that we should not necessarily send our money to a bank account in the country with the highest interest rates. That course of action might only result in sending our money to a bank in the country with the highest expected level of inflation.

Concept Check

1. What does the law of one price say?
2. What is the international Fisher effect?

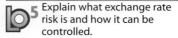

5 Explain what exchange rate risk is and how it can be controlled.

Exposure to Exchange Rate Risk

An asset denominated or valued in terms of foreign-currency cash flows will lose value if that foreign currency declines in value. It can be said that such an asset is exposed to exchange rate risk. However, this possible decline in asset value may be offset by the decline in value of any liability that is also denominated or valued in terms of that foreign currency. Thus, a firm would normally be interested in its *net exposed position* (exposed assets – exposed liabilities) for each period in each currency.

Although expected changes in exchange rates can often be included in the cost–benefit analysis relating to such transactions, in most cases there is an unexpected component in exchange rate changes, and often the cost–benefit analysis for such transactions does not fully capture even the expected change in the exchange rate. For example, price increases for the foreign operations of many MNCs often have to be less than those necessary to fully offset exchange rate changes, owing to the competitive pressures generated by local businesses.

Recall from Chapter 15 that three measures of foreign exchange exposure are translation exposure, transaction exposure, and economic exposure. The three measures of exposure now are examined more closely.

Translation Exposure

translation exposure risk that arises because the foreign operations of MNCs have financial statements denominated in the local currencies of the countries in which the operation are located. These denominations must be translated into the MNCs' home currency at the prevailing exchange rate.

Translation exposure arises because the foreign operations of MNCs have financial statements denominated in the local currency of the country in which the operation is located. But for U.S. MNCs, the *reporting currency* for its consolidated financial statements is the dollar, so the assets, liabilities, revenues, and expenses of the foreign operations must be translated into dollars.

Foreign currency assets and liabilities are considered exposed if their foreign currency value for accounting purposes has to be translated into the domestic currency using the currency exchange rate—the exchange rate in effect on the balance sheet date. Other assets and liabilities and equity amounts that are translated at the historic exchange rate—the rate in effect when these items were first recognized in the company's books—are not considered to be exposed. The rate (current or historic) used to translate various accounts depends on the translation procedure used.

Whereas transaction exposure can result in exchange rate change–related losses and gains that are realized and have an impact on both reported and taxable income, translation exposure results in exchange rate losses and gains that are reflected in the company's accounting books but are unrealized and have little or no impact on taxable income. Theoretically, then, a firm should not have to waste real resources hedging against possible paper losses caused by translation exposure. After all, it's the firm's stock price that really matters. However, there are times a firm may indeed find it economical to hedge against translation losses or gains.

Transaction Exposure

Receivables, payables, and fixed-price sales or purchase contracts are examples of foreign currency transactions whose monetary values are fixed at a time different from the time when these transactions are actually completed. **Transaction exposure** is a term that *describes the net contracted foreign currency transactions for which the settlement amounts are subject to changing exchange rates*. A company normally must set up an additional reporting system to track transaction exposure because several of these amounts are not recognized in the accounting books of the firm.

Exchange rate risk can be neutralized, or hedged, by a change in the firm's asset and liability position in the foreign currency. For example, an exposed asset position (such as an account receivable) can be hedged, or covered, by creating a liability of the same amount and maturity denominated in the foreign currency (such as a forward contract to sell the foreign currency). An exposed liability position (such as an account payable) can be covered by acquiring assets of the same amount and maturity in the foreign currency (such as a forward contract to buy the foreign currency). The objective is to have a zero net asset position in the foreign currency. This eliminates exchange rate risk because the loss (gain) in the liability (asset) is exactly offset by the gain (loss) in the value of the asset (liability) when the foreign currency appreciates (depreciates). Two popular forms of hedges are the money-market hedge and the exchange-market, or forward-market, hedge. In both types of hedge, the amount and the duration of the asset (liability) positions are matched. Note as you read the next two subsections how IRP theory ensures that each hedge provides the same cover.

transaction exposure risk associated with transaction exposure, that is, risk associated with contracts on which the monetary value is fixed at a time different from when the transaction is actually completed and will be impacted by exchange rate changes.

Money-Market Hedge   In a money-market hedge, the exposed position in a foreign currency is offset by borrowing or lending in the money market. Consider the case of the American firm with a net liability position of £3,000. The firm knows the exact amount of its pound liability in 30 days, but it does not know the liability in dollars. Assume that the 30-day money-market rates in both the United States and Britain are, respectively, 1 percent for lending and 1.5 percent for borrowing. The American business can take the following steps:

STEP 1   Calculate the present value of the foreign currency liability (£3,000) that is due in 30 days. Use the money-market rate applicable for the foreign country (1 percent in the United Kingdom). The present value of £3,000 is £2,970.30, computed as follows: £3,000/(1 + 0.01).

STEP 2   Exchange dollars on today's spot market to obtain the £2,970.30. The dollar amount needed today is $4,838.02 (£2,970.30 × 1.6288).

STEP 3   Invest £2,970.30 in a United Kingdom 1-month, money-market instrument. This investment will compound to exactly £3,000 in 1 month. The future liability of £3,000 is therefore covered by the £2,970.30 investment.[3]

Note: If the American business does not own this amount today, it can borrow $4,838.02 from the U.S. money market at the going rate of 1.5 percent. In 30 days the American business will need to repay $4,910.60 [$4,838.02 × (1 + 0.015)].

Assuming that the American business borrows the money, it may base its calculations on the knowledge that the British goods, upon delivery in 30 days, will cost it $4,910.60. The British business will receive £3,000. The American business need not wait for the future spot exchange rate to be revealed because the future dollar payment of the contract is known with certainty. This certainty helps the American business make its pricing and financing decisions.

Many businesses hedge in the money market. The firm needs to borrow (creating a liability) in one market, lend or invest in the other money market, and use the spot exchange

[3]Observe that £2,970.30 × (1 + 0.01) = £3,000.

market on today's date. The mechanics of hedging a net asset position in the foreign currency are the exact reverse of the mechanics of hedging the liability position. With a net asset position in pounds: Borrow in the U.K. money market in pounds, convert it to dollars on the spot exchange market, and invest it in the U.S. money market. When the net assets are converted into pounds (that is, when the firm receives what it is owed), pay off the loan and the interest. The cost of hedging in the money market is the cost of doing business in three different markets. Information about the three markets is needed, and analytical calculations of the type indicated here must be made.

Many small and infrequent traders find the cost of the money-market hedge prohibitive, especially because of the need for information about the market. These traders use the exchange-market, or forward-market, hedge, which has very similar hedging benefits.

The Forward-Market Hedge   The forward market provides a second possible hedging mechanism. It works as follows: A net asset (or liability) position is covered by a liability (or asset) in the forward market. Consider again the case of the American firm with a liability of £3,000 that must be paid in 30 days. The firm can take the following steps to cover its liability position:

STEP 1   Buy a forward contract today to purchase £3,000 in 30 days. The 30-day forward rate is $1.6287/£.

STEP 2   On the 30th day pay the banker $4,886.10 (£3,000 × $1.6287) and collect £3,000. Pay these pounds to the British supplier.

By using the forward contract, the American business knows the exact worth of the future payment in dollars ($4,886.10). The exchange rate risk in pounds is totally eliminated by the net asset position in the forward pounds. In the case of a net asset exposure, the steps open to the American firm are the exact opposite: Sell the pounds forward and on the future day receive and deliver the pounds to collect the agreed-on dollar amount.

The use of the forward market as a hedge against exchange rate risk is simple and direct—that is, match the liability or asset position against an offsetting position in the forward market. The forward-market hedge is relatively easy to implement. The firm directs its banker that it needs to buy or sell a foreign currency on a future date, and the banker gives the firm a forward quote.

The forward-market hedge and the money-market hedge result in an identical future dollar payment (or receipt) if the forward contracts are priced according to the interest rate parity theory. The alert student may have noticed that the dollar payments in the money-market hedge and the forward-market hedge examples were, respectively, $4,838.02 and $4,886.10. Recall from our previous discussions that in efficient markets, the forward contracts do indeed conform to IRP theory. However, the numbers in our example are not identical because the forward rate used in the forward-market hedge is not exactly equal to the interest rates in the money-market hedge.

Currency-Futures Contracts and Options   The forward-market hedge is not adequate for some types of exposure. If the foreign currency asset or liability position occurs on a date for which forward quotes are not available, the forward-market hedge cannot be accomplished. In certain cases the forward-market hedge may cost more than the money-market hedge. In these cases, a corporation with a large amount of exposure may prefer the money-market hedge. In addition to forward-market and money-market hedges, a company can also hedge its exposure by buying (or selling) some relatively new instruments—foreign currency-futures contracts and foreign currency options. Although futures contracts are similar to forward contracts in that they provide fixed prices for the delivery of foreign currency in the future, foreign currency options permit fixed-price delivery to be made anytime *before* maturity. Both futures contracts and options differ from forward contracts in that, unlike forward contracts, which have customized amounts and maturity dates, futures and options are traded in standard amounts with standard maturity dates. In addition, although forward contracts are written by banks, futures and options are traded on organized exchanges, and individual traders deal with the exchange-based clearing organization rather than with each other.

Economic Exposure

The economic value of a company can vary in response to exchange rate changes. This change in value may be caused by a rate change–induced decline in the level of expected cash flows and/or by an increase in the riskiness of these cash flows. **Economic exposure** refers to the overall impact of exchange rate changes on the value of the firm and includes not only the strategic impact of changes in competitive relationships that arise from exchange rate changes but also the economic impact of transaction exposure and, if any, translation exposure.

Economic exposure to exchange rate changes depends on the competitive structure of the markets for a firm's inputs and outputs and how these markets are influenced by changes in exchange rates. This influence, in turn, depends on several economic factors, including price elasticities of the products, the degree of competition from foreign markets, and the direct (through prices) and indirect (through incomes) impact of exchange rate changes on these markets. Assessing the economic exposure faced by a particular firm, thus, depends on your ability to understand and model the structure of the markets for the firm's major inputs (purchases) and outputs (sales).

However, a company need not engage in any cross-border business activity to be exposed to exchange rate changes because product and financial markets in most countries are related and influenced to a large extent by the same global forces. The output of a company engaged in business activity only within one country may be competing with imported products, or it may be competing for its inputs with other domestic and foreign purchasers. For example, a Canadian chemical company that did no cross-border business nevertheless found that its profit margin depended directly on the U.S. dollar/Japanese yen exchange rate. The company used coal as an input in its production process, and the Canadian price of coal was heavily influenced by the extent to which the Japanese bought U.S. coal, which in turn depended on the dollar/yen exchange rate.

Although translation exposure need not be managed, it might be useful for a firm to manage its transaction and economic exposures because they affect firm value directly. In most companies, transaction exposure is generally tracked and managed by the office of the corporate treasurer. Economic exposure is difficult to define in operating terms, and very few companies manage it actively. In most companies, economic exposure is generally considered part of the strategic planning process, rather than a treasurer's or finance function.

economic exposure the impact of exchange rate changes on the value of the firm including both the strategic impact of comparative relationships arising from exchange rate change and the economic impact of transaction exposure.

Concept Check

1. Give a simple explanation of translation exposure.
2. Give a simple explanation of transaction exposure.
3. Give a simple explanation of economic exposure.

Multinational Working-Capital Management

 Identify working-capital management techniques that are useful for international businesses to reduce exchange rate risk and potentially increase profits.

The basic principles of working-capital management for a multinational corporation are similar to those for a domestic firm. However, tax and exchange rate factors are additional considerations for the MNC. For the MNC with subsidiaries in many countries, the optimal decisions in the management of working capital are made by considering the market as a whole. The global, or centralized, financial decisions for the MNC are superior to the set of independent optimal decisions for the subsidiaries. This is the control problem of the MNC. If the individual subsidiaries make decisions that are best for them individually, the consolidation of these decisions may not be best for the MNC as a whole. To achieve global management, sophisticated computerized models incorporating many variables for each subsidiary are utilized to provide the best overall decision for the MNC.

Before considering the components of working-capital management, we examine two techniques that are useful in the management of a wide variety of working-capital components.

Leading and Lagging Strategies

Two important risk-reduction techniques for many working-capital problems are called "leading" and "lagging." Often forward-market and money-market hedges are not available to eliminate exchange risk. Under such circumstances, leading and lagging may be used to reduce exchange risk.

Recall that holding a net asset (long) position is not desirable in a weak or potentially depreciating currency. If a firm has a net asset position in such a currency, it should expedite the disposal of the asset. The firm should get rid of the asset earlier than it otherwise would have, or *lead*, and convert the funds into assets in a relatively stronger currency. By the same reasoning, the firm should *lag*, or delay the collection against a net asset position in a strong currency. Likewise, if the firm has a net liability (short) position in the weak currency, then it should delay the payment against the liability, or lag, until the currency depreciates. In the case of an appreciating or strong foreign currency and a net liability position, the firm should lead the payments—that is, reduce the liabilities earlier than it would have otherwise.

These principles are useful in the management of working capital of an MNC. They cannot, however, eliminate the foreign exchange risk. When exchange rates change continuously, it is almost impossible to guess whether or when the currency will depreciate or appreciate. This is why the risk of exchange rate changes cannot be eliminated. Nevertheless, the reduction of risk, or the increased gain from exchange rate changes via the lead and lag, is useful for cash management, accounts-receivable management, and short-term liability management.

Cash Management and the Positioning of Funds

The positioning of funds takes on an added importance in the international context. For example, an MNC can move funds from a subsidiary in one country to a subsidiary in another country so foreign exchange exposure and the tax liability of the MNC as a whole are minimized.

The transfer of funds among subsidiaries and the parent company is done via royalties, fees, and transfer pricing. A **transfer price** is the *price a subsidiary or a parent company charges other companies that are part of the MNC for its goods or services.* For example, a parent that wishes to transfer funds from a subsidiary in a depreciating-currency country might charge a higher price on the goods and services sold to this subsidiary by the parent or by subsidiaries in strong-currency countries.

transfer price the price a subsidiary or a parent company charges other companies that are part of the MNC for its goods or services.

Concept Check

1. Describe the risk-reduction techniques of leading and lagging.
2. How can a parent company use transfer pricing to move funds from a subsidiary in a depreciating-currency country to a strong-currency country?

 Explain how the financing sources available to multinational corporations differ from those available to domestic firms.

International Financing and Capital Structure Decisions

An MNC has access to many more financing sources than a domestic firm. It can tap not only the financing sources in its home country that are available to its domestic counterparts but also sources in the foreign countries in which it operates. Host countries often provide access to low-cost subsidized financing to attract foreign investment. In addition, the MNC may enjoy preferential credit standards because of its size and investors' preferences for its home currency. For financing purposes, the MNC may be able to access third-country capital markets—countries in which it does not operate but that may have large, well-functioning capital markets. Finally, an MNC can also access external currency markets: Eurodollar, Eurocurrency, or Asian dollar markets. These external markets are unregulated, and because of their lower spreads, can offer very attractive rates for financing *and* for investments. Because of its ability to tap a larger number of financial markets, the MNC may have a lower cost of capital; and because it may be better able to avoid the problems or limitations of any one financial market, it may have more continuous access to external financing compared with a domestic company.

Access to national financial markets is regulated by governments. For example, in the United States, access to capital markets is governed by SEC regulations. Access to Japanese capital markets is governed by regulations issued by the Ministry of Finance. Some countries have extensive regulations; other countries have relatively open markets. These regulations can differ depending on the legal residency of the company raising funds. A company that cannot use a local subsidiary to raise funds in a given market will be treated as foreign. In order to increase their visibility in a foreign capital market, a number of MNCs are now listing their equities on the stock exchanges of many of these countries.

The external currency markets are predominantly centered in Europe, but the majority of their value is denominated in terms of the U.S. dollar. Thus, most external currency markets can be characterized as Eurodollar markets. Such markets consist of an active short-term money market and an intermediate-term capital market with maturities ranging up to 15 years and averaging about 7 to 9 years. The intermediate-term market consists of the Eurobond and the Syndicated Eurocredit markets. Recall from Chapter 7 that Eurobonds are usually issued as unregistered bearer bonds and generally tend to have higher flotation costs but lower coupon rates compared with similar bonds issued in the United States. A *Syndicated Eurocredit* loan is simply a large-term loan that involves contributions by a number of lending banks.

In arriving at its capital structure decisions, an MNC has to consider a number of factors. First, the capital structure of its local affiliates is influenced by local norms regarding that industry and in that country. Local norms for companies in the same industry can differ considerably from country to country too. Second, the local-affiliate capital structure must also reflect corporate attitudes toward exchange rate and political risks in that country. Third, the local-affiliate capital structure must reflect home-country requirements with regard to the company's consolidated capital structure. Finally, the optimal MNC capital structure should reflect its wider access to financial markets, its ability to diversify its economic and political risks, and its other advantages over domestic companies.

Concept Check

1. What factors might an MNC consider in making a capital structure decision?

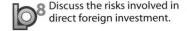 Discuss the risks involved in direct foreign investment.

Direct Foreign Investment

An MNC often makes direct foreign investments abroad in the form of plants and equipment. The decision process for this type of investment is very similar to the capital-budgeting decision in the domestic context—with some additional twists. Most real-world capital-budgeting decisions are made with uncertain future outcomes. Recall that a capital-budgeting decision has three major components: the estimation of the future cash flows (including the initial cost of the proposed investment), the estimation of the risk in these cash flows, and the choice of the proper discount rate. We will assume that the

> **REMEMBER YOUR PRINCIPLES**
>
> Principle Investment across international boundaries gives rise to special risks not encountered when investing domestically. Specifically, political risks and exchange rate risk are unique to international investing. Once again, **Principle 3: Risk Requires a Reward** provides a rationale for evaluating these considerations. Where added risks are present, added rewards are necessary to induce investment.

NPV criterion is appropriate as we examine (1) the risks associated with direct foreign investment and (2) factors to be considered in making the investment decision that may be unique to the international scene.

Risks in domestic capital budgeting arise from two sources: business risk and financial risk. The international capital-budgeting problem incorporates these risks as well as political risk and exchange risk.

Business Risk and Financial Risk

The U.S. MNC needs to be aware of the business climate in both the United States and the foreign country. Additional business risk is due to competition from other MNCs, local businesses, and imported goods. Financial risk refers to the risks introduced in the profit stream by the firm's financial structure. The financial risks of foreign operations are not very different from those of domestic operations.

Political Risk

Political risk arises because the foreign subsidiary conducts its business in a political system different from that of the home country. Many foreign governments, especially those in the third world, are less stable than the U.S. government. A change in a country's political setup frequently brings a change in policies with respect to businesses—and especially with respect to foreign businesses. An extreme change in policy might involve nationalization or even outright expropriation (government seizure) of certain businesses. These are the political risks of conducting business abroad. A business with no investment in plant and equipment is less susceptible to these risks. Some examples of political risk are listed here:

1. Expropriation of plant and equipment without compensation.
2. Expropriation with minimal compensation that is below actual market value.
3. Nonconvertibility of the subsidiary's foreign earnings into the parent's currency—the problem of *blocked funds*.
4. Substantial changes in the laws governing taxation.
5. Governmental controls in the foreign country regarding the sale price of certain products, wages and compensation paid to personnel, the hiring of personnel, transfer payments made to the parent, and local borrowing.
6. Some governments require certain amounts of local ownership in the business.

All these controls and governmental actions put the cash flows of the investment to the parent company at risk. Thus, these risks must be considered before making the foreign investment decision. For example, the MNC might decide against investing in countries with risks of types 1 and 2, whereas other risks can be borne—provided that the returns from the foreign investments are high enough to compensate for them. In fact, insurance against some types of political risks can be purchased from private insurance companies or from the U.S. Government Overseas Private Investment Corporation. It should be noted that although an MNC cannot protect itself against all foreign political risks, political risks are also present in domestic business.

Exchange Rate Risk

The exposure of the firm's fixed assets is best measured by exchange rate changes that affect the firm's future earnings stream: that being economic exposure rather than translation exposure. For instance, changes in the exchange rate can adversely affect sales by making competing imported goods cheaper. Changes in the cost of goods sold can result if some components are imported and their foreign currency prices change. The thrust of these examples is that the effect of exchange rate changes on income statement items should be properly measured to evaluate exchange rate risk. Finally, exchange rate risk affects the dollar-denominated profit stream of the parent company, whether or not it affects the firm's foreign-operations profits.

Concept Check

1. What are some of the risks associated with direct foreign investments?

Summary

The growth of our global economy, the increasing number of multinational corporations, and the increase in foreign trade itself underscore the importance of the study of international finance.

Discuss the internationalization of business.

Under floating systems, exchange rates between currencies vary depending upon supply and demand conditions in the exchange market. Important economic factors affecting the level of exchange rates include the relative economic strengths of the countries involved, the balance-of-payments mechanism, and the countries' monetary policies and interest rates. Several important exchange rate terms are introduced. These include the asked and the bid rates, which represent the selling and buying rates of currencies. The direct quote is the units of home currency per unit of foreign currency, and the indirect quote is the reciprocal of the direct quote. Cross-rate computations reflect the exchange rate between two foreign currencies.

Explain why foreign exchange rates in two different countries must be in line with each other.

The forward exchange market provides a valuable service by quoting rates for the delivery of foreign currencies in the future. The foreign currency is said to sell at a discount relative to the spot rate when the forward rate is lower than the spot rate. It is said to sell at a premium relative to the spot rate when the forward rate is higher than the spot rate. According to the interest rate parity theory, these premiums and discounts depend solely on the differences in the level of the interest rates of countries.

Discuss the concept of interest rate parity.

According to the purchasing-power parity (PPP) theory, in the long run, exchange rates adjust so that the purchasing power of each currency tends to be the same. Thus, exchange rate changes tend to reflect international differences in inflation rates. As a result, countries with high rates of inflation tend to experience declines in the value of their currency. Underlying the PPP relationship is the law of one price. This law is actually a proposition that in competitive markets in which there are no transportation costs or barriers to trade, the same goods sold in different countries sell for the same price if all of the different prices are expressed in terms of the same currency.

Explain the purchasing-power parity theory and the law of one price.

An MNC faces three types of exchange rate risk: transaction exposure, translation exposure, and economic exposure. The company can offset its exposure using various tools, including setting up an offsetting asset or liability of the same amount as the foreign-currency asset or liability, and using money-market and forward-market hedges, futures-market contracts and options, and currency swaps.

Explain what exchange rate risk is and how it can be controlled.

With regard to working-capital management in an international environment, we find leading and lagging techniques useful in minimizing exchange rate risk and increasing profitability. In addition, positioning funds is a useful tool for reducing exchange rate risk exposure.

Identify working-capital management techniques that are useful for international businesses to reduce exchange rate risk and potentially increase profits.

The MNC may have a lower cost of capital because it has access to a larger set of financial markets than a domestic company. In addition to the home, host, and third-country financial markets, the MNC can tap the rapidly growing external currency markets. In making capital structure decisions, the MNC must consider political and exchange rate risks and host- and home-country capital structure norms.

Explain how the financing sources available to multinational corporations differ from those available to domestic firms.

The complexities encountered in the direct foreign investment decision include the usual sources of risk—business and financial—and the additional risks associated with fluctuating exchange rates and political factors. Political risk is due to differences in political climates, institutions, and processes between the home country and abroad. This makes estimating future cash flows and choosing the proper discount rates more complicated than for the domestic investment situation.

Discuss the risks involved in direct foreign investment.

Key Terms

Review Questions

All Review Questions and Study Problems are available in MyFinanceLab.

17-1. What additional factors are encountered in international as compared with domestic financial management? Discuss each briefly.

17-2. What different types of businesses operate in the international environment? Why are the techniques and strategies available to these firms different?

17-3. What is meant by arbitrage profits?

17-4. What are the markets and mechanics involved in generating simple arbitrage profits?

17-5. How do purchasing-power parity, interest rate parity, and the Fisher effect explain the relationships among the current spot rate, the future spot rate, and the forward rate?

17-6. What is meant by (a) exchange risk and (b) political risk?

17-7. How can exchange risk be measured?

17-8. What are the differences among transaction, translation, and economic exposures? Should all of them be ideally reduced to zero?

17-9. What steps can a firm take to reduce exchange risk? Indicate at least two different techniques.

17-10. How are forward-market and the money-market hedges used? What are the major differences between these two types of hedges?

17-11. In the New York exchange market, the forward rate for the Indian currency, the rupee, is not quoted. If you were exposed to exchange risk in rupees, how could you hedge your position?

17-12. Compare and contrast the use of forward contracts, futures contracts, and futures options to reduce foreign exchange exposure. When is each instrument most appropriate?

17-13. Indicate two working-capital management techniques that are useful for international businesses to reduce exchange risk and potentially increase profits.

17-14. How do the financing sources available to an MNC differ from those available to a domestic firm? What do these differences mean for the company's cost of capital?

17-15. What risks are associated with direct foreign investment? How do these risks differ from those encountered in domestic investment?

17-16. How is the direct foreign investment decision made? What are the inputs to this decision process? Are the inputs more complicated than those to the domestic investment problem? If so, why?

17-17. A corporation wants to enter a particular foreign market, but a DFI analysis indicates that putting a plant in the foreign country will not profitable. What other course of action can the company take to enter the foreign market? What are the important considerations?

Self-Test Problem

(The solution to this problem is found at the end of the chapter.)
The data for Self-Test Problem ST-1 are given in the following table:

COUNTRY	CONTRACT	$/FOREIGN CURRENCY
New Zealand—dollar	Spot	0.3893
	30-day	0.3910
	90-day	0.3958

ST-1. You own $10,000. The U.S. dollar rate on the New Zealand dollar is 2.5823 NZ$/US$. The New Zealand dollar rate is given in the accompanying table. Are arbitrage profits possible? Set up an arbitrage scheme with your capital. What is the gain (loss) in dollars?

Study Problems

The data for Study Problems 17-1 through 17-6 are given in the following table:

COUNTRY	CONTRACT	$/FOREIGN CURRENCY
Canada—dollar	Spot	0.8437
	30-day	0.8417
	90-day	0.8395
Japan—yen	Spot	0.004684
	30-day	0.004717
	90-day	0.004781
Switzerland—franc	Spot	0.5139
	30-day	0.5169
	90-day	0.5315

17-1. (*Spot exchange rates*) An American business needs to pay (a) 10,000 Canadian dollars, (b) 2 million yen, and (c) 50,000 Swiss francs to businesses abroad. What are the dollar payments to the respective countries?

17-2. (*Spot exchange rates*) An American business pays $10,000, $15,000, and $20,000 to suppliers in, respectively, Japan, Switzerland, and Canada. How much, in local currencies, do the suppliers receive?

17-3. (*Indirect quotes*) Compute the indirect quote for the spot and forward Canadian dollar, yen, and Swiss franc contracts.

17-4. (*Exchange rates*) The spreads on the contracts as a percentage of the asked rates are 2 percent for yen, 3 percent for Canadian dollars, and 5 percent for Swiss francs. Show, in a table similar to the preceding one, the bid rates for the different spot and forward rates.

17-5. (*Exchange rate arbitrage*) You own $10,000. The dollar rate in Tokyo is 216.6743. The yen rate in New York is given in the preceding table. Are arbitrage profits possible? Set up an arbitrage scheme with your capital. What is the gain (loss) in dollars?

17-6. (*Cross rates*) Compute the Canadian dollar/yen and the yen/Swiss franc spot rate from the data in the preceding table.

Mini Case

For your job as the business reporter for a local newspaper, you are asked to put together a series of articles on multinational finance and the international currency markets for your readers. Much recent local press coverage has been given to losses in the foreign exchange markets by JGAR, a local firm that is the subsidiary of Daedlufetarg, a large German manufacturing firm.

Your editor would like you to address several specific questions dealing with multinational finance. Prepare a response to the following memorandum from your editor:

To: Business Reporter
From: Perry White, Editor, *Daily Planet*
Re: Upcoming Series on Multinational Finance

In your upcoming series on multinational finance, I would like to make sure you cover several specific points. Before you begin this assignment, I want to make sure we are all reading from the same script because accuracy has always been the cornerstone of the *Daily Planet*. I'd like a response to the following questions before we proceed:

a. What new problems and factors are encountered in international, as opposed to domestic, financial management?
b. What does the term *arbitrage profits* mean?
c. What can a firm do to reduce exchange risk?
d. What are the differences among a forward contract, a futures contract, and options?

Use the following data in your responses to the remaining questions:

Selling Quotes for Foreign Currencies in New York

COUNTRY—CURRENCY	CONTRACT	$/FOREIGN
Canada—dollar	Spot	0.8450
	30-day	0.8415
	90-day	0.8390
Japan—yen	Spot	0.004700
	30-day	0.004750
	90-day	0.004820
Switzerland—franc	Spot	0.5150
	30-day	0.5182
	90-day	0.5328

e. An American business needs to pay (a) 15,000 Canadian dollars, (b) 1.5 million yen, and (c) 55,000 Swiss francs to businesses abroad. What are the dollar payments to the respective countries?
f. An American business pays $20,000, $5,000, and $15,000 to suppliers in, respectively, Japan, Switzerland, and Canada. How much, in local currencies, do the suppliers receive?
g. Compute the indirect quote for the spot and forward Canadian dollar contract.
h. You own $10,000. The dollar rate in Tokyo is 216.6752. The yen rate in New York is given in the preceding table. Are arbitrage profits possible? Set up an arbitrage scheme with your capital. What is the gain (loss) in dollars?
i. Compute the Canadian dollar/yen spot rate from the data in the preceding table.

Self-Test Solution

SS-1. The New Zealand rate is 2.5823 NZ\$/\$1, and the (indirect) New York rate is 1/0.3893 = 2.5687 NZ\$/US\$.

Assuming no transaction costs, the rates between New Zealand and New York are out of line. Thus, arbitrage profits are possible.

STEP 1 Because the New Zealand dollar is cheaper in New Zealand, buy \$10,000 worth of New Zealand dollars in New Zealand. The number of New Zealand dollars purchased would be \$10,000 × 2.5823 = 25,823 New Zealand dollars.

STEP 2 Simultaneously, sell the New Zealand dollars in New York at the prevailing rate. The amount received upon the sale of the New Zealand dollars would be:

25,823 NZ\$ × \$.3893/NZ\$ = \$10,052.89

The net gain is \$10,052.89 − \$10,000 = \$52.89.

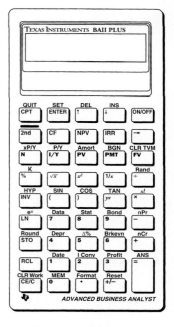

Appendix A

Using a Calculator

As you prepare for a career in business, the ability to use a financial calculator is essential, whether you are in the finance division or the marketing department. For most positions, it will be assumed that you can use a calculator in making computations that at one time were simply not possible without extensive time and effort. The following examples let us see what is possible, but they represent only the beginning of using the calculator in finance.

With just a little time and effort, you will be surprised at how much you can do with the calculator, such as calculating a stock's beta, or determining the value of a bond on a specific day given the exact date of maturity, or finding net present values and internal rates of return, or calculating the standard deviation. The list is almost endless.

In demonstrating how calculators may make our work easier, we must first decide which calculator to use. The options are numerous and largely depend on personal preference. We have chosen the Texas Instruments BA II Plus and the Hewlett-Packard 10bII.

We will limit our discussion to the following issues:

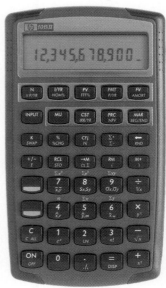

  I. Introductory Comments
 II. An Important Starting Point
III. Calculating Table Values for:
    A. Appendix B (Compound sum of $1)
    B. Appendix C (Present value of $1)
    C. Appendix D (Sum of an annuity of $1 for *n* periods)
    D. Appendix E (Present value of an annuity of $1 for *n* periods)
 IV. Calculating Present Values
  V. Calculating Future Values (Compound sum)
 VI. Calculating the Number of Payments or Receipts
VII. Calculating the Payment Amount
VIII. Calculating the Interest Rate
 IX. Bond Valuation
    A. Computing the value of a bond
    B. Calculating the yield to maturity of a bond
  X. Computing the Net Present Value and Internal Rate of Return
    A. Where future cash flows are equal amounts in each period (annuity)
    B. Where future cash flows are unequal amounts in each period

I. Introductory Comments

In the examples that follow, you are told (1) which keystrokes to use, (2) the resulting appearance of the calculator display, and (3) a supporting explanation.

The keystrokes column tells you which keys to press. The keystrokes shown in a white box tell you to use one of the calculator's dedicated or "hard" keys. For example, if +/− is shown in the keystrokes instruction column, press that key on the keyboard of the calculator. With the Texas Instruments BA II Plus, to use a function printed in a shaded box above a dedicated key, always press the shaded key 2nd first, then the function key. The HP 10bII has two shift keys, one purple (PRP) and one orange (ORG). To use the functions printed in purple (stats) on the keypad, press the purple button first. To use the functions printed in orange (shift) on the keypad, press the orange button first.

II. AN IMPORTANT STARTING POINT - TEXAS INSTRUMENTS BA II PLUS

Example: You want to display four numbers to the right of the decimal.

Keystrokes	Display	Explanation
2nd		
FORMAT	DEC =	
4 ENTER	DEC = 4.0000	Sets display to show four numbers to the right of the decimal
CE/C CE/C	0.0000	Clears display

Example: You want to display two payments per year to be paid at the end of each period.

Keystrokes	Display	Explanation
2nd		
P/Y	P/Y =	
2 ENTER	P/Y = 2.0000	Sets number of payments per year at 2
2nd		
BGN	END	Sets timing of payment at the end of each period
CE/C CE/C	0.0000	Clears display

II. AN IMPORTANT STARTING POINT - HEWLETT-PACKARD 10BII

Example: You want to display four numbers to the right of the decimal. Note that ORG refers to the orange key, which is a "shifted" function used to access the functions printed in orange. There is also a purple shift key that gives you access to the statistical functions in purple.

Keystrokes	Display	Explanation
ORG, C ALL	0.00	Clears registers
ORG, Disp, 4	0.0000	Displays 4 decimal places

Example: You want to display two payments per year to be paid at the end of the period.

Keystrokes	Display	Explanation
ORG, C ALL	0.0000	Clears registers
2, ORG, P/YR	2.0000	Sets payments per year
ORG, BEG/END	2.0000	Sets END mode unless BEGIN enunciator on

III. CALCULATING TABLE VALUES - TEXAS INSTRUMENTS BA II PLUS

A. The compound sum of $1 (Appendix B)

Example: What is the table value for the compound sum of $1 for 5 years at a 12 percent annual interest rate?

Keystrokes	Display	Explanation
2nd		
P/Y	P/Y =	
1 ENTER	P/Y = 1.0000	Sets number of payments per year at 1
2nd		
BGN	END	Sets timing of payment at the end of each period
CE/C CE/C	0.0000	Clears display
2nd		
CLR TVM	0.0000	Clears TVM variables
1 +/−	PV = −1.0000	Stores initial $1 as a negative present value.
PV		Otherwise the answer will appear as negative.
5 N	N = 5.0000	Stores number of periods
12 I/Y	I/Y = 12.0000	Stores interest rate
CPT FV	FV = 1.7623	Table value

B. The present value of $1 (Appendix C)

Example: What is the table value for the present value of $1 for 8 years at a 10 percent annual interest rate?

Keystrokes	Display	Explanation
2nd		
P/Y	P/Y =	
1 ENTER	P/Y = 1.0000	Sets number of payments per year at 1
2nd		
BGN	END	Sets timing of payment at the end of each period
CE/C CE/C	0.0000	Clears display
2nd		
CLR TVM	0.0000	Clears TVM variables
1 +/−	FV = −1.0000	Stores future amount as negative value
FV		
8 N	N = 8.0000	Stores number of periods
10 I/Y	I/Y = 10.0000	Stores interest rate
CPT PV	PV = 0.4665	Table value

C. The sum of an annuity of $1 for *n* periods (Appendix D)

Example: What is the table value for the compound sum of an annuity of $1 for 6 years at a 14 percent annual interest rate?

Keystrokes	Display	Explanation
2nd		
P/Y	P/Y =	
1 ENTER	P/Y = 1.0000	Sets number of payments per year at 1
2nd		
BGN	END	Sets timing of payment at the end of each period
CE/C CE/C	0.0000	Clears display
2nd		
CLR TVM	0.0000	Clears TVM variables
1 +/−	PMT = −1.0000	Stores annual payment (annuity) as a negative number.
PMT		Otherwise the answer will appear as a negative.
6 N	N = 6.0000	Stores number of periods
14 I/Y	I/Y = 14.0000	Stores interest rate
CPT FV	FV = 8.5355	Table value

D. The present value of an annuity of $1 for *n* periods (Appendix E)

Example: What is the table value for the present value of an annuity of $1 for 12 years at a 9 percent annual interest rate?

Keystrokes	Display	Explanation
2nd		
P/Y	P/Y =	
1 ENTER	P/Y = 1.0000	Sets number of payments per year at 1
2nd		
BGN	END	Sets timing of payment at the end of each period
CE/C CE/C	0.0000	Clears display
2nd		
CLR TVM	0.0000	Clears TVM variables
1 +/−	PMT = −1.0000	Stores annual payment (annuity) as a negative number.
PMT		Otherwise the answer will appear as a negative.
12 N	N = 12.0000	Stores number of periods
9 I/Y	I/Y = 9.0000	Stores interest rate
CPT PV	PV = 7.1607	Table value

III. CALCULATING TABLE VALUES - HEWLETT-PACKARD 10BII

A. The compound sum of $1 (Appendix B)

Example: What is the table value for the compound sum of $1 for 5 years at 12 percent annual interest rate?

Keystrokes	Display	Explanation
ORG, C ALL	0.0000	Clears registers
1, ORG, P/YR	1.0000	Sets number of payments per year at 1
ORG, BEG/END	1.0000	Sets timing of payment at the end of each period
		(If BEGIN shows then press ORG, BEG/END again)
1, +/−, PV	−1.0000	Stores initial $1 as a negative present value.
		Otherwise the answer will appear as a negative.
5, N	5.0000	Stores number of periods
12, I/YR	12.0000	Stores interest rate
FV	1.7623	Table value

B. The Present Value of $1 (Appendix C)

Example: What is the table value for the present value of $1 for 8 years at a 10 percent annual interest rate?

Keystrokes	Display	Explanation
ORG, C ALL	0.0000	Clears registers
1, ORG, P/YR	1.0000	Sets number of payments per year at 1
ORG, BEG/END	1.0000	Sets timing of payment at the end of each period
		(If BEGIN shows press ORG, BEG/END again)
1, +/−, FV	−1.0000	Stores future amount as negative value
8, N	8.0000	Stores number of periods
10, I/YR	10.0000	Stores interest rate
PV	0.4665	Table value

C. The sum of an annuity of $1 for *n* periods (Appendix D)

Example: What is the table value for the compound sum of an annuity of $1 for 6 years at a 14 percent annual interest rate?

Keystrokes	Display	Explanation
ORG, C ALL	0.0000	Clears registers
1, ORG, P/YR	1.0000	Sets number of payments per year at 1
ORG, BEG/END	1.0000	Sets timing of payment at the end of each period
		(If BEGIN shows press ORG, BEG/END again)
1, +/−, PMT	−1.0000	Stores the annual payment (annuity) as a negative number. Otherwise the answer will appear as a negative.
6, N	6.0000	Stores the number of periods
14, I/YR	14.0000	Stores interest rate
FV	8.5355	Table value

D. The present value of an annuity of $1 for *n* periods (Appendix E)

Example: What is the table value for the present value of an annuity of $1 for 12 years at a 9 percent annual interest rate?

Keystrokes	Display	Explanation
ORG, C ALL	0.0000	Clears registers
1, ORG, P/YR	1.0000	Sets number of payments per year at 1
ORG, BEG/END	1.0000	Sets timing of payment at the end of each period
		(If BEGIN shows press ORG, BEG/END again)
1, +/−, PMT	−1.0000	Stores the annual payment (annuity) as a negative number.
		Otherwise the answer will appear as a negative.
12, N	12.0000	Stores number of periods
9, I/Y	9.0000	Stores interest rate
PV	7.1607	Table value

IV. CALCULATING PRESENT VALUES - TEXAS INSTRUMENTS BA II PLUS

Example: You are considering the purchase of a franchise of quick oil-change locations, which you believe will provide an annual cash flow of $50,000. At the end of 10 years, you believe that you will be able to sell the franchise for an estimated $900,000. Calculate the maximum amount you should pay for the franchise (present value) in order to realize at least an 18 percent annual yield.

Keystrokes	Display	Explanation
2nd		
BGN	END	Sets timing of payment at the end of each period
CE/C CE/C	0.0000	Clears display
2nd		
CLR TVM	0.0000	Clears TVM variables
10 N	N = 10.0000	Stores *n*, the holding period
18 I/Y	I/Y = 18.0000	Stores *i*, the required rate of return
50,000 PMT	PMT = 50,000.0000	Stores *PMT*, the annual cash flow to be received
900,000 FV	FV = 900,000.0000	Stores *FV*, the cash flow to be received at the end of the project
CPT PV	PV = −396,662.3350	The present value, given a required rate of return of 18 percent. (Note: The present value is displayed with a minus sign since it represents cash paid out.)

IV. CALCULATING PRESENT VALUES - HEWLETT-PACKARD 10BII

Example: You are considering the purchase of a franchise of quick oil-change locations, which you believe will provide an annual cash flow of $50,000. At the end of 10 years, you believe that you will be able to sell the franchise for an estimated $900,000. Calculate the maximum amount you should pay for the franchise (present value) in order to realize at least an 18 percent annual yield.

Keystrokes	Display	Explanation
ORG, C ALL	0.0000	Clears registers
ORG, BEG/END	0.0000	Sets timing of payment at the end of each period (If BEGIN shows press ORG, BEG/END again)
10, N	10.0000	Stores n, the holding period
18, I/Y	18.0000	Stores i, the required rate of return
50,000, PMT	50,000.0000	Stores PMT, the annual cash flow to be received
900,000, FV	900,000.0000	Stores FV, the cash flow to be received at the end of the project
PV	−396,662.3350	The present value, given a required rate of return of 18 percent. (Note: The present value is displayed with a minus sign since it represents cash paid out.)

V. CALCULATING FUTURE VALUES (COMPOUND SUM) - TEXAS INSTRUMENTS BA II PLUS

Example: If you deposit $300 a month (at the beginning of each month) into a new account that pays 6.25 percent annual interest compounded monthly, how much will you have in the account after 5 years?

Keystrokes	Display	Explanation
2nd		
BGN	END	Sets timing of payment at the end of each period
2nd		
SET	BGN	Sets timing of payments to beginning of each period
2nd		
P/Y	P/Y =	
12 ENTER	P/Y = 12.0000	Sets 12 payments per year
CE/C CE/C	0.0000	Clears display

(continues on next page)

Keystrokes	Display	Explanation
2nd		
CLR TVM	0.0000	Clears TVM variables
60 N	N = 60.0000	Stores *n*, the number of months for the investment
6.25 I/Y	I/Y = 6.2500	Stores *i*, the annual rate
300 +/− PMT	PMT = −300.0000	Stores *PMT*, the monthly amount invested (with a minus sign for cash paid out)
CPT FV	FV = 21,175.7613	The future value after 5 years

V. CALCULATING FUTURE VALUES (COMPOUND SUM) - HEWLETT-PACKARD 10BII

Example: If you deposit $300 a month (at the beginning of each month) into a new account that pays 6.25 percent annual interest compounded monthly, how much will you have in the account after 5 years?

Keystrokes	Display	Explanation
ORG, C ALL	0.0000	Clears registers
ORG, BEG/END	0.0000(BEGIN)	Sets timing of payments to beginning of each period
12, ORG, P/YR	12.0000	Sets 12 payments per year
60, N	60.0000	Stores *n*, the number of months for the investment
6.25, I/Y	6.2500	Stores *I*, the annual rate
300, +/−, PMT	−300.0000	Stores *PMT*, the monthly amount invested (with a minus sign for cash paid out)
FV	21,175.7613	The future value after 5 years

VI. CALCULATING THE NUMBER OF PAYMENTS OR RECEIPTS - TEXAS INSTRUMENTS BA II PLUS

Example: If you wish to retire with $500,000 saved, and can only afford payments of $500 at the beginning of each month, how long will you have to contribute toward your retirement if you can earn a 10 percent return on your contributions?

Keystrokes	Display	Explanation
2nd		
BGN	BGN	Verifies timing of payment at the beginning of each period
2nd		
P/Y	P/Y = 12.0000	
12 ENTER	P/Y = 12.0000	Sets 12 payments per year
CE/C CE/C	0.0000	Clears display
2nd		
CLR TVM	0.0000	Clears TVM variables
10 I/Y	I/Y = 10.0000	Stores *i*, the interest rate
500 +/− PMT	PMT = −500.0000	Stores *PMT*, the monthly amount invested (with a minus sign for cash paid out)
500,000 FV	FV = 500,000.0000	The value we want to achieve
CPT N	N = 268.2539	Number of months (since we considered monthly payments) required to achieve our goal

VI. CALCULATING THE NUMBER OF PAYMENTS OR RECEIPTS - HEWLETT-PACKARD 10BII

Example: If you wish to retire with $500,000 saved and can only afford payments of $500 at the beginning of each month, how long will you have to contribute toward your retirement if you can earn a 10 percent return on your contributions?

Keystrokes	Display	Explanation
ORG, C ALL	0.0000	Clears registers
ORG, BEG/END	0.0000(BEGIN)	Sets timing of payments to beginning of each period

12, ORG, P/YR	12.0000	Sets 12 payments per year
10, I/YR	10.0000	Stores I, the interest rate
500, +/-, PMT	500.0000	Stores PMT, the monthly amount invested (with a minus sign for cash paid out)
500,000, FV	500,000.0000	The value we want to achieve
N	268.2539	Number of months (since we considered monthly payments) required to achieve our goal

VII. CALCULATING THE PAYMENT AMOUNT - TEXAS INSTRUMENTS BA II PLUS

Example: Suppose your retirement needs were $750,000. If you are currently 25 years old and plan to retire at age 65, how much will you have to contribute at the beginning of each month for retirement if you can earn 12.5 percent on your savings?

Keystrokes	Display	Explanation
2nd		
BGN	BGN	Verifies timing of payment at the beginning of each period
2nd		
P/Y	P/Y = 12.0000	
12 ENTER	P/Y = 12.0000	Sets 12 payments per year
CE/C CE/C	0.0000	Clears display
2nd		
CLR TVM	0.0000	Clears TVM variables
12.5 I/Y	I/Y = 12.5000	Stores i, the interest rate
480 N	N = 480.0000	Stores n, the number of periods until we stop contributing (40 years × 12 months/year = 480 months)
750,000 FV	FV = 750,000.0000	The value we want to achieve
CPT PMT	PMT = −53.8347	Monthly contribution required to achieve our ultimate goal (shown as negative since it represents cash paid out)

VII. CALCULATING THE PAYMENT AMOUNT - HEWLETT-PACKARD 10BII

Example: Suppose your retirement needs are $750,000. If you are currently 25 years old and plan to retire at age 65, how much will you have to contribute at the beginning of each month for retirement if you can earn 12.5 percent on your savings?

Keystrokes	Display	Explanation
ORG, C ALL	0.0000	Clears registers
ORG, BEG/END	0.0000(BEGIN)	Sets timing of payments to the beginning of each period
12, ORG, P/YR	12.0000	Sets 12 payments per year
12.5, I/YR	12.5000	Stores I, the interest rate
480 N	N = 480.0000	Stores n, the number of periods until we stop contributing (40 years × 12 months/year = 480 months)
750,000, FV	750,000.0000	The value we want to achieve
PMT	−53.8347	Monthly contribution required to achieve our ultimate goal (shown as a negative since it represents cash paid out)

VIII. CALCULATING THE INTEREST RATE - TEXAS INSTRUMENTS BA II PLUS

Example: If you invest $300 at the end of each month for 6 years (72 months) for a promised $30,000 return at the end, what interest rate are you earning on your investment?

Keystrokes	Display	Explanation
2nd		
BGN	BGN	Sets timing of payments to beginning of each period

(continues on next page)

Keystrokes	Display	Explanation
2nd		
SET	END	Sets timing of payments to end of each period
2nd		
P/Y	P/Y = 12.0000	
12 ENTER	P/Y = 12.0000	Sets 12 payments per year
CE/C CE/C	0.0000	Clears display
2nd		
CLR TVM	0.0000	Clears TVM variables
72 N	N = 72.0000	Stores *n*, the number of deposits (investments)
300 +/− PMT	PMT = −300.0000	Stores *PMT*, the monthly amount invested (with a minus sign for cash paid out)
30,000 FV	FV = 30,000.0000	Stores the future value to be received in 6 years
CPT I/Y	I/Y = 10.5892	The annual interest rate earned on the investment

VIII. CALCULATING THE INTEREST RATE - HEWLETT-PACKARD 10BII

Example: If you invest $300 at the end of each month for 6 years (72 months) for a promised $30,000 return at the end, what interest rate are you earning on your investment?

Keystrokes	Display	Explanation
ORG, C ALL	0.0000	Clears registers
ORG, BEG/END	0.0000	Sets timing of payments to the end of each period
72, N	72.000	Stores *n*, the number of deposits (investments)
300, +/−, PMT	−300.0000	Stores PMT, the monthly amount invested (with a minus sign for cash paid out)
30,000, FV	30,000.0000	Stores the future value to be received in 6 years
I/YR	10.5892	The annual interest rate earned on the investment

IX. BOND VALUATION - TEXAS INSTRUMENTS BA II PLUS

A. Computing the value of a bond

Example: Assume the current date is January 1, 2006, and that you want to know the value of a bond that matures in 10 years and has a coupon rate of 9 percent (4.5 percent semiannually). Your required rate of return is 12 percent.

Keystrokes	Display	Explanation
2nd		
BGN	END	Verifies timing of payments to end of each period
2nd		
P/Y	P/Y = 12.0000	
2 ENTER	P/Y = 2.0000	Sets 2 payments per year; end mode (END) assumes cash flows are at the end of each 6-month period
CE/C CE/C	0.0000	Clears display
2nd		
CLR TVM	0.0000	Clears TVM variables
20 N	N = 20.0000	Stores the number of semiannual periods (10 years × 2)
12 I/Y	I/Y = 12.0000	Stores annual rate of return
45 PMT	PMT = 45.0000	Stores the semiannual interest payment
1,000 FV	FV = 1,000.0000	Stores the bond's maturity or par value
CPT PV	PV = −827.9512	Value of the bond, expressed as a negative number

SOLUTION Using the Bond Feature:

CE/C CE/C	0.0000	Clears display
2nd		
BOND	SDT = 1-01-1970	(This will be the last date entered)

2nd		
CLR WORK	SDT = 1-01-1970	Clears BOND variables
1.01.06 ENTER	SDT = 1-01-2006	Stores the current date (month, date, year)
↓	CPN = 0.0000	
9 ENTER	CPN = 9.0000	Stores the coupon interest rate
↓	RDT = 12-31-1990	(This will be the last date entered)
1.01.16 ENTER	RDT = 1-01-2016	Stores the maturity date in 10 years
↓	RV = 100.0000	Verifies bond maturity or par value
↓	ACT	
2nd		
SET	360	Sets calculations to be based on 360-day year
↓	2/Y	Verifies semiannual compounding rate
↓	YLD = 0.0000	
12 ENTER	YLD = 12.0000	Stores the investor's required rate of return
↓	PRI = 0.0000	
CPT	PRI = 82.7951	Value of bond as a percent of par value; i.e., value of bond is $827.95

B. Computing the yield to maturity of a bond

Example: Assume the current date is January 1, 2006, and that you want to know your yield to maturity on a bond that matures in 8 years and has a coupon rate of 12 percent (6 percent semiannually). The bond is selling for $1,100.

Keystrokes	Display	Explanation
2nd		
BGN	END	Verifies timing of payments to end of each period
2nd		
P/Y	P/Y = 12.0000	
2 ENTER	P/Y = 2.0000	Sets 2 payments per year; end mode (END) assumes cash flows are at the end of each 6-month period
CE/C CE/C	0.0000	Clears display
2nd		
CLR TVM	0.0000	Clears TVM variables
16 N	N = 16.0000	Stores the number of semiannual periods (8 years × 2)
1100 +/−	PV = −1,100.0000	Value of the bond, expressed as a negative number
PV		
60 PMT	PMT = 60.0000	Stores the semiannual interest payments
1,000 FV	FV = 1,000.0000	Stores the bond's maturity or par value
CPT I/Y	I/Y = 10.1451	The yield to maturity, expressed on an annual basis

SOLUTION Using the Bond Feature:

CE/C CE/C	0.0000	Clears display
2nd		
Bond	SDT = 1-01-1993	(This will be the last date entered)
2nd		
CLR WORK	SDT = 1-01-1993	Clears BOND variables
1.01.06 ENTER	SDT = 1-01-2006	Stores the current date (month, date, year)
↓	CPN = 0.0000	
12 ENTER	CPN = 12.0000	Stores the coupon interest rate
↓	RDT = 1-01-2003	(This will be the last date entered)
1.01.14 ENTER	RDT = 1-01-2014	Stores the maturity date in 8 years
↓	RV = 100.0000	Verifies bond's maturity or par value
↓	360	
2nd		

(continues on next page)

Keystrokes	Display	Explanation
SET	ACT	Sets calculations to be based on 360-day year
		Verifies semiannual compounding rate
↓	2/Y	
↓	YLD = 0.0000	
↓	PRI = 0.0000	
110 ENTER	PRI = 110.0000	Stores the bond value as a percentage of par value
↑	YLD = 0.0000	
CPT	YLD = 10.1451	Bond's yield to maturity

IX. BOND VALUATION - HEWLETT-PACKARD 10BII

A. Computing the value of a bond

Example: Assume the current date is January 1, 2006, and that you want to know the value of a bond that matures in 10 years and has a coupon rate of 9 percent (4.5 percent semiannually). Your required rate of return is 12 percent.

Keystrokes	Display	Explanation
ORG, C ALL	0.0000	Clears registers
2, ORG, P/YR	2.0000	Sets payments at 2 per year END mode
20, N	20.0000	Stores the number of semiannual periods
12, I/YR	12.0000	Stores annual rate of return
45, PMT	45.0000	Stores the semiannual interest payments
1000, FV	1,000.0000	Stores the bond's maturity or par value
PV	−827.9512	Value of the bond, expressed as a negative number

B. Computing the yield to maturity of a bond

Example: Assume the current date is January 1, 2006, and that you want to know your yield to maturity on a bond that matures in 8 years and has a coupon rate of 12 percent (6 percent semiannually). The bond is selling for $1,100.

Keystrokes	Display	Explanation
ORG, C ALL	0.0000	Clears registers
2, ORG, P/YR	2.0000	Sets payments at 2 per year END mode
16, N	16.0000	Stores the number of semiannual periods (8 years × 2)
1100, +/−, PV	−1,100.0000	Value of the bond expressed as a negative number
60, PMT	60.0000	Stores the semiannual interest payments
1000, FV	1,000.0000	Stores the bond's maturity or par value
I/YR	10.1451	The yield to maturity expressed on an annual basis

X. COMPUTING THE NET PRESENT VALUE AND INTERNAL RATE OF RETURN - TEXAS INSTRUMENTS BA II PLUS

A. Where future cash flows are equal amounts in each period (annuity)

Example: The firm is considering a capital project that would cost $80,000. The firm's cost of capital is 12 percent. The project life is 10 years, during which time the firm expects to receive $15,000 per year. Calculate the *NPV* and *IRR*.

Keystrokes	Display	Explanation
2nd		
BGN	END	Verifies timing of payments to end of each period
2nd		
P/Y	P/Y = 12.0000	
1 ENTER	P/Y = 1.0000	Sets 1 payment per year; end mode (END) assumes cash flows are at the end of each year
CE/C CE/C	0.0000	Clears display

2nd		
CLR TVM	0.0000	Clears TVM variables
15,000 PMT	PMT = 15.0000	Stores the annual cash flows of $15,000
10 N	N = 10.0000	Stores the life of the project
12 I/Y	I/Y = 12.0000	Stores the cost of capital
CPT PV	PV = −84,753.3454	Calculates present value
+/−	84,753.3454	Changes PV to positive
−80,000 =	4,753.3454	Calculates net present value by subtracting the cost of the project
80,000 +/−	−80,000.0000	
PV	PV = −80,000.0000	
CPT I/Y	I/Y = 13.4344	Calculates the IRR

B. Where future cash flows are unequal amounts in each period

Example: The firm is considering a capital project that would cost $110,000. The firm's cost of capital is 15 percent. The project life is 5 years, with the following expected cash flows: $−25,000, $50,000, $60,000, $60,000 and $70,000. In addition, you expect to receive $30,000 in the last year from the salvage value of the equipment. Calculate the NPV and IRR.

Keystrokes	Display	Explanation
CE/C CE/C	0.0000	Clears display
CF	CF$_0$ = 0.0000	
2nd		
CLR WORK	CF$_0$ = 0.0000	Clears cash flow variables
110,000 +/−	CF$_0$ = −110,000.0000	Stores CF$_0$, the initial investment (with a minus sign for a negative cash flow)
ENTER		
↓	CO1 = 0.0000	Stores CF$_1$, the first year's cash flow (with a minus sign for a negative cash flow)
25,000 +/−	CO1 = −25,000.0000	
ENTER		
↓	FO1 = 1.0000	Stores the number of years CF$_1$ is repeated (in this case, 1 year only)
ENTER		
↓	CO2 = 0.0000	
50,000	CO2 = 50,000.0000	Stores CF$_2$
ENTER		
↓	FO2 = 1.0000	
ENTER	FO2 = 1.0000	Stores the number of years CF$_2$ is repeated
↓	CO3 = 0.0000	
60,000	CO3 = 60,000.0000	Stores CF$_3$
ENTER		
↓	FO3 = 2.0000	Stores the number of years CF$_3$ is repeated
2 ENTER		(here, 2 years, so our response is 2 to the FO$_3$ prompt)
↓	CO4 = 0.0000	
100,000	CO4 = 100,000.0000	Stores CF$_4$, $70,000 plus expected $30,000
ENTER		
↓	FO4 = 1.0000	Stores the number CF$_4$
ENTER		
2nd		
QUIT	0.0000	Ends storage of individual cash flows
NPV	I = 0.0000	
15 ENTER	I = 15.0000	Stores interest rate

(continues on next page)

Keystrokes	Display	Explanation
↓	NPV = 0.0000	
CPT	NPV = 29,541.8951	Calculates the project's *NPV* at the stated interest rate
IRR	IRR = 0.0000	
CPT	IRR = 22.0633	Calculates the project's *IRR*

X. COMPUTING THE NET PRESENT VALUE AND INTERNAL RATE OF RETURN - HEWLETT-PACKARD 10BII

A. Where future cash flows are equal amounts in each period (annuity)

Example: The firm is considering a capital project that would cost $80,000. The firm's cost of capital is 12 percent. The project life is 10 years, during which time the firm expects to receive $15,000 per year. Calculate the *NPV* and *IRR*.

Keystrokes	Display	Explanation
ORG, C ALL	0.0000	Clears registers
ORG, BEG/END	0.0000	Verifies timing of payments to end of each period
1, ORG, P/YR	1.0000	Sets 1 payment per year; end mode (END); assumes cash flows are at the end of each year
15,000, PMT	15,000.0000	Stores annual cash flows of $15,000
10, N	10.0000	Stores the life of the project
12, I/YR	12.0000	Stores the cost of capital
PV	−84,753.3454	Calculates present value
+/−	84,753.3454	Changes *PV* to positive
−80,000, =	4753.3454	Calculates net present value by subtracting the cost of the project
80,000, +/−	−80,000.0000	
PV	−80,000.0000	
I/YR	13.4344	Calculates the *IRR*

B. Where future cash flows are unequal amounts in each period

Example: The firm is considering a capital project that would cost $110,000. The firm's cost of capital is 15 percent. The project life is 5 years, with the following expected cash flows: −$25,000, $50,000, $60,000, $60,000, and $70,000. In addition, you expect to receive $30,000 in the last year from the salvage value of the equipment. Calculate the *NPV* and *IRR*.

Keystrokes	Display	Explanation
ORG, C ALL	0.0000	Clears registers
1, ORG, P/YR	1.0000	Sets 1 payment per year END mode
110,000, +/−, CFj	−110,000.0000	Stores CF0, the initial investment (with a minus sign for negative cash flow)
25,000, +/−, CFJ	−25,000.0000	Stores CF1, the first year's cash flow (with a minus sign for negative cash flow)
50,000, CFj	50,000.0000	Stores CF2
60,000, CFj	60,000.0000	Stores CF3
2, ORG, Nj	2.0000	Stores the number of years CF3 is repeated
100,000, CFj	100,000.0000	Stores CF4, $70,000 plus expected $30,000
15, I/YR	15.0000	Stores interest rate
ORG, NPV	29,541.8951	Calculates the project's *NPV* at the stated interest rate
ORG, IRR/YR	22.0633	Calculates the project's *IRR*

Glossary

accelerated cost recovery system (ACRS) depreciation method under U.S. tax law allowing for the accelerated write-off of property under various classifications.

accounting book value the value of an asset as shown on a firm's balance sheet. It represents the historical cost of the asset rather than its current market value or replacement cost.

accounts payable money owed to suppliers for goods or services purchased in the ordinary course of business.

accounts receivable money owed by customers who purchased goods or services from the firm on credit.

accounts receivable turnover ratio a firm's credit sales divided by its accounts receivable. This ratio expresses how often accounts receivable are "rolled over" during a year.

accrual basis accounting a method of accounting whereby revenue is recorded when it is earned, whether or not the revenue has been received in cash. Likewise, expenses are recorded when they are incurred, even if the money has not actually been paid out.

accrued expenses expenses that have been incurred but not yet paid in cash.

accumulated depreciation the sum of all depreciation taken over the entire life of a depreciable asset.

acid-test (quick) ratio a firm's cash plus and accounts receivable divided by its current liabilities. This ratio is a more stringent measure of liquidity than the current ratio in that it excludes inventories and other current assets (those that are least liquid) from current assets.

additional paid-in capital the amount a company receives from selling its own common stock to investors above par value.

agency costs the costs, such as a reduced stock price, associated with potential conflict between managers and investors when these two groups are not the same.

agency problem problems and conflicts resulting from the separation of the management and ownership of the firm.

American depositary receipt (ADR) a security issued in the United States representing shares of a foreign stock and allowing that stock to be traded in the United States.

amortized loan a loan that is paid off in equal periodic payments.

angel investor a wealthy private investor who provides capital for a business start-up.

annuity a series of equal dollar payments made for a specified number of years.

annuity due an annuity in which the payments occur at the beginning of each period.

annuity future value factor the value of $\left[\dfrac{(1 + r)^n - 1}{r}\right]$ used as a multiplier to calculate the future value of an annuity.

annuity present value factor the value of $\left[\dfrac{1 - (1 + r)^{-n}}{r}\right]$ used as a multiplier to calculate the present value of an annuity.

arbitrageur an individual involved in the process of buying and selling in more than one market to make a riskless profit.

arithmetic average return average period return on an investment over multiple periods.

asked rate the rate the bank or the foreign exchange trader "asks" the customer to pay in home currency for foreign currency when the bank is selling and the customer is buying. The asked rate is also known as the selling rate or the offer rate.

asset allocation identifying and selecting the asset classes appropriate for a specific investment portfolio and determining the proportions of those assets within the portfolio.

asset efficiency how well a firm is managing its assets.

average accounting return (AAR) an investment's average net income divided by its average book value.

average collection period a firm's accounts receivable divided by the company's average daily credit sales (annual credit sales ÷ 365). This ratio expresses how rapidly the firm is collecting its credit accounts.

average tax rate the average tax rate on a firm's total taxable income, computed as total tax expense divided by taxable income.

balance sheet a financial statement that shows a firm's assets, liabilities, and shareholder equity at a given point in time.

It is a snapshot of the firm's financial position on a particular date.

bankruptcy a legal proceeding for liquidating or reorganizing a business; also, the transfer of some or all of a firm's assets to its creditors.

benefit cost ratio the present value of an investment's future cash flows divided by its initial cost; also *profitability index*.

best efforts underwriting the underwriter sells as much of a stock issue as possible, but can return any unsold shares to the issuer without financial responsibility.

beta the relationship between an investment's returns and the market's returns. This is a measure of the investment's nondiversifiable risk.

bid rate the rate at which the bank buys the foreign currency from the customer by paying in home currency. The bid rate is also known as the buying rate.

bid-asked spread the difference between the asked quote and the bid quote.

bird-in-the-hand dividend theory the view that dividends are more certain than capital gains.

bond a long-term (10-year or more) promissory note issued by the borrower, promising to pay the owner of the security a predetermined, fixed amount of interest each year.

book value the value of an asset as shown on the firm's balance sheet. It represents the historical cost of the asset rather than its current market value or replacement cost.

budget an itemized forecast of a company's expected revenues and expenses for a future period.

business risk the relative dispersion or variability in the firm's expected earnings before interest and taxes (EBIT). The nature of the firm's operations causes its business risk. This type of risk is affected by the firm's cost structure, product demand characteristics, and intra-industry competitive position. In capital structure theory, business risk is distinguished from financial risk. Compare **financial risk**.

buying rate the rate at which the bank buys the foreign currency from the customer by paying in home currency. The buying rate is also known as the bid rate.

call premium   the amount by which a dealer is willing to pay for a security.

call protection period   a prespecified time period during which a company cannot recall a bond.

call provision   a provision that entitles the corporation to repurchase its preferred stock from investors at stated prices over specified periods.

callable bond (redeemable bond)   an option available to a company issuing a bond whereby the issuer can call (redeem) the bond before it matures. This is usually done if interest rates decline below what the firm is paying on the bond.

capital asset pricing model (CAPM)   an equation stating that the expected rate of return on a project is a function of (1) the risk-free rate, (2) the investment's systematic risk, and (3) the expected risk premium for the market portfolio of all risky securities.

capital budgeting   the decision-making process with respect to investments.

capital gain (or loss)   as defined by the revenue code, a gain or loss resulting from the sale or exchange of a capital asset.

capital markets   all institutions and procedures that facilitate transactions in long-term financial instruments.

capital rationing   placing a limit on the dollar size of the capital budget.

capital structure   the mix of interest bearing short- and long-term debt plus equity funds used by the firm.

capital structure decision   the decision-making process with funding choices and the mix of long-term sources of funds.

cash   cash on hand, demand deposits, and short-term marketable securities that can quickly be converted into cash.

cash budget   a detailed plan of future cash flows. This budget is composed of four elements: cash receipts, cash disbursements, net change in cash for the period, and new financing needed.

characteristic line   the line of "best fit" through a series of returns for a firm's stock relative to the market's returns. The slope of the line, frequently called beta, represents the average movement of the firm's stock returns in response to a movement in the market's returns.

chattel mortgage agreement   a loan agreement in which the lender can increase his or her security interest by having specific items of inventory identified in the loan agreement. The borrower retains title to the inventory but cannot sell the items without the lender's consent

clientele effect   the belief that individuals and institutions that need current income will invest in companies that have high dividend payouts. Other investors prefer to avoid taxes by holding securities that offer only small dividend income but large capital gains. Thus, we have a "clientele" of investors.

collection policy   procedures followed by a firm collecting accounts receivable.

commercial paper   short-term unsecured promissory notes sold by large businesses in order to raise cash. Unlike most other money-market instruments, commercial paper has no developed secondary market.

common stock   shares that represent ownership in a corporation.

common stockholders   investors who own the firm's common stock. Common stockholders are the residual owners of the firm.

common-sized balance sheet   a balance sheet in which a firm's assets and sources of debt and equity are expressed as a percentage of its total assets.

common-sized income statement   an income statement in which a firm's expenses and profits are expressed as a percentage of its sales.

company-unique risk   see **unsystematic risk**.

compensating balance   amount of cash that the firm maintains in its demand deposit account. It may be required by either a formal or informal agreement with the firm's commercial bank. Such balances are usually required by the bank (1) on the unused portion of a loan commitment, (2) on the unpaid portion of an outstanding loan, or (3) in exchange for certain services provided by the bank, such as check-clearing or credit information. These balances raise the effective rate of interest paid on borrowed funds

competitive-advantage period   the number of years a firm's managers believe they can sustain a competitive advantage, given the company's present strategies.

compound annuity   depositing an equal sum of money at the end of each year for a certain number of years and allowing it to grow.

compound interest   the situation in which interest paid on an investment during the first period is added to the principal. During the second period, interest is earned on the original principal plus the interest earned during the first period.

compounding   the process of accumulating interest in an investment over time in order to earn more interest.

contribution-to-firm risk   the amount of risk that the project contributes to the firm as a whole; this measure considers the fact that some of the project's risk will be diversified away as the project is combined with the firm's other projects and assets, but ignores the effects of diversification of the firm's shareholders.

convertible bond   a debt security that can be converted into a firm's stock at a prespecified price.

convertible preferred stock   preferred shares that can be converted into a predetermined number of shares of common stock, if investors so choose.

corporation   an entity that legally functions separate and apart from its owners.

cost of capital   the minimum required return on a new investment.

cost of debt   the return that the lenders require on the firm's debt.

cost of equity   the return that equity investors require on their investment in the firm.

cost of goods sold   the cost of producing or acquiring a product or service to be sold in the ordinary course of business.

coupon rate   the interest rate contractually owed on a bond as a percent of its par value.

covered-interest arbitrage   designed to eliminate differentials across currency and interest rate markets.

credit scoring   the numerical evaluation of credit applicants where the score is evaluated relative to a predetermined standard.

cross rate   the computation of an exchange rate for a currency from the exchange rates of two other currencies.

cumulative feature   a requirement that all past, unpaid preferred stock dividends be paid before any common stock dividends are declared.

cumulative voting   voting in which each share of stock allows the shareholder a number of votes equal to the number of directors being elected. The shareholder can then cast all of his or her votes for a single candidate or split them among the various candidates.

currency swaps   the exchange of principal and interest in one currency for the same in another currency for an agreed period of time.

current assets (gross working capital)   current assets consist primarily of cash, marketable securities, accounts receivable, inventories, and prepaid expenses.

current debt (short-term liabilities)   debt due to be paid within 12 months.

current ratio a firm's current assets divided by its current liabilities. This ratio indicates the firm's degree of liquidity by comparing its current assets to its current liabilities.

current yield the ratio of a bond's annual interest payment to its market price.

date of record date at which the stock transfer books are to be closed for determining the investor to receive the next dividend payment.

debenture any unsecured long-term debt.

debt liabilities consisting of such sources as credit extended by suppliers or a loan from a bank.

debt capacity the maximum proportion of debt that the firm can include in its capital structure and still maintain its lowest composite cost of capital.

debt ratio a firm's total liabilities divided by its total assets. This ratio measures the extent to which a firm has been financed with debt.

declaration date the date upon which a dividend is formally declared by the board of directors.

default-risk premium the additional return required by investors to compensate them for the risk of default. It is calculated as the difference in rates between a U.S. Treasury bond and a corporate bond of the same maturity and marketability.

depreciation expense a noncash expense to allocate the cost of depreciable assets, such as plant and equipment, over the life of the asset.

depreciation tax shield the tax saving that results from the depreciation deduction, calculated as depreciation multiplied by the corporate tax rate.

direct costs see **variable costs.**

direct quote the exchange rate that indicates the number of units of the home currency required to buy one unit of foreign currency.

direct sale the sale of securities by a corporation to the investing public without the services of an investment-banking firm.

discount bond a bond that sells at a discount, or below par value.

discounted cash flow (DCF) valuation (1) valuation calculating the present value of a future cash flow to determine its value today. (2) the process of valuing an investment by discounting its future cash flows.

discounted payback period the number of years needed to recover the initial cash outlay from the discounted free cash flows.

discretionary financing sources sources of financing that require an explicit decision on the part of the firm's management every time funds are raised. An example is a bank note that requires that negotiations be undertaken and an agreement signed setting forth the terms and conditions of the financing.

diversifiable risk see **unsystematic risk.**

dividend payout ratio the amount of dividends relative to the company's net income or earnings per share.

dividend yield the annual dividend per share divided by the current market price of a firm's common stock.

dividends per share the amount of dividends a firm pays for each share outstanding.

Dutch auction a method of issuing securities (common stock) where investors place bids indicating how many shares they are willing to buy and at what price. The price the stock is then sold for becomes the lowest price at which the issuing company can sell all the available shares.

earnings before taxes (taxable income) operating income minus interest expense.

earnings per share net income on a per share basis.

EBIT-EPS indifference point the level of earnings before interest and taxes (EBIT) that will equate earnings per share (EPS) between two different financing plans.

economic order quantity (EOQ) the restocking quantity that minimizes the total inventory costs.

economic profit differs from accounting profit in that it incorporates explicit consideration for opportunity cost of equity financing, as well as debt financing.

effective annual rate (EAR) the annual compound rate that produces the same return as the nominal, or quoted, rate when something is compounded on a nonannual basis. In effect, the EAR provides the true rate of return.

efficient market a market in which the prices of securities at any instant in time fully reflect all publicly available information about the securities and their actual public values.

efficient markets hypothesis (EMH) the hypothesis that actual capital markets, such as the New York Stock Exchange, are efficient.

equity stockholders' investment in the firm and the cumulative profits retained in the business up to the date of the balance sheet.

equivalent annual annuity (EAA) an annuity cash flow that yields the same present value as the project's *NPV*.

Eurobond a bond issued in a country different from the one in which the currency of the bond is denominated; for example, a bond issued in Europe or Asia by an American company that pays interest and principal to the lender in U.S. dollars.

exchange rate the price of a foreign currency stated in terms of the domestic or home currency.

exchange rate risk the risk that tomorrow's exchange rate will differ from today's rate.

ex-dividend date the date upon which stock brokerage companies have uniformly decided to terminate the right of ownership to the dividend, which is two days prior to the date of record.

expectations theory the concept that, no matter what the decision area, how the market price responds to management's actions is not determined entirely by the action itself; it is also affected by investors' expectations about the ultimate decision to be made by management.

expected rate of return the arithmetic mean or average of all possible outcomes where those outcomes are weighted by the probability that each will occur.

external financing needs that portion of a firm's requirements for financing that exceeds its sources of internal financing (i.e., the retention of earnings) plus spontaneous sources of financing (e.g., trade credit).

face value

factor a firm that, in acquiring the receivables of other firms, bears the risk of collection and, for a fee, services the accounts.

factoring accounts receivable the outright sale of a firm's accounts receivable to another party (the factor) without recourse. The factor, in turn, bears the risk of collection.

fair value the present value of an asset's expected future cash flows.

field warehouse agreement a security agreement in which inventories pledged as collateral are physically separated from the firm's other inventories and placed under the control of a third-party field-warehousing firm.

financial distress costs the direct and indirect costs associated with going bankrupt or experiencing financial distress.

financial leverage the use of securities bearing a fixed (limited) rate of return to finance a portion of a firm's assets. Financial leverage can arise from the use of either debt or preferred stock financing. The use of financial leverage exposes the firm to financial risk.

financial markets   those institutions and procedures that facilitate transactions in all types of financial claims.

financial policy   the firm's policies regarding the sources of financing it plans to use and the particular mix (proportions) in which they will be used.

financial ratios   accounting data restated in relative terms in order to help people identify some of the financial strengths and weaknesses of a company.

financial risk   relationships determined from a firm's financial information and used for comparison purposes.

financial structure   the mix of all funds sources that appears on the right-hand side of the balance sheet.

financing cost   cost incurred by a company that often includes interest expenses and preferred dividends.

finished-goods inventory   goods on which the production has been completed but that are not yet sold.

firm commitment underwriting   the underwriter buys the entire issue, assuming full financial responsibility for any unsold shares.

Fisher effect   the relationship between nominal returns, real returns, and inflation.

five Cs of credit   the five basic credit factors to be evaluated: character, capacity, capital, collateral, and conditions.

fixed asset turnover   a firm's sales divided by its net fixed assets. This ratio indicates how efficiently the firm is using its fixed assets.

fixed assets   assets such as equipment, buildings, and land.

fixed costs   costs that do not vary in total dollar amount as sales volume or quantity of output changes. Also called indirect costs.

float   the length of time from when a check is written until the actual recipient can draw upon or use the "good funds."

floating lien agreement   an agreement, generally associated with a loan, whereby the borrower gives the lender a lien against all its inventory.

floating-rate international currency system   a system in which the exchange rates of different currencies are allowed to fluctuate with supply and demand conditions.

flotation costs   the transaction cost incurred when a firm raises funds by issuing a particular type of security.

foreign exchange market   the market in which one country's currency is traded for another's.

forward exchange contract   a forward contract that requires delivery, at a specified future date, of one currency for a specified amount of another currency.

forward exchange rate   the agreed upon exchange currency at some time in the future.

forward transaction   an agreement today to deliver a specified number of units of a currency on a future date in return for a specified number of units of another currency.

forward-spot differential   the premium or discount between forward and spot currency exchange rates.

free cash flows   the amount of cash available from operations after the firm pays for the investments it has made in operating working capital and fixed assets. This cash is available to distribute to the firm's creditors and owners.

future value (FV)   the amount to which your investment will grow.

future value factor   the value of $(1 + r)^n$ used as a multiple to calculate an amount's future value.

future-value interest factor ($FVIF_{r,n}$)   the value $(1 + r)^n$ used as a multiplier to calculate an amount's future value.

future-value interest factor for an annuity ($FVIFA_{r,n}$)   the value used as a multiplier to calculate the future value of an annuity.

futures markets   markets where you can buy or sell something at a future date.

general partnership   a partnership in which all partners are fully liable for the indebtedness incurred by the partnership.

generally accepted accounting principles (GAAP)   the common set of standards and procedures by which audited financial statements are prepared.

geometric average return   the average compound return earned per period over multiple periods.

green shoe provision   a contract provision giving the underwriter the option to purchase additional shares from the issuer at the offering price.

gross fixed assets   the original cost of a firm's fixed assets.

gross profit margin   gross profit divided by net sales. It is a ratio denoting the gross profit earned by the firm as a percentage of its net sales.

gross profit   sales or revenue minus the cost of goods sold.

hedging principle (principle of self-liquidating debt)   a working-capital management policy which states that the cash flow–generating characteristics of a firm's investments should be matched with the cash flow requirements of the firm's sources of financing. Very simply, short-lived assets should be financed with short-term sources of financing while long-lived assets should be financed with long-term sources of financing

high-yield bond   see **junk bond**.

holding-period return (historical or realized rate of return)   (1) the return an investor would receive from holding a security for a designated period of time. For example, a monthly holding-period return would be the return for holding a security for a month. (2) the rate of return earned on an investment, which equals the dollar gain divided by the amount invested.

income statement (profit and loss statement)   a basic accounting statement that measures the results of a firm's operations over a specified period, commonly 1 year. Also known as the profit and loss statement. The bottom line of the income statement shows the firm's profit or loss for the period.

incremental cash flow   the difference between the cash flows a company will produce both with and without the investment it is thinking about making.

indenture   the legal agreement between the firm issuing bonds and the bond trustee who represents the bondholders, providing the specific terms of the loan agreement.

indirect costs   see **fixed costs**.

indirect quote   the exchange rate that expresses the number of units of a foreign currency that can be bought for one unit of the home currency.

inflation-risk premium   a premium to compensate for anticipated inflation that is equal to the price change expected to occur over the life of the bond or investment instrument.

information asymmetry   the difference in accessibility to information between managers and investors, which may result in a lower stock price than would be true in conditions of certainty.

initial outlay   the immediate cash outflow necessary to purchase the asset and put it in operating order.

initial public offering, IPO   the first time a company issues its stock to the public.

insolvency   the inability to meet interest payments or to repay debt at maturity.

interest rate parity (IRP) theory a theory that states that (except for the effects of small transaction costs) the forward premium or discount should be equal and opposite in size to the difference in the national interest rates for securities of the same maturity.

interest rate risk (1) the variability in a bond's value (risk) caused by changing interest rates. (2) The uncertainty that envelops the expected returns from a security caused by changes in interest rates. Price changes induced by interest rate changes are greater for long-term than for short-term financial instruments.

interest rate risk premium the compensation investors demand for bearing interest rate risk.

interest tax shield the tax savings attained by a firm from the tax deductibility of interest expense.

internal growth rate a firm's growth rate resulting from reinvesting the company's profits rather than distributing them as dividends. The growth rate is a function of the amount retained and the return earned on the retained funds.

internal rate of return (IRR) the rate of return that the project earns. For computational purposes, the internal rate of return is defined as the discount rate that equates the present value of the project's free cash flows with the project's initial cash outlay.

intrinsic, or economic, value the present value of an asset's expected future cash flows. This value is the amount the investor considers to be fair value, given the amount, timing, and riskiness of future cash flows.

inventories raw materials, work in progress, and finished goods held by the firm for eventual sale.

inventory loans loans secured by inventories. Examples include floating or blanket lien agreements, chattel mortgage agreements, field-warehouse receipt loans, and terminal-warehouse receipt loans.

inventory management the control of assets used in the production process or produced to be sold in the normal course of the firm's operations.

inventory turnover a firm's cost of goods sold divided by its inventory. This ratio measures the number of times a firm's inventories are sold and replaced during the year, that is, the relative liquidity of the inventories.

investment banker a financial specialist who underwrites and distributes new securities and advises corporate clients about raising new funds.

junk bond any bond rated BB or below.

just-in-time inventory control system a production and management system in which inventory is cut down to a minimum through adjustments to the time and physical distance between the various production operations. Under this system the firm keeps a minimum level of inventory on hand, relying upon suppliers to furnish parts "just in time" for them to be assembled.

law of one price a proposition that in competitive markets in which there are no transportation costs or barriers to trade, the same goods sold in different countries sell for the same price if all the different prices are expressed in terms of the same currency.

limited liability a protective provision whereby the investor is not liable for more than the amount he or she has invested in the firm.

limited liability company (LLC) a cross between a partnership and a corporation under which the owners retain limited liability but the company is run and is taxed like a partnership.

limited partnership a partnership in which one or more of the partners has limited liability, restricted to the amount of capital he or she invests in the partnership.

line of credit generally an informal agreement or understanding between a borrower and a bank as to the maximum amount of credit the bank will provide the borrower at any one time. Under this type of agreement there is no "legal" commitment on the part of the bank to provide the stated credit

liquidation value the dollar sum that could be realized if an asset were sold.

liquidity a firm's ability to pay its bills on time. Liquidity is related to the ease and quickness with which a firm can convert its noncash assets into cash, as well as the size of the firm's investment in noncash assets relative to its short-term liabilities.

liquidity preference theory the theory that the shape of the term structure of interest rates is determined by an investor's additional required interest rate in compensation of additional risks.

liquidity premium the additional return required by investors for securities that cannot be quickly converted into cash at a reasonably predictable price.

lockboxes special post office boxes set up to intercept and speed up accounts receivable collections.

London Interbank Offer Rate (LIBOR) the rate most international banks charge one another for overnight Eurodollar loans.

long-term debt loans from banks or other sources that lend money for longer than 12 months.

majority voting voting in which each share of stock allows the shareholder one vote, and each position on the board of directors is voted on separately. As a result, a majority of shares has the power to elect the entire board of directors.

marginal tax rate the tax rate that would be applied to the next dollar of income.

market risk see **systematic risk**.

market risk premium a risk that influences a large number of assets; also systematic risk.

market segmentation theory the theory that the shape of the term structure of interest rates implies that the rate of interest for a particular maturity is determined solely by demand and supply for a given maturity. This rate is independent of the demand and supply for securities having different maturities.

market value the value observed in the marketplace.

market value added (MVA) the difference in the market value of a firm's total assets and their book value.

marketable securities security investments (financial assets) the firm can quickly convert to cash balances. Also known as near cash or near-cash assets.

maturity the length of time until the bond issuer returns the par value to the bondholder and terminates the bond.

maturity premium the additional return required by investors in longer-term securities to compensate them for the greater risk of price fluctuations on those securities caused by interest rate changes.

money market all institutions and procedures that facilitate transactions for short-term instruments issued by borrowers with very high credit ratings.

mortgage a loan to finance real estate where the lender has first claim on the property in the event the borrower is unable to repay the loan.

mortgage bond a bond secured by a lien on real property.

multinational corporation (MNC) a corporation with holdings and/or operations in more than one country.

mutually exclusive projects projects that, if undertaken, would serve the same purpose. Thus, accepting one will necessarily mean rejecting the others.

net fixed assets   gross fixed assets minus the accumulated depreciation taken over the life of the assets.

net income (earnings available to common stockholders)   a figure representing a firm's profit or loss for the period. It also represents the earnings available to the firm's common stockholders.

net operating loss carryback and carryforward   a tax provision that permits the taxpayer first to apply a loss against the profits earned in the 2 prior years (carryback). If the loss has not been completely absorbed by the profits in these 2 years, it may be applied to taxable profits in each of the 20 following years (carryforward).

net present value (NPV)   the present value of an investment's annual free cash flows less the investment's initial outlay.

net present value profile   a graph showing how a project's NPV changes as the discount rate changes.

net profit margin   net income divided by sales. A ratio that measures the net income of the firm as a percent of sales.

net working capital   the difference between a firm's current assets and its current liabilities. When the term *working capital* is used, it is frequently intended to mean net working capital.

nominal (or quoted) rate of interest   the interest rate paid on debt securities without an adjustment for any loss in purchasing power.

nondiversifiable risk   see **systematic risk**.

non-interest-bearing current liabilities (NIBCL)   current liabilities that incur no interest expense, such as accounts payable and accrued expenses.

operating expenses   marketing and selling expenses, general and administrative expenses, and depreciation expense.

operating income (earnings before interest and taxes)   sales less the cost of goods sold less operating expenses.

operating leverage   the incurring of fixed operating costs in a firm's income stream.

operating profit margin   a firm's operating income (earnings before interest and taxes) divided by sales. This ratio serves as an overall measure of operating effectiveness.

operating return on assets (OROA)   the ratio of a firm's operating income divided by its total assets. This ratio indicates the rate of return being earned on the firm's assets.

opportunity cost of funds   the next-best rate of return available to the investor for a given level of risk.

optimal capital structure   the capital structure that minimizes the firm's composite cost of capital (maximizes the common stock price) for raising a given amount of funds.

order point problem   determining how low inventory should be depleted before it is reordered.

order quantity problem   determining the optimal order size for an inventory item given its usage, carrying costs, and ordering costs.

ordinary annuity   an annuity where the cash flows occur at the end of each period.

organized security exchange   formal organizations that facilitate the trading of securities.

over-the-counter market   all security markets except organized exchanges. The money market is an over-the-counter market. Most corporate bonds also are traded in this market.

par value   on the face of a bond, the stated amount that the firm is to repay upon the maturity date.

partnership   an association of two or more individuals joining together as co-owners to operate a business for profit.

payable-through drafts (PTD)   a legal instrument that has the physical appearance of an ordinary check but is not drawn on a bank. A payable-through draft is drawn on and paid by the issuing firm. The bank serves as a collection point and passes the draft on to the firm.

payback period   The number of years it takes to recapture a project's initial outlay.

payment date   the date on which the company mails a dividend check to each investor of record.

percent of sales method   a method of financial forecasting that involves estimating the level of an expense, asset, or liability for a future period as a percent of the sales forecast.

perfect capital markets   an assumption that allows one to study the effect of capital structure and dividend decisions in isolation. It assumes that (1) investors can buy and sell stocks without incurring any transaction costs, such as brokerage commissions; (2) companies can issue stocks without any cost of doing so; (3) there are no corporate or personal taxes; (4) complete information about the firm is readily available; (5) there are no conflicts of interest between management and stockholders; and (6) financial distress and bankruptcy costs are nonexistent.

permanent investments   an investment that the firm expects to hold longer than one year. The firm makes permanent investments in fixed and current assets

perpetuity   an annuity with an infinite life.

pledging accounts receivable   a loan the firm obtains from a commercial bank or a finance company using its accounts receivable as collateral.

portfolio beta   the relationship between a portfolio's returns and the market returns. It is a measure of the portfolio's nondiversifiable risk.

preemptive right   the right entitling the common shareholder to maintain his or her proportionate share of ownership in the firm.

preferred stock   a hybrid security with characteristics of both common stock and bonds. Preferred stock is similar to common stock in that it has no fixed maturity date, the nonpayment of dividends does not bring on bankruptcy, and dividends are not deductible for tax purposes. Preferred stock is similar to bonds in that dividends are limited in amount.

preferred stockholders   stockholders who have claims on the firm's income and assets after creditors, but before common stockholders.

premium bond   a bond that is selling above its par value.

present value   the value in today's dollars of a future payment discounted back to present at the required rate of return.

present value factor   the value of $\frac{1}{(1 + r)^n}$ used as a multiplier to calculate an amount's present value.

present-value interest factor (PVIF$_{i,n}$)   the value $[1/(1 + r)^n]$ used as a multiplrer to calculate an amount's present value.

present-value interest factor for an annuity (PVIFA$_{r,n}$)   the value used as a multiplier to calculate the present value of an annuity.

price/book ratio   the market value of a share of the firm's stock divided by the book value per share of the firm's reported equity in the balance sheet.

price/earnings ratio   the price the market places on $1 of a firm's earnings. For example, if a firm has an earnings per share of $2, and a stock price of $30 per share, its price/earnings ratio is 15 ($30 ÷ $2).

primary market   a market in which securities are offered for the first time for sale to potential investors.

private placement   a security offering limited to a small number of potential investors.

privileged subscription the process of marketing a new security issue to a select group of investors.

pro forma financial statements financial statements projecting future years' operations.

profit margins financial ratios (sometimes simply referred to as margins) that reflect the level of the firm's profits relative to its sales. Examples include the gross profit margin (gross profit divided by sales), operating profit margin (operating income divided by sales), and the net profit margin (net income).

profitability index (PI) or benefit–cost ratio the ratio of the present value of an investment's future free cash flows to the investment's initial outlay.

profit-retention rate the company's percentage of profits retained.

project standing alone risk a project's risk ignoring the fact that much of this risk will be diversified away as the project is combined with the firm's other projects and assets.

prospectus a legal document describing details of the issuing corporation and the proposed offering to potential investors.

protective covenant a part of the indenture limiting certain actions that might be taken during the term of the loan, usually to protect the lender's interest.

protective provisions provisions for preferred stock that protect the investor's interest. The provisions generally allow for voting in the event of nonpayment of dividends, or they restrict the payment of common stock dividends if sinking-fund payments are not met or if the firm is in financial difficulty.

proxy a means of voting in which a designated party is provided with the temporary power of attorney to vote for the signee at the corporation's annual meeting.

proxy fight a battle between rival groups for proxy votes in order to control the decisions made in a stockholders' meeting.

public offering a security offering where all investors have the opportunity to acquire a portion of the financial claims being sold.

purchasing-power parity (PPP) theory a theory that states that, in the long run, exchange rates adjust so that the purchasing power of each currency tends to be the same. Thus, exchange rate changes tend to reflect international differences in inflation rates.

pure play method a method for estimating a project's or division's beta that attempts to identify publicly traded firms engaged solely in the same business as the project or division.

raw-materials inventory the basic materials purchased from other firms to be used in the firm's production operations.

real rate of interest the nominal (quoted) rate of interest less any loss in purchasing power of the dollar during the time of the investment.

real risk-free interest rate the required rate of return on a fixed-income security that has no risk in an economic environment of zero inflation.

required rate of return minimum rate of return necessary to attract an investor to purchase or hold a security.

residual dividend theory a theory that a company's dividend payment should equal the cash left after financing all the investments that have positive net present values.

residual value the present value of a firm's post-competitive-advantage period cash flows.

retained earnings cumulative profits retained in a business up to the date of the balance sheet.

return on equity a firm's net income divided by its common book equity. This ratio is the accounting rate of return earned on the common stockholders' investment.

revenue total sales dollars.

reverse split stock split under which a firm's number of shares outstanding is reduced.

revolving credit agreement an understanding between the borrower and the bank as to the amount of credit the bank will be legally obligated to provide the borrower.

right a certificate issued to common stockholders giving them an option to purchase a stated number of new shares at a specified price during a specified period of time.

risk potential variability in future cash flows.

risk premium the additional return expected for assuming risk.

risk-adjusted discount rate a method of risk adjustment when the risk associated with the investment is greater than the risk involved in a typical endeavor. Using this method, the discount rate is adjusted upward to compensate for this added risk.

risk-free rate of return the rate of return on risk-free investments. The interest rates on short-term U.S. government securities are commonly used to measure this rate.

S corporation a corporation that, because of specific qualifications, is taxed as though it were a partnership.

safety stock inventory held to accommodate any unusually large and unexpected usage during delivery time

scenario analysis a simulation approach for gauging a project's risk under the worst, best, and most likely outcomes. The firm's management examines the distribution of the outcomes to determine the project's level of risk and then makes the appropriate adjustment.

seasoned equity offering, SEO the sale of additional stock by a company whose shares are already publicly traded.

secondary market a market in which currently outstanding securities are traded.

secured loan sources of credit that require security in the form of pledged assets. In the event the borrower defaults in payment of principal or interest, the lender can seize the pledged assets and sell them to settle the debt.

security market line the return line that reflects the attitudes of investors regarding the minimum acceptable return for a given level of systematic risk associated with a security.

selling rate the rate the bank or the foreign exchange trader "asks" the customer to pay in home currency for foreign currency when the bank is selling and the customer is buying. The selling rate is also known as the asked rate or the offer rate.

sensitivity analysis a method for dealing with risk where the change in the distribution of possible net present values or internal rates of return for a particular project resulting from a change in one particular input variable is calculated. This is done by changing the value of one input variable while holding all other input variables constant.

shelf registration registration permitted by SEC rule 415, which allows a company to register all issues it expects to sell within two years at one time, with subsequent sales at any time within those two years.

short-term notes (debt) amounts borrowed from lenders, mostly financial institutions such as banks, where the loan is to be repaid within 12 months.

simple arbitrage trading to eliminate exchange rate differentials across the markets for a single currency.

simple interest if you only earned interest on your initial investment, it would be referred to as simple interest.

simulation a method for dealing with risk where the performance of the project under evaluation is estimated by randomly selecting observations from each of the distributions that affect the outcome of the project and continuing with this process until a representative record of the project's probable outcome is assembled.

sinking-fund provision a protective provision that requires the firm periodically to set aside an amount of money for the retirement of its preferred stock. This money is then used to purchase the preferred stock in the open market or through the use of the call provision, whichever method is cheaper.

sole proprietorship a business owned by a single individual.

spontaneous financing the trade credit and other accounts payable that arise "spontaneously" in the firm's day-to-day operations.

spot exchange rate the exchange rate on a spot trade.

spot market cash market.

spot trade an agreement to trade currencies based on the exchange rate today for settlement within two business days.

spot transaction a transaction made immediately in the marketplace at the market price.

standard deviation a statistical measure of the spread of a probability distribution calculated by squaring the difference between each outcome and its expected value, weighting each value by its probability, summing over all possible outcomes, and taking the square root of this sum.

Standard Industrial Classification (SIC) code the U.S. government code used to classify a firm by its type of business operations.

stock dividend a distribution of shares of up to 25 percent of the number of shares currently outstanding, issued on a pro rata basis to the current stockholders.

stock repurchase (stock buyback) the repurchase of common stock by the issuing firm for any of a variety of reasons, resulting in reduction of shares outstanding.

stock split a stock dividend exceeding 25 percent of the number of shares currently outstanding.

subordinated debenture a debenture that is subordinated to other debentures in terms of its payments in case of insolvency.

sunk cost a cost that has already been incurred and cannot be recouped and therefore should not be considered in an investment decision.

sustainable growth rate the maximum possible growth rate a firm can achieve without external equity financing while maintaining a constant debt equity ratio.

syndicate a group of investment bankers who contractually assist in the buying and selling of a new security issue.

systematic risk (1) the risk related to an investment return that cannot be eliminated through diversification. Systematic risk results from factors that affect all stocks. Also called market risk or nondiversifiable risk. (2) The risk of a project from the viewpoint of a well-diversified shareholder. This measure takes into account that some of the project's risk will be diversified away as the project is combined with the firm's other projects, and, in addition, some of the remaining risk will be diversified away by shareholders as they combine this stock with other stocks in their portfolios.

tax shield the reduction in taxes due to the tax deductability of interest expense.

taxable income gross income from all sources, except for allowable exclusions, less any tax-deductible expenses.

temporary investments a firm's investments in current assets that will be liquidated and not replaced within a period of one year or less. Examples include seasonal expansions in inventories and accounts receivable.

tender offer a formal offer by the company to buy a specified number of shares at a predetermined and stated price. The tender price is set above the current market price in order to attract sellers.

term loans direct business loans of, typically, one to five years.

term structure of interest rates the relationship between interest rates and the term to maturity, where the risk of default is held constant.

terminal warehouse agreement a security agreement in which the inventories pledged as collateral are transported to a public warehouse that is physically removed from the borrower's premises. This is the safest (though costly) form of financing secured by inventory.

terms of sale the credit terms identifying the possible discount for early payment.

timeline a linear representation of the timing of cash flows.

times interest earned a firm's earnings before interest and taxes (EBIT) divided by interest expense. This ratio measures a firm's ability to meet its interest payments from its annual operating earnings.

total asset turnover a firm's sales divided by its total assets. This ratio is an overall measure of asset efficiency based on the relation between a firm's sales and the total assets.

trade credit credit made available by a firm's suppliers in conjunction with the acquisition of materials. Trade credit appears in the accounts payable section of the balance sheet.

transaction exposure risk associated with transaction exposure, that is, risk associated with contracts on which the monetary value is fixed at a time different from when the transaction is actually completed and will be impacted by exchange rate changes.

transaction loan a loan where the proceeds are designated for a specific purpose for example, a bank loan used to finance the acquisition of a piece of equipment.

transfer price the price a subsidiary or a parent company charges other companies that are part of the MNC for its goods or services.

translation exposure risk that arises because the foreign operations of MNCs have financial statements denominated in the local currencies of the countries in which the operation are located. These denominations must be translated into the MNCs home currency at the prevailing exchange rate.

treasury stock the firm's stock that has been issued and then repurchased by the firm.

triangular arbitrage arbitrage across three markets for three currencies.

unbiased expectations theory the theory that the shape of the term structure of interest rates is determined by an investor's expectations about future interest rates.

underwriter's spread the difference between the price the corporation raising money gets and the public offering price of a security.

underwriting the purchase and subsequent resale of a new security issue. The risk of selling the new issue at a satisfactory (profitable) price is assumed (underwritten) by the investment banker.

unique risk a risk that affects at most a small number of assets; also **unsystematic risk**.

unseasoned new issue a company's first equity issue made available to the public; also **initial public offering**.

unsecured loans all sources of credit that have as their security only the lender's faith in the borrower's ability to repay the funds when due.

unsystematic risk the risk related to an investment return that can be eliminated through diversification. Unsystematic risk is the result of factors that are unique to the particular firm. Also called **company-unique risk** or **diversifiable risk**.

variable costs costs that are fixed per unit of output but vary in total as output changes. Also called **direct costs**.

variance the average squared difference between the actual return and the average return.

venture capital funds made available to start-up companies or companies in the early stages of business, as well as firms in "turn-around" situations. These are risky investments, generally in innovative enterprises and many times in high-technology areas.

venture capital firm an investment firm that provides money to business start-ups.

venture capitalist an investment firm (or individual investor) that provides money to business start-ups.

weighted average cost of capital a composite of the individual costs of financing incurred by each capital source. A firm's weighted cost of capital is a function of (1) the individual costs of capital, (2) the capital structure mix, and (3) the level of financing necessary to make the investment

working capital a concept traditionally defined as a firm's investment in current assets. Compare **net working capital**.

working capital management the management o the firm's current assets and short-term financing.

work-in-process inventory partially finished goods requiring additional work before they become finished goods.

yield to maturity the rate of return a bondholder will receive if the bond is held to maturity.

zero (very low coupon) bond a bond issued at a substantial discount from its $1,000 face value and that pays little or no interest.

zero balance accounts (ZBA) a cash management tool that permits centralized control over cash outflow while maintaining divisional disbursing authority. Objectives are (1) to achieve better control over cash payments; (2) to reduce excess cash balances held in regional banks for disbursing purposes; and (3) to increase disbursing float.

Indexes

Subject